Index to English

Index to English both supplements and augments *Writer's Guide*. It includes entries on grammar, diction, punctuation, mechanics, style, and special kinds of writing, as well as on individual words and phrases—all arranged alphabetically for easy reference. The Correction Chart inside the back cover lists entries that are especially useful in revising papers.

Words

Writing About Literature

The Research Paper

Writer's Guide and Index to English

Seventh Edition

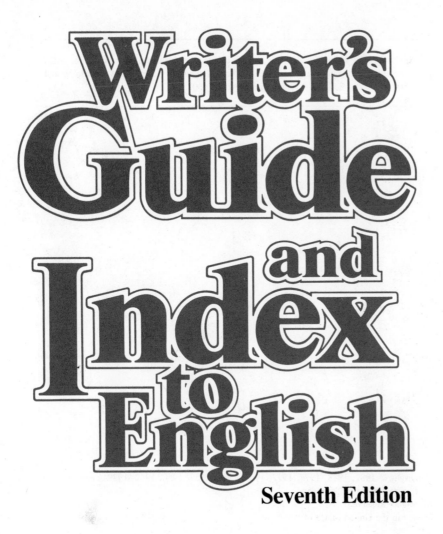

Writer's Guide and Index to English

Seventh Edition

Wilma R. Ebbitt

The Pennsylvania State University

David R. Ebbitt

Scott, Foresman and Company Glenview, Illinois
Dallas, Texas Oakland, New Jersey Palo Alto, California
Tucker, Georgia London, England

An Instructor's Manual is available. It may be obtained through a local Scott, Foresman representative or by writing to English Editor, College Division, Scott, Foresman and Company, 1900 E. Lake Avenue, Glenview, IL 60025.

Library of Congress Cataloging in Publication Data

Ebbitt, Wilma R.
    Writer's guide and index to English.

    First part also published independently as:
Writer's guide. 7th ed. c1982.
        1. English language—Rhetoric. 2. English
language—Handbooks, manuals, etc. I. Ebbitt,
David R., 1919–   . II. Title.
PE1408.E293 1981   808'.042   81-14505
ISBN 0-673-15542-0   AACR2

Acknowledgments of sources granting permission to reprint
copyrighted material appear on pp. 611 ff.

2   3   4   5   6   -   VHJ   -   86   85   84   83   82

Preface

Writer's Guide and Index to English combines a rhetoric, *Writer's Guide,* with a handbook, *Index to English.* In this seventh edition we have given the *Guide* new emphases and a new organization; we have shortened the *Index,* sharply reducing overlap with the *Guide;* and in revising both parts we have tried to produce a more concise, more readable text.

Throughout, our aim has been to offer practical instruction and realistic advice. We have told students that writing well requires concentrated effort, but we have also told them that it needn't be an ordeal, that college papers can give pleasure to the writer as well as to the reader. And college papers generally—not just papers for writing courses—are our concern. To remind students that what they learn in their writing course is applicable beyond the boundaries of that course, we have introduced from a variety of disciplines sample assignments that call on the skills *Writer's Guide and Index* seeks to develop. These skills are equally applicable to the writing tasks students are likely to face in their postgraduate careers.

From the first pages of the *Guide,* we encourage students to assume responsibility for their own progress in writing. We insist that at the heart of the composing process must lie a sense of personal commitment: the student writer must have something that he wants to say, that he believes is worth saying in such a way that it will be understood, accepted, acted upon. To help him achieve that end, we give most of our attention to practical problems of execution—problems that recur in drafting and redrafting papers, in revising and rewriting. Like the earlier editions, the seventh proceeds on the assumption that writing can be most satisfactorily discussed and practiced in the context of a range of choices—rhetorical, syntactic, and lexical—and sets out to present those choices to its readers.

In the first chapter of the *Guide* we have given more attention to prewriting and to techniques of invention, and we have defined the rhetorical situation more fully. In subsequent chapters we have introduced new kinds of assignments, included many more papers written by students, and broadened the range of writing by professionals. Whether by students or professionals, illustrative passages are *not* presented as models of excellent writing, though some of them are very good indeed. Most have been selected to demonstrate particular points made in the text. Others show how students have responded, successfully or unsuccessfully, to particular assignments.

Besides introducing students to the concept of the rhetorical situation and discussing ways of getting started, Chapter One offers an overview of the whose process of writing papers in college—deciding on a manageable topic, arriving at a statement of purpose, gathering material, choosing methods of developing ideas (and in the process generating content), writing drafts, revising, and editing. Chapter One does not formulate *a* procedure, *a* formula for writing. Instead, it outlines various procedures and urges students to experiment, to find out what works for *them.*

Chapter One also introduces the varieties of English. In both *Guide* and *Index* the labels "general," "formal," and "informal" are applied not only to words and phrases but to punctuation, to sentence patterns, to transitions, and to the styles that are the end result of the choices that every writer makes, deliberately or intuitively. So while the varieties of usage are not discussed in detail until Chapter Eight, "Choosing Words," the broad differences between general, informal, and formal styles are introduced in Chapter One and are appealed to throughout the text as a basic element in rhetorical choice.

The methods of developing papers, treated in one very long chapter in the sixth edition, are now divided between Chapter Two, which deals with generalizations and particulars, description, and narration, and Chapter Three, which discusses and illustrates division, comparison and contrast, classification, causal analysis, and definition. Chapter Four, "Persuading Readers," shows how these methods of development work in argument. In addition, the chapter examines the ethical dimension of persuasion and the special rhetorical techniques related to it and includes a brief treatment of the logical underpinnings of argument, formerly given a separate chapter.

Chapter Five takes up the organizing of papers, and Chapter Six the building of paragraphs—both single paragraphs and paragraph sequences. In earlier editions these chapters preceded the treatment of persuasion. We believe that the new order of chapters offers a more teachable progression.

Chapter Seven deals with writing and revising sentences, first with revising for clarity, then with revising for style. Style is also considered in a brief review of punctuation. Students who need to review particular grammatical points are led by a self-test to the item-by-item coverage in the *Index.*

Chapter Eight deals with words, their use and misuse. Again, the material moves from the elementary to the more sophisticated, from finding out what a word means to using words with precision and originality and flair.

Chapter Nine, "Doing a Close Reading," is carried over from the sixth edition. It describes, with an example, a single, specific approach to an extremely broad subject—writing about literature. Chapter Ten, "Writing the Research Paper," includes an up-to-date list of reference works and a new sample research paper. Instruction in documentation conforms to the style recommended in the *MLA Handbook.*

In every chapter of *Writer's Guide* students are given frequent opportunities to test their mastery of the principles of invention, structure, development, and style that are discussed in the text. Sometimes writing tasks are sharply focused; sometimes students are invited to discover and shape their own topics, establish their own rhetorical situations. In addition, they are regularly asked to comment on and sometimes to revise the writing of others, both amateurs and professionals, so that they can develop criteria for judging their own work as they extend their rhetorical horizons. Revising the work of others is the quickest way for students to acquire the objectivity they must have in order to revise their own work intelligently. And, as instructors and students alike must recognize, revising is an indispensable part of the process of writing. While spontaneity has its virtues, for the most part writing that satisfies college standards is rewritten writing.

Supplementary material for class assignments, as well as suggestions for using the *Guide,* will be found in *A Teacher's Guide to the Writer's Guide,* available from the publishers.

In *Index to English,* topics covered in the *Guide* have, with few exceptions, been eliminated. (All these entries will be restored in a separate seventh edition of the *Index.*) Other deletions include out-of-date usage items and entries on grammatical and linguistic matters not immediately applicable to writing. New entries have been added on usage and on words commonly confused. The style of the *Index* has been revised so that it more closely corresponds to the style of the *Guide.*

We have retained the alphabetical arrangement of entries and the extensive system of cross-references that enable users of the handbook to find what they want quickly and easily. There are no dummy references, or blind entries, like *"effect, affect.* See *affect, effect."* Students who look up *effect, affect* will find a sentence or two which may tell them what they want to know. Following this information is a reference to the main entry, *affect, effect.*

To help students write so that what they have to say will be understood, paid attention to, even enjoyed by readers, the *Index* provides them with some rules, reminds them of certain conventions, and suggests some of the uses that can be made of both highly formal and decidedly informal English. Though for practical reasons (outlined in the entry "Usage") we indicate the choices expected in formal styles, our recommendation is that students set out to master general American English, the variety of English that all educated Americans read and that all need to be able to write.

On certain matters students need, and will find, unequivocal advice. In the entries keyed to the correction chart we have made the *Index* as prescriptive as honesty and realism permit. The correction entries answer directly and explicitly such questions as "What mark of punctuation do I need here?" "Should this verb be singular or plural?" "What can I do to improve the continuity of this paragraph?" But they also take into account appropriateness to the writer's subject and purpose and audience and to the writer's self. And in most of the entries relating to usage, style, and rhetorical strategies, appropriateness is the primary criterion students are urged to apply.

In usage entries, after identifying the current status of a locution, we often take up alternatives: the *"pretty* good time" of informal and the *"fairly* good time" of general; the formal *arising* and the general *getting up*. The student who has read the *Guide* knows that the varieties overlap and that on occasion good writers deliberately shift from one variety to another. In a paper that is predominantly in general English, the informal *about* may be used instead of *almost* ("I was about done") as a means of moving a bit closer to the reader. Here and elsewhere we neither deny students a choice nor simply list alternatives and invite them to take their pick. What we try to do is guide them toward making intelligent choices that reflect their awareness of the rhetorical context in which they are writing.

Here, then, is a rhetoric that guides students, by a choice of routes, through the process of writing papers. And here is a handbook they can turn to as they write and revise and as they go over papers that have been corrected and returned, to find solutions to particular problems and answers to specific questions. A general index coordinates the two.

The seventh edition of *Writer's Guide and Index to English* is, we hope, a book worth keeping, a resource for writers not just for the duration of a composition course but through college and beyond. In looking for new ways to help today's college students develop confidence and gain competence in writing, we have been guided by the principles of Porter G. Perrin, who made *Writer's Guide and Index to English* a resource for generations of teachers as well as students.

Before work was begun on this edition, the publisher solicited advice and recommendations from many teachers. The chapters of the sixth edition of the *Guide* were reviewed by William Gibson of Idaho State University, David Hamilton of the University of Iowa, Celia M. Millward of Boston University, Martha Reid of Moravian College, and Robert S. Rudolph of the University of Toledo. The exercises and writing assignments were evaluated by Michael Joyce of Jackson Community College, Carolyn B. Matalene of the University of South Carolina, Carol Simpson Stern of Northwestern University, and James Work of Colorado State University. John J. Ruszkiewicz of the University of Texas at Austin reviewed both the text and the exercises and assignments. Robert S. Rudolph also assisted in the revision of Chapter Ten; Amanda Clark, Vicki Stewart, and Kathleen Lorden of Scott, Foresman were responsible for seeing the entire manuscript through the press. Celia M. Millward provided very helpful criticism of the *Index*.

In response to a questionnaire prepared by the publisher, these teachers expressed judgments about the sixth edition: Mary Ann Aschauer, Susan Baker, Lynette C. Black, Joseph Boles, Alma G. Bryant, Lurene M. Brooks, Howard A. Burton, Jacquelyn B. Carr, Marvin Ching, Valerie Davis, Charles R. Duke, Gail M. Eifrig, Toni Emipringham, Jerry D. Gibbens, Susette R. Graham, Edward D. Gross, Roy A. Helton, Stephen R. ImMasche, Anita Lawson, Elaine McLevie, Collette Mullaney, Francine G. Navakas, Philip D. Smith, Lorene L. Stookey, Elizabeth Wahlquist, Nola J. Wegman, J. R. Wilson.

Our thanks to reviewers and respondents. Our thanks, too, to the many students who gave us permission to reprint their papers and to Jeanne Fahnestock who, as Director of Composition at The Pennsylvania State University, granted us permission to include "A Village by the River," printed in the first issue of *Penn Statements*. Many of the new assignments we owe to the inventiveness of a lively and talented group of composition teachers at The Pennsylvania State University.

Wilma R. Ebbitt
David R. Ebbitt

Contents

3

DIVIDING, COMPARING, CLASSIFYING, ANALYZING CAUSES, DEFINING   56

4

PERSUADING READERS   94

5

ORGANIZING PAPERS 137

6

BUILDING PARAGRAPHS   172

7

SHAPING SENTENCES   202

8

CHOOSING WORDS   244

9

DOING A CLOSE READING 275

10

WRITING THE RESEARCH PAPER 282

Contents

Index to English

The *Index*, pp. 343–610, contains entries in alphabetical arrangement that fall roughly into six categories, with some overlapping:

Entries on particular words and constructions, like *among, between; like, as; not about to; who, whom.*

Entries to be used in correcting and revising papers, signaled by correction symbols in longhand.

Entries on composition, like Beginning, Ending, Organization, Paragraphs, Transition, Unity, and on style, like Abstract language, Diction, Parallelism and style, Nominalization.

Entries offering information and advice on special kinds of writing, such as Business letters and Technical writing.

Entries on grammar, offering definitions and discussions of standard grammatical terms and concepts, such as Collective nouns, Relative clauses, Restrictive and nonrestrictive modifiers, Subjunctive mood, and the parts of speech.

Entries about language and language study, like British English, Origin of words, Sexist language, and Usage.

Writer's Guide and Index to English

Seventh Edition

Writer's Guide

1

Getting Started

The purpose of this book is to help you improve your writing. As a first step, recognize that there is no *one* way to write well. What works for one writer in preparing a paper doesn't necessarily work for another. If one route turns out to be a dead end for you, you'll find there are other routes to travel, and at least one of them will take you where you want to go. Try out different approaches, and settle on the methods of composing that seem to work best for you most of the time. Finding your own way to handle writing projects will increase both your confidence and your competence. And you'll still have plenty of opportunity for improvising, because no two writing projects are exactly alike.

The Rhetorical Situation

Good writing doesn't just happen. It calls for training and practice. Whether writing comes easily to you or not, you'll write better if you pay close attention to the rhetorical situation—the circumstances, or context, in which you're writing.

Whenever you write, you're working within a rhetorical situation that brings together writer, subject, purpose, and audience. You (WRITER) have something you want to say about an incident or person or problem or idea (SUBJECT) for a particular reason (PURPOSE) to one or more people (AUDIENCE). What you write should be determined by your interaction with the other three elements:

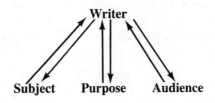

Your subject is what you're writing about, and what you say about it becomes the content of your paper. In the broad sense, then, what you write will be determined by your ideas and feelings about your subject. But in a narrower sense the controlling influence will be your purpose in discussing the subject—to praise, to blame, to inform, to persuade, to amuse, or whatever it may be. Taken together, subject and purpose determine the kind of writing you're setting out to produce, whether it's an account of freshman registration in a letter to your family, or a movie review for the college newspaper, or a term paper in economics.

Subject and purpose are of primary importance in writing. As we'll see in the next section, finding something to write about—a subject—and figuring out what you want to say about it *and why you want to say it*—your purpose—take up much of the time you give to writing in a composition course.

You will make better use of some of that time if you decide what audience you want to reach. In conversation, what you say and how you say it depend to a large extent on who it is you're talking to. If you're asked what college is like, you'll select different information and tell it in different words depending on who asked the question—your mother, a close friend, one of your high-school teachers, a little cousin, or an older person you've met for the first time.

The same thing holds true for writing. To keep you from feeling that you're always addressing the same audience of one—your instructor— many assignments in the first part of this book either set up audiences other than your instructor for you to address or urge you to specify readers you'd like to write for. Here's a small sample of the audiences students have chosen:

Readers of *Family Circle*

Mature television viewers in search of originality on the tube

All those overweight people who run out of breath each morning while walking to the bathroom

A person who has had experience breeding cavies (guinea pigs) but has never exhibited any of his stock

My friend Crystal, to whom I tell *everything*

If you choose an audience you know well, you'll find that your familiarity with their tastes and interests and with what they know and don't know will immediately sharpen your sense of what to say and how to say it.

Clearly, subject and purpose are not all there is to writing a paper. It's only when you have an audience, real or imagined, that you can be said to be operating in a rhetorical situation, for only then can you judge exactly what to say and how to say it. But there's still another element in the rhetorical situation—you, the writer. The way you see yourself and the ways you want different audiences to see you will determine many of the choices you make. You'll speak in different voices and play different roles—some real (son or daughter, sister or brother, friend, lover, student, co-worker) and some imagined (laid-off employee, city manager, reporter). You'll also assume different relationships with audiences—expert addressing experts, expert addressing amateurs, amateur addressing amateurs. The relationship may be characterized by any degree of formality or familiarity, of hostility or affection. Each relationship calls for adjustments in what you say and how you say it.

For Writing and Discussion

1. Write a three-minute talk in which you introduce yourself to your classmates. You can't possibly tell everything about yourself in that length of time, and a recitation of facts—date and place of birth, schools attended, and so on—won't make very interesting listening when you read the paper aloud. So focus on something in your background that will give your listeners an idea of the kind of person you are.

Now write a letter of the same length in response to a "Help Wanted" ad for a part-time job you'd very much like to have. Tell your prospective employer (someone you've never met) just what your qualifications are.

Look closely at the two papers. Explain how the different rhetorical situations have made them differ.

2. Some teachers complain that students today aren't interested in *anything.* Write a page on "What Does and Doesn't Interest Me." Be honest. If you find yourself making a long list of subjects that don't interest you, try to pinpoint the reasons for your lack of interest.

3. Take stock of your strengths and weaknesses as a writer. In a brief paper addressed to your instructor, tell about your experiences in writing. How much writing and what kinds of writing have you done? What's frustrated you? What's given you pleasure? What kind of writing do you think you do best? What, in your judgment, do you need to do to improve your writing?

Your Resources

For your writing, you have rich personal resources to draw on. What you've experienced and observed, what you learn from listening and reading and thinking, give you subjects to write about and things to say about them. Personal experiences not only supply substance for autobiographical papers but provide the basis for an opinion, give authority to an explanation, add conviction to an argument.

Your memory is a unique resource. While it won't hand you a printout at the push of a button, it can be coaxed. When all it comes up with are blurred impressions, keep working on it. Sometimes a snapshot, a souvenir, a song, a clipping, or a few words with an old friend will trigger sharp recall. You'll find that memory often comes through under pressure, sometimes by unusual routes.

In the following paragraph John Updike remembers the summer resort of Martha's Vineyard through the soles of his bare feet.

When I think of the Vineyard, my ankles feel good—bare, airy, lean. Full of bones, I go barefoot there in recollection, and the island as remembered becomes a medley of pedal sensations: the sandy rough planks of Dutcher's Dock; the sidewalks of Oak Bluffs, followed by the wall-to-wall carpeting of the liquor store; the pokey feel of an accelerator on a naked sole; the hurtful little pebbles of Menemsha Beach and the also hurtful half-buried rocks of Squibnocket; the prickly weeds, virtual cactuses, that grow in a certain lawn near Chilmark Pond; the soft path leading down from this lawn across giving, oozing boards to a bouncy little dock and rowboats that offered another friendly texture to the feet; the crystal bite of ocean water; the seethe and suck of a wave tumbling rocks across your toes in its surge back down the sand; sand, the clean wide private sand by Windy Gates and the print-pocked, overused public sand by the boat dock that one picked around in while waiting for friends to be deferried; the cold steep clay of Gay Head and the flinty littered surface around those souvenir huts that continued to beguile the most jaded child; the startling dew on the grass when one stepped outside with the first cup of coffee to gauge the day's weather; the warmth of the day still lingering in the dunes underfoot as one walked back, Indian-file, through the dark from a beach party and its diminishing bonfire. Going to the post office in bare feet had an infralegal, antitotalitarian, comical, gentle feel to it, in the days before the postal service moved to the other side of Beetlebung Corners and established itself in razor-sharp spalls. (When Bill Steward ran the postal annex in his store, it was one of the few spots in the United States that delivered mail on Sundays.) Shopping at Seward's, one would not so carefreely have shelled out "island prices" for such luxuries as macadamia nuts and candied snails had one been wearing shoes; their absence, like the cashless ease of a charge account, gave a pleasant illusion of unaccountability. A friend of mine . . . used to play golf at Mink Meadows barefoot. My children and I set up a miniature golf course on a turn-around covered with crushed clamshells; after treading this surface for a while, it did not seem too great a transition, even for a middle-aged father of four, to climb a tree or go walking on a roof. The shingles stung.—John Updike, *New York Times Magazine*

You can teach yourself to be a better observer. For the most part, we see only what we want to see and what we've been brought up to see; but with conscious effort we can expand the circle of our awareness. By observing with an open mind as well as open eyes, we can literally see more.

Train yourself to see beneath the surface of things. Close, deliberate observation turns up good material. Instead of settling for a general impression, look for parts and the ways they fit together—for example, the way the work of different crafts meshes in a construction job. Single out the specifics that will make your writing concrete and individual.

For Writing

For several days in a row, spend fifteen or twenty minutes looking at and writing about the same thing—a building, a tree, a cat, whatever you choose. Observe it at different times each day, and write down what you see. Each time you look at it, try to see it afresh, and each time you write about it, try to record a sharp image of what you see *that* time.

After a week or so, review the five or six passages you've written. If they all sound much the same, you weren't looking hard enough, or you didn't work hard enough to find the words that would convey exactly what you saw.

Ideas for papers come from listening, reading, and studying—from what you hear in conversations with your friends; from what you read in newspapers, magazines, and books, listen to on the radio, and watch on television; from what you learn in lectures and class discussions and from what you study in course assignments. Ideas also come from talking and writing—from what *you* say and what *you* put down on paper. As you work at converting a vague notion into words, you may find the words themselves sparking a train of thought that leads to a conclusion you'd never considered.

Besides supplying ideas, reading lots of good prose will do more than anything else to help you improve your own use of language. No matter how heavy the reading assignments for your courses, try to read a variety of current magazines and books, both fiction and nonfiction. Paying attention to the ways professional writers organize and express their ideas can help you in presenting your own. In reading, as in observing, you can train yourself to see beneath the surface and examine the ways the parts work together. But first of all read for pleasure. While you're enjoying yourself, you'll be absorbing the rhythms of the written language.

Of all your resources, the essential one is your ability to reason and reflect. Use your papers as testing grounds for the ideas you're incubating, ideas you've formed in response to what you've read and heard. Your mind, which sets you apart from everyone else, gives your writing its individuality. Until your mind begins to work on material, the data remain data and nothing more.

Whether you're drawing on personal experience, observation, discussion, or reading, you need to keep thinking. Think *through* your material, sifting it, sorting it, evaluating it. When you're recalling personal experience, you're the only one who can separate what really happened from what you wish had happened. When you're dealing with what you've read or what you've been told, it's up to you to decide what information is most reliable and which sources are most trustworthy. In the end, *you* must decide what you believe, and why. Writing the truth as you know it or as you see it (without ever forgetting that you may be wrong) is not only the right thing to do in a moral sense; it's also most likely to produce the direct, forceful style that carries conviction.

For Writing

You have still another resource that you shouldn't overlook, and that's emotion. Emotional writing is tricky, because strong feeling often outruns the writer's ability to express it. Its great advantage is that it comes from the heart, or thereabouts. When you write about something you passionately love or hate, there's no doubt about your sincerity or your conviction. Nor do you have any trouble finding something to say or a reason for saying it—you want to be heard! And so long as you stay in control of what you have to say, you have a good chance of being listened to. Even if an audience doesn't share a particular gripe, it does know the feelings of frustration and resentment and the urge to howl.

Here's a complaint by a student who said he had "a great desire to tell those folks off":

> Snow removal is a problem here, but it is one we have blown out of proportion. The citizens of this state pay millions of dollars each year in taxes for snow removal. The University also budgets for this service. The town has even created an ordinance requiring snow removal by property owners. Therefore one could safely assume that our paths are clear to travel, right? Wrong. The state's problems I can understand. There are only so many men and plows for many miles of highway. They have their priorities, and that means some roads just won't get plowed. But the practices of University crews and townspeople I don't understand.
>
> Maintenance crews can salt like hell and plow administration parking lots, but when it comes to the main walkways of campus, forget it. Students and professors alike risk life and limb slipping to class. Sure, salt is effective for melting and breaking up ice, but there's another effective tool that hasn't been on the market for years. Elbow grease. Used in moderate amounts, it has been known to clean sidewalks. Couldn't our president order some for his employees? It might improve the image he talks about so much.
>
> The town walks are just as bad if not worse. It's safe to assume that downtown merchants derive substantial incomes from the student body

(substantial enough for them to ignore the fearsome fine of $3.00 they're threatened with for not cleaning their walks). I would think that their profits are more than enough to pay for snow removal. If not, why don't they raise prices just a hair, collect the money over the year—kind of like a Christmas Club—and then in December go buy a shovel and some salt? If they save wisely, they might even be able to pay someone else to clear their sidewalks for them. Landlords could do the same—raise rents just a little and invest in salt and shovels (tax deductible, I think).

Really, though, it is not the dollars-and-cents aspect of cleaning walks that bothers me. Why can't these people be decent citizens and decent human beings? Needless injuries have occurred—painful falls that could be eliminated if property owners would simply say, "Yes, I care enough about other people to shovel my walks."

Although the writer doesn't get around to the main target of his complaint until he's halfway through and doesn't reach the real core until the last paragraph, his strong feeling holds the paper together and keeps it moving. Try your hand at writing a complaint, specifying your audience.

Prewriting

Looked at from the outside, writing is the act of joining words into sentences on paper. To anyone who's ever tried to write, that's a misleading definition. Certainly a large part of composing takes place in the mind. But if writing isn't just exercising the fingers, neither is it necessarily the act of finding words to express definite, fully formed ideas. For some writers, it is: they "think the whole thing out" before they put words on paper. For others, the physical act of writing stimulates thinking and stirs up ideas. Joan Didion has said, "I write entirely to find out what I'm thinking, what I'm looking at, what I see and what it means." Whatever the action, whether external or internal or both, this initial stage of composing may be called *prewriting*. Without sustained and inventive prewriting, a good paper can only be a lucky accident.

Prewriting is finding a subject and discovering what you think and feel about it; it's deciding on the perspective from which you'll write about it and the goal you'll be working to achieve—your purpose in the rhetorical situation. It includes whatever goes on before you set out to produce a complete first draft. It may even extend into the writing of that draft. And halfway through you may decide that you've been on the wrong track all along and need to start over again.

Depending on your subject and your habits of work, prewriting may be a period of thinking that ranges from daydreaming to active free-associating to hard concentrating. It may include talking, reading, taking notes, making more or less systematic outlines. Or it may mean scribbling away in an attempt to get at a hazy notion that could turn out to be the core of what you write. Some of us think on paper.

Warming Up

Prewriting is the stage at which a good many minds go blank. If you often find yourself unable to get started on a writing assignment, try some of the techniques that have helped others overcome writer's block.

Keeping a Journal

A journal can be the seedbed for the papers you write. It won't be if it's no more than a bare record of what you do from morning to night. It will be if you use it to record, as vividly as you can, anything that impressed itself on you in the course of each day—something you saw or heard or smelled or tasted, or heard about, or thought about, or even something you imagined. Here's a journal entry that captures a vivid impression in a mental snapshot:

> A pimply-faced, dirty, barefooted girl with greasy, stringy hair, smoking a cigarette and eating a peanut-butter-and-jelly sandwich in a crowded elevator while reading a paperback of *How to Win Friends and Influence People.*

And your journal will be a seedbed if you use it to record your thoughts about what you've seen. Another journal entry:

> No bird sits in a tree more proudly than a pigeon. It looks as though placed there by the Lord. The sky was silky blue and white today, and the sun shone through the leaves. But the children's faces, pinched and crooked, made me feel a bit out of love with God.

Use your journal as a place for storing phrases you like or ideas you want to think about:

> "Writing is thinking on paper." That's what my English teacher said in class this morning.

Use it as a place for recording incidents you've observed or taken part in or been told about, descriptions of people who interest you, bits of conversations you've overheard. And by all means use it to conduct dialogs with yourself, with the authors of the books you're reading in your courses, and with your instructors:

> Writing may be thinking on paper, but it's not just that. It's ways of putting sentences together and punctuating them. And SPELLING.

One writer said that his journal was his savings bank, a source he drew on for the essays he published. Look at your journal the same way. When you think you haven't a thing to say, read over the entries you've made. What caught your eye or ear or mind last week or last month is likely to spark interest again and get your thought processes working.

Brainstorming

Another way to get your thought processes working is to give your mind some strenuous exercise. The term *brainstorming* originally meant a group activity in which participants tossed out random ideas, stimulating each other's imaginations. For some class projects such exchanges may be practical as a prewriting exercise. When they're not, storm your own brain. Or, rather, let your mind run. Point it at the subject you want to write on, and turn it loose. Don't try to force it or check it. Jot down the ideas that flash across your mind, however wild they may seem. One thought will lead to another, and the blank page in front of you will gradually fill up with a list of things associated with your topic. Then, after your mind has had its run, go over the list and separate out the items that look promising. Many, probably most, of the items you've listed won't appear in the paper you write, but with luck enough of them will be usable to get you moving.

Here is one writer's list after brainstorming the subject *sleep:*

Sleep.

Dreams.

Getting to bed—big problem.

Beds. Cots. Couches. Sofas. Chairs. Floors. Ground.

Drowsing in class (staying awake big problem).

Lying awake. Lots of people have insomnia. TV ads.

Gloomy thoughts at 3 a.m.

Going without sleep. Went 36 hours at prom time.

Don't need more than six hours a night. Jere seems to need ten.

REMs—rapid eye movements. Cats and dogs dream.

Naps. Fantasizing.

Eight o'clock class—dreary scene.

Noise. Stereos. Traffic. Banging window shades. Faucet drips.

Sound sleepers and light sleepers. My dog snores.

Waking up cold.

Pills for staying awake. Exam time. Truck drivers.

Yawning.

Nightmares.

For Writing

Choose a subject, and then list the ideas that come to mind when you brainstorm that subject for fifteen minutes.

Another method of brainstorming shakes up your way of looking at a subject so that you can see it in a new way. Take any activity you enjoy—singing, swimming, cooking, camping, riding, running, whatever—and see how many resemblances, even accidental and partial ones, occur to you when you think of the activity in terms of another that seems somehow like it. What new perspectives do you gain if you think of singing as painting pictures, of cooking as composing poems, of running as attending a religious service? Such thinking may give you a controlling idea ("A top singing group is like a top basketball team") that will help you say what you feel about your subject. Russell Baker based a newspaper column on "A President should be like a piece of music."

Or try treating the activity as unique. Ask yourself what qualities it has that make it, at least for you, different from everything else. You may find this approach just as effective in opening up the subject: "Designing and making your own clothes doesn't just provide you with a wardrobe you can afford; it lets you feel, and say, 'This is *me*.'"

Free Writing

A third technique that can help you get started is free writing—a matter of getting your fingers working as well as your mind. You sit down with pen or pencil or typewriter and *write,* nonstop, for ten minutes. Nothing to say? Well, "I have nothing to say" is something you can write, and writing that over and over again will be so boring that you'll probably soon shift to something more positive. In any case, keep going, set down thoughts that pop into your head, mark time between thoughts with words or lists or whatever, without paying any attention to spelling or grammar or punctuation or even common sense.

Some students find a warm-up period of free writing good preparation for any writing job. Some use it to discover possible subjects. Others see it chiefly as a way of getting started on a particular topic. Try using it that way. Though the writing will still be spontaneous and unplanned, the subject will be in the back of your mind, and it will make its presence felt. When the ten minutes are up, read over what you've written. You're almost sure to find something that suggests an idea you can build on.

Journal writing, brainstorming, and free writing can do more than get you started. They can also pull you out of the rut of conventional thinking and second-hand opinion. Some of the insights and ideas that surface will be so far out that you can't use them, but a few will have a freshness and originality that will interest your readers and may even delight them.

Settling on a Topic

Assigned topics that don't awaken any immediate interest call for special effort in the prewriting stage. Special effort of a different kind is called for by an assignment that's wide open—a ''free choice''—or by one that invites you to stake out a topic for yourself from a very broad area like education or recreation. For a free choice, don't spend a lot of time deciding what to write about. Recognize that you're a person of many experiences, interests, and talents and that there are probably a dozen topics you can write on with as much authority as anyone else in the classroom, including the instructor. Without wasting time waiting for the ideal topic to suggest itself, you should be able to find a subject that's not only a good one for a paper but the right one for you.

The subject you choose should be close enough to your own experience for you to feel comfortable with it. Or it should be something you've read about and thought about enough so that you can write on it with some confidence. You'll flounder if you launch into a topic that's too big for you, like ''The Outlook for the Twenty-first Century.'' Choose a subject you're capable of handling, but don't settle for one that's trivial. The more your topic stirs your imagination and stretches your mind, the more likely it will be to interest your audience.

Often you'll arrive at a good topic by building up and out from a particular incident—something that amused or stirred you, gave you pleasure or caused you pain. Journal entries are excellent starters for topics, reminding you not just of things you've done and seen but of the impression they made on you and the way you felt about them. When you're faced with a broad, general subject like education, you have to find ways of making it manageable. One way is to cut in on the subject where you've had some personal experience with it. Last summer you tutored some teenagers? Then write about tutoring those teenagers, not about education, or high-school education, or the problem of dropouts, or teaching disadvantaged children. If you want to generalize about reaching unmotivated tenth-graders, let the generalizations develop out of your account of your summer work.

Asking Questions

Another way to explore a general subject is to ask questions about it. Journal entries, brainstorming, and free writing shake up the mind, jolting loose ideas for papers. Probing a subject with questions is a more analytical, disciplined approach. There are many sets of questions you can ask about a large subject. The methods of development we take up in the next two chapters suggest questions like these:

1.   What does the object or scene look like? What are its dimensions, shape, colors, identifying marks? What is the chief impression it conveys? (Description)

2. What happened? *Either:* What happened on that one occasion? How did one incident lead to another? What was the outcome? (Narration) *Or:* What always happens when you go through a certain series of steps or set certain things in motion? (Process)

3. What are the parts of the object, or what are the elements that make up the idea or concept? (Division)

4. What is the object like? What is it unlike? (Comparison and Contrast)

5. What groups or sets can be made from this large collection of items? (Classification)

6. What caused the event or the phenomenon? (Cause) What effect or result has it had or is it likely to have? (Effect)

7. What is it? What are the characteristics or qualities or attributes that set it apart from everything else? (Definition)

The responses you come up with will move you closer to the aspect of the subject that interests you most and that you can write on with knowledge and conviction.

Generating Ideas

Let's see how a less formal approach to these methods of development works. The example will show how naturally and instinctively we use the methods in our thinking and writing.

Suppose you're faced with the broad assignment of writing about the public high school or private school you went to. And suppose you don't feel strongly about your school one way or the other. Your first response is that it had its good points and its bad ones. That's not much to work with. You dig deeper. The bad points come to mind first: "Kid stuff. Routine. Dull classes. The hours dragged. Even the teachers were watching the clock." But there were exceptions: "Mahoney's class. Kapstein's. And good times in the cafeteria—despite that routine menu."

Maybe you could write about the physical surroundings (Description) or give an account of a typical school day (Narration). Or tell about the differences between high-school and college classes (Contrast) or about how your school stacked up against the other high schools in your city (Comparison). It occurs to you that what set your school apart was the unusual mix of students it had. You wonder if you could group them by family income, religion, political party, ethnic background (Classification).

Maybe that's too ambitious. Try another approach. Think of the way courses were grouped in such categories as science, mathematics, social studies, language arts, and so on. You could take one of these—social studies, maybe—and tell what its parts are, what disciplines make it up (Division). Or you might even write a paper on the American public secondary school, using your school as a typical example (Definition). The aim could be simple explanation (addressed to a foreign student, say). Or the aim could be to persuade someone who has an open mind on the subject that attending a public secondary school is better, or worse, than going to a private school.

But maybe the best thing to do would be to go back to that first appraisal—good points and bad—and see if you can explain *why* your school was the way it was. The reasons for its shortcomings, perhaps (Cause). Or, taking another tack, you might argue that, with its well-mixed student body and faculty, your school prepared its graduates for life in a well-mixed society (Effect).

Look again at these last two possibilities—"see if you can explain" and "you might argue that." In the process of settling on your topic, you've arrived at a pretty clear idea of your purpose in dealing with it. That purpose may change as you gather more material or even when you're well along in writing your first draft. But to give direction to your planning and writing and help you spot leads worth following up, you'll need to make at least a tentative decision as to just what it is you're setting out to do.

For Writing

Write three beginnings for a paper on the school you attended before entering college. Each beginning should be at least 75 words, and each should point to a different method of developing your main generalization. One beginning might suggest narrative, for instance, and another comparison. Then, in a paper of about 500 words, complete the beginning that interests you most. Use your paper to make a college friend understand either how lucky or how unlucky you were in going to that school.

Establishing Your Purpose

In different rhetorical situations you will have different purposes. You may want to demonstrate or explain or protest or investigate or ridicule. You may want to entertain or to soothe or to woo your audience. In the papers assigned in most of your college courses, you'll be asked to clarify, interpret, explore, defend, or challenge. That is, most of the papers you write will be explanations (exposition) or arguments (persuasion).

Explaining and Persuading

How do these two kinds of writing differ? Not in the source of the material. Either exposition or argument can be based on reading and research; either can draw on personal experience. You could write a straight autobiographical narrative about your part in a show put on by a community theater group. But you could also use the experience as the basis for an explanation of the process of presenting an original musical. And you could use the same experience to argue that public funds should be used to subsidize the community theater group.

. Nor do exposition and argument necessarily differ in subject. Hundreds of explanatory articles have been written about wildlife conservation, and so have hundreds of persuasive articles. The only sound basis for making a distinction between the two kinds of papers is the use to which the material is put. And use is determined by purpose. In an explanatory paper your purpose is to *inform* your readers, to clarify the subject for them. In a persuasive paper your purpose is to *influence* your readers, to make them think or act in a certain way. Having one of these purposes doesn't mean that you can't also have the other. Informing may be the first step toward influencing. But in a good paper one purpose is usually dominant, and that's the purpose you should spell out to yourself.

Stating Your Purpose

As your prewriting progresses, write out for yourself a statement of the purpose you have in mind. Though it won't appear (at least not in the same form) in the paper you turn in, having it to refer to will keep you on target as you write.

Starting a statement of purpose is simple:

What I want to do in this paper is tell . . .

Who is it that you're going to tell? You need a specific audience. Will it be your instructor? Your classmates? Your parents? Or readers with some special interest in your subject? The audience you choose—real or imagined—will determine in various ways what you say and how you say it.

What I want to do in this paper is tell my classmates about my bicycle trip across Canada . . .

All right, you've named your audience, and you've identified your subject. But *what* are you going to tell your classmates about your trip? And for what purpose? To inform them, amuse them, warn them? Is it to be an explanation, a "how-to" paper? A funny or dramatic narrative? Or do you want to convince your readers that biking is an exhausting, dangerous way to travel, or that biking cross-country in Canada is quite unlike biking in the United States, or that the bike rider comes to know a country and its people better than any other kind of tourist can?

What I want to do in this paper is tell my classmates about my bicycle trip across Canada and how it changed my mind about Canadians.

Then it's to be a personal narrative with a point: the specific effect the experience had on you. In arriving at a full statement of purpose, you've reached decisions that will determine the shape your paper takes and the material it includes. Because you're writing for your classmates, you'll need to provide information about Canada that you wouldn't use if you were writing to friends you'd made on your travels there. Because you're emphasizing the change the experience made in your thinking, you have a criterion for choosing incidents to tell about from among the dozens of adventures you had along the way.

Every statement of purpose should identify not only your subject and what you're setting out to do with it but also your audience. That is, it should specify three elements of the rhetorical situation—subject, purpose, and audience. Sometimes, as in the first of the following statements of purpose, it will characterize the writer as well:

> As the best baker in town, I am going to tell all those interested in good health and good eating how to make better bread than is now available in either bakeries or supermarkets.

> In this paper, addressed to a friend who will be coming here next fall, I am going to give an account of the expenses that face an entering student during the first two weeks of the term, so that she will be better prepared to manage her money than I was.

> My purpose in this paper is to tell college teachers why the writing of entering freshmen often isn't as good as it should be.

Stating a Thesis

The last example introduces a special kind of statement. It strongly suggests that the writer is going to argue, that he intends to persuade his audience to accept a certain thesis, or proposition: "Some freshman write poorly because. . . ." For argumentative papers a statement of purpose called a *thesis statement* is often recommended. As a formal device, it must state the writer's fundamental point precisely:

> One reason some freshmen fail to meet college standards for written work is that high schools provide very little practice in writing.

"One reason" and "some freshmen" limit the writer's assertion. This is not going to be a shotgun attack, blaming poor teachers, crowded classrooms, an unruly student body, or a dozen other possible reasons for the failure of high schools to graduate young men and women who enter college with the ability to write well. The writer more or less promises that he won't drift off into a discussion of such other reasons. The one reason he will discuss is clearly stated: very little practice in writing. The writer commits himself to supporting this generalization with specific evidence. A well-phrased thesis statement, then, guides the writer in producing a paper that is unified by a single, definite idea.

Suppose the writer had limited his statement still further:

I lack the ability to meet college standards for written work because I was not taught to write in high school.

Here, certainly, is a clear, specific assertion. It fails as a thesis, however, because it's not really arguable. Unlike the assertion about "some freshmen," which the writer must work hard to persuade the reader to accept, this assertion is wholly personal. If the writer is telling the truth about his own experience, there's nothing to argue about.

A *because* statement may be a thesis statement, but only if the cause can be questioned. Otherwise, it's simply an explanation, and possibly—as in this case—too limited to build a paper on.

Statements of purpose and thesis statements are primarily for your own guidance, but including them above the title of your first few papers will give your instructor a sound basis for judging your success in doing what you set out to do. You're not likely to include a statement of your purpose in the body of the paper unless you write the kind of technical report that calls for such announcing. But you may very well include a statement of your thesis in an argumentative, or persuasive, paper. You may want to state your position at the very beginning, at the end of your opening, or as your conclusion. Or you may never state it in any single sentence but make it the theme of the entire paper.

Once you've phrased your statement, you're ready to settle on ways of carrying out your intention. Discovering specific things to say may call for reading and research and will certainly mean digging into your experience for details, ideas, and opinions.

All the while your mind has to be active. When you're reading and taking notes, keep asking yourself what function the notes can serve in achieving your purpose. When you're figuring out how to present and develop material, ask yourself what your readers will need in the way of illustration and definition. Don't just think *about* your topic. Think *through* it; make it yours.

For Writing

1. We've said that a statement of purpose should take into account at least three of the four elements in a rhetorical situation—audience, subject, and purpose. Supply the missing element in each of the following.

a. I am writing this to amuse my eleven-year-old sister.

b. I want to explain how to make a first-rate pizza.

c. As the chairman of the Young Republicans, I want to convince the Independents of something.

d. I want my classmates to share some feelings I once experienced.

e. I am writing my parents about switching my major from Physical Sciences to Theater Arts.

f. My purpose is to explore the differences between science fiction and fantasy.

2. Examine each of the following statements. Tell which ones would *not* qualify as thesis statements and why.

a. High-school mathematics was a pleasure.

b. Pocket calculators have made the study of mathematics unnecessary.

c. I find it inconvenient to have grocery stores closed on Sunday.

d. Keeping stores open on Sunday is wrong.

e. The government should dismantle nuclear power plants now in operation and should develop no further plants.

f. Nuclear power plants offer one way of easing the energy shortage.

A Reminder

What we're outlining in this section is a straightforward progression from planning to performing. But not everyone writes that way or can write well that way. Thinking through the topic may lead you to change your mind about your purpose. Writing the first draft of an argument may make you question your thesis. In either case, don't hesitate to back up and take a new route. The essential thing is that you end up writing what you really believe. You can't expect your readers to accept what you have to say if you're not fully convinced of it yourself.

For Writing

1. Your instructor may want you to turn in a proposal for a paper a week or so before the paper is due, for approval or for suggestions for change. Proposals for papers are especially useful in establishing purpose. Whether or not one is asked for, write up a proposal for your next paper, and answer most or all of these questions:

a. What is your subject? Why does it interest you?

b. What particular aspect of the subject do you intend to deal with? (You might tell what broader or narrower aspects of the subject you've rejected, and why. This information will help your instructor make suggestions if the topic you propose isn't satisfactory.)

c. Who is your audience? (A brief description may be useful.)

d. What do your readers know about the subject? What is their attitude toward it?

e. What is the chief purpose of your paper in relation to this audience? Do you want to increase their knowledge? Amuse them? Change their beliefs or attitudes? Make them do something?

f. What are the chief questions you'll ask about your subject in order to develop your paper?

g. How will your purpose influence your tone? Do you want to sound calm and reasonable or lighthearted or sarcastic or angry or what?

2. Choose three of the general subjects listed below and, using whatever technique you prefer—brainstorming, free writing, asking probing questions—narrow each of them to two topics, one for a short paper (400 words or so), the other for a longer one. Consult with your instructor, and write on the one topic you both think is best for you. Predict the thesis the topic would be most likely to lead to, and then try to come up with one that's more original. In a single sentence before the title, make a clear thesis statement or a statement of purpose.

going to college	draft legislation	family life
college courses	health foods	movies
television	finding a job	energy
comic strips	religious faith	science fiction
sex equality	exercise	prestige symbols
discount stores	senior citizens	responsibility

Commitment

Prewriting is a process of discovery—discovering how you view your subject, what meaning it has for you, what you want to say about it, and how you're going to go about saying it. From this it follows that a central requirement of prewriting is, in the words of Gordon Rohman and Albert Wlecke, an "absolute willingness to think one's own thought, feel one's own feeling." Only by becoming involved with the subject will you make it yours.

Making the subject yours doesn't mean that all your writing will be personal. It means that all your writing will be motivated by a kind of personal concern that we'll call the writer's commitment. It's a commitment—intellectual or emotional or both—that's developed during the prewriting stage, an awareness of how you relate both to your subject and to your prospective readers. Writing that lacks such commitment is very likely to be dull stuff, expressing only trite ideas and conventional attitudes. Writing backed up by such commitment will sound as though the writer means what he says. Whether the style is rough or smooth, what comes through is the voice of a living human being.

At times, both in college and later on, you'll have to do kinds of writing that make personal commitment difficult. But with enough effort in the prewriting stage, you can almost always find your way into the subject you're to write about. And the more you get into the subject, the more likely you are to get caught up in it. When that happens, writing becomes a way of learning.

Writing and Revising

Prewriting and writing overlap. Preparing a paper isn't a mechanical, linear process in which each operation is completed before the next one is begun. Instead, each activity continues as the project moves from one stage to another. Some of us prewrite well into the stage of putting sentences on paper.

Even so, once you begin to write, the question of what you want to say leads immediately into the question of how you're going to say it. You need to *reach* an audience, not just say what you mean but say it so that it will interest, inform, perhaps influence others.

Writing a First Draft

Find the way into your paper that suits you best. Will you begin by making a detailed plan for your paper, or will you let the plan develop as you go along? Some writers like to build an organizational framework before they have much to put into it. They start with a few phrases or sentences, arrange them in outline form (see pp. 169–70), and keep working until the outline includes all the main points they want to make in the order they want to make them. Only then do they settle down to writing. Others begin writing and look for an organizational pattern to emerge as they go along. Whatever procedure you follow, leave your mind open to any new possibilities for developing and organizing that the actual process of writing suggests to you.

Use an outline or not, as your instructor recommends, but above all get started. Instead of thinking up reasons and excuses for not getting on with the job, plunge in, and keep going. Don't waste time trying to dream up the perfect opening. Chances are that when you've finished the paper, you'll have a much better notion of what will make a good first paragraph.

Once you've started, stick with it long enough to write several pages— if possible, a complete draft. Writing done in one sitting is likely to have more unity, more consistency, more life than writing that's done in bits and pieces. As Kenneth Clark says, "If words come tumbling out it gives one's style an energy and a rhythm that cannot be achieved by deliberation, and one can enjoy the pleasures of polishing later."

Make your first draft a full one. If you're in doubt about some of your material, include it. When you've finished, you'll be in a better position to decide whether or not a particular passage is relevant. Make your paragraphs full-bodied, too, with plenty of details. In revising, it's easier to reduce an outsize paragraph than to fatten up an undernourished one.

Rewriting

Unless you're the most careful and skillful kind of writer, your first draft will be rough and uneven. A good many sentences will need rewriting, and some will need rethinking. Even if the paragraphs are more or less related to your purpose, they may show little relation to each other. But writing the first draft should have made your ideas clearer. It should also have given you some notion of the shape the paper ought to take and some idea of what needs to be done to produce a strong, unified essay. Possibly you need hard evidence to support your generalizations. Possibly you should build what's now a minor point into a major one. Certainly you should give attention to linking paragraphs to show the connection of ideas, rewriting sentences to make the thought come clear, finding words and images that will sharpen and freshen your meaning. (One of the main objectives of this text is to help you rework early drafts, and several chapters tell you how to go about it.)

As you rewrite, keep your mind open to new ideas. If the process of setting down your thoughts has made you realize that some of them contradict others or that some are plain foolish, it should also have generated sounder, more consistent ones. And keep your mind open to new ways of expressing your ideas. The biggest obstacle to improvement in writing is the notion that once a sentence is written, it's finished, fixed, frozen. Don't guard your first phrasing of an idea as if it's sacred. Take the attitude that anything you write can be improved—or thrown away.

Good writing is rewritten writing. Rework your papers—and the emphasis is on *work*—until you're satisfied that the content, organization, and style represent the best you can do with the subject in the time you have.

Revising and Editing

In the final stage of composition, get outside your paper. Look at it from the perspective of a critical reader. Try to be objective. Drop the role of author and turn yourself into an editor. That usually calls for letting a day or two pass before doing the last revision.

Taking a fresh look at what you've written may persuade you to make further substantial changes in content. A new idea may hit you. For the first time you may see that dropping paragraph 5 and combining paragraphs 4 and 6 will make the organization tighter and more economical. But if you've rewritten the paper enough to produce a version that satisfies you, most of the final editing will consist of revising sentences. Slash unnecessary phrases, the ones you wrote just to get your thinking started or just to fill up space. Pare and prune. Pack more meaning into fewer words. (Much more on this in Chapter Seven.)

As you give your paper this last revision, read it aloud once or twice. Your ear will catch some weaknesses that your eye has missed. You'll stumble over a shapeless sentence. You'll hear clichés and flabby phrases. Even errors in spelling and punctuation sometimes call attention to themselves if you're listening hard. Keep your dictionary open. Check anything you're not sure of.

Finally, type up a clean draft, following the manuscript form your instructor prescribes. Before submitting the paper, proofread it carefully and correct any typing errors.

A Checklist

Before you've established your own habits of composing and developed skill in sizing up the requirements of an assignment, you may find it helpful to have a list of steps to follow in producing a paper. Any division of the writing process into steps is bound to be somewhat artificial and arbitrary, but for most college writing you'll probably go through the stages summarized here. Depending on the method of composing that turns out to be best for you, prewriting may merge into writing as early as the first step or even as late as the fifth.

1. Focus on an assigned subject or on one of your own choosing and locate a specific, manageable topic.

2. Find things to say—from memory or reflection, or from reading or study—and sift and evaluate your material, moving all the while to an understanding of your purpose.

3. Phrase a tentative statement of purpose or thesis statement that acknowledges the rhetorical situation.

4. Organize the material, using an outline or some other method to map out the structure of your paper, and write a first draft.

5. Rewrite until the thought comes clear within a sound structure and until the style fits the rhetorical situation. (During this stage, be prepared to reconsider all the decisions you've made up to this point.)

6. Revise and edit the paper—deleting, adding, rewording to make the meaning clearer and the style smoother; correcting errors in spelling, grammar, and punctuation.

7. Prepare and proofread the manuscript—following prescribed form and correcting any errors made in typing.

About Style

When you write a first draft, you're normally so intent on getting your meaning straight that you may pay little attention to the form in which you express it. In revising, then, you need to work over your sentences carefully to make them say what you want them to say *in the way you want to say it.* So a good part of the process of writing consists of "the pleasures of polishing," revising not for meaning and not for correctness but for *style*—

your choice of words and your syntax, the ways you shape words, phrases, and clauses into sentences.

The basic rule for finding the right style is simple to state: Your style should be appropriate to the rhetorical situation. The informality appropriate in a newsy letter to a younger brother or sister is inappropriate in a letter applying for a scholarship grant. A term paper on the origins of mercantilism should be more formal than a review of a rock concert for the campus newspaper. Most college work neither permits total relaxation nor requires rigid formality. Stylistically, it belongs to that broad middle area represented by what we see regularly in current magazines and nonfiction books, including this one.

Later chapters will deal in some detail with matters of style. Here we'll merely sketch styles that can be called informal, formal, and general and point out some of their more obvious traits.

I. Informal

Once you get off campus, University City is no prize. Pretty horrible, actually. A big, sprawling nothing that could use a load of fresh paint and a lot of soap and water. I guess you could say the U runs this place like a big business runs a company town, but the difference is that here most of the population is just passing through. The kids are investing their time and their dough in their own futures, which will be spent somewhere else. So their main interest in U.C. is getting out of it. And that's the way the place looks.

II. Formal

Westend, a city of medium size in the northeastern corner of the state, differs from University City in a number of significant respects. Although each city is dominated by a single institution—the one industrial, the other educational—the two societies are quite unlike. The great majority of the residents of Westend are permanent; they hold steady jobs at Giant Electric Corporation; they own their own homes; and they look forward to eventual retirement in Westend or its environs. By contrast, the great majority of the residents of University City are temporary: they hold part-time jobs, if any; they rent their living quarters, whether dormitory rooms, apartments, or houses; and they depart as soon as they have received their degrees. These marked differences in the life-styles and attitudes of the populations are reflected in both the physical environment and the ambience of each city.

III. General

Westend, the city I grew up in, is a stable sort of a place compared to University City. Most of the people work in the Giant Electric plant. They start young, and they stick with it till they qualify for their pensions. Unlike University students, who keep their suitcases under their beds, Westenders put down roots. Residential neighborhoods in Westend give an impression of neatness and self-respect, while here off-campus housing is likely to be rundown and dirty.

The first passage might appear in a letter from a student to a hometown friend. Because both know Westend well, the writer can tell the reader a lot about University City by simply suggesting the comparison; there's no need to say what Westenders do instead of "pass through." The style is casual, with some of the flavor of easy talk. The word choice and phrasing—"actually," "dough," "kids," "no prize," "pretty horrible," "like a big business runs," and the abbreviation "U.C."—contribute to a dominant impression of informality. So does the generally loose-jointed syntax and particularly the fragmentary second and third sentences. The writer hasn't gone to any special effort. The reader will catch the tone of voice and get the drift of what's said, and that's enough.

In contrast, the second passage gives the impression that the writer has done a good deal of preliminary planning and then worked over the sentences carefully. The style is about as formal as undergraduate writing ever should be—suitable, perhaps, for a term paper in one of the social sciences. Word choice and phrasing—"eventual," "environs," "depart," "ambience," "a number of significant respects," "dominated by a single institution," "the one industrial, the other educational"—are characteristic of written rather than spoken English. The arrangement of words in the sentence—especially the placing of modifiers and the use of parallel structures—and even the punctuation marks all help point up logical relationships. The distance between writer and reader is much greater than in the informal passage. Although the audience of the second would probably know as much about University City as the audience of the first would know about Westend, the writer of the formal passage has taken no shortcuts. The contrast is balanced throughout.

In the third passage neither word choice nor phrasing nor sentence structure calls attention to itself. If we examine the vocabulary, we find it more precise than in the first passage ("stable," "residential neighborhoods," "neatness and self-respect"), less bookish than in the second ("sort of a place," "there's," "stick with it"). Similarly, the sentences are more carefully constructed than in the letter home, less obviously arranged than in the term paper. It's a kind of straightforward, readable style that we call general, a kind you'll find most useful in the writing you do both in and out of college.

In identifying styles as informal, formal, or general, we go by dominant impressions. In fact, general styles aren't sharply separate from the other two types. When writing in a general style, you can borrow the contractions of informal—*you'll, she's, can't,* and so on—and when you need them, you can take words from the scholarly vocabulary of formal. Thus a style can lean toward either formal or informal while remaining predominantly general. As a college student you'll have few occasions to write in an informal style, except in your diary or journal and in your personal correspondence. In term papers, research reports, and critical essays, you'll probably be expected to write toward the formal end of your range. In most of your writing, a general style will be appropriate.

In writing for college courses, students tend to be unnecessarily formal, often producing stilted, stuffy prose that has no particular relationship to subject or purpose, audience or writer. (They also frequently adopt a pretentious formal vocabulary for humorous writing.) A general style not only is more appropriate than formal but should come much more naturally. This isn't to say that writing good general English is easy. The many options a general style offers are an advantage only if you know how to choose among them. The chief thing to keep in mind is that the stylistic choices you make should fit the rhetorical situation—the interaction of your purpose, your subject, your audience, and yourself. Helping you make the right choices is one major purpose of this book.

For further discussion of informal, formal, and general English, see Chapter Eight.

For Discussion and Writing

1.   Here are three passages from papers written by students. Examine each to determine whether it is predominantly formal, general, or informal. Point out the characteristics of the writing that lead you to classify it as you do.

a. You wouldn't believe what a shy little girl I was. Back in kindergarten, I had a terrific crush on this little boy, Brucie Johnson, who was class president (yes, a president at five years old, my God). I used to play jump rope with my friend Mary, and whenever we jumped to the jingle that goes "I like coffee, I like tea, I love (name of heart's desire), and he loves me," I would always deliberately miss on the word "yes" when I got to the part where missing on the word "yes" or "no" would seal your fate forever, or so all little girls believed. Ah, what love does to even the most honest of hearts. Well, the one day Brucie wanted to sit at my table with me (we had little tables in kindergarten, not desks), what did I do but burst into tears. Here was my dream unfurling, and I blew it with hysterics.

b. Television is big business, and like all businesses it must make money. Programs are designed to garner points in the Nielson ratings. These points attract commercial sponsors, who provide the networks with the money needed to air the various television series. To sponsors interested in hawking their products to as many people as possible, a show with a large viewing audience is naturally most appealing. The people who watch the show are not just television viewers; they are potential buyers of Sanka, Cheerios, Crest, Right Guard, and Pepto-Bismol, all of which supposedly help Americans start each new day feeling great. Those series that accumulate the most ratings points eventually represent millions of dollars for both sponsors and networks.

c. Writing has always been a source of satisfaction to me. At various times in high school, I was first in my English classes; and the quiet exhilaration I experienced made me—in my own eyes—the equal of the illustrious athletic stars who enjoyed the adulation of the crowd. Self-expression through writing gave me momentary status, a feeling that was as rare as it was satisfying.

During my last term in high school, my interest in writing deepened but at the same time narrowed. The course I took in critical report writing discouraged, disconcerted, and disoriented me. Yet my teacher in English literature told me that I was more creative than my peers. I finally came to the conclusion that I was more skilled in composing poetry and fiction than in preparing papers that demanded analytical and argumentative skills. Coming to terms with my own limitations has made me even more determined to cultivate those talents I possess.

2. In a letter to a close friend who doesn't attend your college, describe a current campus fad. Then write an account of the same fad for a national magazine whose readers are mainly college graduates in their thirties, forties, and fifties. For each paper, consider what role you want to play. Are you writing as a participant in the fad or as an observer of it? Are you defending it, attacking it, or simply reporting it? The two papers should probably differ somewhat in content and should certainly differ in style.

2

Developing Papers: Description and Narration

In this chapter we will take a close look at the methods of developing papers that were introduced in Chapter One. But first we are going to discuss generalizations and particulars, the building blocks of all good writing.

Generalizations and Particulars

Looked at in one way, a piece of writing is a story or an explanation or an argument. Looked at in another way, it's a combination of general statements and particular statements.

Some statements can be immediately identified as generalizations ("Italians love music") and some as particulars ("The black-eyed peas were served with bits of bacon"). But the terms *generalizations* and *particulars* are relative: often we can tell which a statement is only in context. "The Olympic Games are ordinarily held every four years" would probably be a generalization in a paper that looked back on the last Olympic Games. It might be a particular in a paper that dealt with the history of amateur and professional sports.

In most writing, particulars—often in the form of examples and details—give support to generalizations, and generalizations give point to particulars. The following passage shows a typical interweaving:

[1] Every house has its own fragrance, or stench, depending. [2] My best friend's house always smelled of his mother's inevitable tuna casseroles and Toll House cookies. [3] My grandparents' home smelled of pine pillows, and cologne, and mildew, and ancestral foundation garments, and mothballs. [4] But our house was distinctive in that its aroma varied dramatically from room to room. [5] The living room smelled of Brasso and floor wax, the dining room of Lemon Pledge, the kitchen of Mr. Clean and bug spray, the bathrooms of Airwick and powdered cleanser. [6] Indeed, the only room in which there

remained some hint of human residence was my father's study, where Lysol could never quite obliterate the lingering overcast from his Burmese cheroots.— Andrew Ward, *Atlantic*

The first sentence is a generalization. (Think about it. Is it true?) That generalization is supported by the more particular statements in sentences 2 and 3. Sentence 4 is another generalization, this one not about "every house" but about "our house." That generalization is particularized by the many details in sentences 5 and 6.

For Writing

Write a six-sentence paragraph modeled on Ward's, with generalizations in the first and fourth sentences and supporting particulars in sentences 2 and 3, 5 and 6. Try to make your last sentence round out the paragraph, as Ward's does.

Choose anything you like for your opening generalization. Then make sure that your second generalization narrows the focus— "America" in the first, for example, and "California" in the second; or "walking" in the first and "walking city streets" in the second.

Generalizations

Generalizations perform many different functions. They may sum up a number of experiences: "Growing up black means growing up angry." They may bring out the meaning of a single experience: "Those first few days in the hospital taught me that there's a time when just surviving is enough." They may express an opinion or a judgment: "All in all, we would have been better off if we had never entered the competition"; "That is certainly the best of all Altman's movies"; "Much of the appeal of country songs is in the stories their lyrics tell."

Because generalizations show relationships, bring out meanings, and draw conclusions, you'll need them in papers that explain or evaluate. On one occasion you may spin an entire essay from the single generalization that's your thesis. On another, everything you write will build toward that generalization.

A dramatic generalization can pull the reader into a piece of writing as nothing else can. Irving Howe's claim for Richard Wright's first novel does just that: "The day *Native Son* appeared, American culture was changed forever." But don't let the urge to be dramatic tempt you into producing a journalistic opener like "Americans love violence" or "Our school totters on the brink of disaster" or "Marriage is obsolete" unless you can support your headline with convincing particulars. Unsupported generalizations are a major cause of weakness in any writing.

Examples

Citing a member of a group or class—using the Labrador retriever as a member of the class *retrievers,* or beets and carrots as members of the class *hardy vegetables,* or "Marriage is obsolete" as a member of the class *generalizations*—is the most common way of bringing in examples. But it's not the only way. The small-scale narratives called anecdotes can serve as examples: an account of an experience you had when you were five might illustrate, or lead to a generalization about, how impressionable children are. Comparisons can serve as examples: a comparison of social dancing in the 1940s and social dancing in the 1980s could support some generalizations about the two periods.

What turns an anecdote or a comparison into an example is its connection with a general statement. In the following passage the connection is made explicit by "a fair example" and "cited as evidence":

> Among the fans of astrology everyone has his or her favorite item of proof. John Dryden's melancholy reading of his newborn son's horoscope is a fair example. He predicted disasters at the ages of eight, twenty-three, and thirty-three. At eight the child was involved in an accident with a stag. At twenty-three he fell from a tower. He drowned at thirty-three.
>
> The amazing batting average of Nostradamus, who appears to have foretold the Great Fire of London, the French Revolution, and the rise of Russian power after World War II, is everywhere cited as evidence of the astrological imperative.—Linda Lewis, *Atlantic*

For example and *for instance* are the familiar introductory tags, and sometimes *include* serves the purpose, as in "Applications of microwave technology include cooking, communication, weaponry," but often no such signals are necessary:

> A possibly significant number of fine singers have had some American Indian blood (Mildred Bailey, Chuck Berry, Johnny Cash, Lena Horne, Waylon Jennings, Loretta Lynn, Johnnie Ray, Kay Starr, and Lee Wiley).—Henry Pleasants, *The Great American Popular Singers*

How many examples you need in a piece of writing depends on the rhetorical situation, especially on how familiar your audience is with your subject and how much authority you speak with. Provide too few examples and uninformed readers will be confused or unconvinced. Provide too many and informed readers will be bored and impatient. (This book presents a great many examples because it's addressed to an audience with widely varied backgrounds and interests.) The number you need depends also on the nature of the subject and the kind of examples it calls for. In the passage by Lewis, two striking examples are enough to support the opening generalization. In the excerpt from Pleasants, nine examples aren't excessive in supporting the generalization about the "possibly significant number," especially when the writer has chosen examples from jazz, rock, pop, and country music in order to make sure that almost any reader will recognize one or more of the names.

Sometimes examples do all the work of conveying a central idea or emotion. The many examples in the following paragraph, the first paragraph in a student's paper, give the reader a clear sense of what "that feeling" is, well before it's given its informal definition:

> I've had that feeling often. Too often. So often that I should have learned. It's the feeling I had at age eight when I called my favorite teacher a witch only to turn to see her standing there, within hearing distance, hearing. It's the feeling I experienced a few years later when, angry with my grandmother, I referred to her as a "fat old lady" just as she walked into the room. It's the feeling I had that same year when, eager to express my indifference, I called the boy I secretly admired "stupid" and "strange," not seeing him a few steps behind me, his hand outstretched to pull my hair. It's the same feeling I had at eighteen when, thrilled to work the few extra hours asked of me but not wanting to seem a workaholic to fellow employees, I complained bitterly and, disregarding the warning glances of my companions, continued to complain bitterly as the boss walked by. It's the feeling of wanting to bite your tongue, of sickness deep in your stomach, of momentary self-hatred, of "Oh, God! How could I have said such a stupid thing?" It's the dismay of wanting to apologize (and ultimately apologizing) while knowing that the person—out of self-respect, anger, hurt, or even hatred—may completely disregard your apology. I should have learned—but I haven't. And though the circumstances have altered as I've grown older, the feeling itself has never changed.

Examples that will be immediately familiar to your audience need only be mentioned: "Freestanding sculpture may be small enough to hold in one's hand or huge, *like the Statue of Liberty*." If your examples are unfamiliar or if you're using them to prove as well as to clarify, you'll want to explain them and support them with details. You would probably want to do that if you based a thesis about high-school education on your own experiences and the experiences of students you've talked with since coming to college.

In revising your papers, examine your generalizations to see if they need to be supported or clarified by examples. If they do, ask yourself whether it would be better to mention half a dozen instances or to develop one or two in some detail. Decide whether, in the particular rhetorical situation, the examples should lead up to the generalization or follow it. And make sure that the relevance of the examples to the generalization is immediately apparent.

Details

You're on the road to writing well if you make it possible for your readers to visualize what you write about and to experience the sounds, smells, sensations, and emotions you've experienced. You can do this if you use appropriate details: the *flashing blue lights* of the police cars, the *saw-toothed blade* of a knife, the *webbed toes* of the Labrador retriever, amplified enough *to make your nose bleed,* walking *arm-in-arm.*

Like examples, details can make your generalizations clear and convincing. And they can do more than anything else to give your writing individuality, immediacy, concreteness. During an actual experience sense impressions predominate. In telling about the experience, you should try to convey those impressions, not just the generalizations that come to mind later. Sensory details extend right through the generalization that concludes this brief description from a student's essay:

> Rat-gray clouds tumble over each other. Chattering sparrows string the wires between telephone poles, readying themselves for flight. The trees pulse and sway, turning the silver bottoms of their leaves against the wind. Winter is whistling her first warning.

Details are essential if your readers are to share your experiences and your feelings about those experiences. They're equally necessary when you're dealing with literary works and with abstract ideas. A review of a novel calls for details of plot, character, style. A discussion of the abstraction *virtue* might use as details the individual virtues honesty, kindness, generosity, and so on. Every subject has its details. Much of the art of writing consists in choosing the right details and making them do what you want them to do. These are matters we'll consider more fully in the next two sections.

For Writing and Discussion

1. Recall an experience you've had, and in two or three substantial paragraphs present it so that the reader will be able to relive it with you. Your purpose is not to tell a story with a beginning, middle, and end but to use sensory details to recreate a scene or recapture the feel of an experience.

Here's a procedure you might follow in preparing the paper. First, choose a scene or an incident from your experiences that, for one reason or another, appealed to your senses. It doesn't have to be dramatic; a particular meal or bus ride or day in the sun may be memorable. Second, decide how you feel about the experience. Third, relive it in your mind, jotting down as many details as you can recall. Try to draw on every one of your five senses. Fourth, select from your list the details that best recreate the feel of the experience, and arrange them so that they work together to give a unified impression. As you write, keep in mind that your aim is to *share* the experience, not just talk about it. Don't tell your readers how you felt; let your sensory details do that.

When you submit your paper, turn in your complete list of details with it.

2. For each of the following passages—the first two by students, the third by a professional—identify the main generalizations and explain why you think the writer's use of detail is or is not satisfactory. Have enough details been used to support the generalizations? Are they the right details?

a. At its best, factory work is merely depressing. The bleak surroundings, the harsh lighting, and the ceaseless din of machinery all combine to dull your senses and cloud your mind. You react like one of Pavlov's dogs, right on cue, to the bell that signals the two ten-minute breaks each day and the half-hour lunch break. It is easy to pick out new workers. They are the ones who prefer to finish the piece they are working on, even if they lose a minute of their break. As soon as the realization hits them that there will be two hundred more where that one came from, and two hundred more where those two hundred came from, from now until the day they quit, they no longer waste precious break time on work.

At its worst, factory work is maddening. You are a nonentity among nonentities; the only thing that makes you better than anyone else is the fact that you have worked there a few months and earn ten cents more an hour than the raw beginner. The mindless routine—endless hours, days, weeks of piece work—is enough to drive you crazy if you dwell on it. At first you look forward to moving up the line and learning the next task, but after a week you have perfected that one, too. Again you look for something new. But there are only so many tasks, and in a month you have learned and perfected them all. So what now? Now you live from hour to hour, from Monday to Saturday, and try not to look ahead.

b. My sister Linda likes to read. All day long she's stretched out on the brown leather sofa, a book in hand, a pillow tucked behind her back, a bowl of Wise potato chips and a glass of Pepsi on the coffee table. She's very particular about what she reads: she doesn't like great English poetry or American folklore or religious literature or historical novels or even *Redbook Magazine*. Along with her potato chips she devours Harlequin Romances. They are short and easy to read, and, most important, they do what the commercials promise they will: they take her into another world. The women in the books are thin and beautiful, they lead glamorous lives, and they are deeply in love. It's hard for Linda to believe that most of them are the same age she is—twenty-five. Once men found her exciting, too. But she was nineteen then. Now she's so fat she hates to take off her robe in the late afternoon and squeeze herself into her clothes. It's only when she's spent an hour putting on makeup that something like the pretty face of the nineteen-year-old reappears, the nineteen-year-old who thought life was going to be one unending Harlequin Romance.

c. I've always had a special liking for old men. Once when as a boy I saw some friends catch a fish and clean it without first killing it, I found myself thinking that an old man wouldn't do such a thing. I listened to the stories strangers told—old people who sat next to me on a bus—and recognized that their pride in what they said was not random boasting, that a man's life story summarizes plainly enough the stamina, concentration and energy he has had over the years, as well as his luck; loyalty, friendship, sanity, imagination—those old words too. Old men are usually joyful men at heart. Ulcers and hypertension have winnowed away the more fretful fellows to the peace of the grave. Old men are those who have bobbed to the surface in time of flood, who have smiled to themselves and let their hurts heal.—Edward Hoagland, *Walking the Dead Diamond River* (appeared originally in *The Village Voice*)

We turn now to methods of developing papers. As Chapter One suggested, your purpose in writing a paper and the chief method you use in developing your material are closely linked. If your purpose in writing is to argue that one book or movie or team or candidate is better than another, you will certainly need to compare the two. If, in cutting "Earning a Living" down to a manageable topic, you decide to tell how you became expert at waiting on tables, then you will be committed to outlining the duties and skills the job demands, and you'll find yourself using the method called division.

The methods you use in carrying out your purpose are central to the writing process in another way: they generate ideas and build content. When you compare and contrast, you immediately ask yourself how the things you're comparing resemble each other and how they differ. When you divide a subject, you break it down into specific parts and go on to discuss each part. Once you start thinking in terms of the methods of development, you can no longer say, "I've got nothing to write about."

In the rest of this chapter and in Chapter Three we'll examine in detail the chief ways of developing explanatory and persuasive papers—description and narration in Chapter Two; division, comparison and contrast, classification, analysis of causes and effects, and definition in Chapter Three. We take up the methods one by one so that we can more easily illustrate the special uses of each and its special problems. There will be times in your writing when you'll focus almost exclusively on one method, as, for instance, in answering an examination question like "Compare and contrast Harry S. Truman's 'Fair Deal' program with the 'New Deal' of Franklin D. Roosevelt." But most college papers of any length call for the use of methods in combination, supporting each other and working together in carrying out the writer's purpose.

Describing: Showing How It Looks

To describe—to show how something looks—observe your subject closely, and in your prewriting build up a store of particulars to draw on. Then, in writing your paper, select details from that store that will make your readers see what you want them to see.

Selecting Details

If your purpose is to picture an object or a place as any careful observer would see it, you'll choose details that supply specific information about size, shape, weight, color, and so on. If it's to have your audience experience the subject as you've experienced it—take *your* view of it—you'll either select different details, or you'll treat the same details differently, choosing modifying words and phrases that convey your mood or attitude or judgment. The objective "sunless day" of literal description could become a "dull sunless day" or a "depressingly sunless day" or a "cool sunless day" or a "sunless day that gave welcome relief from the scorching heat," depending on the way you reacted to it.

If you want your reader to share your impression of your brother, try to capture the features that are unique to *him,* not those that apply equally well to most of his friends. If you want to catch the special flavor of a particular incident or experience, don't bother with the details that apply to whole classes of people or places—the shrill voices of small children, the bustle of shopping centers—but concentrate on what makes the particular person or place distinctive. If, on the other hand, your purpose is to describe in order to define—to tell what a human being is, for example, or what a Sioux encampment was—present details that characterize all human beings, all Sioux encampments.

In choosing details, pay close attention to the rhetorical situation and be guided by your readers' probable knowledge of your subject. If you're describing your basset hound for an audience that doesn't know a basset from a beagle, begin by telling what bassets look like. If your audience already knows what bassets look like and how they act, concentrate on the characteristics that make your dog an individual among bassets.

The two passages that follow show how a writer's purpose governs selection of details:

> The strong electric light was merciless to William Joyce, whose appearance was a surprise to all of us who had not seen him before. His voice had suggested a large and flashy handsomeness. But he was a tiny little creature and, though not very ugly, was exhaustively so. His hair was mouse-coloured and grew thinly, particularly above his ears. His nose was joined to his face at an odd angle, and its bridge and its point and its nostrils were all separately misshapen. Above his small dark-blue eyes, which were hard and shiny, like peb-

bles, his eyebrows were thick and pale and irregular. His neck was long and his shoulders were long and sloping. His arms were very short and very thick, so that his sleeves were like little bolsters. His body looked flimsy yet coarse. There was nothing individual about him except a deep scar running across his right cheek from his ear to the corner of his mouth.—Rebecca West, *The Meaning of Treason*

The head should be large, the skull narrow and a good length, the peak very fully developed. The head should be free from any appearance of, or inclination to, cheek bumps. It is most perfect when it resembles the head of a Blood-hound, with heavy flews and forehead wrinkled to the eyes. The expression when sitting or when still should be very sad, full of reposeful dignity. The entire head should be covered with loose skin—so loose that when the hound brings his nose to the ground the skin over the head and cheeks should fall forward and wrinkle perceptibly.—Arthur Liebers and Dorothy Hardy, *How to Raise and Breed a Basset Hound*

The first of the two passages pictures William Joyce, the infamous "Lord Haw-Haw," as he appeared to a skilled observer at his trial for treason in 1945. The second describes the way the head of a basset should look to any competent observer if the hound is going to compete in dog shows. West wants the reader to see through her eyes the man who made propaganda broadcasts to Britain from Nazi Germany throughout World War II. Liebers and Hardy want the owners of bassets to be able to judge whether their dogs measure up to the standards for the breed. (They go on to present standards for the jaws, ears, eyes, and so on.) To achieve their different purposes, the writers use the same means—concrete details and comparison.

West's details give us the whole man: "a tiny little creature," "exhaustively" ugly, with a body that looked "flimsy but coarse," short, thick arms, a long neck, and long, sloping shoulders. But she concentrates on the head—the thin, "mouse-coloured" hair, the mixed-up nose, and the deep scar from mouth to ear that gives her subject his only individuality.

The basset's head has no individuality at all, for it's not the head of any particular basset but the head all well-bred bassets should have: large, with a long, narrow, peaked skull, free from cheek bumps, and covered with loose skin that's wrinkled above the eyes and hangs in heavy flews (or lips) around the mouth. The expression of the good basset should be "very sad."

Comparison helps do the job of describing in both passages. West's comparisons are with things, "like pebbles," "like little bolsters," making Joyce seem less than human. In the other passage the comparison is simply informative—"resembles the head of a Bloodhound."

As the passages show, generalizations do have a place in description. But when descriptions fail, it's often because the writer relies on generalizations to do the work that should be done by details—saying no more, for instance, than "The park is not old, but it is going to seed." When the same generalization is supported by the details that made it true for the writer, it becomes true for the reader as well. Here's the beginning of a newspaper story:

> The park is not old, but it is going slightly to seed. Grass pushes through the concrete in some places, there's graffiti on the handball courts and benches have boards missing. By the basketball court, some of the slats are broken on the bleachers, and the bolts of one of the baskets have been yanked loose, probably by a future pro practicing his sky-hook slam-dunk—Al Harvin, *New York Times*

For Writing and Discussion

1. For a close friend, recreate in a paragraph of 150–200 words a recent encounter you had with yourself in the bathroom mirror. Choose a specific occasion—just before an early class, after a very late party, before an exam, after changing your hair style or growing a mustache, before a vacation break, after a good night's sleep, before an important first date, in the midst of an attack of flu. Don't include this background in your paper. Your purpose is to make your reader understand what you saw and how you felt, not why you looked and felt as you did.

Here's one student's response to the assignment:

Bleak Beginning

At 7:05 the echo of the alarm still throbs dully in my ears. I grasp the cold, white porcelain of the sink and stare at the face in the mirror, which stares blankly back, mealy-white and blurred, vacant green wall behind. Straggly, broth-colored hair hangs down around the face in wisps and tangles. The eyes are puffed and half-closed, blinking, trying to focus. *Warm bed. Crawl back in, just for a minute.* The face stares indecisively. The distant thunder of trucks echoes, magnified, throbbing in my head, fading into the undercurrent of traffic. My tongue moves leaden in my stale, dry mouth; air whistles faintly through my clogged nose. *There's time. Go back just for a minute.* My whole body feels heavy, as if liquid cement had hardened in my veins overnight. *Too late to go back.* My hand gropes for the cold-water faucet.

2. Now write a paragraph on the Beautiful Face or the Handsome Face. Your aim is to describe a face that most Americans of your generation would consider beautiful or handsome. Though you may have a particular person in mind, concentrate on an ideal type rather than an individual.

3. Write two descriptions of the same thing, each for a different purpose. Example: Describe your desk or your bike. Make one account a "For Sale" paragraph to be posted on a bulletin board. Give particulars that will identify your desk or bike and tell a prospective buyer what he needs to know. Write the other account for a good friend. Describe the desk or bike in such a way that the friend will know how you feel about it. In the first passage your desk or bike is an object. In the second, make it a symbol—beat-up old friend, thing of beauty, comfort or curse, whatever.

4. Describe a place that has some special significance for you—the room you had when you were a child, the park you played in, the candy store you patronized, the church you attended, or the beach or pool you went to in the summer. Select and arrange the details so that the reader will see the place clearly and also understand why you feel about it as you do. So far as possible, make the details do the job of telling the reader how you feel. (To make sure you haven't relied too heavily on generalizations, read your first draft through, skipping all the general statements. If the details don't make you feel you're *there*—in the place you're describing—you need to replace some of your generalizations with particulars.)

In a note at the beginning of the paper, identify the reader you have in mind, preferably someone you want to share your feeling about the place, someone you can count on being a sympathetic audience.

Arranging Details

Once you've chosen your details, your next job is to arrange them so that readers will be able to see what you want them to see. In the description on p. 35 of the park that's going to seed, the writer first calls attention to the cracked concrete, the graffiti on the walls of the handball courts, and the broken benches—things a casual visitor would notice in just glancing around. Then he focuses on the basketball court, its bleachers and one of its baskets, because the subject of his article is the decline of one of the great launching pads for professional basketball stars.

In that description there's no need for the writer to establish a specific viewing point. But sometimes deciding where you are in relation to what you're describing will help you settle on a logical progression of details and keep the scale of the description right—the relation of large elements to small, of more important to less important. In describing the block you live on, you might imagine yourself standing across the street from your home and begin your description with the building on the corner to your left. In describing the statehouse, you could spot yourself at the foot of the steps leading to the front doors and arrange your details in vertical order, either from the steps upward or from the dome of the building downward.

If you change your viewing point—if, for example, you move inside the statehouse—make sure you don't lose or confuse your readers. In presenting what you saw and heard during a Sunday stroll in the park, you might keep a narrative thread running through your description:

> Coming out of my apartment building, I turned left and crossed the bridge into our city's largest park. . . . Enjoying the sunshine, I walked about a mile west through crowds of picnickers to the hill in the center of the park, always the scene of the liveliest action. . . . After an hour or so I moved to a bench near the bandstand at the foot of the hill and waited for the concert to start. . . .

But you can stay out of the picture entirely and still give your readers adequate guidance. In the following paper the student establishes the general location in the first sentence, gets us on the right road in the second, and brings us to the village store in the third. At the beginning of the third paragraph we move inside the store, and at the end of that paragraph we reach the table which is the heart of the store, as the store is the heart of the village.

A Village by the River

Among the rolling hills of Bucks County, settled in a valley formed and bordered by the Delaware River, lies the village of Lumberville. The main and practically only road follows the lazy rolling river and is lined on either side with venerable houses, intimate friends through their generations of owners.

Located along River Road, facing the river and the muddy canal that runs beside it, stands the general store, the social heart of the town. Through this building the entire town passes at one time or another: mothers picking up the mail, husbands grabbing an afternoon newspaper on their way home from work, and little children running over after school for a candy bar or a pack of gum. All day curious tourists, staying at one of the town's two country inns or picnicking for the day by the river, come in to admire the "charming old-fashioned store," buy themselves expensive treats to tickle their tastebuds, and try to pretend they belong in this little country town, far away from the noise of the city.

Inside the store the year seems temporarily lost. The worn wooden floor fits like a comfortable old pair of jeans, and the calendars on the walls show faded pictures of painted young women wearing dresses from the twenties. A big blue box on the shelf brags of "Zud Suds: the newest type of soap for modern wringing washers." In front of the old post office boxes stands an iron woodburning stove, and a big, square, marble-topped table to sit around and pass the time of day.

But the tourists rarely sit there. They're still outsiders in Lumberville. The table is reserved for the owner, with his bushy black beard and his jolly big

belly, and for his friends, who drop in for coffee and sandwiches or hot choc-
olate when it's cold, and for the fat tiger-cat that spends the day wandering
from friend to friend.

The general store has watched for over two hundred years as people came and
went and history went on around it. Yet those of us who have lived in Lumberville will always be a part of the store, as it will be part of us because our town
grew up around it.

In "A Village by the River" we always know where we are. In the
following paper we're never quite certain from one sentence to the next. We
start out somewhere in Queen Victoria Park, come close enough to "the
water" to see snowflakes melt, pull far back for a bird's-eye view of the
Niagara River, its division, and the two falls, move in to look at the bottom
halves of both, pull back again for a long shot of the gorge, and then zoom
in so close we can see the gulls' footprints in the snow.

The Frozen Falls

Although two and a half feet of snow already lie on the frozen ground of
Queen Victoria Park, the gray skies above the falls show no signs that the storm
will end soon. The temperature of the water, slightly warmer than the below-
zero air, causes the snowflakes to melt just as they touch its surface. Many ice
floes have been dislodged by the raging water from the banks of the thirty-six-
mile-long Niagara River, extending from Lake Erie to Lake Ontario. Some of
these floes plummet 160 feet over the crest of the Canadian Horseshoe Falls.
Other masses of ice travel around Goat Island and crash upon the ice and snow-
covered rocks 167 feet below the American Falls. Ice and snow encase the
lower halves of both falls and form many interesting shapes. Below the falls,
the snow-covered ice of the Niagara Gorge extends down the river nearly seven
miles. The fresh snow on this ice, which is said to be between six and eight
feet thick, remains undisturbed except for a few minute footprints of the species
of sea gull that makes its home among the crevices surrounding the magnificent
falls of Niagara.

For Discussion and Writing

1. Study the use of details in each of the following passages. Is the
writer's purpose to show you what he saw or to show you what any
careful (or perhaps expert) observer would see? In answering the
question, define as precisely as you can what the writer is describing
and the point of view from which he's describing it. Then go on to
analyze the kind of detail he uses to accomplish his purpose.

a. The distinctive features of the champion cavy (guinea pig) are its
large size, broad head, deep shoulders, and short, cobby body. In addition, the champion has a short, blunt Roman nose, unlike the slightly

pointed noses of its less successful competitors. Its pink eyes are large, bold, and well set in the sense that they appear to bulge out from their sockets when viewed from above. Just behind them, the cavy's naked ears droop evenly in the shape of rose petals. Behind its ears, the champion displays a prominent muscular hump that extends back over its shoulders. Beneath this hump, the cavy has short, stocky forelegs, ending in four-toed paws. Behind the hump, the cavy's back forms a gently decreasing crescent, extending to its well-rounded, meaty rump. The legs beneath its rump, ending in three-toed paws, are slightly longer than its forelegs and very muscular. Lastly, the champion cavy has no tail stubble.

b. Tuttle's San Francisco studio (he has branches in Los Angeles and Fresno) is situated next to the Greyhound bus station in a district of cheap hotels and racetrack touts. The visitor climbs a long flight of stairs to a brightly lit lobby, the walls of which are covered with numbered examples of Tuttle's tattoo designs, his "flash." Just off the lobby, behind a railing, is an area that has somewhat the feeling of a barber shop, with chairs, mirrors, a sterilizer for tattoo needles, and containers for black, red, green, yellow, and blue India ink. Most of the tattooing is done there, but two private rooms with padded benches are available for working on the less public parts of the body, and for extensive jobs which might take up to five hours at a crack. Pervading the entire studio is the sharp, aseptic smell of surgical soap.—George Leonard, *Atlantic*

c. Just then, I see a tall, powerfully built, khaki-colored young man in skintight shorts and nothing else, a leather belt wrapped around his waist like a bracelet, five or six necklaces around his neck, who has climbed a tree just behind the musicians. Holding one foot in the fork, he slowly stretches his other leg along the branch as he reaches up to the next branch and extends his arms along it until his entire body is stretched taut. Then he begins to flex and writhe to the beat, now and then extending one hand and moving it back and forth, like an exotic benediction. His eyes are as inward as the drummers'. His "dancing" is as dark and potent and on the edge. There is a hint of the jungle here as well as of the San Juan honky-tonks, a mixture of the primitive and the urban, of lust and fear.—Theodore Solotaroff, *New York Times Magazine*

d. For centuries Englishmen and others in temperate climates of Western Europe had been building their wooden houses (or houses with wooden frames) in a certain traditional manner. To insure strength and durability, the house was built on a sturdy frame of heavy timbers about a foot thick. These were held together by cutting down the end of one beam into a tongue ("tenon"), which was then fitted into a hole ("mortise") in the adjoining beam. When there was a pull on the joint, the pieces were held by a wooden peg fitted into an auger hole through the joined timbers. This kind of construction was generally supposed to be the only proper way to build a house. It also required a great deal of skill: shaping tongues and grooves, boring auger holes, making wooden pegs, and finally fitting all these neatly together required the tools and training of a carpenter.—Daniel J. Boorstin, *The Americans: The National Experience*

2. In a paragraph of about 150 words, write a description of an animal, of a shop or laboratory or studio, or of a person in action. Though the subject you choose and your purpose in describing it will certainly determine what details you use, your discussion of *a, b,* or *c* above should give you some ideas about how to organize your paragraph.

3. Describe two houses or apartments you know well—your family's home and the home of another, very different family. Select details that reflect the occupants' personalities, habits, tastes, interests, values. Address your descriptions to an audience that doesn't know either family. Don't *tell* what the occupants are like. If you've chosen the right details, readers will get a clear picture of them.

Dominant Impression

Sometimes the purpose of your description will be to present not a photograph of whatever you're describing but a sketch or cartoon that conveys the dominant impression. The writer of the paragraph about the rundown park made no attempt to cover the park in detail or to map out the relation of its parts. Instead of telling about everything he saw, he chose details that stressed its seediness and arranged them so that they focused the reader's attention on the neglected basketball court. As the following passage shows, precise details about appearance, habitat, habits, diet, and so forth can be coordinated with a writer's personal reactions ("most repulsive," "grotesque," "ridiculous-looking," "absurd," "somewhat crazy," "hard to tolerate") to support the dominant impression of physical ugliness and foolishness. The book, well illustrated with photographs, is written by an expert naturalist for an audience of general readers. From the section on warthogs:

> This, the most exaggerated of pigs, is probably the commonest species alive today and is known to anybody who has ever sat through a travelogue or almost any other film made about or in Africa. Of the most repulsive mien, this squat-bodied, half-naked creature with fragile-looking legs and enormous flattened head, from the sides of which grotesque warts protrude, is found all over Africa south of the Sahara and outside the closed-forests, except in the mountains of Abyssinia and in the Kalahari Desert. It is now also eliminated from the enclosed areas in the Union of South Africa and is rare in West Africa except along a narrow belt between the northern edge of the forests proper and the

southern edge of the deserts. It is not only a ridiculous-looking animal with a topknot of coarse hair and an absurd skinny tail with a small terminal brush that it holds straight up in the air when trotting over the open ground but it is also of somewhat crazy habits—at least to our way of thinking. It lives in large holes which it excavates itself but usually starting with an abandoned Aard-Vark's or other animal's retreat, and into this it backs when retiring to rest or to avoid the heat. Its immense tusks grow outwards, then upwards, and finally inwards over the muzzle and are used much as we use a hoe. Wart-Hogs put on a great show of courage and may carry through their threats but usually retreat, tails on high, with an air of insolence that is hard to tolerate. When they lose their nerve, which is very often, they also lose their wits and become quite hysterical and often run over each other in their eagerness to decamp.—Ivan T. Sanderson, *Living Mammals of the World*

For Discussion and Writing

1. In the following passage a student tells us something about the appearance and habits of his subject. Explain why you think he does or does not create a dominant impression of George.

George Ritchey is a soapmaker, carpenter, landscaper, plumber, horse doctor, beekeeper, butcher, bricklayer, bartender, tree surgeon, taxidermist, farmer, toolmaker, roofer, cook, salesman and inadvertent antique collector. He's seventy years old, shrunken by age to a stout six feet, 230 pounds. His big rounded belly fits the contours of the white, blue, or blue-and-white overalls he always wears—and which he gathers in a pile every other Sunday to stuff into an ancient electric wringer-style washing machine he keeps in the garage. He uses it as one leg of a makeshift work table topped by an old wooden door, which he has to clear off and take down when he does his laundry—or else find a tractor, chair, or roll of wire to use as a substitute leg. He heats the water in a fifty-gallon oil drum over a fire he builds in his driveway. In warm weather he dries his clothes in the sun. In winter he hangs them on a line above the wood-stove he keeps burning in the pantry.

George has a sort of hunt-and-peck attitude toward work. He doesn't actively advertise his skills, but enough people know about him to keep him as busy as he wants to be. He takes only the jobs that he wants. He can and will work on high scaffolds, but at his age he usually declines such jobs unless he wants to prove that he can do it, whether to himself, to a helper, or to a customer.

2. Write a description of a person or an animal in which precise physical details are coordinated with a personal reaction to produce a dominant impression.

Narrating: Telling What Happened

Narration and description occur together more often than not. As we said in the last section, you'll sometimes want to keep a narrative thread running through a description. And every narrative needs a healthy supply of descriptive details. Both narration and description appear in many papers that explain or analyze, and brief passages of both are common in persuasive and critical essays. An argument for improving a neighborhood may open with a description of its present condition. A movie review usually includes a summary of the plot.

Typically, the order of a narrative is chronological. You begin with what happens first and go on from there. That's the order you'd naturally use in telling about the development of an idea, a fashion or a fad, a theory in science, a movement in art or literature or politics, a strategy or technique in sports, a trend in television. You'll also use it in explaining how things work and how things grow and how to do things (how to play tennis, how to cook spaghetti, how to set up a particular experiment), where directions are combined with descriptions of equipment.

Pace

Though you'll normally follow chronological order in your narratives, you'll adjust actual time to suit your purpose. By summarizing one stage and treating another in detail, you can show readers what you regard as less important and more important; and you will perk up your readers' interest with the changes in pace.

If you're a good oral storyteller, you already have the knack of compressing here and stretching out there for dramatic purposes. If you're not a natural storyteller, you can still work on the proportions of the narratives you write when you're revising them. Look carefully at any narrative that goes along at an even pace from beginning to end. If it's an account of a process or the record of an experiment, balanced, comprehensive coverage may be exactly what you intend. Otherwise, you'll want to slow down actual time in some parts by telling about everything that took place and speed it up in others by condensing and generalizing.

Purpose

Purpose is central to the kind of narrative you write. If you want to recreate an event in which you took part—a mini-marathon, for example—you'll tell what you did and what you saw. You'll concentrate on actions and sensations. If you want to report the event so that readers will understand what happened and why and what came of it, you'll give reasons (to raise money for scholarships) and point out significance (college students, as represented by organizers and participants, are willing to contribute time and energy to help others). If you want to explain how to organize a mini-marathon for a good cause, you'll outline a procedure, telling not what happened at a particular race but what should always happen to make such an event a success.

The account that tells what you did and saw is personal narrative. The account that explains what happened is expository narrative. The special variety of expository narrative that tells how something is done is called a process paper. All three may be rooted in the same personal experience; but their purposes differ, and so will the approaches their writers use and the material they include.

Point of View

The technical term *point of view* refers to the writer's relation to the action. Physical point of view locates the writer in space and time. Psychological point of view has to do with the writer's attitude.

Physical Point of View

In a personal narrative you're likely to adopt a *restricted* point of view, reporting only what you could see and hear, and what you could hear about, while the event was taking place. As a reporter giving a comprehensive account of the same event, you might want to use an *unrestricted* point of view, so that you can jump from one incident to another ("Meanwhile, outside the building . . ."). You're then free to be wherever you want to be, both in space and in time ("Two days earlier . . .").

In a process paper the unrestricted point of view allows you to coordinate stages of the process that take place simultaneously: "During this time other members of the committee have been looking for sponsors among the local merchants." But for some processes you may adopt a restricted point of view, identifying yourself with the reader and going through the process with him step by step. In explaining a specific undertaking—making an omelet, changing a tire, setting up lab equipment—your paper will often be clearer and more interesting if you take up the steps in proper sequence, limiting each one to what a person performing the action could do at any one time.

The advantage of the restricted point of view is its realism: you are there, and the reader is there with you. Even when you're writing as an observer rather than a participant, you may want to swap the freedom of the unrestricted point of view for the realism of the restricted. But once you've adopted the restricted point of view, stick to it. Don't suddenly announce that at the very moment you were getting your second wind in the mini-marathon, or standing on the sidewalk taking notes, a big argument was going on over the exact location of the finish line. That argument can enter the narrative only when you first heard about it. If that wasn't until after the race, the argument probably shouldn't be mentioned at all.

The passage that follows is a rather showy example of the restricted point of view, consistently held. The narrator tells in chronological sequence what he heard and saw on a moonless night in the desert as he sat by a campfire. First two yellow lights appeared miles away on the horizon. Soon they illuminated "a swirling, humming cloud of dust." Then:

> The hum became a buzz, a grumble, then a roar; each light split, and now four lights crashed through the dust to reveal an off-white Chevy Blazer. Just when it seemed as if the Blazer was going to stampede through the campsite, the lights bent away and the truck slid to a stop, driver's door next to the fire. The lights flicked black; the hot engine creaked quiet; dust drifted down in the silence and settled over the campsite, on the men. A match was struck inside the Blazer to light a cigarette, and newborn shadows slipped around a felt cowboy hat. The face and body under the hat climbed out of the Blazer and stretched. Pearl shirt snaps glowed like polished mescal buttons, and a sterling silver belt buckle reflected so sharply it seemed to be a tiny window into the man's belly, where a campfire was burning. His filigreed blue cowboy boots had no cow dung on their pointy toes.
>
> The man took a sullen drag on his cigarette, tilted the gray Stetson off his forehead with the side of an index finger and said with a sudden grin, "Damn, I need a tequila."—Sam Moses, *Sports Illustrated*

Attitude

Psychological point of view indicates your attitude toward your subject, the role you've assumed. If you write as a participant, you may be so intensely involved that you pull the reader into the action with you. As a reporter, you may be quite unemotional and objective, but you can also be amused, or bored, or admiring, or disgusted. This applies whether you're reporting something you witnessed or something that took place in Vietnam or the Dakota Territory or czarist Russia or imperial Rome.

Traditionally, process papers stress exactness of observation and clarity of presentation, but that doesn't rule out a personal approach. Given the right rhetorical situation, you may choose to communicate your own curiosity about the subject or your enthusiasm or distaste for it.

As with physical point of view, attitude, once established, should be maintained. Don't make fun of a mini-marathon for two thirds of your paper and then expect readers to believe you when you express great admiration for the organizers and the runners in the final paragraphs. Don't switch back and forth between the invisible, all-knowing reporter of a happening and the "I" who took part in it.

In a process paper you can keep the reader at arm's length with the formal, impersonal "one" ("At this stage one must be careful not to . . ."). Or you can reduce the distance with the less formal "you" ("You would be wise at this point to . . ."). Or you can go arm-in-arm with "we" ("Now let's see if we can run through those steps again"). The rhetorical situation should determine the relationship. Once you've settled on the one you want, stay with it.

For Writing and Discussion

1. For a small group of close friends, write about an incident in your childhood—one that delighted or terrified you, embarrassed you or made you proud. Use the informal style appropriate for such an audience. Then, in another short paper, narrate the same incident in the third person. This time, adopt the role of an interested adult observer addressing general readers. Your style should be different, as well as your physical point of view and your attitude toward what happened.

2. Read the following paper.

A Moving Experience

First came the grand piano, an elegant ebony gleam, slung over the shoulders of two burly men in worn jeans with shirt-tails out and sleeves rolled up. The stares of neighborhood children were punctuated with "oohs" and "ahs." Next came a massive oak table with intricately carved feet, a chandelier of tinkling, sparkling baubles, ivory tables, and a French Provincial bedroom set. The workmen strained while the onlookers gazed in wonder, awe and even fear.

The locusts sang, the stray dogs nervously skittered by—the life in the village continued its slow pace despite this invasion. "Moving day" was extended into four days of sweating and swearing as the movers hauled each treasure past the barefoot children, past the stone gate posts, up the steps, and into the Victorian mansion. Each trip was a new joy to the curious eyes of the watchers.

Sarah was the bravest. She marched over to introduce herself, stammering to herself and finding the familiar sidewalk oddly treacherous, yet confident in all her eleven years. She was secure in her situation—her dog Spikey who didn't even mind being stuffed into ruffly doll dresses for a day, her twin sisters looking after her with eyes of trust and respect, and even the plank bed her father had slaved over "secretly" for many weekends and finally presented to her one Christmas morning.

Sarah's world was different from this confusion, but by gosh she was going to deal with it straight away and make something out of it all. Why shouldn't she—after all, she *was* the head postman's daughter and regular first baseman in the games the kids played after dinner in Pete's side yard, and had even learned how to spell "all-eg-ance" this year (well, almost). I saw her coming and considered my options. I could make a break for the house and hide among the excelsior and cartons until I had mustered sufficient confidence. My ten years had not as yet provided that ease of situation which my older brother had. I decided to stick it out, as much from lack of time to escape as any noble motive.

Now we were within speaking distance and Sarah's bare feet were drawing circles over and over in the loose, warm dust by the road. I opened my mouth to speak, but she was looking down at the time and blurted out:

"Jimmy and Todd and Lynnae all want me to ask, well, where you from an' if you like it here 'cause we'll be your friends if you want an' we know just 'bout everyone here 'cept crazy Mr. Lacy who only likes cats," to which I responded eloquently:

"Um, we're from Rockland County, near New York City. It's pretty here, and *quiet* . . . (pause) . . . um, I'm Kathy."

"My uncle, he lives in that big place, but we can't go 'cause it's filled of fast cars an' lights an' big squashed-together stores. People there must be funny . . . (long pause as the dust circles become smaller and deeper). Are you rich?"

Here was the root of the problem. Were we "too good" for the gang, or even "mean people" like Uncle Tom had told them about? Sarah and the others were wary, judging my reactions. It was all up to me; the pressure was on. I wanted to say the right thing so as not to drive away those potential friends with their curious ways. A thought came to me—cats. I had a cat, so maybe she'd like that. I made the move:

"I have a black cat that had a kitten with too many toes."

No response.

Acute panic was setting in. What if they didn't like me, if they wouldn't talk to me or said bad things about me in school? The introductory lines I had recited in the car for hours had vanished. Why couldn't Mom ever call me at a time like this? These thoughts were paramount in my mind. Both my immediate and future happiness seemed to hang on Sarah's reply. Yes, we were from different worlds, clouded by misconceptions transferred through parents and relatives. We could carry on these attitudes or, with youthful honesty, let down the barriers. At last, a cautious reply:

"Do you want to come with us an' sneak 'round the shed and see Lacy's yeller cat with diff'rent color eyes?"

We ran off together, starting a friendship which transcended furniture styles, grammatical structure, and even the supposedly insurmountable "class" difference.

a. What are your reactions to the paper? Do you understand and share the writer's experience? Does the conclusion seem to be justified?

b. Read what the author has to say about writing the paper.

Writer's Comment

I thought at first that I would write on the subject of discrimination. I found myself making a series of general statements about the basis on which some people discriminate against others (race, color, creed, ways of talking, dressing, eating) and the ways in which they discriminate (depriving people of their rights and keeping them from enjoying themselves).

Though I felt strongly about the subject, I did not find anything original to say on the topic. We had discussed all my points in social science class.

I decided to take a different approach. What group of people discriminates most, I wondered. Do the wealthy discriminate more against the poor than those of moderate income? Do doctors and lawyers discriminate more than plumbers and carpenters? Are the Archie Bunkers in our society the worst discriminators? I couldn't decide.

This was another dead end. I wrote a page or two, taking the position that all of us, consciously or not, discriminate to some extent, but I was not satisfied with it. In my experience, children can find ways to leap over the barrier of discrimination. That was when I decided to write on this subject. The biggest problem I had was with point of view.

What I wanted to do was write about an experience I had when I was ten. But I did not want to restrict myself to how I felt and what I knew at that time. In writing the paper I found it difficult to isolate the thoughts of that early time for my memories were no doubt influenced by my adult perception of how important this moment was in my experience of growing up in a mixed neighborhood.

I have tried to solve the problem by keeping myself out of the picture until the scene has been set. The first two paragraphs give outside observations on the situation on moving day. (I have to say here that I was thrilled when I hit on my title.) In the third paragraph I told about Sarah, giving information about her that I couldn't have known at that time. In paragraph 4 *I* come in with the feelings I had at the time, though those feelings are interpreted from my adult point of view: "as much from lack of time to escape as any noble motive." Then for a space it's just kids talking.

Sarah's question, "Are you rich?" gives me the chance to indicate how important I knew that question was. She was used to the rich discriminating against the poor. If I admitted that my family was rich (we were by comparison with hers, as my first two paragraphs were supposed to show), she would not be my friend.

I hoped the rest of the paper would speak for itself. Sarah and I could leap over the barrier. I didn't know whether to include the last paragraph or not. I finally decided to, even if I'm being obvious.

c. Write the author an evaluation of her work in which you comment on her handling of point of view.

d. Rewrite the paper from a strictly limited point of view, either that of the "I" or that of Sarah, and evaluate the result. Is it better or worse than the original?

Personal Narrative

When you write a personal narrative, you should try to earn a response that fits the nature of the event you tell about. The incident will go dead unless you use enough detail to give the reader the sense of being there. Here a student remembers her first rock concert.

First Love

On February 18, 1973, I experienced my first rock concert. Two hours before show time I met my sister Jane in front of the Tower Theater. My oldest sister, Rosemary, and her husband Cutt had invited us to see David Bowie that afternoon. Rose and Cutt were working backstage.

Cutt rushed Jane and me through the door, past groupies and fans. Their stares inflated my ego, as if I, at thirteen, were important and belonged there. Cutt led us past the candy counter and up the stairway to the balcony. Sitting down with our binoculars, we discovered that the laughter we had heard was not from stagehands. We were alone with David Bowie and the Spiders from Mars, his backup band.

Th-th-th-there he was, in ripped blue jeans, a chrome-green fez perched on his blood-red, Lucille Ball-style, hennaed hair. He looked up and smiled, and the band continued with their sound check. It was here, in the empty Tower Theater, that I first knew love. This was no cliché crush. David Bowie, as I knew him then, was the bisexual King of Glitter Rock, Ziggy Stardust.

Cutt woke me from my daze with an elbowrib and told us that, for the show, we'd have different seats. We followed him—down the stairs, past the candy counter, center-back, center floor, front-center, and into the unmarked seats in the orchestra pit! The very front row. As Cutt handed us cotton balls to protect our ear drums, the audience paraded in. Men? Women? Androgynies? Satin, glitter, theatrical makeup, eight-inch platforms—laughing in their tinseled beauty, eager to see their tortured femme fatale, their dancing sprite, their hero.

Jane elbowribbed me and said the party was just beginning. The Tower, with its art-deco draperies and gilded walls, gave the illusion of a Grand Ballroom. Under the hundred-foot, light-blue ceiling with its star-shaped pinpoint lights, I was in heaven.

The lights went out. Black. Cold. The crowd hushed with anticipation. Then, booming from the speakers, came a synthesized version of Beethoven's "Ode to Joy," the theme from *A Clockwork Orange* (a futuristic tale of rape and madness). I was crushed between screaming David look-alikes and stage guards, frightened and excited to the point of laughing or throwing up or . . . A strobe light began flashing; the band was on stage. David, in a space-age costume with three-foot-wide hooped legs, zoomed across the floor and sang. What an understatement for the mesmerizing magic of Ziggy Stardust!

His voice was that of birds and that of despair and that of youth. His body, alive with animal grace, rolled like a rocker's who was trained as a mime. His face, one eye grey, the other blue, with the bone structure of Katherine Hepburn, was delicately made up. He was talented, versatile, and beautiful. To me, he was divine.

My god offered me his hand, but I held back, entranced, while another devotee quickly reached out for his blessing.

Soon the divine one and his angels departed, leaving behind the old faithfuls and the new converts. The lights came on. Cotton was pulled from my ringing ears. I vaguely remember Cutt asking me, "What do you think? Not bad for your first concert, huh?" I didn't answer. Janie winked.

The writer of the next paper also draws the reader into the experience but makes him share, not star-struck excitement, but acute suffering. Again, the physical point of view is consistently restricted. Note the jump in time in the second last paragraph: "I passed out. Four hours later I came to. . . ."

Down, Down, or The St. Valentine's Day Massacre

I remember it vividly. What time I awoke, my breakfast, new high-top sneakers, straight gray-wool cuffed pants, reversible madras belt, and gray sweatshirt. February 14th, St. Valentine's Day, 1975. I was twelve and into basketball. I played in the school league, the church league, the Y league. No big deal, I just liked to play.

This particular day was a big one. Right after school was our big game—the Clippers versus the Bears for the Cochran School first-half championship. When I excused myself from the homeroom Valentine's party, Mr. Washburn yelled, "Hurry back for refreshments!"

As the homeroom door swung shut, I faked left, double-dribbled right down the empty corridor toward the men's room. My new sneaks squeaked on the shiny waxed floor as I imitated Walt Frazier. Whenever I was alone, it seemed, I was always fake dribbling, shooting, or slam dunking. It was only natural. I played every day, and I wanted to be great.

I dribbled into the boys' room, completed my duties, and turned to leave. Between the urinals and the door was a metal partition intended to block the view into the room. As I walked around the partition, I leaped to slam-dunk over the horizontal supporting rod that ran from the end of the partition to the adjacent wall. I went up, but I didn't come all the way down. For some reason the top of the rod was adorned with sharp, triangular teeth, and the Boy Scout ring on my middle finger caught on one of them.

I hung by my middle finger four long inches from the floor. Flesh split, slowly at first. I struggled to grab the rod with my left hand, but this put more and more strain on my finger. Veins were cut, and blood ran down my arm and over my face, chest, and legs, spotting my new sneakers. Tendons, once tight to the bone, now snapped, springing back in shiny curls. Again I struggled to get my left hand to the bar. If I could grab it, I could pull myself up and release my finger. I swayed back and forth. One final try. I jerked up with my left hand.

A loud snap echoed in the lonely lavatory. I landed on my butt in a pool of blood, looking up at my middle finger. How long had I hung there? I hung till I broke. That is all I know.

I got up, kicked the door open, and rushed to my homeroom, minus half my finger. When I swung the door open, Mr. Washburn cried, "My God!" Thirty twelve-year-olds screamed in horror. Mr. Washburn rushed me toward the principal's office. As we passed the boys' room, I yelled, "Get my finger!" Mr. Washburn disappeared through the door.

I passed out. Four hours later I came to in the recovery room at the hospital. My right arm was in traction, in a heavy cast to the elbow. My finger had been sewed back on and equipped with a plastic knuckle. Recovery took a year and a half, extended by a number of minor operations for nerve damage and skin grafts.

At twelve I knew I was lucky that things turned out as they did, but now I'm even more grateful. I'm involved in music, and I can play the banjo and flatpick a guitar. My finger bends—a miracle in itself.

A personal narrative should make a point. Building that point into your statement of purpose will give direction to your planning and writing. Choose your descriptive details so that they help make clear to your readers the *significance* of what you write about.

You can, of course, spell out the meaning the experience had for you, but if you do, be careful not to claim too much. While "My First Date" should have enough point to be worth writing, no reader will expect it to have more than modest personal significance. And few readers will put up with such lofty moralizing as "That experience taught me a lesson I've never forgotten: Hard work is the straightest road to self-respect."

To avoid sounding preachy, you can work at selecting details that will lead readers to recognize the meaning of the incident for themselves. But one way or another, directly or indirectly, a narrative should carry its own meaning. Whether it's clear to you in the prewriting stage or becomes clear to you only as you write the paper, you should have it firmly in mind as you revise. Weed out incidents and details that blur the impression you want to get across. Keep only those that sharpen the impression. The more superfluous, distracting details you can get rid of, the greater the impact your narrative will have.

For Writing

1. Write an account of an incident that taught you something about an issue or situation or problem you had only heard of: crime in the streets, male (or female) chauvinism, the difference between a public face and a private face. Though the lesson you learned should be clear in your mind, don't spell it out for your readers. Let the narrative tell it for you.

To test your ability to get a point across without preaching, write in a sentence or two just what the point of your paper is. Have a classmate read the paper and write down his impression of what the significance of the incident was. Then compare his interpretation with the meaning you intended.

2. Our lives are often marked by moments of recognition, moments when for the first time we see a person or a situation as it really is. We realize we'll never be famous, or we become aware that a particular acquaintance is someone we can always count on, or we face the fact that when we go home again, things won't be the same. If you've had such an experience, write an account of the incident.

The Process Paper

Process papers are expository narratives that explain how to do something (bake bread, make a hook shot, chair a meeting) or how something works (a combination lock, an antibiotic, a state legislature). In how-to-do-it papers your job is to present the process so clearly and completely that your readers will be able to perform it. Clarity and completeness call for a chronological ordering of *all* the steps in the process, sometimes with warnings against *mis*steps: "Don't touch the wires at this point or you will electrocute yourself." Being clear also means adjusting vocabulary and coverage to the audience. For a reader who doesn't know what a jack or a lug wrench is, you'll have to define more terms and explain steps in much greater detail than for a reader who knows what's in the trunk of his car.

Making the account complete means leaving out nothing that's essential to performance of the operation. So if you're asked to write a process paper, don't choose a process so complicated that you can't cover it adequately in the space allotted. You can't tell anyone how to play tennis in five hundred words, though you may be able to help your readers improve their lobs. (But don't choose a topic that's too simple. Instructions on how to boil an egg belong in a cookbook, not in a college paper.)

If how-to instructions are to be included in a driver's manual or a cookbook or some similar publication, reader interest is no problem. Only people who want to be instructed will seek them out. But with some how-to material and in much other instructional writing, the writer must arouse and sustain the interest of his audience. Clarity will still be the primary goal: make sure you don't baffle readers by using undefined technical terms or confuse them by failing to explain how to get from Step 3 to Step 4. But you'll also need to persuade them that your subject is worth reading about. The best way to do that is to choose a topic that interests you and to have a reason for writing about it.

The good process paper conveys an attitude toward the subject. If you're showing your readers how to do something, the impression you want to convey should be built into your statement of purpose. It might be on the order of "This looks hard, but it's really quite easy" or "Most people think this is simple, but to do it well takes time, skill, and patience" or "Making this will give you a real sense of accomplishment." If you're explaining how something works, the impression you convey might be "Knowing how this works is useful; it could get you out of a tight spot some day."

A paper telling how to shape glass tubing begins with a reason for learning the skill:

> Many failures in chemistry experiments can be avoided simply by using glass tubing that has been properly made. Glass tubing with minute cracks or constricted bends can lead to large quantitative errors in the results of the experiments. To make your own tubing, the only materials required are a glass scorer, a Bunsen burner with a flame spreader, $3/8''$ glass tubing, and an asbestos square. With these materials, you can cut, fire polish, and bend all the glass you will need in about a half hour.

In explaining why the glass must be bent in precisely the right way, the final paragraph echoes the first:

> Although bending glass properly is not a difficult art to master, there are some pitfalls to avoid. If you don't keep the glass in the fire long enough, it will bend only a little. If you keep it in the fire too long, the bend will be looped. If you bend the glass, pause for a fraction of a second to see if it is the desired angle, and then attempt to finish the job, a skewed bend will result. An imperfect bend is weak and can crack under gaseous pressure, leading to gross errors in the experiment.

Thoughtful awareness of the needs and interests of the audience will show up in the body of a good process paper, too. For one thing, the sequence of steps will be made clear by indicators of time: *then, later, next, meanwhile*. For another, reasons for doing something will be supplied by indicators of cause-and-effect relationships: *because, therefore, as a result*. "Telling why" makes "telling what" purposeful. This passage tells anyone shopping for a used car why he should make a careful check of the body:

> Look over the outside of the car—the appearance can tell you a lot about how the previous owner has cared for the car and can also give you warning of trouble to come. Look for unmatching paint; the car was probably in an accident if a section has been repainted. A totally repainted car with paint on chrome moldings and rubber sealing strips may indicate that something had to be covered up. Another tip-off to major body repair is a fresh weld which shows up in the engine compartment, or trunk, or underneath the car. If the car is in a garage, take it outside where the light is better. Sight along the sides of the car to look for uneven places that may mean body work, a result of previous accidents. See that the doors, hood, and trunk open and close properly and fit well. If they do not, the problem could be a bent frame or body. If you or a mechanic conclude that the car has been in a major accident, turn it down at once.— A. M. Pettis, *Basic Car Care*

In the brief how-to paper that follows, the student-author addresses the reader directly, telling the circumstances in which the technique is used and explaining the principle that makes the technique work. With this preparation the reader understands why he does what he does when he executes the maneuver.

The Heimlich Maneuver

Imagine that you're eating in a restaurant and suddenly hear someone at a nearby table gasping loud and hard. He is conscious but cannot speak. His friends are slapping him on the back, but the man continues to gasp. You realize that he is choking on something he was eating. Unless the obstacle is removed, he will die within minutes from lack of oxygen. What can you do?

The answer is to use the Heimlich Maneuver, a technique devised by Dr. Henry J. Heimlich, director of surgery at Jewish Hospital, Cincinnati, Ohio. This technique has proven most effective in forcing large bites of food from the windpipe.

Choking occurs when food is sucked into the windpipe instead of being swallowed. Usually the gag reflex makes a person cough out the food before it becomes lodged, but sometimes—particularly when alcohol has dulled the gag reflex—the big bite of meat or other food "sticks in the throat." Because this can occur only during inhalation, there is normally a small amount of air in the victim's lungs. The principle of the Heimlich Maneuver is that of a piston action—to compress the air out of the lungs with a force that will also propel the food up and out of the mouth.

Stand behind the victim, and instruct him to lean forward, bending at the waist and letting his upper body, arms, and head hang down. Then wrap you arms around him just below his rib cage. (If the arms are wrapped around the rib cage, broken ribs may result.) Make a fist with one hand and grasp it with your other hand. Then exert a sudden, strong, upward pressure, repeating it if necessary. This pressure on the victim's abdomen should force the diaphragm upward, compress the lungs, and cause the air expelled from the lungs to dislodge the chunk of food stuck in the windpipe.

In writing about a process, consider your options. Are you going to use the active voice and tell your audience what to do (a likely choice when you're teaching a skill), or are you going to use the passive voice (a more natural choice when the operation is performed by work crews and machines)? Are you yourself doing the job, perhaps with an assistant? Then use *I* or *we*. As "The Heimlich Maneuver" shows, shifts can be made from an impersonal account (paragraph 3) to a personal one (paragraph 4), but they should be sensible and should coincide with shifts in point of view.

Whatever the point of view, you'll normally use the present tense in giving an account of a process. Unlike pure narrative, which tells what *did* happen ("Once upon a time . . ."), the process paper tells what always happens and always will happen under a given set of circumstances ("Whenever the temperature drops below freezing . . ."). Using the present tense, then, makes good sense, unless you're describing a process that's specifically rooted in the past: "We used to begin our tree-trimming three days before Christmas, when we would bring the boxes of ornaments down from the attic."

For Writing

1. Write a paper explaining how to perform a simple everyday act— putting on a coat, tying a shoe, opening a door and entering a room, shaking hands. Exchange papers with a classmate who has explained a different act. Taking turns, each of you follow the other's instructions precisely, doing everything you're told to do but nothing more. If the instructions don't work, rewrite them so that they accomplish their purpose.

2. Get permission to go behind the scenes in a local restaurant, garage, laboratory, TV repair shop, or fire station, and watch an expert perform a particular job—the chef make a salad, for example. For readers who have never been there, tell what you've observed.

3. In 700–800 words write an account of a process that you consider worth knowing about. It can be a set of instructions (how to upholster a chair, how to play stickball, how to execute a Queen's gambit in chess) or an explanation of how something is done or how it works (how an auction is conducted, how a pinball machine works, how horses are trained to jump, how gypsy moths defoliate a forest). Your statement of purpose, separate from your paper, might indicate how you've acquired your special knowledge of the subject, and it should indicate how much the audience you're addressing knows about it.

4. Certain weaknesses turn up regularly in process papers—dangling modifiers, uncalled-for shifts in pronouns (from "I" to "one" for example), use of the passive voice when the active would be better, lack of connection between sentences, and wordiness. Rewrite each of the following passages from students' papers to correct errors and improve clarity.

> **a.** The injection can be given at a number of sites on the horse: the neck, shoulder, hindquarters and the rump. In this technique, the neck should be used. When giving an injection in the neck, it is important to ensure that the injection is made into the muscle and not between the muscles. To find the correct spot, stand facing the rear of the horse at its head and move to the left side of the neck. Place a hand on the top of the neck above the point of the shoulder blade. Measure about one-third of the way down the neck, from the line of the mane, going toward

the chest. Now feel for the softest area. That is all muscle. That is the place you want.

b. Yawning, you go into the freezer to make an inventory of the number of pies on hand and to bring out a thirty-pound can of frozen egg yolks and a ten-pound can of whites, the yolks for cream pie filling and the whites for meringue. You are in the freezer for ten minutes without any gloves or coat. The experience strengthens and sets your sleepy body for the struggles to come. Thawing your hands the phone will ring and it will be the old man because he wants to know how his pie shop is at eight o'clock in the morning. He will be in at thirteen hundred because he used to be in the army.

c. Batting is relatively easy to take in basic steps. If you are right-handed you stand to the left side of the plate and if you are left-handed you stand to the right side of the plate. There is no prescribed way to choose a bat. I suggest that you select one that is easy to swing and comes to about your hip. While at the plate, spread your legs about shoulder length apart and stand about six inches away and parallel to home plate. Grip the bat as if you were going to shake hands, except wrap your thumb around, so it overlaps your other fingers. Always keep your hands together! To swing, bring your back arm up and back and bend your arm at a forty-five degree angle. Your front arm should be relaxed and relatively straight. While the swinging motion takes place, your weight should be transferred from your back foot to your front foot. The bat should be brought across in an even swing, wrapping itself around the body.

d. Another thing to be considered when collecting firewood is the kind of wood which is needed (birch, oak, etc.). For quick fires to boil use pines, spruces, red maple, basswood, or alder. For lasting fires and good grilling coals, use hickory, the oaks, birch, sugar maple, white ash, beech, or locust. At this point I have a couple of tips to offer concerning firewood collection. If the wood is lying on the ground, it may be partially rotted and therefore undesirable. To test it bend the wood between your hands until it breaks. Good wood will snap and leave a jagged break. Partially rotted wood will break straight across. Another suggestion is that before starting a fire collect enough wood so that it will not be necessary to collect more during meal preparation or during the evening campfire.

e. The most important parts of the ski are the parts that are in contact with the snow. These parts are the bottoms and the edges of your skis. A ski is fabricated in layers starting at the bottom, and adding sheets of varied materials until you reach the final top covering.

3

Dividing, Comparing, Classifying, Analyzing Causes, Defining

In this chapter we'll discuss separately the five other methods of developing a subject that we introduced in Chapter One. Again we remind you that these methods work together; we focus on them one at a time to keep the discussion simple and clear.

Dividing: Finding the Parts

When your purpose is to explain or explore a subject, consider the method called division, or analysis. In dividing, you focus on the *parts* of your subject.

In prewriting your account of a process, you almost certainly thought of the skill or activity as a series of steps, one following another. That is, you divided the process into stages. But division isn't limited to physical processes or chronological sequences. You can divide an object (a computer, a shark). You can divide an institution (a social club, a corporation, a government). You can even divide an abstraction, like courage or capitalism, which doesn't have parts in the sense that an object or an institution does. In such cases, the dividing isn't the result of observing or examining the subject physically; it's a matter of analyzing the subject in your own mind to identify the elements—personal or economic—that are essential to what we call courage or capitalism. Division is also called for by examination questions like this one: "What were the major steps in the process whereby the United States became involved in the affairs of the Pacific area and the Far East from 1899 to 1931?" To answer it you would need to know not only the events of the period but the significant shifts in American policy.

Purpose in Dividing

For a great many subjects—automobiles, human bodies, governments, countries, plays, leagues, and so on—at least one ready-made principle of division suggests itself: mechanical, physical, political, and so on. Automobiles can be divided into their mechanical parts, human bodies into their physical parts. The marching bands that we see performing at sports events can be divided on the basis of the instruments that are played.

Although one principle of division may seem the obvious one, almost any subject can be divided in several different ways, each the result of applying a different principle of division. The choice of a principle depends on the purpose of the person making the division.

The author of a textbook divides his manuscript into chapters and then divides and subdivides the chapters with headings and subheadings. His primary purpose is to present what he has to say so that readers can understand it and learn from it. (Reduced to outline form, the author's division appears as the table of contents, which shows the user what the book contains and where to find it.) For the editor who works out the allotment of pages while the book is being produced, the significant divisions may be front matter (title page, table of contents, and so on), text (the chapters), and end matter (the index, for example). And for the person who estimated the manufacturing budget in the planning stage, the primary purpose was a breakdown, or division, into costs of paper, printing, and binding.

The author's principle is pedagogical—educational. The editor's is physical. The estimator's is financial. When you make an analysis, find a principle of division that reflects your interest in the subject and your purpose in exploring it.

In the article from which the following passage was taken, the author's chief purpose is to examine "the current boom in things parascientific"— certain movies, TV shows, and books. But first he must mark off the area in which, in his opinion, "things parascientific" belong. Concentric circles offer an imaginative way of representing three elements (or parts) of "the situation in science" and showing the status of each:

> One can visualize the situation in science in terms of concentric circles. At the *center* is that body of time-tested, universally accepted ideas that are set forth in school and college texts. The first circle out from the center is the *frontier*, which interacts constantly with the center, feeding it new ideas that the center, after lengthy testing, adopts and assimilates.
>
> If we move beyond the frontier region of a science, however, we come to a hazy outer circle area that I like to call the *fringe*. The fringe is characterized by a scarcity of hard data and by a general fuzziness of ideas that make the average scientist very uncomfortable. It is a zone in which neither accepted scientific writ nor reasonable extrapolations of scientific knowledge seem to apply. For these reasons, it is an area that scientists generally prefer to avoid.
>
> Yet the fringe has its uses, for it feeds ideas to the frontier, much as the frontier feeds ideas to the center. Fifty years ago, the notion that we should attempt to communicate with extraterrestrial intelligences would most emphatically have been a fringe concept. Yet today this idea has moved into the more respectable frontier circle. (Incidentally, this move illustrates an important point about the ideas contained within both the fringe and the frontier: The soundest,

most useful of them keep gravitating inward, ring by ring, toward the orthodox center.)

. . . .

There have of course been thousands of fringe ideas that never made it to the frontier and thousands of frontier ideas that never gained centrist respectability. The basic problems, then, that anyone, scientist or layman, faces when confronted with a new theory are how to decide where it belongs on the concentric-circle scale and how to determine its chances of eventual acceptance.—James S. Trefil, *Saturday Review*

Dividing singles out the topic Trefil wants to investigate; it gives him a context in which to proceed:

With this framework in mind, let's look at some current offbeat theories and the problems they pose for the citizen who is wondering whether to accept or reject their striking claims.

Dividing to Organize

Sometimes, as in the Trefil selection, division is used to arrive at the topic the writer wants to discuss. Sometimes, as in the second sentence of the following passage, it's used to explain the origins of the subject:

"Country" music, though its commercial success came late, was long part of the American popular music tradition. English, Irish, and Scottish ballads, chanteys, and work songs furnished one strand of its development; Protestant hymns, particularly of the evangelical variety, another; the popular sentimental ballad of the turn-of-the-century years a third. Merging these produced music that was predominantly Southern, rural, vocal, and white.—Russel B. Nye, *The Unembarrassed Muse*

Sometimes the division itself (often with subdivisions and always developed with descriptive details) makes up the entire content of the paper. In these cases dividing, or analyzing, the subject does double duty. It produces both the topics the writer discusses and the organization of the paper.

Division and organization are directly related. You use the method of division whenever you read carefully and analytically, trying to see the parts of the discussion and understand how they fit together. You use it every time you outline a chapter in a textbook or one of your own papers. The procedure is familiar. First you divide the material into the main topics; then you divide each main topic into subtopics; and so on. Just as the outline helps you grasp the structure of a chapter or test the organization of your own paper, so making a division of your subject at the beginning of a paper can forecast for your readers the topics you're going to discuss and the order you're going to discuss them in. Especially when your subject is a complex one, this technique will help you as well as your readers. By setting up the organizational scheme for them, you'll plant it firmly in your own mind; and you can then go on to develop each part of the division with appropriate details.

Here's the opening paragraph of a student's term paper on the traits used in selecting beef cattle:

> The goal of commercial beef production is to market animals that return a maximum profit. Just as animals differ in their genetic makeup, they differ in the quality of their meat. Therefore the quality of beef can be improved through selective breeding. Only those traits that increase the rate and efficiency of production as well as the quality of the meat are economically important to the beef cattle industry. These traits, frequently referred to as performance traits, are (1) reproductive performance, (2) longevity, (3) mothering or nursing ability, (4) growth rate, (5) efficiency of gain, (6) conformation, and (7) carcass merit.

There followed a paragraph or two for each of the numbered traits and a concluding summary:

> It is through these seven major traits that beef production is improved. Change through selection is slow but tends to be permanent. These permanent traits increase the quality of beef, meeting consumers' demands, and decrease the production costs, making them economically feasible for breeders.

An undergraduate who described himself as "a knowledgeable science student" first divided an atomic power station into three parts: "the reactor core and its component parts, the power plant, and the safety devices." In his second paragraph he analyzed the nuclear core, discussing the radioactive fuel, the fuel rods, and the control rods and showing how the heat that's produced turns water into steam, which operates the power plant. In his third paragraph he subdivided the power plant into turbine, generator, and condenser, describing each one and explaining its function. In his fourth, he discussed the numerous safety devices that are built into the reactor. In a brief concluding paragraph he summed up: an atomic power station operates on a very simple principle; it has very few major parts; these parts work together to produce electricity.

Thus, through dividing and subdividing, this writer accomplished his purpose—explaining how an atomic power station produces electric power. It's unlikely that any approach other than division would have produced such a clear and economical explanation.

These examples show division generating the entire content of papers. Normally, though, you'll use division as a means to the end you're aiming for. You'll analyze a poem not just to analyze it but to reveal its strengths and weaknesses. You'll set up alternative courses of action not just to set up alternatives but to argue that one is superior to the others. Used in this way, division, the tool of analytical thinking, cooperates with all the other methods of development.

Cautions

Whatever your purpose, your division will be sensible and informative only if it's both consistent and complete.

For some purposes, dividing an apple into skin, pulp, and core would be satisfactory. Simple as the division is, it's consistent (only one principle is applied) and it's complete (it takes in the whole apple). By contrast, a division into skin, pulp, and seeds is incomplete because the seeds are only a part of the core. And a division into skin, pulp, and tartness doesn't work because it's both incomplete and inconsistent. The third part—tartness—results from applying a new principle of division—flavor.

Making a complete and consistent division is easiest when the subject is a physical object, like an apple. It becomes more difficult when the subject is an institution, like a university, and much more difficult when the subject is an abstraction, like patriotism or socialism or love. Discussing the right to commit suicide, one student wrote, "The question involves morals, values, and perhaps selfishness." Since values and morals overlap and selfishness can be considered a kind of value, the division is a muddle.

Muddles occur when you shift from one principle of division to another and end up presenting your reader with parts that can't possibly fit together. Trefil's center, frontier, and fringe make a logical division. Center, frontier, fringe, and the latest Hollywood space spectacular don't. In a paper analyzing the reasons for the popularity of baseball, appeal to players and appeal to spectators make a logical (if extremely simple) division. Appeal to players, appeal to spectators, and the joys of eating hotdogs don't. The hotdogs logically belong in a subdivision of the appeal that baseball has for its fans.

For Writing

1. In an article intended for junior-high-school students, identify the parts of a familiar mechanism—a bicycle, a camera, a cassette recorder, a vacuum cleaner, a lawn mower—and explain how they interact to make the mechanism function.

2. Suppose you have a friend at another college who is very naive about magazine advertising and persists in ordering merchandise that turns out to be disappointing. To try to cure your friend of this expensive habit, write a letter in which you analyze a typical magazine ad, breaking it down into its parts and showing how the parts work together to lure the reader into reaching for his checkbook. Turn in the ad with your paper.

3. Choose a hero (real or fictional, human or nonhuman) that you had as a child and explain what qualities he, she, or it had that you found attractive. Specify the audience you have in mind.

4. Analyze something you strongly like or dislike—a particular movie or TV series, a musical group, a traditional holiday celebration, a current craze. Your purpose is not to describe your subject or to engage in self-analysis to decide why you like or dislike it but to break it down into its basic elements, examine them, and show how they work together to earn your admiration or distaste.

Comparing and Contrasting: Finding Likenesses and Differences

Often you can explore a subject and generate ideas about it by asking how it is like or unlike another subject. In conversation we constantly make comparisons—of movies, teams, books, clothes, and so on. In writing we go through the same procedures more thoroughly and systematically in order to clarify our meaning or make an idea more persuasive.

Whenever your main intention in a paper is to bring out similarities and differences, comparison is naturally central. (Strictly, *comparison* implies likeness and *contrast* implies difference, but ordinarily *comparison* is applied to discovering and presenting either similarities or differences.) Comparison may also be essential in papers with other aims. A good way of explaining how a new mechanism works is to compare it with a similar familiar one, using a known to shed light on an unknown. To establish a generalization about television audiences, you might compare shows that enjoy high ratings with shows the public rejected. And comparison is at the center of many arguments. In controversies about which action should be taken, which policy adopted, which candidate elected, you're bound to use it.

Points of Comparison

A point of comparison is a significant question you can ask about each of your subjects. (What is significant will be determined by your purpose in comparing them.) A question frequently asked about presidential candidates is "What do they plan to do about the three issues that are bothering most Americans—inflation, unemployment, and defense?" These three issues then become points of comparison, topics to be discussed in connection with the candidates.

Skill in dividing will help you in the first stage of comparing, since you arrive at your points of comparison by analyzing each of your subjects. A candidate's economic policy, for instance, is one element of his political philosophy. But what you're looking for in a comparison is not *all* the parts—all the elements of a political philosophy, say—as in a division, but a manageable number that will reveal significant likenesses and differences.

You're most likely to discover relevant points of comparison if you begin by investigating your subjects as fully as possible. Study each one, jotting down all the details and aspects of the subject that occur to you. Keep turning it over in your mind; keep asking questions of it. Once you have two full lists (if you're comparing two subjects), review them, looking for points that suggest relationships worth exploring.

In a brief comparison of two uncomplicated subjects this may not call for any great effort. A student who was interested in finding out why she had come to prefer *Mademoiselle* to *Seventeen* limited her comparison of the magazines' contents to the articles they published and their columns on beauty care, fashion, food, and interior decoration. But if your subjects are more complex, involving ideas, attitudes, and influences, you'll need to examine the relationships between them more closely and make finer distinctions. (Consider, for example, this question on a philosophy examination: "Compare the conception of the self presupposed by Augustine's argument from Truth with the somewhat similar conception in Descartes' *Meditations*.") You'll ask yourself whether the likenesses you've discovered are fundamental or superficial and whether the differences are differences in degree or differences in kind. A difference in degree is expressed in terms of more or less, or better or worse, or stronger or weaker: "Both *A* and *B* are enjoyable, but *A* gives more lasting pleasure." There's a difference in kind between jailing people for their political beliefs and jailing them for stealing cars. A carpenter's producing a cabinet and a woman's producing a baby represent an even stronger difference in kind.

Once you've discovered the points of comparison that have a bearing on your purpose, you have the criteria you need to select from your lists just those characteristics and qualities and details of your subjects that have a bearing on what you want to explain or prove. Then you're ready to consider how you can best organize your comparison.

For Discussion and Writing

An examination question may specify at least some points of comparison, as here: "Critically discuss and compare Rogers' and Freud's positions on the issue of whether, how, and why a therapist should *care* about a patient in order to bring about a cure." Often you're expected to decide what points of comparison are most worth discussing. Initial cost, operating cost, and repair record are points of comparison a prospective buyer might use to evaluate two or more makes of car. What points of comparison would you use to bring out significant similarities and differences between two musicians or groups of musicians (you name them), two of the courses you're now taking, two methods of learning a skill you're qualified to teach? After you've thought through your points of comparison and your purpose, write a paper of 600 words on the subject of your choice. Tell what interest you have in making the comparison—what you're trying to demonstrate or prove—and what audience you're addressing. (In making a comparison of cars for an audience of wealthy readers, you might ignore matters of cost entirely.)

Structuring a Comparison

Although making lists is a practical preliminary step in writing a comparison, simply presenting those lists in sentence form won't produce a comparison worth reading. You need to arrange the points of comparison, filled out with details and examples, so that your audience can grasp the likenesses and differences and understand how you arrive at your conclusion about your subjects. How you arrange the points and supporting information will depend, as usual, on the rhetorical situation—particularly on your subjects, on your audience's familiarity with them, and on your purpose in comparing them.

Three Patterns

Here are three patterns frequently used in balanced comparisons—comparisons in which roughly the same attention is given to each of the subjects being compared. The examples show that the same information can be organized in three ways, each giving the reader a slightly different view. In the first, called *whole-to-whole*, the writer has his say about one of the subjects before turning to the other, presenting each subject as a whole rather than focusing on precise similarities and differences. The *part-to-part* scheme, with its perfect symmetry, highlights specific points of comparison, leaving the reader with a sharp impression of how the subjects relate to each other on each point. (Notice how the symmetry extends even to the individual sentences. Many of them are balanced, the two halves built just alike.) The third pattern, *likeness-difference*, begins with similarities but emphasizes differences; what is given most space and placed last is usually remembered longest.

I. Whole-to-Whole

Thomas Jefferson grew up among the landed gentry of Virginia, and he remained a confirmed Virginian throughout his life. He was a thoughtful man, a scholar and a philosopher, always eager to add to his knowledge of the arts and sciences and to explore the mysteries of the universe and of the human spirit. Though apparently reluctant to take part in the clamor and conflict of politics, he became a powerful political leader, working for the welfare of his nation. A patriot and statesman, he devoted his life to the development of the Republic he had helped to create. His writings reflect a hopeful view of human nature, a belief that under the right conditions men will improve. That faith is implicit in the great Declaration of Independence, of which he was the author. It is the basis of his dream of a happy land of free men, living together in natural harmony. And that faith is, of course, the root of his objection to any kind of government that would stifle individual liberty and hamper individual growth. Both his faith and his dream became permanent parts of American democracy.

Alexander Hamilton came from a background very unlike Jefferson's. He was born out of wedlock on an island in the Lesser Antilles. He became a New Yorker, joining a society of men as competitive and aggressive as himself. A gifted organizer and administrator, he used his brilliant mind as a weapon with which to fight not only for personal success but also for the practical policies he supported. His patriotism was as great as Jefferson's, but his view of the future of the nation was dictated by a very different reading of human nature. He believed that men will act upon the same selfish motives whatever the form of government and that therefore a government with sufficient authority to impose order and stability is always essential. Only through a strong central government, he thought, could America achieve peace, progress, and prosperity. This idea, powerfully expressed in his *Federalist* papers, had great influence upon the organization of the new republic and upon its subsequent history.

II. Part-to-Part

Thomas Jefferson and Alexander Hamilton were two of America's most influential statesmen in the early period of the Republic. Jefferson grew up among the landed gentry of Virginia; Hamilton was born out of wedlock on an island in the Lesser Antilles. Only with apparent reluctance did Jefferson accept a political career, with its accompanying clamor and conflict. A thoughtful man, he would have preferred to spend his life in his native state, free to add to his scholarly knowledge of the arts and sciences and to explore the mysteries of the universe and of the human spirit. Hamilton, on the other hand, found his natural milieu in New York City, in a society of men who shared his competitive, aggressive spirit, and he entered politics with the enthusiasm and efficiency of the born organizer and administrator. His brilliant mind served him admirably in his fight for personal success and for the political policies he supported. His *Federalist* papers are among the greatest documents of the period, ranking in historical importance with Jefferson's Declaration of Independence. Both are the works of great patriots.

Jefferson's political philosophy was optimistic; he believed that, given the right conditions, men would improve. By contrast, Hamilton was convinced that, regardless of environment, human nature does not change. Accordingly, while Jefferson dreamed of a happy land of free men, living together in natural harmony, Hamilton worked for order and stability, for system and organization. The Virginian feared that the machinery of a strong central government would stifle individual liberty and hamper individual growth; the New Yorker believed that government must have authority in order to ensure peace, progress, and prosperity. Regardless of the differences in their views, both men devoted their lives to the welfare of the new nation, which both had helped to create and which both helped to survive. And their different views had permanent influence upon the history of America.

III. Likeness-Difference

Thomas Jefferson and Alexander Hamilton were fellow patriots and fellow statesmen. Men of true brilliance, the powerful influence that they exerted upon the Republic at the beginning of its history had an effect that has persisted to the present day. To them we owe some of our greatest historical documents— to Jefferson the Declaration of Independence and to Hamilton a number of the famous *Federalist* papers. Both were powerful political leaders, working for the welfare of the new nation which they had helped to create and which they helped to survive.

At the same time, their differences were numerous and profound. They were unlike in background, in temperament, in habit of mind, and in political philosophy. Jefferson grew up among the landed gentry of old Virginia; Hamilton was born out of wedlock on an island in the Lesser Antilles. Throughout his life, Jefferson remained a confirmed Virginian, but Hamilton became a New Yorker, flourishing in a society of men as competitive and aggressive as himself. Jefferson apparently shrank from the clamor and conflict of politics; Hamilton had the zeal of a born organizer and administrator. Jefferson was a thoughtful man, a scholar and a philosopher, always eager to add to his knowledge of the arts and sciences and to explore the mysteries of the universe and of the human spirit. Hamilton used his mind as a keen weapon with which he fought not only for personal success but also for the practical policies he supported.

They differed markedly in their views of human nature. An optimist, Jefferson believed that, under the right conditions, men would improve; Hamilton was convinced that, regardless of environment, human nature would never change. Because of their different readings of human nature, they had different views about the role of government. Since he could not believe that a new type of government would result in a new type of citizenry, Hamilton worked for the old objectives—order and stability, system and organization; he sought to build a government with traditional authority, which he considered essential to peace, progress, and prosperity. Just as naturally, considering his philosophy, Jefferson fought against a strong central government, fearing that it would stifle individual liberty and hamper individual growth, seeing it as a threat to his dream of a happy land of free men, living together in natural harmony.

For Writing

This is an exercise—just that. If you approach it the way you approach a jigsaw puzzle or a crossword puzzle, you should have some fun doing it.

What follows is a whole-to-whole comparison of cats and dogs. Using precisely the same material—the same points of comparison, the same details—write two papers, the first a part-to-part comparison and the second a likeness-difference comparison. To produce readable, interesting papers you'll have to do some writing of your own; you can't just shift the sentences of the whole-to-whole comparison around. Make your own transitions and frame your own generalizations, but don't bring in new information or opinion about cats and dogs.

> If your house or apartment is full of mice, a cat will solve your problem. It won't do much else of a practical nature. Cats can be trained to do things, but the training is such an ordeal that few people find it worth while. To their admirers, cats are beautiful to look at and fascinating to have around. Cats don't mind being around so long as it means being well fed, provided with warmth and comfort, and allowed to do pretty much what they want to do, including being let alone. They expect free access to their owners' laps, most comfortable chairs, and beds. Cats that are allowed outside keep late hours, kill songbirds, and ruin the neighbors' gardens. (Cats that are kept inside wreck the drapes and the furniture and force their owners to transport tons of kitty litter.) They also run up huge medical bills, in part because of their violent assaults on veterinarians. Cats have fleas.
>
> Most dogs will make some sort of commotion if a stranger tries to break into the house or apartment they live in. Many can also be trained to do a great variety of things, but if they are house dogs, what they learn has very little practical value. Dog lovers think dogs are great to have around, and most dogs love to be around. If permitted, they will share their owners' meals, chairs, and beds. They like to be patted and praised and demonstrate their own affection by slobbering all over their owners after any separation lasting more than fifteen minutes. Dogs that are allowed to run loose get into all kinds of trouble. Dogs that go out only when leashed cause their owners all kinds of trouble. Vets and dogs love each other: the dogs get attention, and the vets get wealthy. Dogs have fleas.

Modifying the Patterns

Comparisons seldom fall into patterns as neatly balanced as the Jefferson-Hamilton set. If you're comparing the British and American systems of government in order to explain the British system to American readers (or for a course in political science), you'll naturally give the American "whole" briefer coverage. A few generalizations will be enough to remind your readers of what they already know and to open the way for the contrast. The same unequal coverage makes sense if you use the part-to-part structure: whenever you introduce a point of comparison, you'll touch on its application to the American system only briefly, giving much more space to the corresponding details of the British system.

If you use comparison to establish the superiority of public schools over private schools, you'll naturally give most attention to the strong points of public schools—and to the weak points of private schools—since these are what convinced you of the superiority of public schooling in the first place.

If you intend to bring out hidden likenesses between two things normally thought of as strikingly different—tap dancing and ballet, perhaps—there won't be any point in reviewing the differences. You'll acknowledge them very briefly and move on to what you're really interested in—the similarities.

There are valid reasons, then, for giving more attention to one of your subjects or for otherwise modifying the basic patterns of organization. But if you commit yourself to making a full, balanced comparison, you must work at doing just that. And in making a comparison you'll find that each of the patterns poses some problems. In the whole-to-whole the two halves of your paper will drift apart if, in dealing with the second whole, you lose sight of the points you made about the first. Part-to-part has the advantage of keeping the topics in view, but unless they're smoothly related, the paper will seem choppy and disjointed. And if the third pattern is less common than the other two, it's probably because many subjects yield such a random collection of either likenesses or differences that half the comparison turns out to be weak and uninteresting.

Choosing a Pattern

In choosing among the patterns, try to decide which best suits your material, your purpose, and the needs of your audience. Suppose you were writing an article for a popular magazine about the pollution of waterways and you used as evidence a comparison of the Concord and Merrimack rivers as they are today with the rivers as Henry David Thoreau knew them in 1839. Doing a part-to-part comparison probably wouldn't suit your purpose. You'd be more likely to offer a brief sketch of the rivers as Thoreau wrote about them and then move on to a detailed account of their present deplorable state. Your pattern would be *un*balanced whole-to-whole.

When you write an extended, analytical comparison for an audience that knows a good deal about your subjects, you'll probably use the part-to-part pattern. Close analysis of separate points can be sustained longer in that scheme than in the whole-to-whole. A detailed comparison of the techniques and accomplishments of two film directors, supported by examples of their work, would be easier to follow in the part-to-part scheme than in whole-to-whole, and relationships could be stated with greater precision than in the likeness-difference pattern.

Likeness-difference is a good choice when your readers not only know a lot about your subjects but have a strong opinion about them that you want to change. If your purpose is to persuade them that subjects generally regarded as similar are actually unlike, begin with the likenesses and go on to the differences, perhaps showing that the likenesses are more apparent than real. If you want to persuade them that subjects generally regarded as different are actually much alike, acknowledge the differences first and then go on to reveal likenesses that are more significant.

In making a choice of methods, ask yourself questions like these: Will my purpose be best served (and my readers best informed) if I present a general view of each whole? Or should I set certain aspects of each side by side to sharpen the contrast? Or will it be more effective to talk entirely in terms of *like* and *unlike?* Do *like* and *unlike* need equal attention, or should I pass over the likenesses quickly and get on to what really counts—the differences?

Don't focus so closely on the procedures of comparing that you forget the purpose you want the comparison to serve. And remember that though the structure of a comparison must be clear, symmetry doesn't guarantee a good paper. Organization is only a means of calling attention to the similarities and differences. To convince the reader that they are real ones, you must present the details, the examples, the facts that make your subjects alike or different in respects you consider important and interesting.

In the following newspaper article comparison is used to support a thesis:

> Baseball and football nicely reflect, sociologically, their respective eras of inception, development and maturation. They reflect, rather directly, the evolution, or demise, of the American dream. It is no accident that in terms of media popularity, football, a game clearly defined by time and space, is the No. 1 sport in America today. Football in many ways mirrors contemporary America; baseball preserves an image of the America we have lost.
>
> For baseball is a game in which the passage of time is incidental; the season turns, but no clocks run out in baseball games. Baseball is the summer game, reflecting a society still rural and thus fitting perfectly into the languid season between sowing and reaping. Deeds matter in baseball: hits, runs, errors and outs rather than mere time make the inning.
>
> Nor has space, time's twin, much to do with baseball. There were no fences early in the game and even today they are seen as rather arbitrary.
>
> There are home fields but no enemy territory to penetrate, no home territory to defend. The entire field is open to both teams equally. This befits a society in which land is abundant. Baseball is the Homestead Act with bases.
>
> Although there are teams in baseball, there is little teamwork. The essence of the game is the individual with or against the ball: pitcher controlling, batter hitting, fielder handling, runner racing the ball. All players are on their own, struggling (like the farmer) to overcome not another human being but nature (the ball).
>
> This individualism is demonstrated when the shortstop, cleanly fielding the ball, receives credit for a "chance" even if the first baseman drops the thrown ball. It is demonstrated when a last-place team includes a Cy Young Award-winning pitcher or a league-leading hitter. It is perhaps most clearly manifest in the pitcher-batter duel, the heart of the game, when two men face each other.
>
> Baseball is each man doing the best he can for himself and against nature within a loose confederation of fellow individualists he may or may not admire and respect. This reflects a society in which individual effort, drive and success are esteemed and in which, conversely, failure is deemed the individual's responsibility.

Like life itself, baseball is full of surprising twists and turns and there can be no game plans. The season contains all the stuff of the old American dream. Disappointments are softened by the realization that one game, one defeat or even a series of defeats does not spell failure. Such a situation weakens any tendency toward winning at all costs and by any means.

In football, losing is worse than death because after losing there is nothing. In baseball, there is always tomorrow or at least next year. The baseball season ends with harvest time; the football season ends with the plunge into deepest winter.

Baseball is everyman's game; that is, it is not a big man's game: Phil Rizzuto, Bobby Shantz, Pee Wee Reese and Joe Morgan are among the greatest players and not big. Henry Aaron is barely above average in size.

Nor is baseball a specialist's game. Except for pitchers and catchers, many players can readily shift positions, but who ever heard of a utility linebacker?

In baseball we see perpetuated one of the guiding myths of America—egalitarianism, equal opportunity, every man potentially a champion. Neither smallness of stature nor a computer analysis precludes everyman's attempt to make the team and to attain glory. Baseball is perhaps the only team sport in which a good small team can beat a good big team—provided the small team has a superior pitcher.

These factors account in large part for the almost total absence of physical contact, to say nothing of physical violence, in baseball. This rarity of physical violence reflects a time when America itself, as a nation among nations, was incapable of great violence, having neither contiguous enemy or potential enemy states nor a significant standing army.

But America has changed. After World War II, in a clear break with our history, America became a military power of the first order and in the last 25 years we have used that power often: Massive violence, or the threat of it, has been our lot for a generation.

In such a context, football has matured. In football, violence is an essential characteristic; it is a team sport played by specialists who must submerge their personalities for the sake of the corporation; it is a game of big men whom lesser mortals may passively watch but not emulate; it is a game severely circumscribed by time and space factors; it is a game (unlike baseball, of "democratic" origins) that originated among college elites and was purveyed to the masses as a commodity.

Baseball appears as a relic from a simpler, richer, more leisurely past. Its enduring popularity attests to the strength of the myth it re-enacts, of individuals in their lonely struggle against nature. Football is a manifestation of that stage in the evolution of America when highly specialized organization men, inured to violence, confronted a world increasingly limited in economic time, space and resources. Now that "limits to growth" have been perceived, perhaps the situation is ripe for a new American pastime, in which space, time and organization factors are predominant but in which there is room for individualism as well.

Soccer, anyone?—Gerald J. Cavanaugh, *New York Times*

For Discussion and Writing

1. Review the three methods of structuring a comparison, and then write a paper of 600–800 words on one of the following topics.

   a. For the sports section in a newspaper or magazine, compare and contrast two games or sports, like table tennis and paddleball, handball and jai alai, basketball and hockey, baseball and stoopball, golf and tennis.

   b. For a TV magazine, write a comparison of the styles of two performers who appear regularly on television, with a view to demonstrating that one is more talented or more entertaining than the other. Audience: TV fans.

2. Write a comparison of your own family and another very different family that you know well. In making the comparison, rely chiefly on details about their homes—furniture, drapes, color schemes, pictures on the walls, knickknacks, and so on—that seem to you to reflect the occupants' personality, tastes, interests, and values. (The details you chose for assignment 3 on p. 40 could be used for this comparison.) Your audience is acquainted with both families but hasn't visited their homes.

3. Think about a practice or way of behaving that you don't like: a teacher's methods, a parent's way of dealing with a son or daughter, a partner's behavior on a date, a roommate's life style, an advertising campaign. In a carefully structured essay, pinpoint the inadequacies or weaknesses of this way of behaving by comparing it with a better way.

4. Some experiences measure up to our expectations, some surpass them, and some fall short. For a friend, write an account of what you expected of a place, an event, or a person and how the experience actually turned out. Shape your paper so that it implies some generalization about your outlook on life.

5. For a sympathetic audience such as an old friend or a school counselor, discuss your relations with your parents. Indicate how similarities and differences in your values and attitudes affect the relationship.

6. Read the following paper, written in response to assignment 5.

   a. What purpose does the comparison serve? Is it intended simply to show likenesses and differences, or is it used to support a thesis?

   b. What method of comparison has the student used? Is it a good one for the purpose, or would another have been better?

   c. Are the details well chosen? Do they make the generalization believable?

   d. Are the style and tone appropriate to the audience proposed in 5? Why or why not?

Old is Right?

Many members of the older generation are under the impression that their values and ways of life are the only right ones. They think that their children must inherit these qualities or they, the parents, have failed. They refuse to acknowledge that teenagers might have some legitimate ideas of their own. I am tired of having my opinions put down by my parents simply because of my youth and relative lack of experience.

Family ties are extremely important to my father and mother. They feel that their children should prefer to do things with the family rather than on their own. Unfortunately, their attitudes make me unwilling to spend time with them.

"Conservative" is a good word to use to describe my parents. They find it hard to accept any sort of change. When I was growing up, all the girls were wearing pants to school, but I wasn't allowed to until the seventh grade, and even then I was restricted to dress pants. It was my senior year in high school before I was permitted to wear jeans—once a week. I consider myself a liberal to a certain extent. At least I see nothing wrong in dressing in a casual, comfortable way.

My father and mother are very straitlaced Protestants who firmly believe that going to church every Sunday is an integral part of religion. I see religion as a more personal thing. I feel that I can be just as close to God, if not closer, through my own private, nightly prayers. Although I believe strongly in the love of God, I am not interested in organized religion. Rather than accepting and respecting my views, my parents are constantly trying to convert me to their way of thought.

Politics is another sore point. My parents are devoted Republicans and always vote for the party's candidate because they are sure he must stand for Republican principles and ideals. I chose to register as an Independent, believing that I should vote for the candidate whose personal qualities I most admire, regardless of his party label. My parents disapprove.

My father and mother are convinced that one of the most important things in life is working to earn money for later years. For them, work has nothing to do with enjoyment or even interest. It is a duty you must perform for yourself and your family. I feel that work is part of life but that life is something to be relished. So I would rather work for low pay in a job I like than be stuck in a high-paying dull job. My parents can't understand this. One of the worst shocks of their lives was when my sister dropped out of college, leaving behind a relatively secure career in fashion merchandising, to become an apprentice sailor on a square-rigged ship.

I don't mean to sound like my parents are inhuman. My mother and father have always been more than generous, giving me everything I ever needed. I love them both dearly and don't mean for it to appear otherwise. They have taught me many valuable lessons. But though I appreciate their efforts to give me the best upbringing possible, according to their standards, I think we would get along much better if they would only try to understand my feelings and remember that I am an independent adult with ideas of my own, however different they may be from theirs.

Classifying: Making Groups

As a method of developing and organizing papers, classifying is closely related to dividing and also requires skill in comparing. In dividing you analyze *one* thing or *one* concept to see what it's made up of. In classifying you deal with several things or concepts: you sort a collection of individual things—jobs, stereos, people, sports, foods, books, coins, wars—into groups or classes on the basis of likenesses. Grouping makes it easier for us to understand and talk about large numbers of things. Much of human knowledge is organized by classification, in the humanities as well as in the physical sciences and the social sciences (note this classification). So is much human prejudice, as in racial, ethnic, regional, social, and sexual stereotypes (note this classification).

In some college courses you'll be asked to demonstrate your familiarity with an existing classification: a question on a physiology examination asks students to name and describe the three main body types. In some courses you'll be expected to demonstrate the existence of a group: in a sociology paper a student argued that cowboys—"a species that most Americans think is extinct, preserved only in caricature in Hollywood Westerns"—are "very much alive and well" in Montana.

In some papers you'll need to fit your subject into an established classification. If you're writing a review of a movie, you may want to start by placing it in its class—comedy, melodrama, musical, satire, whatever. That will open up the way to comparing it with others like it and may lead to evaluation. In still other papers, including those you write for a composition course, you may be asked to take a collection of items, sort them into groups, and make clear the chief characteristics of each group. Original classifying of this sort requires the ability to observe, to generalize, and to differentiate.

In the following passage the author takes a huge group, the people who immigrate to Southern California. She first establishes the characteristic that sets them off from the natives (in the second sentence) and then goes on to divide them into three groups:

I have often tried to imagine what people who come to this place feel. I know they feel compelled to judge, to embrace or deride, an impulse which by its very nature marks them as outsiders. Some who immigrate become wildly happy; they feel uncaged. They maneuver the freeways like veterans, not knowing whether they are passing Pacoima or Pasadena, not caring, not missing the old perimeters of any kind. Their marriages become blurry, at least for a while. Out West, under the sun, the Puritan ethic at last relaxes its grip. They defend their new land with a vehemence foreign to the natives. It is hard not to like the energy with which they fall into this or that, the completeness with which they fall out of their past lives. The people I know who have hot tubs were born elsewhere.

Others who come never stop feeling lost even when they know their way around. They seem to recoil from Southern California, to cling to their pallor, unable to find in the splay of suburbs and shopping malls any center, any historical monument save for a few stars in the sidewalk of a seedy boulevard. They band together like expatriates, trying to make a neighborhood out of their grievances. They blame their discomfort on the size of Los Angeles, its sunshine, its sybaritic tilt, its taco stands and pool boys. Nobody reads, they say; everyone is so tan, so intent on beauty. They set themselves up as the imported intellectuals and in that role find some happiness.

I guess that the most difficult adjustment is left to those who come to try to be stars, people who mean to matter in a business as precarious as the land on which it was built. More hearts are broken here than are not broken. But, oh, those first days in Hollywood are something: the sun, the nearness, at last, of the camera, days akin to the first days of loving someone. I have seen that love. I know the contours of those lives.—Anne Taylor Fleming, *New York Times Magazine*

Observers with an eye for new trends and new variations on old themes are constantly creating classifications or making fresh uses of existing ones. You can find new ways of looking at the world, too. In the prewriting stage, when you're mulling over possible approaches to a subject, you can often generate good ideas by putting your subject into as many classes as you can think of. So long as things are in the process of changing—and they always will be—there are endless opportunities for inventing fresh classifications. In the rest of this section we'll suggest the criteria you should keep in mind as you make new groupings.

Consistency

Like division, classification should be consistent—that is, only one principle of classification should be applied at a time. You can classify cars by make or by size or by price, people by age or by body type or by nationality, and so on. Once you've classified your subject according to one principle, you can classify it by another; but don't shift principles in mid-classification.

For your classification to be reasonably sound, the classes must be reasonably separate and distinct. In a paper describing the football fans at his college, a student set up four groups: alumni, students, serious fans, and "the ones that party." As a classification this is a mishmash. Both alumni and students may attend tailgate parties, and whether they do or not, they may be serious fans. Beginning with a single principle of classification—main purpose in attending—would have permitted a division into those who come primarily for love of the game, those who come primarily for love of the school, and those who come primarily for social reasons. Then these groups could have been subdivided. For example, those who come primarily for love of the game would probably include people who have no connection with the college.

In classifying a subject you're personally associated with—sorority or fraternity members, for example—you may make the mistake of using individuals you know as the basis for establishing groups. If you do, your classification is likely to emerge as a series of character sketches. As a classifier you must concentrate on types, not individuals. Your main concern is not the idiosyncracies that set one person apart but the characteristics that two or more share when they're looked at from a particular perspective—as students, perhaps, or as voters or as consumers of junk food. As a classifier you say, in effect, that, *for the purpose you have in mind,* some people can be grouped. Though they may be very different in respects unrelated to your point, they're alike in terms of your principle of classification.

Completeness

The classifier's interest in the type rather than the individual often makes necessary some relaxation of the rule that a classification must be complete—that is, that it must assign a place to every item in the collection of items being classified. Formal classifications, like those used in the sciences, seek to organize all the available data according to objective criteria. But making your classification all-inclusive when its aims are modest and its criteria personal may be unwise as well as unnecessary. For most purposes the rule can be modified to something like this: A classification should be as complete as your knowledge of the subject permits and as your purpose requires.

In classifying a large group of people, there's no necessity for pigeonholing every last individual. A too-conscientious effort to do so may result in the major groupings getting lost among minor divisions and catchalls with labels like "borderline" and "miscellaneous" and "other." The writer who says that there are four types of students or five types of statesmen or three types of singers is not saying that *every* student or statesman or singer fits comfortably into one of these groups. He'd admit that some might straddle groups. What he is saying is that four (or five or three) classes can be differentiated in ways that are significant for the purpose he has in mind. If the classification is relatively inclusive, if each class is identified fully enough to make it a real one, and if the classes are adequately differentiated from one another, the reader will be satisfied.

Here's a student's classification of "distracting types." Note the formal vocabulary and the identifying labels—both overused devices in classifications that are intended to be funny.

Distracting Types

Over the course of sixteen years of sitting in classrooms, study halls, and libraries, it has been my distinct misfortune to situate myself next to or near some of the most despicable and distracting characters imaginable. With their various idiosyncracies, they make it difficult for even the most stoical person to remain calm and attentive. Fortunately, I have developed an ability to distinguish these various delinquents from the normal student, thereby avoiding their annoying diversions.

Perhaps the most obvious of these rapscallions is the chronic toe-tapper. From the waist up, he is the picture of calm, usually sitting slumped and relaxed in his chair. Only his foot is alive, as if a thousand volts were racing from heel to toe. Often his beat is supplemented with an interjection from his other foot. Due to the inherent nature of this activity, toe-tappers prefer aisle seats, which enable both feet to move unrestrained. Although the motion may be slight, it is usually forceful enough to shake an entire row of connected seats. A seat in front of one of this type can be equally affected if his tapper is rubbing against it.

Similar to the toe-tapper is the pencil-tapper. Driven by some inaudible, internal rhythm, these frustrated minstrels drum a beat which Ringo Starr would be hard-pressed to match. They have no seating preference and no visible distinguishing marks, making them impossible to detect and avoid. Fortunately, a throaty "un-humm!" is sufficient to snap them back to normalcy—at least for a while.

The nail-biter is the most unscrupulous of all. These varlets are liable to sit anywhere. Once seated, they look their fingers over as they might inspect a spare rib for that last meaty morsel. A persistent gnawer can groom a whole handful of nails and cuticles in a single period. Compounding the nauseating effect of such unsanitary activity is an occasional elbow to the side of your head as the biter jockeys for the perfect angle on that last hangnail.

Sleepers offer a relatively mild distraction. They are distinguishable by pronounced bags under their eyes and a proclivity for sitting in the back row. Some sleep erect in their seats and move from consciousness to oblivion and back without a sound, presenting no problem at all. Others are not so restrained. Their breathing is heavy, with an occasional muffled snort. Their elbows have been known to slide suddenly off desks and chair arms, often disconnecting their owners from their seats. Worst of all, sleepers are prone to drool.

The rarest of all these deviants are the rockers. They often grow to be six feet tall and three feet wide but can look quite ordinary. Wasting no time, this frivolous varmint bobs forward and back from the moment he sits down until he again stands up. Apparently there is some primordial, subconscious appeal to rocking, because four or five others soon join in, usually in time with the original rocker. I can foresee the day when an entire class will rock uncontrollably.

There are others, of course, such as hummers, snifflers, and late-arrivers, to name but a few. With a keen eye for detail and an acute sense of the obvious, the discerning student can successfully outmaneuver the aforementioned horde of irreverent twits. Away from such multitudinous activity, he is free to lose himself in *War and Peace,* ponder the theory of relativity, or just gradually . . . peacefully . . . fall . . . asleep.

Many informal classifications have a highly personal flavor. In her book *The OK Boss,* for example, Muriel James classifies types of bosses as the critic, the coach, the shadow, the analyst, the pacifier, the fighter, and the inventor. This is certainly not a logical classification, but it is refreshingly original. Another classifier of bosses might come up with a completely different set of labels. In establishing a classification, you may find that you're learning (and telling) something about yourself as well as about your subject.

For Discussion

Examine the following groupings. Identify the basis or bases of classification. Explain why you think each grouping is or is not logically sound (or as sound as the subject permits). If you find a grouping satisfactory, tell what it's useful for. If you think a grouping is unsatisfactory, suggest a better one.

1. Apples: good for pies, good for sauce, good for eating, good for cider, good for nothing

2. Personal habits: the compulsively neat, the compulsively sloppy

3. College students: those who want an education, those who want a job, those who want a diploma

4. Clothes: those that feel comfortable, those that are made of natural fabrics, those that are made of synthetics, those that are in style

5. Political extremists: the ultraconservatives, the ultraliberals, the terrorists, the know-nothings

6. Churchgoers: the devout, the insecure, the socialites

7. TV programs: news, sports, sitcoms, movies, specials

8. Courses: essential, nonessential but valuable, nonessential but fun, worthless

Writing a passage or a whole paper that offers a classification calls on many of the skills you use in comparing. Similarities join; differences separate. So as you classify, keep your emphasis on the similarities that bring some things into one group and the differences that push other things into separate groups. And make your groups convincing through the use of descriptive details.

For Analysis and Writing

1. Propose five different principles or bases for classifying four of the following subjects: religions, campus activities, vegetables, songs, humorists, sports, feminists, attitudes toward feminists, supermarket shoppers, standards of physical attractiveness. (Example: Students might be classified on the bases of their reasons for being in college, their study habits, their recreational choices, their places of origin, and their manner of dress—not necessarily in that order.) Not every principle need be serious. Use your imagination. Once you have your five principles, set up the groups that each principle yields. (Your instructor may want you to write a paper that makes use of one of the groupings.)

2. Choose a class or type of novel (horror, science fiction, romance), movie (catastrophe, supernatural, comedy), or TV program (melodrama, situation comedy, children's show), and write a paper about it, dividing it into subclasses with illustrative examples.

3. Group the people you went to high school with according to some principle of classification that interests you. Write for a specific audience—your high-school counselor, a student who will be attending your high school next year, your parents. In developing your paper, use contrasts that will keep the groups distinct and descriptive details that will make them real. Make your classification support a generalization—some point or some conviction you want to express about your high-school classmates.

Analyzing Causes and Effects: Finding Out Why and What Then

I'm disorganized because my mother's always been super-organized.

We wouldn't have lost if she hadn't fouled out.

If they win the election, taxes will go up.

All of us are constantly crediting or blaming *A* for causing *B* or predicting that *C* will result in *D,* and in ordinary conversation this free-swinging approach usually goes unchallenged. When you write, though, your readers have time to examine and think about what you have to say. If the causal (*not* casual) connection you assert doesn't make sense, they'll reject it. If it's sensible enough but you provide no evidence to back it up, they'll treat it as no more than an opinion.

Whatever the situation, we all have a passion to know *why.* An article reporting on the widespread habit of talking in movie theaters classifies the different kinds of talkers (the Describers, the Forecasters, the Analyzers, and so on) and then raises the crucial question and considers several answers:

What is the cause of this curse to the modern moviegoer? A breakdown in our sense of community? A simple lack of consideration? A new trend of attendance at movies by people who do not really want to see them but merely want to get in out of the heat or the cold or the light?

No, these are considered but minor factors. The main reason for the babble, many people believe, is that old archenemy of the movies: television. People have become so used to talking in front of the television set that the cinema becomes merely an extension of their living room.

"It's all because of the habit of chatting while you're watching television," a securities analyst said. "After a while it just seems natural to talk while you're watching the screen."

The socio-artistic level of the movies . . . is also an important factor. Nancy Reynolds, a dance writer and author of "Repertory in Review: Forty Years of the New York City Ballet," pointed out, "At the opera or the ballet, if enough people say, 'Shush,' they're kind of cowed into submission and they stop talking. But the movies are a popular art and people feel they can do whatever they like. You ask people at a movie to be quiet and they say, 'I'm gonna talk if I want to.' "—Larry Miller, *New York Times*

Here a scientist, puzzling over why he and a colleague draw different conclusions from data regarding life on Mars, finds the reasons in their scientific backgrounds and interests:

Since Sagan and I respect each other greatly as scientists and find much stimulation in each other's thoughts, why should we find it so difficult to read the record similarly? One can look first to our scientific backgrounds. He aimed at the planets and research from his undergraduate days. My first love was—and is—the Earth, and my initial postgraduate activities were of an applied nature. I didn't return to a university for a research career until I was twenty-nine years old. Carl has emphasized synthesis and conjecture about how things are, might be, or could be beyond the Earth. If he is lucky, his great passion, the search for extraterrestrial life, especially intelligent life, will blossom during his lifetime. I, on the other hand, have been mainly concerned about distinguishing fact from fiction in a subject moldy with misconceptions and inherited prejudices. My passion is to understand how things *really* are on Earth as well as in space.—Bruce Murray in *Mars and the Mind of Man* by Ray Bradbury and others.

A passage of causal analysis often brings to a close a paper that's been developed by description or comparison or classification. When you write a narrative or a description of a process, discussions of cause are likely to run through your paper, for causal statements are one chief means of giving coherence to material that's organized chronologically. In a paper on soil drifting, for example, you can't give your reader understanding of the process without providing answers to a whole series of *why* questions.

Examination questions frequently call for causal analysis, even though the word *cause* may not appear:

How do we account for the rise of towns in the eleventh century?

How do you respond to the character of the Duke in the poem "My Last Duchess"? Justify your response.

Explain how a label such as "delinquent," "criminal," or "insane" affects society's perception and treatment of an individual.

In a paper where cause-effect analysis is the chief method of development, the writer searches out the causes of (or reasons for) an event or situation or policy or belief. Or he traces the effects (or results or influences) it has had or will have. Or he does both, first telling what has led to a certain state of affairs, then telling what has resulted or predicting what will result. Notice the focus of attention. In discussing the *causes* of student apathy toward politics or the psychological *effects* of rape, the writer's interest is centered not so much on the situation itself as on what led to it or on what it led to or will lead to. His main concern is to present, and perhaps argue for, the relationships and connections he's arrived at by reasoning about origins and results.

In the following paper the student's interest centers not on the fact of consumerism or on advertising but on showing the connection between the two:

Consumerism

In our sociology class the other day we discussed consumerism in America. At first I felt very much above it all. I honestly thought that I was free of the disease. But I have come to realize that I am just another consumer at the mercy of the advertiser. Even though I'm not an impulse buyer, nor a constant buyer, I do have the consumer attitude.

What is this attitude and why does it affect millions of Americans, including me? It's the belief (often held subconsciously) that to buy and own in large quantities is the equivalent of finding happiness. Its most general cause is the use of the mass media to control the minds of Americans. We are daily bombarded by advertisements on radio and television, in magazines and newspapers, on signs and billboards, pushing the millions of products on sale each year. Advertisers mold our conceptions of what the necessities of life are. They plant their view of a decent standard of living in our subconscious. Advertisements accomplish this by insisting that we will suffer inconvenience or miss out on the fun unless we purchase a product which common sense would tell us is a luxury, not a necessity. Under the influence of advertising, we experience a constant feeling of need, which is only temporarily satisfied by a new purchase.

Through the mass media, advertising teaches us what we want to believe— that life should be lived in luxury. Television shows us that "real" people do live that way. Furthermore, we must constantly strive for this life of luxury or we won't be "with it." What we see in the ads teaches that society recognizes those who work hard in order to buy much. Therefore, so do we. Our lives turn into a struggle for acceptance—and acceptance is earned by regular shopping sprees.

What we shop for is determined by the producers' needs, not ours, so what the ads tell us to buy is constantly changing. This neither surprises nor bothers us. Our fast-paced society allows for it, making us believe it to be natural. We depend for security on the changing demands on our pocketbook because such change is a part of our everyday lives. Tomorrow, two cars—even two houses—per family may be too few.

Is there any way to stop this craziness? It can be resisted only by the individual. Because of the great complexity of business operations, no group of people, no set of legislation, can curb the endless flow of advertising. What is needed is an intense effort on the part of individuals to recognize the mind control exerted by TV for what it is. We must make each other aware of it, too, and we must be able to point to our own silly behavior as consequences we deserve for not distinguishing fake reality from true.

We have to take control of our own minds. Instead of letting the media manipulate us, let us manipulate the media. Once we pause, once we examine advertising and see it for what it is, we can put the brakes on the fast-paced society we live in. We can even get off the merry-go-round of consumerism.

Causal analysis frequently leads to a program for action, as it does in "Consumerism." Note the change in tone and content in the last two paragraphs of the paper.

A word of caution: Like any other kind of reasoning, reasoning in terms of cause and effect can be done well or badly. If you make a cause-effect analysis without giving it enough thought, you're almost sure to oversimplify: "government" is to blame for high taxes; slavery caused the Civil War; the poor representation of women in top executive positions is the result of male chauvinism; vitamins will prevent head colds. You'll match one cause to one effect, often without providing any evidence that your one cause is, in fact, a cause at all, and in that way turn what should be a reasoned discussion into a dogmatic statement of opinion.

Instead of oversimplifying, you may go to the opposite extreme and refuse to commit yourself. Playing safe, you include all sorts of qualifications, present an endless list of "possible" causes, or trace the "possible" immediate causes back to such remote and virtually meaningless causes as "civilization," "chance," or "human nature." Thus World War II (or World War I or the Trojan War or the Vietnam War) was caused by human nature. If you have a tendency either to oversimplify or to overqualify, you need to develop a more realistic approach to answering *why* questions: Why did this happen? Why didn't that work?

Discovering Causes

The procedure in answering *why* questions always involves two steps—investigating the facts and reasoning from the facts to a causal explanation. In scientific experiments that set out to see if *A* causes *B,* a laboratory worker tries to isolate all variables and then puts strict controls on one variable after another until eventually he determines what condition or set of conditions operates as a cause. He runs experiments again and again until he either verifies or disproves his hypothesis—his hunch or guess that *A* is the cause of *B*.

In attempting to answer many of the *why* questions that matter most to us, we can't set up controlled laboratory experiments. We can't call into existence the actual circumstances in which a fatal accident took place or a game was lost or a war was won. And even if we could rerun such happenings, we would rarely be able to isolate a single cause that inevitably led to the given effect. An investigation into the collision of two cars may have to take into account such *necessary* antecedents as weather, traffic, and road conditions, the mechanical condition of the cars, and the competence of the drivers. The investigator may be able to demonstrate that one of many *contributory* causes had a more immediate connection with the accident than the others and was in itself *sufficient* to have caused the accident. But he may have to be satisfied with listing three or four contributory causes, none of which can be said to have been decisive.

When you write about social and moral problems like alcoholism, drug addiction, or the divorce rate, you'll probably want to list several causes, not just one, and distinguish immediate causes from remote ones. In a thoroughgoing causal analysis you may show that a commonly accepted cause can't be held solely responsible, distinguish between those conditions that made an event likely to occur and those that triggered the event, perhaps rank contributory causes in order of importance—any or all of these.

Merely asserting causal connections isn't enough: you must supply enough details to join cause to effect. Causal analysis usually has an argumentative edge. There's no point in writing about cause-effect relations that are obvious to everyone (touching a hot stove causes pain). There *is* some point in exploring probable relationships that can increase a reader's understanding of a subject or suggest solutions to a problem. (Why do so many students have difficulty with math? Why has the Midwest lost industries to the Sun Belt? Why have there been a number of collisions on Amato Road within a period of weeks?) It is demonstration, not mere assertion, that establishes probability—demonstration in the form of concrete, relevant details and facts that knit cause to effect.

Here is the beginning of a student's account of his search for a cause:

Making Marks

Living in Philadelphia, a person learns to accept and overlook a variety of things that outsiders might consider unusual. One of these is graffiti. My home is in the far northeast section of the city, so whenever I go into town, I have to ride two trains and a bus. As the trains advance from the suburban northeast, the graffiti thicken rapidly, soon becoming the dominant scenic feature, covering station walls and benches, marring the sides of buildings, defiling poles, windows, houses, trucks, blotting almost everything that can be spray-painted or scribbled on.

Naturally, I was always aware of the phenomenon, but I'd taken it for granted, like the screeching turns, jarring stops, and expressionless faces that characterize such rides. It was just there. I saw it, but it registered as little more than vandalism. It wasn't until two months ago that I began to think of graffiti as something else.

The occasion was a wet night in the town where he was attending college. He took shelter from the rain in an underpass and found graffiti all over the walls.

There were two things about the graffiti that interested me. First, this was a college town, and the graffiti were the work of college students, a supposedly intelligent group of people. Secondly, I noticed that most of the writings were just single names—''Bill,'' ''Mary,'' ''Jill,'' ''Lou.'' I wondered why anyone in college would write his name on a wall.

Then he and a friend stopped at a bar, and there he came upon the name ''Ted Roethke'' carved on a table top.

Later I learned that when he carved his name at the Shandy Gaff, the famous poet Theodore Roethke was just another professor, with unlived dreams. Something else occurred to me. I remembered that Hector Berlioz, the French composer, had attributed his desire for success to a wish to be remembered after his death. He wanted to leave something behind. George Orwell made a similar statement in his essay, ''Why I Write.'' He said that one of the main reasons for writing was sheer egoism and that a characteristic of that egoism was the desire to be remembered after death.

Then I understood. As the artist, like Orwell and Berlioz, strives for a sort of immortality, so, too, does the graffitist. For him, as for Roethke the night he carved his name, it is the attempt to plant something permanent, to leave a mark, to have an effect. Roethke eventually achieved this with his poetry. But when he cut those ten letters into the wood, he was just one person among millions, another graffitist suffering the same insecurities that we all feel. He was another person trying to leave a little of himself somewhere.

Finally I thought again of the people in the lower-income neighborhoods of Philadelphia, the areas where the graffiti are thickest. They are the people whose chances are most limited. They are the most frustrated, the most insecure. Their effect on society is as limited as their prospects. So they are even more desperate than the college student, than the artist, to make a mark somewhere, to know that their names survive on some dirty wall, no matter where they go.

Of course, there are other reasons for graffiti. People spray or scribble them to be funny, to vent their anger, to pass time. But the most common form, the single name, is neither funny, abusive, or time-consuming. It is the individual's attempt to make his mark. That's why, in Philadelphia as elsewhere, the name prevails as the most common graffito, and even the most elaborate graffiti are usually signed.

For Discussion

A student wrote, "The prime culprit for the slump in the record industry is OPEC, because record vinyl is a petroleum derivative, and
when the cost of a barrel of oil goes up, the record manufacturers
increase the price of a record." What's the missing connection between the price of records and the slump in the industry? Is the chain
of reasoning convincing, or is it unconvincing? Why?

Attributing Effects

You're primarily concerned with effects in two situations. In one you work
from a current state of affairs or a current policy to its effects (the effects of
draft registration, for example), with a view to arguing that since the effects
have been desirable, the state of affairs or the policy should be continued,
or that since the effects have been undesirable, the state of affairs or the
policy should be changed. Here, the procedure is much like the one you use
in discovering causes and in persuading readers that your analysis was plausible. As in identifying causes, you must take care not to attribute to one
cause a condition that might just as logically be the effect of another cause.
Good relations in a housing unit may be less the result of social arrangements than of pleasant surroundings and a fair distribution of responsibilities.

In the second writing situation you *predict* effects as part of your argument for accepting or rejecting a proposed policy. When you predict, you
need to bring in all the evidence you can to show that the results you project
are likely to occur. We're all familiar with predictions about the bad consequences that will flow from courses of action or habits that the speakers
or writers don't approve of—continued busing will destroy the American
educational system; rock concerts will deafen a generation; anti-pollution
legislation will wreck the economy; television will wipe out literacy; and so
on. To make sure your analysis of effects is taken seriously, provide enough
detailed evidence to establish reasonable links between the policy or event
or situation and the results you say it will bring about.

Tracing a sequence of probable effects, linking one effect to another, is
a natural way of making predictions. The following passage gives a good
idea, in summary fashion, of how a scientist interprets a phenomenon, reasoning from a limited effect to a much more sweeping one.

Modern man's impact on butterflies, as well as other harmless insects, is of
deep concern to many scientists today. Their reasoning goes something like this:
About the only way man can totally eliminate a butterfly or moth species from
the earth—intentionally or accidentally—is by destroying its habitat (which
contains its food plant), leaving no possibility for regeneration in the foreseeable
future, as when a meadow is paved for a shopping mall, a woodland cleared for
a subdivision or a marsh drained for an industrial site. This habitat, however,

is not the butterfly's alone. It is something the butterfly has shared with other living creatures, including man. And when man thus molds a habitat to his exclusive use, asserting his claims there over those of all the other life forms in it, he is destroying *his* natural environment as well as theirs.

So it isn't just a question of the butterfly's world going down the drain; the world in which man in his present form has been able to flourish so successfully for half a million years or so is going down the drain, too, leaving in its place a very dubious synthetic substitute. It is with such a set of interlocking relationships in mind that Robert M. Pyle, the Xerces Society's executive director, has called butterflies "excellent monitors of environmental change and of rises in pollution levels." From this viewpoint, moths and butterflies are the barometers of our industrial civilization; their elimination from our human habitat is a danger signal we must heed.—Paul Showers, *New York Times Magazine*

For Writing

1. "At night the noise in the dorm makes sleeping, as well as studying, almost impossible." Take this statement or a similar one based on your own experience and develop a paper in which you first investigate the causes of the situation and then discuss its effects. You might go on to propose a remedy. Your audience is the director of housing on campus.

2. Take the general topic "Why I Am What I Am" and narrow it down to something you can treat in 500–700 words: Why I Am a Believer (*or* a Republican *or* a Bigot *or* a Feminist), for example. For an audience of your choice, you should explain how you came to fit into that category. Caution: your paper should not be an apology for what you are nor a glorification of the category in which you place yourself; it should be a causal analysis.

3. This topic requires some work in the library. Read the first page or two of the issue of the *New York Times* (or another newspaper with national circulation) that came out the day you were born. Select a story dealing with an event of major importance and do some research to discover the causes of the event, its outcome, and its long-range effects.

4. "In the world of reality," a logician observes, "there is no such thing as *the* cause of anything. There are many causes, or necessary antecedents, for everything that happens." And a historian says, "Any search for causes, if it is persistent, as in the case of the fall of the Roman Empire, becomes comic—such is the abundance of causes discovered." Take something from your own experience—an accident, a celebration, a failing grade in a course—and in a paper addressed to an audience of your choice analyze it to show the variety of causes or antecedent conditions that led to that happening.

Defining: Telling What It Is

College courses devote a good deal of time to defining terms and explaining concepts. Because mastering the vocabulary of a subject is essential, examinations often ask for the meaning of key terms. You'll be expected to recall, from lectures and textbooks, definitions of terms like *superego, deduction, occlusion, naturalism, macroaggregate.*

It's not only new terms that you need to master in your course work. Most branches of study give specialized meanings to terms that are in ordinary use. A sociology text points out that a definition of *group* must cover "such diverse phenomena as a Bantu family, a New York street gang, the board of directors of IBM, the International Red Cross, the U.S. Army, the British House of Commons, and even whole communities and societies." It goes on to establish its definition: "a group is a number of individuals who interact recurrently according to some pattern of social organization" (De Fleur, D'Antonio, Nelson, *Sociology: Human Society*). For the sociologist, a group isn't just "a number of people assembled together" or "a number of individuals who have something in common," definitions that would serve in everyday contexts.

And even words in everyday contexts may need defining. *Sexist, racist, ethnic,* and scores of other words are used in so many different ways that a careful writer will specify the meaning he intends. In discussing the ethnic revival of the seventies, Andrew M. Greeley says:

> The word *ethnic* has come to have many different meanings. . . . It is not that the word means nothing, but rather it means whatever the user wants it to mean. Sometimes it stands for "minority" and refers primarily to black, brown, native American, and Asian American, as in "ethnic studies" programs at universities; other times it is a code word for Catholics, as in "the white ethnic blacklash." . . . When the national news magazines or journals of opinion speak of ethnics, they mean Catholics, as when the *Nation* announced Daniel P. Moynihan as "ethnic." When I use the word, I normally refer simply to the variety of American subcultures whether that variety be based on race, religion, nationality, language, or even region.—*Harper's*

The sociologists' definition of *group* and Greeley's definition of *ethnic* are *stipulative* definitions: they tell how the word is being used in the particular context. In your papers you will sometimes need to stipulate the meaning you intend. When you do, be sure the meaning you stipulate is plausible. Nobody will pay much attention to a writer who decides, like Humpty Dumpty in *Alice in Wonderland,* that *glory* is to mean "a nice knock-down argument."

Among terms that need defining are the new words that are constantly entering the language, spawned by technological developments, hobbies, forms of entertainment. The definitions that follow, for example, are part of an article that begins by establishing the need for a rock-and-roll glossary. The author points out that many of the terms he uses as a rock-music critic are unfamiliar to readers of a general-interest newspaper and that the dictionaries aren't much help to them. So he provides the glossary for those who might be interested in the subject "if only because their *children* are interested and they feel vaguely curious about it."

> The difference between *rock-and-roll* and rock is a fine one, but generally the former means rock in the 1950's and the latter, rock in the 60's and 70's. *Hard rock* is loud and aggressive, usually more so than *mainstream rock*, which by the 70's turned softer and mellower. Even harder than hard rock is *heavy-metal rock*, brutally aggressive music played mostly for minds clouded by drugs and often performed by *power trios*, meaning guitar, bass and drums with as much amplification as they can afford.—John Rockwell, *New York Times*

These are informal definitions, which the writer concedes are "shorter and vaguer than any self-respecting dictionary would permit." But they suit his purpose.

A good grasp of the rhetorical situation will help you decide when to define and when not to. If you don't supply a definition your readers need, you'll lose touch with them. If you keep on providing definitions they don't need, you may lose them altogether. Awareness of your audience, its needs and capabilities, should also determine how you phrase a definition. Don't confuse a general audience by defining a technical term in language that's exclusively technical. Don't insult a well-informed audience by simplifying so much that your definition lacks precision. So far as you can, harmonize the definition with its context. Scientific terminology is required in a course paper for Zoology 101 but out of place in a letter to your cousin describing the attractions of the local zoo.

Except in situations where you want to fix the reader's attention on the meaning you're giving to a term, you don't need to rear back and announce that you are about to offer a definition. There are many ways of working a brief definition into a sentence or a paragraph. In these passages the explanations are slipped in without delaying the forward movement:

> Docudramas—made up of supposed scenes from the lives of living or recently deceased public persons—are proliferating on television, on the stage, and in fiction.—Carll Tucker, *Saturday Review*

> The *caciques* symbolized Spanish backwardness. These rural bosses controlled land and local political life.—Robert W. Kern, *Red Years/Black Years*

> The basis of the [Greek architectural] style was the lintel, that is to say, the horizontal wooden beam resting on two or more uprights, but on this simple foundation had been raised the subtlest, the most complete and the most purely logical style of architecture that the world has ever known.—Osbert Lancaster, *A Cartoon History of Architecture*

At first glance, the idea of taking deliberate aim at cities appears a barbarian thing to do, for the people who live in those cities are innocent of aggressive designs. But under deterrence theory, aiming at cities, called by the experts in these matters "countervalue," makes more sense than the alternative of "counterforce": aiming at the enemy's own missiles.—Alan Wolfe, *Nation*

Dr. King was a radical in the truest sense: he insisted at the same time upon the terrible reality of our problems and upon their solubility, and he rejected everything that was irrelevant to their solution.—*New Yorker*

"Mad Max" is the "Apocalypse Now" of exploitation movies. An exploitation movie, of course, is a pure commercial product—a polyurethane-wrapped package of sex, or violence, or horror, or all three flavors swirled together. "Mad Max" is a straight fix of violence.—Jack Kroll, *Newsweek*

Formal Definitions

Unlike a *lexical*, or dictionary, definition, which tells how a word is used in different contexts, or a stipulative definition, a variety of lexical definition that tells how a writer is using a word in a particular context, a *formal* definition points to the class of objects or events that a term names. While the noun *check* is used for many different things, there can be only one formal definition of the piece of paper we rip from a checkbook. It goes something like this: "A check is a written order directing a bank to pay money as instructed." The definition first places the class of things we call checks in the larger class (the *genus* or set) that it belongs to ("A check is an order") and then differentiates it from other classes in the set. A check is a written order, not a spoken one; it is addressed to a bank and only a bank; it instructs the bank to pay a specified amount of money from a specified account. For some terms, one differentiating characteristic, or *differentia*, is adequate ("A ballad [term] is a song [genus] that tells a story [differentia]"); for others, like *check*, several differentiae are needed.

Framing definitions on the pattern of genus-plus-differentiae gives excellent practice in precise, formal statement. In college courses, logical definitions are the kind you're most often expected to learn and to recall. But for some purposes the pattern is too confining and smacks too much of textbook or encyclopedia style. There are other ways of conveying your sense of the meaning of a term.

For Discussion

1. Using textbooks, unabridged dictionaries, or encyclopedias, construct formal definitions of several terms on the model of

term-to-be-defined = genus + differentia(e)

Suggestions: *superciliousness, dilemma, winter, technology*

2. Now consider these additional ways of building brief definitions:
   a. Etymology, or the history of a word, may or may not tell you something that will help explain the current meaning of a term. Does it help to know that *supercilious* comes from *supercilium,* a Latin word meaning "eyebrow"? Write a definition of *superciliousness* that takes that information into account.
   b. We often rely on synonyms, or "something-likes," in defining. Though no two words mean exactly the same thing, several words may have roughly the same meaning. In what circumstances might you find it useful to open a discussion of *dilemma* by listing such terms as *predicament, quandary, plight,* and *jam?*
   c. We use connotations—the associations a word has—to convey an emotional response to the subject. Compare a formal, impersonal definition of *winter* that gives the denotative meaning ("the season between autumn and spring, extending in the northern hemisphere from the December solstice to the March solstice") with definitions that rely on connotations: "When my brother hears the word *winter,* he thinks of exhilarating skiing trips and lodge fires; for my father it means a perpetual cold in the head and chronic depression." In a sentence or two, indicate what connotations *winter* has for you. (Connotation is discussed in Chapter Eight.)
   d. In almost all writing situations, examples support definitions, and frequently they stand in for them. For an audience of sixth-graders, write a paragraph built around three examples that show what we mean by the term *technology*.

Extended Definitions

Brief definitions, consisting of one or two sentences, occur in all types of writing. But definition can also be the chief means of explaining a subject or persuading an audience to respond to it in a particular way.

In some papers you may find that the question you're raising about your subject can best be answered by explaining what a term means or by asserting what it ought to mean. Is the world at peace when there's violent conflict in a number of small—that is, economically, politically, and militarily weak—countries? (Note the definition of *small*.) That depends on what you mean by "the world" and by "peace." Is violence a legitimate form of protest? That depends on your conception of both violence and protest. Should universities adjust their course offerings to the job market? That depends on what you believe a university's function should be.

In writing an extended definition, you can't simply report on how a term is used—though you may need to do that, too. You have to single out the distinctive characteristics or qualities or functions of the class of things or events that the term refers to—the world, peace, violence, universities.

As you explore your subject, you'll find yourself drawing on several of the methods of development we've discussed in this chapter and the last.

A student writing a paper on buck fever begins by dismissing some notions of what the term might mean: "It is not a yearning for money, nor is it a fictitious disease that young boys in high school contract during the first week of deer season." Treating it as a real "disease," he describes the symptoms—"the 'knocking knees' syndrome, a sudden increase in the blinking and watering of the eyes, a loss of equilibrium, tremors that affect the entire body"—symptoms that interfere with a hunter's ability to fire his rifle accurately.

For the benefit of nonhunters, the student compares buck fever to "situations that everyone should be capable of relating to":

> For instance, suppose that a young man who has had only modest success with the opposite gender sees a very attractive young lady who falls into the classification of "bombshell." After much deliberation, the young man decides to strike up a conversation with the young lady, expecting to be ignored. But to his surprise, the young lady responds to his queries. The young man immediately loses the ability to speak coherently. This is the equivalent of buck fever in interpersonal relations.
>
> Another example can be taken from the world of sports. In the bottom of the ninth inning of a championship game, the home team is losing by three runs. With the bases loaded and two outs in the inning, the next batter is the home run leader of both leagues. As he confidently approaches the batter's box, he suddenly begins to sweat profusely. As he swings at the first pitch, the bat flies out of his hands, and the batter ends up on his derriere. The nervous feeling preceding and the embarrassment following are the same as those experienced by a hunter with buck fever.

In the remainder of the paper the student takes issue with a dictionary definition that limits buck fever to inexperienced hunters (no hunter, he says, is immune) and tells of the attack he suffered.

"Buck Fever" examines a common malady and argues that it afflicts more hunters than most people realize. The following excerpt shows a similar attempt to alter the reader's understanding of what a term stands for. Borland wants to break down the boundaries we create when we think of ourselves as separate from nature and from animals. To do this, he relies less on logical definition (though he gives one in the second sentence of the second paragraph) than on a series of identifications at the end of paragraph 1 and a series of comparisons at the end of paragraph 2. The upshot of the discussion is that man is an animal and that *all* animals make up the "life principle" that is nature. If Borland has succeeded, his readers will leave the piece with a new understanding of what nature is and of how we relate to it.

> The words we use so readily are vague. We talk of nature and what we mean is life, the whole life principle. We too often think of nature, and even of life,

as apart from ourselves. Biologically we are animals, capable of procreation, needing food and drink, tolerant of a relatively narrow range of temperature and humidity, physical weaklings subject to injury and disease, organisms that eventually wear out and hence of limited life-span. Yet we talk of "the animals" apart from ourselves, and of "nature" as apart from this environment where we live. Actually, nature is you and me and the air and water around us, wherever we are, and the soil underfoot. Nature is a mouse, a rat, a bear, an earthworm, a louse, a flock of geese, a child and its parents.

I suspect that we set ourselves apart because nature is so unforgivably impartial—nature is no more concerned with the welfare of mankind than with that of rabbits or snapping turtles or periodic locusts. So far as dispassionate inquiry has yet determined, nature is a complexity of impersonal forces and materials whose only purpose is to sustain and perpetuate life on this planet. Not one particular form of life, but the basic life-force whether expressed in algae or slime mold or daffodils or buzzards or tigers. There are countless life-forms, from microscopic bacteria to elephants and whales and giant redwoods. And men. Man just happens to be one of those forms, a relatively minor one and a conspicuous physical weakling at that. Man is bigger than a fox, smaller than a cow, lacks fangs, claws, horns, and poisonous saliva, is so naked of skin that he sunburns in summer, is frostbitten in winter, and is an open feast for fleas, gnats, mosquitoes, and all manner of hungry insects.—Hal Borland in *What We Save Now*

In the preceding passage the writer has spent a good deal of energy trying to dislodge misconceptions. So that we can fully understand what nature is, what man is, and what the proper relation between them is, we must be brought to reject our mistaken ideas. Negation, then, or contrast, has an essential place in definition: defining is the process of limiting and excluding until you're down to those characteristics or properties that set apart the class you're concerned with. You tell what the class is *not* in order to better explain what it *is*. Sometimes you may find it useful to begin a paper with a single explicit negative like "A composition text is not a book of etiquette" or "Loyalty is not conformity."

In the following passage, negation is one of several means the writer uses to define the concept of protest:

How does protest differ from revolution? The word "revolution" is often used for any radical change in an aspect of government or society, but in its strict and more correct historical usage revolution is the great exception, whereas protest is the norm. Protest is an attack on the prevailing system in an intellectual or organized way. Revolution is a sickness in society, a breakdown of the social order, the kind of general demoralization and civil war that the ancient Greek philosophers called *stasis*. Protest uses violence, but it is strictly controlled and specific in its purposes—the seizure of a building, a riot, a political assassination—designed to shock and bewilder the elite and to advertise a grievance. Revolution is unchecked violence in which social groups war against one another for dominance, although violence usually becomes an end in itself and the groups often lose sight of their original purposes.

Revolution occurs only when an old regime defends itself against protest by becoming more reactionary and oppressive but, once having radicalized the middle class and stirred the workers and the poor to involvement, is too inefficient or guilt-ridden to carry out the necessary slaughter and imprisonment of protesters. The political and legal system then splinters, and uncontrolled violence takes over. Finally, some army or police leader takes advantage of middle-class fear of extermination and working-class hunger and establishes a new tyranny. Protest in the twentieth century has led to social change and, more often than not, to social melioration: revolution has been the road to chaos, civil war, and new tyranny.—Norman F. Cantor, *The Age of Protest*

Cantor uses not only standard ways of defining—stipulative definition (the strict historical use of the term *revolution*) and formal definition (in the third and fourth sentences)—but comparison and contrast, analysis of causes (government responses that lead to revolution), process (the stages in the fall of a regime), and attribution of effects (the contrasting results of protest and revolution). Clearly, there are many ways of building an extended definition.

Which ways you use in writing papers where definition is central will depend on your subject. You may want to investigate its origin or its history or what it's made of or what it looks like or what it's used for. You'll define a physical object like a lathe in different ways from a concept like responsibility, and a concept in different ways from a course of study.

Which ways you use will also depend on the rhetorical situation. Nowhere more than in defining is it essential for you to understand your relation to your audience. Expert addressing expert can confidently define in ways that would be disastrous if expert were addressing layman.

Whatever your subject and whatever the rhetorical situation, you have a great variety of resources at hand when you define—not only etymologies, synonyms, connotative and denotative meanings, and examples but also description, narration, comparison, contrast, classification, division, analysis of causes and effects. Choosing wisely among these techniques of defining will help you make clear the properties or characteristics of your subject— those distinctive features that set it off from everything else. And this is why we use definition.

For Discussion and Writing

1. Choose a slang term that you enjoy using, explain its meaning, illustrate its use, and offer some reasons for its popularity. Your audience is your grandparents—or your future grandchildren.

2. New attitudes, new outlooks, new policies require new terms. Here are two examples:

Somehow this nation has been caught in what I call the mire of "tech-nofix": the belief, reinforced in us by the highest corporate and political forces, that all our current crises can be solved, or at least significantly eased, by the application of modern high technology.—Kirkpatrick Sale, *Newsweek*

The word is *intermodality*. Not in standard dictionaries, it is increasingly common in the travel industry. As applied to travel it means combining modes of transportation—air, rail, bus, ship, car—to enhance a vacation. The term, commonly applied to fly/drive and rail/drive packages and air/bus and rail/bus tours, encompasses almost limitless possibilities. It is especially important in times of high gasoline prices because it can vir-tually eliminate the need to travel by car.—Paul Grimes, *New York Times*

Look around you. In what new ways are people acting or talking or thinking? Invent a word and then explain what it means. Your expla-nation should show that your new word fills a need.

3.   Explain what you mean when you speak of sin (or pain or toler-ance or courage or prejudice or any other concept that can mean different things to different people). Your audience is someone you want to help understand you better.

4.   Without attempting to make converts of your readers, define a political "ism" you favor (conservatism, liberalism, radicalism, or any other).

5.   Write a paper on some group you're familiar with, one that can be identified or defined by its habitual activities; its moral or social standards; its dress, language, or ceremonies. Make clear through concrete details the distinguishing characteristics of the group, its typical behavior, and the shared attitudes that give it unity and ex-plain its actions. Address your paper to readers who are *not* familiar with the group.

6.   In which of the following passages is *rhetoric* used favorably? In which unfavorably? In which is the connotation neutral? You should be able to answer these questions by examining the contexts in which the word appears. But does the word *rhetoric* communicate a precise meaning in each passage? In *b, d,* and *e,* substitute for *rhetoric* a word or phrase that expresses the meaning you think the writer had in mind.

a. Over and over again he made clear his detestation of rhetoric, of word-spinning, of heartlessness and frivolity; nor had he greater patience with the safe and commonplace.—Robert Towers, *New York Review of Books*

b. When the action is hot, keep the rhetoric cool.—President Richard M. Nixon in a television address, May 1970

c. Rhetoric, therefore, is the method, the strategy, the organon of the principles for deciding best the undecidable questions, for arriving at solutions of the unsolvable problems, for instituting method in those vital phases of human activity where no method is inherent in the total subject-matter of decision.—Donald C. Bryant, *Quarterly Journal of Speech*

d. ". . . do you think back on the fight?"

"Not as much as I thought I would," Ali answered. "Fighting is more of a business now than the glory of who won. After all, when all the praise is over," and he shifted into the low singsong voice that he uses for rhetoric and poetry, "when all the fanfare is done, all that counts is what you have to show for. All the bleeding; the world still turns."— George Plimpton, *Sports Illustrated*

e. Unlike typical writings on this subject, all of these public documents are remarkably free of the usual rhetoric and imprecations.—George W. Bonham, *Change*

f. Rhetoric, we argued, is concerned primarily with a creative process that includes all the choices a writer makes from his earliest tentative explorations of a problem in what has been called the "prewriting" stage of the writing process, through choices in arrangement and strategy for a particular audience, to the final editing of the final draft.—Richard E. Young, Alton L. Becker, and Kenneth Pike, *Rhetoric: Discovery and Change*

4

Persuading Readers

A persuasive paper doesn't just explore or examine a topic. It asserts something about the topic. It sets forth and supports a proposition. An expository paper about a college club may explain how the club's activities are related to its purpose. A persuasive paper about the club may use the same material to support the proposition that, because the club performs valuable functions, it should be subsidized by the college administration; or that, because of certain activities, it should be censured; or that, because the membership rules discriminate against certain groups, it should be disbanded. A book report for a high-school course may do no more than summarize the contents of the work. In a college course the student is likely to be asked to offer his interpretation and his judgment of the work. The summary is descriptive; the critical analysis is argumentative.

For Discussion

The differences between informing and persuading an audience are illustrated in three papers written in response to the following assignment:

Choose any subject that you're interested in and that you feel competent to write about. Write three brief papers (200–250 words each) about your subject, naming for each one the audience you're addressing.

1. In the first, give a neutral, informative account.
2. In the second, give an unfavorable view of your subject.
3. In the third, give a favorable view of it.

Finally, write a short account of how you went about writing the three versions, and tell which you think is most successful and why.

Read the papers and the author's comments and be prepared to discuss the ways in which writing to inform readers differs from writing to persuade them.

1.

Audience: Readers of my local newspaper, who know very little about running.

The Popularity of Running

Today more people run than ever before. Tall, short, fat, thin, runners can be found in the city and the country. Some run laps around quarter-mile tracks, some run established routes on local streets, still others ad lib, crossing whatever street or field they come to.

Not every runner has the same purpose. Some train for long-distance races, some hope to get in shape, some try to stay in shape. For one, running is the core of a strict exercise regimen; for another, it is just something to do.

The dedicated runner often seeks coaching to help improve his form, which includes everything from stride to arm position to breathing pattern. Informal joggers, on the other hand, just start running without giving serious thought to form.

The growing interest in running has led to more publicity for track and field, which in turn leads to more runners. Perhaps because it might be fun, perhaps because it might be healthy, running has become an activity that more than 10 percent of all Americans now share. Its popularity has led to the publication of many books on running, some of them best-sellers. It has also produced new lines of running gear, including running shoes and sweat suits. This highly individual, unregimented activity has therefore had an impact on the national economy.

2.

Audience: Jack, my hard-core running friend, whose motto is "Every week another quarter of a mile."

America's Latest Craze Runs Rampant

Like any other fad, running has become bloated with self-importance. Runners, cluttering the shoulders of America's roads, have formed their own cult. The gods they worship are the authors of books on running, dealers in running gear, and even doctors who specialize in treating runners' injuries.

Ten years ago running was simply exercise. Today it has exploded into a multimillion-dollar business. It used to be that you could slip on any old pair of sneakers and run. Now, thanks to the writers and dealers, runners buy zillions of shoes, a different pair for every conceivable running surface, every conceivable temperature and weather condition. Today's runner eats, sleeps, and talks running. He is a pawn in the Color-Coordinated Sweat Suit Empire.

Running does have its place—at bus stops and train stations, for instance. But there are better sports. Informal tennis, basketball, and touch football provide exercise, camaraderie, and a chance to *think*. (Deciding to run around a mud puddle hardly compares to developing a winning touch football stratagem.) And there are better exercises. Mowing the lawn, shoveling snow, and chopping wood (all of which runners are too worn out to do) are constructive ways to rev up the body. Even walking has advantages over running. Not only is it good exercise, but you can enjoy it longer and you don't smell like a locker room when you stop.

So why would anyone want to run? You run and sweat and stink and ache—and when you stop you're right back where you started, with the lawn still not mowed. Yes, why *should* anyone want to run? It must be those pretty shoes.

3.

Audience: Those people (including my father) who frown on running.

Run for Your Life

The fact that more people run today than ever before is a testament to the vast benefits to be gained from running, most obviously the physical benefits. Regular running is the best exercise there is, the key to staying fit. It used to be that only dedicated athletes were trained in the science of running, but today its popularity is widespread. Books steer the beginner away from bad habits, like overdoing it, toward a sensible regimen tailored to his needs. Shoes have been painstakingly designed to protect his feet from every kind of terrain, almost precluding strains and blisters. And to treat those few, usually minor injuries that do occur, skilled doctors have been specially trained. Running hones the body, then keeps it in shape.

Running has immeasurable psychological benefits as well. It's true that a healthy body makes a healthy mind. Group-joggers develop uniquely close friendships and the tight camaraderie that comes with sharing a common cause. But running has it over other sports in that it can be done alone. A runner takes himself from one piece of life to another—from city sidewalks to neighborhood lawns to country roads. It's an escape that no other activity provides, a euphoria that comes only when the body fulfills the mind's image of it. A stimulated body stimulates the mind; there's no greater satisfaction than completing a run, no more powerful confidence than that developed in one who has carried physical endurance over to other aspects of life.

Comment

I thought of my first paper as something that ought to be published in a newsmagazine. Accompanied by pictures, it might be in the Sunday paper. I wanted to give readers who don't run some idea of the great popularity of running today, so I gave a general picture first and then discussed why different kinds of people run. This is one main point that I wanted to make—that people have many different reasons for running. The other main point comes at the very end. Running has become big business. This should interest even those who for some reason or other never can or never will run.

The second paper was easiest to write. I'm a runner myself, but I'm not a fanatic like Jack, and I can see how ridiculous the Serious Runner can seem in the eyes of an anti-runner. Jack can't be reached if you talk about him and his obsession, but I thought by making fun of *all* runners I might get to him. I feel strongly about some of the things I write about too; I've been burned up by how much my shoes cost me. That gave me the idea for the second paragraph and for the last sentence, which I think is a neat way to end the paper. It's the best of the three, in my opinion. It was certainly the most fun to write.

The third one I couldn't get going on. Though it is the shortest, it took longest to write. I couldn't get the same flow I had in the second. My father is pretty serious in his opposition to running. He thinks it can be harmful, not just faddish. So I wanted to be serious too. The language is more formal, with words like "terrain" and "precluding" and "euphoria." I like "A runner takes himself from one piece of life to another." That is smoother than most of the paper. I had a lot of trouble with the last sentence. Even though the writing doesn't satisfy me, the ideas in the paper do, and I think I have accomplished my purpose, which was to show that running gives two different kinds of benefits, both of them important.

The Ends and Means of Persuasion

When we think of attempts to persuade, the first examples that come to mind are likely to be television commercials or, if it's around election time, campaign speeches—all-out efforts to sell products or candidates. What we're concerned with in this chapter is persuasion of a more reasoned and reasonable sort. The persuasive papers you write may, like commercials and campaign speeches, urge your audience to *do* something—go out and buy, get out and vote—or they may simply try to win a hearing for an opinion you hold or earn respect for a theory you advance.

When your purpose is to persuade, the papers you write should grow out of ideas you believe in, principles you hold to be true. You should make every effort to show your readers that you have good reasons—the best reasons—for believing as you do. Don't try to win arguments by slanting the evidence, by blustering and brawling, or by ignoring common sense. That persuasion can be dishonest, we all know. It can also be fallacious— that is, based on faulty evidence or illogical reasoning. What you should aim to do is to write *honest* arguments that are *logically sound* and, at the same time, as persuasive as you can make them.

Issue, Thesis, Proof

In choosing a topic for a persuasive paper, you must first of all see an *issue* in it. An issue exists when there is disagreement, and the best kind of issue for you is one you have convictions about.

Given a live issue, the two essential elements in a persuasive paper are the *thesis* and the *proof*. The thesis, or central proposition, represents your stand on the issue. The proof is the evidence you offer to support it. Thesis and proof make up the "what" and the "why" of argument.

Proof in persuasive papers is not the same as scientific demonstration. If we could settle a dispute by demonstrating conclusively that one side was right and the other wrong, presumably there would be no further debate. But the things we argue about from week to week and even from generation to generation (questions of morals and ethics, of priorities, of policies, of taste) can't be proved in that way. When sensible people of good will honestly disagree about whether a particular course of action is just or wise— or whether this person is better than that one at a certain skill or job or profession, or whether a movie or play or poem or painting is good—it's because the evidence very often can't be conclusive.

From the point of view of the writer, proving means giving reasons why a belief should be held or an action taken—reasons strong enough to lead readers to share the belief or agree that the action is wise. Not all such reasons are *logical* proofs, proofs that are addressed to the intellect. Some are *emotional* appeals. Appeals to the emotions are not necessarily inferior to appeals to the intellect. They are *alogical*—not illogical, but simply outside the province of logic. (The term *illogical* refers primarily to mistakes in reasoning.) In most great arguments—speeches or essays that argue with compelling power for a course of action or a principle or a belief or a judgment—logical and emotional appeals work together, reinforcing each other. The crucial distinction is not between the kinds of appeal but between the ways either kind is used. Unethical or immoral arguments as well as ethical and moral ones can be logically sound. Good arguments as well as bad ones may make deliberate appeals to the emotions.

The two paragraphs that follow support the same thesis and use the same basic approach: they argue that the government must institute programs to help the poor meet rising energy costs. Both are persuasive. But the methods of persuasion differ. The first asks for our understanding of a situation that is leading to serious problems for the whole economy; the appeal is to reason. In the second, the appeal is to emotion, to sympathy for those trapped in a situation they didn't create.

> We must have government programs to help the poor meet rising energy costs. Already thousands of families have been forced to give up their cars simply because they cannot afford the price of gas. Those who can pay the fares use public transportation to get to their jobs; but as we all know, public transportation is often inadequate, inconvenient, or nonexistent. So in many cases lack of transportation has meant loss of jobs. Increased unemployment, in turn, means loss of productivity and additional welfare costs at a time when our economy is in deep trouble. If that trouble is not to worsen, we must immediately take steps to halt this ripple effect at its source.

> Without government programs to help them meet rising energy costs, millions of poor Americans face bitter hardship. Those who have cars (invariably ancient, dilapidated gas and oil guzzlers) are being forced to give them up and rely on public transportation—if it exists and if they can afford the fares—or on their own two feet. For many, lack of transportation has meant loss of jobs, with all the financial and psychological damage that involves. For both urban and rural poor, it can mean a weary hike to reach stores in order to obtain the food and medicines necessary for survival. Meanwhile, ever-higher utility bills further constrict pitifully tight household budgets. Cold weather brings sickness and suffering for the poor of all ages. For thousands of the very young and the very old, it brings death. We cannot permit this human tragedy to continue.

Working Within the Rhetorical Situation

How should you go about persuading others to accept your views, to share your beliefs, to act in ways you think right? To begin with, size up the rhetorical situation, and then work in that context. Aim for a paper that will exhibit adaptation *by* a writer *to* an audience *of* an argument *on* a specific subject. The whole art of persuading consists of maintaining the right balance among these elements.

The "I" of Argument

In situations that require judgment, the qualities and qualifications of the person who is judging are the most powerful of the alogical (*not* illogical) arguments in favor of that judgment. Logically, the worth of an idea has nothing to do with the character of the person advancing it; but in areas where differences of opinion exist among people of good will, it *is* a matter of importance for the audience to have confidence in the writer. Indeed, it has such weight that some students of rhetoric, following Aristotle, give a separate label to this dimension of the rhetorical situation: they use the term *ethical proof* for all those appeals that relate directly to the character and authority of the person who's attempting to persuade.

In the persuasive papers you write, in and out of college, you should have no problem making clear the ways in which you're qualified to argue for a particular thesis. As for character, you should present yourself in your writing as you present yourself in person to someone whose respect and attention you value. By creating a favorable impression, you make your readers want to identify with you, and identification opens the way to agreement. In general, what wins confidence is a discussion conducted with intellectual vigor by a person who knows the subject, has a good grasp of the issue being debated, is fair in examining alternatives, but at the same time shows a strong commitment to the solution he's convinced is right.

Beyond that, different circumstances call for different strategies and different voices. In one situation, crisp, incisive, confident arguing is appropriate; in another, a tentative searching out of the truth works better. In one situation your tone will be forceful; in another it will be restrained. Sometimes you'll open an argument by telling readers what they want to hear. Other times you'll begin by telling them what they *don't* want to hear. Tough talk sometimes succeeds where sweet talk does not. Readers may be moved to grudging admiration for the writer who's not afraid to stand up for an unpopular idea, and grudging admiration may make them receptive to arguments on the issue itself. But if you do come out swinging, in the course of the argument you must find ways to bring yourself and your readers around to the same side. Your goal is not to win an argument but to persuade your readers that the position you support is the position that deserves their support as well.

You should be able to make your presence felt in your papers without either insulting your audience or harping on your own tastes, feelings, and attitudes and relating all your arguments to your own ego. Don't simply announce that you know what you're talking about ("As an expert on digital sound . . . "); earn the respect and trust of your audience. The "I" dimension of persuading is one more of the rhetorical matters that call for the right balance between two much and too little.

For Discussion and Writing

1. Below are passages from papers on vegetarianism—one spurning it, one supporting it. What tone of voice comes through each passage? How do the writers present themselves? What kinds of people do they seem to be?

When I look at a cut of beef in the supermarket, I don't see a piece of a murdered steer, cut down (and cut up) in the prime of life. To me it is a potentially satisfying meal wrapped in plastic. It is something my body will enjoy, and my mother may even derive a certain warm feeling cooking it for me. Should I deny her this little happiness? I can honestly say that my conscience has never bothered me after a double pepperoni and sausage pizza, though my innards sometimes have. The fault lies not in the food but in the gluttony of the eater, and a person can be just as intemperate with bread, or beans, as with hamburg or venison or duck.

A vegetarian diet makes sense both biologically and economically, but my reason for becoming a vegetarian was ethical. Representatives of the meat industry claim that the cruel methods used in slaughtering have been made more humane with the use of the modern electric stunner. They claim that this instrument makes an animal insensitive to pain at the moment of death. Unfortunately, the stunner doesn't always work. A butchering plant reeks of death, and an animal senses death and feels fear when he is being hoisted up in the air on his way to die. The living conditions of these animals are also horrendous. Veal calves, which incidentally are made anemic so that their flesh stays tender, are sometimes so weak that they never make it to the modern electric stunner. They drop dead when they are taken from their pens. Thus the vegetarian diet is not only a healthier and cheaper way to eat but a more humane, guilt-free way as well.

2. Write a one-page argument for or against vegetarianism. On the back, in a sentence or two, tell what tone of voice you intend the reader to hear. If you feel there's nothing new to say on the subject of vegetarianism, write your argument on health foods or junk foods.

The "You" of Argument

The better you know your readers, the more likely you are to speak directly to them. In accommodating your argument, take into account the general state of their knowledge, as well as their grasp of the particular issue. Do they know anything about it? As much as you do? More? What attitudes, values, and prejudices do you expect them to have? What is their response to your thesis likely to be—hostile, critical, skeptical, open-minded, tolerant, sympathetic? Do you need to overcome apathy? Relieve tension? Get rid of fears?

If you can judge how well acquainted with the issue your readers are, you'll know how much background information you should provide and how much specialized data you can include. If you know what their values and prejudices are, you'll be able to avoid insulting or irritating them. In general, it's prudent to show respect for old loyalties and prejudices even as you urge the need for change and for an unprejudiced stand on the particular issue. At times a direct appeal to self-interest is necessary (as in urging parents to oppose construction of a power plant that could be a threat to the health of their children). At other times an audience needs to be urged to rise above self-interest (as in persuading the elderly and childless to vote for higher taxes to improve schools).

When circumstances call for action as well as intellectual conviction, don't hesitate to supplement logical proof with honest appeals to your readers' hopes and fears, their sense of what's right and just, their sentiments of love and pity. Rational responses alone, and rational commitment alone, may stop short of any action. In some situations—particularly where self-sacrifice is involved—moral exhortation has its place. Readers may need to be told not only that they *can* take a certain action—contributing to famine relief, for example—but that they *should* take it.

Your sense of your audience's mood and convictions will help you decide how much space you should give to refutation—to attacking opposing views. Others have lined up in support of the counter proposition, or there wouldn't be any need for you to press your argument. If they've made a strong case for it, you'll need to give that case your serious attention. Whether you need to make refutation a major part of your paper or an incidental one depends in part on how much your audience has been swayed by the opposition. Anticipating and dealing with objections your readers are likely to raise is an excellent rhetorical technique. (Refutation is discussed on pp. 132–35).

Take into account the special characteristics of your audience. Every appeal for funds to support the university library gives primary attention to the library's need; but an appeal to one alumnus may emphasize school pride, and an appeal to another may stress the financial advantages of a tax write-off. Both appeals are legitimate attempts to accommodate an argument to a particular audience.

For Discussion and Writing

1. Use a local issue you're interested in as the basis for two papers, about 500 words each, in which you try to persuade two distinctly different audiences to share your judgment or support your recommendation. (An illustration—but only an illustration: Write to the curriculum committee asking that specific changes be made in a college course you've taken. Write to a friend urging him not to sign up for the course until these changes have been made.)

Though your two papers will present the same general views about the issue, they should differ in the space you give to each reason, the order in which you present your reasons, the way you open and close, and the general style and tone. Your task is to adapt the same argument to two very different audiences and to lead them both to the same conclusion.

2. Read the following passage.

What joins all languages, and all men, is the necessity to confront life, in order, not inconceivably, to outwit death. The price of this is the acceptance, and achievement, of one's temporal identity. So that, for example, though it is not taught in the schools (and this has the potential of becoming a political issue) the south of France still clings to its ancient and musical Provençal, which resists being described as a "dialect." And much of the tension in the Basque countries, and in Wales, is due to the Basque and Welsh determination not to allow their languages to be destroyed. This determination also feeds the flames in Ireland for among the many indignities the Irish have been forced to undergo at English hands is the English contempt for their language.

It goes without saying, then, that language is also a political instrument, means, and proof of power. It is the most vivid and crucial key to identity: It reveals the private identity, and connects one with, or divorces one from, the larger, public, or communal identity. There have been, and are, times, and places, when to speak a certain language could be dangerous, even fatal. Or, one may speak the same language, but in such a way that one's antecedents are revealed, or (one hopes) hidden. This is true in France, and is absolutely true in England: The range (and reign) of accents on that damp little island make England coherent for the English and totally incomprehensible for everyone else. To open your mouth in England is (if I may use black English) to "put your business in the street": You have confessed your parents, your youth, your school, your salary, your self-esteem, and, alas, your future.

Now, I do not know what white Americans would sound like if there had never been any black people in the United States, but they would not sound the way they sound. *Jazz,* for example, is a very specific sexual term, as in *jazz me, baby,* but white people purified it into the Jazz Age. *Sock it to me,* which means, roughly, the same thing, has been adopted by Nathaniel Hawthorne's descendants with no qualms or hesitations at all, along with *let it all hang out* and *right on! Beat to his socks,* which was once the black's most total and despairing image of poverty, was transformed into a thing called the Beat Generation, which phenomenon was, largely, composed of *uptight,* middle-class white people, imitating poverty, trying to *get down,* to get *with it,* doing their *thing,* doing their despairing best to be *funky,* which we, the blacks, never dreamed of doing—we *were* funky, baby, like *funk* was going out of style.

Now, no one can eat his cake, and have it, too, and it is late in the day to attempt to penalize black people for having created a language that permits the nation its only glimpse of reality, a language without which the nation would be even more *whipped* than it is.—James Baldwin, *New York Times*

Here is a reader's comment on the passage:

Baldwin first presents himself as a student of language who is making a detached, impersonal analysis. But something happens toward the end of the second paragraph. The Baldwin of the second half of the passage speaks in a different tone and adopts a different attitude toward his audience.

Do you agree or disagree with this interpretation of the passage? In either case, point to the words and phrases that give clues to Baldwin's sense of the "I-You" relationship, and explain how you as audience respond to Baldwin's argument, and why.

The Limits of Accommodation

You don't accommodate an argument to an audience just by adding a few personal remarks or some emotional appeals. Accommodation involves the method and manner of developing the entire argument—what evidence you use and how you use it, what appeals you make and how you make them, the way you organize your material, even the style you use.

Finding common ground, however limited, is a necessary first step. That doesn't mean that you should start by buttering up your readers or making them laugh or impressing them with what a noble character you have. Such tricks sometimes work, but they don't represent honest, ethical persuasion. Accommodation in this sense means finding ways to make your readers feel the force of the reasons that have led you to believe your thesis. Probably the best protection against a temptation to adopt the con man's techniques is to remind yourself that whether you win the argument or not, you're trying to lead your audience to see the truth as you see it. The right procedure is to find good reasons for supporting the position you've taken and then to use all the resources of *responsible* communication to persuade your readers to assent to it.

The criterion of responsible communication puts limits both on what you say and how you say it. In accommodating your argument to your audience, don't compromise either your best self or your best arguments. We give our serious attention to the writer who, as we say, knows his subject (meaning that he knows more about it than we do) and who gives solid reasons why we should accept the position he's taken. The position may be a minority one; his views may be unpopular. But we read what he has to say if we have the impression that he is testifying to the truth as he sees it. In honest persuasion the writer adjusts neither his thesis nor his evidence to his notion of what his audience wants to read. Though he adapts his arguments to a particular audience, he doesn't alter his basic beliefs. He doesn't write in support of a point of view for an audience favorably disposed toward it and then write against that point of view when he's addressing an audience he knows is strongly critical of it. Accommodate your argument to your readers, yes. But don't accommodate it out of existence.

Discovering Proof

To win readers over to your position, you have to give them compelling reasons to believe that it's the right one. Discovering good reasons calls for effort. You don't stumble onto arguments ready-made. You need to hunt for them, both in the subject itself—the internal sources of argument—and in external sources, those that lie outside the subject.

Internal Sources of Argument

A real issue will yield any number of lively arguments. You can generate some of them by studying the nature of what you're arguing about, by investigating its causes and effects, and by finding out what it's like and unlike. To see how, we'll refer again to some of the methods of developing ideas discussed in Chapter Three. Definition, example, classification, division, causal analysis, and comparison can all be given an argumentative thrust that shapes them into support for a belief or a proposal.

Argument from the Nature of the Subject

If you take the position that college students should have certain privileges and if you offer as a reason the assertions that college students are mature and that mature people deserve these privileges, you're drawing your argument from the nature of the subject—here, the nature of college students. A vital part of the argument is the case you make for putting students into the class of mature people: you need to give evidence about their habits, attitudes, and so on. (For the moment we're not concerned with the details of the proof but only with the general lines of the argument.)

Making a similar approach to a different issue, you might argue that a high-school diploma should guarantee competence in the basic skills—reading, writing, arithmetic—on the ground that the public schools are responsible for developing such skills. Or you might argue that tuition fees should be abolished in all schools supported by public funds, on the ground that, according to our democratic principles, every citizen has the right to be educated to the limit of his intellectual ability. In each case you're saying that something—the something your thesis is about—is a member of a class: college students are mature people; teaching competence in fundamentals is the responsibility of the public school system; free tuition is a right of citizens in our society. It follows that any assertion you can make about the class as a whole, you can make with equal confidence about your subject—so long as you've persuaded your audience that your subject is indeed a member of the class.

In arguing from the nature of the subject, your essential task is to fit your subject into a class that your audience will accept and respond to. Maturity (in connection with privileges), responsibility (in connection with the public schools), rights (in connection with American citizenship)—relating your particular subject to classes like these assures you at least of a hearing, if not of agreement with your thesis.

In building your argument, work hardest at supporting the proposition that your readers are least likely to find acceptable. In most rhetorical situations, arguing that college students are mature would be more to the point than arguing that mature people deserve specific privileges. It would usually be more telling to argue that a high-school diploma should guarantee competence in fundamentals than to argue that the public schools are responsible for teaching fundamentals.

But sometimes the proposition on which you base your thesis may need defending. If you did some investigating before writing a paper on the right of every citizen to be educated to the limit of his intellectual ability—that is, before arguing that no one who is qualified intellectually should be denied an education for economic or other reasons—you might find that some of your prospective readers believed only that all young people should have the *opportunity* to be educated to the limit of their ability—that is, that schools should be open to all who can meet their intellectual requirements *and* pay their fees. Those who viewed as a right not education but the opportunity to be educated would be trying to dislodge your subject from the class you put it in. So if you were committed to arguing the issue on the ground of citizens' rights, you would in this case first need to persuade your audience that those rights do indeed include free tuition.

A student's paper, "Live Free," opens with an argument based on his highly individual interpretation of the nature of his subject:

> "As long as possible live free and uncommitted," Thoreau urges us. "It makes but little difference whether you are committed to a farm or the county jail." Free and uncommitted! But what does it mean to be free or to live free? What is freedom? A free man is one who will not allow himself to be locked into safety and security, no matter how promising, at the expense of the opportunity to *live*. Freedom is essentially the chance to become better; enslavement of any kind dooms one to become worse.
>
> What is a farm or a marriage or a job but a respectable form of enslavement? To be locked into a farm is to be committed to a prison. The mortgage keeps the farmer in a cell; the bankers, the sellers of seed and farm equipment, and the buyers of farm produce are the guards that keep him from escaping. Yes, a farm is a prison.

The definition of a free man, the definition of freedom, and the classification of a farm as a kind of prison all contribute to an argument rooted in the nature of the subject. Anyone wanting to refute it would have to challenge its definitions and its position that any form of commitment is a kind of slavery.

Though arguments from the nature of subjects can often be stated concisely, the beliefs they reflect are so much a part of your thinking that you may scarcely be aware of them. These beliefs—about human nature, ethics, government, education, and so on—shape your convictions on issues and stand as unstated *assumptions* behind every serious argument you take part in. (Anyone who argued that the availability of pocket calculators made the teaching of mathematics unnecessary would be revealing questionable assumptions about the nature of calculators, the nature of mathematics, and the nature of education.) As a writer, be sure you recognize what your assumptions are. In some rhetorical situations you'll also want to state them to your audience. Readers who begin by opposing your position on an issue but share your basic assumptions can be led to see that your position follows logically from those assumptions. And even when you know that your readers don't share your assumptions, stating them may clarify your stand.

The bare statement of a shared assumption can have great rhetorical force. Consider this assertion by John T. Rule: "To punish all to prevent the transgressions of the few is, on the face of it, unjust." In the context, "on the face of it" clearly indicates that the writer believes no proof is needed. Any reasonable person, he says in effect, will accept as truth, or at least as an assumption he can go along with, that it's unjust to punish everyone in order to prevent a few from breaking the law. Another unstated assumption stands behind this one: A policy that's unjust shouldn't be pursued. Again the writer takes it for granted that any reasonable person would accept that assumption.

To the extent that evidence is offered in support of them, assumptions take on the character of definitions or statements about membership in a class. Typically, in an argument based on classification, you refer the specific issue to a larger context. You discuss a question about university policy in the context of what a university should be. You refer a question about the quality of a particular dictionary to the question of the nature and function of dictionaries. Once you've supported your belief about the larger question, you can turn to the particular instance with confidence that your argument is solidly grounded.

Working in terms of definitions and classes isn't the only way of conducting an argument based on the nature of the subject. Examples (see pp. 28–29) are often powerful persuaders, as in this passage from a student's paper in support of the metric system:

> Not long ago, my father asked me to figure out a way to tell him how much fuel oil was in our oil tank by measuring the height of the oil. After some hasty measurements of the tank, a little thought, and some algebraic manipulation, I came up with a formula which gave the volume in cubic feet. "But I need to know how many gallons of oil I have, not how many cubic feet," my father commented upon the results. Neither he nor I knew how many gallons were in a cubic foot.
>
> "Now you know why we're going metric," was my only reply. Had the measurement been taken in centimeters, the answer would have been in cubic centimeters, which can be converted to liters merely by moving the decimal three places to the left. Such simplicity is unheard of with the English system. Metric may take all the fun out of solving problems for some people, but it sure can save time.

Division (see pp. 56–60) opens the door to two common, if sometimes risky, ways of arguing. One is to make inferences about part-whole relationships—to argue that what is true of a part is true of the whole ("The recall of thousands of cars with defective door latches indicates that this is a poorly designed model, carelessly constructed of shoddy materials'') or that what is true of the whole is true of a part (''In a university with a fine reputation, you can be confident that the faculty is first-rate''). The other is to examine each part in turn and come to some judgment. The parts may be constituent elements, as plot, character, and theme are constituent elements of a novel; or they may be two alternative courses of action, in which case the typical procedure is to show that since one course is impracticable or unwise or impossible, the other should be adopted.

For Discussion and Writing

1. Analyzing publications designed to persuade can help you sharpen your own skill in writing persuasive papers. The practice is particularly useful when the techniques of persuading are not blatant—when you are nudged rather than pushed to adopt certain attitudes. Magazine advertisements are sometimes blatant, sometimes subtle. The same can be said of the persuasive techniques of the magazines in which they appear. Several American magazines are aimed at the population in a particular region, among them *Sunset* (subtitled *Magazine of Western Living*), *Southern Living* (for the South), and *Yankee* (for New England). Each of them, in its articles, special columns, and advertisements, creates a certain image of the region it's concerned with. After examining several issues of one of these periodicals, or any other regional magazine, write a paper describing the way of life, including the values, that the publication presents as admirable.

If a regional magazine isn't available, choose any magazine that sets out to help its readers create a domestic environment—indoors and perhaps outdoors as well—which represents the Good Life. Examples: *Better Homes and Gardens, Apartment Living, Good Housekeeping.*

Your paper should be rich in specifics drawn from the magazines; it should pull these specifics together into interesting and persuasive generalizations. You may want to move beyond analysis to comment on the connection, or lack of connection, between life as the magazine presents it and life as it's actually lived.

2. In a study of the importance of physical appearance, a group of business students of both sexes were asked to judge applications for a managerial and a nonmanagerial job. Each student was given four application forms, two from men and two from women, with photographs attached. All four were equally qualified, but one man and one woman were attractive, the other two ordinary in looks. The good-looking men were chosen more often for both jobs. The good-looking women were preferred for the nonmanagerial job, but the plain woman was picked for the managerial job.

a. Analyze the results of the study to determine what assumptions guided the judgments.

b. Write a paper arguing either for or against the basis of judgment. Should looks be a criterion in hiring when job performance has no connection with appearance? Why or why not?

c. Do you or don't you agree that plain women should be chosen over attractive women for managerial jobs? Support your position with the best evidence you can come up with.

Argument from Causal Relations

Often a productive line of argument will open up if you inquire into the causes or the effects of a situation or a policy or an action. Here the main emphasis is not on the nature of the subject but on its origins or its consequences—how it came about or what it will lead to and sometimes, though not always, what should be done about it.

An argument from causal relations (or consequences) is the natural approach whenever you're urging that a new policy be adopted or an old one changed. Typically the argument moves through four stages: an analysis of conditions ("Among teenagers in our central city, unemployment has reached 60 percent . . ."); an investigation of causes ("With no incentive to stay in school, these young people enter the job market lacking any real qualifications . . ."); a proposal designed to correct, control, or improve conditions ("What we need are tax adjustments that will enable companies to provide job training . . ."); and a call for action to put the proposal into effect ("So write your representative in the legislature, urging support for immediate revision of the tax structure so that . . .").

That's the *proposal* argument in its classic form. Sometimes you may have to deal with a whole network of causes instead of a single cause. And even when the cause can be pinpointed, you may become convinced that eradicating it isn't feasible. When the cure is worse than the disease, you may conclude that the wisest course of action is to treat the symptoms— make the effects less harmful or expensive or unpleasant. (A secretary of agriculture was quoted as saying that the effect of a ban on nitrites in curing foods would be "the world's worst case of food poisoning: thousands of people would die of botulism." In such a situation the dangerous effects of using nitrites must be balanced against the dangerous effects of not using them.)

So the crux of a proposal argument may not be identifying the cause of a situation but deciding how best to correct the situation. One familiar example is the debate over the use of nuclear power as an energy source by public utilities at a time when an adequate supply of oil depends on imports.

When a situation is familiar enough to need no detailed analysis, the writer may plunge into his remedy immediately and concentrate his argument on its feasibility. Such is the procedure of Edward Abbey in what he describes as one of his "constructive, practical, sensible proposals for the salvation of both parks and people." His argument in support of the proposal is made succinctly in paragraph 1: Automobiles are not driven into holy places; parks are holy places; therefore, automobiles should not be driven into parks. (Note how much hangs on the concisely stated argument from the nature of the subject—the park as holy.)

Paragraphs 2–4 work out the proposal in detail. Paragraph 5 dismisses in a vigorous, assured tone the claims of the very young and the very old. The last two paragraphs deal with objections to the proposal. Again, the tone is brisk, even impatient: "But this is nonsense." Yet Abbey doesn't just dismiss the complaints. In dealing with them, he shows that his proposal may have long-term beneficial effects as well as short-term ones.

[1] No more cars in national parks. Let the people walk. Or ride horses, bicycles, mules, wild pigs—anything—but keep the automobiles and the motorcycles and all their motorized relatives out. We have agreed not to drive our automobiles into cathedrals, concert halls, art museums, legislative assemblies, private bedrooms and the other sanctums of our culture; we should treat our national parks with the same deference, for they, too, are holy places. An increasingly pagan and hedonistic people (thank God!), we are learning finally that the forests and mountains and desert canyons are holier than our churches. Therefore let us behave accordingly.

[2] Consider a concrete example and what could be done with it: Yosemite Valley in Yosemite National Park. At present a dusty milling confusion of motor vehicles and ponderous camping machinery, it could be returned to relative beauty and order by the simple expedient of requiring all visitors, at the park entrance, to lock up their automobiles and continue their tour on the seats of good workable bicycles supplied free of charge by the United States Government.

[3] Let our people travel light and free on their bicycles—nothing on the back but a shirt, nothing tied to the bike but a slicker, in case of rain. Their bedrolls, their backpacks, their tents, their food and cooking kits will be trucked in for them, free of charge, to the campground of their choice in the Valley, by the Park Service. (Why not? The roads will still be there.) Once in the Valley they will find the concessionaires waiting, ready to supply whatever needs might have been overlooked, or to furnish rooms and meals for those who don't want to camp out.

[4] The same thing could be done at Grand Canyon or at Yellowstone or at any of our other shrines to the out-of-doors. There is no compelling reason, for example, why tourists need to drive their automobiles to the very brink of the Grand Canyon's south rim. They could *walk* that last mile. Better yet, the Park Service should build an enormous parking lot about ten miles south of Grand Canyon Village and another east of Desert View. At those points, as at Yosemite, our people could emerge from their steaming shells of steel and glass and climb upon horses or bicycles for the final leg of the journey. On the rim, as at present, the hotels and restaurants will remain to serve the physical needs of the park visitors. Trips along the rim will also be made on foot, on horseback, or—

utilizing the paved road which already exists—on bicycles. For those willing to go all the way from one parking lot to the other, a distance of some sixty or seventy miles, we might provide bus service back to their cars, a service which would at the same time effect a convenient exchange of bicycles and/or horses between the two terminals.

[5] What about children? What about the aged and infirm? Frankly, we need waste little sympathy on these two pressure groups. Children too small to ride bicycles and too heavy to be borne on their parents' backs need only wait a few years—if they are not run over by automobiles they will grow into a lifetime of joyous adventure, if we save the parks and *leave them unimpaired for the enjoyment of future generations*. The aged merit even less sympathy: after all they had the opportunity to see the country when it was still relatively unspoiled. However, we'll stretch a point for those too old or too sickly to mount a bicycle and let them ride the shuttle buses.

[6] I can foresee complaints. The motorized tourists, reluctant to give up the old ways, will complain that they can't see enough without their automobiles to bear them swiftly (traffic permitting) through the parks. But this is nonsense. A man on foot, on horseback or on a bicycle will see more, feel more, enjoy more in one mile than the motorized tourist can in a hundred miles. Better to idle through one park in two weeks than try to race through a dozen in the same amount of time. Those who are familiar with both modes of travel know from experience that this is true; the rest have only to make the experiment to discover the same truth for themselves.

[7] They will complain of physical hardship, these sons of the pioneers. Not for long; once they rediscover the pleasures of actually operating their own limbs and senses in a varied, spontaneous, voluntary style, they will complain instead of crawling back into a car; they may even object to returning to desk and office and that dry-wall box on Mossy Brook Circle. The fires of revolt may be kindled—which means hope for us all.—Edward Abbey, *Desert Solitaire*

For Writing

Write a page or two supporting or attacking Abbey's proposal. If you support it, you'll need to find further good reasons for banning cars and further good consequences that would result. If you attack it, you might take issue with his view of parks as holy places. Or you might argue that the proposal is undemocratic or that the bad effects would outweigh the good. For this paper, your audience is Edward Abbey.

In writing proposal papers, take care not to exaggerate your case. It's natural to express cause-effect arguments in unqualified assertions and in strong language. If you're tentative in suggesting the cause of a situation, your reader may not see the need for change. But rash claims don't convince, either. In your eagerness to press for *your* solution, don't rule out all alternatives. The only possible excuse for doing so is an absolute personal conviction that the situation dictates *one* course of action. Essentially what you tell your audience is that, given the circumstances, there's just one thing we can do—not because it's a good or wise or appealing action but because the only alternative is disaster. This variety of causal argument, called the argument from circumstances, is often justly criticized for blocking off rational discussion.

For Discussion and Writing

1. The following excerpt shows a typical use of the argument from circumstances—first the situation, then the solution, then the call for action. Do you find the argument convincing? Why or why not?

> Ten percent of the human beings ever born are now alive and breeding like bacteria under optimum conditions. As a result, millions live at famine level. Yet even with the fullest exploitation of the planet's arable land—and a fair system of distribution—it will not be possible to feed the descendants of those now alive. Meanwhile, man-made waste is poisoning rivers and lakes, air and soil; the megalopolis continues to engulf the earth, as unplanned as a melanoma and ultimately as fatal to the host organism. Overcrowding in the cities is producing a collective madness in which irrational violence flourishes because man needs more space in which to *be* than the modern city allows. . . .
>
> To preserve the human race, it is now necessary to reorganize society. To this end, an Authority must be created with the power to control human population, to redistribute food, to purify air, water, soil, to repattern the cities. . . .
>
> These, then, are the things which must now be done if the race is to continue. Needless to say, every political and economic interest will oppose the setting up of such an Authority. Worse, those elements which delight in destroying human institutions will be morbidly drawn to a movement as radical as this one. But it cannot be helped. The alternative to a planned society is no society. If we do not act now, we shall perish through sheer numbers, like laboratory rats confined to too small a cage.—Gore Vidal, *Esquire*

2. Note the form of this statement:

> If capital punishment is ever necessary for the preservation of public welfare, and it is at times necessary for that end, then according to reason capital punishment is lawful.—John J. Ford, *Catholic Mind*

Using that statement as a model, build several sentences that move through the three stages "If . . . , and . . . , then. . . ." Some samples are:

> If a standing army is ever necessary for national defense, and it is sometimes necessary for that purpose, then a standing army must be maintained.

> If government seizure of all interstate transportation is ever necessary to safeguard the public welfare, and it is at times necessary for that end, then it stands to reason that such seizure is constitutional.

Then choose one of your sentences and write a paragraph that supports the proposition phrased in the "and" stage.

3. Write a proposal for correcting a situation or changing a course of action. You may want to follow the organization outlined on page 109—analysis of conditions, investigation of causes, proposal, call for action—or you may hit upon some other organization that seems likely to accomplish your purpose. In any case, sketch the rhetorical situation in a sentence or two above your title, specifying in particular the probable attitude of your audience about the need for change.

You may get some ideas for a subject from these theses supported by students who have written on this assignment:

a. For health, nutrition, and economy, we should all include soy foods, especially tofu, in our diets.

b. To reduce the stresses of everyday living and to increase creativity and general well-being, Americans should follow a regular program of Eastern meditation techniques.

c. The traffic in various brands of Oriental "meditation techniques" poses a substantial threat to the mental health of our citizens.

d. A three-party political system in this country would result in better officials being elected and, consequently, in better government.

e. The physical and psychological benefits of regular exercise make it a "positive addiction."

f. Everyone planning to go to college should take at least a year off after high school to travel and work.

4. Write a persuasive paper in which you demonstrate that either good effects or bad effects followed from an action you took despite the objections of your parents, your adviser, your employer, or some other person of authority. In the course of your paper, make clear what the objections were. Identify your audience. If you're arguing that good effects resulted, your audience might be whoever raised the objections. If you're arguing that the effects were bad, your audience might be a sister or brother or a friend who is tempted to take the same action.

Argument from Likenesses and Differences

Ideas about what a thing is like and what it's unlike can provide you with a
lead-in to productive argument. The main function of difference arguments
is to make distinctions among things normally thought to be the same. And
the main function of likeness arguments is to persuade the reader that things
not normally thought of as alike are, in fact, alike in important respects that
bear directly on the point at issue. Likeness and difference relations enter
into a great many arguments where the aim is not to establish good or bad,
or right or wrong, or to propose solutions but to make a comparative judgment: to argue that one book is better than another, to show that one candidate is stronger than another, and so on.

A typical use of likeness arguments is to argue that a program or policy
be adopted—or rejected—because the same program or policy, or a similar
one, has—or has not—been successful in a comparable situation. One argument for some universal form of health insurance in the United States is
that socialized medicine functions well in Great Britain. (And one argument
against universal health insurance in the United States is that the British
medical system does *not* function well.) The proposal that criminal behavior
be treated medically, as physical and psychological ailments are, makes
sense if it is based on a strong argument that criminal behavior stems from
a disorder of the personality.

In opposing government aid to a private corporation faced with bank-
ruptcy, an economist uses a major difference between the private enterprise
system and a government-controlled system to support his argument:

> The private-enterprise economic system is often described as a profit system.
> That is a misnomer. It is a profit and *loss* system. If anything, the loss part is
> even more vital than the profit part. That is where it differs most from a gov-
> ernment-controlled system. A private enterprise that fails to use its resources
> effectively loses money and is forced to change its ways. A government enter-
> prise that fails to use its resources effectively is in a very different position. If
> Amtrak loses money, it is more likely to get a larger appropriation from Con-
> gress than to be forced to change its ways. Indeed, Congress may even instruct
> it to expand.—Milton Friedman, *Newsweek*

Differences are often used effectively in refutation. Here, the proposition that violence against women in the United States is caused by the availability of pornography (as argued by Susan Brownmiller and others in a
colloquium at New York University Law School) is dismissed by a persuasive argument from difference:

> Of course, the ideologically rooted suspicion that there is a causal relationship
> is buttressed in the United States by the plentifulness of both pornography and
> violence against women. That can make it seem that there is a connection,
> providing credibility for Brownmiller's catch line: ''Pornography is the theory;
> rape is the practice.'' But that impression is quickly dissipated when one looks

at the situation in other countries. For example, violence against women is common in two countries I had occasion to visit during the past year, Ireland and South Africa, but pornography is unavailable in those countries. By contrast, violence against women is relatively uncommon in Denmark, Sweden and the Netherlands even though pornography seems to be even more plentifully available than in the United States. To be sure, this proves little or nothing except that more evidence is needed to establish a causal connection between pornography and violence against women beyond the fact that both may exist in the same place. But this evidence, as the American commission concluded ten years ago and as the British committee decided last year, simply does not exist.—Aryeh Neier, *Nation*

The variety of likeness-difference argument called analogy is extremely common in argument. We argue from analogy when we say that because the period we're living in is strikingly similar to some period in the past, we should adopt a policy now that proved successful then. We argue from analogy when we say that methods used to solve an economic or social problem in an industrial city in Italy can be successfully applied in Seattle, or that blacks can work their way out of the slums as white ethnic minorities have done. Some years ago, members of the women's liberation movement who saw the position of women as analogous to (comparable to) that of an exploited racial or ethnic group called for a program of action like the one then being pursued by black militants. These are all *literal* analogies, in which things of the same class are compared—historical periods, industrial problems, people. When you use a literal analogy, your argument will be persuasive if the similarities between the two cases have a direct bearing on the point at issue.

In other analogies, sometimes called figurative, the writer sees a relationship that involves members of different classes—governments and families, for example. He may argue that just as a family can spend no more than its wage-earners bring home, so a government should spend no more than it takes in, keeping its budget in balance. An analogy of this kind doesn't argue from similarities between two things; it argues from a similarity of *relationship*. Nobody would say that a family is significantly like a government. But some believe that the relationship between the government and the federal budget is, or should be, comparable to the relationship between a family and its budget. (Some disagree—or point out that most families are in debt.)

In the example we've just discussed, the analogy takes the form A:B::C:B (A is to B as C is to B). *B* (the budget) is the common term. More often there is no common term, and the analogy takes the form A:B::C:D, as in "The university is for learning as an airplane is for flying" (McGeorge Bundy). Here, the relationship is function: just as an airplane is built to serve the function of flying, so a university is established to serve the function of learning.

In argument, an analogy may be a single assertion like those just quoted, or it may be developed throughout a lengthy passage:

> The appeal for [economic] restraint must be based on ground rules that spell out what decision makers are being asked to do. "Drive carefully" is just not an effective substitute for a posted speed limit. Speed limits on wages and prices will inevitably share some of the imperfections of posted speed limits on the highways. They will contain an element of arbitrariness, just as a fifty-mile speed limit is arbitrary in the sense that it is not demonstrably superior to forty-nine or fifty-one. Just as a passing lane is needed on the highways, so a "passing lane" must be provided for wages and prices, allowing relative shifts over time in response to the signals of the market. Just as some speeders will escape the eyes of the traffic patrol, so some violators of the price and wage standards will not be identified. Despite these imperfections, posted speed limits on the highways serve the nation well and so can speed limits on prices and wages— Arthur M. Okun, Henry H. Fowler, and Milton Gilbert, *Inflation*

You can use figurative analogies to throw new light on a subject, to open up an avenue of speculation, to give colorful support to an argument.

Like the argument from difference, analogy is a useful means of refutation:

> Even if human sexual capacity could be said to be for the purpose of generation, the argument that it is therefore sinful to use it for any other purpose is fallacious. There can be no good reason for saying that if a thing was designed for one purpose it is wrong to use it for some other purpose instead or in addition. It is not sinful to use a screwdriver for opening a pot of paint, though that is not what screwdrivers were meant for. It is not sinful to use one's teeth for untying knots, one's breath for cooling one's porridge, or one's intelligence for solving crossword puzzles, though it cannot be maintained that these are the purposes for which these gifts were conferred upon us. It is equally absurd to argue that, because the gift of sexual potency was conferred upon us for the purpose of producing children, it is therefore wicked to use it for some other purpose, such as the giving and receiving of sensual pleasure.—C. H. Whiteley and Winifred M. Whiteley, *Sex and Morals*

Seeing similarities between things is essential to thinking, and seeing similarities that others have overlooked can open the way to a fresh, inventive approach. In offering an analogy, you don't claim that two things are alike in all respects or even in most respects. You only say that they're alike in some respect that's relevant to the point at issue. And you may, quite fairly, make an inference based on that one resemblance. An analogy isn't fallacious because it ignores differences; it's fallacious when the differences it ignores are highly significant. An analogy between a bird and a plane wouldn't serve much purpose in an argument about the consumption of petroleum products. Though a bird and a plane are alike in certain respects, there is no relationship so far as the point of the argument goes. (For common weaknesses in the use of analogy, see p. 129.)

For Writing

1. Write an argument of 800–900 words supporting or attacking the position taken in the passage below. In this paper you'll probably want to draw on arguments based on the nature of the subject (both college work and professional basketball) and on consequences as well as on similarities and differences.

> If a kid has the talent to play [basketball] professionally, neither transcript irregularities nor low grades nor complete illiteracy should bar him from college, because college ball is a generally necessary stepping-stone to a career he is qualified to pursue. People don't have to go to college to become professional dancers, stockbrokers or photographers. They almost always have to to become professional basketball players.—Roy Blount, Jr., *Esquire*

2. You have a friend (or relative) in another country who has asked you to explain the nostalgia craze in the United States. Write a letter saying why you think Americans—particularly young Americans—have been attracted by the songs and movies, fashions and styles of the 1960s or the 50s or 40s or 30s or 20s. Some questions to consider: Does it reflect discontent with the present? Were those happier times? Is it simply human nature to look back with longing on earlier times? In your paper, make clear whether or not you share the current fascination with some past decade.

3. In your own words, reproduce the train of reasoning in each of the following excerpts and explain why you do or do not find it convincing. Then try composing a different argument to prove the point each excerpt makes.

> **a.** Every winter those of us who attend plays at the Auditorium come away with only a faint notion of what the actors were saying. This is because of the endless hacking and coughing that makes hearing the actors' lines almost impossible. During last night's performance, however, there was a sudden silence that lasted for minutes. It occurred during the nude scene. Here, then, is the solution to our problem. From now on, let's have all plays presented in the nude. While eye strain may increase, ear strain and throat irritation will be wiped out. And everyone will be happy.

> **b.** Everyone would agree that poetry needs rhythm, but some people still cling to the notion that a poem is not a poem unless it has rhyme as

well. In connection with this, one is reminded of a woman wearing an extraordinary diamond necklace. The necklace enhances her costume, but whether or not she *needs* it is questionable. The jewelry may be so distracting that perhaps we will not notice the fact that she is not attractive. If she is really beautiful, the necklace will serve only as a charming incidental. Similarly with poetry. If the work is a piece of great writing, rhyme acts only as an incidental. If, however, the work is poor, the rhyme may serve to distract us from that fact.

c. A farm is not merely a different kind of prison; it is actually the worst kind. A jail can incarcerate the body only, while the mind and spirit may roam and wander. The farm, on the other hand, occupies and dominates a man's mind with such burdens as when to plant, what to plant, will the weather be favorable, will the crops sell, and if so at what price. All of a farmer's time and thoughts are devoted to making his farm successful, and this leaves his mind unreceptive to higher, more important thoughts. The farm is the farmer's master, and he is its slave.—From "Live Free," p. 106

d. The main reason I believe that a perfect society is impossible is that it would have to be made up of perfect people. A society is just a group of people, and one could not have a perfect society made up of imperfect people any more than one could have a perfect diamond made up of imperfect crystals. The faults and variations in people would cause fissures in a perfect society just the same as faults and variations in crystal structure would cause fissures in a diamond. Something cannot be truly perfect if its basic components are not perfect.

e. On the Noche Triste in Mexico, the Spaniards with the most gold in their pockets sank quickly to the bottom of the swamp; those with some gold lasted a bit longer but eventually drowned; but those with no gold made it to shore and survived. Be a poor Spaniard and live.

External Sources of Argument

Internal arguments grow out of the issue itself or, rather, out of the writer's development of his views on the issue. The case is decided on its merits: a product should be used because it's well made and serviceable; a policy should be adopted because it's wise and humane. External arguments don't relate directly to the issue or the writer's analysis of it but to evidence brought to bear on it from the outside—the testimony provided by documents or by statistics or, most commonly, by other people: a certain type of tennis racket should be used because the Wimbledon champion uses it; a foreign-aid bill should be enacted because the secretary of state has spoken in its favor.

Argument from Authority

In structure, the argument from authority could hardly be simpler: it asks for the reader's assent or belief on the basis of the recommendation of somebody (or a number of somebodies) presumed to be better informed or wiser than either the writer or his audience. To use this kind of argument responsibly, you must first of all be sure that your authority *is* an expert. If you ask your readers to take his word on a factual matter, they have the right to assume that he has access to the relevant information and that his integrity guarantees honest reporting. If you ask them to accept his opinion, they should be able to count on his ability to form sound judgments. Thus the ethical dimension of argument bears as strongly on the external sources you use as it does on the internal ones. You must carefully choose authorities whose integrity and competence on the particular issue are generally recognized.

When equally respected authorities offer testimony supporting different sides of the same issue, you have to go beyond the simple use of authority. You need to make clear to your readers why you find this expert's view more convincing than the opposing view, why you've chosen this expert rather than that one.

Argument from authority is so frequently abused that it must be handled with special care. It's misused, logically and ethically, when it's substituted for reasoned discussion: "Dr. Rogers says so, and that settles the matter." Authority and issue must be precisely matched: not only can a television star's opinion of toothpaste or an evangelist's opinion of fiscal policy be inexpert and irrelevant, but a mechanic who works on pickup trucks may have no expert knowledge of jet engines, and a psychologist may lack authority in psychiatry. In addition, the right authority must not be used in the wrong way. Don't misrepresent the views of an authority by selective quotation or other distortion in order to strengthen your argument.

One of the common abuses of argument from authority is to cite not any identifiable individual but a vague, general class: "Scholars tell us . . . ," "Scientists say . . . ," even "Everybody knows. . . ." The next step is the fallacy known as *hypostatization* or *reification*—appeal to an abstraction: "Science tells us . . .," "History says . . .," "Democracy teaches. . . ."

Sometimes you may want to present testimony from a respected or revered document like the Bible or the Constitution. The effectiveness of such testimony will depend on the attitude of your audience toward the document you quote, but it's well to remind yourself that the Constitution is open to conflicting interpretations on many points, and that "the devil can cite Scripture for his purpose." In general, quotations, maxims, proverbs, and platitudes are unreliable grounds for arguments. An alert reader can usually find another bit of wisdom that directly contradicts the one he's been asked to accept: "Look before you leap," but remember that "He who hesitates is lost."

Use of Statistics

The testimony of statistics is used so widely that it deserves special consideration. The basis for its persuasive appeal is the maxim that figures don't lie. But of course they do lie—when opinion polls are not representative, when rating systems have biases built into them, when the figures are irrelevant, or incomplete, or when they are misinterpreted, either deliberately or through error or ignorance. Like the human authorities you appeal to, your statistical authorities must be carefully examined and responsibly presented. Announcing that 274 students signed a petition may help your argument, but if you hide the fact that 742 refused to sign it, you're grossly distorting the situation.

Even when accurate statistics are honestly presented, an argument based on them is not necessarily sound. Establishing the fact that a sizable majority agrees with you proves only that a sizable majority agrees with you— not that your audience should therefore agree. Use of the *bandwagon* fallacy—vote for the candidate who's going to win, buy the product that "everyone" buys, read the best seller, join the crowd—is an appeal not to authority but to the herd instinct.

So far as everyday matters go, it's advisable to use authority and testimony only as supporting evidence. As such, it can strengthen a paper whose main substance has been drawn from internal sources of argument. In research projects, where the use of authority and testimony is essential, wise and scrupulous use is of first importance not only in doing justice to the subject but in convincing the reader of your own fairness and accuracy. (See Chapter 10.)

Some acquaintance with the sources of argument, both internal and external, will help you size up realistically what you have to do to prove your thesis. In skeleton form, proof consists of a chain of related propositions, one anchored to another and all giving support, direct or indirect, to what needs to be proved. Once you've visualized your argument as a series of key assertions moving from *here* (the problem) to *there* (the solution), you can turn to the question of proof in the particular context, asking which of your assertions can stand unsupported and which, without support, are likely to strike your readers as arbitrary or shaky or unreliable. Good judgment at this point is important. If you prove what doesn't need proving, you'll bore your readers. If you simply assert as truths what they regard as debatable issues, you'll outrage them.

For each of your key assertions, then, ask yourself these questions:

Is this a basic assumption I can count on my audience sharing, or does it need support?

If it needs support, how will I go about making a convincing case?

What possibilities open up when I try to support the assertion by analyzing the nature of the subject? By investigating causal relations? By making comparisons?

What concrete evidence will convince my readers that the definition is reasonable? The causal analysis sound? The comparison legitimate?

For what instances, what particulars, can I draw on my own knowledge and experience? What kind of support can I find in the writings of others? If authorities disagree, how shall I choose among them?

Good answers to these questions will generate the substance of your paper.

So far we've stressed the value of the sources in discovering arguments when you're writing papers based largely on your own experience. They can also be of great help in responding to examination questions. Whatever the subject matter, you're likely to be asked to cite evidence, to support positions. Examinations often begin with directions like these: "Compose an essay—a structured argument of several paragraphs built around a clearly stated thesis—in response to each of the questions that make up this examination."

The following questions from examinations ask for careful attention to argument, including skill in using the sources of argument discussed in this section:

> Many of the major changes that have taken place in Middle Eastern countries during this century were carried out by powerful, often dictatorial leaders. Comparing Ibn Saud, Reza Shah, and Ataturk, which one do you think benefited his country the most? Why?

> What goals and strategies do you think will be most fruitful for the black movement in the coming years?

> Compare and contrast Plato's idea of ignorance with the Christian idea of sin. What causes ignorance? What causes sin? Which of these "diagnoses," in your view, most adequately explains human failings? Give reasons for your view.

> In Euripedes' *Medea*, the character Medea says, "Of all things which are living and can form a judgment, we women are the most unfortunate creatures." Discuss the status and life of women in classical Greece. Were things really so bad?

For Discussion

1. From each of two newspapers or magazines that are known to have basically different political viewpoints (*National Review* and *The Nation,* for instance), make a copy of an editorial or column dealing with an important topic. (If possible, choose articles on the same topic.) Or check through back issues of weekly magazines *(Newsweek, Time, The New Yorker)* until you find two sharply conflicting reviews of the same movie. Submit them with a paper in which you compare and contrast the two articles. Give the best explanation you can for the differences in the opinions you find stated in the articles, in the assumptions underlying these opinions, in the kinds of arguments used, and in the style and tone. Be objective; don't express your own opinion on the issue.

2.   From the subjects below, choose one that interests you. Specify an issue related to it, and when you've committed yourself to a thesis, write a persuasive essay for an audience of your choice. For some of the subjects you may want to support your thesis by offering the testimony of experts. If you do, give some attention to establishing their credentials.

love and marriage	psychiatry
drinking	sex discrimination
a college education	work and the workweek

Keep asking questions about your subject until you can see a problem in it. For example, about work and the workweek: What are the psychological effects of working? Of not working? If you found you could meet expenses by working only ten hours a week, would you choose to work only ten hours? Would a three-day workweek be desirable? What should a person do whose job brings him a good paycheck (which he wants and needs) but no satisfaction? What should a person do whose job brings him great satisfaction but not enough money to live on?

3.   From the areas of education, politics, social reform, art, and popular culture, draw up a list of assertions or propositions that you're prepared to support—for example, that students should have a voice in promoting and firing faculty members, that voting rights in the United States should be restricted to property owners, that adults should be made legally responsible for the welfare of their aged parents, that transistor radios should be banned from public transportation, parks, and beaches. (The propositions can be more specific— that the management of the cafeteria or the bookstore should be replaced, that Instructor X was treated unjustly because of sex discrimination.) Settle on a proposition that your instructor approves. Write two short papers (about 400 words each) on the same topic, one addressed to a neutral audience, one to an audience that's at least mildly opposed to the action you suggest or the judgment you make.

The Logical Underpinnings

In gathering evidence in support of your thesis, anticipate the questions a skeptical reader will raise: Is this assertion true? Is this generalization convincing? Does this statement follow from that one? Is the conclusion justified by the evidence?

Let's start with the last question. Traditionally, the terms *induction* and *deduction* identify two ways of reaching conclusions. In argumentative writing, inductive reasoning and deductive inference mix freely; but because different methods are used to test the conclusions they lead to, we'll discuss them separately.

Testing Induction

An inductive inquiry is grounded in particulars. It moves from the observation and analysis of facts, characteristics, attitudes, or circumstances to an inclusive statement or generalization. It has its origin in a puzzle or a question. (Why was Cortez with a few hundred men able to conquer the Aztec nation?) Essentially it's a search for a pattern or an explanation. The inquiry is set in motion by a hunch or guess—a hypothesis (something had weakened the Aztecs)—that is then tested by further investigation (the Aztec capital was being ravaged by smallpox, to which the Spaniards were immune).

The generalization that's the outcome of an inductive inquiry may describe and classify, or express a causal relation, or make a comparison. Induction is the procedure you're most likely to use when you approach your subject from the various perspectives we discussed as the internal sources of argument (pp. 105–17); it's the pulling together of evidence that will make your particular assertions convincing. When you base your argument on external sources, you're asking your readers to accept the results of the inductive investigations that were carried out by others—the authorities you cite (pp. 118–20).

Establishing Inductive Generalizations

What makes a sound induction depends, first of all, on what's being asserted. When the hypothesis takes the form of a generalization that can be shown to be true or false, it's easy to state the criteria for reliability and easy to assess whether or not the generalization is sound. If the assertion "All our entering students graduated from high school with averages of B or better" is based on an examination of the grade records of all the freshmen, and if the calculations are accurate, the statement is true. (This is actually nose-counting rather than rhetorical induction.) But significant arguments seldom rest exclusively on factual statements that can be definitely confirmed or contradicted. The evidence is less certain, less "hard," and altogether more difficult to weigh when you're generalizing, say, about campus attitudes toward international affairs or about the merit of a musical group or about the extent of regional bias in the United States. Even when you can examine all the data (listen to all the recordings of the musical group, for example), inspection alone won't produce a sound generalization. You need to interpret and judge.

For the vast majority of the generalizations that figure in persuasive writing, you can't examine all the data. At some point you make the *induc-*

tive leap—a shift from a descriptive or statistical observation about this item, that item, and the next one to an assertion about the whole class of items, including those members of the class not available for inspection. Look back at the passage by Baldwin on pages 102–03. "So that, for example" in the first paragraph signals an induction—a list of places where a language is linked with a sense of identity. In paragraphs 3 and 4 the writer builds another induction, this one consisting of a dozen instances of Black English words and usages that have moved into the language of white Americans. On the basis of those instances Baldwin expects us to go along with him in his leap to the generalization that the language of white Americans is significantly different from what it would have been if there had been no blacks in the United States.

Whenever unexamined data are included in a generalization—and no one has ever examined all men or all women or all robins or all Toyotas or all the words in the language—the logician insists that the inference (in contrast to the nose count) is not certain, however high its degree of probability. Even death and taxes, according to this principle, may not be inevitable. Such skepticism is a useful reminder that inductive generalizations in your papers need the best support you can give them.

Take a relatively simple generalization: "Students on this campus have practically no interest in international affairs." Unsupported, it doesn't convince. Backed up by well-chosen examples, it may be highly persuasive. But how many examples, and what kind? Probably no reader would be persuaded by a single instance—"My roommate doesn't even watch the news on TV" or "The Political Science Club had to disband this year for lack of members" or "Only a handful turned out to hear Senator Patch talk on foreign relations." Nor will a reader be impressed by a quantity of evidence if he has reason to believe that the instances you cite are not representative. To decide that students are apathetic about world affairs on the basis of the indifference shown by your roommate would be premature: the sample is too small and the generalization *hasty*. To base the judgment on the indifference shown by all students majoring in music or in forestry would be unwise: because the sample is unrepresentative, the generalization is *faulty*.

In moving toward a key generalization, don't brush aside contradictory evidence. Suppose you want to follow up a hunch that your roommate's apathy toward international affairs is an attitude shared by a great many other students. On the basis of that hunch, or hypothesis, you start to investigate—carefully reading the campus newspaper, including letters to the editor, and talking to as wide a range of students as you can, particularly to those who've made attempts to stir up interest in international affairs or in talks by visiting statesmen. The hypothesis is necessary; without it you could hardly launch an inquiry. But if your investigation doesn't turn up support for your hypothesis, abandon it, no matter how much you wish it were true.

This doesn't mean that all the evidence you turn up must support your hypothesis. Inductive generalizations offer only probability, not certainty. So if you come upon some negative evidence, acknowledge it in your paper.

Admitting that exceptions exist can damage a persuasive paper less than ignoring them. And if you offer plausible reasons for the exceptions, your generalizations will be all the sturdier.

Establishing Causes

Inductive inquiries that set out to establish causal relations need to be handled with special care, particularly when they're presented as guides to future action. Some causal relations are indisputable: no one who puts a plastic dishpan on a very hot burner will consciously do it a second time. But in other situations causal connections are much harder to establish.

Suppose you hear that not one of the last ten students to come to your college from the high school you attended managed to graduate. Upset by the information, you decide that you haven't a chance of ever earning a diploma. You've formed a causal connection between coming-from-Monitor-High and failing-in-college.

Are you right? Probably everyone would agree that the causal connection is less sure than the one established between the hot burner and the ruined dishpan. The capacity to withstand heat isn't likely to vary much from one plastic dishpan to another. But you can't count on such uniformity when you're dealing with the quality of instruction in a high school from year to year or with the capacity of individual students to succeed in spite of poor instruction.

Did the ten students who preceded you fail *because* they came from Monitor High? The evidence might be enough to suggest this as a hypothesis, but it can do no more than that. You need to go on to make inquiries about the students who failed, about Monitor High, and so on. Such inquiries might make it possible for you to confirm the hypothesis about the ten students, or they might force you to alter it or reject it altogether. Determining cause is the most rigorous stage of any inductive inquiry, for only a good deal of analytical skill can distinguish coincidental circumstances from genuine causes. (See pp. 77–82.)

Even if you found strong support for a causal relation between attendance at Monitor High and failure in college for the other ten students, you'd have difficulty convincing others that *you* were therefore doomed to failure. A prediction of future effects is much more difficult to support with evidence than an assertion of past causes.

Most of the issues you'll debate in college papers are too complex to be argued on the basis of a single cause. You can acknowledge the complexity by ranking causes in terms of probability, by classifying different kinds of causes, and by proposing solutions that take into account a variety of causes.

Testing Deduction

In reasoning inductively we pull particulars into an inclusive generalization that describes or explains them. In reasoning deductively we draw a conclusion from propositions that we accept as true or that we have already proved to be true, or probable, by inductive procedures. We reason deductively when we say, ''If this is true, that *must* be true.'' If Jack is a National Merit finalist, he must be smart. Why *must?* Because we take it for granted, or are convinced on the basis of our own inductive inquiries, that all National Merit finalists are smart. The essence of the deductive process is the *must*—drawing an inevitable conclusion from propositions known or assumed to be true. Logicians label as the major premise the proposition ''All National Merit finalists are smart''; the minor premise is ''Jack is a National Merit finalist.'' These two premises and the conclusion that follows from them make up the three-part structure known as the *syllogism* in formal logic.

Some assertions can be proved both deductively and inductively. A cluster of examples, each giving evidence of Jack's braininess, would lead inductively to the same conclusion as the deductive inference. For sound induction you would have to know a lot about Jack. For sound deduction you would need to know only the one fact about him, so long as you could get agreement on your general principle, or major premise, about *all* National Merit finalists.

To test the conclusions arrived at deductively, you ask two questions: Are the premises true? Is the reasoning valid—that is, does the conclusion follow logically from the premises? Only if you can answer *both* questions affirmatively is your argument sound.

Are all National Merit finalists smart? Is the generalization true beyond a doubt, or is it only highly probable? The question is a complex one, involving among other things the meaning of *smart*. But if you could win agreement that all National Merit finalists are smart, and if you knew in addition that Jack was a National Merit finalist, your conclusion that Jack is smart would be valid as well as true.

It would not be valid, however, to argue that because Jack's brother Frank was *not* listed as a National Merit finalist, he is *not* smart. From the statement that all the finalists are smart we cannot move to the statement that the only smart students are those who are National Merit finalists. The question of logical implication, or how much it's valid to infer from a premise, is addressed in this passage:

> Teachers of writing courses in which a good deal of time is spent analyzing readings assume that there's a significant connection between the ability to read and the ability to write. There is. But it's important to get straight the logic of that relation. If a student can't read well, he can't write well. But it does not follow that if he can read well, he can write well.

A negative cause-effect sequence (poor reader = poor writer) can't be turned into a positive one (good reader = good writer). Nor can a cause-effect sequence be reversed. People who have college degrees expect to earn (and often do earn) higher salaries than people who don't. But it doesn't follow that everybody who earns a big salary in a given company has a college degree. (It doesn't follow either that someone who doesn't have a college degree won't get a job that pays a big salary.)

From the proposition that all those who eat a certain food are healthy, can you infer that those who don't eat the food will be unhealthy? No. That would require beginning with the proposition that all those who don't eat the food are unhealthy. Nor can you infer from a person's good health that he eats that particular food. That would call for the proposition that *only* those who eat the food are healthy.

From the proposition that all American flags are red, white, and blue, you can't infer that every red, white, and blue flag you see is American. That would require beginning with the proposition that *only* American flags are red, white, and blue.

If you accepted the proposition that all good citizens are nature lovers, would logic then convince you that a thief (who is certainly not a good citizen) couldn't love nature? No, not unless you found a way to support the proposition that all nature lovers are good citizens.

Non sequitur ("does not follow") covers all those errors in reasoning in which the stated conclusion doesn't follow from the premises of the argument. Normally it's easy enough to detect the logical flaw in someone else's argument. "But that doesn't follow!" you splutter, when a friend goes beyond the limits of legitimate inference—assuming, perhaps, that because you don't want to see a certain movie, you're a prude, or that because you like contact sports, you're an animal. But it sometimes takes real effort to recognize unjustified leaps and irrational zigzags in your own thought processes. In revising your papers, try to play the role of the skeptical reader who doesn't automatically accept the facts and generalizations an argument presents but insists on examining the relationships that are asserted or implied between this fact and that one, between this generalization and that one, between this fact and that generalization.

Certainty versus Probability

Logical inference offers general guidance but no sure criteria for the arguments we most often use in persuading. In everyday arguments our reasoning isn't grounded in universals—*all* or *none*—and does not yield, or claim to yield, certainty. More often we argue and act on the basis of probability: "The Corner Bookstore carries a good stock of new novels, so I'll probably find Rogers' latest one there." To say that you'll undoubtedly find the novel you want is illogical. To say that you'll probably find it is a reasonable inference. Weighing the probabilities is the crucial test for most of the deductive inferences we make as well as for our inductive generalizations.

For Writing

1. Drawing evidence entirely from your own experience and investigations, write a substantial paragraph in support of whichever of these generalizations you believe to be true:

a. Students who can't read well don't write well.

b. Some students who can't read well do write well.

c. Students who read well normally write well.

d. Some students who read well do not write well.

2. For the preceding assignment you were asked to rely on inductive reasoning—from facts about the ability to read and write that you observe in yourself and others. Now write a paragraph or so in which you reach a conclusion by reasoning deductively. You might proceed this way:

a. Describe the skills and qualities that make a "good reader."

b. Describe the skills and qualities that make a "good writer."

c. Now argue that good readers are likely to be good writers *or* that poor readers are likely to be poor writers *or* that there's no causal connection between the two skills.

Fallacies

When arguments go wrong, it's because of faulty evidence (mistakes in fact or inaccurate generalizations), or faulty reasoning, or irresponsible or misleading use of language—occasionally all three. Sometimes these faults are unintentional; sometimes they are deliberate attempts to deceive. Collectively, they're known as *fallacies*.

Below is a listing of the more common fallacies, arranged in groups. Some have been mentioned earlier in the chapter, in connection with particular kinds of argument. The categories frequently overlap; and it's well to remember that recognizing an argument as fallacious is much more important than labeling the fallacy precisely. Even so, the names can help remind you of what to check as you revise your own arguments and what to look for as you read the arguments of those you disagree with.

1.   *Hasty generalizations* are based on inadequate, scanty evidence. *Faulty generalizations* are based on weak, unrepresentative, or irrelevant evidence, or on emotion rather than evidence. Deliberately slanting or suppressing or disguising contradictory evidence is a variety of faulty generalizing known as *card-stacking, special pleading,* or *dealing in half-truths*. Generalizations that don't stand up under careful examination represent one of the most common of all fallacies in argument.

Stereotyping is the practice of applying group labels to persons or things without regard for individual differences and sometimes without regard for the significant characteristics of the group. There are popular stereotypes for hundreds of groups—scientists, schoolteachers, Swedes, redheads, athletes, Baptists, bird watchers, Rotarians, Texans, New Yorkers, "the enemy," and so on—including college students and young people generally. Stereotypes in your thinking, or non-thinking, may reflect unexamined assumptions that weaken your entire argument. You can guard against stereotyping by citing numerous examples and by recognizing contradictory evidence.

2. *False cause* embraces all the fallacies relating to causal reasoning—
post hoc, mistaking an accompanying circumstance for a cause, failing to
recognize multiple causes. Logicians give the label *post hoc, ergo propter
hoc* (''after this, therefore because of this'') to the fallacy of assuming that
what comes after an event is necessarily a result of it. The mere fact that
one event follows or precedes or accompanies another in time doesn't
necessarily indicate any causal relationship. *Post hoc* is the most common
fallacy of causal relations.

3. *Faulty analogy* results from making comparisons that aren't relevant to
the issue, from pressing an analogy beyond legitimate similarities, from
treating a figurative analogy as a literal one, or from insisting that
analogical resemblances constitute adequate proof. The fallacy of the
perfect analogy occurs when you reason from a partial resemblance to an
entire and exact correspondence.

4. *Either-or* fallacies (sometimes called false dilemmas) occur when you
fail to see that other alternatives exist or refuse to recognize their
existence: ''We must choose between inflation and recession''; ''You're
either for me or you're against me.'' It's possible to have both inflation
and recession. And between pro and con, there's neutrality.

5. *Non sequitur* (''does not follow'') refers to errors in reasoning in
which the conclusion doesn't follow from the premises supplied. You
should not only avoid committing this fallacy; you should avoid giving the
impression that you have committed it. You give that impression when you
skip a step in your argument and leave the reader confused about how one
assertion connects with another.

6. *Begging the question* means assuming the truth of a proposition that
you actually need to prove. ''This unfair method of voting'' assumes that
the method is unfair. (''Unfair'' is a question-begging epithet.) Though the
writer who uses that phrase hopes to take advantage of a general
preference for virtue over vice, in begging the question he is himself
engaging in an unethical tactic. One common form of begging the question
is *arguing in a circle.* At its simplest, the circular argument asserts that X
is true because X is true: ''In our society it is necessary to keep up with
the latest styles because it is essential to be fashionably dressed.'' This
evasion is often hard to recognize when it's buried in a long chain of
argument; but in developing an argument, you should be sufficiently aware
of the steps you take to avoid tripping over your own heels.

Another version of begging the question is the *false* or *complex
question.* ''When is the Administration going to stop bankrupting the
country with its illegal expenditures?'' begs at least two questions—
whether the Administration is bankrupting the country and whether its
expenditures are illegal.

7. *Ignoring the question* is a broad label for various kinds of irrelevant
argument. It consists in shifting the grounds of the argument from the real
issue to one that's not under consideration. In one characteristic form,
argumentum ad hominem, the attack is not on the issue itself but on those
who support the view that's being opposed: ''It should be mentioned that

this champion of freedom of the press recently had his license suspended for driving while intoxicated.'' The trial lawyer's tactic of seeking to discredit hostile witnesses usually depends on *ad hominem* argument. Related to it is the tactic of *damning the source*—dismissing the opposing view because of its origin (''After all, that was Hitler's line''), sometimes called *poisoning the well* (or *spring*).

To set up a *straw man* is another form of ignoring the question. The strategy is to argue not against the opposing point of view but against a caricature of it which supports propositions it does not support and may even expressly condemn—that is, to attack an opposition that doesn't exist. To use a *red herring*—still another form—is to introduce an issue that diverts the discussion from its proper course: ''Before we permit this rock festival to be held in our town, let us remember that many young people have threatened to leave the country rather than ever be drafted.''

Two more forms of ignoring the question are the *argumentum ad populum* and *name-calling*. The *argumentum ad populum* (which usually incorporates a variety of other fallacies) speaks to the jealousies, hatreds, fears, resentments, prejudices, and passions of audiences: ''Are you going to continue to allow your hard-earned tax dollars to be handed over to a bunch of immoral bums who are too lazy to work?'' Name-calling includes not only insulting racial epithets and crude slurs like *commie, fascist, bum,* and *pig* but labels chosen for their connotations for particular audiences: *liberal, controversial, Eastern, Southern, conservative, intellectual, foreign.* Irrelevant emotional appeals can take many forms and can be subtle or blatant. Epithets may be slanted to arouse admiration, sympathy, anger, disgust. Propaganda regularly substitutes diabolical abstractions for human beings. Vocabulary may be deliberately used to impress: sometimes a parade of technical terms will hoodwink an audience into accepting claptrap.

8. In the fallacy known as *shifting the burden,* the writer asserts his case and dares the audience to prove him wrong. All manner of beliefs and superstitions fall into this category, from the Great Conspiracy theory of national and international affairs to the conviction that toads cause warts.

In testing your arguments, be sure to examine all the appeals you've used to support your thesis—the alogical ones as well as the logical ones. Appeals to emotions and ideals—to pride, to justice, to morality—can be extremely persuasive. They are properly used when they're brought to bear on the real issue. To use them to cloud or misrepresent or smother the issue is to argue unfairly and dishonestly.

For Discussion and Writing

1. Examine these brief bits of reasoning and decide whether or not the conclusions are sound. If a conclusion is unsound, tell how the reasoning went wrong.

a. Of course the book is a best-seller. Look at the sex in it.

b. Parents have no right to criticize the public schools. After all, they don't tell their surgeons how to operate.

c. Philosophy 12 isn't teaching me anything I'll need to know to be a research chemist, so I think I should be allowed to drop it.

d. The reason for all the trouble with our young people can be identified in two words: permissive parents.

e. The sexual revolution has finally freed America from the repressions and inhibitions that formerly made it a nation of hypocritical neurotics.

f. Style is choice, and choice reflects personality. Writers differ in their personalities, so they differ in their styles.

2. Analyze the train of reasoning in each of the following excerpts (the last one from a student's paper) and explain why you find it sound or unsound. If it's sound, is it also convincing?

a. The universe creates certain problems that mankind can't really do much about, but we try to do something about those things that we can. We can't stop rain, but we do manufacture umbrellas.—Arthur Okun

b. I see no reason in morality (or in aesthetic theory) why literature should not have as one of its intentions the arousing of thoughts of lust. It is one of the effects, perhaps one of the functions, of literature to arouse desire, and I can discover no ground for saying that sexual pleasure should not be among the objects of desire which literature presents to us, along with heroism, virtue, peace, death, food, wisdom, God, etc.—Lionel Trilling, quoted by Kenneth Tynan, *Esquire*

c. All life and property are now in jeopardy because the foreign policies of the national sovereignties produce total anarchy. It is necessary, therefore, for people to stretch their minds, their concepts and their demands in order to bring about a government over governments. Anything else is irrelevant to their safety and indeed to their destiny.—N[orman] C[ousins], *Saturday Review*

d. The newspaper should stop reporting local incidents of rape and assault. Such reports arouse fear in our citizens and do harm to the image of our town as a safe, pleasant place to live. The ill effects of such news items certainly outweigh any benefits.—Letter to the Editor

e. The college administration has gradually recognized that dorms are private residences of students who may see whom they wish, when they wish, in their homes. Administrators have ceded their right to restrict our personal actions in dorms except in the most destructive or violent cases. Drinking is neither.

Granted underage drinking is illegal in this state, and the college is bound to obey state law. But a second Prohibition will be no more successful than the first. Most of us demand liquor. If we're denied it, the dorm supervisors will all have writer's cramp from filing disciplinary charges, the bureaucratic gears will grind to a halt when faced with their processing, the administration will have its back to the wall, and the students will still be merrily boozing it up.

All students, whether "wet" or "dry," should oppose any attempt to force us back into a childhood we have outgrown.—Adapted from a college newspaper editorial

f. We're all aware of the problem. Our natural resources are limited, and if we continue to deplete them at our present rate, they are going to run out. What should be done, however, is another matter. It's easy to say, as many people do, that Americans must reevaluate their ideals and limit consumption. But that, I think, is no solution. The economic effects of mass conservation would be catastrophic. America's capitalist system thrives on consumption. Our already struggling economy could not sustain a massive reduction in expenditures on natural resources. The results would be disastrous. If we use the fuel oil industry as an example, it's obvious what would happen. People would stop buying gasoline. The companies would lose money. They would compensate by limiting investment and laying off labor. So unemployment would go up, while spending would decrease. Less money would be fed into the economy, and other businesses would suffer. Soon these businessmen would be forced to lay off workers. Eventually the trend would grow until the economy spiraled downward into depression.

3. From the six excerpts in 2 (above), select any assertion that interests you and write an argument supporting or attacking it.

Refuting Arguments

In the background of every piece of persuasion lurks the opposing thesis. And very often it looms in the foreground. In fact, the procedures you follow in revising your persuasive papers—testing the logical relationships in your argument and checking for fallacies—are the same procedures you'll follow when you set out to correct a misinterpretation or to refute an opinion, though then you'll be probing logical relationships and searching for fallacies in the writings (or speeches) of others.

Refutation may be your main purpose or only incidental to it. In some of the papers you write, you'll simply be correcting a mistaken notion. The author of the following passage rejects one explanation for the decline in movie attendance after World War II and argues for an explanation he considers more valid:

> When the artist, in whatever medium, provides *all* the stimuli necessary to keep his audience awake and fully informed, the audience, having nothing to do, goes limp. This is not to say that audiences at today's sound films, which blaze with color and screech with car-skids, are limp. But there was a time when they were. In the late 1940's and early 1950's, audience attention at films dropped so spectacularly that thousands of film houses closed and the studio system itself was destroyed. The decline is normally attributed to television. But in certain Rocky Mountain states where television was not yet available, the falloff was exactly as precipitous. Filmmakers had put their audiences to sleep. They had done it by taking care of everything—smoothing the way with slow dissolves that made transitions plain, firmly ending sequences with fade-outs followed by a few seconds of blankness to indicate the passage of time, beginning new sequences with fade-ins that made adjustment easy, *always* indicating shifts of time and place with calendar leaves slipping from the wall, candles burning down, railroad wheels racing. Movement within a scene, no matter how many shifts of position the camera might record, was complete: long establishing shot in which we could identify the room and see a character entering it, pickup shot from the doorway as the character moved deeper into the room, reaction shot from another character watching him come closer—the whole clock accounted for moment by moment. Of course there were graceful elisions, interesting camera-made metaphors, as there always had been. But if film had nearly, and too literally, ground to a halt, it was partly because it had learned to be too helpful.—Walter Kerr, *The Silent Clowns*

In preparing any argument, find out what's been said on the other side or figure out what might be said. Even if you give no explicit recognition to the opposing view in your paper, knowing what arguments its proponents present will help you decide what kind and quantity of evidence you need, what reasons give strongest support to your thesis, and how they can best be organized. In some of your papers you may limit yourself to constructive argument—affirmative support of your thesis—but in others you'll probably want to meet objections, demolish misconceptions, and in general strengthen your own thesis by showing the weaknesses in the counter-thesis. (Recall Abbey's dealing with the opposition, pp. 110–11.)

Especially when you have reason to believe that your readers lean to the opposing view, you may find it useful to open your paper by analyzing that view and exposing its weaknesses. Launching a brief and temperate offensive at the start can clear away obstacles to a sympathetic hearing for your own view. On the other hand, it's ordinarily a bad tactic to recognize and deal with the opposition at the very end of the paper, no matter how briefly. The conclusion should strongly reaffirm your own thesis.

Refutation is an attack on the evidence and the reasoning that make up the proof for the other side. In most cases attack isn't enough; you must bolster it by building an affirmative argument for your own thesis. But the term *refutation* properly applies only to proving the opponent wrong. Full-scale refutation goes to the roots of the opposing argument. If it's to be convincing, it must attack the fundamental assumptions or the crucial premises of the argument, not merely its conclusions. If it's to win respect, it must scrupulously avoid those tactics that it criticizes the opponent for using.

In the following passage the writer comes close to full-scale refutation. She is not attacking a particular argument but is challenging fundamental premises, or assumptions, that have developed over a period of time:

> If we step back a little from the fevers of the moment, we must be astonished at how easily it has been established, particularly in the press, that a certain group of issues belong exclusively within the province of women's concern; that they are issues best dealt with through the political process, and, last but not least, thay they are definable for the vast majority of women in the terms so vehemently set forth by women's lib. In only a little more than a decade the movement has succeeded in planting the idea that the needs and desires of American women are spoken for by its particular brand of "feminism." And this idea has in turn influenced the language and conduct of a growing number of political campaigns.
>
> Just how women's lib accomplished this will one day be a fascinating question for cultural historians. A more pressing question for today is what the movement's agenda says to and about women, as political actors and as citizens in general. The issues about which the movement seeks to convince politicians, male *and* female, that there is a women's vote are mainly issues of sex and family, such as abortion, rape, day care. The assumption here is a twofold one. First, that decisions about sex and family are the special concern of women. The issue of abortion, for instance, has been defined as the problem of whether "society" will grant or refuse a woman "control over her own body." Similarly, government sponsorship of day-care centers has been urged on the ground that she has the same "right" as her husband to pursue a career unhampered by the need to offer full-time care to the babies she does decide to give birth to. The second assumption is that women are agreed: to oppose abortion on demand or day-care centers (I have yet to encounter anyone in favor of rape) is to oppose the social needs and political demands of American womanhood.
>
> Both these assumptions are wrong and dangerous. Problems of family are the problems of men as well as women; indeed, it is impossible to think about the welfare of one group separate from the welfare of the other. A pregnancy, for instance, is the creation of two sexes. Whether or not, and under what circumstances, to sustain it, and how to raise the baby that ensues, is thus the respon-

sibility of a man no less than a woman. To define this problem as one of "women's rights" has the ironic effect of making fatherhood secondary. (Nor is this effect being lost on American men: the idea that women's bodies and the fruits thereof are women's own business has led to growing abdication by young men of responsibility for the young they have sired.)

Most pernicious of all, however, is the idea that women are some kind of bloc, that they have reached a consensus on at least a number of major issues and can be expected to vote accordingly. Not only is this idea false—witness the difficulty in ratifying even so vaguely symbolic a statement as ERA, with the vast number of women voters in this country, let alone the increasing electoral strength of the Right to Life movement—it is subversive of the very equality that the women's movement claims to embody. For genuine equality means just that. It means that women will be distributed along the political spectrum, as along the intellectual, the moral, the social, in about the same proportions as men. They will be left wing and right wing and in the center; they will be doves and hawks, for heavy government regulation and free marketeers, and they will be for and against abortion and somewhere in between, for and against preferential treatment, *depending on their underlying political attitudes,* in about the same proportions as men.—Midge Decter, *Newsweek*

For Discussion

How does Decter's own argument stand up logically? Can you spot flaws in her reasoning?

There are other ways of refuting an argument besides attacking its premises. Refuting by analogy often involves *reductio ad absurdum*—pushing the thesis or the proposed course of action to an illogical extreme, as in this excerpt from a call for more "realistic risk/benefit decisions":

> Everything we do in life involves some element of risk. Nitrite use is just one of many. Smoking, drinking, flying in an airplane or driving an automobile are other examples. Of course, our Government could legislate away some of these risks. For example, when the speed limit was reduced to 55 miles an hour during the energy crisis, we discovered that it saved lives. By limiting speed still further, more lives could be saved. And by reducing the speed limit to 10 miles an hour we could virtually eliminate all of the 50,000 traffic deaths that occur each year on our highways.—James G. Affleck, *New York Times*

Drawing out the implications of a proposal is an effective technique in refutation and, if it's done fairly, a reputable one. If used unscrupulously, it will distort and misrepresent the original argument, creating a straw man.

Making a lucid, accurate statement of the view that you're refuting is the best protection against misrepresenting it in the course of your paper. Caricaturing comes easy in refutation because normally anyone who undertakes a rebuttal has been stirred—emotionally as well as intellectually—to disagree. But setting up a straw man or distorting the position that's being opposed means there will be no real debate. Ask yourself: Have I represented my opponent's case in such a way that he would find it an acceptable statement of his position?

It's also easy, when feelings are strong, to berate and scold and ridicule. But no one who's seriously interested in dealing with the issue, as contrasted with cowing the opposition, uses language as a club. A temperate tone in refutation isn't incompatible with strong, incisive assertion of a different point of view. Most important for responsible refutation, perhaps, is to have respect for your opponent. Unless you *know* him to be otherwise, assume that he's the kind of person you'd like to think you are—open, intelligent, reasonable. And as you proceed with your refutation, remember that the purpose of argument is to get closer to the truth. Much sound refutation is devoted not to rejecting the opposing position outright but to refining and modifying it.

For Discussion and Writing

1. Make a copy of a newpaper editorial or column or a magazine article that expresses an opinion or makes a recommendation you strongly disagree with. Make a careful analysis of the selection, singling out the premises on which the argument hinges and examining the evidence offered in support of it. Then write a "Letter to the Editor" in which you make clear exactly why you disagree with the position advanced in the editorial, column, or article. Depending on what the issue is, you may or may not decide to go on to make a constructive argument for the position you favor.

Submit the selection you're refuting along with your own paper.

2. Here is a passage from a student paper. If you agree with the writer's position, extend and develop it through two or three pages. If you disagree, make the best case you can against it.

> Inflation is strangling our country, unemployment is breeding crime, government corruption is increasing, chances of nuclear war are growing frightfully, six inches of ice are covering all the walks on campus— and I don't care.
>
> What? All these atrocities and she doesn't care? How un-American! But in eighteen years of watching people try to cure social ills, I have noticed one thing all these valiant attempts have in common—they've all failed. So I've finally come to the conclusion that one should not commit oneself to any cause or to any side of an argument. Since nothing ever comes of trying to change a major problem in the world, people shouldn't spend their time trying.

5

Organizing Papers

In the last three chapters we have been chiefly concerned with invention—with developing content for papers—but we have said some things about arranging content as well. In this chapter we'll focus directly on arrangement—on how to organize papers. As we do, we'll suggest that you take another look at some of the illustrative passages in the preceding chapters, examining them this time not so much to see how incidents or ideas have been developed as to note the pattern, the shape, the structure that the writer has given the material.

When you read a successful piece of writing, you're seldom conscious of its organization. If you do consider it, it seems inevitable. "This is the way it should be," you think; "this is the way it had to be." But when you're prewriting, organizing is nothing more than an attempt to pull together a collection of facts and a jumble of ideas. And even when you begin writing, you may still be trying to detect a pattern in your material.

In your search for order you should be guided by two considerations—what you've thought out and found out about your subject and what you want to say about it to the particular audience you're addressing. As you write and rewrite, compressing here and expanding there, you may find yourself changing the order of your material. Such shifts are a natural part of the writing process. What you're looking for is the structure that shows to best advantage the thoughts and feelings you want to convey. When you find it, your reader will recognize it as the right structure for your purpose, because the expectations you've created will have been fulfilled.

Types of Order

There are two basic types of order for material. The first is related to the order that exists in space or in time. So it includes *spatial* order, which occurs most commonly in description, and *chronological* order, which occurs most commonly in narration.

Rhetorical order, the second type, is a pattern that the writer thinks out or invents. In most explanatory and persuasive papers there is no natural or obvious way to arrange the material, as there often is in description and narration. The writer has to work out an order. The good writer works out an order that helps him accomplish what he wants to do in the rhetorical situation.

Spatial Order and Chronological Order

Because we've already discussed the arranging of details in description (pp. 36–38) and such matters as pace and point of view in narration (pp. 42–44), here we'll simply suggest some choices you have when the structure of your paper is rooted in the space order or time order of the material.

When you're writing a physical description, you may proceed systematically from left to right, or from top to bottom, or from inside to outside, or from suburbs to city, and so on. Or you may decide that you can give a clearer, more unified account of the same subject by describing it in a chronological framework, which may follow the sequence of your own observations: first the major features, visible from a distance, then successively smaller details as you (and your readers) come closer. See, for example, "A Village by the River," pp. 37–38.

When you're using description to support a thesis, the thesis will influence the way you order your visual impressions. If you found registration day a confusing mess, you'll want to describe it so that your reader sees it that way. If it impressed you as an efficient operation, you'll describe it differently. In either case, if you're presenting a factual account, the spatial arrangements you indicate in your paper should be recognizable to anyone who was present, even though someone else's interpretation may be totally unlike yours.

For material presented in a time sequence—an account of a process, a summary of a plot, a personal narrative—the typical movement is chronological: raw material to product, opening to closing, March to September. But you can modify the actual sequence in various ways. You can describe the finished product before giving the instructions for making it. You can begin with the climax of a plot and then work backward and forward from it. You can start with the concluding episode of a personal narrative and use flashbacks to fill in the action. Whatever the modifications, the order should make sense, and the reader should be able to reconstruct the actual order of events.

And whether or not you spell out your point of view, it should be consistent. Organizational weaknesses in descriptive and narrative papers can often be traced to a physical point of view that shifts for no good reason or to an unexplained change in the writer's attitude toward his subject. If, in describing the scene on registration day, you abruptly changed your physical point of view from that of an observer on the sidelines to that of a student enduring the long delays—or if you changed your attitude from detached to disgusted—the organization of your paper would be weakened. When such shifts occur, the reader simply can't tell where you stand, literally or figuratively, in respect to the subject.

In the following paper the structure is clear and firm.

How to Deliver a Calf

[1] Ordinarily, cows give birth very easily. But every once in a while a cow does have trouble calving, and human assistance becomes necessary to save the life of the cow or her calf—sometimes both. A cow gives signals of an approaching birth by walking lazily away from the rest of the herd, by becoming uneasy and excited, and finally by bellowing incessantly. Within three hours, a violet "water bag" should appear at her vulva (or genital opening). This bag should then burst, spilling its watery fluid to the ground and forcing out the calf's forelegs. If the forelegs do not present themselves at the vulva twenty to forty minutes after the bag bursts, the cow needs to be examined.

[2] Before making the examination itself, you must sterilize a pair of heavy steel chains with large triangular links on one end by boiling them in water for at least twelve minutes. You will use these chains only as a last resort, but since time is important, it is best to get them ready now. Once they are sterilized, place the chains in a clean bucket of lukewarm water. They will cool to a temperature close to the cow's by the time you need them. Thus they will neither burn nor shock her internal genital organs if they are needed.

[3] Next, strip to your waist, for now you must disinfect your own tools— your hands, your arms, and your shoulders. Do this by scrubbing with warm water and a mild soap—preferably with Dettol, a soap designed to prevent any irritation to the internal surfaces of the expectant mother. Make sure that you wash your entire arms well, to guard against causing infection.

[4] Now move slowly toward the nervous cow, talking to her quietly and soothingly. Give her posterior a few gentle pats to let her know where you are. Then smear your arms with an antiseptic lubricant designed for vaginal use or, if no such lubricant is handy, with Vaseline Petroleum Jelly. Gently insert your hand into the cow's genital passage and explore whatever presents itself to your hand.

[5] Using your hand as your eyes, you should be able to distinguish the two forefeet of the struggling fetus in that part of the passage which lies lowermost when the cow is standing. Above and slightly behind them, you should be able to feel its nostrils and its mouth. If so, you need do nothing further; the cow will calve normally, given more time. It may happen, however, that you cannot locate one or both forefeet or the nose. In this case, reach in farther until you discover those parts. By gently pulling and readjusting the leg or head, you can bring it to its normal position.

[6] If, by exploring, you discover that the calf is positioned backward—as indicated by the difference between the knees of the forelegs and the hocks of the hind legs—it is best not to try to maneuver the fetus to the front position. That takes time—time that can make the difference between respiration and

suffocation. Now you need the chains. Remove your arm, then re-insert it holding the triangular links of the two chains in your hand. Slip the triangles around the hocks of each hind leg. Then, grasping the chains with both hands, pull with all your might until the calf flops to the ground.

[7] As soon as the little animal is born and free from its mother, remove any fetal membranes that may cling to its nostrils or mouth, obstructing its breathing. If, after you've removed these membranes, the calf still can't breathe, grab its hocks and hold it upside down, so that any mucus in the air passages will drain. If this also proves unsuccessful, swing the calf over your head. With this motion, centrifugal force will undoubtedly clear these blocked passages, and finally the little creature will take its first shallow breath.

[8] Now it is up to the calf itself to do the rest of the work. Within a half hour it should be standing on its own feet—although it is shaky at first. You can encourage it by briskly rubbing it dry with a clean towel. Once the newborn calf is standing, your work is done, for instinct will lead it to its mother's udder for its first rich meal of milk in its brand new life.

The author of "How to Deliver a Calf" has a good sense of pace and maintains a consistent point of view. Chronology dominates, as it usually does in an account of a process. Where necessary, causal explanations are introduced, supplying information without drawing attention away from the instructions. Most of paragraph 5 is spatial description; and here the writer faces an unusually difficult task, for she's deprived of the direct observation we normally consider indispensable for accurate description. "Using your hand as your eyes" acknowledges the difficulty and tells how it's overcome.

Rhetorical Order

Except when it clearly lends itself to spatial order (as in physical description) or to chronological order (as in narration), a subject seldom suggests a definite order of discussion. There's no necessary arrangement of material, for instance, in a criticism of a movie or an argument about sexist language or an analysis of the problems of adjusting to college life. The structure of any paper that explains or argues is an outgrowth of the writer's purpose and his estimate of the rhetorical situation. The writer decides what aspects of the subject to discuss, in what sequence, and with what emphasis. Rhetorical order is thought-out order.

Rhetorical arrangement includes a great variety of organizational patterns. But whatever the pattern, the good paper has direction and destination. The thought moves. It gets somewhere. Sound organization reveals the relation among details or between ideas and carries the readers from one stage of the discussion to another. It doesn't make the readers puzzle over the relation, say, of the sixth paragraph to the fifth or leave them wondering why a topic is treated here, not there—or why it's treated at all.

Let's look at three basic patterns commonly found in explanatory and persuasive papers—the *support* structure, the *discovery* structure, and the *pro-and-con,* or *exploratory,* structure.

Support Structure

In the support structure the paper develops *from* the central idea—an assertion, a generalization, a thesis. Early in the paper the writer advances the idea or cluster of ideas that he intends to analyze or defend or attack. Read this opening paragraph:

> Baseball and football nicely reflect, sociologically, their respective eras of inception, development and maturation. They reflect, rather indirectly, the evolution, or demise, of the American dream. It is no accident that in terms of media popularity, football, a game clearly defined by time and space, is the No. 1 sport in America today. Football in many ways mirrors contemporary America; baseball preserves an image of the America we have lost.

Now reread the whole article by Cavanaugh beginning on page 68. Notice that paragraph 1 introduces in a compressed and abstract way all the topics that receive detailed treatment in the rest of the article.

The opening paragraph below is equally informative in forecasting the content that follows. The reader is told that a commonly accepted generalization has been tested and has been shown to be true for one group but not for another.

> One would suppose, in view of all the household appliances that have been introduced over the past 50 years, that American women must spend considerably less time in housework now than their mothers and grandmothers did in the 1920's. I have investigated the matter and found that the generalization is not altogether true. Nonemployed women, meaning women who are not in the labor force, in fact devote as much time to housework as their forebears did. The expectation of spending less time in housework applies only to employed women.—Joann Vanek, *Scientific American*

The reader expects, rightly, that the article will proceed by giving the evidence on which the findings are based.

As we saw in the section "Dividing to Organize," pp. 58–60, the whole plan of a paper may be laid out in the opening paragraph—the topics to be discussed and the order of discussion. This is support structure in its purest form. You'll find many examples in textbooks and technical journals.

Discovery Structure

In the discovery structure the paper develops *toward* a generalization, a thesis, a solution. Using this structure, you can start a paper small and end broad, building an inverted pyramid. You move from one detail to another, unfolding your subject as you go and arriving at a conclusion that tells the reader something he couldn't have predicted from the way the paper started. Narratives that are written to illustrate a thesis—like "A Moving Experience" (pp. 45–46)—are usually built on a discovery structure. So are causal analyses like the inquiry into why people talk at the movies (pp. 77–78), where the minor causes are glanced at before the major ones are discussed in some detail. And so are some arguments, like Decter's (pp. 134–35).

One common application of the discovery pattern is the problem-solution (or question-answer) structure. The student's paper on graffiti (pp. 81–82) opens with an account of a practice the writer puzzled over and later solved to his own satisfaction. A magazine article begins: "Are we experiencing an epidemic of cancer, or of cancerphobia—or both?" The occasion for such papers lies in a problem that needs solving, a question that needs answering, an issue that needs settling, a happening or situation that needs explaining. The paper comes to a close when the solution has been offered, the course of action shown to be wise or unwise, the happening or situation explained. In such a paper you may move directly from your analysis of the problem to your solution, or you may explore alternative proposals, showing them to be inadequate and all the while piling up evidence for the solution you're going to propose. Though the content of papers that follow this pattern may be complex, the bare structure can often be reduced to some such simple formula as

To solve *X*, we need to take steps *A*, *B*, and *C*.

or

What caused *X?* Not *A*. Not *B*. Not *C*. But *D*.

or

What is the right course of action? Not *A*. Not *B*. Not *C*. But *D*.

Because the sense of investigation is strong in the problem-solution structure, you'll find the approach particularly useful for persuasive papers. It's also suitable for expository papers in which you present various other explanations before offering your own.

Pro-and-Con, or Exploratory, Structure

You set out to write an evaluation—of a movie, a book; a musical group, a team; an actor, a singer, an athlete, a poet, a political candidate; a policy, a theory, a technique. You're familiar with your subject, but you quickly become aware that you've never reached any firm conclusion about it. Just how good or bad is the work, how competent or incompetent the performer, how wise or unwise the idea? In the prewriting stage you find your opinions zigzagging, with a "yes, but" or an "and yet" following immediately after each point for or against: "She did an excellent job in Movie *A* . . . but in *B* she overacted. Maybe comedy just isn't her thing . . . though two years ago she almost won an Oscar for her performance in that very funny picture called *C*." So it goes, as you explore the subject and finally reach a judgment, with strengths balanced against weaknesses and your own system of values determining the decision, or perhaps end up still undecided but with a much clearer understanding of the reasons for your indecision.

When you write a paper based on such internal conflict, or ambivalence, reproducing the zigzag movement of your thoughts may create a good pattern of organization. And you can use the same pattern when the conflict is external—when you begin with the opinions of two critics, one strongly pro and the other con, or the differing interpretations of two historians, or the projections of two economists, or the theories of football coaches or astronomers or psychologists. In all these cases you first undertake to present the opposing points of view and then give your support to one of the positions, explaining why you find it superior, or identify the common ground that makes it possible to reconcile them, or tell why you can't choose between them.

Though the pro-and-con, or exploratory, structure resembles an organizational pattern used in comparisons, the purpose of these papers is not simply to compare but to arrive at a decision or a conclusion: Good or bad? Strong or weak? Right or wrong? The question can be phrased as a generalization to be examined and tested: Team *X* is the best in the league; Writer *Y* is a mediocre poet; Admissions policy *Z* is turning this college into a joke. When two opposing generalizations are involved—Sociologist A says that young people today are more religious than their parents; Sociologist B says that, for college students, religion is largely a fad—a question is still implicit: Who's right? The exploration should lead to a judgment, an answer. In some cases the conclusion may be that the question can't be answered, that the problem can't be solved, or that the truth isn't found in either point of view. But you shouldn't use pro-and-con as a cover-up for fence straddling. In the end you must make up your mind about the subject, and the reader should be able to see how you reached that judgment.

An article about the effect of television on American sports begins with a series of charges against TV, each one followed by a rebuttal offering evidence or opinion that contradicts the accusation. Then the writer summarizes:

> Rounding out the pros and cons of TV's impact on sports, the plus side of the ledger should include the following:
> TV aroused the sleepy hinterlands, transmitting images that conveyed reality as radio never could. ("Not only does it provide big revenue," argues Baltimore Orioles manager Earl Weaver, "but it gives people all over the U.S. a chance to see all the big players.") TV created a new appetite for big-league sports, and the major leagues—to nearly everyone's satisfaction—were willing and able (in the jet age) to supply a new diet of big-league franchises. And besides contributing to the expansion of existing leagues, TV helped create entire leagues out of whole cloth (the AFL, the ABA, etc.). It raised pro football to a par in popularity with baseball. It introduced millions to tennis and golf (particularly women). It turned pro sports into a socially acceptable profession, and a desirable one.
> On the minus side, though, TV turned most of those 488 minor-league baseball stadiums into supermarkets and parking lots. And TV has legitimized such

pseudo sports as demolition derbies and wrist-wrestling, by presenting them, as one critic puts it, "with all the solemnity of the British Open."—Don Kowet, *TV Guide*

The writer concludes that there is a "tenuous balance" of pros and cons but "no guarantee" that the balance won't "tip toward the negative" as the investment and influence of TV networks grow.

The opening of an essay, "The Two Faces of Vermont," sets up the kind of pro-and-con situation that people as well as places have to face. Of two conflicting sets of values, which should prevail?

[1] When you cross the bridge from Lebanon, New Hampshire, to Hartford, Vermont, practically the first thing you see on the Vermont side is a large green and white sign. This bears two messages of almost equal prominence. The top one says, "Welcome to Vermont, Last Stand of the Yankee." The bottom one says, "Hartford Chamber of Commerce."

[2] Only Vermont could have a sign like that, I think. Vermont makes a business of last stands. Consider just a few. It is the last stand of teams of horses that drag tanks of maple sap through the frosty snow. It is the last stand of farmers who plow with oxen and do the chores by lantern light. Together with New Hampshire and maybe a few places in Ohio, it is the last stand of dirt roads that people really live on, and of covered bridges that really bear traffic. It is the last stand of old-timers who lay up stone walls by hand, of weathered red barns with shingle roofs, of axmen who can cut a cord of stove-wood in a morning—of, in short, a whole ancient and very appealing kind of rural life. This life is so appealing, in fact, that people will pay good money to see it being lived, which is where the trouble begins. There's a conflict of interest here.

[3] On the one hand, it's to the interest of everyone in the tourist trade to keep Vermont (their motels, ski resorts, chambers of commerce, etc., excepted) as old-fashioned as possible. After all, it's weathered red barns with shingle roofs that tourists want to photograph, not concrete-block barns with sheet aluminum on top. Ideally, from the tourist point of view, there should be a man and two boys inside, milking by hand, not a lot of milking machinery pumping directly into a bulk tank. Out back, someone should be turning a grindstone to sharpen an ax—making a last stand, so to speak, against the chainsaw.

[4] On the other hand, the average farmer can hardly wait to modernize. He wants a bulk tank, a couple of arc lights, an automated silo, and a new aluminum roof. Or in a sense he wants these things. Actually, he may like last-stand farming as well as any tourist does, but he can't make a living at it. In my town it's often said that a generation ago a man could raise and educate three children on fifteen cows and still put a little money in the bank. Now his son can barely keep going with 40 cows. With fifteen cows, hand-milking was possible, and conceivably even economic; with 40 you need all the machinery you can get. But the tourists don't want to hear it clank.

[5] The result of this dilemma is that the public image of Vermont and its private reality seem to be rapidly diverging.—Noel Perrin, *First Person Rural*

Toward the end of the essay Perrin writes:

> In the last five years the balance has perceptibly tipped in favor of moderniza-
> tion. Most people agree that the last stand is likely to end in about one more
> generation. What will happen then? Let me present an admittedly partisan view.

And his partisan view begins:

> Most of Vermont will look like—well, it will look like central New Jersey
> with hills.

In a pro-and-con structure the writer investigates his subject by weighing its strengths and weaknesses, its advantages and disadvantages, or by
looking at it from different points of view. The reader of a paper organized
according to the pro-and-con pattern is like the Vermonter in Perrin's essay
who has to decide where he wants to be ten years from now. By contrast,
the reader of a paper organized according to the support pattern starts out
for a definite destination with his itinerary and guidebook in hand. And the
reader of a paper that follows the discovery plan is the traveler who buys a
ticket for a bus tour that takes him into country he hasn't seen before and
doesn't know about.

Support, discovery, and pro-and-con are basic structures that are useful
to keep in mind when you're planning a paper. One of them will be more
suitable than the others in view of your purpose, your thesis, and your estimate of the needs and interests of your audience. Sometimes you won't stick
to one pattern from start to finish. Indeed, you're not likely to in a long
paper made up of several sections. But even then the movement within each
section is likely to approximate one of these patterns:

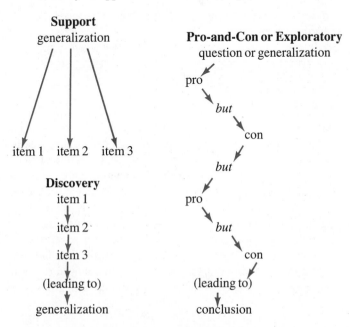

Within each of the structures you'll need to arrange your examples or details or pieces of evidence in a sequence that makes sense—chronological, simple-to-complex, order of increasing importance, or whatever suits your purpose. But once you know the general shape your paper is to take, you'll find it easier to make these choices.

For Discussion and Writing

1. Review the three short papers on running, pp. 95–96.
a. Which one comes closest to the support structure in organization, and how could it be shaped into a clear example of that structure?
b. Which one has elements of pro-and-con in it? What are they? How could they be further developed?
c. Which one is closest to the discovery pattern? Can you explain why the rhetorical situation, as defined by the student, makes discovery a good choice for this paper?
2. Americans of all ages worry about being overweight. Write three brief papers (4–5 paragraphs each) to an audience of decidedly chubby teenagers.
a. Open the first with a paragraph that warns your readers about the dangers of obesity and promises a program for reducing. Follow through on the promise.
b. Make the second the story—personal or otherwise—of the unhappy life of a fat teenager and the improvement, psychological as well as physical, that came with thinning down by following a weight-reduction program.
c. Open the third with a paragraph that recognizes both the pleasures of overeating and the desire to look attractive. Work through a pro-and-con pattern that will leave your audience convinced that it's better to look good than to gorge.

Associational Order

Instead of basing your paper on a perceived order in time or space or on an order that another writer could invent and impose on the same material, you can follow a pattern suggested by the associations the subject sets off in your own mind. Associational writing is sometimes not much more than free writing that's been pruned. Though not often suitable for college papers, it can work well when a distinctly personal flavor is appropriate. Instead of giving a chronological account of the building of a house or using a space order in describing its interior, you might begin a paper with a description of the house as it looked to you when your family first moved into it, perhaps, and then drift from one memory to another as you recall the years you lived there. Such a paper would probably end up telling more about you and what your memory clings to than about the house and what it looked like, but if done well it could have charm, drama, humor, tragedy. Unless it's handled skillfully, however, associational order may be confusing, and the paper as a whole may seem rambling and pointless.

Strategies of Ordering

The structure of a paper is always strongly influenced by the nature of the material and the writer's purpose. In most writing the third major influence should be the audience. With the audience in mind you decide whether to organize your material according to the rhetorical strategy of *announcing* or the rhetorical strategy of *disclosing*.

Announcing and Disclosing

In announcing, you let the reader know early in the paper what approach to your subject you're taking. Sometimes you list the topics you'll discuss; sometimes you open with a direct statement of purpose of the "This-paper-will-attempt-to-show" type. As further guidance you may introduce sentences throughout the paper that summarize and forecast, reminding the reader of what ground has been covered and giving clues to what lies ahead.

When you announce, you either reveal what the structure of your paper will be or strongly suggest which organizational pattern you'll follow. You use the strategy of announcing when your opening paragraph contains a statement like this:

> Critics of feminism give several reasons why the movement has limited appeal for American women (reader knows the reasons will be given)

or

> Five accomplishments of the women's movement seem to me to be most significant (reader expects discussion of the five accomplishments)

or

> Feminists rely too much on stereotypes in their pronouncements about the sexes (reader anticipates examples of stereotypes).

Announcing is strong in the opening of Abbey's article (pp. 110–11). It is equally strong in this opening:

> Violence is not only "as American as cherry pie," it is likely to remain à la mode for some time to come.
>
> At its simplest, it arises from two basic causes: too many people and too many weapons. The population explosion simply creates too many people rubbing up

against too many others; and every species from rats on up finds more to fight about when there is less room.

The availability of weapons—both firearms (the favorite of amateurs) and explosives (the historic preference of professionals)—is an unchecked scandal in our country. And the sale of weapons internationally has never known a boom period like the present. It points to a dangerous, deeper possibility of which the spread of weapons may be both a cause and a symptom: the breaking up of the modern nation-state.—James Billington, *Newsweek*

Though the announcing is less strong in the following paragraph, there's a definite promise that the article will tell us about the giant water lily:

There is a tropical plant that blooms white one day and turns purple the next, heats up at night and imprisons its insect pollinators, but is most often remarked on for quite a different quality. That quality is size, a size so out of proportion with what we are accustomed to that it unsettles our perspective. The plant is the legendary giant water lily of the Amazon, and recently, where the cola-colored water of the Rio Negro meets the chocolate-pudding water of the Amazon near Manaus, I was privileged to see some myself.—Thomas E. Lovejoy, *Smithsonian*

The first paragraph of "Old Is Right?" (p. 71) makes a protest that sets the tone of the paper and lets the reader know the general position that will be developed. Again, in the paper "Distracting Types," the first paragraph (p. 75) announces unmistakably what the nature of the paper will be. Both these papers announce; both are developed in a modified support structure. (In a pure support structure the charges in paragraphs 3–6 of "Old Is Right?" would be summarized early, and the classes in "Distracting Types" would be listed early. Neither paper would be improved by the change.)

In the strategy of disclosing, your beginning doesn't forecast your ending, and you proceed from stage to stage without revealing to the reader just how each is related to the point you'll eventually make. When you use the strategy successfully, the subject unfolds as you proceed, and the climax sometimes brings in an element of surprise. (In the good paper the surprise is immediately followed by a "Why, of course!")

Normally, though not always, descriptions and narrations open with a disclosing rather than an announcing paragraph. The description of George Ritchey (p. 41) is an example, and so is the narrative "Down, Down, or the St. Valentine's Day Massacre" (pp. 49–50). "Making Marks" (pp. 81–82) is an example of disclosing in expository writing.

Announcing would seem to be the likelier strategy for a paper that moves *from* a generalization and disclosing for a paper that moves *toward* a generalization, but this is not always the case. A problem-solution paper may begin with an announcement of what procedures are being followed, what alternatives excluded, and so on. Or it may be handled in such a way that the reader is gradually brought to realize that a problem exists and then given a sense of sharing in a joint inquiry that leads to a solution.

Choosing a Strategy

For some of your papers it will seem natural to adopt one strategy rather than the other. But often you can use either. In making your choice you should be guided by your estimate of the needs, interests, and attitudes of your audience. If the material is difficult or the organization has to be complex, you may decide that readers will find the paper hard going unless you announce at some length, offering a blueprint to show how each topic or section fits into your scheme. Or you may decide instead that you should begin with the material your readers are familiar with and gradually work up to the more complicated aspects of the subject, disclosing your full scheme only toward the end of the paper.

If you can count on your readers having a strong interest in the subject, you may decide to plunge in without offering any guidance to the structure. Or you may conclude that sketching the course of your discussion in an opening paragraph will make it easier for readers to concentrate on the content as they move through the paper. If you suspect that they're not much concerned, you have a harder decision to make. Can announcing be a promise of interesting things to come? Or does the strategy of disclosing seem more likely to capture their attention? If you're writing an argument, size up the probable attitude of your audience. If it's opposed to your position, will announcing increase the opposition or reduce it?

Answers to particular questions like these depend on the individual writing situation. Few rhetorical problems are solved by formulas. Handled well, either strategy can result in strong, satisfying organization. But each has its drawbacks. Though announcing ensures that readers know where they're going, it may make the structure seem too mechanical. The strategy of disclosing escapes this danger; but unless the parts of the paper have a tight, organic connection, making the logic of a shift from one part to another immediately clear, readers may not see what direction the paper is taking. And if they have difficulty detecting the general drift, they'll probably miss the significance of many of the details. A good writer always provides clues to structure, even if he plants them deep.

One strategy doesn't rule out the other. In long papers you may use both. For example, you might use announcing in introducing and describing a problem and then shift to disclosure in proposing a solution. Whether you choose to announce or to disclose or to announce and disclose by turn, your motive should be to get your readers involved in your subject. You want them to take an intelligent interest in it, to understand what you have to say about it, and finally to accept what you have to say as worth reading.

Whether or not the organization of a paper has been signaled, it should be firm. These instructions on examinations (none of them for English courses) give evidence of the importance college faculty place on organization:

> Your answers will be graded not only on the quantity and accuracy of their factual content but also on their organization, coherence, and relevance to the questions asked.

> Pay close attention to clear writing, logical organization, clear and useful illustrations, and full and correct documentation of material from outside sources.

These instructions ask further that the organization be signaled from the start:

> The topics given are general; you will need to limit them further to make a tight and coherent paper. Be sure to establish in your opening paragraph exactly what point you are going to make about the topic you select; a vague, general, unfocused paper is a poor one.

> From the beginning of your essay, make sure that your reader knows what you intend to do and how you intend to do it. Then lead your reader through the argument, step by step, making sure that there are no breaks in the logic. Finally, conclude in such a way that your reader is in no doubt about the main points you have made.

Announcing alone won't guarantee a good examination answer. A history professor writes in the margin of a first paragraph: "Here you *tell* me you are going to do three things—first, second, third. But look at your essay. Nowhere do you take up your second point, and the third wanders off from the point you said you were going to make. What use is it to outline your paper if you don't follow the outline?" Good question.

Parts and Paragraph Sequences

Let's look at a complete article to see what we can learn from its organization.

Barbed Wire

[1] If you grew up in a city, it is possible that you have never had occasion to look closely at a barbed wire fence. In that case, it might be fun to try to invent it, in imagination, for yourself. It sounds easy. You only have to set two posts in the ground and string between them wires, fitted with barbs at about six-inch intervals. The problem is to fix the barbs so firmly that a heavy animal brushing against the fence will not break them off, or slide them along the wire. If they slide, you will soon have all the barbs shoved up against one post or the other, with a naked wire in between. Another problem is to figure out a way to make your wire cheaply and fast—that is, with machinery requiring a minimum of hand labor.

[2] You might think of soldering on the barbs, but that quickly turns out to be a poor idea. The soldered join is inherently weak, and since each one has to be made by hand, the process would be prohibitively expensive. Another possibility is to take a ribbon of steel about one inch wide, cut zigzags along one side to form sharp points, and then twist the ribbon as you string it. This, too, has been tried and found impractical. The ribbon can be rolled, and cut by machinery, but it is too heavy to handle easily, uses too much expensive steel per foot, and is too weak to resist the impact of a charging bull. Another abortive scheme involved spiked spools strung on a wire.

The two opening paragraphs indicate that we can expect a problem-solution variety of the discovery structure. The author doesn't tip his hand by announcing what's to come. Plainly he's alert to a rhetorical situation that includes among the audience city folks who ''have never had occasion to look closely at a barbed wire fence.'' He uses the ingenious tactic of inviting them to invent barbed wire. In outlining what's needed and telling what won't work, he gets across a lot of information.

[3]According to the Bivins Museum in Tascosa, Texas, 401 patents for barbed wire have been recorded, and more than 1,600 variants have been catalogued. Out of all these attempts, only two proved successful. Both were patented at nearly the same time by two neighbors in De Kalb County, Illinois: Joseph F. Glidden and Jacob Haish. Whether they got their ideas independently, and who got his first, are questions that have provoked much expensive litigation. Their concepts were quite similar. Each involved clasping barbs around a wire at appropriate intervals—and then twisting that wire together with another one, so that the barbs are tightly gripped between the two. The only essential difference, to the eye of anyone but a patent lawyer, was in slightly variant methods of clasping the barb.

Paragraph 3 marks a turn, as the writer moves from the hypothetical inquiry into information about how the problem was actually solved.

[4] Whether or not Glidden was the original inventor, he certainly was the more successful businessman. He made his first wire in 1873, forming the barbs with a converted coffee grinder and twisting the twin wires in his barn with a hand-cranked grindstone. He sold his first wire, and took out his patent, in 1874. That same year he formed a partnership with a neighbor, I. L. Ellwood, and built a factory in De Kalb. Before the end of the next year, their factory was turning out five tons of wire a day, using improved, steam-operated machinery. In 1876 Glidden sold a half interest in his invention to the Washburn and Moen Manufacturing Company of Worcester, Massachusetts, which had been supplying him with plain wire; in payment he got $60,000, plus a royalty of 25 cents for every hundredweight of barbed wire sold.*

[5] How profitable this deal proved to be can be glimpsed from the following figures. In his first year of manufacture, Glidden sold 10,000 pounds of wire. Two years later, Washburn and Moen sold 2.8 million pounds. Within the next

five years, sales mounted to more than 80 million pounds a year—yielding Glidden an income of more than $200,000 annually, the equivalent of at least $1 million today, and that was before the era of income taxes. The manufacturers' profits amounted to many times that.

[6] Much of his wire was being shipped to Texas. Glidden and his money followed it, leaving a permanent impress on the settlement of the High Plains and especially on its main city, Amarillo. There I came across his traces nearly sixty years later.

*Washburn and Moen eventually merged with the American Steel and Wire Company, a subsidiary of U.S. Steel. American Steel and Wire's museum in Worcester is the prime source of information about barbed wire.

Paragraphs 4–6 begin with a generalization about the inventor Glidden, which is supported by details of his spectacularly successful career. Paragraph 6 concludes the section with a sentence that joins present to past.

[7] But in the meantime I had a chance to become well acquainted with his product. When I was eleven years old, my grandfather John Fischer taught me how to string wire during a summer I spent on his homestead near Apache, Oklahoma. To my eyes he seemed a very old man, but he was still wiry, lean, hard-muscled, and accustomed to working from sunup till long after dark.

[8] Like inventing barbed wire, stringing it is a more complex business than you might think. First you find your posts. My grandfather insisted that they be either cedar, locust, or bois d'arc, also known as Osage orange. These woods will last in the ground for many years, while cottonwood or pine will rot quickly unless creosoted—and we had no creosote in those days. Some he cut himself along a little creek that ran across one corner of his 160-acre farm; others he bought or bartered from neighbors. Each post had to be exactly six feet long.

[9] When the posts were all collected, with a mule team and wagon, he stacked them near the edge of the pasture he planned to fence, and then marked his line. This he did with a borrowed surveyor's transit, a handful of stakes, and a few rolls of binder twine. At thirty-foot intervals he scratched a mark on the hard prairie soil to indicate where he wanted each post to go. One of my jobs was to make a hole in the ground with a crowbar at each mark, and fill it with water from a five-gallon, galvanized-iron milk can, thus softening the earth for my grandfather, who followed me with his post-hole digger.

[10] The first post set, to a depth of precisely two feet, was of course at a corner of the tract he was going to enclose. It had to be braced in both directions of the future fence lines. For braces he used two other posts planted diagonally in the earth with their feet anchored against heavy stones; their top ends he sawed at the proper angle and fastened to the corner post with tenpenny nails. Then we set about the weary labor of digging holes and setting intermediate posts until we came to the place he had marked for his next corner. We had to do only three sides of the forty-acre pasture, because the fourth side abutted a field enclosed years earlier; but at that, the post-setting took us the best part of two weeks.

[11] Then we drove the wagon into Apache to get a load of wire. It came on big wooden spools, so heavy that the hardware dealer had to help us load them. Grandfather let me drive back, a proud and nervous assignment for me, although the mules—named Pete and Repeat—were gentle enough.

[12] At the rear end of the wagon bed he rigged a pole, crosswise, to serve as a spindle on which a spool of wire could be mounted and easily unwound. We drove the wagon close to a corner post, twisted the end of the wire around it one foot above the ground, and stapled it fast. Next we drove along the line of posts for about 200 yards, unreeling wire on the ground behind us. There Grandpa stopped, unhitched the team, blocked three wheels of the wagon with rocks, and jacked up the fourth wheel, the rear one next to the fence line. He cut the wire and twisted the loose end around the axle of the jacked-up wheel, fastening it to a spoke for additional security. By turning the wheel, we wound the wire around the axle until it was taut. (There were patent wire-stretchers, but Grandpa did not own one. The wheel-stretching method worked just as well, and saved money.) After he had lashed the wheel to maintain the tension, we went back down the line and stapled the wire to each post. Then we repeated the process, time after time, until we had the pasture enclosed with a standard fence of four strands, spaced a foot apart. We finished up by making a wire gate at the corner nearest the house.

[13] Three tips for fence-stringers:

—Wear the heaviest leather gauntlets you can find. Even so, you are bound to get your hands and arms torn, so carry some iodine and bandages with you.

—Staple the wire on the side of the posts facing into the pasture. When a heavy animal runs into the fence, he will press the wire against the posts, not the staples. If the wire were on the other side, the staples might pop out.

—Hang the expense, and use two staples for each fastening of the wire. One of them might someday rust or work loose.

This section (paragraphs 7–13), which follows a discovery structure, is subdivided into three parts:

Paragraph 7 brings the writer into the picture; "in the meantime" takes him back to a time long before he had heard of Glidden.

Paragraphs 8–12 open with a strong transitional sentence that carries back to the second sentence in the first paragraph. From here on, we have the description of a process, told clearly and efficiently yet with details that fit the point of view of the eleven-year-old apprentice.

Paragraph 13, with its briskly stated tips, is set somewhat apart from the process, summarizing and pulling together.

[14] I haven't seen that fence in decades, but my brother told me a few years ago that it was still standing and tight. Probably it is the most nearly permanent thing I have ever worked on. Certainly its useful life has been far longer than that of any article or book I have written.—John Fischer, *Harper's*

The last paragraph makes a definite conclusion. Looking at the process of stringing wire from the perspective of several decades, the author finds it a deeply satisfying experience.

Some readers might argue a bit about where lines should be drawn in the article. Is paragraph 3 more closely related to 1–2 or to 4–6? Is 6 closer to 4–5 or to 7–13? Is 13 separate from 7–12, or does it belong to the process? The questions are worth raising, but for the moment there's no need to agree on firm answers. The main point we want to make is that all but the shortest and simplest papers move through stages. In a paper of some length you can keep tighter control of the organization if you think of it as consisting of, say, five parts rather than of fifteen separate paragraphs. The beginning is a part, whether it's a single sentence, several sentences, a paragraph, or three or four paragraphs in sequence. The ending of a paper is a part, no matter how long or short it is. Each bridge between one stage of the discussion and the next is a part. And each paragraph or sequence of paragraphs that forms one of those stages is a part.

In revising a paper, you can work more efficiently once you've identified the paragraphs that belong together, that perform one main function in the total scheme. You can make sure that such paragraphs are grouped in a sensible order, and you can shift or drop any paragraph that appears in a sequence where it doesn't belong. Revising one sequence, or block, of paragraphs before turning to the next is more likely to produce a paper that has direction and point than simply revising paragraph by paragraph without paying attention to these groupings.

Once you have the parts of your paper mapped out, you should be able to answer such basic questions about its structure as these:

Are the parts in an order that makes the best sense in terms of my purpose?

Will the connections between the parts be clear to my readers?

Are the beginning and ending suitable in this rhetorical situation?

Are the proportions satisfactory? Have I given most space and emphasis to what's most important?

These matters we'll consider in the remainder of this chapter.

Signals of Transition

Strong organization demands that the parts of a paper be in an order that permits you to say what you want to say to your particular audience. It also requires that the order be apparent to the audience and that it seem at least reasonable, at best inevitable. Though what you write may meet the first requirement, it will fall short of the second if you don't provide connecting links. Remind yourself regularly that while *you* know how the parts fit together, your readers don't have your inside information.

Sometimes the connections are in the material, and the movement from one part to another seems entirely natural and necessary. More often they're in your understanding of the subject, the way you feel about it, the way you approach it. You *make* the connections, and in composing your paper you must be sure they come clear to your readers. At the structural breaks where one stage of a discussion ends and another begins, you should consider using explicit transitions, bridges that will carry your reader from one topic to the next.

Explicit Signals

Explicit transitions spell out relationships and establish connections. Often they comment directly on the structure of the essay, as in the transitional paragraph below (beginning ''I suppose''), which looks back to the end of the paragraph that precedes it by repeating ''good taste'' and then announces the approach to be taken:

> . . . Our readers know that change is natural and essential. So long as change does not involve a departure from good taste you will find them cheering you on.
> I suppose we could spend a good deal of time attempting to arrive at a definition of good taste without being satisfied. Let me go at it therefore in terms of what good taste is not.
> In recent years, sleaziness has invaded the culture. . . .—Norman Cousins, *Saturday Review*

The machinery of transition is also visible in the following key paragraph, which comes exactly in the middle of the article. The first sentence summarizes the discussion to this point; the last forecasts what's to come:

> These, then, are the negative effects of the scientific literature I have observed in the course of teaching scientific writing. I am glad to say that there are also definite positive findings. The most striking observation is that by teaching writing you can actually strengthen students' ability not only to write but also to read more attentively and to think more logically and rigorously.—F. Peter Woodford, *Science*

Paragraphs like these announce their function directly. Other transitional paragraphs are less obvious; only in context can they be seen to be gathering up and pushing on. In the article ''Barbed Wire'' paragraphs 3 and 7 are of this type. They make a turn in the discussion without saying that's what they're doing.

Because transitional paragraphs are a little like police officers directing traffic, they should be used only to mark major turns in a discussion. In short papers their function can be performed by single sentences, which gather up less material and usually provide gentler guidance. The transitional sentence normally comes either at the beginning or at the end of a paragraph. It signals a shift from one idea to another, indicates that the discussion is to take a new turn, or marks a digression from the main thread.

> But finally, of course, we come back to the musicians themselves, for this is the book they wrote.—Nat Shapiro and Nat Hentoff, *Here Me Talkin' to Ya*

> But even this is not the whole story.—Karen Rothmyer, *Nation*

> In order to examine this state of affairs, I shall have to touch first on a few preliminary matters.—Roger Shattuck, *New York Review of Books*

Transition can be provided by a question:

> Where does that leave man?—Arthur C. Clarke, *Profiles of the Future*

A question like this one structures the discussion very clearly. Though it doesn't disclose precisely what the writer's position is, it does promise an answer. Used sparingly, the question is a good transitional device. Overused, it quickly becomes tiresome (as does any other transitional device). Misused—as when the question doesn't rise naturally out of the discussion—it's clumsy and distracting.

Explicit transitions serve you well when they point out connections that your readers wouldn't otherwise see. If you use too few, your writing will seem disconnected, and readers may fail to see relationships you count on their recognizing. But if you use too many, you'll weigh your writing down, slow its movement, and make the machinery of expression seem to be more important than what's being expressed. When the direction of your paper is clear and the order of its parts readily apparent, announcing is wasteful and sometimes annoying.

Most transitional paragraphs and some transitional sentences are like road signs: they tell readers where they're going and perhaps where they've been. Other transitions indicate connections readers must make and relationships they must recognize if they're to follow the discussion. A good many words and phrases perform this function, among them *but, however, moreover, therefore, on the contrary, on the other hand, likewise, consequently, incidentally, as a result, nevertheless, in the first place, in short*. The function of such transitional words and phrases in achieving coherence within paragraphs will be discussed in some detail in the next chapter (see pp. 194–95).

Implicit Signals

A skillful writer uses explicit transitions where he needs them—especially to mark a sharp turn in the discussion and to relate paragraphs in which the ideas aren't obviously consecutive. The skillful writer also knows the value of less obvious means of establishing continuity. Instead of standing outside his material and pointing readers in the right direction, he makes the language of the discussion do the work. These implicit transitions, called lexical because they depend on vocabulary and meaning, include repeating or echoing key words and phrases. A phrase at the beginning of a paragraph ("The notion that busing could be a 'remedy' for official school segregation was encouraged by . . .") may allude to a use of *remedy* three paragraphs earlier. Or, in moving from one paragraph to another, the writer may carry over a key word or synonym that echoes the idea. Here "peerless moments" accomplishes the transition:

> Special-effects sequences have not only performed well at the box office as substitutes for star names, but the arrival of the giant space ship at the end of "Close Encounters" has been called by Pauline Kael "one of the peerless moments in movie history."
>
> She's right, of course; but most of the other peerless moments have depended primarily on the presence of actors speaking or relating to one another.—Richard Shickel, *New York Times Magazine*

In "Barbed Wire" the author relies much more on implicit signals of transition than on explicit ones:

> Whether or not Glidden was the original inventor, he certainly was the most successful businessman. (Sentence 1, paragraph 4)

> How profitable this deal proved to be can be glimpsed from the following figures. (Sentence 1, paragraph 5)

> There I came across his traces nearly sixty years later.
> But in the meantime I had a chance to become well acquainted with his product. (End paragraph 6, beginning 7)

> Like inventing barbed wire, stringing it is a more complex business than you might think. (Sentence 1, paragraph 8. This transitional sentence is unlike any of the preceding ones. Harking back to the opening, it marks a shift into the second half of the essay. It has very much the function of a transitional paragraph.)

The first sentences of paragraphs 9, 10, and 11 are closely linked to the ends of the preceding paragraphs.

Organic transitions—those that depend on meaning—bind a discussion together without stopping its flow. These lexical means of establishing continuity, as well as such grammatical means as the use of pronouns and parallel constructions, will be discussed in greater detail in the next chapter.

For Discussion and Writing

1. Identify the transitional devices in this opening passage from a student's paper. Tell how you expect the paper to continue and why.

> America is a death-denying society. Most Americans refuse to acknowledge that dying is an inevitable part of living. This is an unhealthy attitude. To live life fully, we must be able to think and talk openly about our own deaths and those of our friends and families. We can make a beginning by paying attention to what psychologists have to say about death and the effects of grief. One of them, Elizabeth Kubler Ross, interviewed more than one thousand terminally ill patients, their families, and their doctors for her book, *On Death and Dying.* She found that all three groups approach death in five stages.
>
> In the first stage the patient and his family deny that death is even a possibility.

2. List three or four points you might make in a paper describing a course you either liked or disliked in high school. Then list three or four related points you might make in a paper describing one of your current college courses. Write a brief transitional paragraph (three or four sentences) that links these two subjects, leading the reader smoothly from the first to the second.

3. This is an exercise to be done with a classmate. Each of you starts by making a photocopy of a magazine article or an essay from a book of readings. Choose one that's at least eight paragraphs long, and be sure it's something your partner has never read. Cut the paragraphs apart, and put them in random order. Exchange the batches of paragraphs.

Each of you should now read what's on each piece of paper you received and then put the pieces in the order you think they originally appeared in. When you're both finished, compare your versions with the originals and discuss the results. If either of you duplicated the original order, identify the clues that led you to decide where to put each paragraph. (This will show you how transitions work.) If you produced a different order, decide whether your version is as satisfactory as the original. (If the original was loosely organized, your version might be as satisfactory, but you'll probably find that you missed a clue.)

The exercise should convince you that the order of paragraphs—in your own writing as well as in that of professional writers—has a great deal to do with the reader's understanding and appreciation of an essay or article.

Beginnings and Endings

The beginning of a paper may be a paragraph, less than a paragraph, or—if the paper is a long one—several paragraphs. The same is true of endings. How your paper opens and how it closes have a decided bearing on the reader's interest in what you have to say.

Beginnings

For most readers, interest and understanding are closely related. If they don't understand what a writer is up to, they won't be much interested in what that writer says. If an opening captures their interest, they'll work harder to understand what follows. If it doesn't interest them, all the clarity in the world won't help much. Your beginnings should be clear, then, for understanding, and they should catch the attention of your readers, for interest.

You might think that the sure way of achieving clarity would be to use the strategy of announcing. But a labored statement of what's to follow can kill off a reader's interest: "This paper is going to discuss. . . . The four chief topics to be treated are. . . . First in importance is. . . ." This sort of blueprinting works in some kinds of writing, as in technical reports, where the only considerations are accuracy and system; and in special circumstances it can be dramatic, as when a trial lawyer begins, "I am going to prove to you that. . . . First, I will describe. . . . Second, I will trace. . . . Third, I will expose. . . . And finally I will demonstrate. . . ." But for most purposes the announcing should be less direct and less obvious.

And it need not be done in the first sentences of a paper. In a long paper the paragraph that does the announcing is often the last in the sequence of paragraphs that makes up the opening section; sometimes it's the first paragraph of the second section. In such cases the announcing paragraph is preceded by a stretch of material that brings the reader into the paper less formally and less abruptly—a short anecdote, a passage of descriptive details (giving, say, the look of clouds on a summer day as a way into a precise account of what causes cloud formations and how clouds are classified).

When beginnings can be recognized as attempts to whip up interest and no more than that, they do more harm than good. Sensational details, forced enthusiasm, and chitchat actually draw attention away from the subject, not toward it. One trouble with a wildly exciting opening is that it robs you of the opportunity to build to a climax; the paper can only run downhill. And concentrating on grabbing the reader's attention often produces an opening that has little connection with the real subject of the paper and therefore misleads the reader. The short, dramatized narrative used as a standard opening in popular magazines is sometimes relevant to what follows, often no more than a gimmick. Remember: A good beginning arouses expectations that the body of the paper satisfies.

Common types of openings include the anecdote, often in the dramatized form already mentioned; the generalization followed by a quick narrowing down to the specific subject; the quotation; the citation of statistics; and the question. Here are some examples:

Anecdote

The strapping rodeo bull rider grabbed Jerry Jeff Walker's arm in a vicelike grip and stared angrily at the singer, who bore a beatific, faraway expression on his face. "Didn't you hear me, boy?" he growled. "I told you to play that song about red-necks. Now play it. Fast."

Stoned and drunk and uncertain if he was in a honky-tonk in Austin or in Oklahoma City, Walker struggled to concentrate on his dilemma. If he played the song, which he knew the cowboy hated, he would probably be beaten up. If he refused the request, he would also be beaten up. Finally, he began to play. The cowboy hit him three times, smashed his guitar and left him bloody. "Situations like that," Jerry Jeff explains cheerfully, "are what being an outlaw is all about."

The outlaws of country music need all their dark memories these days; tales of brawls, drug busts and rejection slips seem to be their best means of coping with the fact that they are suddenly rich and fashionable.—Pete Axthelm, *Newsweek*

Generalization

More and more people are seeking out islands, I read in the newspaper recently, in the hope of finding freedom from neighborhood blight, crime, atmospheric pollution, noise, and the general fears and insecurity of a troubled world. The law of supply and demand having asserted itself, the article continued, habitable islands are becoming almost impossible to acquire.

I live during the more moderate months of the year on a small island close to the coast of Maine, and perhaps I can furnish a footnote on the prizes—and shortcomings—of island life.—Caskie Stinnett, *Atlantic*

Quotation

"Public education is the last great stronghold of the manual trades," John Henry Martin, superintendent of schools in Mount Vernon, New York, recently told a congressional committee. "In education, the industrial revolution has scarcely begun."—Charles E. Silberman, *Fortune*

Statistics

In the abysmal silence of interplanetary space, 2.8 billion kilometers from the life-giving warmth of our sun, lies a strange and alien world: the planet Uranus. Completely unknown to the early civilizations on Earth, Uranus has circled the sun more than 60 million times since its birth about five billion years ago.— Dennis L. Mammana, *Smithsonian*

Question

Remember the great tumult during the Sixties about talking dolphins? Because a dolphin brain is larger than ours, could it be that porpoises are potentially as bright as we are, maybe more so? John C. Lilly seriously tried teaching English to these clever little whales and for a time actually believed he had taught dolphins to mimic human speech. Like the black races of Africa, Lilly once said, porpoises are on the brink of becoming Westernized, a revolution with unpredictable consequences. "If dolphins come to understand our cold war," he warned, "we don't know how they will proceed to operate."—Excerpt from "Monkey Business" by Martin Gardner in *The New York Review of Books*, March 20, 1980, p. 3. Copyright © 1980 NYRev. Inc. Reprinted with permission from *The New York Review of Books*.

English teachers and editors who have been swamped with openings that are phony or plodding or pointless sometimes advise throwing away all first paragraphs and letting second paragraphs stand as openings. It's true that a short paper scarcely needs a paragraph that can be identified as a separate, distinct "beginning." But every piece of writing requires some context, and both writer and reader must have a sense that the starting point is a logical or natural one. Besides, throwing out the first paragraph doesn't guarantee that the next one will make a strong start.

The best course is to cut in on your material at a point that has caught your own interest and *get started*. It's much better to build up some momentum than to sit around trying to compose the perfect opening. Try writing your introduction last. Then you can gear it to the rest of the paper. Or you may discover that you don't need a separate introduction.

Endings

Short papers seldom need formal conclusions. When the process has been described, the narrative completed, the problem solved, nothing more remains be said. But discussions that move through several stages need recognizable endings if they're not to give the impression that they've been cut off or that they've simply run down. You can turn this necessity to your advantage. The ending is your last chance to win acceptance for your ideas—to establish your generalization, to drive home your thesis, to clinch your argument.

When you've built up evidence throughout a paper, you can end by asserting confidently what you presented at the start as no more than a possibility. Or you may finish up by recapitulating only the strongest of the points you've made. Even when it's little more than a summary, your ending can take on freshness from a slight change in style—a sharpening of the tone or a relaxation of tension or a touch of humor.

Your ending should make clear that the paper has arrived at its destination. It should strike a note of finality and completeness. Don't use it for apologies, for afterthoughts, for bringing in ideas that should have been treated in the body of the paper, or for introducing a brand-new issue. Make it as affirmative and positive as your discussion justifies. Point to broader implications, indicate the significance of your findings, make predictions or recommendations, or throw out a challenge to your readers. An ending that brings a paper to a totally satisfying conclusion may at the same time generate a follow-up paper.

One good way to test the effectiveness of an ending you've written is to see how well it fits the beginning of the paper. In the following paired passages, the conclusion expresses a belief that the subject's love for America—established in the opening—would have survived the worst of times:

> They still tell in our family how the 14-year-old, my father, came off the boat with a rope around his waist to hold up his pants. When he bent to kiss the ground, the rope loosened and his pants fell down. ''America!'' he cried.
>
> •   •   •   •
>
> The cataclysmic assaults upon faith and myth, innocence, invincibility all came after my father's death. I cannot imagine what he would think today, but I suspect that he would still hear America singing. It was a sound so sweet that he could never have borne to relinquish it.—Martha Weinman Lear, *New York Times Magazine*

In the next pair the opening narrative raises the question of why the ''deadly device'' had been planted. The last one-sentence paragraph is a reminder, in a play on words, of the opening. The substantive conclusion, which makes up the second last paragraph, is characteristic of inquiries of this kind. It both indicates the limits of our present knowledge and points the way to investigations that urgently need to be made.

> It was just after dawn on a chilly November morning, and the three surveyors were scratching about the barren earth southwest of Fort Stockton, Texas, looking for the old cedar stakes that would give them their bearings. The men were members of a seismic team, jolting and bullying the earth out of its geologic secrets on behalf of a major petroleum company. One of them, 49-year-old Raymond Medford, reached down to tug at a gray pipe protruding from the chalky soil; as he did, there was a sharp report and something tore upward into the fleshy part of his hand. ''What happened?'' one of the other men shouted. Medford, confused and shocked, was running in circles. Then he calmed and

said, "That thing went off! It had an explosion, whatever it was." A doctor in Fort Stockton looked at the bloody hand, administered first aid and sent the surveyor off to bed. An hour later Medford was dead.

Investigation showed that the pipe in the earth was a so-called "coyote-getter," a deadly device loaded and cocked and set to shoot a cyanide charge into the mouth of any animal that pulled at its aromatic wick.

• • • •

One comes away from a discussion with this plain-spoken biochemist—and other experts in the field—with the uneasy feeling that there are serious gaps in the toxicological profile of sodium fluoroacetate. Whole tables and booklets have been prepared on such practical matters as the exact amount of 1080 required to kill kangaroo rats, ferruginous rough-legged hawks, Rhode Island red hens and Columbian ground squirrels, but no one seems to have done much research into an equally practical matter: What is the total amount of 1080 and other poisons that the sodden soils and polluted waterways of the West can absorb without becoming lethal agents themselves? One asks, and one is told: "Nobody knows."

Someday we may be dying to find out.—Jack Olsen, *Sports Illustrated*

Here a brief, generalized anecdote opens a discussion and evaluation of eyewitness testimony. The paragraph that concludes the article indicates that the "impressive testimony" in the opening should not impress jurors as much as it does.

The woman in the witness box stares at the defendant, points an accusing finger and says, loudly and firmly, "That's the man! That's him! I could never forget his face!" It is impressive testimony. The only eyewitness to a murder has identified the murderer. Or has she?

Perhaps she has, but she may be wrong. . . .

• • • •

It is discouraging to note that the essential findings on the unreliability of eyewitness testimony were made by Hugo Münsterberg nearly 80 years ago, and yet the practice of basing a case on eyewitness testimony and trying to persuade a jury that such testimony is superior to circumstantial evidence continues to this day. The fact is that both types of evidence involve areas of doubt. Circumstantial evidence is tied together with a theory, which is subject to questioning. Eyewitness testimony is also based on a theory, constructed by a human being (often with help from others), about what reality was like in the past; since that theory can be adjusted or changed in accordance with personality, with the situation or with social pressure, it is unwise to accept such testimony without question. It is up to a jury to determine if the doubts about an eyewitness's testimony are reasonable enough for the testimony to be rejected as untrue. Jurors should be reminded that there can be doubt about eyewitness testimony, just as there is about any other kind of evidence.—Robert Buckhout, *Scientific American*

For Discussion

Describe and evaluate the beginnings and endings of the student papers in each set quoted below. What expectations does the beginning arouse? How do you know the ending is an ending?

1. Making a bassoon reed is certainly not the first thing that might come to mind when pondering what to do on a rainy Saturday afternoon, but if you ever plan to take a basic course in Woodwinds or date a bassoonist, you may find it fun and a helpful thing to know. The process is intricate and lengthy, but the result, when you hear the mellow bass tones a bassoon with your reed can produce, is worth the effort.

•   •   •   •

If you aren't a bassoonist, don't date a bassoonist, and don't even plan on taking any Woodwinds courses, this talent you've just acquired may seem to have little value for you. Well, you're wrong, because there is a profit to be made in good bassoon reeds. Consider the fact that all the materials and tools except the cane can be reused and that the cane costs only about thirty-nine cents. Add to that the fact that pre-made bassoon reeds bought in a music store cost from six to ten dollars *a reed,* and you might decide it worth while to take up reed making. Good bassoonists are as common as the cold, but a good reed-maker could be very valuable to an orchestra, music store, or conservatory, and with the profit per reed at least five dollars, a good reed-maker could also be very rich.

2. Our nation, this once great country, is in a bad state. Look around you, and you will see a countryside marred by industrial wastes. Our air is no longer good to breathe nor our water good to drink. Our legislators don't seem to realize that if we wish to sustain our lives, we must protect our plants and animals. Constantly, our policy-makers choose in favor of further industrialization rather than in favor of Mother Nature. This they justify by the bad economic situation, which is in itself just another example of how we have failed to maintain a stable nation. Recently we've been faced with corruption in government. It is on such a scale that it baffles the average voter as to whom to trust. But can we elect representative leaders at all? A further examination of the presidential elective process shows even this hallowed institution to be a farce at heart.

Our choice of candidates is limited to those individuals rich enough to afford a campaign with all the trappings. They need money for travel, advertising, debates and bribes. In the case of the presidency, even if you like the policies of one candidate and vote for that person, in the end it is the electoral college that elects the president. Under our democratic system minorities can never have a proper say no matter how large their numbers. They are taken into account only as tokens. There is one minority which deserves and has deserved better than this. They are the original owners of this land—the American Indians—and my policy of reform will focus on them.

•   •   •   •

By turning the government over to a small group of people who would have tight control of the country, I would hope we could perhaps reverse some of our destructive tendencies and expand our progressive ones. Ya-tahe! (Friendly Indian greeting.)

3. A year ago, like you, I would never have turned on a soap opera. If by some dreadful accident I happened to be in the same room with a television set turned to "Edge of Night" or "Search for Tomorrow," I would have snickered or shaken my head with amazement. "How," I would have wondered, "can people waste their time on such tripe?"

•   •   •   •

Obviously there is something to be said for the "daytime drama." And I could certainly say more. But right now I really want to see what this mysterious disease is that's filling the isolation ward at General Hospital. Has Vicki Riley's old split-personality problem come back, leaving her with Two Lives to Live? And who killed Marco Dane, anyway?

Proportion and Emphasis

A paper needs to have shape as well as direction. If you let a minor point get out of control and take up more space than it deserves, the paper will bulge where it shouldn't. Good proportions depend on your own sense of the relative significance of your ideas about your subject, modified by your sense of the needs of your audience. If your readers are unfamiliar with the subject, spend time introducing them to it. If they're likely to reject one of your ideas, pile up evidence on that point. If your discussion has been complicated, be especially careful to pull things together at the end.

Proportion is related to emphasis. What deserves most emphasis should get most space. Position can provide emphasis too: beginnings and endings offer major opportunities. Beginnings can arouse curiosity and overcome resistance, and endings—of sentences and paragraphs as well as of whole papers—can serve as clinchers. If you use a comparison to prove that one product is superior to another, put its strongest claim either at the beginning or at the end—the beginning if you feel the need to break down resistance, otherwise the end for climax.

Failures in proportion and loss of emphasis often result from writing by association and from excessive qualifying. Associational thinking may be a great help in prewriting (writer in search of a topic) and in rough notes. One idea or image or word can remind you of another. At this early stage you aren't selective. You follow your subject through related pictures in your mind, even through puns and other kinds of word play. You're hospitable to all ideas. Approaching a subject this way helps get you into a first draft. But a paper isn't a duffel bag. You can't stuff everything into it. At some point you've got to select and shape. Otherwise you'll never focus on a single theme. As your real topic becomes clear, you've got to throw out the extraneous material that free associating produced and arrange the relevant material with attention to proportion and emphasis.

Some of us don't do enough qualifying when we write. We generalize about "people," "men," "women," "students," and so on, without a "some" or a "many" or a "most" to indicate that our statements aren't all-inclusive. As you work for accuracy and truth in what you write, you'll need to qualify some of your generalizations, take note of exceptions, ward off unwarranted inferences. Simply adding "based on my own experience" or words to that effect will often make acceptable a statement that readers might otherwise reject: "On the basis of my own experience, I'd say that women bosses are harder on women employees than men bosses are." This kind of qualifying is reasonable, often admirable. But don't carry it so far that you weaken your organization and deaden your style. There are always exceptions if you hunt for them hard enough (just about every statement on writing in this book could be qualified); but introducing them when they have little point or significance will slow your paper to a crawl and make you sound like an overly cautious bore.

Aids to Organizing: Outlines

Opinions differ sharply on the value of outlining in the prewriting stage. Some writers never make outlines of any kind. Others can't write without an outline. Of those who use outlines, some work from sketchy notes, others draw up extremely detailed plans, and still others *think* the whole thing through, so that they have a complete structure in mind before they write a word.

What sort of writer are you? If your papers—particularly the longer ones—are criticized for being disorganized, you probably need to try outlining before you write. Developing an outline can help you find gaps in your material or twists in your thinking—in the way you're fitting your material together. Once you've constructed an outline and repaired its flaws, it can serve as a kind of blueprint for your paper.

But never let an outline freeze a paper. As you write, always be prepared to move away from your plan. The act of writing down one recollection may spark another that throws a different light on the event; a new example may point toward a conclusion quite unlike the one that originally seemed logical. Whenever you have to choose between following your outline and following your ideas, go with your ideas. Change your outline. Keep your mind open and active.

Types of Outlines

The working outline (or scratch outline or informal outline) is a private affair—subject to constant revision, made without attention to form, and finally tossed into the wastebasket. But enough working outlines have been retrieved from wastebaskets that something can be said about them.

A working outline usually begins with a few phrases and some descriptive details or examples. From them grow fragmentary sentences, tentative generalizations, guesses. One or two of these take on prominence and are shaped into statements that seem worth developing. New examples bring to mind new ideas, and these find a place in the list of phrases, canceling out some of the original ones. The writer keeps inserting and crossing out, juggling and shifting, until he has his key points in an order that makes sense to him. He scribbles a sentence, works in a transition, adds examples.

Depending on his habits, he may discard his working outline as soon as it has served the purpose of getting the direction and shape of his essay clear to him. Or he may keep it beside him as he writes, checking off points as he covers them, rejecting ideas that prove unsatisfactory, taking time to rethink and reorder before finishing the first draft. By then, if he has kept expanding and correcting it, his outline comes close to being a rough summary of the essay itself.

Here, minus cross-outs and general untidiness, is the first rough outline for a paper about a made-for-television movie that the writer has just seen and greatly enjoyed. As it stands, it's little more than a plot summary, jotted down while her memory of the film is fresh and her enthusiasm high.

A TV movie that moves you. Laughter and tears, as they say.

Great job by John Yule as Frank—ex-janitor, ex-drunk, half-blind old man who can't settle down to wait for death.

Director Susan Kolb ducks all—well, almost all—the sentimental clichés. Frank not broke (couple of pensions). Not alone. Has younger brother, nieces, who help him out, try to look after him. Not in a home or a slum. High-rise housing project for elderly. Popular there despite lying, bragging, swearing, etc. (Frank is NOT a Grand Old Man.) Other old people all around him. Great faces for camera to work with.

Seems like comedy at first. Only gradually recognize Frank's fears—of losing things, losing memory, losing sight, losing mind, losing life. Stares at TV. Walks streets (straddle-legged for balance). Never misses a wake or a funeral. Has tantrums.

Betting on numbers a lifetime habit. Legal now. $5 a day on state lottery. Boasts of near misses. Then hits for $5000! Wild excitement. Tells everyone in project. Roams neighborhood to spread the news. Then tiredness sets in. Not much interested in collecting. (What can money solve?) Show leaves him in front of TV. Glare of tube shows grim smile on his face.

From this rough outline of the plot a more coherent and more compact version was developed:

1.   The excellent TV movie *Lottery* is the story of Frank Gilman, a half-blind old man who is finding it hard to settle down to wait for death.
2.   The director of *Lottery,* Susan Kolb, refuses to make Frank either pitiful or heroic: he is neither broke nor friendless; he is a braggart and a liar; and he has a rotten disposition.
3.   Only gradually do we realize that Frank—beautifully played by John Yule—lives in growing fear of the disabilities of old age and the approach of death.
4.   Frank's hour of glory comes when he hits the state lottery for $5000 and becomes the hero of the housing project and the surrounding neighborhood.
5.   The wild excitement soon gives way to weariness, and without collecting his winnings, Frank returns to his TV, to sit and stare—smiling.

For a short paper that set out to do no more than tell the story of *Lottery* and praise the movie, this outline would be adequate. With the help of the details in the rough outline and the other details in the writer's memory, each sentence could generate a paragraph, and the job would be done. But for a more ambitious analysis and evaluation, a formal outline might be desirable.

A formal outline is orderly and neat. Particularly when it's intended for eyes other than the writer's, it should follow certain conventions. Beneath the title of the paper there should be a thesis statement. The outline form represents a process of logical division. The statement of the thesis is broken down into its parts, each represented in the outline by a main heading. The main heads are in turn divided into their parts, with subdivisions indented to show relationships of coordination and subordination. The process continues according to this formula:

    I.   (Main, or first-level, head)
       A.   (Second-level head)
          1.   (Third-level head)
             a.   (Fourth-level head)

On the logical principle that division always produces at least two units, there should be two or more headings at each level: if a I, at least a II; if an A, at least a B; if a 1, at least a 2; and so on. I, II, III, etc., are coordinate with each other, as are A, B, C, etc.; 1, 2, 3, etc.; and so on. A, B, C, etc., are subordinate to the first-level head they follow; 1, 2, 3, etc., are subordinate to the second-level head they follow; and so on.

Unless a paper is long and complex, the subdividing seldom needs to be carried beyond the third level. Keep in mind that the purpose of an outline is to help you produce a good paper. Time spent in constructing an elaborate outline for its own sake is time stolen from your main job.

One of the advantages of making a formal outline is that it can quickly show up a flaw in the thesis statement. Let's say that in the prewriting stage our writer has settled on this statement: ''Breaking away from the usual film formulas, a TV movie called *Lottery* find humor, excitement, and temporary triumph in a public housing project for old people.'' On the basis of notes she's scribbled and ideas she's generated, she begins her outline this way:

   I. Most American movies—theater or television—fall into familiar categories.
       A. Comedies
           1. Hip urban comedies
           2. Corny rural comedies

And she goes on to add headings for ''Catastrophes,'' ''Horror shows,'' ''Space extravaganzas,'' and so on, until she realizes she's building much too big a frame for her limited subject. So she backs off, rethinks her thesis, and begins her outline once more.

Two versions follow—one a *topic* outline, the other a *sentence* outline. The first uses single words and phrases for headings; the second uses complete sentences. In the topic outline heads that are coordinate should be presented in matching grammatical structures. In a paper on running, for example, subheads under ''II. Reasons for running'' might be ''A. To lose weight,'' ''B. To improve health,'' ''C. To enjoy the out-of-doors.'' They should *not* be ''A. To lose weight,'' ''B. Good health,'' ''C. Nature.''

The topic outline:

Lottery: A Winner

Breaking away from the usual film treatment of old people, a TV movie called *Lottery* finds humor, excitement, and temporary triumph among the tenants in a public housing project for the elderly.

   I. Old-age stereotypes in movies
       A. Indomitable old ladies; funny, or wise, old men
       B. The old as separate species
  II. Exception: *Lottery*
       A. Setting
       B. Characters
       C. Plot
 III. The achievements of *Lottery*
       A. What it doesn't do
           1. Setting
           2. Characters
           3. Plot
       B. What it does do
           1. Honesty
           2. Understanding
           3. Performance

The sentence outline:

Lottery: **A Winner**

Breaking away from the usual film treatment of old people, a TV movie called *Lottery* finds humor, excitement, and temporary triumph among the tenants in a public housing project for the elderly.

I.   On the big screen and the small one, old people are usually sterotyped.

    A.   Favorite stereotypes are the spunky, indomitable little old lady and the funny, or wise, old man.

    B.   More generally, old people are treated as a species separate from the rest of the human race.

II.   A major exception to this rule is the movie *Lottery,* which treats old people as ordinary human beings who have lived a long time.

    A.   Most of the action takes place in a high-rise housing project for old people with low incomes.

    B.   The characters are the tenants, their visitors, the staff, and a few neighbors.

    C.   Frank Gilman, a half-blind old man, wins $5000 in the state lottery, glories in his good fortune, then again faces his certain future.

III.   With these modest materials, Director Susan Kolb has put together a film that packs more laughs and more honest emotion than any other movie I've seen in years.

    A.   *Lottery* gives great pleasure by what it *doesn't* do.

        1.   It does not make the housing project a hell-hole.

        2.   It does not make the characters stereotypes: the staff members aren't monsters; the tenants aren't victims; Frank is neither broke and alone in the world nor a Grand Old Man.

        3.   It does not tell a story that ends with all problems solved, either by a happy miracle or by a four-alarm fire.

    B.   *Lottery* wins, and moves, the viewer by offering honesty *and* understanding *and* some great performances by a first-rate cast.

        1.   It gives us a clear-eyed view of the aged—warts, worries, and all.

        2.   It gives us the view, not of a "documentary" camera, but of an intelligent, compassionate individual—Susan Kolb.

        3.   It gives us outstanding performances by all involved: the star (John Yule), the supporting actors (particularly Dean Morrow as Willie's brother and Ann Rice as his niece), and the bit players.

The topic outline is the usual choice in preparing short or medium-long papers. A sentence outline is always the best choice for long papers, and especially for research papers, when you plan to ask your instructor for advice and criticism before proceeding with the project. Because the ideas are expressed in complete sentences, inconsistencies and lapses in logical progression are more obvious in the sentence outline than in the topic outline or the working outline. And when you have to write complete sentences, you're sure to examine the *purpose* of each paragraph or other subdivision of your paper. Though a sentence outline takes time to prepare, it remains the most informative of all outlines for the writer as well as for the reader.

Testing Organization

Whether or not they find it helpful to prepare an outline in the prewriting stage, most writers would probably agree that reducing a completed essay or article to an outline is an excellent way to expose its structure and test the progression of ideas. Making a detailed outline on the model of the sentence outline is the surest means of gaining control of any difficult reading you're assigned. And making an outline, however rough, of your own papers is one of the best ways to determine whether they have unity and continuity. For this purpose, begin by making a paragraph-by-paragraph summary (a sentence for each paragraph is enough).

Unless your paper is very short, this first step will make clear that not all your paragraphs are of equal importance. It will also show you that many of your paragraphs fall into groups, each of which performs one main function in the total scheme. Bracket the sentences representing such paragraph sequences, to show that the block as a whole is one of the parts into which your paper is divided, and compose a sentence that states the point of each of these stages in the discussion. Indent the sentences that state supporting points. A paper twelve to fifteen paragraphs long may fall into three or four sequences of closely related paragraphs, connected either by transitional paragraphs or by transitional sentences that stand at the end of one sequence or the beginning of the next.

Once you've made this rough approximation of a sentence outline, including the formal statement of a thesis, you can move quickly to close gaps, improve sequences, and in general give your rewrite a stronger, firmer organization. Unquestionably, bad papers are sometimes written from splendid outlines; but accurate outlining does expose structural weaknesses, and exposure clears the way for intelligent revision.

6

Building Paragraphs

A *content* paragraph—the kind of paragraph that does the work of conveying ideas rather than, say, making a transition—is a group of related statements that a writer presents as a unit in developing a subject. It strikes the eye as a unit because it's set off physically from what precedes and what follows, either by indention or by spacing above and below. It strikes the mind as a unit because the sentences that make it up are logically connected. Each of these clusters of related statements forms a stage in the flow of the writer's thought (as this paragraph defines the subject and the next one expands on the function of paragraphing).

Experience leads readers to expect that each new paragraph will either add to what's already been said—supply further supporting evidence, perhaps—or take a somewhat different tack. They read indention as a signal that some kind of shift, minor or major, is going to occur, and they adjust their attention accordingly. If you do your job well, your paragraphing will help them follow the movement of your ideas. If you do it carelessly, your paragraphing will confuse them.

Function and Length

If you've had a lot of practice writing single paragraphs, you may have come to think of them as complete little papers—"compositions in miniature." Though the label may be accurate for the one-paragraph assignment, it seldom is valid when applied to paragraphs in context. Pulled out of tightly organized papers, many paragraphs are obviously incomplete. And even when a paragraph makes perfectly good sense standing alone, it usually doesn't say precisely what it says when it speaks in company with its neighbors. In a good paper every paragraph performs a definite function.

Function

As the examples in this chapter and preceding ones show, you can make paragraphs work for you in a variety of ways. You can write a sequence of three linked paragraphs, using the first to make a major point and the next two to illustrate and support it. You can write another three that stand in a first-second-third relationship, all of roughly the same importance. You can write pairs of paragraphs that complement each other—one cause and the other effect, one positive and the other negative, one posing a problem and the other offering a solution, one listing advantages and the other disadvantages.

In the opening paragraph of a long paper you can lay the groundwork for a discussion that you'll carry on through the next five or six paragraphs. Then you can move to a new topic by way of a transitional paragraph—one that serves as a structural guide rather than a conveyor of ideas (see pp. 155–56). Or, before you move ahead, you can help your reader by restating in a short paragraph a complex or difficult part of your discussion.

Length

How long should your paragraphs be? That depends on two things: function and convention. A transitional paragraph is typically very short. A good content paragraph will be longer, because it presents a succession of logically related sentences that add up to something. Such a paragraph focuses on a single subject or part of a subject; it gives a reader the sense that it's a logical unit. Does that mean three sentences or thirty? In the abstract the question is impossible to answer. A three-sentence paragraph *could* be all right—particularly if the sentences were packed with ideas and information. But in most college writing, a three-sentence paragraph would be skimpy. The three sentences could be in logical order, and they could make a single, sensible point; but the result wouldn't be satisfying. The point wouldn't be sufficiently developed, or the problem wouldn't be explored in enough detail.

A thirty-sentence paragraph *could* be all right, too. Certainly in a long paper—say a twenty-page term paper based on research—thirty logically ordered sentences could form one unified phase of the subject. But whether the thirty sentences *should* be presented as a single unit would depend not only on the continuity through the stretch of sentences—the flow of thought from sentence to sentence—but also on the audience. Long paragraphs demand sustained concentration. While a succession of very short paragraphs gives a choppy, jerky effect, a short paragraph is easier to read than a long one. And very long paragraphs look forbidding. Convention and consideration for the reader call for breaking them into manageable bites.

If a first draft of yours includes a thirty-sentence paragraph, examine it carefully. Does it hold together? Does it proceed logically? Does it convey the message you intend, with the emphasis you want? If so, good. But you should also ask yourself whether your readers will be able and willing to make their way through it without getting lost or bored. If you're doubtful, look for a satisfactory dividing point. Two paragraphs that your audience can read comfortably are better than one paragraph that intimidates or overwhelms. (The two paragraphs that precede this one could be joined. They're separated to make the tone brisker and the reading easier.)

For Analysis and Writing

1. Count the words in each of three complete paragraphs (other than opening and closing paragraphs) and calculate the average number of words per paragraph
   a. in this chapter
   b. in two essays in a scholarly journal such as *Science, American Psychologist, American Historical Review, PMLA*
   c. in two nonfiction articles, without dialog, in one or more of the following: *The Atlantic, Saturday Review, The New York Review of Books, The New Yorker, Scientific American*
   d. in *Time, The Nation, National Review,* or *U.S. News & World Report*
   e. on the front page, on the editorial page, and in the sports pages of a newspaper.

2. Do you see a relationship between paragraph length and what is being written about? Between paragraph length and the kind of audience being addressed, as indicated by the nature of the publication? Do your findings in *b* and *c* suggest that writers for the same publication use paragraphs of roughly the same length or very different lengths? Through further sampling try to estimate the relative importance of content, expected audience, and a writer's individual style and taste in determining paragraph length.

3. Make a word count for paragraphs 2, 3, and 4 in a recent paper of yours. Write a brief report comparing the average length of your paragraphs to the average lengths you found in 1. Which is yours closest to—*a, b, c, d,* or *e*? Which should yours be closest to, considering the rhetorical situations in which you've been writing?

Unity and Development

As you write college papers, it's helpful to visualize each content paragraph as an organic unit built around a nucleus, linked to what precedes and what follows but with its own center, a core of meaning that justifies including the paragraph in your paper. Every paragraph must *do* something for the sequence of paragraphs it belongs to or for the paper as a whole or for both—make a point, convey an idea, create an impression. It *will* do something only if all the sentences that make it up contribute to its meaning and if that meaning is an integral part of the stream of ideas that flows through the essay.

You can make a point in different ways. You may want to express your core of meaning in a single sentence called the *topic* sentence. You may need two sentences to give it adequate expression. You may develop it through several sentences. And sometimes, instead of stating your main point in a single sentence or sequence of sentences, you can get it across by making sure it's what all the particular statements of the paragraph add up to. In the expository paragraph that follows, for instance, the core of meaning is the idea or observation that major changes have taken place in the study of philosophy. That meaning receives full expression in no single sentence of the four that make up the paragraph yet is present in every one of them and comes through strongly in the paragraph as a whole.

> Those unaware of what is happening in philosophy today may be surprised to learn that few academic philosophers address the sort of problems one studied in college: death, the existence of God, the cardinal virtues, the external world, or the prospects of happiness. Instead, if one walks into a classroom or lecture hall, one is likely to find brief discussions dealing with an odd assortment of issues about such things as time machines, adverbs, pains, possible worlds, sexual perversion. Even the language has changed. In many cases, English prose has been replaced by codes, symbols, and dialects incomprehensible to those outside the profession and not much better known to some of those inside.—Kenneth Seeskin, *American Scholar*

Topic Sentences and Pointers

Every content paragraph you write should contain a core of meaning. Whether the paragraph has a topic sentence is secondary; normally the question won't enter your mind. When you're intent on formulating and expressing ideas, you don't think in terms of topic-sentence-and-support-for-it any more than you consciously decide that you're going to develop a paragraph by definition or by causal analysis or whatever. You follow the flow of your ideas. But when the flow is down to a trickle, you'll probably start trying to figure out what general point you want to make next. In the process, you'll review your purpose, skim over what you've already written, and choose from among the major points you still plan to make. Hitting on a central idea gives you the sense of direction you need, and framing a sentence that expresses the idea gives you something to work toward or away from. Once you have a topic sentence—either in mind or on paper—you'll find it easier to write a paragraph that's a meaningful unit, not just a collection of statements.

Whether you keep the topic sentence in your final draft or allow the meaning to emerge without one depends on the rhetorical situation—your subject and what you want to do with it, your relation to your readers, and so on. Ordinarily your readers won't be any more concerned with spotting topic sentences than you are with writing them, but if the material is difficult, they may look for some guidance. Topic sentences are one means of providing guidance.

Topic Sentences

A topic sentence gives the gist of the discussion or states the central proposition to be explained or defended. It's the clearest single statement the writer makes of a paragraph's core of meaning. And it's the rack on which all the other sentences in the paragraph (except transitional ones) are hung. To see the relationship of a topic sentence to the other sentences in a paragraph, review some of the paragraphs we've quoted in earlier chapters. As you do, you'll find that the topic sentence can take any position in a paragraph. You'll also find that some paragraphs (roughly half, according to a survey made by one scholar) don't have topic sentences.

In the first paragraph of the selection on pages 26–27 the topic sentence is in lead position: "Every house has its own fragrance, or stench, depending." The topic sentence opens the second paragraph of the paper on page 41: "George has a sort of hunt-and-peck attitude toward work." (Note that the first paragraph of that paper has no topic sentence. Many descriptive and narrative paragraphs have none.) In passage II on page 64 the topic sentence is the first sentence of paragraph 1, but in paragraph 2 it's the next to last sentence. It's also next to last in the passage quoted on page 141: "Nonemployed women, meaning women who are not in the labor force, in fact devote as much time to housework as their forebears did." In the opening paragraph of "Consumerism," page 79, the topic sentence stands last: "Even though I'm not an impulse buyer, nor a constant buyer, I do have the consumer attitude."

Topic sentences like these are the sentences you'd quote or paraphrase if you were asked what the author was getting at, what point he was trying to make. They represent, more or less fully, the paragraph's core of meaning. In an explanatory or argumentative paper a well-phrased topic sentence is useful to the writer: it gives him a nucleus to build around. It's useful to the reader, too, for it gets him to the heart of the matter.

Pointers

You have another means of controlling and directing the reader's attention in a paragraph. You can use *pointer statements*. Instead of telling the reader the central idea—what the paragraph says—a pointer tells what the paragraph is going to do. Pointers are part of the strategy of announcing, as in this paragraph opener: "Here is what happens when you heave to" (William F. Buckley, Jr., *New Yorker*). The reader doesn't learn from this sentence what happens when you heave to, but he knows he's going to find out. Pointers include some questions and many transitional statements. Most often they come at the beginnings of paragraphs. Here are some pointers from paragraphs quoted earlier:

> How does protest differ from revolution? (p. 90. This paragraph has no topic sentence.)

> The word *ethnic* has come to have many different meanings. (p. 85. The topic sentence is the last one in the paragraph.)

> I have often tried to imagine what people who come to this place feel. (p. 72. The sentence that follows this one is the topic sentence for the sequence of three closely related paragraphs.)

Their function as guideposts makes pointers extremely useful in organizing a paper. When the material you're dealing with is complex and you know your readers will welcome all the help they can get, you may want to use both topic sentences and pointer statements to characterize and control the content of a paragraph or of a sequence of paragraphs. Notice how these two pointer statements, which stand at the beginning of a paragraph, together give readers a good deal of guidance to what follows:

> A word is needed at this point to explain in fuller detail what is meant by the *structure* of a subject, for we shall have occasion to return to this idea often in later pages. Three simple examples—from biology, from mathematics, and from the learning of language—help to make the idea clearer.—Jerome S. Bruner, *The Process of Education*

Though at this point the reader doesn't know the outcome of the discussion—what structure means—he does know, as he reads on, what purpose the example from biology is intended to serve. And at the close of the paragraph he finds the promised definition, expressed in a topic sentence and then—for clarity and emphasis—restated:

> Grasping the structure of a subject is understanding it in a way that permits many other things to be related to it meaningfully. To learn structure, in short, is to learn how things are related.

These twin topic sentences sum up the content of the paragraph just as the opening pointers predict it.

Expanding the Core

Even when you've expressed the central idea of a paragraph in a topic sentence, the real work remains to be done. A topic sentence may be the most inclusive sentence in a paragraph but also the least interesting. In this paragraph, the opening one of the paper quoted on page 95, the first sentence makes an adequate topic sentence, but the other two are the ones that catch the reader's attention:

> Today more people run than ever before. Tall, short, fat, thin, runners can be found in the city and the country. Some run laps around quarter-mile tracks, some run established routes on local streets, still others ad lib, crossing whatever street or field they come to.

The openers of the two paragraphs quoted on page 31—"At its best, factory work is merely depressing" and "At its worst, factory work is maddening"—do their work as topic sentences; but it's the details that follow them that the reader remembers. What convinces, then, is not so much the bare idea a topic sentence expresses as the clarification and dramatization of the idea by the other sentences in the paragraph—sentences that support it and expand on it with anecdotes, descriptive details, and examples.

In Chapter Two we said that writing is weakened by the habit of relying on generalizations to do the work that should be done by details. Precisely the same weakness shows up in papers where topic sentences are allowed to stand without adequate support: the paragraphs are undeveloped and the papers unconvincing.

Recall the differences between an article or a chapter you've read and the outline you've made of it. Reviewing the outline several times while the complete reading is fresh in your mind is an excellent way to get control of the material. But if you go back to the outline a few weeks later, you're not likely to get much help. In the interval you'll have forgotten the particulars—the details, the examples, the evidence—that originally supported the key statements in your outline. Topic sentences are like those key statements. Bare assertions—"Going to college is worth the cost in time, money, and effort"; "Going to college isn't worth the struggle"—don't begin to convey the thought processes by which the writers arrived at the assertions. If readers are to share in your thinking and find their way to the same conclusion you reached, you must lead them over some of the same ground.

The following paragraph is both abstract and undeveloped:

> It is wrong to think that the murderer is an average gun owner. It is also wrong to think that taking guns away from the murderer would make much difference in murder rates.

Fleshed out as it was originally written, it's a good deal more interesting and more persuasive. What persuades are not sentences 3 and 7, which, as the most general statements of the author's position, qualify as topic sentences. What persuades are the definition in sentence 4, the comparison in 5, the statistics in 8, and the predicted effects in 9 and 10.

[1] It is certainly true that only a little more than 30 percent of murders are committed by robbers, rapists, or burglars, while 45 percent are committed among relatives or between lovers. [2] (The rest are a miscellany of contract killings, drug wars, and "circumstances unknown.") [3] But it is highly misleading to conclude from this that the murderer is, in any sense, an average gun owner. [4] For the most part, murderers are disturbed, aberrant individuals with long records of criminal violence that often include several felony convictions. [5] In terms of endangering his fellow citizens, the irresponsible drinker is far more representative of all drinkers than is the irresponsible handgunner of all handgunners. [6] It is not my intention here to defend the character of the average American handgun owner against, say, that of the average Swiss, whose government not only allows, but requires, him to keep a machine gun at home. [7] Rather it is to show how unrealistic it is to think that we could radically decrease homicide by radically reducing the number of civilian firearms. [8] Study after study has shown that even if the *average* gun owner complied with a ban, the one handgun owner out of 3,000 who murders (much less than the one in 500 who steals) is not going to give up his guns. [9] Nor would taking guns away from the murderer make much difference in murder rates, since a sociopath with a long history of murderous assaults is not too squeamish to kill with a butcher knife, ice pick, razor, or bottle. [10] As for the extraordinary murderers—assassins, terrorists, hit men—proponents of gun bans themselves concede that the law cannot disarm such people any more than it can disarm professional robbers.—Don B. Kates, Jr., *Harper's*

In expanding the core of a paragraph, you have two obligations. One is to keep the paragraph unified. All the statements in it must have a bearing on its main point. The second obligation is to develop that point adequately. A broad assertion may be a good start for a paragraph and may often serve as its topic sentence. But if left to stand alone, it's likely to be unsatisfactory. To improve the paragraph, ask yourself why you made the assertion in the first place. Once you're clear on that, figure out what kind of support the assertion needs to make it convincing or memorable for the reader—specific details, examples, definitions, comparisons, and so on. Some of the dozens of ways of supporting a generalization were introduced in Chapter One (pp. 11–13) and discussed in Chapters Two and Three.

For Discussion and Writing

1. Compose a generalization about yourself, about college life, about some issue that interests you—or, if you prefer, choose one from the list below. Treat it as your main point, and develop it in a sequence of three or four paragraphs. After you've written the sequence, examine the paragraphs and underline any topic sentences or pointers.

a. The three-day visit consisted of one amazing event after another.

b. When he got back, the house was a shambles.

c. Doing mathematics is like playing chess.

d. Apes are like human beings in all respects but one.

e. I have some ideas about why drug addiction became a national problem.

f. My mother doesn't seem to know what fear is.

2. When the next two paragraphs were examined in class, students were interested in the content but dissatisfied with the development of the main point. If you disagree with that criticism, explain why you find the paragraphs satisfactory. If you agree with the criticism for either paragraph or both, decide exactly what's wrong. Then, putting yourself imaginatively into the skin of the writer of either *A* or *B*, rewrite to produce a paragraph that you consider more satisfactory.

Paragraph A

Camping with my family always gives me the time to think about myself. I walk through the towering trees believing I'm as high as the tops. Sitting beside a silent pond, I see the reflection of an outgoing yet very self-conscious person. A pebble thrown in—and I see the uncertainty of my future wavering in front of me. A small family of rabbits rapidly hops by, and I realize how great it is to be with my family. Camping provides the time for me to get to know myself a little better.

Paragraph B

Early this term I had a good dose of the spirit of competition, and it left me with a bitter taste in my mouth. My roommate and I were taking exactly the same courses. She was so competitive that she would actually snicker when I did worse on an exam than she did. She seemed to get nourishment out of my failures. For a few weeks I played the same game, always aiming to beat her instead of aiming to learn. It wasn't one of my favorite experiences.

3. For each of the paragraphs in this passage, pick out the topic sentence or pointer, or, if the paragraph has neither, compose a sentence that expresses the topic idea. Then identify in class discussion the chief method used in developing the paragraph. (A checklist: Description, Narration, Examples, Division, Comparison and contrast, Classification, Causal analysis, Definition.)

Whatever is different about the scientist must begin with the particular kind of intelligence such a man possesses. It is said that the scientist must have an inquiring mind—which is true; and that he must also be one of those people who take deep pleasure in learning—which is also true, and also superficial; because both these qualities are demanded also by any number of other disciplines. The particular kind of sensibilities required by a scientist are more complicated.

Begin with his intense awareness of words and their meanings. While the poet's affinity for words makes him sensitive to their sound, emotion, and rhythm, the scientist uses them as instruments of precision. He must be capable of inventing new words to express new physical concepts. He must be able to reason verbally by analogy—to explain "how this thing is like that thing," and to be able to fit the many resemblances into one single generalization that covers them all.

The scientist must also think graphically, in terms of dynamical models, three-dimensional arrangements in space. The dynamical model of a bacterial cell, for example, is a hollow rigid capsule that may be either spherical or tubular, containing an otherwise shapeless living cell enclosed within a soft sac, the plasma membrane. Niels Bohr's dynamical model of an atom is a miniature solar system with relatively enormous electrons orbiting about an almost inconceivably small sun—the atomic nucleus—a tremendous distance away. Scientists keep these three-dimensional pictures in mind as vividly as if they were actually seeing them. Formulas and equations printed on a two-dimensional page have three-dimensional meanings, and the scientist must be able to read in three dimensions to "see the picture" at once. There is nothing "abstract" about a scientist's thinking.

This visualization is so vivid that a scientist examining a theoretical problem is really like a jeweler peering through his loupe at a gem which he holds close to his eye, turning it over and over in his fingers. To Einstein, there was nothing abstract about his theory of relativity. Even the slightest apparent deviation from the hard world of physical reality made him intellectually uncomfortable. For more than a decade, meeting at international science conferences, he and Bohr, by then both in middle age, had monumental arguments over the meaning of the uncertainty principle, with Einstein the one who stuck stolidly to the basic mechanistic principle of cause and effect. "I cannot believe that God throws dice," he said.—Mitchell Wilson, *Atlantic*

Paragraph Structure

Worrying about the structure of your paragraphs while you're writing a first draft inhibits more than it helps. It's when you turn to revising and rewriting that you should ask whether each paragraph is constructed so that it does the job you want it to do and whether the sentences in it track one another logically and smoothly.

Ask yourself, too, whether each paragraph will satisfy whatever expectations it arouses in the reader. Does the opening of the paragraph promise an account of an episode? Does it commit you to give examples, justify a generalization, attack or modify a position? Once you recognize the obligation you've assumed, you can see what underlying structure the paragraph should have. As in a whole paper, the order in a paragraph can be chronological or spatial, rhetorical (support, discovery, pro-and-con), or associational. Recognizing that you've committed yourself to a certain structure in the opening sentence or two is the first step toward repairing a paragraph that heads one way at the start and midway through veers off without warning in another direction.

Functional Units

To test the structure of a paragraph, you'll naturally look closely at individual sentences, asking whether and in what way each one advances the main point. Does each one make it more specific by illustrating it or comparing it or supporting it in some useful way? If the function of a sentence—what it's doing in the paragraph—isn't clear to you, ask yourself whether you should omit it or move it to another position in the paragraph where its purpose will be obvious, or revise it so that it contributes to the work done by neighboring sentences.

Here's a student's paragraph as originally written:

> [1] Since I was the youngest person and only available female there, I was an easy target for some of the "confirmed bachelors." [2] Not all of the attention I got was exactly what I welcomed. [3] I was bombarded with questions, and offers to get me another drink or a piece of cake. [4] My uncle had to rescue me from being taken out "dancing" at 2 a.m. [5] Everyone paid a lot of attention to me.

As a result of class discussion, the writer decided to move the last sentence into second place. The new order—1, 5, 2, 3, 4—made the development of the point more sensible and the continuity smoother. Then she went on to consider another order: 1, 5, 3, 2, 4. This, she decided, was the best order of all, for it indicated both the pleasure and the embarrassment she had felt. She revised her original second sentence to mark the contrast:

> Since I was the youngest person and only available female there, I was an easy target for some of the "confirmed bachelors." Everyone paid a lot of attention to me. I was bombarded with questions, and offers to get me another drink or a piece of cake. Not all the attention was exactly welcome, though. My uncle had to rescue me from being taken out "dancing" at 2 a.m.

As you try to strengthen the continuity of a paragraph, you'll find it useful not just to look *at* sentences but to look *for* functional units. Just as a long essay like "Barbed Wire" (pp. 150–53) is divided into parts or paragraph sequences, so most paragraphs have their parts. The group of related sentences that make up a part is a functional unit. The paragraph that follows is made up of just two units—a generalization that's a topic sentence (the first) and particulars that illustrate it (the other five):

> If an American city is named after a foreign city, chances are it is pronounced differently. In Minnesota, Montevideo is "Montevi-DEE-oh," not "Montevi-DAY-oh." In Idaho, it's "Moscoh," never "Mos-cow." Sample the Wienerbrot in "VY-enna," not Vienna, Ga., and try the pasta in "MY-lan," which is the way they pronounce Milan in Ahia [Ohio]. In South America, Lima, Peru, may be "Lee-ma, Per-OO," but in Ohio, it's "LY-ma," and in Indiana, it's "PEE-ru." Similarly, say "CAY-ro," not Cairo, Ill.; "New BURR-lin," not New Berlin, Pa., and "Del-high," N.Y., not "Del-hee," as in India's New Delhi.—William Safire, *New York Times Magazine*

The format is open-ended, in the sense that illustrations could be put in or pulled out and the paragraph shortened or lengthened without changing the basic structure.

When you write such a paragraph, ask yourself questions like these: Do the examples really bear on the opening statement? Is each one interesting in its own right? Are there enough examples? Too many? Are they of roughly the same significance, so that the order doesn't matter much, or is one of them so much more convincing than the others that it should be placed first or last? Should I leave the paragraph open-ended, or should I close it out with an example so strong or so dramatic that it clinches the generalization?

The paragraph that follows also has a two-part structure. The "roles" of the first sentence are elaborated on in the next three. But because the sentences lengthen and the details become increasingly specific, this paragraph has a more climactic effect than Safire's:

> [1] In the media, women appear primarily in supportive roles as housewives, secretaries and girl friends. [2] They usually are incapable of initiating actions of their own: they get into difficulties from which they must be extricated by their men. [3] When not treated as weak and scatter-brained, women are likely to be portrayed as devious, dehumanized sex objects, the ornaments of male egoism. [4] In media advertisements women seem exclusively concerned with getting a fluffy glow shampooed into their hair, waxing "their" floors, making yummy coffee for hubby, getting Johnny's clothes snowy white, and in other ways serving as mindless, cheery household drones.—Michael Parenti, *Democracy for the Few*

The simple two-part structure of topic + illustration or topic + development can be extended by adding functional units. In a paragraph of three units—topic + restriction (or development) + illustration—the middle stage modifies or restricts the topic idea, narrows and limits it, defines it, or extends it. The following paragraph has three related units—topic (sentence

1), specification or development (sentences 2 and 3), illustration (sentences 4–6):

> [1] Once in a great while, a man all of a sudden finds himself completely happy and content. [2] His stomach feels good; he's breathing fine and easy; there's nothing whatever bothering him in his mind; the sun is shining, perhaps, but it doesn't have to be; a breeze is blowing gently, perhaps, but it doesn't need to be; and nearby there is something or somebody he has a deep fondness for. [3] What he's fond of can be a boat, or a woman, or a horse—anything at all. [4] About eleven o'clock in the morning on Tuesday, April 14th, I was silently grateful to find myself in that pleasant fix. [5] At that hour, I was sitting alone in a warm and comfortable room no more than thirty yards away from the stall in which stood the race horse Native Dancer. [6] I have a deep fondness for Native Dancer.—John McNulty, *New Yorker*

The General Plan

The three paragraphs quoted in the preceding section (from Safire, Parenti, and McNulty) are all built on the *support* plan. This is the favorite plan in exposition and argument because it offers the easiest way of keeping the reader informed about what's coming next. Probably most of the expository paragraphs you write will follow this order. The opening sentence more or less establishes the dimensions of the discussion by telling either what the subject is or how the paragraph will develop. Then come statements that illustrate, interpret, extend, explain, qualify, or refute. (Sentences that "support" an opening generalization don't necessarily back it up or prove it. They may even contradict it. The point is that in one way or another they're all related to it.) The supporting statements may be roughly equivalent to each other, as in Safire, or they may be built one upon another to reflect a train of reasoning or to move to a particular situation, as in McNulty.

In writing a paragraph on the support plan, you can leave it open-ended or move clearly to a "therefore" conclusion or end with a statement that's in tune with the opening one but adds more information or emphasis. The following paragraph opens by telling what Los Angeles in the twenties was not and closes by telling what it was:

> Nor did Los Angeles in the late twenties resemble in any way the city we know now. It was before the Age of Air Conditioning. The houses of the rich were built with thick walls and small windows, as the Spanish had done for centuries, to keep the heat and sunshine out. When the dry Santa Ana wind began to blow, igniting brush fires in the hills and sending the local suicide rate soaring, half the city retired to nurse a migraine, while the rest huddled in bars seeking relief in heavy drinking and the occasional murder. Before the widespread adoption of air conditioning, the whole sweep of the Southwest, from Palm Springs through Las Vegas and on to the Rockies—now covered with

homes, swimming pools, motels, casinos and shopping centers—remained the preserve of a few scattered Indian tribes and the occasional crazed dirt-rancher, a searing, hot wasteland which served to reinforce the feeling of isolation. Los Angeles was a series of loosely connected, sleepy and sometimes bizarre townships, clustered around a center so shabby and rundown that it seemed to decay as it was built.—Michael Korda, *Charmed Lives*

In some rhetorical situations the *discovery* structure—the paragraph that leads the reader through a series of particulars to a generalization—has distinct advantages. You may want to withhold the main idea until the end of the paragraph to make readers feel they're sharing in the process of discovery, to make it easier for them to understand a complicated or difficult generalization, to break down their hostility to what you're going to propose, or to achieve dramatic impact. In any case, when the movement is *toward* a generalization, it's especially important that the particulars lead logically into one another and so into the generalization. The readers won't know just where the discussion is heading, but they should have a sense that every detail is moving it toward a destination.

The following passage shows the discovery pattern in one of its typical forms. The bulk of the paragraph consists of details that, taken together, justify the writer in presenting a "new view" of the tiger, a view that's summarized in the second and third sentences of the following paragraph:

For centuries man has viewed the tiger with fear, as the "embodiment of devilish cruelty, of hate and savagery incarnate," as one author put it. I had come to Kanha to remove some of the mystery that surrounds the habits of this nocturnal and solitary wanderer. Days sometimes passed without my meeting one of the elusive cats, but over the months I encountered the same individuals again and again, recognizing them by the distinctive stripe patterns on their faces, until slowly they revealed some of the secrets of their society. For instance, one day I found a tigress with four small cubs. She had killed a bull gaur, a remarkable feat considering she weighed about three hundred pounds and he two thousand. Five days the family camped in a ravine by the kill. During mornings the cub sometimes played, stalking each other and wrestling and chasing, but during the heat of the day all rested, the tigress often cooling herself by reclining with her hindquarters submerged in a pool. As the forest grew dark, the family resumed its meal, and I watched them from the branches of a nearby tree, fleeting shadows under a crescent moon. Early one morning, at 4:30, the tigress roared twice, and an answer came from far away. Since this tigress shared her range with three other residents, two tigresses and a male, and transients also wandered through the area, I wondered who the caller was. At 8:00 a.m. the male tiger suddenly appeared, a massive fellow with a short ruff of hair on his neck. From many previous encounters I knew that he claimed the whole center of the park as his own, although he shared it with several tigresses. Now he was visiting one of them, amicably checking on her and her cubs before resuming his solitary rounds. One night, at another kill, the same tigress and cubs, the male, and a second tigress, a total of seven, ate together, but by morning the group had split again. Similarly, two tigresses, each with cubs, fed together on a large kill several times.

From these and other observations, a new view of the tiger emerged. Far from being asocial, irascibly avoiding contact, tigers may meet, sometimes casually on a trail, at other times to share a kill. Solitary but not asocial, the tigers are part of a small community in which all resident members know each other and retain contact by roaring and leaving their scent on bushes and tree trunks.— George B. Schaller, *Stones of Silence*

The *pro-and-con* movement has a more complex structure than those illustrated so far. After opening with a generalization, which is given support, the paragraph takes a turn in another (but related) direction, signaled by *but*, *still*, *however*, or some similar contrast. This two-stage movement is well suited to balancing a positive against a negative—advantages against disadvantages, say—and it's a natural choice for a paragraph in which you set out to challenge a widespread notion.

Here a student adapts the pro-and-con technique by opening with a series of challenging questions, making a turn with her "If you do . . . " sentence, and then going on to assert the real situation as opposed to the ideal one the questions implied:

How do you decide who you're going to vote for? Do you pore over the records of the candidate's previous work? Do you determine his position on a variety of issues? Do you compare levels of experience? Do you look for consistency? For managerial competence? Do you spend a tenth of the time checking the qualifications of the person you're about to elect president that you would checking the qualifications of someone you were going to hire as an administrative assistant? If you do, you're probably one of those diligent souls who spend New Year's Day preparing their tax returns. Most of us make our decisions based on impressions, not primary source material. We don't actually read those speeches the newspapers thoughtfully reprint in their entirety. We watch television reports that have already been edited by someone, the very process of which means that a point of view has been imposed on the material. (By choosing which thirty seconds of a four-hour debate is going to make it onto the evening news, the editor decides whether the candidate is going to look serious or foolish.) We buy the impressions we're given and make our decisions based on this tainted, fragmented, second-hand information. Anything else would require work on our part, and we don't have time for that.

Handled well, a paragraph organized on the pro-and-con pattern suggests that you've explored the subject thoroughly. Handled badly, it can give the impression that you're sitting on the fence, evading the responsibility of making clear what your own ideas on the subject are. Usually a pro-and-con paragraph needs to end with a forceful, positive statement that leaves the reader in no doubt as to where you stand.

Not every content paragraph you write will follow one of the patterns we've illustrated, but every paragraph you write should have some discernible pattern. Each should be built in such a way that your readers will be able to follow your thought and end up with a feeling of comprehension and satisfaction. In all but the shortest papers you'll naturally vary the structure of your paragraphs to accommodate your material.

For Discussion and Writing

1. Describe and evaluate the structure of each of the passages below. Consider these questions: (a) What are the main functional units in the paragraph? (b) Is the paragraph tightly unified, in the sense that all the sentences in it bear directly on the core of meaning? Or do some of the sentences relate to the core only loosely? (c) Is the paragraph tightly structured, in the sense that the order of sentences couldn't be altered without damaging the continuity of the paragraph, or could some of the sentences be interchanged? (d) If you find that one paragraph is less unified than the others or looser in structure, can you justify the difference in terms of the subject and general style? Rewrite the paragraph you judge to be weakest to improve the structure.

a. A great swindle of our time is the assumption that science has made religion obsolete. All science has damaged is the story of Adam and Eve and the story of Jonah and the Whale. Everything else holds up pretty well, particularly the lessons about fairness and gentleness. People who find those lessons irrelevant in the twentieth century are simply using science as an excuse for greed and harshness.—Kurt Vonnegut, Jr., *Wampeters, Foma & Granfalloons*

b. For a chicken that grows up to have such exceptional good looks, the peacock starts life with an inauspicious appearance. The peabiddy is about the color of those large objectionable moths that flutter about light bulbs on summer nights. Its only distinguishing features are its eyes, a luminous gray, and a brown crest that begins to sprout from the back of its head when it is ten days old. This looks at first like a bug's antennae and later like the head feathers of an Indian. In six weeks green flecks appear in its neck, and in a few more weeks a cock can be distinguished from a hen by the speckles on his back. The hen's back gradually fades to an even gray and her appearance shortly becomes what it will always be. I have never thought the peahen unattractive, even though she lacks a long tail and any significant decoration. I have even once or twice thought her more attractive than the cock, more subtle and refined; but those moments of boldness pass.—Flannery O'Connor, *Mystery and Manners*

c. One of the biggest reasons there are so many hunters is because it is a great sport. It is a real challenge to get a deer nearly on its own terms. Every year approximately one out of every eleven hunters succeeds in getting a deer. To do this, the only legal advantage the hunter has is the weapon. The main advantage the deer has is that the deer knows every inch of the woods. It also has a keen sense of smell, sight, and hearing. Also, a hunter can't use dogs, any kind of trap, bait, a flashlight, a silencer, a semi-automatic or automatic gun, or a vehicle to hunt from, and he can't shoot a deer that has taken refuge in the water. The hunters that don't get a deer at least succeed in having fun while hunting and on the way to and from the hunting grounds. Some of the best times of my life have been spent in a car joking with fellow hunters and telling of the deer that got away. Some "hunters" who go to their camps in the mountains supposedly to hunt don't even make it out of their cabins but instead relax, play cards, joke and drink their troubles away.

d. An opinion often expressed these days is that today's young generation is becoming functionally illiterate. Many blame overworked teachers, unsatisfactory high school English courses, and, of course, television for the decline in the quality of high school students' ability. Although it is true that some students may be adversely affected by these conditions, it is not fair to generalize and condemn all high school graduates for their poor backgrounds in English. It has been found that in watching television, the eyes remain fixed, while in reading, the eyes are constantly flickering back and forth across the page. Thus the child who grows up watching TV for many hours every day simply does not have the same physical training as the child who grows up reading books. The TV watcher has to learn a new skill—eye movement—when reading is taught in school, and he must keep practicing this skill if he is going to be a good reader.

e. Americans are opposed to illegal aliens for a variety of reasons. The fact that Mexicans are entering illegally is reason enough for many. Others see them as depriving deserving Americans out of jobs, latching on to free welfare and education, perpetrating crime, and upping the population of an already overcrowded country. Americans should take a look at their own roots. America was founded by immigrants. Immigrants built the railroads, tilled the land, mined the coal, populated the cities, and conquered the west. Every family in America immigrated from somewhere. The only differential is time. Some arrived before others. Throughout our history the earlier arrivals have hated and feared the later. Today, they are called wetbacks. Yesterday, they were micks, wops, guineas, kikes, polacks, etc. Supposedly, the Statue of Liberty is a symbol of our ideals. We should live by what it says: "Give me your tired, your poor, your huddled masses yearning to breathe free, the wretched refuse of your teeming shores." Today's immigrants, legal or not, perform a valuable service for our country. Namely, they come to work. They do the dirty work that Americans refuse. They follow the crops, wash the dishes, sweep the floors, empty the bed pans, and fill the factories. For the illegal immigrant a job in itself is a privilege.

2.   Comparing a paragraph requires you to, among other things, find the structure that best suits what you want to say to your readers. Now and then it's good practice to find material that fits into a structure worked out by another writer. Drawing on a subject of your own choosing, write a paragraph that follows closely the *structure* of one of the following paragraphs, all quoted in this chapter:

> Safire, p. 183
> McNulty, p. 184
> O'Connor, p. 187
> Schaller, pp. 185–86
> Student paragraph, p. 186

3.   Compose a paragraph that sets forth both the advantages and the disadvantages of a proposed course of action. Make sure that by the end of the paragraph the reader will know whether you do or do not support the proposal.

Paragraph Coherence

A paragraph is coherent if it hangs together as a whole (if it has unity) and if the thought flows smoothly and consecutively from sentence to sentence (if it has continuity). To give your writing coherence, you can use a variety of techniques—repeating, partially repeating, or echoing key words and ideas; repeating grammatical patterns; introducing transitional words like *but* and *therefore*; and, on occasion, announcing what the preceding paragraph (or sequence of paragraphs) has done and what the next one will do. But to use these various ways of linking sentences and paragraphs so that they convey the relationship among your ideas, you must first find what those relationships are. You must know what it is you want to say.

If you don't think through what you want to say, you're likely to produce paragraphs like this one:

> Many good citizens find it hard to convince themselves that their vote will make any difference. Men of good will have been voting for generations with little effect. The same hacks and manipulators seem to get into office every time, and the same corrupt Establishment runs the show. When a young person becomes eligible to vote in a national election, he should either acquaint himself with the issues and the policies of the candidates or use the day to catch up on lost sleep. Voting Republican or Democratic because that's how your parents vote is irresponsible if not stupid. A thoughtless vote can cancel an intelligent one, and this country has no intelligent votes to spare.

Three sentences on one topic, three on another—the structural gap suggests that the writer made two different stabs at his subject. That might have turned out all right if he had thrown one away, settled down to work on the other, and developed it adequately, but instead he simply jammed the two together. The result: an incoherent paragraph. And tinkering with it won't help. Merely inserting transitional words, for instance, would be useless. Before he can revise it sensibly, the writer must decide what he wants to talk about and what he wants to say. Coherent writing requires logical thinking.

Unified content and orderly movement are necessary for coherence, but they don't guarantee it. Even if every sentence in a paragraph has a bearing on the central point, and even if the order of the sentences is sensible, the paragraph may fail to give readers an understanding of how one thought relates to another. The following paragraph is hard to read because the sentences seem to be sealed off from one another; the reader gets no help at all in trying to move from one statement to the next.

> [1] Parson Weems' story about George Washington and the cherry tree is really about the little boy's willingness to accept responsibility. [2] The ability to say, "Yes, that was my fault" is a sign of true maturity. [3] Not many people are mature. [4] We try to avoid taking the blame for the things we do. [5] People don't even like to share blame. [6] We are partly responsible if the side we vote for in an election wins and then makes a mess of things. [7] Not voting is safer. [8] People are often dishonest with themselves. [9] Someone else is always to blame for what they did. [10] If we admitted the truth, we would hurt our self-image.

Here is the paragraph rewritten to improve coherence:

> [1] The moral of Parson Weems' fable about George Washington and the cherry tree is not just that the little boy is unable to tell a lie but that he is willing to accept responsibility. [2] Such willingness—the ability to say, "Yes, that was my fault"—is the sign of a maturity that too many of us lack. [3] At every age, we try to find ways to avoid taking the blame for our foolish or cowardly or selfish action. [4] In fact, we duck even a share of blame, if we possibly can. [5] For example, we know that if the side we support wins an election and then makes a mess of things, we are partly responsible for the mess; so some of us don't vote at all. [6] Fear of accepting responsibility may reflect our concern about what others think of us, but it also reflects our reluctance to face up to our own faults. [7] We convince ourselves that we weren't "really" to blame, that somehow or other someone or something else—our roommate, our parents, the person we hurt, our alarm clock, luck—was "really" responsible. [8] Accepting responsibility means having the guts to be honest, even when honesty damages our self-image.

"Such willingness" in sentence 2 of the rewrite echoes "willing" in sentence 1. In sentence 4 "a share of blame" picks up "the blame" in sentence 3, and in sentence 7 we find the verb "to blame." "Fear of accepting responsibility" in sentence 6, "responsible" in 7, and "accepting responsibility" in 8 all look back to "willing to accept responsibility" in the opening sentence.

In addition to repeating or echoing key words, the rewrite uses transitional phrases to join sentences, most noticeably at the beginning of sentences 4 and 5. All these are lexical means of making the paragraph coherent. The writer also relies on grammatical means: notice that *we* is the subject of four sentences. Continuing the same subject through several sentences contributes to coherence by keeping the focus of the paragraph sharp. Contrast the consistency of the subject in the revised paragraph with the frequent shifts of subject in the original.

Repetition and Parallelism

As the preceding example shows, one of the ways you can make your paragraphs coherent is by repeating key words and grammatical patterns. Repetition of both kinds is marked in the paragraph that follows. Note the number of times "rhythm," "rhythms," and "rhythmic" occur; the similarity of pattern in sentences 3–6 and again in 8–9; the long series that opens sentence 2 and the shorter one ("the next step," "the next beat") in the final sentence:

> [1] Our lives are completely dominated by the fundamental rhythms. [2] My breathing, my pulse, my unconscious processes of digestion, my hearing, my eyesight, my sense of touch, my speech, my thought—all are matters of rhythm. [3] Life is governed by the rhythms. [4] The female animal has rhythmic periods of fertility. [5] The sex act of fertilization is rhythmic. [6] Birth is accomplished in rhythmic labor. [7] And all the rhythmic processes in us, pulse to speech, are a part of growth, maturity, life's continuation. [8] When they cease, a unit of life has come to its physical end. [9] When my pulse stops, I die. [10] But my progeny, in whom the rhythm continues, live on, the next step, the next beat, in the rhythm of life.—Hal Borland in *What We Save Now*

In college papers you won't often write on subjects that lend themselves so well to repetition as Borland's does, but if you're like most writers, you can strengthen the coherence of your prose, whatever your subject, by repeating key words and their synonyms and by putting into parallel grammatical structures ideas or details that are logically coordinate. (Parallelism is discussed in detail on pp. 226–33). In revising your first drafts, introduce whatever grammatical and lexical repetitions will help make clear the focus you intend and guide readers through the sequence of ideas you're presenting. Meanwhile, look out for—and get rid of—unintentional repetitions that make your prose boring to read and may suggest connections in meaning where none exist.

The combination of a key word and its related pronouns and synonyms—all the words and phrases that in the context have roughly the same meaning or that refer to the same thing—creates an *equivalence chain*. In this example the words in italics show how a dominant equivalence chain can link all the sentences of a paragraph:

No other living writer has yielded himself so completely and recklessly as has *Isaac Bashevis Singer* to the claims of the human imagination. *Singer* writes in Yiddish, a language that no amount of energy and affection seems likely to save from extinction. *He* writes about a world that is gone, destroyed with a brutality beyond historical comparison. *He* writes within a culture, the remnant of Yiddish in the Western world, that is more than a little dubious about *his* purpose and stress. *He* seems to take entirely for granted *his role* as a traditional *storyteller* speaking to an audience attuned to *his* every hint and nuance, an audience that values *storytelling* both in *its* own right and as a binding communal action—but also, as it happens, an audience that keeps fading week by week, shrinking day by day. And *he* does *all this* without a sigh or an apology, without so much as a Jewish groan. It strikes one as a kind of inspired madness: here is a *man* living in New York City, a sophisticated and clever *writer*, who *composes stories* about Frampol, Bilgoray, Kreshev AS IF THEY WERE STILL THERE. *His work* is shot through with the bravado of a *performer* who enjoys making *his* listeners gasp, weep, laugh, and yearn for more. Above and beyond everything else *he* is a great *performer*, in ways that remind one of Twain, Dickens, Sholom Aleichem.—Irving Howe, Introduction to *Selected Short Stories of Isaac Bashevis Singer*

In the fifth sentence, "his role," one item in the dominant chain, initiates the sequence "storyteller," "his," "storytelling, "its," "all this," "composes stories." In the same way, "his work" introduces "performer." These words and phrases, all stemming from the key word "Singer," make a network of relationships linking the ideas. The paragraph contains another chain initiated by "audience" and continued in its equivalent, "listeners." Parallelism of verbs strengthens continuity not only by the repetition of "writes" in three successive sentences but also by the consistent use of the present tense: "seems," "does," and so on. And parallelism of other words and phrases plays a role in keeping the emphasis where the author wants it. But by far the strongest cohesive force in the paragraph is the recurrence of the same grammatical subject, or its equivalent, from sentence to sentence. A new subject is introduced only when it's needed to mark a shift in the point of view ("It strikes one" in the third-to-last sentence).

In your own writing, work to avoid shifts in point of view that are unnecessary and illogical—the changes in person, voice, tense, and structural pattern classed as shifted constructions. Consistency in these matters contributes to the grammatical cohesion of a paragraph; lack of consistency detracts from it and gives even a well-unified paragraph a general air of incoherence.

Though using similar grammatical subjects is a dependable means of maintaining continuity, it's not always feasible. The process of reasoning from premises to conclusion or of relating causes to effects calls for a different procedure. Instead of invariably returning to the one subject (or a related subject), a writer may knit sentences together by having the subject of one sentence grow out of the predicate of the preceding sentence. In the following paragraph the strongest links occur not between grammatical subject and grammatical subject but between the end of one sentence and the beginning of the next.

> The evidence is clear that we should rely, for the immediate future, on ethanol as the only sensible, quick alternative to fossil fuels. It is the route that Brazil took five years ago. This year, some 250,000 Brazilian cars will be built to run on pure ethanol, and an additional 70,000 existing cars will be converted to run on unblended alcohol. Why hasn't the United States, with all its vaunted technology, adopted a similar program?—Fred J. Cook, *Nation*

For Discussion and Writing

1. What methods does Perrin use to achieve coherence in the passage on page 144?

2. Rewrite the following paragraphs to make them more coherent. Pay special attention to improving the continuity and getting rid of unnecessary shifts in grammatical structure and in point of view.

a. I was just about to enter junior high when my parents were divorced, and it surprised me to see that my school work and grades were not affected at all. Maybe it was because I worked harder at school to forget my family problems. In the days that followed, there was a strange sensation in my stomach that was probably due to nerves. I was really in a sensitive state, and whenever I thought about it, an uncontrollable urge to cry resulted (which was embarrassing if someone found me). This situation touched on my nerves so much that whenever I expressed my feelings about an emotional subject, it would take only seconds for tears to form. This was the most upsetting time that my young mind and body had ever lived through, and I was afraid that I wouldn't be able to handle it without some special counselling. My friends knew nothing about how I felt at home because in school I was a different person. My feelings continued to build up until they reached a point where I had to talk to someone. I had a long discussion with my father, and he finally convinced me that there was no hope of us ever becoming a whole family again.

b. At the opening whistle the two sides burst into action. They had been preparing themselves for this for weeks. Many long hours of tiring practice were behind us, and now was the time to prove just how much endurance we had built up. Sweat began flowing in streams and breath came in gasps. The first time the ball sailed through the air, the clean swish of the net was met with deafening applause. Every bounce, twist, and turn of the orange sphere was alertly followed by all eyes. The players felt the pressure more and more as the game progressed and the figures on the scoreboard remained ever so close. "Push yourself harder, harder!" I kept repeating to myself as my limbs began to ache with tiredness.

Transitions

In Chapter Five, pages 155–56, we saw how transitional paragraphs help readers move from part to part in a paper and how transitional sentences help them move from paragraph to paragraph. Within paragraphs, as between them, connecting words, phrases, and clauses spell out relationships and establish connections. In so doing, they help make the paragraphs coherent and they help readers follow the line of thought. Most common of these signals are the coordinating conjunctions (*and, but, or, nor, for, so, yet*), the conjunctive adverbs (*however, indeed, moreover*, and so on), the phrases like *of course, for example, in the first place.* Subordinating conjunctions (*because, since*) and simple adverbs (*then, here*) may also mark transitions.

Transitional words, phrases, and clauses all share the function of calling the reader's attention to the role played by what follows. In this way they bind ideas together and bring out connections in the material. In the following paragraph of tightly knit prose, transitional words and phrases are italicized. Note that the favorite position for transitional markers is at the beginning of sentences or clauses. Note, too, that colons can do the work of transition, as in the third sentence.

> The intensified use of capital equipment, and of the energy needed to run it, typically results in an increased output of goods. *However*, the increased output is not necessarily proportional to the increased inputs of capital and energy. *Indeed*, the added costs for capital and energy may well yield a proportionally smaller increase in output, *and* this is particularly true in respect to the development of modern technology: capital productivity and energy productivity decrease. *Obviously*, if nothing else changed, it would make less and less economic sense to introduce more costly, more energy-intensive capital equipment. *But* something else does change: the productivity of labor, which, in contrast to the productivity of capital and energy, typically increases as new technology is introduced. *Indeed*, the expectation of increased labor productivity is normally the chief motivation for introducing new technology into a production enterprise.—Barry Commoner, *New Yorker*

Simple as transitional markers are, using them well calls for care and discrimination. An *and* shouldn't suggest a logical connection when there isn't any. A *therefore* shouldn't indicate that an argument has been settled when nothing relevant has been proved. If you use too few markers, your sentences may seem unrelated to one another, as in the example on page 190, and the train of thought will be hard to follow. If you use too many, your style will be heavy-handed. *For example* is the typical marker to indicate that what follows illustrates what has come before or particularizes it in some way; but if you use *for example* to signal every such instance, readers will feel you're lecturing them. You can often expect readers to make the connections you might signal by *that is, likewise, as well as, for example*. By contrast, you normally have to guide readers through the relationships expressed by such words and phrases as *but* (and *however, yet, nevertheless*), *instead, on the other hand*.

The need for explicit signals of transition also depends on your subject and your purpose. When the thought drives straight ahead—when one idea clearly builds on another—explicit transitions are unnecessary. When the thought is complex, it's your responsibility to mark the path. You'll probably use more explicit transitions when your purpose is to inform or instruct than when your aim is simply to suggest a possibility or to make a tentative proposal.

In a paragraph that has consistent focus and well-made equivalence chains, logical relationships may not have to be indicated by connectors. When readers get their clues from the language of the discussion itself, they'll prefer not to be elbowed from one sentence to another by a *therefore* or an *as a result*. And some clues are wordless: as in this sentence, a colon can do the work of *for example*. Just placing one sentence immediately after another can signal a relation of addition or, in other contexts, of contrast or cause-effect. Transitions can be implied.

The following paragraph needs no explicit signals of transition to show the relationship of one idea to the next:

> The influence of the modern medical school on liberal-arts education in this country over the last decade has been baleful and malign, nothing less. The admission policies of the medical schools are at the root of the trouble. If something is not done quickly to change these, all the joys of going to college will have been destroyed, not just for that growing majority of undergraduate students who draw breath only to become doctors, but to everyone else, all the students, and all the faculty as well.—Lewis Thomas, *The Medusa and the Snail*

In selecting a transitional marker, be sure first of all that you need one. If you're convinced you do, then be sure the one you choose expresses the logical relationship you intend.

For Discussion and Writing

Identify and explain the function of the transitional words and phrases in the passage by Mitchell Wilson on pages 180–81. For each of the paragraphs after the first, propose a different way of moving in from the preceding paragraph. Explain why your method would or wouldn't be an improvement.

Development and Coherence in Paragraph Sequences

As we've seen, there are many techniques for developing paragraphs and for binding ideas together, in paragraphs, in paragraph sequences, in whole papers. Which ones you should choose will depend chiefly on the complexity of your subject and on your purpose in dealing with it.

The complete article reprinted below is a good example of the way a professional writer handles a very large subject for a general audience of readers who are interested in keeping up with what's going on and who are therefore presumably familiar with the major events of the recent past. (Allusions to "Potomac fever" and the Gulag Archipelago are probably safe. Reference to Kossuth is more of a gamble.) Though the article is short, it has a distinct movement. The author's ideas progress through stages—represented by parts, or paragraph sequences—and the means of achieving coherence are adjusted to the methods used to develop and organize the discussion. In the commentary S stands for "sentence," Ss for "sentences."

¶1 [1] The United States is a nation consciously conceived, not one that evolved slowly out of an ancient past. [2] It was a planned idea of democracy, of liberty of conscience and pursuit of happiness. [3] It was the promise of equality of opportunity and individual freedom within a just social order, as opposed to the restrictions and repressions of the Old World. [4] In contrast to the militarism of Europe, it would renounce standing armies and "sheathe the desolating sword of war." [5] It was an experiment in Utopia to test the thesis that given freedom, independence and local self-government, people, in Kossuth's words, "will in due time ripen into all the excellence and all the dignity of humanity." [6] It was a new life for the oppressed, it was enlightenment, it was optimism.

¶2 [1] Regardless of hypocrisy and corruption, of greed, chicanery, brutality and all the other bad habits man carries with him whether in the New World or Old, the founding idea of the United States remained, on the whole, dominant through the first 100 years. [2] With reservations it was believed in by Americans, by visitors who came to aid our Revolution or later to observe our progress, by immigrants who came by the hundreds of thousands to escape an intolerable situation in their native lands.

¶s 1–2 form the first part, or paragraph sequence. ¶1 defines the United States as an idea. The definition is built by contrast (Ss 1, 3, 4) and, more important, by division. The "idea" is partitioned into its elements, and beginning with S2, coherence is achieved through the use of "it" as subject of every sentence. Ss 2, 3, 5, and 6 are all on the same level of generalization. S4 particularizes S3. Parallelism, used throughout the article, is especially noticeable in the three clauses that end ¶1.

¶2 uses the same devices as ¶1: "it," the subject of S2, makes "idea," the subject of S1, the center of the paragraph. The simple series of nouns in S1 and the more elaborate parallelism of S2 provide the writer with very economical ways of qualifying and particularizing in S2 the assertion that "the idea" remained dominant for "the first 100 years."

¶3 [1] The idea shaped our politics, our institutions and to some extent our national character, but it was never the only influence at work. [2] Material circumstances exerted an opposing force. [3] The open frontier, the hardships of homesteading from scratch, the wealth of natural resources, the whole vast challenge of a continent waiting to be exploited, combined to produce a prevailing materialism and an American drive bent as much, if not more, on money, property, and power than was true of the Old World from which we had fled. [4] The human resources we drew upon were significant: every wave of immigration brought here those people who had the extra energy, gumption or restlessness to uproot themselves and cross an unknown ocean to seek a better life. [5] Two other factors entered the shaping process—the shadow of slavery and the destruction of the native Indian.

¶4 [1] At its Centennial, the United States was a material success. [2] Through its second century, the idea and the success have struggled in continuing conflict. [3] The Statue of Liberty, erected in 1886, still symbolized the promise to those "yearning to breathe free." [4] Hope, to them, as seen by a foreign visitor, was "domiciled in America as the Pope is in Rome." [5] But slowly in the struggle the idea lost ground, and at a turning point around 1900, with American acceptance of a rather half-hearted imperialism, it lost dominance. [6] Increasingly invaded since then by self-doubt and disillusion, it survives in the disenchantment of today, battered and crippled but not vanquished.

¶5 [1] What has happened to the United States in the twentieth century is not a peculiarly American phenomenon but a part of the experience of the West. [2] In the Middle Ages, plague, wars and social violence were seen as God's punishment upon man for his sins. [3] If the concept of God can be taken as man's conscience, the same explanation may be applicable today. [4] Our sins in the twentieth century—greed, violence, inhumanity—have been profound, with the result that the pride and self-confidence of the nineteenth century have turned to dismay and self-disgust.

¶6 [1] In the United States we have a society pervaded from top to bottom by contempt for the law. [2] Government—including the agencies of law enforcement—business, labor, students, the military, the poor no less than the rich, outdo each other in breaking the rules and violating the ethics that society has established for its protection. [3] The average citizen, trying to hold a footing in standards of morality and conduct he once believed in, is daily knocked over by incoming waves of venal-

¶s 3–4 form a second paragraph sequence. ¶3 opens with a transitional sentence, with "idea" pointing back to ¶s 1–2 and the second clause ("it was never . . .") introducing the notion of opposing forces. These are dealt with throughout ¶3. S2 and S3 are closely linked, S3 particularizing S2 and establishing a causal relation. S4 and S5 are on the same level of generalization as S2. Mainly because S1 promises an enumeration, sentence-to-sentence connectives are unnecessary in this paragraph. S5, however, does have two devices for maintaining coherence: "other" (in "other factors") and "the shaping processs," which repeats in another way the verb "shaped" in S1.

¶4 takes up the "opposing force" introduced in ¶3. S2 sets up the conflict between the "idea" and "material success." A chronological thread makes time indicators of first importance: "through its second century," "in 1886," and so on. In S5 "but" provides transition to the decline of the "idea." Second in importance in maintaining coherence is an equivalence chain ("idea," Ss 4–5; "it," Ss 5–6), like the one in ¶s 1–2.

¶s 5–6 form a third paragraph sequence. ¶5 consists of an explanation or causal analysis of the onset of "self-doubt and disillusion" (¶4, S6). Related terms, "dismay and self-disgust," occur in the last sentence of ¶5. While ¶1 stressed the uniqueness of the new nation, ¶5 uses comparison to show it is no more immune from the consequences of its acts than were Old World countries.

¶6 extends and particularizes the sins of greed, violence, inhumanity (¶5, S1). S2 particularizes S1. (The "average citizen" of S3 prepares us for ¶7 by indicating that while lawlessness pervades our society, most of us struggle against the breakdown in ethical behavior.) Ss 4–6 make an attack on the government,

ity, vulgarity, irresponsibility, ignorance, ugliness, and trash in all senses of the word. [4] Our government collaborates abroad with the worst enemies of humanity and liberty. [5] It wastes our substance on useless proliferation of military hardware that can never buy security no matter how high the pile. [6] It learns no lessons, employs no wisdom and corrupts all who succumb to Potomac fever.

¶7 [1] Yet the idea does not die. [2] Americans are not passive under their faults. [3] We expose them and combat them. [4] Somewhere every day some group is fighting a public abuse—openly and, on the whole, notwithstanding the FBI, with confidence in the First Amendment. [5] The U.S. has slid a long way from the original idea. [6] Nevertheless, somewhere between Gulag Archipelago and the featherbed of cradle-to-the-grave welfare, it still offers a greater opportunity for social happiness, that is to say, for well-being combined with individual freedom and initiative, than is likely elsewhere. [7] The ideal society for which mankind had been striving through the ages will remain forever beyond our grasp. [8] But if the great question, whether it is still possible to reconcile democracy with social order and individual liberty, is to find a positive answer, it will be here.—Barbara Tuchman, *Newsweek*

with "government" and "it" creating a minor equivalence chain.

¶7, the last part of this four-part article, opens with the conjunction "yet," marking a contrast with what precedes. S1 takes us back to the end of ¶4, where "the idea" was last mentioned. Ss 2–4 support S1 with increasing specificity ("Americans" in S2, "we" in S2, "some group" in S3). S5 repeats in a new way the case against America that has been made in ¶6. Again, the assertion is followed by a transitional conjunction marking a contrast ("nevertheless") and introducing a comparative statement. S7 makes a generalization. S8 restates the point made in S5 and ends appropriately with the word "here"—taking us back to the opening words of the article and the references to the United States in ¶s 2, 4, 5, 6, 7. This last paragraph has a pro-and-con structure that achieves coherence chiefly through conjunctions that contrast or qualify.

For Discussion and Writing

1. When a paragraph is unsatisfactory, the trouble may be caused by (1) lack of development—not enough details; (2) lack of unity—no controlling idea; (3) lack of continuity—insufficient indication of the relationship between statements; (4) lack of consistency in point of view or tone or style. Using this checklist as a guide, identify the weaknesses in each of the following, and rewrite to improve the paragraphs. In rewriting you may find it necessary to choose just one of the points made and develop that.

a. Have you ever thought of traveling abroad but, being a student, felt you did not have the time or money? Through the many programs offered in studying abroad, a college student can now afford to travel while earning a degree. Those students enrolled in Liberal Arts and Business at my university are offered a wide variety of International Student Exchange Programs—in Europe, Asia, and South America. These programs are no longer limited to members of the elite social class who once considered studying abroad to be a sign of wealth, intelligence, and social status. Today, any student who can meet the academic and financial requirements can apply for a position in an International Exchange Program. Although studying abroad can provide many benefits, some facets of the program can be disadvantageous.

b. Football is a money game, even when it comes down to covering a game on television. Try to imagine how much money changes hands in the process of putting on a game. You know the fancy commercials we see between replays, like the ones for Exxon and Gulf Oil, the ones with that extra kick per tankful. They pay the television networks about $100,000 for sixty seconds of prime-time viewing during the Christmas holidays. We see a forest scene with deer and raccoons nibbling on bushes while they tell us how they are protecting our environment and speeding up sapling growth rates. At the same time they are stockpiling oil and gas to raise prices so they can afford to pay for more fancy commercials. So many people are exposed to football on television, but no one forces them to watch it. What is it that interests so many people? The person who can answer that question will be or already is a millionaire.

c. All controversies in education start from dissatisfaction with what our children are being taught or with what they are not being taught. What should we teach and why is a question that arises on the very threshold of intelligent concern with the process of schooling. The easiest way to answer this question is also the most deceptive. We should teach those subjects that embody the great truths of our human tradition, the accumulated knowledge, skills, and wisdom which are the inalienable heritage of every child. This answer is deceptive because it assumes that there are educators or others, for that matter, who assert that we should not teach these things. Nothing can be taught which does not at one point or another involve the use of some tradition. Nothing can be learned which is not continuous with something already known. So why are many colleges and universities adopting programs to teach college students what they already know but don't put to use? The answer is very simple. Many colleges and universities believe students need the teaching of the basics. Therefore, the effort and time put toward these programs is useless. Useless because students view these programs as a setback. They know that they know most of the basics, and they therefore don't get a true outlook of how college really is. That is to say, the justification for teaching or learning anything must be observable consequences within the student's experience. Whatever other world an individual will inhabit, his life will be spent in this one. Whatever may be the society of the future, either it will be continuous with the society in which he now lives or it will develop out of its conflict and problems.

d. I personally prefer prose over poetry, for reasons I'll explain later. I enjoy fiction and non-fiction very much. I do like non-fiction better, though. Nothing can beat a well-written biography, or autobiography.

The details and explanations in someone's life are fascinating, and elucidate the human spirit in the individual, and in all of us. *The Diary of Anne Frank* is a good example of this. Her problems with adolescence, combined with her Jewish identity in Nazi Germany, while living in hiding, are written with sensitivity and insight, making her diary a famous autobiography, and wonderful reading material. At the same time, however, I derive great enjoyment out of novels and short stories. I have been concentrating on novels for the past few months, and am now realizing the beauty of the novel. I have said that I prefer non-fiction: I like to read about reality. However, I now recognize the power fiction has in expressing truth and reality. The more abstract forms of human emotions, such as freedom and guilt, are beautifully portrayed in such novels as *1984* and *The Scarlet Letter,* two books that held me spellbound this summer. One book I read, *The Fox in the Attic,* was a combination biography/ novel based on the facts of pre-WW II Europe, but developing fictitious characters. It was a tremendous book, and showed to me the overlapping of fiction and nonfiction can be successfully done.

2. Below is part of a paper analyzing a neighborhood for someone who is trying to decide whether to retire there. The writer analyzed the subject into three parts: "socializing, property responsibility, and recreation." This paragraph is the complete part on "socializing."

Examine the paragraph to see how it could be improved. Are all the details necessary and useful? If not, cut the ones that aren't. Should details be added? If so, make up some and add them. Is the movement of thought from sentence to sentence clear and smooth, or should you introduce transitions? Revise or rewrite to produce a better paragraph.

Socializing with neighbors will only be accomplished if you make the first move toward friendship. Many people will not bring themselves to you, but once you show that you want to know them, then their hearts are warmed. We have had neighbors move in before who have alienated themselves completely by never showing or trying a friendship with the family next door. Our neighborhood will keep to themselves unless you make the initial move. You will find them quite friendly. Since you are a senior citizen, you will find that my neighborhood is mostly adult-oriented. I'm sure you wouldn't prefer a teenage hangout outside your driveway every night. This is not the case. Only three teenagers live in the development, and that is with their parents. However, your tolerance for kids may be tested at times. You might love kids and no problem will exist. I'm stating this because I learned you were never married. Some of the older couples are quite rich and show it off. But most others are middle income families. We have no poverty problems and like to keep it that way.

3. In a paper of 500–750 words, contrast the version of love and marriage presented by popular TV programs with the version presented in recent movies you've seen. Or explain how your own view of love and marriage conforms to or conflicts with your parents' view of them or the view of your friends, your church, TV, Hollywood, or any other individual, group, or institution. Instead of love and marriage, your subject can be women, religion, goals in life, or bringing up children.

In writing the paper, pay particular attention to relating the paragraphs to each other. Whether your transitions are explicit or implicit, make sure that the movement from paragraph to paragraph is clear.

7

Shaping Sentences

Whether the sentences you compose turn out to be clear or fuzzy, limp or emphatic, rhythmical or stumbling depends on how skillful you are in putting them together and particularly in revising and rewriting them for your final draft. This chapter will focus on individual sentences; but remember what we said in Chapter Six about the need for relating sentences to one another and grouping them in paragraphs. It's always better to think in—and write—blocks of sentences rather than single sentences. No matter how well made a sentence is, unless it works well with its neighbors, it doesn't do what it should for your paper.

When we compare two versions of a sentence in this chapter and indicate that one is better than the other, we're saying that *in most contexts* it would be better. The important thing is for you to be in control of a variety of ways of expressing your ideas, so that you can meet the rhetorical demands of the immediate context. Satisfying these demands is part of your job when you sit down to prepare a final draft.

When you're revising, don't just look at individual sentences and decide to cross out words in one or add them to another. Concentrate on separating, combining, and regrouping *ideas*. More often than not, your purpose in breaking up one sentence or combining two will be to get rid of an inconsistency, to introduce a qualification, to give a statement the right emphasis—most of all, to bring out logical relationships.

The next two sections deal with combining sentences and breaking up sentences, two of the major options available to you as you revise your work. Later sections apply these options in a variety of contexts.

Combining Sentences

In revising, you may find that you've used too many sentences in your first draft. Perhaps you've given a full sentence to an insignificant detail, or said the same thing twice, or separated ideas that belong together. If your sentences are consistently short—say under seventeen words—you're probably fragmenting your ideas.

To make sure we have a vocabulary for discussing syntax, the order and relation of sentence elements, we'll briefly review the traditional system of classifying sentences:

Sentences are classified according to the number and kind of clauses (subject-predicate combinations) they have. Clauses may be independent or dependent. Grammatically, an independent clause can stand alone as a complete sentence. A dependent (or subordinate) clause can't. Dependent clauses are introduced by subordinating conjunctions like *if, when, although* or by relative pronouns like *that, who, which,* though these relative pronouns may sometimes be omitted from the clauses they introduce ("I knew [that] you would come").

A *simple* sentence, like this one, consists of one independent clause. It's often short but needn't be. Like the other three sentence types, a simple sentence can contain compound subjects, compound verbs, compound objects, and compound modifiers; prepositional phrases; verbals and verbal phrases; adjectives, adjectives in series, and adjective phrases; and nouns and noun phrases used as appositives. Grammatically, the long sentence you've just read is a simple sentence.

A *compound* sentence consists of two or more independent clauses. The clauses are usually joined by coordinating conjunctions like *and, but, or,* but sometimes two clauses are joined by a pair of correlative conjunctions like *either . . . or* or *not only . . . but also.* (The preceding sentence is a compound sentence.) They may also be linked by a semicolon; in such cases the second clause often begins with a conjunctive adverb like *however, nevertheless, hence.* (The preceding sentence, too, is compound.)

A *complex* sentence consists of one independent clause and one or more dependent clauses. When you write a complex sentence, you can often place the dependent clause either before or after or inside the independent clause, as you choose. (The preceding sentence is a complex sentence.)

A *compound-complex* sentence consists of two or more independent clauses and one or more dependent clauses. A compound-complex sentence can be very long, or it can be as short as "If he did it, find him guilty; if not, set him free."

For Writing

Using as models the examples you've just read, compose three simple sentences, three compound, three complex, and three compound-complex. That's a warm-up exercise.

Now write a long paragraph (10–12 sentences) on any topic you choose. When it's done, identify each sentence in the margin, labeling it simple, compound, complex, or compound-complex. How many of each kind do you have? Comparing your figures with those of your classmates will reveal whether you're unusually dependent on any single pattern.

Coordinating and Subordinating

Sentences can be combined most easily by coordinating clauses or by subordinating one of them. The simplest way is to join them with a coordinating conjunction:

> The United States is a conservative country. Its working class is one of the anchors of its conservatism.

> The United States is a conservative country, and its working class is one of the anchors of its conservatism.—Richard Hofstadter, *Harper's*

Often, though, simply tying two sentences together won't work. Take these two sentences:

> The principal urban characters in the comic strips—Maggie and Jiggs, Moon Mullins, Dick Tracy—were Irish. These were early comic strips.

Turning them into a compound sentence—"The principal urban characters . . . were Irish, and these were early comic strips"—wouldn't make sense in most imaginable contexts. Instead, the second sentence could, with some minor revisions, be converted into a dependent clause and placed first:

> When the comic strips began, the principal urban characters—Maggie and Jiggs, Moon Mullins, Dick Tracy—were Irish.—Nathan Glazer and Daniel Patrick Moynihan, *Beyond the Melting Pot*

Sensible subordination of separate sentences puts information together that belongs together, gives writing a brisker pace, and makes it sound more adult, less like the prose in grade-school readers. The two sentences

> She left without Jack. He was the man she had come with.

can be rewritten as a single sentence in various ways:

> She left without Jack, the man she had come with.

> She left without Jack, though she had come with him.

> Though she had come with Jack, she left without him.

Making Choices

When you combine sentences, what you want to say will ordinarily determine whether you use coordination or subordination. But often you can say what you mean in either a compound sentence or a complex sentence, and then you choose one rather than the other in order to make a smoother transition, to break up a succession of sentences with the same structure, or for some similar reason. Though there may be slight differences in emphasis and degree of explicitness, in some contexts either of these paired sentences could be used:

He shouted, *but* the crowd paid no attention.

Although he shouted, the crowd paid no attention.

You must enroll for the course, *or* you will not receive credit.

Unless you enroll for the course, you will not receive credit.

She appealed the decision, *for* everyone advised her to.

She appealed the decision *because* everyone advised her to.

Both coordinating and subordinating offer further choices. Take these two statements:

They were targets for angry criticisms.

Their parents stood by them.

If you want to point up the contrast, you can coordinate them in any of these ways:

They were targets for angry criticism, but their parents stood by them.

They were targets for angry criticism; however, their parents stood by them.

They were targets for angry criticism; their parents, however, stood by them.

Or you might have reason to reverse the order of the clauses:

Their parents stood by them, but they were targets for angry criticism.

And so on. Instead of *but* or *however,* you might use any one of a number of other connectives that indicate contrast: *yet, still, nevertheless, in spite of that* are examples.

If you want to point up the contrast by subordinating, you have to decide which clause should be the independent clause—where the emphasis in the sentence should fall—and also whether it should follow or precede the dependent clause. If you settle on *though* as the subordinating conjunction, you have these possibilities to choose from:

Though they were targets for angry criticism, their parents stood by them.

Their parents stood by them, though they were targets for angry criticism.

Though their parents stood by them, they were targets for angry criticism.

They were targets of angry criticism, though their parents stood by them.

Choices should be made largely on the basis of context—what the neighboring sentences call for, what emphasis is needed. Compare:

> Though they were targets for angry criticism, their parents stood by them. So they persisted. That support was all they needed.

> Though their parents stood by them, they were targets for angry criticism. The community was almost unanimous in opposing their stand.

The first passage begins by emphasizing the loyalty of the parents and thus points the way to the third sentence, which has *support* as its subject. The first sentence of the second passage acknowledges the support but puts emphasis on the hostility. The second sentence again emphasizes opposition.

Placing Clauses

In subordinating, it's good stylistic practice to experiment with the position of the dependent clause. You'll find that some kinds of clauses are more mobile than others and that some shifts in the position of clauses will clarify your meaning while others will obscure it. At times the position of an adverbial clause (introduced by words like *when, if, although, because*) makes no difference in the meaning:

> When he spoke in support of the bill, he was in Washington.

> He was in Washington when he spoke in support of the bill.

The adverbial clause could also come in the middle of the sentence—"He was, when he spoke . . . , in Washington"—but not without sounding a bit strained.

In other sentences the placing of the adverbial clause makes a decided difference in meaning:

> While he was in Washington, he argued that the bill should be passed.

> He argued that the bill should be passed while he was in Washington.

Note, too, that the second of these sentences can be interpreted in at least three different ways: Was he arguing that the passage of the bill should be accomplished during the time that he was in Washington, not after he had left? Was he two-faced—arguing for the bill in Washington but against it elsewhere? Or does the sentence mean that though he argued for the bill while he was in Washington, he soon had to leave the capital? Although context could probably be counted on to resolve the ambiguity, the adverbial clause should be placed so that the meaning is unmistakable. If that's impossible, the sentence should be rewritten.

Clauses used either as nouns or as adjectives (usually introduced by *who, which, that,* though the introductory word is sometimes omitted) are less mobile than adverbial clauses. When a clause used as an adjective is placed near a word it can't logically modify, there's not so much a change in meaning as a loss of sense:

No one was interested in meeting Oscar or his new bride, who had come to the reunion only to show her off. [The *who* clause doesn't modify ''bride.'']

We drove over an old bridge into the village, which grumbled under the weight of our camper. [The *which* clause doesn't modify ''village.'']

In cases like these, simply shifting the clause either creates confusion:

No one was interested in meeting Oscar, who had come to the reunion only to show her off, or his new bride.

Or it causes an awkward interruption:

We drove over an old bridge, which grumbled under the weight of our camper, into the village.

In both cases, the best solution is to rearrange the sentence so that the word being modified and the clause that modifies it come together at the end:

No one was interested in meeting Oscar's new bride or in meeting Oscar, who had come to the reunion only to show her off.

We drove into the village over an old bridge, which grumbled under the weight of our camper.

In other cases, shifting the clause to a different position in the sentence will make the intended meaning clear:

The stanza in the poem that I prefer is only two lines long.

The stanza [that] I prefer [in the poem] is only two lines long.

The bracketed words can be omitted.

When a dependent clause can come before, after, or in the middle of the independent clause without altering the meaning, weigh the advantages of one position against another as you revise your draft. Putting the clause first usually produces a neater sentence:

When we finally got to her house, she was packed and ready to leave.

Putting it last produces a looser, more casual style:

She was packed and ready to leave when we finally got to her house.

When it's placed first, readers have the circumstance or qualification or concession in mind while they're reading the main assertion; and this is often an advantage. But you may decide to put the dependent clause last or in the middle so that you can make a smoother transition into or out of the sentence. What's important is to recognize the difference between a situation in which you have a choice and one in which you don't and, when you have a choice, to select the alternative that helps you say best what you want to say.

Choosing Conjunctions

In either subordinating or coordinating, the choice of conjunction is often automatic, but in revising your early drafts you should keep reminding yourself of the context. Out of context, *and* clearly adds and *but* contrasts. Just as clearly, the *and* of the first passage below conveys a different meaning from the *and* of the second:

> Yesterday I had news of the two Smith boys for the first time since they left home. John is a bank manager in New Orleans, and James is a forest ranger in Idaho.

> Although he modeled himself on his brother for years, James Smith finally showed some independence. Now John is a bank manager in New Orleans, and James is a forest ranger in Idaho.

In conversation, the clause introduced by the second *and* would have something of a "what-do-you-know" effect, with the *and* close to the usual meaning conveyed by *but*.

Context, then, can give an overlay of meaning—even a new meaning—to the commonest of conjunctions. What causes trouble is the use of *and* in contexts that call for decidedly different conjunctions:

> He went to church every Sunday, and he never put a cent in the collection plate.

The sentence seems to cry out for *but* instead of *and*. If the first clause was subordinated, *although* would be the natural choice of conjunction, expressing the same contrast that *but* does.

Here the reader has to puzzle over the illogical *however:*

> Admittedly the high cost of automobile liability insurance is a real burden to some drivers. However, the protection it affords is so limited that the insured may still be stuck with tremendous bills.

Furthermore or *besides* would be a logical choice.

Even when a conjunction isn't misleading, it may be less precise than it should be. In this pair of sentences, *because* makes explicit what *and* can only imply:

The film upsets traditional notions about morality, and conservatives are agitating to have its audience restricted.

Because the film upsets traditional notions about morality, conservatives are agitating to have its audience restricted.

While cause shouldn't be assigned casually, use *because* whenever you have good reason to do so. Explicit conjunctions give combined sentences a strength and vigor seldom found in their separate parts.

For Discussion and Writing

Revise the items below according to the instructions that follow each one.

1. After the battle of Waterloo, Napoleon's carriage fell into the hands of the Prussians. Napoleon had left it to go ahead on horseback. (Make one complex sentence.)

2. At first he found her attractive. She wore a bit too much makeup. Underneath it, her facial bone structure was strong and pleasing. (Rewrite as one or two sentences, using conjunctions to bring out a sensible relationship among the observations.)

3. The main reason I began college in the summer term is that it will take me several years to complete my formal education. The sooner I start, the sooner I will be through. (Join the two sentences so that the causal relation is clear and logical.)

4. Scientists face many conflicts between their work and moral standards that seem insoluble. (Revise to make clear what *that* modifies.)

5. A reporter's news stories must be unemotional. They must be objective. A reporter at the scene may be bored. He may also be amused. Or he may be admiring. At the scene he may even be disgusted. (Rewrite as a single sentence.)

6. I worked hard and produced a good paper, and I got it in two days late and my teacher lowered the grade from A to B. (Rewrite in one sentence, using subordination to make clear the logical relations between the ideas.)

7. From the beginning I liked math. It wasn't easy for me. There was great satisfaction in coming up with the right answers. (Rewrite as one or two sentences, using conjunctions to bring out a sensible relationship among the observations.)

8. With a bedroom, a kitchen, a living room, and a bathroom up the hall that rented for $250 a month, the apartment was a bargain. (Make clear what rented for $250 a month.)

9. There are also study lounges in the library if you don't want to leave the building where you can study. (Shift the position of the *if* clause for clarity and smoothness.)

10. The class became overcrowded. Solutions were found. They permitted writing workshops to continue. (Rewrite as one complex sentence.)

Embedding Words and Phrases

Combining sentences needn't involve either coordinating or subordinating. Sometimes in revising you'll reduce one sentence to a few words and add them to, or embed them in, another sentence:

> Parts of the world are becoming overrun by tourists. They are the most beautiful parts.
>
> *The most beautiful* parts of the world are becoming overrun by tourists.

You can also make subjects, verbs, and modifying words compound. In the following example the single sentence that expresses the content of the separate sentences has a compound subject ("Both radio and TV") and compound adjectives (''short, unrelated'') as well as the compound adverbs (''between and within'') that appear in the first version:

> Radio offers short programs, interrupted between and within by commercials. They are often unrelated. TV does this too.
>
> Both radio and TV offer short, unrelated programs, interrupted between and within by commercials.—Edmund Carpenter, *Explorations in Communication*

Verbs and objects may also be made compound when words from one sentence are embedded in another in this way:

> Too much sun dries out the skin. It causes wrinkles. It may even result in skin cancer.
>
> Too much sun dries out the skin, causes wrinkles, and may even result in cancer.
>
> Too much sun can cause dry, wrinkled skin and even skin cancer.

Often, in combining sentences, you'll find that you have to change the form of a word you're transferring. Frequently you'll change verbs to verbals—gerunds, participles, and infinitives—and embed them either singly or in phrases, as in these examples:

> I *read* the book. It was a shock, a thrill, a wild adventure.
>
> *Reading* the book was a shock, a thrill, a wild adventure.

> This flood of rhetoric had an effect. It *befuddled* the outside world with the view that China was indeed being aggressive, as the West already assumed.
>
> The effect of this flood of rhetoric was *to befuddle* the outside world with the view that China was indeed being aggressive, as the West already assumed.— John K. Fairbank, *New York Review of Books*.

And you will shift some adjectives from predicate position and turn them into modifiers of the subject:

Yaks are bulky. They are black and shaggily clad. They convey a rugged elegance.

Bulky, black, and shaggily clad, yaks convey a rugged elegance.—George B. Schaller, *Stones of Silence*

When you combine sentences, you can also use nouns—singly or in series or in phrases—as *appositives*, words that name or further identify or describe the other nouns or the pronouns they refer to. In this example the series of nouns in apposition to "those" specifies who is hunted:

And none of those he hunts—thieves, drug pushers, Murphy men, assault and robbery men, killers—wants to confront him on anything resembling even terms.—James Mills, *Life*

Separation into two sentences would produce something flatter, like

He hunts thieves, drug pushers, Murphy men, assault and robbery men, and killers. None of them wants to confront him on anything resembling even terms.

For Discussion and Writing

Revise the items below according to the instructions.

1. They made their first homes in dugouts or sod cabins. These dugouts or cabins were dark. They were badly ventilated. The windows were covered with blankets or hides. So were the doors. (Combine into one sentence.)

2. We heard it everywhere. We heard it around campus. We heard it in the corridors and in the classrooms. We heard it in the cafeteria. We heard it in the dormitories. (Reduce to a single main clause followed by phrases.)

3. Teachers who are interested in their subjects do the best work. The same is true of students. (Make one sentence, first by joining these two and then by reducing one of them to a phrase and embedding it in the other.)

4. A few years later I was taking my older brother to Norfolk. My brother had enlisted in the navy. He was to meet his first ship. We decided to stop by the park. We had played in the park as children. (Rewrite as a complex sentence.)

5. Laguna Diablo is about 175 miles down the Baja California peninsula. It is surrounded by mountains of brown rock. It is dry. It is desolate. It is miles from the nearest plumbing, the nearest freeway.—Sam Moses, *Sports Illustrated*. (Combine into one simple sentence.)

6. Because the mainland was convulsed in civil war, news of the massacre received little world attention. The news was reported by a few foreign journalists on the spot. (Make one sentence by reducing one of these sentences to a dependent clause or phrase.)

7. Flour has gone up in price. Honey costs more than it did. The price of raisins is higher. Eggs are more expensive. The four main ingredients in the recipe have all increased in price. (Reduce to one simple sentence.)

8. Being able to earn a living is one of the things that increases the well-being of women today. Another thing is being able to play a number of roles at the same time. Just living in this period of feminist progress helps, too. (Reduce to one sentence.)

9. "Horrid" was the name of the basset who appeared on the stage in "Camelot." Horrid played the part of King Pellinore's hound. (Rewrite as a single sentence that tells who played the part of King Pellinore's hound.)

Breaking Up Sentences

In revising your first drafts you may come upon sentences that need breaking up. And in going over revisions in which you've combined sentences, you may find that at times you've stuffed in more than you should have. The sentences that most urgently need breaking up are those that join unrelated ideas and so lack unity. The two assertions in the following sentence belong in separate—and separated—sentences:

> The desert country of New Mexico presents a striking contrast to the mountain beauty of Colorado, where the citizens are strongly opposed to any increase in the state income tax.

It would be hard to imagine any possible connection between the attitude of Colorado's citizens toward a state income tax and the geological contrast between Colorado and New Mexico. So simply turning the subordinate clause ("where the citizens . . . ") into a separate sentence ("The citizens of Colorado are . . . ") wouldn't improve things. The new sentence probably belongs in a different paragraph.

Less obviously illogical but still troublesome is the sentence that brings together ideas that have some relationship but not one close enough to justify joining them. These two examples show that the lead sentence of a book review or news story can be too heavily loaded for clarity:

> Without its storytellers, any nation would be reduced to the moral equivalent of a trading post, and after two generations of spinning the tales that have literally created the Delta country and the Natchez Trace (but not Yoknapatawpha County, which is another world also unto itself) for us outsiders—shy for one reason or another of Mississippi—it is sensible and honorable to regard Eudora Welty as a great national resource.—Carole Cook, *Saturday Review*

> Mr. Nader's criticism of pollution caused by Union Carbide's Ferro Alloy Division here, which results in a 24-hour pall of black, yellow and orange smoke and soot that nearly blots out the sun and has forced the Roman Catholic Church to enclose an outdoor statute of St. Anthony in a transparent plastic case, was contained in a letter to . . . the Carbide board chairman in New York.—*New York Times*

The first example would be much easier reading without the parenthetical allusion to William Faulkner's fictional Yoknapatawpha County and without the description of "us outsiders" as shy of Mississippi. Even with these interrupters gone, the name of the tale spinner, Eudora Welty, remains some distance from its modifiers. The clause could be rewritten this way:

> . . . after two generations of spinning tales that have literally created the Delta country and the Natchez Trace, Eudora Welty can sensibly and honorably be regarded as a great national resource.

In the second example the details about pollution compete so strongly for attention that the reader is distracted from the main point. Separating out some of the details about the pollution would improve sentence unity. But the main point is hard to grasp for still another reason: the grammatical subject ("criticism") is separated from its verb ("was contained") by a long string of phrases and dependent clauses. Reordering the main elements and replacing abstract "criticism" with an active verb ("criticized") would make the sentence clearer and more direct:

> In a letter to the Carbide board chairman . . . Mr. Nader criticized the pollution caused by. . . .

Long modifiers that break up the basic structure of a clause can so interfere with the forward movement of a sentence that the reader loses track of the really important assertion. And when repeated embedding places two verb phrases side by side, the reader has to go back over the sentence to match the right verb to the right subject:

> All these forces, added to the other deterrents which combinations of Powers, great and small, ready to stand firm upon the front of law and for the ordered remedy of grievances, would have formed, might well have been effective.— Winston S. Churchill, "The Munich Agreement"

The sentence would be easier to read if the modifiers of "Powers" were dropped:

> All these forces, added to the other deterrents which combinations of Powers would have formed, might well have been effective.

or if all the interrupters were shifted to the beginning:

> Added to the other deterrents which combinations of Powers, great and small, ready to stand firm upon the front of law and for the ordered remedy of grievances, would have formed, all these forces might well have been effective.

But perhaps the best reordering would join the main verb, "might well have been" to its subject:

All these forces might well have been effective if added to the other deterrents which combinations of Powers, great and small, ready to stand firm upon the front of law and for the ordered remedy of grievances, would have formed.

Even short interrupters can spoil a sentence if they're allowed to create an erratic, jerky movement. Here the parts of the verb phrase are separated:

> And I would have, as they did in 1948, gone over to the conquering Communists.—Theodore H. White, *In Search of History*

In this sentence by a student, the interrupter is itself interrupted:

> The technological revolution, which brings us more breakthroughs—both for the benefit as well as the detriment of mankind—every day, had a slow start.

The first sentence would read more smoothly with "as they did in 1948" placed either before "I" or after "Communists." In the second, one interrupter should be completed before another is begun:

> The technological revolution, which brings us more breakthroughs every day, both to the benefit and to the detriment of mankind, had a slow start.

Embedding would help:

> The technological revolution, which daily brings us both beneficial and detrimental breakthroughs, had a slow start.

If you find yourself writing sentences that contain several paired commas or dashes or parentheses, examine the elements they enclose to see, first, whether the qualifications you're making are necessary. Repeated interruption to qualify can make you sound indecisive or evasive or prissy. And if the enclosed elements are no more than asides or extraneous details (often in the form of prepositional phrases), they overload your sentences and slow them down.

Be sure you haven't produced a sentence so long or so complicated that the reader gets lost in it. For a house-that-Jack-built sentence that stitches several dependent clauses together, separation is often the best remedy. This one, with its ten dependent clauses—most of them built one upon the other—needs to be separated into at least two sentences and, in the process, reduced to its essential meaning:

> He admitted that the course of study which he was taking was the wrong one for him because it could never lead to a job that would give him the kinds of satisfaction that he would expect if he agreed to put up with the restrictions on his time that would certainly be the result of taking a position in the field for which he was currently preparing himself.

He admitted that the course of study he was taking was the wrong one for him. It could only lead to a job that would restrict his freedom and deny him the satisfactions he sought.

And so sentences string together one independent clause after another, flattening out logical relationships so that everything seems to have equal importance. Unless there's a rhetorical justification for this effect—unless, that is, you have a reason for wanting to give just that impression—restructure any *and so* sentence you find in your writing. Ordinarily a stringy sentence like the following will strike the reader as unemphatic, imprecise, and tiresome:

I found my eyes blurring, and so I took my usual headache pills, and after a couple of hours my head didn't hurt so much and my vision cleared, and so I went back to work.

In revising, look for natural breaking points (here after ''and so I took my headache pills''), and then consider whether using subordination to bring out chronological and causal relations would improve the sentence. In revising the preceding example, you might end up with something like:

When I found my eyes blurring, I took my usual headache pills. After a couple of hours my head didn't hurt so much, and since my vision had cleared, I was able to go back to work.

For Writing

• Reshape each of these sentences from student papers to make it easier to read and understand.

1. Before the church service and the burial, a viewing, in which people come to look at the body in an open casket, is held. (Make the sentence end with "casket.")

2. Two birds are killed with one stone, so to speak, by my choosing nuclear engineering as a major. I can perhaps help man in his search for new or better sources of energy, which will give me a sense of satisfaction with my life, not to mention a sense of purpose, and I am most likely to feel at ease with the type of work required to become, and to be, a nuclear engineer— mathematical and scientific work—because that has always been my strong area scholastically. (Make the movement brisker, perhaps by reducing the interruptions, possibly by breaking the second sentence in two.)

3. If you get in there and hustle and if while you're doing that, without losing your concentration and with your goal clearly in mind, as it should be at all times in a highly competitive situation like this one, you figure all the angles and settle on the most efficient way of getting ahead of the guy at the next machine, you'll be what society calls a success. (Reduce the interruptions.)

Emphasis, Directness, Economy

As you revise and rewrite, keep trying to make your sentences say what you want them to say with the emphasis you intend. For the most part, this means expressing yourself directly and economically.

Achieving Emphasis

In reviewing your early drafts, examine your sentences to see that you've placed emphasis where it belongs. Decisions about such matters as whether to combine or separate sentences and where to place elements within sentences determine what's emphasized and what isn't.

Separating for Emphasis

In speaking, a pause allows what's just been said to sink in or throws emphasis on what follows. In writing, something of the same effect can be gained by separating. Consider this sentence:

> The trouble with modern English spelling is that it does not spell or even approximately spell modern English but instead spells the English of the Late Middle English period around 1470 A.D.

Here is the much more emphatic form in which it originally appeared, as three separate sentences:

> The trouble with modern English spelling is that it does not spell modern English. It does not even approximately spell modern English. What it does spell is the English of the Late Middle English period around 1470 A.D.—Harold Whitehall, *Structural Essentials of English*

Now contrast this pair of sentences:

> It promises and delivers a civilized, casual, and colorful account of a phenomenon unfamiliar to many of us but important to our times.

> It promises a civilized, casual, and colorful account of a phenomenon unfamiliar to us but important to our times; and it delivers.—Dan Wakefield, *Atlantic*

In the second version Wakefield's use of two clauses instead of one and his choice of a semicolon (instead of a comma) between them give "delivers" an emphasis that's completely lacking in the first.

In smaller units, repeating the conjunction or preposition in a series of parallel items isolates and emphasizes each item. Here, in an article on the position of women in America, the repetition of *her* underlines the division of the sexes:

It is not exactly a posture in which she has much of a chance to enjoy her life, her liberty, or the pursuit of her happiness.—Clare Boothe Luce, *Saturday Review/World*

Ordering for Emphasis

The natural points of emphasis in a sentence are the beginning and the end. You'll waste them if you launch your sentences with empty introductions or let them run down into trivial detail. In revising sentences (or paragraphs) for emphasis, look for ways to build to some sort of climax. It may be simply a matter of making your point at the end, or of making the last word one that has impact (*victory, disaster, ridiculous, magnificent*—if the context justifies such words), or of using a short, punchy sentence to bring a paragraph to a close. When you list items, order them in some logical way—either the order of climax, with the biggest, oldest, richest, or most-something coming last, or possibly in order of diminishing importance, moving down the scale.

Often, of course, a list may offer no rationale for ordering the items. But when there's an opportunity to provide a logical order, failing to do so may result in a flabby, boneless sentence or sometimes in silly anticlimax:

> The driver of the other car was in much worse shape, with a sprained ankle, a crushed pelvis, a severe concussion, and a bruised elbow.

In this case, as in many others, the items should be pruned as well as reordered. The bruised elbow should be eliminated as a trivial detail and probably the sprained ankle as well: "The driver of the other car was in much worse shape, with a crushed pelvis and a severe concussion."

The introductions *It is, It was, There is, There were* are properly criticized as sentence openers when they substitute unnecessary filler for strong subject-verb combinations:

> [There is] a small group of eccentric individuals [who] attend college because they have no other plans or interests.

> [There is] a long chain of events, set off by oil prices, [that] led to the present situation in the record industry.

The words in brackets could be omitted—and should be, unless the context provides some excuse for the longer version. In revising your papers, check every sentence that you've begun with *It is* or *There is,* and unless the opener is serving some real function, drop it. Breaking the habit of beginning sentences with these words is one of the quickest and easiest ways to improve a writing style.

This doesn't mean you'll never open a sentence with *It is, It was, There is,* or *There were,* but when you do, it will be for a purpose. These openers can perform useful—even necessary—functions. They may assert the existence of what follows: "There are six major martial arts." They may provide special emphasis: "Quarreling about words is silly" emphasizes *silly;* "It's silly to quarrel about words" emphasizes *words*. And using the expletive *It is* to begin one sentence often opens the way for a smooth transition into the next one:

> It is important to the purposes of history to remember that the twenty blacks who arrived in Jamestown in 1615 were not, strictly speaking, slaves. They were permitted to become "indentured servants."—Larry L. King, *Confessions of a White Racist*

An alternate version of the first sentence—"Remembering that the twenty blacks . . . is important to the purposes of history"—would shift the emphasis to "the purposes of history" and blur the transition to the following "They."

Mechanical Devices and Word Choice

You can indicate emphasis by underlining, by capitalizing, and by using exclamation marks, but depending on these methods is primitive practice— like shouting to gain attention. If your content is strong and you're expressing yourself well, the mechanical devices aren't necessary. If your content and style are weak, the devices won't help.

Slightly less obvious are the adverbs commonly tacked onto adjectives (*very* beautiful, *extremely* successful, *terrifically* loud); the adjectives that once carried real force but now, through overuse in conversation, do little more than express approval or disapproval (a *wonderful* time, a *terrible* exam, a *horrible* day); and the superlatives most of us overuse in speech (the *greatest* game, the *wildest* time, the *craziest* driver). In serious writing, reliance on any one of these weakens rather than strengthens what's said. Nouns that are themselves emphatic in meaning—the *victory* and *disaster* we cited earlier, *triumph, genius, tragedy, sensation*—have their legitimate uses, but when applied indiscriminately ("The new sweater was a sensation"), they make a writer sound silly.

The emphasis you achieve by means of mechanical devices and exaggerated word choice isn't likely to convince your readers. Rely instead on words that are appropriate to the context and the rhetorical situation, placed where you want the emphasis to fall.

Repetition

Thoughtless, accidental, or lazy repetition always weakens style, but consciously repeating words and phrases that are genuinely significant emphasizes ideas. (The function of repetition in binding sentences together and making paragraphs cohere has been discussed on pp. 189–92.) Controlled repetition of the key terms in a paper keeps the reader's attention focused and makes for clearer writing than shifting from synonym to synonym does ("the Supreme Court . . . the high court . . . the highest tribunal").

In the first sentence of the passage that follows, James Baldwin makes careful discriminations in word choice ("chilling," "cruel," "bitter"); in the second he uses repetition deliberately and purposefully:

> He could be chilling in the pulpit and indescribably cruel in his personal life and he was certainly the most bitter man I have ever met; yet it must be said that there was something else in him, buried in him, which lent him his tremendous power and, even, a rather crushing charm. It had something to do with his blackness, I think—he was very black—with his blackness and his beauty, and with the fact that he knew that he was black but did not know that he was beautiful.—James Baldwin, *Notes of a Native Son*

Notice that both nouns ("blackness," "beauty") and adjectives ("black," "beautiful") are involved in the repetition.

Often, as here, the effect of verbal repetition is enhanced by the repetition of sounds. Together the two sentences offer many examples of alliteration—in addition to the insistent *b*'s, the patterns of sound in "indes*cri*bably *cru*el," "*cru*shing charm," and so on. But like aimless repetition of the same word, aimless repetition of the same sound can become obtrusive and distracting, as in the hiss and clatter of "excessively successful executives." So can unintentional rhymes and off-rhymes, as in "I treated the wound, but the *pain* re*main*ed the *same*." Generally, in prose, words that rhyme shouldn't be allowed to come close enough together to create accidental comic effects (or bad verse). To find out how your own writing sounds, read your papers aloud or—better—have someone read them to you.

Repetition must be controlled. Like repeated drum beats or high notes or dramatic gestures, emphases that come in bunches soon stop being emphatic. To make your writing genuinely emphatic, use emphasis sparingly.

Long and Short Sentences

Besides combining some first-draft sentences and splitting others to make them clearer, you may want to reshape sentences to improve them stylistically. At their best, short sentences have a simplicity and directness that makes them easy to understand and a briskness and drive that carries the reader along. But they can become choppy and jerky, breaking ideas into units too small to be followed easily; and several in succession can result in monotony and a loss of emphasis. Long sentences, on the other hand, can be so complicated or so rambling that the reader (if not the writer) loses track of the main idea. But handled well, a long sentence—even a very long one—can gather up and convey the full meaning of a complex thought, with all its distinctions and qualifications.

If there's no special virtue in either long sentences or short ones, there *is* a virtue in making the length of your sentences appropriate to what you're saying. Especially in narrative, you may want to use short sentences to separate details. Keeping them apart gives each one significance, as in this account of an imagined earthquake:

City church bells aimlessly ringing announced the temblor. Waves formed on the ponds in John McLaren Park. In a block of Victorian houses on Union Street, the chimneys snapped off at the roof-line. Approaches to the Bay Bridge and the Golden Gate collapsed. Concrete slabs of freeway spun through the air like Frisbees. Overpasses to highways 101 and 280 crumbled. The Candlestick causeway was under six feet of water. San Francisco was closed off.—Ted Morgan, *New York Times Magazine*

A long sentence coming after a series of relatively short ones can pull particulars together into an inclusive statement that summarizes or interprets or evaluates, rounding off a paragraph or a stage in the discussion or the discussion itself. Here the long sentence gives illustrations of the general point made in the two short sentences that precede it:

Rod Carew is like every great craftsman in history. What he does requires great concentration, painstaking attention to detail. There are times when the rest of life must seem like an imposition, an annoying distraction, just as Beethoven must have considered the Napoleonic wars as a distraction; or like the ballet impresario who, when asked if the ballerina could take the night off to say goodbye to her fiancé going to the front in the war, said, "My dear, I am not interested in troop movements."—Jim Murray, syndicated columnist

A short sentence following one or more long ones can often bring a paper to a dramatic close:

I would expect an instant rebuttal by the anthros. They will say that my sentiments do not represent the views of all Indians—and they are right, they have brainwashed many of my brothers. But a new day is coming. Until then, it would be wise for anthropologists to climb down from their thrones of authority and pure research and begin helping Indian tribes instead of preying on them. For the wheel of karma grinds slowly, but it does grind fine. And it makes a complete circle.—Vine Deloria, Jr., *Custer Died for Your Sins*

The preceding excerpt illustrates another principle of sentence style: Except for special effects, don't use an unbroken series of sentences of roughly equal length. The sentences in Deloria's passage follow this sequence: short, long, very short, very long, medium, very short. Though your paragraphs may not show as much variety as Deloria's, they should show *some*. The following paragraph from a student's paper indicates how monotonous a stretch of medium-length sentences can be:

Obesity, or an abnormal accumulation of fat in body tissue, leads to numerous social, economic, and psychological problems. Most often the initial gain in weight results from failure to make a good social adjustment. Rejection by one's peers is compensated for by food, setting off the vicious cycle of increased weight and further rejection. Obesity limits participation in active sports like tennis and social activities like dancing, and reduced physical activity encourages weight gain. Obese people endure economic disadvantages, too, because those jobs in which appearance is important are closed to them. Besides the loss of income from better-paying jobs, there is the further expense of having to buy outsize clothes. Psychologically, obese individuals often have undesirable personality characteristics, including withdrawal, passivity, and a sense of inferiority. The habit of blaming all failures and disappointments on one's weight is another unattractive characteristic of the obese.

The range in these sentences is very narrow—from sixteen to twenty words. For almost all purposes, that range is too narrow.

Achieving Directness

Most good expository writing is direct and economical. It says what it has to say without being stuffy or roundabout or long-winded. This doesn't mean that it's always best to use the fewest possible words or that it's always wrong to repeat yourself. But *unnecessary* words and *pointless* repetition work against clarity and directness and create a style that bores and frustrates readers.

In most good writing, sentences are built on concrete subjects and active verbs. While changing a whole clause to a noun or a noun phrase is a great help in combining sentences, a heavy dose of abstract nouns can ruin a prose style. If you get in the habit of relying on abstract nouns to do most of the work of a sentence, you'll find yourself writing this kind of foggy, pompous prose:

> While the diversity which characterizes people might be said to enhance the quality of human existence, this selfsame characteristic may be cited as a causal factor in many of the negative facets of humanity, including prejudice, hostility, exclusion, and other social obstacles to the happiness and well-being of the individual. This problem is perhaps most blatantly manifested in the negative social consequences which individuals with certain variations in physical characteristics have encountered.

The following revision gets rid of some of the fog as well as some of the bulk:

> Although the differences among people might be said to improve the quality of life, they may also give rise to prejudice, hostility, feelings of exclusion, and other obstacles to individual happiness and well-being. Differences in physical appearance are especially likely to arouse such reactions.

In sentences like this one, we hear the voice of a committee, not of an individual:

There was an affirmative decision in regard to the implementation of a policy concerning a reduction in employment levels on the part of management.

Either of these short sentences captures the gist of that long-winded pronouncement:

The Board of Directors has decided to employ fewer workers.

The Company is going to fire some of you.

It could be argued that the writer of the first version, with its abstract nouns and its string of prepositional phrases ("in regard to . . . of . . . in . . . on the part of . . ."), accomplished his rhetorical purpose—to muffle the unpleasant truth in a cloud of abstraction. But much writing of this kind results not from conscious choice but from a failure to assign action to the active—that is, a failure to make *people* the doers, the subjects of your verbs:

A state of fury existed among the ticket-holders after their learning of the failure of the stars to appear.

Simply by asking yourself "Who did what?" you come around to this rewrite:

The ticket-holders became furious when they learned that the stars hadn't shown up.

If you find yourself using abstract nouns, especially nouns ending in *-ence, -ity, -ment, -tion,* every six or seven words, make a habit of asking yourself "Who did what?"

Asking yourself that question will also help you avoid overuse of passive verbs. Passives can't be, and shouldn't be, avoided entirely. In describing an industrial process or recording a laboratory experiment, there may be good reason to keep the focus solely on what takes place, ignoring the operators or researchers or other human agents involved. There are times when the doer of the action isn't important or can't be identified: "The oil is loaded aboard tankers in the Gulf of Aden"; "For a week no garbage was collected." And there are times when being acted upon is what you're writing about: "I was laughed at by every kid on the block." But despite these exceptions, the general rule holds: Use active verbs to make your writing direct and vigorous—and honest. Active verbs are more likely to assign responsibility; instead of reporting that tuition was increased, they state that someone raised tuition. Hiding behind passives is a rhetorical strategy of cowardly or dishonest bureaucrats.

When you're revising your papers, four steps will make your sentences more economical.

1. Reduce subject-verb combinations by combining and embedding.

The leaves covered the ground. *They looked* like a carpet.

The leaves, which looked like a carpet, *covered* the ground.

The leaves covered the ground like a carpet.

The leaves carpeted the ground.

Each of the first two versions contains two subject-verb combinations; each of the last two contains one. Which is the most appropriate sentence would have to be decided in context. From the point of view of economy, the last two versions are better.

2. When you have a choice between long and short constructions, use the shorter form unless the rhetorical situation demands a formal style.

The man [whom] I spoke to is my counselor.

He knew [that] the cause was lost.

Political success was limited to those [who were] skilled in public debate.

You can often make deletions in a series of parallel structures:

A light rain was called a bird sweat, a sprinkle was a shirttail shower, a heavy rain a frog-strangler.—Helen Bevington, *The House Was Quiet and the World Was Calm*

"Was called" in the first clause is reduced to "was" in the second and omitted altogether in the third without loss of clarity.

3. Choose direct phrasing instead of circumlocution. "Have the idea that" instead of "believe," "in rather short supply" instead of "scarce," "destroyed by fire" instead of "burned"—these are typical circumlocutions. As a characteristic of style, they create pomposity or flabbiness or both. And they may hide, or at least blur, the central subject-predicate idea. In each of the following pairs, the action statement comes through less clearly in the first version, with its circumlocution, than in the second:

The way psychologists measure ability is by the use of tests.

Psychologists use tests to measure ability.

As far as the mission is concerned, there is no question that it was a success.

The mission succeeded.

My answer is in the affirmative.

Yes.

Like the overuse of abstract nouns, prepositional phrases, and passive verbs, circumlocution is a characteristic of institutional prose—the kind of writing churned out by government agencies, corporations, and administrative offices, sometimes to inform, sometimes to mislead.

4.   Reduce wordiness. The bracketed words in the following sentences can be omitted with no loss in meaning and, of course, with a gain in economy:

> Thinking persons [these days would] probably agree [with the conception] that the world has gone mad.

> Anyone familiar with violin-making knows that the better the wood is seasoned, the better [the result will be as far as] the tone [of the instrument is concerned].

> Having the right camping equipment is [one of the most] important [phases of camping].

Wordiness is particularly annoying when it repeats what's already been said, as when *size* is added to a word that can only mean size—"large *in size*"—or when an unnecessary adverb doubles the meaning of a verb: continue *on,* repeat *again,* return *back.* And it's especially wasteful when it takes the emphasis from more important words. Giving a sentence an empty introduction ("What I would like to say is that . . .") means losing the chance to make a firm assertion: "I hate running."

Pruning what you write is part of the job of revising, and usually ridding it of wordiness results in stronger as well as leaner prose. Though writing can be so compressed that it's hard to follow, most writers need to work for economical expression rather than for expansion. Length in a paper should come from building content—from working out ideas—not from piling up words. The right kind of economy means using no more words than you need to say what you want to say in the way you want to say it.

For Writing

Rewrite each of these passages according to the instructions.
1.   Many of her fox-hunting friends included several crowned heads of Europe. (Omit the words that make the sentence illogical.)
2.   The first thing to do is choose the right pack for your size and weight. Do not buy a pack that is bigger than you are, because you will have an extremely hard time carrying it. The best idea is to get a pack with a frame. The frame will spread the weight of the pack across your body better than a pack without a frame, making your load much easier to carry. (Make the passage more economical and direct, the connections between the statements clearer.)

3. When you start living in a fraternity, you have to pay house fees and social dues. The cost usually amounts to about the same amount you would have been charged for living in a dorm. (Rewrite as one compact sentence, getting rid of unnecessary words and careless repetition.)

4. In college an exposure to many views of government, morality, and society is beneficial not only because weaknesses can be detected but also because strong points might also be discovered that can be borrowed and incorporated into the American way of life. (Begin the sentence with "College students" and turn passive verbs into active ones.)

5. A good indication that the human animal is still a brute at heart is to be found in the fact that there is an endless stream of books and articles on manners and etiquette, in all of which the purpose is to urge on us the desirability of introducing into our lives some of the amenities of gracious living. (Condense and make the phrasing more direct. Start by finding out what the real subject of the sentence is.)

6. The central character is admirable: she is conscientious, she is marvelously sensitive and humane, and she is considerate of her associates. (Make the sentence more emphatic.)

7. When someone suggested in late afternoon to the several hundred students who waited almost five hours in intermittent sleet and snow to receive the . . . Committee's response to their demands for a budget review that the group sing, "We Shall Overcome," the new activists made an embarrassing discovery: hardly anyone knew the lyrics.—*Brown Alumni Monthly.* (The dependent clause is too long, with far too many prepositional phrases. Rewrite, correcting these flaws. Making two sentences might be the best solution.)

8. As this record was slipped across this reviewer's desk, the initial response was: ". . . You're kidding! . . ."

But, knowing an assignment is an assignment and seeing that the "Alma Mater" was the first selection, solace was taken in the prospect of becoming one of the apparent few who actually know the "G-- ---- words" to that hallowed dirge. . . .

As the record spun through the last "dear old State, dear old State," first impressions seemed to be confirmed. . . .

However, the sardonic smile began to fade after awhile as the mellow timbre of blended male voices caressed one of the more delicate selections on the album. An appreciation grew for the extra touches and a seductive urge to harmonize began to well in the throat.—Charles C. Dubois, *Centre Daily Times.* (Rewrite in the first person, using active verbs.)

9. Wanumetonomy Golf Club and St. Columba's Cemetery were passed at a speed of about 10 mph. At places the Burma Road could be seen, and motorists waved at us. Other landmarks, usually seen by most of us from the West Main Road, were observed from the water level route.—*Newport Daily News.* (Turn passive verbs into active ones.)

10. There are very few cities in Latin America. In most of the countries (excluding Brazil, Colombia, and Ecuador) there is only one major city. In most of Latin America there are small towns; there is practically no transportation between these towns or between towns and cities. (Revise to reduce wordiness and the number of *There is/There are* openers.)

Parallelism and Order

From the discussion of types of sentences, you know that the compound sentence joins an independent clause to an independent clause. You also know that in the complex sentence the order of elements may be dependent-independent or independent-dependent. Here we'll have more to say about balance and order and about the relation between how you shape your sentences and what you want your sentences to say.

Using Parallelism

Early in this chapter we combined two simple sentences to make a single compound sentence:

> The United States is a conservative country,
>
> and
>
> its working class is one of the anchors of its conservatism.

The coordinating conjunction *and* joins two independent clauses that follow the same pattern: "The United States is . . . and its working class is. . . ." When clause is matched to clause in this way—or phrase to phrase, noun to noun, verb to verb, and so on—they are said to be parallel. As you work to untangle a confusing first-draft sentence or to smooth a ragged sentence in a second draft, you'll often find that the best way to bring together related details and ideas is to put them into grammatically similar, or parallel, structures.

Grammatical Uses

Our speech and writing are full of parallel structures:

young and *old*	*laughing* and *crying*
red, white, and *blue*	*for richer, for poorer*
men, women, and *children*	*come rain* or *come shine*

She is more at home *with gladness* than *with gloom*.

In an economic summit that has become a ritual annual event, the leaders of the industrialized world again agreed *that inflation is the principal threat, that oil imports must be reduced, that poor nations deserve increased aid* and *that free trade is desirable.—Newsweek*

All of us use parallelism all the time without even thinking about it.

Because we're so accustomed to it, its absence where we expect it can bother us. Try reading this sentence:

> Some people have their hearts set on marriage, finding someone they can live with happily is all others ask for, and there are some who don't want to get tied down at all.

With some effort we can figure out what the writer means; but the way he's expressed it is garbled, and the sentence is certainly no pleasure to read.

Before we try to improve it, let's see what we're trying to say. We're contrasting three different attitudes people have toward the same thing, so joining them together in a single sentence is sound. But for easy reading as well as for sense, three things that have something in common need to be set up as a series. And a series calls for parallelism. Let's try using our first unit as the pattern:

> Some people have their heart set on marriage.

What next? To parallel "Some people" as subject of the first unit, we need "other people" or "others" as subject of the second:

> Others just want someone they can live with happily.

But here we have two clauses—two subject-predicate combinations—instead of one. To get rid of the extra clause ("[whom] they can live with happily"), we need a word that will parallel "marriage" in the first unit. "Partnership" will do, with "stable" before it to get across the meaning of "live happily with"; and we can add "with or without marriage" to make the contrast clear:

> Others just want a stable partnership, with or without marriage.

What about the rest? To be in step with the first two groups, they must be made the subject of a single clause that states their attitude directly:

> Still others don't want to get tied down.

Now we have

> Some people have their hearts set on marriage.
>
> Others just want a stable partnership, with or without marriage.
>
> Still others don't want to get tied down.

For close parallelism the third unit needs something to balance "marriage" in the first unit and "partnership" in the second. An exclusive relationship is what these people don't want. But following "others just want" with "still others don't want" would be awkward, and "still others want to avoid" would be worse. So we rephrase:

Still others shy away from any kind of exclusive relationship.

Now we combine the three units with their parallel forms:

Some people have their hearts set on marriage;

others just want a stable relationship, with or without marriage;

and

still others shy away from any kind of exclusive relationship.

And we have a smoother, clearer, more unified sentence. Because the second clause contains a phrase set off by commas, semicolons are a good choice to separate the units except in informal contexts. "But" might be used instead of "and" to emphasize the contrast between the first two attitudes and the third.

Since parallelism is a form of coordination, failures in parallelism may occur in pairs of any kind or in series of three or more items. Faulty parallelism is a variety of shifted construction: you use a different form to fill a specific position in a sentence that seems to call for matching structures. What goes with what is the key question. Here are a few examples:

Parallel: Her hobbies were *swimming* and *playing the piano.*

Parallel: *To swim* and *to play the piano* gave her great pleasure.

Not parallel: *To swim* and *playing the piano* were her hobbies.

Parallel: I've heard about her *swimming* every day and *playing the piano* every evening.

Parallel: I've heard that she *swims* every day and *plays the piano* every evening.

Not parallel: I've heard about her *swimming* every day and *that she plays the piano* every evening.

A more drastic failure in parallelism is illustrated here:

The best way to prevent choking is to avoid excess talking or laughing when eating and do not indulge in too much drinking before meals.

By the time she got to "and," the student who wrote this sentence had forgotten how she'd started it. If she'd looked back, she would have realized that what was called for was "and not to" instead of "and do not." ("And not to drink too much before meals" would have reduced wordiness.)

So far we've examined sentences that would be clearer and stronger if parts of them were made parallel. But parts that are made parallel must be logically related. You'll confuse your readers if you put into matching structures ideas or details that can't sensibly be paired. What do you make of this sentence?

> Though spectator sports are often criticized, the viewers do gain some recreational advantages, including release from daily routine, getting outdoors, and providing an exhilaration that has a tonic effect.

Of the three elements put into a series, the first two belong together, but the third, which is parallel in form to the second, doesn't belong with them. The writer has shifted from what the spectators gain—release from routine and getting outdoors—to what the sports provide—exhilaration. Consistency of point of view would provide a logical parallelism that could be emphasized by parallel structures:

> Though spectator sports are often criticized, the viewers do gain some recreational advantages, including fresh air, exhilaration, and release from the daily routine.

Besides keeping order in a sentence, parallelism can contribute to economy. By using parallelism, the author of the following passage was able to put into one sentence (the second) what otherwise might have taken as many as seven or eight:

> As an educator I am unhappy about the rise of vulgarity disguised as freedom. I refer here to intellectual and esthetic vulgarity, to aggressive coarseness in speech and manners, to contempt for grammar and indifference to logic, to sloganeering as a substitute for thought, to hatred of culture, antipathy to history and release into fashionable nihilism.—John Bunzel, *Newsweek*

For Writing

Introduce parallelism or strengthen it in those items that you think need improving.

1. I was told to report to the supervisor and that I was to bring a note from my doctor explaining my absence.

2. You can go by plane or bus or now an Amtrak trip is possible.

3. I have very little background in English literature, but all of the major American poets were studied in my senior literature course.

4. Cessation of breathing may be caused by drowning, electrocution, suffocation, drug intoxication, or auto accident.

5. Not only did her writing skills develop but also her interest in books, magazines, and other literature was stimulated.

6. You need to know when to begin the job and knowing what to do in which order.

7. I was fortunate enough to attend a small school in which my largest class contained twenty-five students and in the smallest only eight students were the subject of the teacher's attention.

8. The resort was quiet. There was not much to do besides taking walks or the local movie house.

9. Early training in grammar, a concerned composition teacher, and being interested in books provide an excellent foundation for a writing career.

10. He said that we should either live according to our beliefs or that we were hypocrites and ought to face the fact.

11. As for myself, I have to admit that I am guilty of watching too much TV and not enough time reading.

12. The law serves a double purpose: first, it protects the people, and second, the capture of criminals.

13. I knew what I wanted from college. I expected to concentrate on my major, and all other "nonrelated" courses would be entirely incidental.

14. Because he had failed the course, and having no chance of graduating, he packed up and left.

15. Malamud creates characters that are real yet eccentric, and his recurring themes of suffering and poverty are presented with a twist of absurdity that tickles and also horrifies.

16. We can only conclude that either there are going to be drastic changes made by English teachers, or parents are just going to have to pull the plug on the tube.

17. Considering the low rent, the house is a bargain even though the roof leaks, some window panes are missing, and it is not what you would call modern plumbing.

18. The university grew so rapidly that it was short of facilities, instructors, and was faced with a discipline problem.

19. Besides basketball, field hockey, and tennis, she keeps in shape by running up three flights of stairs instead of using the elevator.

20. Everything in college was new to me—buying books, registering, spending only a few hours a day in class, people from backgrounds different from my own, classmates older than myself, no restrictions on my hours, no obligations to my family.

Rhetorical Uses

Parallelism can do its work casually and unobtrusively, keeping order in a sentence and making reading easier. It can also be planned and carried out so deliberately that it calls attention to itself and becomes a feature of style. If you don't use parallelism for stylistic effect, you're not making an error in grammar or syntax, but you're neglecting a resource that could help you achieve your purpose.

The careful patterning in this sentence by Samuel Johnson becomes clear when the matching structures are made visually parallel:

> The mind is exercised either by recollection
> or   inquiry;
> either something already learned is to be retrieved,
> or   something new   is to be examined.

When used deliberately and insistently, parallelism is one of the most common persuasive devices. Close to the end of an article about the absence of heroes in our society, Henry Fairlie deplores the "central lack of belief" which, he thinks, is largely responsible for our refusal to "make heroes":

> We no longer believe in the mission of our civilization. We once believed that it should explore, so that we could see Lindbergh as a hero, but we no longer do: Hillary was not a hero. We once believed that it should go to the bounds of the earth, but we do not believe in it going to the boundaries of the universe, and so we regard our astronauts as little more than acrobats. We once believed that it should teach and heal, so missionaries such as Livingstone and Schweitzer were heroes, but now when we read that some missionaries have been massacred we tend to think that they may have deserved it. We once believed in our science, so that in the Golden Age of Physics, men such as Einstein and Rutherford and Bohr were heroes, but now we do not believe in it, and out of all the scientific advances of recent years not one scientist's name is a household word. We used to think that our civilization should be guarded, and even at times that it should advance, so that our soldiers were heroes, but now we think of our generals only as stupid and knavish and war-hungry. We used to think that our civilization should act with great authority in the world, so that we found heroes among our politicians to speak for it, but now we regard our politicians only as petty and self-serving. We once believed that our writers and artists should speak of and to the common values of our civilization and be bearers of it, so that we found heroes among them even down to the 1930s, but now we think that our writers and artists should stay on the margins and entertain us.—Henry Fairlie, *Harper's*

If you look closely at every sentence after the first, you'll find that though they vary in the number and kinds of clauses they contain, their basic structure is the same. This parallelism both illustrates and emphasizes the author's thesis that our loss of faith in our civilization has led us to a rejection of heroes, as represented by leaders in a wide range of human endeavor:

We once believed	so that	but we no longer do
We once believed	but we do not	and so we regard
We once believed	so	but now
We once believed	so that	but now
We used to think	so that	but now
We used to believe	so that	but now
We once believed	so that	but now

Though you may never have occasion to build so much parallelism into a passage of your own, conscious use of parallelism can give your writing more impact, as in this passage by a student:

> My parents complain that I am *arrogant, thoughtless,* and *rebellious.* I tell them they misunderstand me. *What they see as arrogance* is my attempt to be a person in my own right. *What they see as thoughtlessness* is usually just forgetfulness. *What they see as rebelliousness* is a drive to be independent.

In each of her parallel concluding sentences, the student defends herself against what she considers her parents' misinterpretations of her conduct. The same opening for three sentences in a row is justified because each has the same purpose.

When the parts of a sentence are matched to a noticeable extent in grammatical form and even in vocabulary, as in the sentence by Samuel Johnson on page 231 or in this one by Abraham Lincoln, the sentence is said to be *balanced:*

> The world will little note nor long remember what we say here
> but
> it   can never forget   what they did here.

Grammatically, the balanced sentence is made up of parallel structures. Rhetorically, the parallelism points up the similarity or the opposition of ideas. Balance can match a positive statement with a negative one, an abstract statement with a concrete expression of the same idea. You can use it, as it's used here, to give an assertion a forthright, authoritative tone:

> They have been educated to achieve success; few of them have been educated to exercise power. —Walter Lippmann, *A Preface to Morals*

In formal contexts, parallelism may be sustained and deliberate. (Balanced sentences are a hallmark of formal prose and particularly of oratory.) In informal contexts, where the series is just as common as in formal contexts—though the structures are usually not so elaborate—the writer may give a sentence a twist that signals to the reader that he's *not* working at matching word with word or phrase with phrase. Here, for example, the writer achieves economy and rhythm with a fast-moving series but rejects a dramatic climax with the closing, informal "whatever":

> He carried his faith into the country like baggage and hung onto it, with that fierce urgent immigrant's grip, through the sweatshops, through the Crash, through the wars, the political scandals, the Coughlins, the Ku Klux Klanners, the lynchings, whatever. —Martha Weinman Lear, *New York Times Magazine*

As usual, then, context counts. Though sustained parallelism within and between sentences is appropriate in writing situations that call for gravity, for judiciousness, for carefully thought-out pronouncements, and for stirring emotional pleas, in more relaxed situations parallelism can be treated more casually:

> What made the house a home was the runaround porch, a screen that stuck or slammed, a wire basket of dead ferns, a swing that scuffed the paint off the clapboards, a rail to lean on when you threw up, a stoop to sit on when you watered the grass.—Wright Morris, *God's Country and My People*

There's enough parallelism here to hold the sentence together and give it an easy, casual rhythm but not so much that it becomes monotonous or seems contrived. (If you try attaching a *that* clause to each of the nouns after "was"—"porch," "screen," "basket," "swing," "rail," "stoop"— you'll see how stiff and affected parallelism can make everyday material sound.) Today's writers often feel no need to press parallelism to the point of exact symmetry:

> Warsaw to many who arrive from Paris is drab and joyless; to those who arrive from Moscow it is colorful, joyous, swinging.—David Halberstam, *Harper's*

Would the sentence be any better if "drab and joyless" had been matched with "colorful and joyous"?

Making a fetish of parallelism will hurt any style. Regardless of context, the parallelism in the following passage falls flat:

> Although some of the graduating seniors frowned, awed by the solemnity of the occasion; although some beamed, responsive to the praise heaped upon them; although some grinned, anticipating the end of deadlines, requirements, and examinations, there was a difference between them and their parents in the audience.

The parallelism of the three introductory clauses builds up the reader's expectations, but the writer fails to deliver. The independent clause makes all the careful structuring that precedes it seem pointless.

Use parallelism for clarity. Use it for rhetorical effect when the ideas you're expressing justify the emphasis parallelism gives. But don't construct a series of parallel clauses when what you have to say can be expressed more simply and casually. If you do, the elaborate structure will only emphasize the contrast between form and content.

For Writing

A good way to broaden your range of sentence patterns is to imitate patterns that occur in other writers' prose. Using whatever details and ideas you wish, build three sentences on the model of each of the following:

1.   The scientist or artist takes two facts or experiences which are separate; he finds in them a likeness which has not been seen before; and he creates a unity by showing the likeness.—J. Bronowski, *Science and Human Values*

2.   Around the buoys and on the open sea, in match races and fleet races, in boats large and small, they have both been consistent front-runners, progressing ever upward, sometimes on collision courses, sometimes on diverging ones.—Coles Phinizy, *Sports Illustrated*

3.   He developed airports and encouraged rural electrification and was probably the most successful Health Minister Ireland has had, commissioning new hospitals, psychiatric hostels, and old people's homes, encouraging home-help schemes for the aged, increasing the number of district nursing posts, establishing area health boards, and giving medical card holders (generally the less well off) the right to choose their doctors, thereby removing an element of social discrimination.—Anthony Bailey, *Acts of Union*

Composing Cumulative Sentences

The fully balanced sentence represents sentence form at its most symmetrical. Two other patterns—the cumulative sentence and the periodic sentence—may both make good use of parallelism, but they contrast sharply with the balanced sentence and with each other.

The *cumulative,* or loose, sentence opens with a base structure—usually a short independent clause—and then adds modifiers:

> Each *palazzo* was like a secret, hard to find in the maze of canals, unreachable except by gondola, presenting to the outside world a facade of crumbling stone, stained marble and decay which concealed astonishing rooms that seem to have been kept in darkness for centuries, hidden behind the shutters, draperies and blinds that covered every window.—Michael Korda, *Charmed Lives*

Here the base structure consists of the first six words. It's followed by modifiers of various kinds, each adding details. Because the meaning is in some sense complete at the end of the base structure, the sentence would remain coherent if it were cut off at various points along the way—after "secret," for instance, or after "canals" or "gondola" or "stone" or "decay" or "rooms" or "centuries" or "shutters." And possibly the sentence could go on, adding modifiers to "window."

When you use cumulative sentences in description and narration, your modifiers will typically add details. If you use the pattern in exposition or argument, your modifiers will probably serve to interpret, illustrate, or qualify your main assertion.

Because it follows the normal order of speech—main statement first, then qualifications and particulars—the cumulative sentence can give the impression of being natural and spontaneous, of following the movement of the writer's eye or the workings of his mind. But writing a good cumulative sentence calls for control over both content and structure. If your modifiers don't strengthen your original assertion, if they wander away from it, if they get into a tangle, you've written a bad sentence. See how this one drifts, as detail is added to detail:

> It was a new experience for us, waking before sunrise, the wind quiet then, the countryside still except for the first bird calls, the blackbirds whistling in the bushes, the pale light streaking the windows on the east side of the cabin, facing the barn, empty now, unused for years, its doors nailed shut to keep out tramps, waiting for the day to begin.

When modifiers are stacked the way these are, their grammatical relations must be clear. The sentence drifts grammatically with its final verbal phrase, "waiting for the day to begin," which belongs just after "waking before sunrise." In any position after that, the phrase dangles.

In brief, then, you can achieve an impression of ease and flexibility with the cumulative sentence, but you must arrange your modifiers carefully to keep your meaning clear.

Shaping Periodic Sentences

Because its base structure stands first, the cumulative sentence can be cut off after the initial assertion (and often at several points beyond that) and still be intelligible. Because its base structure stands last, the *periodic* sentence is intelligible only when it's complete, or very nearly so. The reader has to hold the elements of a periodic sentence in mind as he goes along, instead of getting the central message and then adding to it, detail by detail, as he does with the typical cumulative sentence.

In a simple example, this is no great burden:

> Tired, cold, and hungry, and discouraged by my failure to find a job, I crawled into bed.

In a long sentence the elements must be related to each other so that the reader can easily keep them in mind as he moves toward the main assertion:

> Through all the decades since Chaplin's arrival in Hollywood in the early years of motion-picture history; through all the changes and developments that have taken place in the industry with the advent of sound, color, new cameras, new dollies, the wide screen, stereophonic sound, big studios, no studios, big budgets, little budgets, big and rich producers, little and poor producers, big-star pictures, no-star pictures, big agents, the bankers in the background, the tie-ins with books, the tie-ins with records; through the rise of the director, the rise of the movie writer, the rise of movie-theory jargon, the rise of intellectuals as custodians of the art of "film," the rise of college courses in "film," the rise

of the lecture circuit on "film," the rise in the power of the stars, and the superpower of the superstars; through the strain to compete with television, the strain to cooperate with television; and through the countless technological advances—through everything, Charlie Chaplin has persisted as a gigantic, incomparable figure.—Lillian Ross, *New Yorker*

Largely through her skillful use of parallelism, Ross keeps her very long sentence under control. It's held together by the series of six *through* phrases, with "through everything" drawing the preceding five into the single independent clause. Four of the six *through* phrases contain series; some contain series of series.

A periodic sentence achieves its effect by withholding its full meaning until its last words; and as the Ross example shows, building a long one can be a tour de force, with the reader kept in suspense as to how both structure and meaning are going to come out. Unless there's a good reason for withholding the full meaning (unquestionably, Ross's sentence ends up impressing the reader with how very long Charlie Chaplin persisted), a long, complicated periodic sentence may seem decidedly artificial. And unless parallelism provides order among the elements piled up before the final clause, both sense and grammar become tangled.

Cumulative and periodic sentences sometimes offer alternative ways of expressing the same idea. As you revise a paper, you may decide to make a loose sentence periodic so that it will be more emphatic, or you may make a periodic sentence cumulative so that your writing will have a less formal, more open style. Ordinarily it's the long cumulative sentence or the long periodic sentence that calls attention to itself; and when any sentence calls attention to itself, it should do so for the right reason—because its form not only fits but strengthens the idea it expresses.

The study of good cumulative sentences and good periodic sentences suggests one simple, practical rule: Keep your main assertion short and direct. Whether you place your modifiers early or late or spread them through the sentence, your writing will be clearer if your main assertions—your action statements—are short clauses rather than long ones.

For Writing

Compose cumulative and periodic sentences according to the instructions.
1. Begin a cumulative sentence with "This will be your dream vacation," adding three or more details.
2. Write a periodic sentence ending with "the concert ended" or "the game was over."
3. Begin a periodic sentence with "Although most of my friends long to have lots of money."

4. Begin a cumulative sentence with "College courses are demanding."

5. Begin a cumulative sentence with "The storm broke."

6. End a periodic sentence with "the storm broke."

Imitating Sentence Patterns

Analyzing sentence patterns shows you how many choices you have. Imitating the patterns makes you feel at home with the wide range of options that you might otherwise never try out. In this chapter you've been asked to build sentences that follow one pattern or another. Continue the practice on your own. Choose any sentence that's put together in a way that pleases or puzzles you. Then, using your own content, compose a sentence that matches it in structure. Move on to two or more sentences, and imitate not only their structures but the ways they're linked. Finally, imitate a complete paragraph. This book is full of useful ones for the purpose. Or pick a paragraph from a book you're reading for another course or for your own enjoyment.

Below, a paragraph from Chapter 2 of *Walden* by Henry David Thoreau is followed by imitations written by three students. Examine the imitations to see how faithful they are to the original, and then try one of your own.

I went to the woods because I wished to live deliberately, to front only the essential facts of life, and see if I could not learn what it had to teach, and not, when I came to die, discover that I had not lived. I did not wish to live what was not life, living is so dear; nor did I wish to practice resignation, unless it was quite necessary. I wanted to live deep and suck out all the marrow of life, to live so sturdily and Spartan-like as to put to rout all that was not life, to cut a broad swath and shave close, to drive life into a corner, and reduce it to its lowest terms, and, if it proved to be mean, why then to get the whole and genuine meanness of it, and publish its meanness to the world; or if it were sublime, to know it by experience, and be able to give a true account of it in my next excursion. For most men, it appears to me, are in a strange uncertainty about it, whether it is of the devil or of God, and have *somewhat hastily* concluded that it is the chief end of man here to "glorify God and enjoy him forever."

Why I Kept On Dancing

I finished the Dance Marathon because I had resolved to do so previously, to face the task with determination and strength, and see if I could not prove I have what it takes to endure, and not, when I would be revived three days later, discover that I had not completed this forty-eight-hour test of my will power. I did not wish to endure what was not important to me, a goal should be worthwhile; nor did I wish to practice masochism but pain was part of the contract.

I wanted to dance in this marathon and grab everything I could from it, to program my plan of attack so carefully and conservatively as to prove wrong all who did not believe in me, to start out steady and dance slow, to let others tire themselves out, and finish with a flourish, and if it proved to be painful, experience the torturous mind-twisting agony of it, for this was an integral part of the marathon, and if it was worth the pain, to know it from dancing this year, and perhaps be able to endure forty-eight more hours of "stayin' alive" next year.

Why I Took This Course

I took this course because I wished to write deliberately, to use only essential words and phrases, and see if I could not learn to express myself better, and not, when I came to graduate, discover that I could not write well. I did not want to fail the course, my grade point average is so dear; nor did I wish to drop the course, unless it was quite necessary. I longed to write brilliantly and turn out the best possible essays, to write so perfectly as to put an end to all of the corrections on my papers, to cut out unnecessary words and produce clear prose, to try to bring any writing ability I possessed into the open, and expose it to criticism, and, if I proved to be a poor writer, why then at least I would have tried, and I would have no misconceptions about my skills, and if my writing were satisfactory, to gain confidence through my course experience, and be able to give an even better account of myself in my next English class. But many members of the class, it appears to me, are in a strange uncertainty about the course and its goals, whether it has been of benefit to them or not, and have *somewhat hastily* concluded that the chief purpose of the course is to "glorify Thoreau and enjoy him forever, whether you like it or not!"

What I Grew and Why I Grew It

I cultivated my beard to assert my independence, to show my family and friends that not only was I master of my own cheeks and chin, but of my life as well, and not, as they had thought, merely to enhance my appearance by natural cosmetic. I did not wish to hide my natural features, for I usually don't fret about things that aren't my fault or cannot be effectively changed; nor did I wish to sow the seeds of family discord for a few paltry hairs. I wanted to say to my parents at all times without having to talk incessantly, that I would not necessarily be molded by commonly held notions of respectability, that I would not necessarily marry respectably, if it all, get a respectable job, or live the proper life; but if I did, all would know that it was by my own hand, of my own mind, and for my own reasons; and if I didn't, it would also be of my own choice and no reflection on them. I would not require nor owe apologies. Few men and fewer women know why they grow their beards; or if they know, they grow them for the wrong reasons: appearance, rebellion, prospective employment in a circus, or just a lack of concern for looks and hygiene. My beard was a subtle declaration that was either misinterpreted or ignored altogether. Now my mustache is another story.

Punctuating Sentences:
Convention and Choice

Punctuation marks separate sentences and indicate the relationships of words and word groups within sentences, joining them, separating them, or setting them off. Properly used, punctuation controls and emphasizes meaning. Misused, it distorts meaning and confuses the reader. Though accurate punctuation can't redeem a mixed-up sentence—one that requires rewriting—it may save a weak sentence from ambiguity, and it can make the meaning of a complicated sentence precise and clear.

Some punctuation marks are substitutes for, or reminders of, elements in speech for which we have no written equivalents—a pause, for example, or a raising or lowering of the voice's pitch. But though we should listen to what we're writing and punctuating, the correspondence between punctuation and features of speech is by no means complete. We can't always hear the difference between a pair of commas and a pair of dashes, nor can we hear the apostrophe in an apostrophe-*s* like "Bill's." Some uses of punctuation marks must be learned as arbitrary conventions—rules for writing that have become established through practice.

The conventions governing the apostrophe and such matters of mechanics as capital letters are so well established that every careful writer observes them. But you still have a considerable range of choice. In deciding whether to use a particular mark of punctuation, you may be guided by the emphasis, tone, and movement in a sentence or perhaps by the intention of a whole paragraph. Some uses of punctuation marks are almost entirely stylistic. For example, when either a comma or a semicolon can be used before the co-ordinating conjunction in a compound sentence, the semicolon is the more formal choice:

> He deplores the Easter Rising as willful and unnecessary; [a comma would be equally correct] but in deploring it he sounds as if he thought that an Irishman in, say, 1914 should have been content to find himself represented by the squires of the Irish National Party.—Denis Donoghue, *New York Review of Books*

Besides making specific choices in specific contexts, you can choose between two styles of punctuation—open and close. Close punctuation puts a comma before the conjunction in every compound sentence and a comma after an introductory clause or phrase. Open punctuation does not, except to prevent misreading. Close punctuation typically encloses interrupters like *however, of course, too.* Open punctuation seldom sets off *too,* often leaves *of course* unpunctuated, and may omit commas around other interrupters.

Although punctuation in general is more open than it was a generation ago, good writers adjust their punctuation to their subject matter and to their audience. The difficult concept probably won't be expressed in such elaborate, heavily punctuated sentences as it would have been in 1900, but it still may call for complicated sentence patterns with supporting punctuation. Casual general-to-informal writing can usually get by with a minimum of punctuation, but the writer needs to keep his audience in mind. A sophisticated reader skims such writing rapidly, and if a lack of punctuation invites even momentary confusion, he may quit rapidly, too. An unsophisticated reader needs the help that conventional punctuation can provide.

In punctuating as in writing generally, the claims of your readers should come first. Use punctuation marks to help readers understand what you have to say. Beyond that, a good rule of thumb is to use no more punctuation than *current* convention calls for. Punctuation marks that are too numerous or too heavy—as colons and semicolons may be in a relaxed style—call attention to themselves just as words that are too heavy or too pretentious do. But limiting yourself to a subsistence budget of commas and periods is no more essential to good writing than sticking to one- and two-syllable words.

Self-Test

This self-test is a review of trouble spots in grammar and sentence structure. In some of the items a plural subject may have a singular verb; the reference of a pronoun may be unclear; a modifier may be placed so that it doesn't seem to be related to the word it's meant to modify or may be punctuated so that the intended meaning doesn't come through; and so on. A "sentence" may be less than a sentence, or it may be two sentences inaccurately punctuated. Revise the unsatisfactory items to make them satisfactory in college writing. Then see the comments on pp. 242-43 and, when necessary, read the articles in *Index to English* that are referred to there.

1. Why don't people give their pets warm food before they leave for work on these cold mornings?

2. Reaching sixteen, my parents agreed to let me drive.

3. A big effort is put forth to meet people most of the students are ready to be friends.

4. The major fault of the black powder were the dense clouds of smoke it generated.

5. The problem of doing all the assignments and meeting all the deadlines make freshman year especially difficult.

6. Since sponges are capable of consuming food, making cells, and reproducing its own kind, they are living organisms.

7. She was pleased to be offered a salary higher than a trainee.

8. Women swimmers are helped not only by their body fat, which gives them buoyancy, but their narrow shoulders make it easier for them to cut through the water.

9. Many people take pills without a doctor's prescription. This is unwise.

They begin by taking habit-forming sedatives only when they cannot sleep or when they are tense. But it is not long before they can't do without them, and they increase the dose until all it does is make them worse.

10. The only correct standard of English is that which is appropriate to the occasion and accepted by the people with whom you are.

11. He asked me who I thought would win the election.

12. From the attic window of our home, one can command a view of our entire neighborhood. Situated in the northeast corner of this quiet suburb, it is a perfect spot from which to observe the community.

13. Hanging out on the corner all the time, it was not long before I got into trouble.

14. They think they should get some credit because they done the best they could.

15. Many childless couples want to adopt babies, they must proceed with great caution.

16. These two stories deal with Americans in Europe who suffer conflicts of love and questioning of the standards of European society.

17. Things have changed considerable since the seventies.

18. The Democratic organization, as many other organizations, are concerned about young people's lack of interest in politics.

19. Residents object to the cutting down of trees which the officials say is necessary.

20. Having worked all day in the hot sun, their favorite way of spending the evening was lying around watching TV.

21. If you get in there and hustle, on the other hand, and if, while you're doing that, without losing your concentration, and with your goal clearly in mind, as it should be at all times in a situation like this one.

22. They invited my roommate and I for the next weekend, but we decided it would be safer to refuse.

23. In the final minutes of the trial, he clenched his fist and shouted. Actions that showed how concerned he was for the welfare of his children.

24. If the mixture tastes bitterly, dump it down the sink. You made a mistake in your measurements.

25. Even though she drunk more than I did, she was full of pep the next morning.

26. When he left the building he was so tired that he was thankful he brought his bike to ride home on.

27. It has always been felt by me and by my friends that to study the subject of physics is to waste a lot of time on material which will soon be outdated.

28. His choice of audience could not have been better selected.

29. He seemed to think that the most promising fuel for the future was solar energy, and which was cleaner, safer, and more dependable than other energy sources.

30. Preparing the equipment for the experiments takes a long time, and another course I am taking is Business Administration.

Comments on Self-Test

1. Change "before they leave" to "before leaving" to avoid any suggestion that the pets are employed. See **Reference of pronouns 1a**.

2. Change "Reaching" to "When I reached." See **Dangling modifiers**.

3. Put a period after "people" and begin "most" with a capital letter. See **Fused sentence**.

4. Change "were" to "was." See **Agreement 1a**.

5. Change "make" to "makes." See **Agreement 1a**.

6. Change "its" to "their." See **Agreement 2**.

7. Change "trainee" to "trainee's." See **Comparison of adjectives and adverbs 2**.

8. For parallelism, change to "but by their narrow shoulders, which make it easier for them to cut through the water." See **Parallelism and style 1**.

9. A clutter of pronouns. "This" in the second sentence isn't ambiguous, but for economy that sentence might well be embedded in the first one: "Many people unwisely. . . ." Similarly, though the reader can sort out the *them*s, the chore should be made less difficult. The shift from "cannot" to "can't" is a needless inconsistency. "All it does" in the last sentence brings the vagueness and fuzziness to a climax. A general rewrite is needed. See **Reference of pronouns 1d, 2, 4**.

10. Ending with a preposition ("the people you are with") would make the sentence less awkward. Changing "The only correct standard of English" to "Good English" would reduce the wordiness. See **Prepositions and style 4; Wordiness**.

11. OK. If you changed it, better see **who, whom**.

12. Loose. "It" refers to "attic window," but it's the house that's situated; and so forth. One revision would reverse the sentence order: "Situated in the northeast corner of this quiet suburb, our house is a perfect spot. . . . From the attic window I [*or* you] can. . . ." Or: "Our house is situated. . . . The attic window gives a view. . . ." See **Reference of pronouns 3; Point of view 1; one**.

13. Though there's no real problem here, the conservative reader would be troubled by "it was not long before" coming between the modifier "Hanging out on the corner all the time" and "I." Such a reader would prefer "Hanging out on the corner all the time, I soon got into trouble." See **Dangling modifiers**.

14. Change "done" to "did." See list in **Principal parts of Verbs**.

15. Put a period after "babies" and begin "they" with a capital letter. See **Comma splice 1**.

16. Make the coordinate items grammatically similar: ". . . who suffer conflicts of love and who question the standards of European society." See **Shifted constructions**.

17. Change "considerable" to "considerably." See **Adverbs and style 1a.**

18. Change "as" to "like" and "are" to "is." See **like, as; Agreement 1a.**

19. Change to: ". . . trees, but [*or* though] the officials say it is necessary." At the very least, put a comma between "trees" and "which." See **Reference of pronouns 2; Restrictive and nonrestrictive modifiers 2.**

20. Although this type of dangling modifier, in which the word the writer means to modify is in the possessive, now appears fairly often in print, conservative stylists would insist on making the participle modify "they," not "their favorite way," and that would call for rewriting. See **Dangling modifiers.**

21. If you can complete this unfinished sentence, good for you. One alternative would be to cut it back to "Get in there and hustle, and while you're doing that, keep your goal clearly in mind." See **Fragment.**

22. Change "I" to "me." See **Case 2a; Hypercorrectness.**

23. Replace the period after "shouted" with a comma and begin "Actions" with a small letter. See **Fragment.**

24. Change "bitterly" to "bitter." See **Predicate adjectives.**

25. Change "drunk" to "drank." See list in **Principal parts of verbs.**

26. Change "brought" to "had brought." See **Tense 2.**

27. Get rid of the weak opener and the unnecessary words: "My friends and I have always felt that to study physics. . . ." See **Passive voice 1; Wordiness 1.**

28. Delete "selected." See **Repetition 2.**

29. Delete the "and" before "which." See **Subordination 2.**

30. The two statements don't belong in the same sentence. See **Coordination 1.**

8

Choosing Words

In Chapter One we spoke of the need to fit the language in a paper to the rhetorical situation. Now we turn to the question of how to find the right words. Though at times in our discussion we'll treat words in isolation, keep in mind that the most important qualities and powers of words come alive only *in context*—the immediate context of the sentence, the larger context of the paper, and the still larger context of the rhetorical situation.

As we've said, your prime objective in writing should be to express your ideas as clearly and directly as possible. Choosing words that will help you achieve that objective calls for careful attention to differences among words of roughly the same meaning.

Some problems in choosing words stem from the difference between your recognition vocabulary, the words you understand when you read them or hear them, and your active vocabulary, the words you speak and write with confidence and assurance. When a word is in your recognition vocabulary but not in your active vocabulary, it may come out sounding not quite right—"the dominating cause," for instance, instead of "the dominant cause." Or it may come out sounding quite wrong—"dominant parents" instead of "domineering parents," or "the element of mysticism" when you intend "the element of mystery," or (as in a campus newspaper story) "the utmost in human suffrage" instead of "the utmost in human suffering." To increase your control of these borderline words—to keep words moving from your recognition vocabulary into your active vocabulary—listen, read (and read and read), and get into the habit of using dictionaries. Own a good dictionary, and open it often.

Using Dictionaries

There's no such thing as *the* dictionary, one that can be quoted to settle every question about words. But there's a real difference between a dictionary that's newly compiled or that's kept up to date and a dictionary that's patched together from older dictionaries. The following dictionaries, appropriate for the personal libraries of college students, are listed alphabetically: *The American Heritage Dictionary of the English Language* (Houghton), *Funk & Wagnalls Standard College Dictionary* (Funk), *The Random House College Dictionary* (Random), *Webster's New Collegiate Dictionary* (Merriam), *Webster's New World Dictionary of the American Language* (Collins and World). When you buy a dictionary, get the newest edition. And don't ever choose a dictionary simply because it has "Webster's" in its title. While the two in the preceding list will serve your needs, some others won't. "College" and "text" editions are designed especially for students.

Entries

To make good use of your dictionary, first read the introductory material. Lexicographers—dictionary makers—have to resort to space-saving devices wherever possible. The shortcuts they have used, as well as their general policies and purposes, will be explained in the front matter of the dictionary.

After you've read the introductory sections and acquainted yourself with the arrangement of material, read a page or two of consecutive entries. Then look up a few words that you know and a few that you've heard or seen but aren't certain about. Try pronouncing some words, familiar and unfamiliar, to see how the pronunciation key works. Work through some entries carefully. In most dictionaries you'll find the following information:

Spelling and Division of Words

A word is entered in a dictionary under its most common spelling. When more than one spelling is given, both are in good use: *esthetic, aesthetic; judgment, judgement.* The entry shows where a word should be hyphenated at the end of a line, as in *mor•ti•fi•ca•tion, dis•par•ag•ing•ly.*

Pronunciation

Dictionaries respell words in specially marked letters to show their pronunciation. The key to the sounds represented by the symbols is usually printed at the bottom of the page and further explained in a discussion of pronunciation in the front matter. If more than one pronunciation is given without qualification, as in the following example, each is acceptable:

> **bo·vine** (bō′vīn, -vin, -vēn), *adj.* **1.** of the ox family, *Bovidae.* **2.** oxlike; cowlike. **3.** stolid; dull. —*n.* **4.** a bovine animal. [< LL *bovīn(us)* of, pertaining to oxen or cows = L *bov-* (s. of *bōs* ox) + *-īnus* -INE¹] —**bo′vine·ly,** *adv.* —**bo·vin·i·ty** (bō vin′i tē), *n.*
>
> From *Random House College Dictionary*, Revised Edition. Copyright © 1975, 1980 by Random House, Inc. Reprinted by permission.

Linguistic Information

A dictionary entry indicates the part or parts of speech, the transitive or intransitive use of a verb, the principal parts of irregular verbs, plurals of irregular nouns, and any other distinctive form a word may take. An entry may also give the history of the word—its etymology. Sometimes this is merely a statement of the language from which the word came into English; sometimes, using such abbreviations as *L* for Latin and *OE* for Old English, it traces a chain of sources and identifies words in other languages that are related to it, as here:

> **sil·ly** \\'sil-ē\ *adj* **sil·li·er; -est** [ME *sely, silly* happy, innocent, pitiable, feeble, fr. (assumed) OE *sǣlig,* fr. OE *sǣl* happiness; akin to OHG *sālig* happy, L *solari* to console, Gk *hilaros* cheerful] **1** *archaic* : HELPLESS, WEAK **2 a** : RUSTIC, PLAIN **b** *obs* : lowly in station : HUMBLE **3 a** : weak in intellect : FOOLISH **b** : exhibiting or indicative of a lack of common sense or sound judgment <a very ~ mistake> **c** : TRIFLING, FRIVOLOUS **4** : being stunned or dazed <scared ~> <knocked me ~> *syn* see SIMPLE — **sil·li·ly** \\'sil-ə-lē\ *adv* — **sil·li·ness** \\'sil-ē-nəs\ *n* — **silly** *n or adv*

From *Webster's New Collegiate Dictionary.* © 1981 by G. & C. Merriam Company, Publishers of the Merriam-Webster Dictionaries. Reprinted by permission.

Definitions

The definitions of words take up most of the space in a dictionary. When you check an entry to find out what a word means or to sharpen your understanding of a word that's only in your recognition vocabulary, keep three points in mind. First, a dictionary doesn't authorize or forbid a particular sense of a word but records the various senses in which people use the word. It reports facts about words, including perhaps the fact that a word is acquiring a new sense or that its customary sense is being altered. Second, the purpose of the definition, together with any examples or illustrations, is to help you understand what, in the world of objects and ideas, the word refers to—its *denotation*. Third, as we shall see later, a dictionary definition can barely hint at the associations or overtones a word has—its *connotations*. Since these overtones are what can make a word just right in one context but not in another, it's unwise to use a word solely on the basis of what you learn about it from a dictionary. Before using it, you should hear it or read it in various contexts and so know it in part through experience.

The order in which most dictionaries offer definitions of a word is either oldest meaning first or oldest last. A third form of entry begins with the "central" meaning:

> **style** (stīl) *n.* **1.** The way in which something is said or done, as distinguished from its substance. **2.** The combination of distinctive features of literary or artistic expression, execution, or performance characterizing a particular person, people, school, or era. **3.** Sort; kind; type: *a style of furniture.* **4.** A quality of imagination and individuality expressed in one's actions and tastes. **5. a.** A comfortable and elegant mode of existence: *living in style.* **b.** A particular mode of living: *the style of a gentleman.* **6. a.** The fashion of the moment, especially of dress; vogue: *out of* (or *in*) *style.* **b.** A particular fashion. **7.** A customary manner of presenting printed material, including usage, punctuation, spelling, typography, and arrangement. **8.** *Rare.* A name, title, or descriptive term. **9.** A slender, pointed writing instrument used by the ancients on wax tablets. **10.** An implement used for etching or engraving. **11.** The needle of a phonograph. **12.** The gnomon of a sundial. **13.** *Botany.* The usually slender part of a pistil, rising from the ovary and tipped by the stigma. **14.** *Zoology.* Any slender, tubular, or bristlelike process. **15.** *Obsolete.* A pen. **16.** A surgical probing instrument; stylet. —See Synonyms at **fashion.** —*tr.v.* **styled, styling, styles. 1.** To call or name; designate: *"whatever is mine, you may style, and think, yours"* (Sterne). **2.** To make consistent with rules of style. **3.** To design; give style to: *style hair.* [Middle English, from Old French, from Latin *stilus†,* writing instrument, style.] —**styl′er** *n.*

© 1980 by Houghton Mifflin Company. Reprinted by permission from *The American Heritage Dictionary of the English Language.*

The front matter of your dictionary will tell you which order is followed in the entries.

Labels

Words that are unlabeled in a dictionary are assumed to belong to the general vocabulary; other words, or senses of words, may be labeled *dialectal, obsolete, archaic, foreign, informal, colloquial, slang, British,* or *United States* or may be referred to some field of activity—*medicine, aeronautics, law, astronomy, baseball, printing, electronics, philosophy.* (Labels may be abbreviated—*dial., colloq., U.S., aeron.,* etc.) Subject labels indicate that a word is restricted to one field or has a special meaning in that field, as in the following example:

---

push·er (-ər) *n.* **1.** a person or thing that pushes **2.** an airplane with its propeller or propellers mounted behind the engine: also **pusher airplane** ☆**3.** [Slang] a person who sells drugs, esp. narcotics, illegally

From *Webster's New World Dictionary,* Second College Edition. Copyright © 1980 by Simon & Schuster, Inc. Reprinted with permission.

Because labels can be only rough guides to usage, you need to supplement the advice they offer with your own judgment of the appropriateness of a word in a particular rhetorical situation. While the labels *nonstandard, substandard, illiterate,* and *vulgar* can be taken as fair warning that the words or word forms would not normally be appropriate in college writing, you'll sometimes find that the dictionary editors' point of view is out-of-date. Some words marked *dial.* or *colloq.* or *slang* may fit perfectly well not only in informal writing but also in general styles. On the other hand, many words that carry no label are rarely used (*pursy, lucubration*) and would be out of place in most writing.

The labels themselves are descriptive. *Colloq.,* for example, simply means that the word is characteristic of ordinary conversation and of general rather than formal writing, though some readers persist in interpreting it as condemning the words or word forms it's attached to. Because dictionaries vary in the labels they use and in the amount of labeling they do, you'll often want to consult several when you're trying to determine the status of a word.

Besides providing usage notes, *The American Heritage Dictionary* reports the preferences of a usage panel. As a rule, the recommendations represent what this text would call formal choices.

Synonyms

Most dictionaries gather words that are used in similar senses into a group and show in what ways the words are alike and in what ways different, as here, under *SYN:*

> **ex·clude** (iks klo͞od′) *vt.* **-clud′ed, -clud′ing** [ME. *excluden* < L. *excludere* < *ex-*, out + *claudere*, CLOSE²] **1.** to refuse to admit, consider, include, etc.; shut out; keep from entering, happening, or being; reject; bar **2.** to put out; force out; expel —**ex·clud′a·ble** *adj.* —**ex·clud′er** *n.*
> **SYN.**—**exclude** implies a keeping out or prohibiting of that which is not yet in [to *exclude* someone from membership]; **debar** connotes the existence of some barrier, as legal authority or force, which excludes someone from a privilege, right, etc. [to *debar* certain groups from voting]; **disbar** refers only to the expulsion of a lawyer from the group of those who are permitted to practice law; **eliminate** implies the removal of that which is already in, usually connoting its undesirability or irrelevancy [to *eliminate* waste products]; **suspend** refers to the removal, usually temporary, of someone from some organization, institution, etc., as for the infraction of some rule [to *suspend* a student from school]
> —**ANT.** admit, include
>
> From *Webster's New World Dictionary*, Second College Edition. Copyright © 1980 by Simon & Schuster, Inc. Reprinted with permission.

Unabridged and Specialized Dictionaries

For reading and writing in special fields, you'll need to supplement your desk dictionary.

Unabridged Dictionaries

The most complete dictionaries of present-day English are called unabridged, meaning that they are not selections from larger works as, in effect, many desk dictionaries are. The three most widely used American unabridged dictionaries are *Funk & Wagnalls New Standard Dictionary of the English Language* (Funk), the unabridged edition of *The Random House Dictionary of the English Language,* and *Webster's Third New International Dictionary of the English Language* (Merriam).

Historical Dictionaries

The twelve-volume *Oxford English Dictionary* is the great storehouse of information about English words. It traces the various forms of each word and its various senses, with dates of their first recorded appearances and quotations from writers to illustrate each sense. Supplements give material on new words and evidence on earlier words not found in the original work. The complete work is also available in the two-volume *Compact Edition.*

The Dictionary of American English, four volumes on the same plan as the *OED,* is especially useful in reading American literature, for it gives the histories of words as they have been used in the United States. An entry begins with the first use of the word by an American writer and continues, with quotations, to 1900. The more recent *Dictionary of Americanisms* presents only those words and word meanings that have entered the language in this country.

Dictionaries in Special Subjects

For the vocabularies of special fields, you can find dictionaries in education, law, business, medicine, philosophy, psychology, sociology, economics, mathematics, and so on.

For Discussion and Writing

1. Examine your dictionary and write out answers to these questions: What is the title, the date of original copyright (on the back of the title page), the date of the latest copyright? Who is the publisher? Do the editors say what they believe the function of a dictionary is? What sections precede and follow the main body of your dictionary? Approximately how many entries does it have? Is there a supplement of new words? Where are biographical and geographical names listed? Where is the key that explains the symbols used in giving pronunciations? When several definitions of a word are given, in what order do they appear—in historical order, in order of frequency, or in some other order? What labels does your dictionary use, and what does each label mean? Are profanity and obscenity labeled?

2. Look up the following words to see what usage labels, if any, your dictionary applies. Then examine other desk dictionaries to see what labels they apply. How do you account for differences?

bobby	deadhead	honky-tonk	old-timer	T formation
boss	death duty	hush puppy	pester	turn on
clepe	dinkum	joint	snide	whiz
clime	fain	laid back	snoot	yare

3. Does your dictionary include synonyms and antonyms? If so, where in the entry are they placed? Does your dictionary discriminate among synonyms, explaining the differences between words that have similar meanings? Does it help you distinguish among *argue, dispute,* and *contend*? Does it help you decide in what situations you would use *done in, tired,* and *fatigued*?

4. Would your dictionary help a writer who was trying to make a choice between each pair of words in parentheses? If not, why not? Select what you consider to be the better choice and be prepared to defend it.

He had the (temerity, timidity) to suggest that he alone could solve the (issue, problem). As it turned out, his solution was (ingenious, ingenuous) but showed no (perceptive, perceptible) difference from one that had (failed, faltered) last year. What he was counting on was the (affect, effect) of the special appeal he directed to the (new, novice) voters—those who had just turned eighteen.

Are the choices offered by these seven pairs all of the same kind? If not, how do they differ?

5. Use the word *dog* with a different meaning in each of six or more sentences. Do the same with *bug, run, horse,* or *cast.*

6. Although *lucid* means "clear" in such contexts as "lucid instructions" and "a lucid speaker," we don't talk about "a lucid liquid" or "a lucid day." We say "humid day" but not "humid towel." Explain why a dictionary would or would not help a person who had not grown up speaking English to avoid lapses like "lucid day" and "humid towel."

7. Choose the word in parentheses that's most closely synonymous with the italicized word. Then test your answer by checking with your dictionary. Does it permit you to say with confidence that you've made the best choice?

    a. The speaker's remark was entirely *apposite* (foolish, fitting, irrelevant, unintelligible, to the point).

    b. The date of the ceremony was left *tentative* (indefinite, undecided, provisional, uncertain, contingent).

    c. The well-dressed guest seemed strangely *diffident* (indifferent, shy, fearful, evasive, embarrassed).

    d. Many causes have been suggested to explain the *deterioration* of moral standards in Roman society (degeneration, decadence, lowering, decline, decay).

    e. The essay was badly written, but it was *sincere* (candid, simple, honest, guileless, frank, plain).

    f. The affairs of the nation have now reached a *crucial* stage (dangerous, decisive, critical, ticklish, difficult, delicate).

Connotation

Your dictionary can keep you from using a "wrong" word—a word that doesn't convey your meaning. It can help you distinguish between look-alikes (*insidious, invidious; incredible, incredulous*) and sound-alikes (*write, right; born, borne; bridle, bridal*). It can give you some help in finding synonyms, words with such a large overlap of meaning that in at least one of their senses they are interchangeable in some contexts. But it can't tell you all you need to know to make the best choice between words that are very similar in meaning.

    Scarcely any words in the language duplicate each other to the extent of being interchangeable in all contexts. *Shiver* and *quiver* are very close and can often be substituted for each other, but the overlap isn't complete. Though we say "She quivered with rage," we don't ordinarily say "She shivered with rage." *Pail* and *bucket* are used in different parts of the country to refer to the same thing, but people who normally use *pail* find *bucket* old-fashioned. The difference between the words in each of these pairs lies not in their denotations—they refer to the same action or things—but in their connotations, in the associations they have for speakers and hearers, for writers and readers. In a column written while George Bush was a contestant for the Republican presidential nomination, George F. Will made the point:

Thirteen months ago, I described George Bush as "skinny." Silly me. I now realize that what Bush actually is is *lean*. Now, as then, he is a string bean. But then he was just plain George, merely a verteran of distinguished careers in business, politics and diplomacy. . . . To call him skinny now would be lese majesty. He deserves a more dignified adjective: lean.—*Newsweek*

English is rich in words that carry different shades of meaning:

joke/jest average/mediocre childish/childlike flashy/striking cheap/inexpensive intelligent/smart

obedient/dutiful/amenable/docile/yielding/compliant

old-fashioned/antiquated/passé/dated/out-of-date/old hat

What sometimes makes it difficult to discriminate among synonyms is that though the related words have a common core of meaning, their different connotations make it inappropriate to substitute one for another freely in all contexts. A dictionary may define *mediocre* as "average," but normally the connotations of *mediocre* are derogatory, while *average* is sometimes derogatory, sometimes favorable, often neutral, depending on the context. You say, "He's an average student" with no derogatory intention; but "As a driver, he's no better than mediocre" means you don't have much respect for his skill behind the wheel. Making the right choice between words you're not entirely familiar with requires care and thought and information. A thesaurus—a book of words and their synonyms—may offer a dozen words with the same general denotation, but to make a wise choice among them you need to know what their connotations are.

The context in which a word has been regularly used, the variety of usage to which it belongs (standard or nonstandard; formal, informal, or general), and the prevailing social attitude toward what it refers to and toward the people who generally use it (politicians, prizefighters, secretaries, writers of television commercials, college students, teachers, children, seamen)—all these things contribute to a word's connotations. And connotations change with changing attitudes. The associations of much slang and profanity have altered in recent years with their widening use by adults of high social and economic status and by respected publications. Historically, connotations change as the people, things, or actions the words refer to move up or down in social esteem: *Methodist* and *Quaker* originally had derogatory connotations but are now either simply denotative or approving. For the general public, *drugs* has acquired wholly new connotations in the last generation, though these connotations differ from group to group.

Words that are heavily connotative are sometimes referred to as emotive, evaluative, intentional, loaded, or slanted. As these labels suggest, such words are often regarded with suspicion; and it's true that slanting—in headlines, in advertisements, in political speeches, in discussions of social problems—can be deliberately malicious and deceptive. But connotation is inescapable, and used wisely it can greatly enrich our writing. We use words not only to give information about things but to express our attitudes toward them and our feelings about them and to influence the attitudes and feelings of others. It's natural for us to apply words that have favorable connotations to actions we honestly admire *(courageous)* and to apply words with unfavorable connotations to actions we deplore *(foolhardy)*. Doing so is irresponsible only if we assume that by giving a name to the action, we've proved that it is indeed courageous or foolhardy or whatever.

If we're to be persuasive, we need to make good use of connotation, not to evade it by trying to find words that are as purely denotative as possible. To describe a family in desperate need, *penniless,* with its emotional connotations, may be a more responsible choice than the flatly factual *without funds*.

Words pick up associations not only from the way we regard what they refer to but from the contexts in which they're commonly used. Connotation provides much of the basis for classifying words as standard and nonstandard and for dividing standard English into formal, general, and informal. The words *stasis* and *eschew* are so unfamiliar to most of us that we probably have no particular emotional response to them, only a sense that they're formal (itself a kind of emotional response), and so we would find them out of place in everyday contexts. Whenever you ignore the social side of connotation by using a formal word where the rhetorical situation calls for a casual one, or the reverse, you distract your readers from what you're trying to say—amusing them, perhaps, or annoying them, but in any case creating a barrier to communication. Like style in the broad sense, diction should call attention to itself only if, by doing so, it strengthens what's being said.

For Discussion and Writing

1. Explain what these words have in common and how they differ: *svelte/slender/slim/lean/thin/skinny/scrawny.* Compose sentences to show which you would use and how you would use them if you wanted to be complimentary, neutral, insulting.

2. Explain, with sample sentences, why the words in each of the following pairs are not interchangeable in all contexts: *brave/bold; fair/objective; polite/courteous; clamor/uproar; stubborn/obdurate.*

3. What connotations or associations does each of these words have for you: *soul, booze, politics, hunter, business woman, science?* Which of the connotations do you believe to be generally shared (at least by your contemporaries)? Which are private associations of your own, and what are they based on?

4. In a newspaper or magazine, find a discussion of a current issue in which words are, in your opinion, deliberately slanted. Rewrite the article, removing the slant. (Be careful that your own feelings about the issue don't lead you, instead, to reslant in another direction.) Turn in both the original and your rewrite.

5. Write three one-paragraph descriptions of the same building (your home, your dormitory, your church, a skyscraper, a city hall, a shack). In the first be as objective as you can. In the second be affectionate or admiring. In the third be hostile or contemptuous. Each paragraph should include the same details, but the language in which they're presented will surely differ.

The Varieties of English

Even if you keep a stack of good dictionaries on your desk, the right answer to the question "What word should I use?" is usually "It depends." *Request* and *ask* are both correct; which one is preferable depends on the style of your paper, and that in turn depends on your purpose and your audience. Both *can't* and *cannot* appear regularly in print; in a specific context, one would be better—more appropriate—than the other. (In a paper in which *can't* is stylistically appropriate, *cannot* might be introduced to provide special emphasis.)

Questions about usage arise because there are different varieties of English and because these varieties don't fit equally well into every social and rhetorical situation. What's appropriate in casual talk isn't always appropriate on paper. What sounds natural to an audience of teenagers may baffle an audience of old people. What amuses readers in one context antagonizes them in another. Knowing what kinds of English there are and recognizing how and why the alternatives differ puts you in a position to suit your style to your subject and to your audience and to the occasion. When you write English that's appropriate to the rhetorical situation, you're making the right use of language. Good English isn't just arbitrarily "good." It's good because it's right for the job. (In these last few sentences, *right* is used in a functional, not a moral, sense. If your purpose in writing is dishonest, then your use of language—whatever it may be—is morally wrong.)

Standard and Nonstandard English

There are many ways of classifying the Englishes we use, both the spoken and the written. This book is concerned primarily with written varieties of the language in their edited form—that is, with writing that's been gone over with some care. Its purpose is to help you increase your skill and confidence in writing standard English.

Standard English is the dialect approved by the middle class, the dominant class in American society. The other cultural variety of English is *nonstandard* English, which includes usages from numerous regional and social dialects. In speech the distinction between standard and nonstandard hinges on a fairly small number of pronunciations, words, word forms, and grammatical constructions habitually used by people whose educational backgrounds and social standings are noticeably different from those of members of the middle class. In writing, the distinction is chiefly based on a carry-over of those speech habits, with spellings taking the place of pronunciations:

> He et a apple.
>
> Youse guys ain't wrote us in months.
>
> She seen them kittens get drownded.

Nonstandard English, which appears in published writing chiefly in dialog and in other prose that attempts to reproduce nonstandard speech patterns, is inappropriate in the writing that you'll normally be expected to do in college.

In Chapter One, where we introduced informal, general, and formal styles of writing, we showed how they differed in sentence structure and punctuation as well as diction. Here we'll talk mainly about informal, general, and formal as varieties of standard English—categories of usage that correspond broadly to the social and rhetorical situations in which the stylistic varieties commonly occur. Since they shade into each other, with large areas of overlap, the categories shouldn't be rigidly interpreted nor the labels rigidly applied. While some words are clearly more formal than others— *disputatious,* for example—and some more informal—like *hassle*—many can be labeled only in context. A word that stands out as inappropriately formal in one paper might, in a different paper, pass as general. To say that a passage is formal, then, doesn't mean that the vocabulary and sentence structure are exclusively formal. It means that there are enough traits usually associated with that variety of the written language to give the passage a formal feel or tone, even though much of it—perhaps most of it—may be general in style.

The boundaries between the varieties continue to shift, as they have been doing for hundreds of years. Today's good formal English is close to what would have been considered general English in the essays of a half century ago, while what might be called the High Formal of the 1800s has almost disappeared. General English, meanwhile, has become increasingly relaxed, taking in more and more words, phrases, and constructions from informal. Even short periods of time bring changes in the status of individual usages. A word or phrase that's looked on as informal one year may appear often enough in well-edited publications to be considered general a year later, as the verb *bug* (to plant a secret listening device) did in the early 1970s. A word from the formal vocabulary may catch on in general English (as *charisma* and *détente* did), enjoy a vogue, and then either return to its original, restricted use or become a permanent part of the general vocabulary. Given such short-term change, the best way to keep in touch with what's going on in the language is not by relying on dictionaries and guides to usage, which are inevitably out of date, but by reading current books and newspapers and magazines and by listening to all the voices that reach your ear, directly and by way of radio and television. As you do, you'll become increasingly aware that the language is a living, changing thing; you'll expand your range of choices; and if you read and listen intelligently and critically, you'll also increase your ability to choose well.

Formal English

Old-fashioned formal English—what we've referred to as High Formal—survives today chiefly in oratory: in some political speeches, some sermons, some eulogies and other ceremonial addresses, as at graduation time. At its best, old-fashioned formal demonstrates that the English language can not only disseminate information with clarity and precision but also spark the imagination, stir the emotions, lift up the heart. At its worst, it's empty verbal posturing, a pompous parade of ''big'' words and stilted phrases.

Formal written English is found today in some textbooks—particularly those for advanced courses—and in some learned journals. Outside academic circles it appears in books and articles addressed to well-educated audiences willing to make a greater intellectual effort than is called for by a newspaper or a popular magazine. Formal is appropriate (though not obligatory) for writing on philosophy, religion, aesthetics, literature, theoretical science, and so forth. Though its subject matter is likely to be intellectual, its tone need not be solemn. Wit and formal English are often happily allied.

The vocabulary of formal English smacks of the literary, the scholarly, the philosophical. It includes words seldom used in ordinary conversation *(desultory, ubiquitous, importunate)* and a high proportion of nouns like *hiatus, resurgence, synthesis,* which generalize about experience rather than present it directly. For those familiar with them, the words are often rich in suggestion *(omen, luminous, transcend)* or have some special appeal of sound or rhythm *(immemorial, quintessence),* while the abstract nouns and technical terms permit the exact and concise statement of ideas.

Though formal English uses short, compact sentences for emphasis, its typical sentence is fairly long, and the elements in it are carefully ordered. Here's an example:

> The children, we hear, are badly taught and cannot read, spell, or write; employers despair of finding literate clerks and typists; the professions deplore the thickening of jargon which darkens counsel and impedes action; scientists cry out in their journals that their colleagues cannot report their facts intelligibly; and businessmen declare many bright people unemployable for lack of the ability to say what they mean in any medium.—Wilson Follett, *Modern American Usage*

Such deliberate, studied arrangement of elements in a series (''employers despair . . . ; the professions deplore . . . ; scientists cry out . . .''), as well as word choice that shows careful consideration ("the thickening of jargon which darkens counsel and impedes action"), characterizes formal writing, making its impact quite different from that of most general and all informal styles.

When you set out to write a paper in a formal style, you run some risks. The bad imitations of formal English called officialese are prize exhibits of unreadable prose, while literary efforts are plagued by words selected more to impress than to inform and by styles so self-conscious that they divert attention from the content. And there is the problem of sustaining a formal style—not writing just one or two neatly balanced sentences but continuing to show control of phrases and clauses, mastery of the rules of close punctuation, informed conservative taste in usage, and a vocabulary adequate to the demands of the subject and the style. In short, writing a successful essay in formal English is a challenging undertaking. Meeting the challenge when the occasion arises is one measure of your sophistication as a writer.

Informal English

Informal written English is the variety of standard English that most of us use naturally in letters to members of our families and to close friends, in diaries and journals, and in other kinds of personal, intimate expression. Some elements of informal are also used—sometimes appropriately, sometimes not—when writers who share no intimacy with the readers they're addressing try to reduce the distance between themselves and their audiences.

Although it actually differs a good deal from the English we use in casual, spontaneous conversation, informal written English suggests speech in several of its characteristics. It swings over a wide range, sometimes mixing vocabulary from formal English with verb forms from nonstandard. It makes free use of slang and draws on the shoptalk that develops in every occupation and the ingroup vocabulary that attaches to every sport. The writer takes many syntactic shortcuts, sometimes omitting subjects, usually skipping optional relative pronouns ("I hear he's in town" instead of "I hear that he is in town"), regularly using contractions. Some of the sentences of informal are short and elliptical ("Bet I won more than you" instead of "I'll bet that I won more than you did"); others are unusually long, with asides and afterthoughts keeping the structure loose and rambling. The following passage from an autobiography keeps the feel of informal even when its vocabulary and its sentences are within the range of general English:

> A year went by. With time we got badder and cooler. I stopped counting the scores. We hit small bars, East Side, West Side, all around the paddy town. I took a room on my old block with an old lady for a few bucks a week. She was all right. I gave her a lot of hell, but she loved me like a son—she said. I believed her, so I acted like most sons do in Harlem—I paid her no mind.—
> Piri Thomas, *Down These Mean Streets*

In published nonfiction the extended use of informal English is mostly limited to some periodicals addressed to special audiences (rock fans, surfers, motorcyclists), to the columns of determinedly personal columnists in more general publications, and to letters from readers. Often, published informal represents the hyped-up "Hey, there, you guys and gals" school of artificial intimacy, but it may also echo the flatness of much ordinary speech, as in these excerpts from campus newspapers:

> I can't see why girls should be given a free ride. They're just being used as the window dressing and guys are being played for suckers.

> The hell a nuclear explosion isn't that awful.

In small doses, however, informal English appears in a great variety of newspapers, magazines, and books, where writers of general English use informal words and phrases to move closer to their readers. The following excerpts, from a range of sources, share the feel of informal and the personal note that's one of its chief characteristics:

> When I was 10, gangs of hoods would stone us Jewish kids.—Audrey Gellis, *Ms*.

> The average Samoan makes Bubba Smith of the Colts look like a shrimp. They start out at about 300 pounds and from there they just get *wider*. They are big huge giants.—Tom Wolfe, *Radical Chic and Mau-Mauing the Flak Catchers*

> Around 3:30 in the afternoon, he'd been fooling with his hair, spraying, setting, combing, until it was perfect.—Lawrence Gonzales, *Playboy*

> Zelda's occasional accusations that Fitzgerald was homosexual have usually been put down to the fact that she was either off her rocker or, mounted on that rocker, she was eager to wound Fitzgerald. . . . In any case, Zelda managed to so bug her husband on the subject that one day in Paris . . . he suddenly let go.—Gore Vidal, *New York Review of Books*

> A single outing with one dame when he was 60 later cost him a couple hundred grand in paternity suit fees.—Tony Hiss, *New York Times Book Review*

If you have a chance to write a paper in an informal style, don't make the mistake of assuming that it won't be any more of a problem than writing to your kid sister or your best friend. Your readers probably won't include your sister or your friend, but they will include your instructor and your classmates. And while no one should be applying the standards of formal written English or even the more relaxed ones of general English, all of them have a right to insist on being able to understand what you say. In a letter to family or hometown friends, you can take a lot for granted: they

know the local places and people and happenings you refer to without needing to have everything spelled out in detail; they know the special connotations of some of the words you use; they know your regional and social
dialects. But it's certain that not everyone in your class knows these things,
nor will everyone be as willing as family and friends to puzzle over what
you're getting at.

So your job will be to put informal English to work for you—to preserve its easy, casual tone while ridding it of its sloppiness and vagueness.
That takes some doing.

General English

Occupying the broad middle ground between formal and informal is general
written English. It's the variety of standard English that educated people
most often read and that they themselves most often write. The words in its
vocabulary include *spacious* as well as *roomy, precipitation* as well as *rainfall, nutty* as well as *eccentric, rip off* as well as *steal;* but unless there's a
special reason for using the formal or informal words, *roomy, rainfall, eccentric,* and *steal* will be its choices. Writers of general English are likely
to use words that are concrete, close to experience, referring to things, people, actions, and events more than to abstractions. The turns of phrase reflect those of speech *(look into, give up, take over);* coordinating conjunctions like *and* and *so* are much more common than conjunctive adverbs like
furthermore and *consequently.* Typical sentences are moderate in length,
with few interrupting phrases or elaborate constructions.

General written English is much less conservative than formal, more
controlled than informal. Though it's more likely than informal to follow
strict conventions of subject-verb agreement, it doesn't do so as consistently
as formal does. It often ignores formal distinctions, as between *can* and
may, raise and *rear.* Yet it's slower than informal to accept slang. And
while the writer of general English is less conservative than the writer of
formal English, he may be quite as careful. Indeed, because his style is not
so restricted by conventions, he has more choices to make than the formal
writer does.

General English is the most versatile and the most serviceable of the
three varieties of standard written English this book deals with. It's the variety we use in this book, because general English can reach more people
than formal or informal can. For the same reason, it's the variety you'll use
in most of your writing while you're in college and after you've graduated.
But keep alert to the opportunities informal and formal English offer you.
Mixing the varieties of English is common practice in current writing. Note
the mixture as this writer recalls the *Godfather* movies:

> There was a kind of golden aura about Brando's Don Corleone, even as he
> was plotting to destroy half the population of Harlem. He was a luminous goon.
> There, but for a few wrong turns of fate, one felt, goes a real sweetie pie of an
> Italian poppa. One could imagine being caressed by his caring; he was the

prototypical daddy of our nursery dreams—the powerful man of the world who wipes the tears from the eyes of his babies and acts always, and only, to protect his cherished family. He was, literally, the God/Father.—Barbara Grizzuti Harrison, *Off Center*

In many magazine articles, you'll find an informal phrase dropped into a passage whose predominant tone is general or formal—possibly for shock effect, possibly because the writer wants to show a new side of himself, possibly because he wants to wink at his own seriousness or an attitude held by his audience. Or an essay that's been light and casual may move to a thoughtful, measured, formal conclusion.

Sudden shifts in style that have no apparent motive distract the reader and suggest that the writer has lost control. Sometimes he has. But a good writer knows what he's doing: by calling attention to *what* he's saying by the *way* he says it, he makes shifts in style perform double duty. Even though most of your writing may be general, then, the more you acquaint yourself with the alternatives that formal and informal English offer, the better you'll be able to use them for rhetorical effects that rely on contrasts in style.

Barriers to Communication

No word, no type of word, is in itself good or bad, right or wrong. As Justice Oliver Wendell Holmes wrote:

> A word is not a crystal, transparent and unchanging; it is the skin of a living thought and may vary greatly in color and content according to the circumstances and time in which it is used.

All kinds of words can be put to good use. You'll have reason to use abstract words like *rage, honor, symmetry, evil* as well as concrete words like *show, onion, motorcycle, flower.* You'll need to decide, in a particular context, whether you want to use the broad term *headache* or the more specific *migraine,* the broad term *typewriter* or the specific *my Olympia portable.* You'll have to decide whether a highly connotative word would be better or worse than a relatively neutral one. You'll have to decide whether to choose from the formal or the general or the informal vocabulary. Whether a word is actually put to good use can be judged only in context, for good diction is diction appropriate to the rhetorical situation. But something can be said about ways of using words that are likely to weaken writing and handicap you in your attempts to communicate.

Pretentiousness

You throw up a barrier to communication when you try too hard—when you set out to impress readers rather than to inform them. Perhaps this means using five words where one would do *(prior to the time that* instead of *before);* perhaps it means choosing a formal word where a general one is more suitable *(ameliorate* instead of *improve);* perhaps it means adopting the special vocabulary of a subject—the jargon of literary critics or sociologists or psychologists or economists, for example—when doing so is unnecessary or inappropriate.

Many of the words selected more to impress an audience than to express meaning are what are sometimes called "big" words—*emulate* for *imitate, inculcate* for *teach, valiant* or *intrepid* for *brave.* Though "big" words are often long, length alone doesn't make them objectionable. Long words are the only words for some things: *polyunsaturated* and *sphygmomanometer* have their place. Short or long, "big" words are words that are too heavy for the subject, too pretentious for what the writer is saying. In the proper rhetorical situation, they may be exactly the right words. Where they don't fit, they're "big" words.

Triteness

You throw up a barrier to communication by not trying hard enough—not working to find the words that express your ideas and feelings. It's easy to slide into the ready-made expression, the phrase that's on everyone's lips. It takes less effort to use a trite phrase, a cliché, than to find your own words to express your meaning.

A word or a combination of words isn't trite simply because it's familiar. Phrases like "in the first place" and "on the other hand" can be used again and again (though *not* in the same paper) without attracting attention to themselves, and the names of things and acts and qualities don't wear out from repetition. But unlike transitional devices and nouns and verbs that perform essential functions, formulas like "a sunny smile," "a necessary evil," "a tower of strength," "the acid test," "the crack of dawn," "a whole new ball game," and scores of similar expressions have become almost meaningless. A phrase doesn't have to be ancient and corny to be trite. Thanks to the saturation made possible by the mass media, last year's vogue expressions can be as thoroughly drained of substance as frayed quotations (and misquotations) from Shakespeare and the Bible. *Massive* has been so widely applied since the late 1960s that it's lost all its former impact. Often there's an inverse relation between how widely a word or phrase is used and its rhetorical strength.

If you turn in a final draft that's littered with clichés, your readers are going to sense that you didn't bother hunting for words that would accurately express what *you* thought. And if you write in all seriousness that "there are two sides to every question" or that "life is what you make it," your readers will have reason to suspect that you didn't bother to think. Triteness is a matter not only of using worn-out words but of using worn-out ideas. When the word comes before the idea, the trite expression can lead to the trite thought. If you write in clichés, you'll think in clichés. And vice versa. Here's an example of trite ideas tritely expressed:

The world of fashion shows free enterprise in action—the good old American way. Spending six months as a salesgirl in a dress shop made me realize that most women are slaves to fashion, that few know the value of a dollar, and that there's lots of truth in the old saying "It takes all kinds." Some of the customers made my life miserable. On more than one occasion I had to bite my lip to keep from giving them a piece of my mind, and sometimes it was difficult to keep from crying. But there was laughter as well as tears, and I learned many valuable lessons in interpersonal relations. After all, getting along with others— even featherheaded spendthrifts—is a must if we want to make this old world a better place to live in. And if our economy is to stay healthy, we'll have to put up with women (and men too) breaking down the doors to grab up bargains that aren't bargains and making fools of themselves as they adjust to the winds of fashion, season after season.

One reason the paragraph lacks focus is that the writer follows the lead of clichés instead of expressing her own perceptions and substantiating them from her own experience. Even when she's talking from her experience, the phrases she uses—"bite my lip," "a piece of my mind," "laughter as well as tears"—have been repeated so often that they carry no personal flavor. When she deals in generalizations, she's so locked into clichés—"world of fashion," "free enterprise in action," "good old American way," "interpersonal relations," "healthy" economy, "winds of fashion"—that whatever ideas she may have had are lost in the blizzard of trite words and phrases.

If triteness is a problem in your writing, the cause isn't necessarily laziness. Perhaps you're simply unaware that the phrases you use are worn out. Possibly you haven't read enough or listened carefully enough to know that your figures of speech are stale. The first step in replacing stock phrases and senile images is to recognize them for what they are. Compare these three descriptions:

I.

A grey mist overhung Nature like a pall. The somber shroud wrapped in oblivion lifeless forms which had been so beautiful in their summer splendor. The branches of the trees, shorn of their green raiment, appeared like spectral fingers reaching up to the somber, low-hanging clouds. Stunted shrubs, less bold, groveled to the ground. Closer still to the earth huddled withered blades of grass, corpses of the gallant, green-clad knights of early May. The staunch little soldiers of spring and summer were no more; they had succumbed in the battle with wind and storm. Faded autumn leaves stirred restlessly with every puff of wind, but seemed unwilling to leave the protection of Mother Earth's embrace.

II.

A tall lonely tree in the distance remained silent in the calm night breeze. The tree stood like a proud mother with her branches reaching out welcoming arms into the darkness. She had a straight stately trunk which was surrounded by her children. The small pines, dressed in white, stood close together under her outstretched arms to be protected by her. Their branches touched each other, holding hands for comfort in the darkness. The mother and her children stood against the horizon, and above them the stars shone brightly in the clear sky. The hilltop, which was their home, smelled crisp and clean.

III.

The oak trees on our street were honest and forthright. The bark was not just a grey skin but a solid dark coat. In the winter they stood heavy and black against the sky, while other trees threw up mere bundles of twigs. In the spring, they did not creep out in pale green mistiness, like the other trees; they waited until they were sure, and then they put out their leaves in great confident clots. When summer winds blew, the oaks never trembled. They surged mightily, sighing fiercely. And in the fall, their leaves felt like stiff wrapping paper, and their seeds, which were not of membrane and cotton but of wood, bounced smartly when they fell on the sidewalks, and popped loudly in the fires.

In the first passage the clichés—including much old-fashioned personi-fication—make the description both flat and pretentious. The student who wrote it had done some reading and had been much influenced by it. And that's the trouble: The description is derived not from life but from litera-ture. If the student kept on reading, she'd find that generations of writers have used the same similes and metaphors. But even without doing any further reading, she could expose the artificiality of her description simply by being honest with herself. Has she ever seen a pall? A shroud? Knights, "green-clad" or otherwise? Does she wear "raiment"? Does she really pic-ture plants as "staunch little soldiers"? Does she spontaneously think of "Mother Earth" embracing anything? The whole paragraph smells of the library, not of nature with or without a capital N.

The writer of the second passage began with a single cliché—the per-sonified tree—and then got all tangled up in triteness and sentimentality. The "lonely," "silent" tree turns into a "proud" mother with "welcom-ing" arms. Next the loneliness is forgotten: a whole family of "children" is disclosed, holding hands. The mother's welcoming arms become protec-tive. The stars are bright; the sky is clear; the hilltop smells crisp and clean. The inspiration in this case seems to be, not literature and certainly not nature, but a combination of Walt Disney, greeting cards, and television commercials. There's no sign of a controlling idea, no coherent attitude, no consistent emotion.

In the third passage personification persists; but here it's fresher because the student has looked squarely at what he's writing about and presented it as *he* sees it, in forceful prose.

The ways to avoid triteness, then, are first of all to do your own think-ing and your own seeing and then to say what *you* think and to record what *you* see. A good deal can be accomplished by simply rejecting combinations that come to mind automatically: "godless communism," "capitalist imperialism,'' ''male chauvinism,'' ''the weaker sex,'' ''crooked politicians,'' and so on. Often the phrase that comes to mind without active thought performs no function in the context. The ''godlessness'' of communism may have no relevance to the thought in the passage you're writing. And even if you want to express the idea a stock phrase stands for, you'll do better to express it in a different way so that, in fresher form, it can make some impression on your readers.

Jargon

You throw up a barrier to communication when you hide your meaning in jargon—language that combines the pretentiousness of ''big'' words and the deadness of cliché with a degree of abstraction that isolates what's said from the world of living beings:

> One of the prominent factors in marital discord is economic.

If the writer of that sentence stopped to ask himself what he really had to say, he might come up with ''Many husbands and wives fight over money''—a sentence with its feet on the ground.

Abstract terms are essential in all kinds of writing, and language that's predominantly abstract is capable of great precision. But it's annoying when it's substituted unnecessarily for concrete expression, and it can cripple communication by forcing readers to guess at the meaning. The literature of the social sciences often suffers from a lack of clarity because of its fondness for impersonal constructions (''It is generally agreed that . . . '') and for abstract and general terms that deny the reader images of human activity:

> Conflict within and between groups in a society can prevent accommodation and habitual relations from progressively impoverishing creativity.

Here, from an article on jargon, a jargon-ridden passage is followed by an attempt to reduce it to plain, clear prose:

> It has been observed that the offspring of familial units in the lower economic brackets demonstrate a frequent tendency to sublimate status-anxiety by means of organized aggression against societal mores, such aggression taking the form of vandalistic assaults upon institutional properties.
>
> . . . the children of poor parents often try to smother their sense of inferiority by throwing rocks at the schoolroom windows.—Robert Gordon, AAUP *Bulletin*

The original passage creates no images at all; it is only when the abstract terms are replaced by concrete ones and the general terms are made more specific that we ''see'' what the writer is talking about. Notice that one abstraction remains, and properly so: the concept of insecurity. Yet here, too, the change from jargon—"status-anxiety"—to the normal English of "sense of inferiority" is an improvement.

Just as the use of cliché expressions can lead to cliché ideas, so the application of laboratory jargon to human affairs can lead to a kind of thinking that ignores people. The children of poor parents just about disappear in "the offspring of familial units in the lower economic brackets." Many other collectives hide the particulars they stand for. *Doublespeak* is a handy term for language that obscures meaning rather than communicates it. *Urban renewal* that means "removal of blacks," *inner city* for "slums," *correctional institutions* for "prisons" are examples.

Jargon is hard to avoid. All of us are exposed to it constantly. Daily, on radio and television, in newspapers and magazines, we hear and read the jargons of politics and economics, the arts and sciences, the professions and the academic disciplines. In every college classroom words are regularly used for which simpler, more direct, more concrete, often more honest substitutes could be found. Indeed, for college students jargon presents a unique problem. Their instructors use the specialized vocabularies of the various disciplines and defend them as necessary:

> Developing an adequate terminology for sociological concepts is an exacting—and sometimes exasperating—task. It is complicated not only by the fact that almost all of the concepts in the field are undergoing continuous revision and refinement but also by the fact that many of them deal with aspects of social behavior already understood in part by the lay person. Often a new name must be invented to symbolize some newly discovered property of a familiar societal phenomenon, or a term already in popular use must be assigned a new meaning so that it can be used to signify properties of social events which have not previously been studied. Thus, in their search for adequate tools of conceptualization, social scientists often find it necessary to manipulate language in ways that are puzzling or even irritating to members of the general public, some of whom charge that sociological terminology is a hopeless jargon that obscures communication instead of clarifying it. Sociologists are aware of this difficulty, but they rightly insist on the need for using the symbols of language in whatever way is necessary to define the concepts they need as tools for systematically exploring the nature of social reality.—Melvin L. DeFleur, William V. D'Antonio, and Lois B. DeFleur, *Sociology: Human Society*

The style of the following excerpt from a tongue-in-cheek "college essay," a combination of sociologese and educationese, is meant to reflect unfortunate parental influence:

> First, let me say that I understand why you want to know as much as you can about me before your institution decides whether to enter into a commitment situation with respect to my enrollment. You prefer healthy, well-rounded individuals as students. I believe that, thanks to nurturing and careful parenting by my father, a sociologist, and my mother, a high-school curriculum expert,

combined with an innovative education in which all subjects were taught as a cohesive, interrelated whole, I am such an individual. So, indeed, are my siblings.

I do have a special interest, based on what I hope is a creative self-perception. It is to upgrade my potential. When I prioritize my goal/objectives, that comes first. I have other goal/objectives, of course, and my view of my development perspective is not rigidized. Far from it. Members of my peer group say that I have a propensity for exuding enthusiasm, and I know that at times I may overdo it, so that my ambitions appear to lack integration. Nonetheless, with me, the core programmatical element is upgrading my potential, and in realizing that goal/objective, I am sure that I will not require achievement motivation. I need only the academic tool concepts that will enable me eventually to achieve and attain at my full potential.—Edwin Newman, *New York Times Magazine*

Some students are able to switch from jargon to jargon as they shift from class to class. They recognize the changing rhetorical situations and speak and write accordingly. But many students lack the versatility to match jargons to audiences. And they often suffer for it. For most, the best advice is to learn the essential vocabulary of each discipline—what's shoptalk in the discipline but jargon outside it—and, beyond that, to stick to the vocabulary of general English.

Finding the right substitute for jargon isn't always easy. In reading over the first draft of a paper you've written, you're likely to come upon some "big" words you can't translate. They sound right in the context. You have a general notion of what they mean. You think most readers will understand what you intend. But in fact you don't know exactly what you're saying. The right thing to do in such a situation is to ask yourself, "What am I talking about, and what do I want to say?" Then, using words you *can* define, say it as clearly as you can, no matter how many ordinary words it takes.

For Writing

Rewrite each of the following sentences to make it clearer and more direct. This may mean using more than one sentence.

1. Among the many alterations in life-style that require adjustment on the part of the freshman the most important are environmental changes, which range from a lessening of restrictions in socializing to greatly extended opportunities for intellectual development.

2. The artificiality of the collective conscience has so dehumanized society that nobody has guilt feelings about the difference between his conduct and the principles he professes allegiance to.

3. Governmental mandatory regulation of wages and prices cannot be implemented without consequent disaffection of powerful voting interests.

4. The cost reduction campaign was the most prominent factor in the decision not to augment the work force.

5. Doomed by a poor field position situation and an intimidating opposition that defensed with unremitting savagery and zeal, the Zips found themselves incapable of achieving the momentum that might have muffled the expressions of frustration and discontent to which the occupants of the stands were giving vent with increasing volume and unanimity.

Euphemism and Overkill

You throw up a barrier to communication when you use words to hide or distort the truth—either pale euphemisms chosen to disguise injustice and brutality and stupidity, or invective intended to insult or incite without regard for fairness or reason.

A *euphemism* is a substitute for a word that is direct and explicit—the *departed* for the *corpse*. The substitute is milder, less disturbing, more neutral in connotation, perhaps less harsh in sound, usually less precise in meaning than the term it displaces. Many euphemisms have their origin in prudishness, as substitutes for the vigorous monosyllabic names of physical functions: *perspire* for *sweat, expectorate* for *spit, odor* for *stink* and *smell,* and so on. Others originate in a desire to gloss over social situations or facts of life that might be regarded as distressing. Old age becomes *golden years;* the poor and oppressed are the *underprivileged,* the *culturally deprived* or *disadvantaged.* Some of these terms are so firmly established in current usage that you'll find it hard to avoid using them in your writing, but you should never lose sight—or let your reader lose sight—of the reality behind the label.

Euphemism, like the language it supplants, is a relative matter: whether a word sounds genteel or neutral or blunt depends on the ear that hears it. And people differ in their attitudes toward specific euphemisms. Though *senior citizens* is widely deplored by those who are not so labeled, many old people prefer it to *old people.* Deciding whether to use or to avoid euphemism therefore calls for attention to the rhetorical situation. In everyday life the motive for euphemism is usually tact or consideration for the feelings of others. Euphemism is also used in public situations (sometimes justifiably, sometimes not) to dilute the audience's emotional response to a potentially explosive situation—as when a riot is reported as a "disturbance." But it can backfire. Many people prefer *slum* or *ghetto* to the euphemistic *ethnic neighborhood,* especially if they think the euphemism is being used to mask an ugly reality. So there are two sides to the relation between euphemism and good taste: even a well-intentioned attempt to avoid giving offense can itself be offensive.

Because a responsible writer faces facts, he doesn't seek out euphemism in a deliberate attempt to hide the truth. But neither does he use verbal overkill, bludgeoning readers with language that exaggerates where euphemism minimizes. The usual motive for overkill is to blind the audience to all but the emotional aspects of an issue. Besides being irrational, verbal violence, including the use of obscenities, is often ineffective. An overkill expression quickly becomes a cliché and, like every cliché, loses most of its original force.

Renewing Words

Word choice poses a dilemma. If you always use words in just the way everyone is accustomed to seeing and hearing them used, you'll sound like an echo. Yet if you strain for original turns of phrase, you'll sound affected or odd. So you need to look for ways of expressing yourself that fall somewhere between the thoroughly conventional and the idiosyncratic. Try to make familiar words take on freshness.

Giving words new life is partly a matter of perception, of how you see what you see, and partly a matter of controlling the context so that a word is freed from its routine associations. You can use metaphor and allusion to make a new reading of experience, to reinforce or sharpen meaning, or simply to give the reader the pleasure that comes from finding words used in fresh and distinctive ways. Or—and this is worth remembering—to give yourself the fun of capturing on paper the odd connections that pop into your mind. For all kinds of writers, from poets to sports columnists, word play is sometimes a private game that brings some pleasure into the hard work of composing:

> It is as though the Great God Muzak has beserked out of the dentist's office and ran amuck with all the decibels exposed.—Frank Trippett, *Time*

> We aren't out of the woods yet. The wage-price crunch is fueling inflation, there are eight million Americans without jobs and the stock market is as nervous as a pregnant cat.—Judd Arnett, *Detroit Free Press*

> I took the precaution of draping a poncho over myself and the entire ensemble and then wobbled off toward the frontier looking like a greenish-brown lump of ambulatory Jell-O.—Robert Pilpel, *Harper's*

> [In defeating Sandy Koufax in Koufax's last game Jim Palmer] had a complete lack of a sense of history. What he did was on a par with throwing a brick through a Rembrandt, . . . bulldozing the log cabin Lincoln was born in, writing graffiti in the Vatican. . . . He painted the full moustache on the Mona Lisa. He snored at the opera. . . . Not since Stephen Foster died in a flophouse had there been a bigger shame.—Jim Murray, syndicated columnist

While awful puns and outrageous exaggerations won't often be appropriate in your college papers, write down any that occur to you. Sooner or later the right rhetorical situation may come along, and meanwhile you'll have something to turn to when you need a laugh.

Metaphor

There are many different kinds of figures of speech, each with its own label. But since naming them is a lot less important than putting them to work, we'll use the term *metaphor* here for any nonliteral use of words.

Metaphors have greatly extended the meanings of many words. *Head* still has its old literal denotation as part of the body, but it's also applied to the top or principal part of a wide variety of things—of a nail, pin, screw, bay, news story, stalk of grain, bed, golf club, beer, boil, barrel—not to mention parts of a number of machines, the leaders in all sorts of institutions and governments and movements, the users of addictive and nonaddictive drugs, and a ship's toilet. *Head* for the head of a nail has become one of the senses of *head*: there's no other word for it, and it's one of the regular definitions listed in dictionaries. The language is full of such petrified, or dead, figures of speech. What we're interested in here is live figures, extensions of words to new referents.

Functions of Metaphor

Metaphor can be used to please or to persuade or to explain. The simplest of its functions is to enliven style: "Into even a newspaper paragraph phrases are flung the way a teen-ager flings socks into a closet, and half of them inside out" (Hugh Kenner, *New York Times Book Review*). But metaphor can also make an idea more interesting, more amusing, easier to understand, as in these passages:

It's a sobering experience to learn that for years your mind has been blocking out something that should be obvious. It's like realizing there's been a blown fuse in part of your upstairs wiring.—Thomas H. Middleton, *Saturday Review*

Great luck and catastrophe are equal dawdlers. Good news comes down the road like a herd of snails, and disaster wheezes and coughs along and finally arrives when you are sick of waiting for it.—William A. Emerson, Jr., *Newsweek*

The faces that passed me were like dull thuds, like slow, rhythmic taps on a loose drumhead.

And metaphor can make an idea memorable, as in this comparison of the correspondence between Thomas Jefferson and John Adams to an instrumental duet,

an eighteenth-century music of the mind, in which the two men trade off themes, challenge and echo each other, swell and fade in the give and take of ideas and memories. If Jefferson prefers trim little violin tunes, while Adams more often chuckles or grumbles along on the bass, the marvel is their final mutual deference.—Garry Wills, *New York Review of Books*

Metaphor can become the means of investigating a subject. Analogies to natural objects or processes are often used to trace movements or to analyze intangibles. Following out the implications of a metaphor—if the stirrings of an independence movement are compared to germinating seeds, what caused the germination? how will the plants develop?—may provide new insights into the subject. If using clichés can lead to thinking trite thoughts, using original metaphors can lead to making discoveries. The following passage goes beyond a simple analogy between the facts in a theory and the tumblers in a lock to introduce a metaphorical family that embraces both love and physics and a metaphorical friendship that extends to the universe:

> A theory is a wonderful thing. Beginning with a handful of mere facts, it moves them about like the tumblers in a lock, until there is a click in the mind and a deep feeling of satisfaction: the lock has opened; the facts have abandoned their lonely oddity and become part of the family of relationships, such as the law of gravity, or $e = mc^2$, or eros, or the death instinct, or other explanatory schemes that, at one time or another, have helped us to make friends with the cosmos.—Paul Zweig, *New York Times Book Review*

Metaphor provides us with ways to express what we couldn't otherwise express or, at least, couldn't express as well—not only feelings but ideas and concepts. The wave theory of light in physics and the concept of the watershed in the history of ideas—these represent more than ways of describing a subject or investigating it; they represent ways of knowing it. Good metaphors open doors to perception and understanding.

Controlling Metaphor

The figures you use in your papers should represent *your* way of perceiving your subject. If a borrowed figure fits the context, it's usually so general and time-worn that it can't contribute much. Now and then the homely comparisons of everyday speech—"fresh as a daisy," "cold as ice"—can be used effectively in writing, but only now and then. The strength of metaphor lies in its power to evoke images and emotions, to make the reader experience and not just comprehend. And a stale or trite figure—including the pseudo-literary cliché (see pp. 261–62)—simply doesn't stir the reader's imagination.

The risks in using metaphor are greatest when you're working too hard at enlivening your prose. If a figure doesn't represent a way of thinking about the subject that's natural to you, you may lose control of it and produce a conspicuously mixed metaphor. Probably the most common variety results from the meeting of two figurative expressions that have lost most of their metaphorical life. In one context a worn-out figure calls no attention to itself, except as a cliché:

> The voters made it clear they didn't want to switch horses in midstream.

In another context it will show just enough life to clash with a similarly enfeebled neighbor. Here the mixture of horses, stream, and limb encourages a mental picture of cowboy acrobatics:

> If we switch horses in the middle of a stream, we'll find ourselves out on a limb.

Here, two metaphors that relate to the same referent are permitted to collide:

> She was more sheepdog than chaperone, herding us onto the bus. When, at last, all her chicks were counted, she clucked contentedly.

But the dangers of mixing metaphors can be exaggerated. While the transformation of a metaphorical sheepdog into a metaphorical mother hen is too incongruous to go unnoticed, many good writers introduce one figure after another, each one yielding pleasure for the reader without calling undue attention to the logical inconsistency: "Consider Walter Kerr, a highly visual critic steeped in the silent movies, who turned his back on the talkies to find more nourishment in, God help us, the Broadway stage" (Wilfrid Sheed, *New York Review of Books*).

Whether or not a figure works depends in part on the rhetorical situation. The better you know your audience, the less likely you'll be to stumble into an inappropriate metaphor. And to be sure a figure fits your subject, you need to be aware of all the connotations of the term you're using metaphorically. "Game plans," with connotations of sport, might be acceptable when used in connection with political campaigning but objectionable in the context of the nation's military or economic policies.

Allusion

Sometimes you can add interest or clarity or emphasis to what you're discussing by alluding to something outside your topic. A brief reference to literature, to history, to a public figure can contribute to your meaning and also have a distinct stylistic effect.

An allusion leaves the reader some work to do. Instead of referring directly to an event, the writer refers to the place where it occurred. (Hundreds of political writers have used "Munich" to allude to the attempt to appease Nazi Germany that was made by French and British statesmen at a conference in that city in 1938.) Instead of quoting and naming the source of his quotation, he refers to the source indirectly. Often he incorporates familiar phrases from the Bible or from Shakespeare or suggests such phrases, as "We all know that Britain is awash in a sea of adversity" (Roland Gelatt, *Saturday Review*) suggests Shakespeare's "sea of troubles" (*Hamlet*, III.i.59). Thus a literary or historical allusion may be no more than a word or two (*summer soldier, honorable men*), a place name (*Hiroshima, Times Square, Gethsemane*), or a name (*Pocahontas, Canute*). By summoning up in the reader's mind the context in which the phrase or name originally appeared, an allusion of this kind can add a new level of meaning to the discussion. This reference to Diogenes, the Greek philosopher who supposedly searched Athens for an honest man, makes a very strong claim for the function of news analysts:

> We are not in the business of winning popularity, and we are not in the entertainment business. It is not our job to please anyone except Diogenes.—Walter Cronkite, *Saturday Review*

Unless the rhetorical situation demands formality, you can sometimes draw allusions from advertising slogans, popular songs, gag lines. A well-chosen topical allusion may convince the reader that the writer knows what's going on; but the topical allusion quickly becomes dated. On the other hand, the obscure, esoteric allusion may be taken as a sign of the show-off—and may baffle the reader completely. Allusions, then, should be appropriate to the rhetorical situation, giving the reader the pleasure of recognition, adding richness to the idea, and at the same time expressing something of the writer's personality.

Some allusions have made themselves so much at home in the language of every day that we no longer think of them as allusive; but recalling that what hangs over the head is the sword of Damocles can give a little more zest to both writing the phrase and reading it:

> Drawing a daily comic strip is not unlike having an English theme hanging over your head every day for the rest of your life.—Charles M. Schulz, *Saturday Review*

For Discussion and Writing

1. Make a list of things, experiences, and activities that interest, amuse, please, or annoy you. Then write a brief figurative passage that shows how you perceive each item in the list and (perhaps) how you feel about it. Sample list: walking, skiing, sunrises, beagles, birthday celebrations, word play, Chinese food.

2. Examine each of these excerpts (those unidentified are by students) and explain why you do or do not find it an effective expression of the idea. Try your hand at rewriting the figurative passages that you consider weak, incongruous, overdone, or otherwise unsatisfactory.

a. The furnace-beast is making hungry noises down in its cellar lair. I can hear its teeth crunching the black coal and feel its hot breath hissing up through the vents.

b. When it comes to television, we are all guinea pigs in a living room laboratory.—Kark E. Meyer, *Saturday Review*

c. The branches are grey, smooth, while the trunks are black, shaded with green lichen and moss, like mildew on an old lady's dress.

d. I loved the freshmen dearly, as one loves a docile child who takes all one's time and love. They were like puppies. They swirled and barked around me like the hellhounds of remorse.—Helen Bevington, *The House Was Quiet and the World Was Calm*

e. School is the workhouse of education. At the tender age of six, the young are sentenced to twelve years' hard labor and begin their incarceration.

f. For the last few years in the Middle East, Western Europeans have been content to sit like wallflowers at a dance, watching Egypt and Israel waltz around clumsily while the United States chaperoned and other Arabs tried to trip them up.—Christopher S. Wren, *New York Times*

g. As I started on my second pack of cigarettes, I could see my cell membranes laughing at me.

h. To call out the National Guard at the first hint of trouble means inflicting a permanent wound on the fabric of our national life.

i. Like a factory ship in the whaling season, [Theodore Roosevelt] combined the principles of maximum production and perpetual motion.—Edward Morris, *The Rise of Theodore Roosevelt*

j. It is a situation which puts the film people in a particularly awkward position. They let TV have their movies but at the same time they object when they find that most stations regard a movie as simply a thread on which to string as many profitable beads as possible. The more commercials, the more money. The movies and TV are, it seems, destined for a shotgun marriage—two spheres locked in combat, yet each realizing in the other the fattening of its pocketbook.

k. America is experiencing a cultural revolution, headquartered in New York's Metropolitan Museum. The grande dame of art, regally perched on an edge of Central Park, has a jazzy glass-and-steel wing that celebrates our native art forms in a spectacular way.—Kellee C. Reinhart, *Horizon*

l. I found I had only nibbled at the vast edifice of sociology.

m. The clouds sit high in the coal-rich mountains and hurl long, jagged, vicious, bright lightning bolts into the peaks. On the valley bottom, each bolt of lightning is like a gigantic flashbulb, bouncing brilliant blue light off the houses, stores, trucks and coal tipples.—Tom Price, *Reporting: The Rolling Stone Style*

n.   The roof of the cottage is like a patchwork quilt—decades of repairs, made with whatever materials were at hand, have left it with a dozen different textures and colors.

o.   The island, shielded from the throb of Kowloon by the harbor and Victoria Peak, is necklaced by a road that vistas down over fishing villages like Aberdeen, with its famed double-decker floating restaurants—sweet and sour upstairs, mahjong below decks—and shifting water carpets of sampans.—Carol Wright, *Providence Journal*

p.   It was as if he were contained still in a kind of spiritual amniotic sac, comfortable, no more than shadowily touched by the actual wonder and terror and exhilaration of what it finally, fully means to be a human being.—Marshall Frady, *Billy Graham*

q.   Most students seem to feel, as I did, that the selection of a major field of study is a miraculous phenomenon similar to falling in love. This expectation accounts for the feelings of guilt and anxiety that many of us experience when we realize we have made a wrong choice. It's like feeling unfaithful.

r.   The ultimatum was issued in the wake of a rash of outbreaks of violence.

s.   When they write about women, the young whippersnappers turn on the reptilian charm, oozing gallantry from every pore.—James Wolcott, *Esquire*

t.   In his first few years with the Bureau, he climbed right to the top of the pecking order. His colleagues, all busy in their own affluent anthills, scarcely recognized what was happening.

u.   State College, even on the weekends, runs like a Timex: smoothly, consistently, predictably.

v.   Art reflects the events of the time. It is a mirror of political and social history. When its creators are gone, it stands as the guidebook to what we were.

w.   The creatures who most enjoy themselves may be the 15-year-old girls on the beach who all day squeeze lemon juice on their hair and lazily brush it to make blond streaks; their faces as they do it are as perfectly empty as certain August afternoons.—Lance Morrow, *Time*

x.   All the great goals of humane and just government, all the hopes of citizens and leaders may count for nothing if the clanking machinery of the executive branch is simply unequal to the tasks laid upon it.—John W. Gardner, *Newsweek*

y.   The rewriter is as one who packs his thought for a long journey. Having packed the garment, he does not merely straighten out the folds and close the paragraph. Instead, he unpacks completely and repacks again. And again; and again and again. Each time, he tucks just one more thought into this or that pocket. When he quits, there are more of them than of words. So many labors of love on a single sentence, that many rewards for the rereader. On the surface, one teasing half-reward; others at successively greater and greater depths, so that each reading finds one more. . . .

Conceivably those successive depths might be achieved in one writing; but more probably the genius is simply the man who can do the repacking inside his skull. In any case, there must be repacking with more ideas insinuated into the wording. The rewards will lie at successive depths only if they were packed into the text in successive repackings. That is simply the kind of wits we have.—Martin Joos, *The Five Clocks*

9

Doing a Close Reading

For one or more papers in your writing course, you may be asked to do a "close reading" (or explication) of a literary work. For such an assignment you're expected to write a paper explaining the work in detail and some-times—depending on the instructions you receive—evaluating it as well. As the term "close reading" indicates, this project tests your ability both as a reader and as a writer. During the prewriting stage you'll be working out ways to report the understanding you achieved through concentrated study of the poem or short story, the essay, novel, or play.

Reading the Work

Your first step in writing a critical paper about a literary work is to read the work, and read it, and read it again. Begin by getting a sense of the work as a unified whole. Study what the author set down on paper until you know what he *said*. If you're reading a short story or a novel or a play—or a poem with a narrative line—find out what happens, who does what. If you're reading an essay, find the line of logic or emotion that runs through it and follow where that leads, so that you can infer and can demonstrate how the author reaches his conclusion. Once you've done that, you're ready to look at individual sentences, phrases, words—to listen to rhythms and sounds—and see what they contribute to the total effect.

You can't jump into a literary work and achieve instant understanding. Fight against a temptation to skim, to race through the work, and then to leap to an explanation and evaluation of it. And fight down any urge to quit—to struggle through it once and decide then and there that you'll never be able to figure out what the author is talking about. Read carefully, and concentrate on what you're reading. Make notes, ask yourself questions, circle words (and look up those you're not sure of), underline sentences.

Just as you should read your own papers aloud to see if they sound the way you want them to, so you should read aloud any literary work you're going to write about. A literary work is more than a plot line or a train of thought; it's also a work of art—or an attempt to be one—and you need to take its style into account when you set out to understand it and judge it. Reading poetry aloud is absolutely essential. Unless you can hear what a poet says and describe what you hear, you don't really know a poem.

Each time you read a work, you become more conscious of its elements, the way its author put them together, and the reasons he put them together the way he did. From knowing what happened in a story, you'll move on to why it happened and begin to wonder about its significance. Is the author saying no more than "John and Mary loved each other," or is he saying something about the relationships between men and women, or about the nature of love? Is the poet writing about springtime, the four seasons, a flower, a dead animal, or about a kind of immortality? What's the generalization, the theme, the comment about life or some phase of life that the work embodies?

Deciding what the author's purpose was—what he set out to do—is necessary because only after you've decided what that was can you judge whether he failed or succeeded. In reaching your decision, rely on the work itself. Some students develop an ability to come up with interpretations that are remarkably clever and imaginative but, when tested, prove to have little basis in the text—that is, in what the author wrote. Often such interpretations are built instead on what the reader suggests is a web of images or a pattern of symbols. Images and symbols are important devices that writers use to communicate their meaning; and sometimes a writer will underline a symbol to make its significance unmistakable. The bursting buds of spring, for example, is a popular symbol of rebirth. But remember: A bursting bud may be no more than a bursting bud.

Writing the Paper

When you've done all you can to understand what the author wrote, when you've decided (or at least done your best to decide) what he wanted to accomplish, and when you've arrived at a judgment of his work, then remind yourself of what you've learned about writing as you've moved through this book. All the time you were reading and rereading the literary work, you should have been engaging in the prewriting process. The rhetorical situation suggests a rather formal approach, unless you're writing on a work that itself makes formality seem out of place. Whatever method of development you use, generalizations and details will make up the bulk of your explication. Support, discovery, and pro-and-con are all possible organizational patterns; pro-and-con would be particularly appropriate if you should find yourself torn between two possible interpretations of the work.

A critical essay has to meet the criteria for any piece of good persuasive writing. To convince your readers that your interpretation is justified and your evaluation sound, you must do more than assert. You must demonstrate. Fortunately, your evidence is the work itself. You have that to draw on to make your case. In doing so, remember what's been said about building paragraphs, shaping sentences, choosing words. Strive for continuity, clarity, precision. The labels we all toss around so freely in conversation—"beautiful," "wonderful," "great"—can be an embarrassment when they're attached to quotations that most readers don't find particularly impressive.

Writing a good critical paper demands time, concentration, and hard thought. But as you're writing the paper, don't be concerned primarily about having the "right" answer. While some close readings are unquestionably more valid, more acceptable, than others, it can be argued that for many works there is no single "right" reading. Be careful not to confuse the writer's intention with your own experience ("I grew up on the Plains and know what a tornado does to a community") or bias ("Poems about death are morbid") or personal needs or private emotions. Say what the work means to you, but keep your emphasis on the *work*, not on *you*. Your interpretation may not be the one generally accepted by literary scholars. It may not be what the author has announced as his intended meaning. But if you support it with adequate evidence from the work itself, and if your paper shows that you've read the work thoroughly, thought about it long and hard, and then written about it to the best of your ability, you will have earned a fair hearing.

For Analysis

Read the poem printed below. First read it silently; then read it aloud three or four times. In these readings, try to do two things simultaneously or nearly so. Put your main effort into grasping the plain sense of the poem—what the poet is saying to you—but at the same time *listen* to what you're reading as you'd listen to a piece of music.

The Explosion

On the day of the explosion
Shadows pointed towards the pithead:
In the sun the slagheap slept.

Down the lane came men in pitboots
Coughing oath-edged talk and pipe-smoke,   5
Shouldering off the freshened silence.

One chased rabbits; lost them;
Came back with a nest of lark's eggs;
Showed them; lodged them in the grasses.

So they passed in beards and moleskins,   10
Fathers, brothers, nicknames, laughter,
Through the tall gates standing open.

At noon, there came a tremor; cows
Stopped chewing for a second; sun,
Scarfed as in a heat-haze, dimmed.   15

The dead go on before us, they
Are sitting in God's house in comfort,
We shall see them face to face—

Plain as lettering in the chapels
It was said, and for a second   20
Wives saw men of the explosion

Larger than in life they managed—
Gold as on a coin, or walking
Somehow from the sun towards them,

One showing the eggs unbroken.   25

—Philip Larkin

A Close Reading

Here's a paper that a student wrote in response to this assignment: "Do a close reading of Philip Larkin's 'The Explosion.' Quote freely from the poem to support the assertions you make as you explicate the poem and advance your interpretation of it. Directly or indirectly express your own opinion of 'The Explosion.' Your analysis of the poem should warrant your evaluation of it."

"The Explosion" by Philip Larkin

"The Explosion" is a short, extremely powerful poem that deals with an explosion in a mine. The language is simple and direct, the poetic images few. There are no unnecessary words, no frills. The result is a haunting work of great emotional impact.

Larkin isn't coy with us. He begins matter-of-factly with "On the day of the explosion" (line 1), and we therefore know (as we do also from his title) what is going to happen. At the scene, however, there are no warning signs. Although we can read something ominous into the shadows that "pointed towards the pithead" (line 2) or something sinister into the slagheap that slept in the sun (line 3), in fact the shadows and the slagheap are doing what they always do. All appears to be normal.

The three short lines of the second stanza offer some fine examples of

Larkin's power with words. He captures the gruff, masculine world of the miners: "Down the lane came men in pitboots" (line 4). The harshness of the sounds they make—"Coughing oath-edged talk and pipe-smoke" (line 5)—reminds us of the stale, dead, dust-filled air they must breathe in the mine and of the brutal lives they lead. But as we hear the early morning quiet broken by the rough voices of the men heading for the pit, we are also reminded of their comradeship: "Shouldering off the fresh-ened silence" (line 6).

The third stanza is important on several levels. It reemphasizes the absence of any threat of impending catastrophe. The miners walk to work in early morning innocence: "One chased rabbits" (line 7). It demonstrates the reverence for life that they share: "Came back with a nest of lark's eggs;/Showed them; lodged them in the grasses" (lines 8–9). The eggs are not dropped or tossed away but are set down gently. The stanza also lays the groundwork for what I feel is the theme of the poem. "The Explosion" is not a poem of death but rather a poem of life. More explicitly, it is a poem about the cycle of life celebrated and made complete by the event of death. The concept of the egg as the symbol of life will be echoed in the last line.

The warm feeling of brotherhood that is so evident in the fourth stanza adds to the positive tone: "So they passed in beards and moleskins,/Fathers, brothers, nicknames, laughter" (lines 10–11). Larkin shows us the tight-knit fellowship of men bound both by the blood of kinship and by the bonds of shared labor and shared danger. Every day they pass together "Through the tall gates standing open" (line 12). Today they will pass together through the gates of death.

The description of the explosion in stanza five is subdued and almost casual. The world above the mine is barely affected: "At noon, there came a tremor; cows/Stopped chewing for a second" (lines 13–14). Death, symbolized by the explosion, is only a tiny interruption in the day's (life's) events. Down below all may be fire and pain and death, but above there is only slight evidence that something out of the ordinary is taking place: "sun,/Scarfed as in a heat-haze, dimmed" (lines 14–15).

When people live as close to death as miners and their families do, they must have an easy, trusting relationship with their God, one that will make death less fearful. The people in Larkin's poem have such a faith, as is demonstrated by the litany of the sixth stanza. Belief in a tangible afterlife is present in the words, *"The dead go on before us, they/Are sitting in God's house in comfort"* (lines 16–17). Death does not mean permanent loss. It is only a transition from one life to another: *"We shall see them face to face"* (line 18). Although Larkin's poem is about a catastrophe, there are no scenes of horror, no blood and gore. The dead men have gone home to God. Life will go on.

The last three stanzas describe a transcendental vision experienced by the widows of the dead miners. At the moment of the explosion, the images of the dead men, "Plain as lettering in the chapels" (line 19), are seen. By using this particular example, Larkin emphasizes that this is a spiritual experience. The "men of the explosion" (line 21) have made the transition from this life. They have achieved immortality and become like gods, "Larger than in life. . . /Gold as on a coin, or walking/Somehow from the sun" (lines 22–24).

The dead appear to the living, and their message is one of life: "One showing the eggs unbroken" (line 25). We sense the wonder at life in that last line, the childlike awe, and the acknowledgement that life will continue in spite of this horrible interruption. The last line is a beautiful affirmation of life. The egg, the universal symbol of life, is fragile yet somehow durable. Life continues, life survives to bring forth new life, in spite of its fragility and the ever present threat of death.

"The Explosion" uses the occasion of death to emphasize life—survival, continuity, and order in the face of chaos. The poet's stress is on the "eggs unbroken"—life uninterrupted in its cycle.

In producing this close reading of the poem by Philip Larkin, the student first offers an evaluation of the poem in a brief opening paragraph, then leads his audience through "The Explosion," stanza by stanza. He explains what happens in the poem, discussing the action in his own words but keeping in close touch with the poem by citing lines that illustrate and justify his commentary. He's not simply giving a prose paraphrase but providing interpretation ("it is a poem about the cycle of life") and critical reaction ("fine examples," "beautiful affirmation"). He finds a symbol ("the egg, the universal symbol of life") and assigns it a central position in the meaning of the poem. This "discovery" is announced in the discussion of the third stanza and supported with evidence thereafter.

A major strength of the paper is the student's obvious familiarity with Larkin's poem; this does a good deal to win our confidence and hold our attention. A serious weakness of the paper is its failure to deal with the sound of the poem and the effect of sound on meaning. The student makes no mention, for example, of the way Larkin controls the tempo—the single pauses in the first and second stanzas; the rhythmic tread of the miners in the second stanza; then the jagged movement in the third, with four punctuation breaks to mark the activity of the lively miner; and so on. And doesn't the *sound* of "In the sun the slagheap slept" invite reading something sinister into the line? The student gives every evidence of knowing the work except the evidence that only his ear could provide.

For Writing

1. Reread "The Explosion." Do you disagree with any of the assertions made about it in the paper, either interpretations or judgments?

Are there ways in which you would have handled the assignment differently? If so, write a short paper stating specifically where and why
you disagree and explaining what you would do instead. Or rewrite
the student's paper according to your own ideas of what it should say
and how the content should be expressed and organized.

2. Choose a poem or a short story and, once it's been approved,
do a close reading of it. Your instructor will tell you whether to limit
yourself to analysis or go on to evaluate the work.

10

Writing the Research Paper

Although in college you can't learn everything about everything, you should learn how to find out about almost anything. You should know where to look and how to find what you want quickly and efficiently. This chapter deals with a special form of expository writing, the research paper, which grows out of the writer's efforts to find information, reclaim it, and use it for his special purpose. As such, the research paper—sometimes called the reference paper, library paper, term paper, or source paper—has a place in many college courses. To write a satisfactory one calls for resourcefulness in using the library and other facilities of scholarship, critical judgment in transforming a collection of data into cogent support of a thesis, and skill in organizing and writing a paper of some length.

Preparing a research paper in your writing course will give you practice in finding material, taking notes on it, evaluating its reliability and its relevance to your topic or your thesis, ordering it, and presenting it. Advanced study, especially in literature, history, and the social sciences, depends on this sort of work, and in the physical sciences a laboratory experiment is often supplemented by research in records of previous experiments. These same methods, more elaborately developed, are used in writing monographs, theses, and dissertations in graduate school and in preparing many business reports and industrial studies. Your reference paper, then, is an introduction to scholarly activity and practice for the research that you may do later.

The Nature of the Research Paper

A research paper is an ambitious and complicated undertaking; every stage takes time, patience, and judgment. At first your personal contribution may seem negligible. Most of the material will come from sources outside your immediate experience, the style you write in will probably be more impersonal and formal than you normally use, and your primary objective will be to inform and interpret rather than to express your feelings. But serious work on the project will show that the range and direction of your research offer considerable scope for originality. And though the methods of gathering material have been worked out by thousands of researchers before you and the form of the manuscript has been standardized, the actual content, organization, and style of your paper will be the product of your thought and judgment and imagination.

It would be wrong, then, to regard the research paper as totally unlike other kinds of writing we've discussed. While following the conventions of proper note form is an indispensable obligation in writing a research paper, meeting that obligation doesn't guarantee that the paper will be worth reading. To produce a really effective paper, you must first find a subject that stirs your curiosity, one that you'd like to know more about. Beginning with such curiosity can turn what might be a tiresome canvassing of sources into an investigation that interests you and will ultimately interest your readers. Your research may simply add to your own store of knowledge and supply information that you can present to your audience in an expository paper— for example, "Acid Rain: Problem and Solutions." Or it may support convictions that you'll want to argue for: "Why Acid Rain Must Be Stopped." Regardless of the topic or the approach, your paper is not likely to be satisfactory unless it gives the impression that in writing it you found out something *you* consider worth knowing.

Research and Writing Procedures

If you're to produce a good research paper, your intelligence and your intellectual curiosity must dominate your research. Wearied by long hours in the library and confronted by a stack of notecards, you may find yourself losing both your confidence and your enthusiasm (they're related), and you may be tempted to fit together mechanically the bits of information you've collected. A paper composed in this way is bound to be unsatisfactory—the proportions bad, the continuity rough and awkward, the focus unclear or nonexistent. What your readers are mainly interested in is what your research led you to—the store of information or the interpretation that's the outcome of your inquiry. Only if they see clearly how you move toward that goal can they judge the pertinence and value of the facts you present.

One note of caution about the methods outlined in the following pages. During the time you spend on the project, you'll need to strike a balance between your interest in the subject for its own sake and your interest in the procedures of research. Exclusive absorption in either is costly and unwise. At first you may feel a certain impatience at having to follow a rather rigid pattern in preparing and documenting your paper, particularly if you begin by simply wanting to know more about the subject. Meticulousness in recording bibliographical data and taking notes may seem to be a waste of good hours. But in the long run what you learn about the procedures and standards of scholarship will probably be more valuable to you than the paper itself.

This is not to say that the writing of the paper can be treated lightly. It's as unwise to concentrate solely on method as it is to slight it. In the end, converting material gathered from many sources into a paper that has its own integrity presents more challenges and offers more rewards than hunting for the material. If you become absorbed in the details of preparing extensive bibliographies and taking full notes, you may exhaust your interest and enthusiasm as well as your time before you begin to cope with the central task of the whole project—writing a paper that reflects discriminating use of a variety of sources to arrive at a point worth making.

The Focus of the Research

You begin work on a research paper by gathering material—looking up references, examining books and articles, taking notes. In most cases you're not entirely sure where your research will take you. You think you know what you want to write about, but until you've done some reading and collected some notes on what you've read, you can't know what you're going to say. Even if you know what you *want* to say, your research may make you change your mind.

Still, you'll probably find it helpful to make an outline—a *tentative* outline—fairly early in the note-taking stage. In the first few days of looking for material, you'll no doubt have in mind a few points you want to develop or some problems you want to solve; but if you let them control your note-taking, you may overlook many interesting alternative approaches to your topic. On the other hand, if you have only the haziest notion of your subject—if you haven't begun to ask questions of it—you can hardly take notes intelligently or economically. And because your full notes will represent a sizable investment in time and energy, you may later find yourself struggling to incorporate in your paper a miscellany of information. Some notes are bound to be wasted; every researcher duplicates information and jots down some irrelevancies. But you can reduce the duplications and irrelevancies if you keep a tentative outline beside you as you take notes and if you revise it regularly. After every lengthy session of reading, while your notes are fresh in your mind, spend some time studying, modifying, and developing your outline, trying always to arrive at what will be the justification for writing the paper, its *statement of purpose* or *thesis sentence*.

In a research paper, with its considerable length and numerous details, an exact formulation of the thesis or purpose is especially important. Often writing the paper calls for a good deal of juggling and testing of ideas. The point is to force yourself, as soon as your research permits, to define the purpose of your paper to *yourself*. It may help to conceive of the thesis sentence or statement of purpose as a response to a question—for example, "Does our correctional system do a better job in discouraging crime or in reforming criminals?"

A possible response and thesis sentence might be:

Since the crime rate continues to rise and most prison inmates return to prison at least once, our correctional system is failing either to discourage crime or to rehabilitate criminals.

You may never use this sentence in your paper, but it will serve its purpose in focusing your ideas and your source materials during the preliminary stages of your research and writing. Without it your selection of material would be aimless and your organization would be diffuse, with innumerable supporting details in search of something to support.

For Writing

1. The subject areas in the following list are too broad or too general for successful treatment in a reference paper of moderate length. Select two that interest you, and narrow each into at least three topics that could be treated adequately in papers of the length assigned in your course. If you are not well informed about your chosen subject area, you may have to do some initial reading before you can narrow down topics for research.

Acid rain
Acid rock
Alternative fuels
American Civil War
American family
Anarchism
Appalachia
Astrology
Black American literature
Buddhism
Caffeine
Censorship
Chicano literature
Civil rights
Coal mining
Computer culture
Deserts
Detective stories
Disposal of toxic wastes
Dolphin language
Electoral college
Eskimos
Feminism

Gold rush of 1848
Gun control
Islam
Kung-fu
Lasers
Lewis and Clark
Malthusian theory
Mass media
Meditation
Mideast
Modern art
Nuclear power plants
Nuclear warfare
Pet population boom
Political scandals
Pollution
Primitive peoples
Prison conditions
Productions (on film, videotape, or stage) of a particular play
Radar
Rights of the dying
Satellites

Southern American writers	Test-tube babies
Space exploration	Third World
Stereophonic sound	Trains
Styles of marriage	Utopias
Televised political debates	Witchcraft
Tennis	World War II

2. Choose one of the topics you listed in 1 above as the topic of your research paper; then prepare brief statements on the following:

a. Your reason for choosing the topic and your purpose in writing the paper.

b. Your present knowledge about the topic and the gaps you have to fill.

c. The audience you have in mind and the information you assume this audience already has about the topic.

d. Some sources that you plan to include in your bibliography— the list of books and articles you'll draw on in writing your paper.

e. The main points you now think you'll make and the methods you'll use to develop them.

Gathering Material

Reading and learning more about your subject area, searching out sources in the library, discovering the most useful references for your topic, selecting data that support the points you want to make, and recording the data in properly documented notes—these are the important early steps in preparing your research paper.

Sources of References

Almost everyone begins compiling references for a research paper with some sources in mind—a discussion in a textbook, a magazine article, the name of a writer, the title of a book. Very often, preliminary reading furnishes references to other works, and these make a natural starting point for the working bibliography. But to assemble a fairly comprehensive list of possible sources, you must make informed use of the resources of the library. There are several aids planned specifically to direct you to books and periodicals. No matter what your choice of topic, you'll want to consult your library's card catalog, its periodical indexes and special bibliographies, and its other general and special reference works.

The Card Catalog

The library card catalog lists all the books in the library by author and usually by title and subject as well (sometimes under more than one subject heading). This means that most books in the library can be located in three ways. If you know the name of the author of a book you think will be useful to you, look it up in the card catalog. If you know the title of a book dealing with your topic, look up the title. And if you don't yet know of specific books or authors, look up the subject you're interested in.

Besides finding books listed under the subject heading, you may also find cross-reference cards that will give you clues to other places to look. There are two kinds of cross-reference cards, *see* and *see also*. For example, if you looked up scuba diving in the card catalog, you might find a card reading "SCUBA DIVING, see SKIN DIVING." This would tell you that all books in the library dealing with scuba or skin diving are listed under SKIN DIVING. If you looked under SKIN DIVING you might find several cards for books on that subject and perhaps also a card reading "SKIN DIVING, see also UNDERWATER EXPLORATION." "See also" suggests a closely related subject that may provide further useful information.

If you don't find anything under the first topic you look for, try to think of synonymous or related subject headings. Since no card catalog can possibly have every imaginable cross-reference, you may have to try two or three alternatives before you find the right one. Don't assume the library has nothing on the subject just because you don't find sources listed under the first heading that comes to mind.

The library subject card below illustrates the information given about a book. In preparing your working bibliography (see p. 298), you would transfer the library call number, author, title, and publication information to a bibliography card (pp. 299–301). The entry on the bibliography card should follow the form prescribed for the final bibliography (pp. 317–20) so that making the bibliography will be simply a matter of arranging the cards alphabetically and copying the entries, inserting conventional punctuation.

Library Subject Card

```
┌─────────────────────────────────────────────────────────────┐
│        UNITED STATES--SOCIAL CONDITIONS--1960-               │
│  HM      Tallman, Irving.                                    │
│  136         Passion, action, and politics : a              │
│  .T32    perspective on social problems and                 │
│          social-problem solving / Irving                    │
│          Tallman. -- San Francisco : W. H.                  │
│          Freeman, c1976.                                     │
│              xxi, 299 p. : ill. ; 24 cm.                    │
│              Bibliography: p. 265-283.                       │
│              Includes indexes.                               │
│                                                              │
│              1. Social conflict.  2. Social                 │
│          psychology.  3. Sociology.  4. Problem             │
│          solving.  5. United States--Social                 │
│          conditions--1960-       6. Social                  │
│          problems.  I. Title                                 │
│                                                              │
│  OTU      13 MAY 81 ME           TOLLnt      75-37959        │
└─────────────────────────────────────────────────────────────┘
```

Periodical Indexes

Next to the card catalog, your most useful source of references will probably be periodical indexes. You may have already used one of these, *Readers' Guide to Periodical Literature*. In *Readers' Guide*, articles from more than 150 general interest magazines are indexed by author and subject.

In using periodical indexes, start with the most recent and move backward in time for several years. To locate the article you want in your library's periodical collection, carefully note the author's name (if given), the title of the article, the name of the journal or magazine in which it appears, the date of the issue, and the page numbers of the article. Look for references under your subject heading and cross-headings. Index entries often employ abbreviations and symbols to save space. These are explained in a "how to use" section at the front or back of the index.

Readers' Guide

The *Readers' Guide* is one of the most useful indexes. Here is a representative series of entries from the May 10, 1980, quarterly issue of *Readers' Guide:*

FASHION shows
  Autumn looks from Paris. il N Y Times Mag
    p 126-31 Ap 5 '81
  From Milan, a first look at fall. C. Donovan.
    il N Y Times Mag p 106-11 Mr 22 '81
  Look out, Paris, it's chic to chic in Milan. M.
    Demarest and L. Bentley. il por Time 117:
    64-5+ Ap 6 '81
  Show [O. de la Renta's summer styles] New
    Yorker 56:32 F 16 '81
FAST food restaurants
    See also
  McDonald's Corporation

          France
  Life in the fast-food lane [croissanteries] M.
    McDonald. il Macleans 94:32-3 Mr 16 '81

Here is an explanation of how to read a typical entry in *Readers' Guide*:

Emergency seizings. B. Beavis. il Motor B & S 145:118 F '80

The entry contains seven elements:

1. *Emergency seizings*—title of article.
2. *B. Beavis*—author's name.
3. *il*—an abbreviation indicating that the article contains illustrations.
4. *Motor B & S*—the abbreviated name of the magazine in which the article appears. In *Readers' Guide,* "Motor B & S" stands for *Motor Boating & Sailing.*
5. *145*—volume number.
6. *118*—page number. (A plus sign after the page number means article is continued on some other page of the same issue.)
7. *F '80*—the date of the issue: February 1980.

Newspaper and Specialized Indexes

In addition to magazines and journals, newspapers can often provide current information on topics. *The Wall Street Journal, The Christian Science Monitor,* and some other daily newspapers have indexes. Most important is *The*

New York Times Index. Although it lists only articles appearing in *The New York Times*, it serves as a rough general index to material in other newspapers, since the dates indicate when news stories were breaking. Through this index you can find the text of important speeches and documents carried in *The New York Times* as well as news coverage of important events.

For more specific information, you may need to turn to articles listed in specialized indexes such as the following (a † means "most generally useful"):

†*Applied Science and Technology Index*, 1958–date (that is, from 1958 to the present). Subject index to a selected list of engineering and trade periodicals. Before 1958 see *Industrial Arts Index*.

Art Index, 1929–date. Author and subject index to fine arts periodicals and museum bulletins.

Bibliographic Index, 1937–date. Subject index to bibliographies in books and periodicals.

†*Biography Index*, 1946–date. Subject index to biographical material in books and periodicals.

Biological and Agricultural Index, 1964–date. Subject index to a selected list of periodicals, bulletins, documents. Before 1964 see *Agricultural Index*.

†*Book Review Digest*, 1905–date. Author, subject, and title index to published book reviews. Gives extracts from reviews and exact references to sources.

†*Business Periodicals Index*, 1958–date. Subject index to a selected list of business periodicals. Before 1958 see *Industrial Arts Index*.

Catholic Periodical and Literature Index, 1968–date. Author and subject index to a selected list of Catholic periodicals. Before 1968 see *Catholic Periodical Index*.

†*Education Index*, 1929–date. Subject index to educational periodicals, books, and pamphlets.

Engineering Index, 1884–date. Subject index to technical periodicals; transactions and journals of engineering and other technical societies; reports of government bureaus, engineering colleges, research laboratories.

Guide to the Performing Arts, 1957–date. Annual index to articles and illustrations pertaining to the performing arts in selected American and foreign periodicals.

†*Humanities Index*, 1973–date. Author and subject index to periodicals in the humanities. Issued as part of *Social Sciences and Humanities Index* from 1965 to 1973. Before 1965 see *International Index to Periodicals*.

Music Index, 1949–date. An index to music periodicals arranged by author, composer, subject, and country.

Philosopher's Index, 1957–date. An international index to philosophical periodicals. Abstracts about 150 journals, including many foreign-language as well as English-language publications.

Public Affairs Information Service Bulletin, 1915–date. Subject index to books, periodicals, pamphlets, and other materials on economics, government, and other public affairs.

†*Social Sciences Index*, 1973–date. Author and subject index to periodicals in the social sciences. Issued as part of *Social Sciences and Humanities Index* from 1965 to 1973. Before 1965 see *International Index to Periodicals*.

United States Government Publications, Monthly Catalog, 1895–date. A bibliography of publications issued by all branches of the government.

This list is by no means complete. If you're unsure about which index to use, ask the reference librarian for help.

Indexes to Books, Pamphlets, and Collections

A few of the periodical indexes listed above cover material published in books, pamphlets, and collections as well as in periodicals. Miscellaneous indexes that concentrate specifically on books, pamphlets, or collections include the following:

Books in Print, 1948–date. Author and title index to books currently in print in the United States.

Cumulative Book Index, 1898–date. An author, subject, and title index to books printed in English.

Essay and General Literature Index, 1900–33. Supplements, 1934–date. Author and subject index to essays and articles in collections and miscellaneous works.

Granger's Index to Poetry, 6th ed., 1973. Supplement (1970–77), 1978. Author, title, and first-line index to poetry in collections.

Play Index, 1949–52, 1953–60, 1961–67, 1968–72, 1973–77. Author, title, and subject index to plays in collections. Brief information about each play is also included.

Ottemiller's Index to Plays in Collections, 6th ed., 1976. Author and title index to plays in collections from 1900 to 1975.

Popular Song Index, 1975. Supplement, 1978. Index to 301 songbooks published between 1940 and 1972.

Short Story Index, 1953. Supplements, 1950–54; 1955–58; 1959–63; 1964–68; 1969–73; 1974 and 1975. Author, title, and, in many cases, subject index to stories in collections.

Vertical File Index, 1932–date. Subject and title index of pamphlets, booklets, leaflets, and mimeographed materials.

General Reference Works

General reference works offer a good starting point for compiling a bibliography because they almost always refer you to authoritative specialized works. Comprehensive guides to reference works of all kinds include:

Finding Facts Fast (Todd), 1972.

Guide to Reference Books (Winchell, rev. Sheehy), 9th ed., 1976.

How and Where to Look It Up: A Guide to Standard Sources of Information (Murphey), 1958.

Reference Books: A Brief Guide for Students and Other Users of the Library (Barton and Bell), 8th ed., 1978.

Reference Books: How to Select and Use Them (Galin and Spielberg), 1969.

General encyclopedias are helpful in early stages of research, offering basic information in a given subject area and often referring you to more complete specialized sources. The major American encyclopedias vary in size from the single-volume *Columbia* to the multivolume *Britannica* and *Americana*. Though by no means infallible and always in need of revision (the larger ones revise some articles for each new printing), they contain information on a vast number of subjects.

Dictionaries and books of quotations are other standbys of the general reference section of the library. For dictionaries of the language, see pp. 244–45, 248. For books of quotations, the following are generally helpful:

Familiar Quotations (Bartlett and Beck), 15th ed., 1980.

The Home Book of Bible Quotations (Stevenson), 1977.

The Home Book of Quotations, Classical and Modern (Stevenson), 10th ed., 1967.

The Home Book of Shakespeare Quotations (Stevenson), 1965.

The Oxford Dictionary of Quotations, 2nd rev. ed., 1978.

Special Reference Works

Even more important for college papers than general reference books are the reference works in specific fields. The following list includes useful books in art and architecture, biography, education, literature, music and drama, philosophy, psychology, religion, science and technology, and the social sciences.

Art and Architecture

Art Books: A Basic Bibliography on the Fine Arts (Lucas), 1968.

Art-Kunst: International Bibliography of Art Books. Annual.

Art and Architecture: Including Archaeology (Besterman), 1971.

Britannica Encyclopaedia of American Art: A Special Educational Supplement to the Encyclopaedia Britannica, 1976.

Encyclopedia of the Arts (Read), 1966.

Encyclopedia of Modern Architecture (Pehnt), 1964.

Encyclopedia of World Art, 15 vols., 1959–68.

Guide to Art Reference Books (Chamberlin), 1959.

A History of Architecture on the Comparative Method (Fletcher), 18th ed., 1975.

Index to Reproductions of American Paintings (Monro and Monro), 1948. Supplement, 1964.

Index to Reproductions of European Paintings (Monro and Monro), 1967.

McGraw-Hill Dictionary of Art (Myers and Myers), 5 vols., 1969.

Mallett's Index of Artists, 1940. Supplements, 1948 and 1977.

Oxford Companion to Art (Osborne), 1970; rpt. 1971 with corrections.

Who's Who in American Art, 1936–date.

Biography (General)

Chambers's Biographical Dictionary, rev. ed. with supplements, 1978.

Current Biography, monthly since 1940, with annual cumulative volume.

Index to Women of the World from Ancient to Modern Times (Ireland), 1970.

International Who's Who, 1935–date.

McGraw-Hill Encyclopedia of World Biography, 1973.

Twentieth Century Authors (Kunitz and Haycraft), 1942; Supplements, 1955 and 1973.

Webster's Biographical Dictionary, rev. ed., 1980.

Who's Who in the World, 1971–date.

Biography (American)

Dictionary of American Biography, 14 vols, 1927–72.

Encyclopedia of American Biography (Garraty), 1974.

National Cyclopaedia of American Biography, 53 vols., 1893–1971.

Notable American Women, 1607–1950 (James), 3 vols., 1971.

Notable American Women: The Modern Period (Sicherman and Green), 1980.

Webster's American Biographies, 1979.

Who Was Who in America (since 1897), 5 vols., 1951–73. Historical volume, 1943, covers the years 1607–1896.

Who's Who in America, 1899–date.

Who's Who of American Women, 1958–date.

Who's Who Among Black Americans (Matney), 2nd ed., 1978.

Biography (British)

Dictionary of National Biography, 22 vols., 1885–1901. Supplements through 1960.

Who Was Who, 6 vols., 1952–62.

Who's Who, 1849–date.

Education

Dictionary of Education (Good), 3rd ed., 1973.

The Encyclopedia of Education (Deighton), 9 vols., 1971.

Encyclopedia of Educational Research (Ebel), 4th ed., 1969.

Literature (General)

Cassell's Encyclopedia of World Literature (Buchanan-Brown), new rev. ed., 3 vols., 1973.

Columbia Dictionary of Modern European Literature (Smith), 2nd ed., 1980.

A Concise Bibliography for Students of English (Kennedy and Sands, rev. Colburn), 5th ed., 1972.

Contemporary Authors, 1962–date.

Dictionary of World Literature (Shipley), new rev. ed., 1972.

A Handbook to Literature (Thrall, Hibbard, and Holman), 4th ed., 1980.

Reader's Guide to English and American Literature (Wright), 1970.

Selective Bibliography for the Study of English and American Literature (Altick and Wright), 6th ed., 1979.

Literature (American)

American Authors, 1600–1900 (Kunitz and Haycraft), 1938.

Articles on American Literature, 1900–1950 (Leary), 1954; 1950–67 (Leary et al.), 1970; 1968–75 (Leary et al.), 1979.

Bibliography of American Literature (Blanck), 6 vols., 1955–73.

Contemporary American Authors (Millett), 1940; rpt. 1970.

Literary History of the United States (Spiller et al.), 4th ed., 2 vols., 1974.

The Oxford Companion to American Literature (Hart), 4th ed., 1965.

The Reader's Encyclopedia of American Literature (Herzberg), 1962.

Twentieth Century Authors (Kunitz and Haycraft), 1942. Supplements (Kunitz, Haycraft, and Colby), 1955; (Kunitz and Haycraft), 1973.

Literature (Black)

Afro-American Writers (Turner), 1970.

Black American Fiction Since 1952 (Deodene and French), 1970.

Black American Literature (Whitlow), rev. ed., 1976.

Encyclopedia of Black Folklore and Humor (Spalding), rev. ed., 1978.

From the Dark Tower: Afro-American Writers from 1900 to 1960 (Davis), 1974.

Literature (British)

British Authors Before 1800 (Kunitz and Haycraft), 1952.

British Authors of the Nineteenth Century (Kunitz and Haycraft), 1964.

The Cambridge History of English Literature (Ward and Waller), 15 vols., 1963–65.

The Concise Cambridge Bibliography of English Literature, 600–1950 (Watson), 2nd ed., 1965.

The Concise Cambridge History of English Literature (Sampson), 3rd ed., 1972, rpt. 1979.

A Literary History of England (Baugh), 2nd ed., 4 vols., 1967.

The New Cambridge Bibliography of English Literature (Watson), 5 vols., 1969–76.

The Oxford Companion to English Literature (Harvey, rev. Eagle), 4th rev. ed., 1974.

Twentieth Century British Literature (Temple and Tucker), 1968.

Literature (Mythology and Classics)

Larousse Encyclopedia of Mythology, new ed., 1974.

Mythology of All Races (Gray et al.), 13 vols., 1916–32.

The Oxford Classical Dictionary (Hammond and Scullard), 2nd ed., 1977.

The Oxford Companion to Classical Literature (Harvey and Heseltine), 2nd ed., 1937; rpt. with corrections, 1974.

Music and Drama

Black Image on the American Stage: A Bibliography of Plays and Musicals 1770–1970 (Hatch), 1970.

A Concise Oxford Dictionary of Music (Scholes), 2nd ed., 1964; rpt. with corrections, 1977.

The Dance Encyclopedia (Chujoy and Manchester), rev. and enl. ed., 1967.

Harvard Dictionary of Music (Apel), 2nd rev. and enl. ed. with corrections, 1978.

A History of English Drama 1660–1900 (Nicoll), 6 vols., 1952–59; rpt. 1961–65.

The International Cyclopedia of Music and Musicians (Thompson, rev. Bohle), 10th ed., 1975.

McGraw-Hill Encyclopedia of World Drama, 4 vols., 1972.

Music and Drama (Besterman), 1971.

The New Grove Dictionary of Music and Musicians (Sadie), 20 vols., 1980.

New Oxford History of Music (Westrup et al.), 10 vols. In progress.

Reader's Encyclopedia of World Drama (Gassner and Quinn), 1969.

Theater Dictionary: British and American Terms in the Drama, Opera, and Ballet (Granville), 1974.

The Theatre: Three Thousand Years of Drama, Acting, and Stagecraft (Cheney), 1972.

Voices of the Black Theatre (Mitchell), 1975.

Philosophy

The Concise Encyclopedia of Western Philosophy and Philosophers (Urmson), 1960.

The Dictionary of Philosophy (Runes), 1970.

The Encyclopedia of Philosophy (Edwards), 4 vols., 1973.

Guide to Philosophical Bibliography and Research (DeGeorge), 1971.

A History of Philosophy (Copleston), new rev. ed., 1962.

Psychology

A Comprehensive Dictionary of Psychological and Psychoanalytical Terms (English and English), 1958, rpt. 1976.

Dictionary of Psychology and Related Fields (Beigel), 1974.

Encyclopedia of Psychology (Eysenck), 1972.

Encyclopedia of Human Behavior (Goldenson), 2 vols., 1974.

Psychological Research: An Introduction (Bachrach), 3rd ed., 1972.

Religion

The Concise Encyclopedia of Living Faiths (Zaehner), 3rd ed., 1977.

Dictionary of the Bible (Hastings), rev. ed., 1963.

Dictionary of Comparative Religion (Brandon), 1970.

A Dictionary of Non-Christian Religions (Parrinder), 1973.

Encyclopaedia Judaica (Roth and Wigoder), 16 vols., 1971.

Encyclopedia of Religion and Ethics (Hastings et al.), 2nd ed., 13 vols., 1962.

The Exhaustive Concordance of the Bible (Strong), 1894; rpt. 1980.

The Interpreter's Bible (Buttrick), 12 vols., 1951–57.

New Catholic Encyclopedia, 15 vols. and index, 1967. Volume 16, 1974; Volume 17, 1979.

The New Schaff-Herzog Encyclopedia of Religious Knowledge, 12 vols. and index, 1908–12; rpt., 13 vols., 1949–50; Volumes 14 and 15, 1977.

The Oxford Dictionary of the Christian Church (Cross and Livingstone), 2nd ed., 1974; rpt. with corrections, 1978.

Shorter Encyclopedia of Islam (Gibb and Kramers), rev. ed., 1965.

Twentieth-Century Encyclopedia of Religious Knowledge (Loetscher), 2 vols., 1977.

Science and Technology (General)
American Men and Women of Science, 13th ed., 7 vols., 1976.

Dictionary of Science Terms (Speck and Jaffe), 1965.

Dictionary of Scientific Biography (Gillispie), 14 vols., 1970–75; Supplement, Volume 15, 1978.

Harper Encyclopedia of Science (Newman), rev. ed., 1967.

McGraw-Hill Encyclopedia of Science and Technology, 4th ed., 15 vols. and supps., 1977.

The New Space Encyclopedia, 2nd ed., 1973.

Reference Sources in Science and Technology (Lasworth), 1972.

Technology (Besterman), 2 vols., 1971.

Understanding Technology (Susskind), 1973.

Van Nostrand's Scientific Encyclopedia, 5th ed., 1976.

Science and Technology (Biology)
Biological Sciences (Besterman), 1971.

A Dictionary of Biological Terms (Henderson and Henderson), 8th ed., 1963.

Encyclopedia of the Biological Sciences (Gray), 2nd ed., 1970.

Student Dictionary of Biology (Gray), 1973.

Science and Technology (Chemistry)
The Encyclopedia of Chemistry (Hampel and Hawley), 3rd ed., 1973.

Hackh's Chemical Dictionary (Grant), 4th ed., 1969.

How to Find Out in Chemistry (Burman), 2nd ed., 1966.

Lange's Handbook of Chemistry (Dean), 12th ed., 1979.

Thorpe's Dictionary of Applied Chemistry (Thorpe and Whitely), 4th ed., 12 vols., 1937–56; rpt. 1980.

Science and Technology (Engineering)

Dictionary of Modern Engineering (Oppermann), 3rd ed., 2 vols., 1972–73.

Engineering Encyclopedia (Jones and Schubert), 3rd ed., 1963.

How to Find Out About Engineering (Parsons), 1972.

Science and Engineering Reference Sources (Malinowsky), 1967.

Science and Technology (Geology)

A Dictionary of Geology (Challinor), 5th ed., 1978.

Geologic Reference Sources (Ward and Wheeler), 1972.

Science and Technology (Mathematics)

How to Find Out in Mathematics (Pemberton), 2nd rev. ed., 1969.

Mathematics Dictionary (James and James), 3rd ed., 1971.

Universal Encyclopedia of Mathematics, 1964.

Science and Technology (Physics)

Encyclopaedic Dictionary of Physics (Thewlis), 9 vols., 1961–64; Supplement, 4 vols., 1966–71.

Encyclopedia of Physics (Besancon), 2nd ed., 1974.

How to Find Out About Physics (Yates), 1965.

New Dictionary of Physics (Isaacs and Gray), 2nd ed., 1975.

Social Sciences (General)

Encyclopedia of the Social Sciences (Seligman and Johnson), 15 vols., 1930–35.

How to Find Out in the Social Sciences (Burrington), 1975.

International Encyclopedia of the Social Sciences (Sills), 17 vols., 1968.

Sources of Information in the Social Sciences (White et al.), 2nd ed., 1973.

Worldmark Encyclopedia of Nations, 5th ed., 5 vols., 1976.

Social Sciences (Black Studies)

A Bibliography of the Negro in Africa and America (Work), 1965.

Black American Reference Book (Smythe), 1976.

Black Studies (Irwin), 1973.

Index to Periodical Articles By and About Negroes, 1960–date.

International Library of Negro Life and History, 10 vols., 1970.

The Negro in America: A Bibliography (Miller and Fisher), rev. ed., 1970.

Social Sciences (Economics)

Dictionary of Economics and Business (Nemmers), 4th enl. ed., 1978.

Encyclopedia of Banking and Finance (Munn; rev. Garcia), 7th ed., 1973.

How to Find Out About Economics (Parsons), 1972.

The McGraw-Hill Dictionary of Modern Economics (Greenwald), 2nd ed., 1973.

Social Sciences (Geography)
Goode's World Atlas, 15th rev. ed., 1977; 3rd prt., 1979.

How to Find Out in Geography (Minto), 1966.

Webster's New Geographical Dictionary, 1972.

Social Sciences (American History)
Dictionary of American History (Adams), rev. ed., 7 vols., 1976.

Encyclopedia of American History (Morris and Morris), 5th ed., 1976.

Harvard Guide to American History (Handlin et al.), rev. ed., 1974.

Historical Statistics of the United States, Colonial Times to 1970, 2 vols., Bicentennial ed., 1975.

The Oxford Companion to American History (Johnson), 1966.

Social Sciences (General History)
The Cambridge Ancient History (Bury et al.), rev. ed., 12 vols., 1961–73.

The Cambridge Medieval History (Bury et al.), 2nd ed., 8 vols., 1975.

The Cambridge Modern History (Ward et al.), 13 vols. and atlas, 1902–26.

Encyclopedia of World History (Langer), 5th ed., 1972.

How to Find Out in History (Hepworth), 1966.

Guide to Historical Literature (Howe et al.), 1961.

The New Cambridge Modern History, 14 vols., 1957–75.

Rand McNally Atlas of World History (Palmer), 1965.

Research Guide in History (Wilson), 1974.

Shepherd's Historical Atlas, rev. and enl. ed., 1976.

Social Sciences (Political Science)
American Political Terms (Sperber and Trittschuh), 1962.

The New Language of Politics (Safire), rev. and enl. ed., 1972.

Political Handbook of the World (Banks et al.), 1928–date. Annual.

Political Science: A Bibliographic Guide to the Literature (Harmon), 1965; Supplements, 1968–74.

Research Guide in Political Science (Kavelage and Segal), 1976.

United States Government Manual, 1935–date. Annual.

Social Sciences (Sociology)
Dictionary of Sociology and Related Sciences (Fairchild), 1970.

Encyclopedia of Social Work (Morris), 1965–date.

Handbook of Modern Sociology (Faris), 1966.

A Modern Dictionary of Sociology (Theodorson and Theodorson), 1979.

The Uses of Sociology (Lazarsfeld et al.), 1967.

Yearbooks and Almanacs

Various publications can direct you to the facts you need:

The Americana Annual, 1923–date. Annual supplement to the *Encyclopedia Americana*.

The Annual Register of World Events, 1758–date. Summary of events which emphasizes Great Britain and the Commonwealth.

Britannica Book of the Year, 1938–date. Annual supplement of *Encyclopaedia Britannica*.

Facts on File, 1940–date. Weekly digest of world and domestic news, with index.

Information Please Almanac, 1947–date.

McGraw-Hill Yearbook of Science and Technology, 1962–date.

Reference Shelf, 1922–date. Reprints of articles, bibliographies, and debates on topics of current interest.

The Statesman's Year Book, 1864–date. Descriptive and statistical information about world governments.

Statistical Abstract of the United States, 1878–date. Summary of statistics on the industrial, social, political, and economic organization of the United States.

Women's Rights Almanac, 1974–date.

United Nations Demographic Yearbook, 1948–date.

United Nations Statistical Yearbook, 1948–date.

University Debater's Annual, 1915–date. Annual survey of debates in American colleges.

The World Almanac and Book of Facts, 1868–date.

You'll always find some important references indirectly, unexpectedly, by hunch or by chance. Almost every article or book will refer to some other source or give you a clue to follow up. (Check the bibliographies you'll find at the end of many of the books you consult.) Your instructor and specialists in the field will offer suggestions. If you combine orderly work habits with a certain alertness and ingenuity in following up clues, the sources of material on your topic will begin to spread out before you like a river system, with one stream leading into another.

Since one of the values in undertaking a research paper is to become self-reliant in the use of research methods, you should do as much as possible on your own. The library has trained reference librarians, and you should ask their help when you're stumped, but you'll learn most by not asking for help until you've exhausted your own resources.

The Working Bibliography

Before you concentrate on gathering material for your topic, you should compile a working bibliography of sources you expect to consult. Check reference works of the kind described in the preceding section, and consult the appropriate subject headings in the card catalog and the periodical indexes. To make sure that enough material on your subject is available in the library, compile the working bibliography before you start to take notes. This preliminary survey of materials will save you time and worry when you begin reading and will help you make an intelligent selection of books and articles.

Everyone should have a consistent method for keeping track of references and for taking notes. For casual study, notebooks and odd sheets of paper may do, but for large projects standard filing cards, either 3″ x 5″ or 4″ x 6″, are most efficient. To begin with, you should prepare a separate bibliography card for each reference. Later you'll add note cards on the content of the reference.

The bibliography card records all the facts you need to identify a book or an article, to find it in the library when you want it, and to make the formal bibliography that will appear at the end of the paper. Each card should carry these facts:

For the formal bibliography:

1. The *author's* or *editor's name,* last name first, *ed.* after editor's name. If no author or editor is given, omit this item and start with 2.

2. The *title* of the article (in quotation marks) or of the book (underlined to represent italics). Keep your bibliography cards in alphabetical order according to author or, if no author is given, according to title.

3. *The facts of publication*

    a. Of a book: the city, the name of the publisher, and the date.

    b. Of a magazine: the name of the magazine (underlined), the volume (if given), the date, the pages on which the article appears.

    c. Of a newspaper story: the name of the paper (underlined), the date, the section if the pages are numbered by sections, and the page. You may also include the edition and the column number.

For your own use:

4. *The library call number* or location of the source—"Per." for Periodical Room, for instance—preferably in the upper left corner, as it is in the card catalog. If you're working in two or more libraries, put an identifying symbol before the call number.

5. *Any other facts* that relate to the use of the reference, such as the pages that treat your subject or the value of the source—preferably at the bottom of the card.

6. *A subject heading,* a phrase for the particular part of your topic that the reference pertains to, at the top center of the card. This label is known as a *slug*.

7. *A code reference* in the upper right corner. This reference may be a number, a letter, or the author's last name. Using it instead of a full citation on each note card taken from this source will save a great deal of needless copying.

Samples of bibliography cards for a book, a magazine article, and a newspaper article are on page 301. Numbers on the cards correspond to the items in the preceding list.

The number of references depends on the nature of the topic. An undergraduate paper should represent adequate coverage of the subject; that is, the writer should locate and consult the most important and influential commentary, especially by modern authorities, and not merely use the first three books he comes across, regardless of their dates or their quality. On the other hand, most undergraduate research projects, by their nature, impose a limit of some sort: there comes a time when sleuthing must give way to the critical job of reading, evaluating, and note-taking.

Evaluating Sources

Sources are classed as *primary* (or *original*) and *secondary*. A primary source is a first record of facts or the closest a person now writing can come to the subject he's discussing. A secondary source is something written by someone else using original sources. In a paper on an author, for example, the primary sources are the works written by the person you're discussing and the letters, diaries, and so on written by him and by others who knew him. The secondary sources are what critics and historians have written about this author on the basis of these materials. In a science, primary sources are records of observations or experiments; secondary sources are discussions and analyses of such records. In history, primary sources are records and artifacts of all sorts; secondary sources are historians' accounts based on this evidence. Most textbooks and reference works are secondary sources. Don't go beyond secondary sources to *tertiary sources*—that is, to material that is itself drawn entirely from secondary sources, as in popular magazines and newspaper supplements. Any information that is third-hand is obviously of limited use and value.

Particularly in research papers on works of literature, you should try to come to grips with the major primary sources before immersing yourself in commentary. A study of the theme of corruption in language in George Orwell's *1984* and *Animal Farm* should begin with a reading of these books. Without this informing experience you'll have no way to evaluate the critics' views when you take up the substantial body of Orwell criticism.

Because preparing a reference paper is largely an exercise in critical judgment, you must evaluate the sources you use. "I found a book in the library that said . . . " is a confession of uncritical work. Some sources are better—more comprehensive, more accurate, more penetrating—than others. Your aim should be to find the best books and articles, the most

Bibliography Card for a Book

HM Theory of Social ⑦ Tallman
④ 136 ⑥ Problems
.T32

① Tallman, Irving.
② *Passion, Action, and Politics.*
③ San Francisco: W.H. Freeman
  and Company, 1976.
⑤ pp. 130-40 — emotion about social
  problems arises from a mixture
  of hope and frustration.

Bibliography Card for a Magazine Article

④ Per ⑥ Consumer Education ⑦ Monsma

① Monsma, Charles.
② "Educating Consumers: Whose
  Responsibility?"
③ *Current History*, 78 (1980),
  214-17 and 228-30.
⑤ Avoids forming judgment about
  proper role for consumers, business,
  and government in providing
  consumer ed.

Bibliography Card for a Newspaper Article

④ Per ⑥ Women's attitudes ⑦ Klemesrud

① Klemesrud, Judy.
② "Survey Finds Major Shifts in
  attitudes of Women."
③ *New York Times*, March 13, 1980,
  Sec. C, p. 1, col. 1 - p. 6, cols. 1-3.
⑤ Virginia Slims poll results—
  marriage: sharing of
  overlapping roles.

recent and most reliable material on your subject. When you come upon contradictions or differing estimates in two sources, you should investigate to determine which is more accurate or more probable. At first you'll have to rely on the judgment of others. In your reading you may find that the author of one of your sources is generally accepted as the authority in the field but that the scholarship or the fairness of another has been questioned. You should note judgments like these and, if possible, substantiate or disprove them through further investigation.

For recent books it's often possible to find reviews that give some indication of their quality. The best sources of reviews of scholarly works are the learned journals of the various academic disciplines. *Book Review Digest* will lead you to reviews of less specialized works.

After you've worked on a subject for a while, you can evaluate a good deal of the material yourself, and your informed judgment should guide your further choice of materials. If you're impressed by a psychologist's report on a study of high-school students, you may decide to examine his book on adolescent behavior.

Taking Notes on Reading

Good notes are crucial in the preparation of a reference paper. Illegible handwriting, meaningless phrases (clear when the note was taken but not a week or so later), and inadequate labeling of the source may send you back to the library when you should be settling down to write. As you become experienced in note-taking and comfortable with your topic, you'll learn to evaluate the importance of a source quickly and to vary the kind, length, and number of your notes accordingly. From some sources you may need only a few facts or statistics; from others you'll want not only direct quotations but careful summaries of whole paragraphs, sections, or even chapters; for a few you may simply jot down a sentence or two describing and briefly evaluating the content. In the beginning, of course, you'll be taking notes partly on faith, feeling your way note by note toward a thesis. Once you've defined your thesis, it will determine what material should be recorded.

Form of Notes

Notes on 4″ x 6″ or 5″ x 8″ cards are easy to sort, discard, and rearrange; they can be accumulated indefinitely and kept in good order in an indexed file box. (Notes may also be taken on the pages of a loose-leaf notebook.) The three essential parts of a note card are: (1) the *material*—the facts and opinions to be recorded; (2) the exact *source*—your bibliographical code reference to the source and the page numbers from which the material is taken; (3) a *subject label,* or slug, for the card, showing what subject it treats. Avoid weak, general subject labels like "causes" or "cures." A sample note card follows.

Sample Note Card

The sample note card above shows a convenient form. In the upper right-hand corner put the author's name and the source—just enough to make reference to the full bibliography card easy and sure. Before writing the note, set down the exact page on which the material was found. Inclusive pages (such as 87–92) should not be used unless the note actually describes or summarizes what those pages say. Put the slug in the upper left corner so that you can easily sort the cards when you shape up your outline before writing.

A single card should contain only one point or a few facts that bear on one point. If unrelated bits of information are included (the temptation is always strong), you'll find when you sort the cards that one bit belongs here and another there. One hundred items of information on one hundred cards can be organized and reorganized speedily and efficiently; fifty items on ten cards will lead to confusion, exasperation, and error.

It's good practice to use only one side of each card. If only a few words remain at the end of a statement, they can be written on the back, but the signal OVER should be put on the front as a reminder.

Not all notes need be taken in full sentences. Words, phrases, and topics are enough if you're not quoting directly and if you're sure the note will be meaningful after you've laid it aside for a while. Take notes in ink as you do the reading, but don't bother to recopy them except for some very good reason. They're only means to an end—a good paper.

Suggestions for Note-Taking

It's impossible to give exact rules for taking notes. As you gain experience, your judgment will improve, and you'll probably formulate your own special rules as you go along. But it's wise to begin by reading through the article or chapter rapidly to see what it contains for your purpose. Then go over it again, this time taking notes. From your first few sources you'll probably take a good many, but after you've accumulated material covering the major points of your topic, a new reference may give only a few additional facts.

In taking notes, distinguish between the author's facts and his opinions. If there's any chance of confusion, label the opinions "So-and-so thinks. . . . " In general, pay most attention to the *facts* presented, unless you're writing on a topic for which the sources are chiefly expressions of critical opinion. You'll need facts as the basis of your own interpretations and as evidence to support them in the paper.

You should also distinguish carefully between direct quotation and summarizing notes. Anything you quote should be taken down exactly as it appears in the original and enclosed in quotation marks. If you omit a word or more from a quoted passage, indicate the omission with three spaced periods (. . .) called an ellipsis. After an obvious error in the source, write *sic,* meaning "thus," in brackets—[sic]—to indicate that the error was in the original.

In the early stages of note-taking, before you have a clear perspective on your subject, you may want to quote rather fully. Many of these quotations won't appear in the final draft, but having a quotation before you as you write can help you work the summary of it into your discussion more smoothly. (It can also prevent unintended plagiarism.) In the later stages of note-taking, quotations should be copied out only for good reason: material that's crucial for your paper; controversial or difficult material that you want to think about; a striking statement that you want to quote for its pithiness or its authority.

Finally, distinguish between what you take from a source and comments of your own. Either bracket your own comments or circle them and write your initials alongside. "Notes to myself" often prove very valuable when you begin to write. Indeed, as you take notes, it's a good idea to keep a running log of questions, notions, and leads on a separate pad.

Taking notes on literary works may require some changes in method. As each work is a developing whole, it can't be broken down into "main points" as an article or chapter can; so you may find it best to take running notes (on paper) of your impressions and questions while you read and then go back over these comments to find out what lines of interpretation are worth pursuing in detail.

The Summarizing Note

Use the summarizing note when an argument or explanation in one of your sources seems crucial to your project. Doing a good summary tests your ability to read critically. Read the material several times. Watch for the main ideas and see how each is developed. Move from the general to the specific. Try to determine the overall meaning or purpose, then the main points, and then the subdivisions supporting each main point. The author's transitional expressions give clues to the pattern of his ideas. As in any other note-taking, you must be sure you understand and record the author's ideas, not your own, even when you disagree violently with his point of view. Don't interrupt or distort a summary by including your personal opinions. They'll come into play later.

Your success in producing a good summary will depend partly on the care with which you read the original and partly on your skill in cutting unnecessary passages and in condensing. A good summary reproduces as faithfully as possible the ideas and the emphasis of the original—and if incorporated in the final paper must credit the original. Condense by eliminating nonessentials—anecdotes, descriptive details, digressions, illustrations, and all kinds of repetition—and by using appositives, series, and verbals to make the phrasing more compact.

Though you won't always be able to avoid using words from the original in your summary notes, do your best to put the information into your own words. If you use a phrase exactly as it appears in the original, enclose it in quotation marks and cite the page number in parentheses. Leaving out or changing a few words or phrases while otherwise repeating the words of the original is not an adequate way to write notes. This procedure will lead to your being charged with plagiarism. The following illustrations show how a summarizing note relates to the original passage and how it differs from a plagiarized note.

Original Passage

The value of cemetery evidence to an archaeologist is considerable. Not only does it provide a wealth of domestic material reflecting on the life-styles of the different communities but it enables the composition of populations to be assessed—physical types, nutrition, diseases, and death rates. Moreover, by observing their attitudes to death we can begin to come closer to the people themselves, to their fears, hopes, and aspirations.—Barry Cunliffe, *The Celtic World*

Summarizing Note

The findings from burial sites tell archaeologists much about the physical condition of a people, their eating habits, and even some of their feelings.

Plagiarized Note

Not only does cemetery evidence provide domestic material showing the life-styles of the different communities but it enables the composition of populations to be revealed—physical types, nutrition, diseases, and death rates. Also, by observing their attitudes toward death, we come closer to the fears, hopes, and aspirations of the people themselves.

Original Passage

Rapid population growth is no more equitably distributed than food. Even as a baby boom swelled populations in the developed nations following World War II, it accounted for but 20 percent of the growth in world population. Today population growth in the United States is near zero. In West Germany and much of the Soviet Union, population is declining. More than 90 percent of all future population growth will occur in the world's poorer countries.—Lowell Ponte, *The Cooling*

Summarizing Note

Population is growing much more quickly in underdeveloped countries than in industrialized countries.

Plagiarized Note

Population growth is no more evenly distributed than food. More than 90 percent of all future population growth will occur in the poorer countries of the world.

For Writing

Write a summarizing note for each of the following passages:

Some of the same ideas carried out to keep humans more comfortable and healthy have been found to be beneficial for animals as well. Earlier we mentioned that hens are more productive in a cool environment. Hogs eat more and gain weight faster when they are protected from the scorching of an Iowa summer. Cool, contented cows produce more milk.—Louis J. Battan, *Harvesting the Clouds*

Despite its success, the nonviolent civil rights movement failed to touch many areas important in the South and neglected issues vital to blacks in northern urban ghettos. In the North overt legal discrimination (Jim Crow laws) had not really been much of a problem for blacks in the twentieth century. Northern whites had discriminated against blacks almost as severely and rigidly as had their southern counterparts, but they did so less openly and as a matter of custom rather than law. This discriminatory pattern was a great deal more difficult to combat than was the legal discrimination in the South.—Robert L. Church, *Education in the United States*

Even if we ignore the introduction of fleets of jumbo jets, trucks, cars, trains, subways and the like, our social investment in mobility is astonishing. Paved roads and streets have been added to the American landscape at the incredible rate of more than 200 miles per day, every single day for at least the last twenty years. This adds up to 75,000 miles of new streets and roads every year, enough to girdle the globe three times. While United States population increased during this period by 38.5 percent, street and road mileage shot up 100 percent.—Alvin Toffler, *Future Shock*

Another pro-marriage argument, occasionally encountered, is based on demographic statistics that married people live longer than the unmarried. But this finding can be readily explained without recourse to the proposition that marriage causes longevity. For example, the statistics do not take into account the likelihood that ill individuals may decide not to marry or may not be able to find partners. As long as such selective factors are ignored, the demographic data will remain difficult to interpret.—Lawrence Casler, *Is Marriage Necessary?*

Unlike judo, aikido has no rules, no static opening positions; the throws are more fluid, the movements more like a dance. The nonaggressive nature of this art is reflected in its terminology. The defender is known as the *nage* (pronounced nah-gay), from a Japanese word meaning "throw." The attacker is called the *uke* (oo-kay), from a Japanese word associated with the idea of falling. Thus, in aikido, he who attacks takes a fall.—George Leonard, *The Ultimate Athlete*

"Renewable marriages" they have been called. A five-year commitment, or a ten-year commitment, or a three-year commitment would be made. The partners would promise to maintain the marriage at least for this limited period of time. If at the end of that period they felt that the relationship was not a good one, they could renege. Alternatively, if they felt that it was a good one, they could recommit themselves to it.—Jessie Barnard, *The Future of Marriage*

Writing the Paper

Writing a research paper doesn't differ essentially from writing other papers in which the purpose is to explain or persuade, interpret or criticize, but some of the procedures discussed in earlier chapters have special pertinence. For one thing, it's imperative to budget your time and to work systematically at every stage of the project. However thorough your research and however lucid your report on your findings, your paper won't be satisfactory if the documentation is inconsistent and the proofreading careless. And however elegant the documentation, shoddy basic research will undermine its effect. A good reference paper shows deliberate care in all its aspects— enough evidence of care that the reader feels he can take the accuracy of text, documentation, and mechanics for granted and concentrate on the thesis, the evidence, and the movement of ideas through well-constructed sentences, paragraphs, and sections.

Planning and Writing

Although the quantity of material and the length of the paper make it advisable to have your outline on paper before you begin writing, consider several possibilities before you commit yourself to one plan. Your material will fall into blocks, probably from five to eight. The order of these blocks, which turn out to be paragraph sequences as you write, should grow logically out of your material, your approach, and your purpose.

The Outline

When you survey the notes you've taken, you'll probably revise the tentative outline you've used as a guide in gathering material. For your final outline you'll sort your facts into those that must be used, those that will probably be used, those of incidental interest that may be used, and those that clearly don't belong. To avoid wasting time in planning and writing, you may want to sort your cards into four groups: *Must, Probably, Maybe,* and *No.* Throw out *No.* Once you've done that, you can draw up an outline in standard form so that your instructor can examine it and offer suggestions.

The Writing Process

Perhaps because it's long, some of the typical problems of writing any paper occur in more exaggerated form in the research project. Many writers waste an alarming amount of time making a beginning. The usual advice holds: Pull yourself out of a bogged-down introduction and get on with the rest of the paper. After the whole paper has begun to take shape, go back and compose an introductory passage. This advice assumes that you're in command of a workable thesis. Sometimes floundering at the outset is caused by vagueness of purpose. If you're in that predicament, the thing to do is admit the problem and think through the material again, working toward a thesis that you believe in and find manageable.

As you write, you'll almost certainly encounter unexpected problems. What seemed like intersecting avenues of meaning will become blind alleys. Authorities you took to be unshakable will totter and fall. But as you struggle with a deskload of material, you'll often surprise yourself by coming up with new connections between ideas, new alignments of facts, new interpretations of evidence. The important thing is to cultivate an attitude of openness to such possibilities as you write—and to proceed with the deliberateness of a writer to whom each sentence and paragraph is a matter of rhetorical calculation. Given the nature of the subject, the audience, and your own intentions, what strategies of language, method, organization, and argument will produce the most clarity and persuasiveness?

Even when you're well launched into the writing and feel thoroughly at home with your material, it's wise to review all your notes periodically. Much of your paper will be a digest of sources in your own words, and you need to have a good grasp of the ideas and facts so that you won't rely too heavily on what you wrote on the cards. A great deal of rephrasing of even your best summaries will be necessary if they're to fit comfortably into the paper and harmonize with your own style.

Use of Quotation and Paraphrase

You'll need to decide when it's better to paraphrase and when to quote directly from your sources, and how you can best integrate the material you're citing. Use direct quotation rather sparingly—keeping it within, say, 10 percent of your final manuscript. A research paper shouldn't be a string of quotations knotted together with transitional sentences; too many quotations betray an overdependence on sources and reveal a failure to assimilate the material into your own thinking. What you are expected to do is give the material a form and a thrust of meaning of its own.

Quote directly from sources when the exact words in the passage illustrate or support your point more effectively than a restatement of the idea could. A short quotation—of a sentence, a phrase, key words—should be run into your text in quotation marks and documented (see p. 328). If what you quote contains quotation marks, change the double quotes of the original to single ones, since they now indicate a quotation within a quotation. A quoted passage that's more than four lines long when you type it out should be set off from the rest of the manuscript. Unless your instructor wants you to single-space, type it double-spaced. Indent each line ten spaces from the left-hand margin, using an additional five-space indention for new paragraphs (at the opening or within the passage). Don't use quotation marks around passages set off in this way. Place the note number at the end of the last word of the passage. This procedure is illustrated in the sample research paper, on the page numbered 1. (See p. 327.)

As you write, you'll paraphrase many of the facts and interpretations you've recorded in your notes. In restating the idea in your own words and fitting it into the context of your paper, recheck your notes to be certain that in using the material you're remaining true to the sense of the original, that it provides the support you want in developing your subject, and that you're crediting it properly.

Often you'll mix paraphrase with brief quotations—integrating ideas and key words from your sources into the pattern of your own presentation. Go over these portions of your paper to achieve a smooth blending of elements, and be sure to give proper credit to your sources. (See pp. 2, 3, and 6 of the sample research paper for examples of brief quotation, paraphrase, and a longer quotation.)

Because the finished paper gives credit in notes to the sources used, you'll want to indicate these sources in your first draft. You can put an abbreviated reference to the source in parentheses after a statement (see the draft reproduced on p. 329) or in the margin. Either method enables you to transfer the data to a note when you make your final copy.

Type your rough draft triple-spaced or write it with wide margins to leave room for revisions.

For Writing

Write a rough draft of the first four or five paragraphs of your paper. Don't try to write an introduction to the whole paper; just begin with the substance of your discussion. Submit the draft to your instructor with a trial outline.

Style and Point of View

The conventional style of research papers is formal and impersonal. Usually the writer doesn't refer to himself extensively—though there's no good rhetorical reason why the first person pronoun shouldn't be used for special emphasis (it's certainly preferable to the stuffy "the present writer" or the editorial "we"). Writing that strives for accuracy and objectivity in its treatment of a subject doesn't have to be dull, nor does it require total self-effacement. Just keep in mind that your reader will be more interested in what you've done with your material than in what it's done to you—and try to write prose that's concise, specific, readable, and calculated to reach your audience.

What assumptions should you make about your reader? This question, like others about rhetorical strategy, should be discussed with your instructor. A safe general rule is to pitch your essay at the brightest members of your class—intelligent, critical readers who know little about your subject but want to know more. Assume that you'll be asked to read parts of the paper aloud to them.

Beginning and Ending the Paper

Although there's more reason for a research paper to have formal introductory and concluding sections than for a short essay to have them, most professionals studiously avoid the kind of beginning that self-consciously announces what is going to be said and the kind of ending that solemnly sums up point by point what *has* been said. Instead, the best practice involves finding a provocative angle in the research material and building an introduction around that—one that succeeds in stirring interest and at the same time defines the nature of the inquiry. An essay on ideas about the political significance of language in George Orwell's novels might, for instance, begin with the image a friend has given of Orwell propped up in bed in his final illness, happily cutting out newspaper articles that confirm his fears about the general decline of English through political misuse and propaganda.

As for the conclusion, a skilled writer will generally resist the urge to grandly recapitulate his argument one more time, choosing instead to end the paper with a final, clinching point that grows directly out of the body of the paper. If he offers a summary at all, it will be brief and straightforward, a final demonstration that the paper's argument speaks for itself.

Proofreading

Proofreading is not just a matter of striving to please your instructor—"profreading" one student called it. It's essential in all writing and particularly crucial in the writing of a research paper. The attention you give to it is a courtesy to your readers and a basic way of serving your paper's best interests. What would you think of the authority and dependability of an essay on, say, pollution in Lake Ontario that spelled *effluent* three different ways, omitted several notes, put Chart I where Chart III should have gone and vice versa, and added three zeros to the 1970 population of Rochester, New York? You might not be especially impressed to find all such errors *avoided* in a paper, to be sure; but the positive virtues of an essay rest in part on such negative virtues, the result of careful proofreading.

In proofreading a research paper, it's especially important to check the accuracy of your source references. Does the information used in the paper actually come from the page of the source on which you say you have found it? To make sure, check your reference to sources against your original note cards or even against your sources themselves.

Documentation: Endnotes or Footnotes

Any paper based on the writings of others should acknowledge the sources used. Common courtesy and honesty require that credit is given where credit is due, and a scrupulously documented source allows the reader to judge for himself the evidence an assertion is based on. It also allows the reader to turn to the sources for further information. College students are expected to draw their materials from various sources, but they are also expected to make a frank acknowledgment of these sources.

In formal academic papers, it's conventional to give exact source references in endnotes or footnotes. These notes record in a brief and consistent form the author, title, facts of publication, and exact page from which each quotation and each fact or opinion is taken. Your instructor will prescribe the style of documentation you should follow. The style of notes and bibliography suggested in this section follows the recommendations of the *MLA Handbook*.

Documentation is needed for all direct quotations, except for lines from the Bible, proverbs, and other familiar sayings. Documentation is also needed for all important statements of fact, interpretations, opinions, and conclusions that you've derived from the work of other writers—*even if you phrase this material in your own words*. You need to give the source for all statistics, descriptions of situations, scientific data, and the like that are neither common knowledge nor the product of your own investigation. (Common knowledge includes not just facts like the location of San Francisco but undisputed matters—the dates of Theodore Roosevelt's birth, marriage, and death, for example—that anyone can find without difficulty.) If you have any questions about what to document, consult your instructor.

Placement of Notes

To document your source of information, insert a note number slightly above the line immediately *after* the quotation or summary. This number refers to a footnote at the bottom of the same page or a corresponding endnote located on a separate page at the end of the paper. The *MLA Handbook* recommends endnotes; some teachers prefer footnotes. Follow your instructor's directions.

If you are using endnotes, type them all on a separate page at the end of the paper. Double-space endnotes and double-space between them. The endnote number should be slightly raised, and there should be one space between the number and the first word of the note.

If you are using footnotes, type all footnotes for each page at the bottom of that page. Triple-space between the text and the first note. Single-space footnotes, but double-space between them. The footnote number should be slightly raised, and there should be no space between the number and the first word of the note.

Form for the First Reference

The first time a source is identified in a note, the documentation must be complete. As you'll see in the examples below, you'll need to vary the form according to the kind of source you're citing—books, compilations, translations, articles in journals or newspapers, unpublished dissertations, and so on. Examine each form carefully to see what elements are included, in what order they appear, and how they're punctuated.

A book by a single author:

[1] Truman A. Hartshorn, <u>Interpreting the City: An Urban Geography</u> (New York: Wiley, 1980), p. 322.

A book by more than one author:

[2] Eric Dunning and Kenneth Sheard, <u>Barbarians, Gentlemen, and Players</u> (New York: New York Univ. Press, 1979), p. 73.

(Use "et al." or "and others" when there are more than three authors: Mary Beth Sullivan and others, *Feeling Free*.)

A book with a corporate author:

[3] Organization for Economic Cooperation and Development, <u>Adverse Weather, Reduced Visibility, and Road Safety</u> (Paris: OECD, 1976), p. 62.

(A corporate author is an organization, legislative body, committee, or any other group that is cited as a book's author.)

A work in more than one volume:

[4] John Lyons, <u>Semantics</u> (Cambridge: Cambridge Univ. Press, 1977), I, 96.

(The roman numeral is the volume number. When the volume number is given, page numbers are not preceded by "pp.")

An edition other than the first:

⁵ James F. Engel, Martin R. Warshaw, and Thomas C. Kinnear, Promotional Strategy, 4th ed. (Homewood, Ill.: Irwin, 1979), pp. 19-20.

(If the city where the book was published is not well known, the name of the state or country should be included. This technique is sometimes used to avoid confusion between places with the same name: Toledo, Spain.)

An edited work:

⁶ Ralph Waldo Emerson, Emerson's Literary Criticism, ed. Eric W. Carlson (Lincoln: Univ. of Nebraska Press, 1979), p. 205.

A compilation:

⁷ Michael Steinman, ed., Energy and Environmental Issues (Lexington, Mass.: Lexington Books, 1979), pp. iii-iv.

A selection, chapter, or other part of a compilation:

⁸ P. A. M. Dirac, "Developments of Einstein's Theory of Gravitation," in On the Path of Albert Einstein, ed. Arnold Perlmutter and Linda F. Scott (New York: Plenum, 1979), p. 6.

A translation:

⁹ Immanuel Kant, Lectures on Ethics, trans. Louis Infield (Gloucester, Mass.: P. Smith, 1978), p. 153.

A book in a series:

¹⁰ Edmund Reiss, **William Dunbar**, Twayne's English Authors Series, No. 257 (Boston: Twayne, 1979), p. 69.

A reprinted book:

¹¹ William Godwin, Life of Geoffrey Chaucer, 2nd ed. (1894; rpt. New York: AMS, 1974), II, 271.

A signed article in a newspaper:

¹² Fox Butterfield, "Religions Flower as China Eases Rules," New York Times, 27 May 1980, Sec. A, p. 12, col. 1.

An unsigned article in a weekly magazine:

¹³ "Robots Join the Labor Force," Business Week, 9 June 1980, p. 62.

An article in a monthly magazine:

[14] Glyn Daniel, "Megalithic Monuments," <u>Scientific American</u>,
July 1980, pp. 75-76.

(No volume numbers are used for weekly or monthly magazines. Notice the form
for citing the date of the issue.)

An article in a journal paged continuously through the annual volume:

[15] Sherle L. Boone and Alberto Montari, "Aggression and Family
Size," <u>Journal of Psychology</u>, 103 (1979), 69.

(In some journals pages are numbered continuously from issue to issue throughout
the year. For such journals, cite the volume number and the year of publication of
the annual volume but not the number of the issue or the month of publication.)

An article in a journal with separate pagination for each issue:

[16] Fred L. Fry, "The End of Affirmative Action," <u>Business
Horizons</u>, 23, No. 1 (1980), 36.

(For a journal that does *not* number pages continuously through the issues of each
annual volume, the issue number must be given in addition to the volume number
and the year.)

A signed encyclopedia article:

[17] C. L[ockard] C[onley], "Blood, Human," <u>Encyclopaedia
Britannica: Macropaedia</u>, 1978 ed.

(When an article is only initialed, the rest of the author's name as cited in the list
of contributors is placed between square brackets.)

A book review:

[18] June Sochen, rev. of <u>Children of Fantasy: The First Rebels of
Greenwich Village</u>, by Robert E. Humphrey, <u>American Historical Review</u>,
84 (1979), 576-77.

An unpublished dissertation:

[19] Frances Nicol Teague, "Ben Jonson's Stagecraft in His Four
Major Comedies," Diss. Univ. of Texas 1975, p. 71.

A government document:

[20] U.S. Dept. of Labor, <u>Work Attitudes and Work Experience:
The Impact of Attitudes on Behavior</u> (Washington, D.C.: GPO, 1979), p. 3.

A pamphlet:

21 Sex Equality in Educational Materials, American Assn. of
School Administrators Executive Handbook Series, IV (Arlington, Va.:
AASA, n.d.), 12.

(When citing pamphlets, imitate the form of a book citation as closely as possible, using appropriate abbreviations if facts of publication are missing. The "n.d." in this entry means "no date." The meanings of other common abbreviations are explained on pp. 316–17 of this chapter.)

A lecture:

22 Richard Ruland, "American Literature in Europe Since World
War II," American Literature Section, MLA Convention, San Francisco,
28 Dec. 1979.

An interview:

23 Personal interview with Jean Del Gaudio, Writer/Editor,
Technical Communications Services, Owens-Corning Fiberglas Corp.,
18 July 1980.

(Begin an interview entry by designating the type of interview, personal or telephone.)

A TV or radio program:

24 Washington Week in Review, mod. Paul Duke, PBS, 25 July 1980.

The citation of an unusual source that doesn't fit any of the conventional forms (a phonograph record or record jacket or a personal letter, for example) should conform as closely as possible to the style used for other notes:

25 R. A. Randall, letter to the author, 23 April 1981.

Form for Later Reference

A shortened note form is used for subsequent references after the first full citation. Use the author's last name or—if the author's name is not given—use a shortened form of the title. The following notes illustrate the proper form:

26 Dirac, p. 8.

27 Lyons, p. 103.

28 "Robots Join," p. 65.

If more than one work by the same author is used, then subsequent references must include at least the key word in the title:

> [29] Hartshorn, <u>Interpreting</u>, p. 83.

> [30] Hartshorn, <u>Metropolis</u>, p. 101.

When two or more notes in order refer to the same work or even the same
page, simply repeat the short form:

> [31] Reiss, p. 72.

> [32] Reiss, p. 72.

Ibid., which used to appear regularly in notes to indicate "in the same
place," is now out of fashion.

Split Note

If the author's name is given in full in the text, it can be omitted from the
note. This does not apply to the title of a work, however. If title and author
both appear in the text, the title should still begin the note.

Informational Note

In some scholarly publications, an additional fact, a statement of a different
opinion, a quotation, or a reference to other sources is sometimes given in
a note. In college writing you may occasionally want to use an informational
note for useful material not directly pertinent to the discussion; but be careful not to use the device for digressions that, however interesting, are irrelevant to the discussion.

You can also use informational notes to explain special documentation
and thus save notes. For example, a paragraph containing a number of statistics from a single source interspersed among the writer's own comments
would need only a single note if the note explained that it applied solely to
the statistics.

Common Abbreviations

The following abbreviations are commonly used in notes. Although you're
not likely to use more than a few of them, you should know what they
mean. The *MLA Handbook* notes that practice varies in italicizing abbreviations of Latin words. Of the following only *sic* is italicized in *A Manual of
Style,* 12th ed. (Chicago: Univ. of Chicago Press, 1969). The practice in the
Handbook is not to italicize *sic* or any other common Latin terms.

art.	article.
c. or ca.	for *circa:* around a given date (ca. 1480).
cf.	for *confer:* compare
ch. or chap.; chs. or chaps.	chapter; chapters.

col., cols.	column, columns.
comp.	compiler, compiled by.
ed.	editor, edition (2nd ed.), edited by.
e.g. (set off by commas)	for *exempli gratia:* for example.
et al.	for *et alii:* and others (used in MLA style when there are more than three authors; but the English words are also widely used: Walter S. Avis and others).
f., ff.	and the following page (386f.), and the following pages (286ff.). Exact references are preferable: pp. 286–87, pp. 286–91 (MLA style); or pp. 286–287, pp. 286–291.
ibid.	for *ibidem:* in the same place. (No longer in fashion.)
l., ll.	line, lines.
loc. cit.	for *loco citato:* in the place cited. (No longer in fashion.)
MS, MSS	manuscript, manuscripts.
n., nn.	note (to refer to a footnote in a source: p. 135, n. 2), notes.
n.d.	no date of publication.
n.p.	no place of publication; also, no publisher.
NS or N.S.	new series of a periodical.
op. cit.	for *opere citato:* in the work cited. (No longer in fashion.)
OS or O.S.	old series of a periodical
p., pp.	page, pages
passim	throughout the work.
sic	thus, so (used to indicate that erroneous or doubtful information or a misspelling has been quoted exactly).
trans. or tr.	translator, translation, or translated by.
vol., vols.	volume, volumes (vol. and p. are not used when figures for both are given: Vol. III *or* p. 176; but III, 176).

The Final Bibliography

The bibliography of the sources actually used in the preparation of a reference paper comes at its end. It contains not all the sources consulted but only those that have actually furnished material. (Your instructor may, however, ask you to supply a supplementary list, ''Other Works Consulted.'')

Its purpose is to enable a reader to see at a glance the range of works cited in the notes; therefore, entries begin with the authors' last names. When no author is given, the first important word of the title is used as the key word for alphabetizing.

The first line of each entry in a bibliography is begun at the left margin, and succeeding lines are indented five spaces. The sample entries that follow are double-spaced as recommended in the *MLA Handbook*. The sample entries here are for the same works used earlier to illustrate note form. Comparison will make clear how the two differ.

A book by a single author and a second book by the same author:

Hartshorn, Truman A.   Interpreting the City: An Urban Geography.

New York: Wiley, 1980.

----------.   Metropolis in Georgia: Atlanta's Rise as a Major

Transaction Center.   Cambridge, Mass.: Ballinger, 1976.

(Instead of repeating the author's name, use ten dashes followed by a period.)

A book by more than one author:

Dunning, Eric, and Kenneth Sheard.   Barbarians, Gentlemen, and Players.

New York: New York Univ. Press, 1979.

(Do not reverse the names of co-authors following the first author's name: Bryant, Barbara, William Jensen, and Ann Wagner. Separate "et al." or "and others" from the first name with a comma: Sullivan, Mary Beth, and others.)

A book with a corporate author:

Organization for Economic Cooperation and Development.   Adverse

Weather, Reduced Visibility, and Road Safety.   Paris: OECD, 1976.

A work in more than one volume:

Lyons, John.   Semantics.   2 vols.   Cambridge: Cambridge Univ. Press, 1977.

An edition other than the first:

Engel, James F., Martin R. Warshaw, and Thomas C. Kinnear.

Promotional Strategy.   4th ed.   Homewood, Ill.: Irwin, 1979.

An edited work:

Emerson, Ralph Waldo.   Emerson's Literary Criticism.   Ed. Eric W.

Carlson.   Lincoln: Univ. of Nebraska Press, 1979.

A compilation:

Steinman, Michael, ed. <u>Energy and Environmental Issues</u>. **Lexington,**
    Mass.: Lexington Books, 1979.

A selection, chapter, or other part of a compilation:

Dirac, P. A. M. "Developments of Einstein's Theory of Gravitation."
    In <u>On the Path of Albert Einstein</u>. Ed. Arnold Perlmutter and
    Linda F. Scott. New York: Plenum, 1979, pp. 1-13.

A translation:

Kant, Immanuel. <u>Lectures on Ethics</u>. Trans. Louis Infield.
    Gloucester, Mass.: P. Smith, 1978.

A book in a series:

Reiss, Edmund. <u>William Dunbar</u>. Twayne English Authors Series,
    No. 257. Boston: Twayne, 1979.

A reprinted book:

Godwin, William. <u>Life of Geoffrey Chaucer</u>. 2nd ed. 1804; rpt.
    New York: AMS, 1974.

A signed article in a newspaper:

Butterfield, Fox. "Religions Flower as China Eases Rules." <u>New
    York Times</u>, 27 May 1980, Sec. A, p. 12, cols. 1-6.

An unsigned article in a weekly magazine:

"Robots Join the Labor Force." <u>Business Week</u>, 9 June 1980,
    pp. 62-65, 68, 73.

(All the pages on which the article appears are listed in the bibliography, not just
those pages that were actually used.)

An article in a monthly magazine:

Daniel, Glyn. "Megalithic Monuments." <u>Scientific American</u>, July
    1980, pp. 64-67, 70-76.

An article in a journal paged continuously through the annual volume:

Boone, Sherle L., and Alberto Montare. "Aggression and Family Size."
    <u>Journal of Psychology</u>, 103 (1979), 67-70.

An article in a journal with separate pagination for each issue:

Fry, Fred L. "The End of Affirmative Action." Business Horizons,
    23, No. 1 (1980), 34-40.

A signed encyclopedia article:

C[onley], C. L[ockard]. "Blood, Human." Encyclopaedia Britannica:
    Macropaedia. 1978 ed.

A book review:

Sochen, June. Rev. of Children of Fantasy: The First Rebels of
    Greenwich Village, by Robert E. Humphrey. American Historical
    Review, 84 (1979), 576-77.

An unpublished dissertation:

Teague, Frances Nicol. "Ben Jonson's Stagecraft in His Four Major
    Comedies." Diss. Univ. of Texas 1975.

A government document:

U.S. Dept. of Labor. Work Attitudes and Work Experiences: The
    Impact of Attitudes on Behavior. Washington, D.C.: GPO, 1979.

A pamphlet:

Sex Equality in Educational Materials. American Assn. of School
    Administrators Executive Handbook Series, IV. Arlington, Va.:
    AASA, n.d.

A lecture:

Ruland, Richard. "American Literature in Europe Since World War
    II." American Literature Section, MLA Convention, San
    Francisco. 28 Dec. 1979.

An interview:

Del Gaudio, Jean. Writer/Editor, Technical Communications Services,
    Owens-Corning Fiberglas Corp. Personal interview. 18 July 1980.

A TV or radio program:

Washington Week in Review. Mod. Paul Duke. PBS, 25 July 1980.

For Writing

1. Put the following references to source material in consistent note form as they would appear on the Notes page of a research paper. Keep them in the present order.

a. To page 14 of Marketing Principles, 3rd edition, by Ben M. Enis, published by Goodyear Publishing Company of Santa Monica in 1980.

b. To an unsigned article called Did the Earth Once Have a Ring? published in the July 7, 1980, edition of Newsweek. The entire article appears on page 75 of the issue.

c. To pages 323–24 of Personal Selling: Foundations, Practice, and Management, by Ben M. Enis, published by Goodyear Publishing Company of Santa Monica in 1979.

d. To pages 98–99 of the book mentioned in *a*.

e. To an initialed article entitled Islam in the Encyclopaedia Britannica: Macropaedia, the 1978 edition. The initials, F. R., belong to Fazlur Rahman.

f. To page 41, volume one, of The Printing Press as an Agent of Change by Elizabeth L. Eisenstein, published in 1979 by Cambridge University Press of England. This book is published in two volumes.

g. To page 54, volume one, of the book mention in *f*.

h. To pages 347–48 of an article Let's Get Realistic About Career Paths by James Walker. The article was published in Current Issues in Personnel Management, a book of readings edited by Kendrith M. Rowland, Manuel London, Gerald R. Ferris, and Jay L. Sherman. This book was published in 1980 by Allyn and Bacon of Boston. The entire article appears on pages 347–55.

i. To an article in the Wall Street Journal entitled The Latest Thing in Condominiums Is Merely an Open Piece of Land. Written by David P. Garino, the article is found in the August 1, 1980, issue, in columns 1 and 2 on page 13. Material for the note comes from column 1.

j. To an article entitled Regionalism in the 1976 Presidential Election. Written by John Swauger, the article appears on pages 157–66 in The Geographical Review, volume 70, 1980. Material for the note comes from page 159. This periodical is paginated continuously throughout the volume for each year.

k. To page 162 of the article mentioned in *j*.

2. Put the items above in proper form and order for a bibliography.

In short bibliographies like those you'll prepare for most of your college papers, all the items are run in one list, alphabetically arranged. Very long bibliographies are sometimes grouped by type of material: primary sources, secondary sources; works by an author, works about him; and so on. They should not be grouped according to type of publication, such as books and periodicals, except in a list of the works of a single writer.

Divisions of a Completed Paper

The completed research paper is usually made up of the following units:

1. *Title page.* Give the title of the paper, your name, the date submitted, and any other required information, such as your instructor's name and the course and section number.

2. *Outline and table of contents.* Make the type of outline assigned. Be sure it conforms to the order of material in the finished paper. Check its form by referring to the models on pp. 169–70. The outline can serve as a table of contents if you give at the right of each main topic the page on which it begins.

3. *Text of the paper.* This is the final copy of the paper, complete with diagrams or any other illustrative material used. Put the title at the top of the first page. Follow the manuscript form required by your instructor.

4. *Endnotes.* The first page of endnotes should be titled "Notes." Follow the note forms illustrated on pp. 312–16 of this chapter.

5. *Bibliography:* On a separate page, list in the form suggested on pp. 317–20 the books and articles you actually used in writing your paper.

6. *Appendix.* Occasionally a paper needs a table of statistics too long to work into the body of the essay, or it may require a long quotation, such as part of a treaty or other document that much of the paper is based on. Such material can be placed in an appendix, but in student research papers it generally should be abridged and included in text.

Sample Research Paper

The sample research paper included here follows the guidelines for research and writing set forth in this chapter and the style of documentation described on pp. 311–17. Comments in the margin and questions are designed to help you identify particular details of form to be followed and alert you to specific problems that you may encounter in writing your paper.

For comparison with the final typed version, samples are included of material from the early stages of preparing the paper: preliminary version of the outline (p. 324), note cards (p. 333), rough draft (p. 329), and bibliography cards (p. 341).

Talking Apes?

by

Eric Kelly

English 102-27
Ms. Kathleen Taylor
May 15, 1981

Preliminary Outline

Talking Apes?

Experiments in teaching apes to use American Sign Language (ASL) show that apes can name objects and can even combine symbols, but these experiments have failed to show that apes have the ability to combine signs grammatically.

  I. Apes can use symbols accurately.

     A. Test scores--Washoe and Koko.

     B. Washoe's errors.

  II. Extensive vocabularies.

     A. Nim--125 signs; Koko--245; Washoe--300.

  III. Symbols are not combined grammatically.

     A. Apes can use sign-combinations to convey wants and needs.

     B. However, taken out of context the signs can mean various things, which would not be the case if they were combined grammatically.

  IV. Criticism of the training methods should result in a reevaluation of evidence. However, there is other evidence that these apes do use signs meaningfully.

Sentence Outline

Talking Apes?

Although experiments in teaching apes to use American Sign
Language (ASL) show that apes can use gesture-symbols to name
objects and can even combine symbols to express meanings, these
experiments have failed to show that apes share with human beings
the ability to combine symbols in grammatical patterns.

I. Apes trained in American Sign Language (ASL) have shown that
    they can use the correct gesture-symbols to name objects.

    A. Washoe and Koko scored well on tests in which they
        were asked to identify objects by signing.

    B. Even Washoe's errors showed that the gesture-symbols
        had some meaning for her.

    C. Some of the apes trained in ASL have developed fairly
        extensive vocabularies of signs.

II. Although apes trained in ASL can put signs together into
    combinations, these combinations fail to show that apes
    share with human beings the ability to relate language
    symbols grammatically.

    A. These apes can use combinations of gesture-symbols to
        express their wants and needs to their trainers.

    B. However, these combinations convey clear meaning only
        in context--in the immediate situation.

**Compare with
preliminary
outline on
facing page.**

III. On the basis of his own studies, Herbert S. Terrace has
concluded that the sign-combinations are simply imitations
of trainers' signs--not attempts to convey meaning.

    A. Videotapes and films show that the signs were a response
to signs that had just been used or that were being
simultaneously used by the trainers.

    B. Terrace's criticisms should lead to a reevaluation
of the testing methods.

    C. His criticism should not overshadow the evidence that apes
have used the signs spontaneously and meaningfully.

IV. Although apes have some ability to use a language system,
that ability--as far as the experiments show--will never
develop beyond that of a two-year-old child.

For Analysis

Compare the sentence outline with the preliminary version and
analyze the differences. What changes were made in the revision to
regularize the form? What changes were made in the thesis statement? Do the changes in the thesis statement improve it? How?

Talking Apes?

As far as we know, possession of human language is
associated with a specific type of mental organization,
not simply a higher degree of intelligence. There seems
to be no substance to the view that human language is
simply a more complex instance of something to be found
elsewhere in the animal world.[1]

These words of Noam Chomsky express the belief that only human
beings can use language, because language is the unique product of
the human brain. During the 1960s and 1970s, several American
psychologists working with chimpanzees and gorillas conducted experiments that challenge this belief. They taught a number of these
animals the sign language used by many deaf people, a system called
American Sign Language (ASL). The researchers wanted to see whether
apes could be taught to use gestures to name objects and concepts.
More important, they wanted to see whether apes could be taught to
combine symbols in patterns similar to those in human languages.
Questions about their testing methods have raised doubts about the
accuracy of some of their findings. But some of their observations
do seem trustworthy. These apes seem to be able to use ASL symbols
to communicate intentions, observations, and elementary ideas.

**Note numbers
are placed
slightly above
the line
following a
quotation or
summary of
information
taken from a
source.**

**Compare with
rough draft on
facing page.**

Apes trained to use ASL have shown that they can associate
specific gesture-symbols with objects. In one vocabulary test
of this ability, the apes were asked to give the correct ASL sign
for a familiar object that was placed in a box or shown in a
slide-picture projected on a screen. According to trainers Beatrice
and Allen Gardner, the chimpanzee Washoe used the correct sign
fifty-three out of ninety-nine times when given this test.[2] In another
instance, the gorilla Koko scored an even better 62 percent.[3]

While the ability of the apes to use ASL was obviously far from
perfect, the tests show that apes can learn to connect symbols with
the objects those symbols stand for. Their use of signs is not
merely random. Statistically, given the number of signs she could make
at the age when she took these vocabulary tests, Washoe would have made
only three correct choices out of ninety-nine through chance. Even her
mistakes suggest some understanding of what the ASL symbols mean.
Often, her incorrect sign was actually the sign for another object in
the same class of objects. Take, for example, her performance in
making the correct signs for grooming objects. Thirty of the tests
of her vocabulary involved giving the sign for comb, or brush, or some
other object used in grooming. Washoe made the correct sign only
eighteen times. But, according to the Gardners, "7 of the 12 errors
were the signs for other items in the category of grooming articles."[4]
In other words, she might sign "comb" when she saw a brush in the box.
This type of error suggests that she at least perceived the category

Rough Draft

¶ apes trained to use ASL have shown that they can associate specific gesture-symbols with objects.

^ ~~These apes can associate symbols with objects.~~ In one vocabulary test of this ability, the apes [were] ~~are~~ asked to give the correct ASL sign for a familiar object [that was] placed in a box or [shown in] a slide-picture ~~of such an object~~ projected on a screen. [According to trainers Beatrice and Allen Gardner,] ~~In a test on recognizing ninety-nine objects Washoe gave the correct sign for fifty-three, far beyond the mere chance of three correct. Her errors were often to give the sign~~ the chimpanzee Washoe used the correct sign fifty-three out of ninety-nine times when given this test.[2] In another instance, the gorilla Koko scored an even better 62 percent.

~~of something in the same class of objects like "comb" instead of "brush" (Gardner, Two-way, p. 160). On a test similar to Washoe's Koko at age four scored an even better 62 percent. Her errors were to sign to have the box containing the object opened; to give the sign for something else in the same class; to make again a sign she had previously made; to use a sign similar to the correct one (Patterson, Ling., pp. 179 and 181).~~

¶ While the ability of the apes to use ASL was obviously far from perfect, the tests show ~~These tests show that the apes have some ability to connect symbols with objects.~~ that apes can learn to connect symbols with the objects those symbols stand for. Their use of signs is not merely random. ~~Given the vocabulary she possessed at the age when she was given the box test,~~ Statistically, given the number of signs she could make at [the age when she took these vocabulary tests,] Washoe would have ~~posted~~ [made] only three correct [choices] out of ninety-nine through ~~random~~ chance. (Gardner, Two-way, p. 160). Even her mistakes [suggest] ~~show that she has~~ some understanding of what the ASL symbols mean. Often, her incorrect sign was actually the sign for another object in the same class of objects. Take, for example, her performance in making the correct signs for grooming objects. Thirty of the ~~ninety-nine~~ tests [of her vocabulary] involved giving the sign for comb, or brush, or some other object [used] ~~involved~~ in grooming. Washoe made the correct sign only eighteen times. But, [according to the Gardners,] "7 of the 12 errors were the signs for other items in the category of grooming articles." (Gardner, Two-way, p. 160). In other words, she might sign "comb" when she saw a brush in the box. This type of error suggests that

A brief citation in parentheses records the source. As a result, material can be omitted or the order of material can be changed without ruining an established sequence of note numbers.

3

"grooming item" as a link between object and sign.

These results show that apes can learn the meanings of ASL symbols. Some of the apes used in the experiments learned to use well over a hundred symbols with some degree of accuracy. At forty-four months, the chimpanzee Nim knew 125 signs, ranging from symbols for nouns, like "dog," to symbols for verbs, like "drink," and including symbols for adjectives and adverbs.[5] Koko's vocabulary is thought to include 245 signs,[6] and one researcher estimates the number of signs in Washoe's vocabulary to be "close to three hundred."[7]

A more important issue, however, is whether apes can be taught to put symbols together in the patterns we use in speaking and writing. For if they can be shown to have this ability, Chomsky's theory that human language requires a unique kind of brain would be disproven. The brain of an ape would have to be considered as also having the ability to do what only a human being has been thought capable of doing—perceiving grammatical relationships.[8]

The apes trained in ASL do use short combinations of signs. For example, Nim has been recorded as having used the following: "eat grape," "food Nim," "eat tickle," "food there," "green color," "clean there," "Nim out," and others. One of his most frequently made sign-combinations is "play me" or "me play."[9]

A number of incidents make it clear that the apes can communicate with their trainers using such short sign-combinations. Nim loved to help his trainers with the wash. When he wanted them

Although the information about Nim comes from more than one page of the source, a single note is sufficient documentation here.

4

to get clothes to put in the washer, he signaled "give me." When

he wanted the door to the washing machine opened, he signaled

"open" and then signaled "wash" or "give wash" to get soap.[10]

Similarly, Washoe used short sign-combinations to make one of her

trainers, Susan, remove her foot from Washoe's rubber doll. (Susan

had deliberately stepped on it to test whether Washoe would rely on

her symbol system to make Susan stop.) Some of her sign-combinations

were "up Susan," "Susan up," "mine please up," "please shoe," "more

mine," "baby down," and "baby up."[11] In such situations as these,

the trainers responded appropriately. Given the situation and the

chimp's behavior, they could understand what the animal meant.

However, the apes' use of sign-combinations to communicate their

desires does not show that apes can perceive grammatical relation-

ships. In fact, the combinations of individual signs form no

clear language patterns.[12] This lack of grammatical relation-

ship is evident from the vagueness of the messages when they are

read out of context. Only a few sign-combinations like Washoe's

"Naomi good" and "Washoe sorry" are understandable to someone who

does not know the situation in which the signs were made. Most of

the sign-combinations can have several possible meanings. Take,

for example, Nim's "play me." This combination could mean "play

with me," or it could mean "I want to play," "I am playing," or

"play for me." Similarly, Nim's "baby chair" could mean "the baby

5

**Compare the
information
for notes 13
and 15 with
the note cards
on the facing
page.**

is in the chair," "the baby fell off the chair," "the baby's chair,"
and so forth.[13] Only someone who knew the context in which the
signs were made could say which meaning was probably intended.
In making these sign-combinations, the apes seem merely to be
giving individual signs of important elements in the situation.
The elements, the Gardners admit, are related by the context
rather than by grammatical patterns.[14]

In their use of signs, then, the apes do not produce the kind
of evidence that would disprove Chomsky's theory. Language still
seems to be the product of a unique kind of brain that can perceive
grammatical relationships. Human beings have such a brain. Therefore, they can move beyond a basic level of language usage. By
the age of three, human beings are making up sentences in which
phrases and clauses are grammatically related.[15] No matter how
long they have been trained in ASL, apes have never gone beyond
the level of "play me" and "food Nim."

Just as disturbing a thought for people engaged in teaching
ASL to apes is the real possibility that most of the apes' sign-
combinations are not genuine evidence of any language ability
whatsoever. This possibility has been raised by one of the
leading researchers in the field, Herbert S. Terrace. Terrace
observed videotapes of the work done under his direction with
Nim and the training sessions between other apes and their
trainers. On the basis of these observations he charges that
the short sign-combinations may be mere imitations rather than
genuine attempts to convey meaning.

Note Cards

Nim: Two-Sign Combinations   Terrace,
                                                Nim

191 eat grape   out pants
       drink tea   green color
       food tea   clean there
       food Nim   tickle there
       ice Nim   Nim out
       baby chair   me open
       food there

Washoe's Sign-Combinations: Limber,
not Grammatical   "Language"

285 While not random, Washoe's sign-
       combinations are not result of
       grammatical rules such as those
       known even by children of three
       years of age. The grammar of such
       children has a "recursive hierarchi-
       cal constituent structure."
       [They can make up sentences with
       grammatically related clauses and phrases.]

Use square
brackets for
your own com-
ments and
explanations.

In the work done with Nim, Terrace discovered that the chimpanzee's sign-combinations were almost always a response to the signs that had just been used or were simultaneously being used by the trainer. Forty percent of his signs merely repeated the signs of the trainer, while only 10 percent were produced spontaneously.[16] Children at approximately the same level of language development imitate their parents' words far less frequently than this. When Nim used signs that did not repeat the trainer's, they were often signs like "hug" and "eat" that were irrelevant to the situation.[17]

In the work done with other apes, as recorded in the films The First Signs of Washoe (produced for television by Nova) and Teaching Sign Language to the Chimpanzee: Washoe, Terrace found evidence of the same overdependence on the signs of the trainer:

Long quotations (more than four lines) are indented ten spaces, double-spaced, and set apart from the text by triple-spacing above and below.

> Each of Washoe's multisign sequences (24 two-sign, 6 three-sign, and 5 four-sign sequences) were preceded by a similar utterance or a prompt from her teacher. Thus, Washoe's utterances were . . . imitative of her teacher's utterances. The Nova film, which also shows Ally (Nim's full brother) and Koko, reveals a similar tendency for the teacher to sign before the ape signs. Ninety-two percent of Ally's, and all of Koko's, signs were signed by the teacher immediately before Ally and Koko signed.[18]

7

These findings suggest that apes' multisign sequences may not
reveal their ability to use signs meaningfully so much as their
ability to play clever games with their trainers.

Terrace's criticism is too serious to be shrugged off. At
the least, it should lead to a reexamination of the evidence
produced by the experiments in training apes to use ASL. If
possible, the influence of the trainer's behavior might have to
be separated from the apes' spontaneous use of signs. Perhaps
a different system of reporting results will have to be adopted
in which the behavior of both the trainer and the ape are made
known.

On the other hand, Terrace's criticism should not be allowed
to overshadow the positive evidence that on some occasions apes
have used sign language spontaneously and meaningfully. For
example, Washoe would occasionally make the correct sign for
something she noticed outside her window--a cat or some other object.
After her training had been completed and she had gone to live with
other chimpanzees in a compound, she was observed to signal "come,
hurry up, dear" to another chimpanzee she was trying to alert to
the presence of a snake.

Koko, too, showed an ability to use signs meaningfully and
spontaneously. When her fellow gorilla Michael, who had also
learned ASL, was about to have his picture taken, Koko, who loves

cameras and even takes her own snapshots, signed "smile" to him. Another time Koko prompted Michael with the right answer to his trainer's question. And on yet another occasion, when out in the car with her trainer, Koko pointed to a girl who had passed them on a bicycle and signed "catch, hurry, hurry."[21] While arranging her sleeping place, Koko often signs "me sleep" to herself.[22] These bits of evidence show that Terrace's criticism needs to be qualified. While he does raise valid questions about the genuine-ness of much of the data reported from the experiments with these apes, there is also significant evidence that the apes can combine signs meaningfully without being prompted by trainers.

What, then, have these experiments in teaching ASL to apes shown? Basically, they have shown that apes have only a small ability to use a language system. They can learn to use individual gesture-symbols with something less than 100 percent accuracy. They can even produce short combinations of these symbols and occasionally will use them to express their desires, intentions, and observations. But their language ability--at least so far as these experiments show--remains at the level of a two-year-old child. When the child wants a drink of juice, it will hold out its hand and cry "Juice!"[23] If the evidence of these exper-iments is trustworthy, the chimpanzee who wants to eat a grape can learn to signal "eat grape."[24] But while the child, having

9

a human brain, will go on to learn how to say "Me want
drink juice" and then to say "I want a drink of juice" and
"I would prefer to drink juice at breakfast if you don't
mind," the ape trained in ASL, lacking the unique mind of
the human being, will remain forever at the level of "eat
grape," "play me," and "baby chair."

Evaluate the
way the writer
ends this paper.
Is the conclu-
sion too much of
a summary of
points? Does the
ape/child con-
trast effectively
emphasize the
paper's main
point?

Notes

[1] Noam Chomsky, _Language and Mind_, enl. ed. (New York: Harcourt, 1972), p. 62.

[2] Beatrice T. Gardner and R. Allen Gardner, "Two-way Communication with an Infant Chimpanzee," in _Behavior of Nonhuman Primates_, ed. Allan M. Schrier and Fred Stollnitz, Modern Research Trends, IV (New York: Academic, 1971), 160.

[3] Francine Patterson, "Linguistic Capabilities of a Lowland Gorilla," in _Sign Language and Language Acquisition in Man and Apes_, ed. Fred C. C. Peng, AAAS Selected Symposium, 16 (Boulder, Colo.: Westview, 1978), p. 179.

[4] Gardner and Gardner, p. 160.

[5] Herbert S. Terrace, _Nim_ (New York: Knopf, 1979), pp. 137 and 264.

[6] Patterson, p. 181.

[7] Fred C. C. Peng, "Linguistic Potentials of Nonhuman Primates," in _Sign Language and Language Acquisition in Man And Apes_, p. 214.

[8] John Limber, "Language in Child and Chimp?" _American Psychologist_, 32 (1977), 281.

ii

[9] Terrace, pp. 191 and 212.

[10] Terrace, pp. 76-77.

[11] Gardner and Gardner, p. 167.

[12] Limber, p. 285.

[13] Terrace, p. 191

[14] Gardner and Gardner, p. 175

[15] Limber, p. 285.

[16] Terrace, p. 218.

[17] Herbert S. Terrace, "Can an Ape Create a Sentence?" Science, 23 Nov. 1979, p. 900.

[18] Terrace, "Can an Ape?" pp. 897-99.

[19] Beatrice T. Gardner and R. Allen Gardner, "Evidence for Sentence Constituents in the Early Utterances of Child and Chimpanzee," Journal of Experimental Psychology (General), 104 (1975), 246.

[20] Georges Mounin, "Language, Communication, Chimpanzees," Current Anthropology, 17 (1976), 3.

[21] Francine Patterson, "Conversations with a Gorilla," National Geographic, 154 (1978), 450-51 and 465.

[22] Patterson, "Linguistic Capabilities," p. 195.

[23] Limber, p. 283.

[24] Terrace, Nim, p. 191

When you've cited more than one work by the same author, subsequent references must include a title.

Bibliography

See sample
bibliography
cards on facing
page.

Chomsky, Noam. Language and Mind. Enl. ed. New York: Harcourt,
1972.

Gardner, Beatrice T., and R. Allen Gardner. "Evidence for Sentence
Constituents in the Early Utterances of Child and Chimpanzee."
Journal of Experimental Psychology (General), 104 (1975),
244-67.

----------. "Two-way Communication with an Infant Chimpanzee." In
Behavior of Nonhuman Primates. Ed. Allan M. Schrier and Fred
Stollnitz. Modern Research Trends, IV. New York: Academic,
1971, pp. 117-84.

Limber, John. "Language in Child and Chimp?" American Psychologist,
32 (1977), 280-95.

Patterson, Francine. "Conversations with a Gorilla." National
Geographic, 154 (1978), 438-65.

----------. "Linguistic Capabilities of a Lowland Gorilla." In
Sign Language and Language Acquisition in Man and Ape. Ed.
Fred C. C. Peng. AAAS Selected Symposium, 16. Boulder, Colo.:
Westview, 1978, pp. 161-201.

Peng, Fred C. C. "Linguistic Potentials of Nonhuman Primates."
In Sign Language and Language Acquisition in Man and Ape.
Ed. Fred C. C. Peng. AAAS Selected Symposium, 16. Boulder,
Colo.: Westview, 1978, pp. 204-24.

Terrace, Herbert S. "Can an Ape Create a Sentence?" Science,
23 Nov. 1979, pp. 891-202.

----------. Nim. New York: Knopf, 1979.

Bibliography Cards

Location   Slug   Code

> Per   Ape Sign-Combinations: Limber,
> Grammar?   "Language"
>
> Limber, John. "Language in Child
> and Chimp?"
> <u>American</u> <u>Psychologist</u>,
> 32 (1977), 280-95.
>
> sign-combinations -- no grammatical
> relationships

Call number   Slug   Code

> QL   Research methods: Terrace,
> 737   description and   <u>Nim</u>
> .P96T47   criticism
> 1979
>
> Terrace, Herbert S. <u>Nim</u>.
> New York: Alfred A. Knopf, 1979.
>
> critique of training methods
> recorded on videotape and film.

For Analysis and Writing

1. Evaluate "Talking Apes?" as a piece of writing. Does the opening quotation make an effective beginning? Is there sufficient evidence to support the generalizations made in the paper? Are the transitions between and within paragraphs effective? What is your evaluation of the paper's organization? Is the section on criticism of research methodology in the right place? How about style? Are there places where the word choice could be improved or where more variety in the length and structure of sentences is needed? What things are done well here? What things could be improved?

2. Write a brief report on one of the following topics:

a. Lessons about selecting and narrowing a topic, finding source materials, taking notes, and writing a research paper that you have learned while completing your own paper.

b. Different ways you could have developed your paper, and why you chose the one you did.

c. Problems you encountered in finding a suitable beginning and ending for your paper and how you solved them.

d. What you have learned about the subject of your paper and what ideas you have for further research in this area.

Index
to
English

Introduction

Index to English applies the principles of style discussed in *Writer's Guide*. Because it deals with English as it exists—in publications addressed to moderately well-educated and to well-educated audiences, as well as in students' papers—many of its entries don't offer a simple Right and Wrong, Do and Don't. Often they give both the formal choice and the general choice, sometimes the informal choice as well. When you have a particular job of writing to do, with a particular audience in mind, the relevance of the choices will come clear.

The entries in the *Index* are alphabetically arranged. They fall roughly into six categories, with some overlapping:

1. Entries on particular words and constructions, like *among, between; like, as; not about to; who, whom.* Information about the standing of a locution in current usage is often supported by examples quoted from newspapers, popular magazines, scholarly journals, and books. (The fact that something is printed doesn't mean that it's recommended; bad writing may appear in respectable publications.) Read the entry to see where the locution is placed among the varieties of English, and then decide whether it fits your style in the particular rhetorical situation. The titles for entries on words and phrases are the only ones that are not capitalized.

2. Entries to be used in correcting and revising papers. Signaled by correction symbols in longhand, these entries are listed in the correction chart on the inside back cover of this book. They offer straightforward advice—practical *do*s and *don't*s. Go to them when your corrected papers have been returned to you, but also get in the habit of consulting them before you submit your papers, while you're in the process of revising your first drafts. Checking what you've written against their instructions and illustrations will help you decide whether you've punctuated a sentence correctly, used the expected case of a pronoun, made clear what a modifier relates to.

3. Entries on composition, rhetoric, and style. Many of the entries in the second category also belong in this group. Beginning, Ending, Organization, Outline form, Paragraphs, Coherence, Transition, Emphasis, Unity— these and other entries carry you through the stages of writing a paper. Style is treated more directly in such entries as Abstract language, Adjectives and style, Adverbs and style, Conjunctions and style, Diction, Infinitives and style, Nominalization, Parallelism and style, Phrases and style, and Prepositions and style.

4. Entries offering information and advice on special kinds of writing, such as Business letters and Technical writing.

5. Entries on grammar, offering definitions and discussions of standard grammatical terms and concepts—Collective nouns, for example, and Relative clauses, Restrictive and nonrestrictive modifiers, Subjunctive mood, and the parts of speech.

6. Entries about language and language study, such as British English, Origin of words, Sexist language, and Usage.

Refer to the *Index* when you're faced with a writing assignment, as you write, as you revise what you've written, and when your corrected essay is returned to you for further revision. Besides following up the cross-references that most entries contain, look up any term you come across that is new or unclear to you—*modal auxiliaries,* for example, or *deep structure.* Most such terms are explained in entries of their own.

A word about editorial procedure: In order to keep the topic of each entry in sharp focus, unnecessary material has been deleted from illustrative quotations; and when what remains is grammatically a complete sentence, it is printed without opening or closing ellipses.

a, an

Use *a* before all words beginning with a consonant sound: a business, a *D*, a European trip, a usage. Use *an* before all words beginning with a vowel sound, including words that begin with an *h* that's not pronounced: an apple, an *F*, an uncle, an honor, an hour.

In words beginning with *h* that are not accented on the first syllable, like *histo' rian, hyster' ical,* the *h* used to be silent, so *an* preceded such words. Today, though Americans often pronounce the *h,* some still say and write "an historian," "an hysterical witness," "an habitual set of choices" (Josephine Miles, *CCC*). Even if you hurdle the *h* when you speak, *a* is the better choice in writing: The Jews had a historic task.

When you use a series of singular nouns, you may want to repeat *a* or *an* before each one in order to give emphasis to each—"a hound, a bay horse, and a turtle-dove" (Henry David Thoreau, *Walden*)—or you may run them together with *a* or *an* before only the first noun: Soon she had bought a skirt, shirt, and scarf.

See **awhile, a while; half; kind, sort 2.**

Abbreviations

Write in full the word or words inappropriately abbreviated. Or use the correct form of the abbreviation marked.

1. Appropriateness. Abbreviations are used to save space in manuals, reference books, business and legal documents, scholarly footnotes, and some other kinds of writing. You can also use them in informal writing— notes for your own use, letters to friends. In general and formal writing, use only those abbreviations that are fully established in standard usage (see **2**) or that regularly occur in discussions of a particular subject.

2. Standard abbreviations. Always use the abbreviations *Dr., Mr., Mrs.* with names. (A comparable term, *Ms.,* is technically not an abbreviation but a combination of *Miss* and *Mrs.*) A number of abbreviations, such as *St.* (see **saint**), *B.C.* and *A.D., a.m.* and *p.m., Jr.* for Junior, and initial letters for government agencies like *CIA* and *SEC,* are standard. In formal writing, titles like *Reverend, Professor, President,* and *Senator* are not abbreviated, nor are naval and military ranks. In general writing they may be abbreviated when initials or given names are used: Professor Hylander *or* Prof. G. W. Hylander (*but not* Prof. Hylander).

3. Period with abbreviations.   Where standard practice requires a period after an abbreviation, omitting it (*p* instead of *p.* for *page* in a footnote) is a careless slip. Use only one period at the end of a sentence: The abbreviation for both *saint* and *street* is *St.*

Increasingly, periods are omitted from abbreviations that are used in place of the words they stand for *(FBI, AFL-CIO, CBS, GNP, ID, IQ, hp, kwh, 780 rpm).* In addressing letters, don't use periods with the two-letter abbreviations for states adopted by the Postal Service *(PA, TX).*

Abbreviations that are pronounced as words *(WASP, UNICEF)* are called acronyms. Dozens entered the language during World War II *(Nazi, Gestapo, radar, sonar, Wac, Wave),* and thousands have been created since *(NATO, SALT, laser).* The acronym *OPEC,* from Organization of Petroleum Exporting Countries, gained worldwide prominence in the 1970s.

For abbreviations of dates, see **Months.** Compare **Contractions, Numbers, Origin of words 3c.**

ability to

The idiom is *ability* plus a *to*-infinitive (ability *to do*): He has the ability to design (*not* of designing) beautiful buildings. You can often express the idea better with an adjective or a verb: He is able to (*or* He can) design beautiful buildings; He designs beautiful buildings.

able to

Avoid using a passive infinitive (like *to be done* or *to be ended*) after *able:* This was not able to be done because of lack of time. Instead write: This could not be done because of lack of time. Or: They were not able to do this because of lack of time (*or* because they didn't have time).

about

About has a variety of uses. Check the following for trouble spots:

1. about–around.   In describing physical position, *about* and *around* are nearly interchangeable, though *around* is the more common (about the tree—around the tree). In the sense of "nearly" or "approximately," *about* is more common (about 70°), but both are standard American usage. In telling time, *around* (around two o'clock) is considered more informal.

2. about–almost.   In the sense of "almost" (about finished), *about* is standard but mainly informal.

3.   at about.   In formal English *at about* is avoided on the grounds that something must be either *at* or *about*. But *about* in *at about* is being used as an adverb, and the preposition-adverb pattern is well established: at approximately noon; in about ten minutes.

4.   about to.   *About to* is a convenient idiom for "on the point of": She was about to make a third try. The negative *not about to* (an emphatic "not going to") is more informal: I'm not about to sign up for a class at that hour.

above

Using *above* as an adverb in such phrases as "the evidence cited above" and using it as an adjective (the above prices) and as a noun (the above is confirmed) are fully established as standard but are not accepted by everyone. Some careful writers avoid using *above* as an adjective; others use it: "for a comment on the above use of the word 'claims' . . ." (Theodore Bernstein, *Watch Your Language*). In many business, legal, and other technical contexts, all three uses of *above*—as adverb, adjective, and noun— would be entirely acceptable. In general and formal writing they would bother some readers.

Absolute phrases

An absolute phrase modifies all the rest of the sentence it appears in, not just a word or group of words: *The battle lost,* the army surrendered.

Absolute phrases are economical, offering a compact way of singling out details of a scene or relating parts to a whole: He came downstairs looking much the worse for wear, *eyes bloodshot, shirt rumpled, tie askew.* But their somewhat formal quality makes them seem out of place in casual writing: *The long day finally at an end,* the kids went to bed. And absolute phrases that contain auxiliaries (*being, having, having been*) may be heavy and awkward: *The description of the scene having been completed,* the stage is set for the crucial action. A dependent clause is often smoother and sometimes more precise: After the scene has been described. . . .

Some absolute phrases have been used so often that they've become fixed formulas, or idioms: all things considered, this being the case, God willing.

See **Dangling modifiers, Idiom.**

Absolutes, comparison of

Logically, absolutes like *perfect* and *final* can't be more or most, less or least. But see **Comparison of adjectives and adverbs 4.**

abst Abstract language

Make this word or passage more concrete or more specific.

Abstract words refer to emotions, qualities, concepts, relationships: *love, courage, square root, symmetry.* They contrast with concrete words like *kiss, lion, computer, hoop,* which refer to things we can see or touch or otherwise perceive with our senses.

Abstract terms are essential in communicating ideas, and abstract language can be just as precise as concrete language. But if you rely too much on abstract vocabulary, your papers may seem to lose contact with human experience. To keep your rhetorical feet on the ground, follow these suggestions:

1. Provide concrete examples. If you're writing about courage, describe a brave act, or contrast a brave act with a cowardly one. The shift from the concept to the example will make it natural to use concrete terms. Or follow an abstract statement with a concrete expression of the same idea:

> The survey's assumption that the bodily symptoms in question are indicators of psychological distress leads to the conclusion that the working class tends to somatize its emotional troubles, whereas the middle class experiences them more directly. In other words, clammy hands and upset stomach are apt to be the poor man's substitute for angst.—Charles J. Rolo, *Atlantic*

2. Replace general terms with specific ones. *General* and *abstract* are sometimes used interchangeably, and so are *specific* and *concrete.* But the match-ups are not exact. Though we can easily classify a word as concrete or abstract, we can say that a term is specific or general only if we compare it with a related term. In the series *Volvo, car, vehicle,* all the words are concrete, but judged in relation to each other, *car* is more general than *Volvo* and more specific than *vehicle.* In the series *emotion, love, lust,* all the words are abstract, but *love* is more specific than *emotion* and more general than *lust.* So a concrete term is not always specific, and an abstract term is not always general.

Prose that strikes the reader as abstract often contains a high proportion of general terms, both abstract and concrete. Instead of using the general, abstract term *immorality,* specify the kind of immoral act you have in mind (*adultery, bribery, robbery*). Instead of the general, concrete term *lawbreakers,* use *speeders, vandals, muggers, burglars, rapists*—naming the kind of lawbreakers you're writing about.

3. Choose your abstract terms with care. What often causes trouble isn't the use of abstract terms but the particular terms chosen. If every sixth or seventh word you write is a noun ending in *-ence, -ity, -ment,* or *-tion* (*permanence, responsibility, management, utilization*), your style will be abstract and heavy. Many abstract nouns are related to verbs: *intention (in-*

tend), refusal (refuse), response (respond). Given a choice between representing an action in an abstract noun or in a full verb, you'll generally write a livelier, clearer sentence if you choose the verb:

> The achievement of clarity of thought has a definite dependence on the correctness of the formulation of the problem.

> *Better:* To think clearly, you need to formulate your problem correctly.

Though neither sentence contains any concrete words, the second is a lot more direct and easier to read than the first. Its style, we say, is more concrete.

See **Details, Nominalization.**

accept, except

Accept means "receive" or "say yes to." *Except,* as a verb, means "leave out," "exclude." See **except, accept.**

Accusative case

The object of a verb or a preposition is said to be in the accusative (or objective) case. Six distinctive pronoun forms are often called accusative (or objective) forms: *me, her, him, us, them, whom.* (*You* is both accusative and nominative.) See **Case 2; Gerunds 2; Infinitives and style 2; it's me; Objects; who, whom.**

acquiesce

If you have reason to use the formal verb *acquiesce,* be sure to follow it with the right preposition. You can agree *to* or *with* a decision, but you acquiesce *in* a decision.

Acronyms

Abbreviations pronounced as words are called acronyms *(OPEC, SALT).* See **Abbreviations 3.**

Active voice

All verbs except those consisting of a form of the verb *be* and a past participle (is cooked) are in the active voice. See **Voice.** Compare **Passive voice.**

actually

Like *basically, definitely,* and *really, actually* is seldom necessary in writing, even when it's meant literally: "My nomination for the 'most neglected
book' is actually a trilogy" (Carlos Baker, *American Scholar*). (All four
words are overused in conversation as fillers or as weak attempts to provide
emphasis.) In revising your papers, delete every *actually, basically, definitely,* and *really* that isn't serving a useful purpose, particularly if it appears
at the beginning of a sentence: [Actually] we lost the game.

ad

Ad, the clipped form of *advertisement,* is appropriate in all but formal writing. It's not an abbreviation, so it shouldn't be followed by a period.

A.D.

A.D. stands for *anno Domini,* "in the year of the Lord," and logically,
therefore, should precede a year (A.D. 107) and should not label a century.
But there's a strong tendency to treat *A.D.* as if it meant "after Christ" (as
B.C. means "before Christ"), and phrases like "in the second century
A.D." have appeared regularly in the works of respected writers for many
years. Some conservative stylists condemn this usage. Some more liberal
stylists (and Latinists) hold that *A.D.* and *B.C.* should be treated as non-
translated adverbials, applying to both years and centuries. Consider your
audience.

adapt, adopt

To *adapt* is to adjust so as to fit or conform: Immigrants often have difficulty adapting their ways to American customs and values. To *adopt* is to
accept, to choose, to make your own: The motion was finally adopted; The
engineers adopted the third alternative; They adopted three children in two
years.

Adjectivals

Phrases, clauses, and words that are not adjectives may function like adjectives. That is, they may restrict or limit a subject, object, or indirect object.
When they do, they can be called *adjectivals.*

1.   Phrases and clauses used in adjectival function:
The man *with the hat on* is Harry.
I like the one *on the end* best.

Everyone *who agrees* should raise his right hand.
That was the summer *we went to Bermuda.*
He asked the first man *he met.*

2.   Other parts of speech in adjectival function.   Participles, which are derived from verbs, function as adjectivals: a *coming* attraction, a *deserved* penalty. And one of the most characteristic traits of English is the use of nouns in the adjectival function: a *glass* jar, the *Roosevelt* administration, *adjective* modifiers, *high-school mathematics* test. But see **Adjectives and style 2.**

Adjectives

An adjective modifies—that is, restricts or limits—a subject, object, or indirect object. *Good* performs this function in the sentence ''A good dancer isn't just any dancer but a dancer who's better than others.''

1.   Forms.   Many adjectives don't have a form that sets them off from other parts of speech *(high, civil)*. Other adjectives consist of a noun or verb plus a suffix such as *-able (bearable)* or *-ible (reversible), -al (critical), -ed (chilled), -ful (playful), -ish (childish), -less (harmless), -ous (joyous),* or *-y (dreamy).*

Many adjectives are compared by adding *-er* or *-est* to the positive, or base, form or by putting *more* or *most* before it: *warm, warmer* or *more warm, warmest* or *most warm.* See **Comparison of adjectives and adverbs.**

Proper adjectives are capitalized, like the proper nouns they're derived from: *French* restaurants, *Italian* wines, *Elizabethan* drama, *Victorian* furniture. When used frequently enough in a merely descriptive sense, a proper adjective becomes an ordinary adjective, written without a capital: *diesel* fuel, *india* ink.

2.   Functions.   The main function of adjectives is to modify a subject or object, but when preceded by *a, an,* or *the,* some adjectives serve as subjects or objects: the *just,* the *rich,* a new *high.* When so used, words that are ordinarily adjectives function as nouns and can be called *nominals.* See **Adjectivals, Nominals.**

adj Adjectives and style

Reconsider your choice of the adjective marked.

The adjectives you use should make your statements more precise or more forceful.

1. Adjectives that fail. Some adjectives are redundant. In "briny ocean," *briny* adds nothing because all salt water is briny. (Adjectivals can be similarly redundant, as in "wandering nomads.") Very general adjectives like *good, bad, beautiful, wonderful, terrible, terrific, fantastic, incredible, awful,* and so on communicate attitudes rather than specify characteristics. The reader who finds someone described as "good" wants to know the particular kind of goodness. Is the person agreeable? kind? virtuous? talented? generous? Many adjectives that are specific enough have been teamed so often with particular nouns (*beady* eyes, *fond* farewell) that the combinations have become trite. In writing, think twice before using any combination of adjective and noun that comes automatically to mind. See **Triteness.**

2. Adjectives that clutter. Sometimes in reading over what you've written, you'll find that you've piled up adjectives. Deleting most of the adjectives and adjectivals from the following passage would improve it considerably.

> My blurred, aching, stinging eyes focused not on the shiny, slippery, polished, golden oak floors that reflected the frilly-white sparkle of the neat, spandy-clean room of my long-gone childhood but on the ugly lumps of dirty, worn-out jeans, decrepit, sagging jogging shorts, and gray, smelly, mud-caked sweat socks that littered the dingy, dusty, ragged old rug.

The stylistic effect is particularly bad when the words in adjectival position are nouns. Piling nouns in front of nouns produces prose that's heavy and hard to understand. "The chairman selection committee progress report date has been changed" needs to be translated into "The date for the progress report of the committee on selecting a chairman has been changed." A string of prepositional phrases isn't very graceful, but it's better than the rear-end collisions of a string of nouns.

3. Adjectives that work. Used sensibly and sensitively, adjectives reinforce meaning and improve style. If your material is technical and your audience is familiar with the technical vocabulary, you need only be careful to use the right term—*biaxial,* perhaps, or *extravascular,* or *granular.* But if you're writing on a technical subject for readers who lack the technical vocabulary, or if you're dealing with a subject that has no special vocabulary of its own, then you have to make choices. Choose your adjectives with the needs of your subject matter and your audience, as well as your purpose, in mind. Chosen well, they'll seem to fit, to belong, as in this account:

> A few miles from Southampton I saw the real sea at last, head on, a sudden end to the land, a great sweep of curved nothing rolling out to the invisible horizon and revealing more distance than I'd ever seen before. It was green, and heaved gently like the skin of a frog, and carried drowsy little ships like

flies. Compared with the land, it appeared to be a huge hypnotic blank, putting everything to sleep that touched it.—Laurie Lee, *As I Walked Out One Midsummer Morning*

According to E. B. White, "The adjective hasn't been built that can pull a weak or inaccurate verb out of a tight place." True enough. And Carl Sandburg is said to have warned a writer, "Think twice before you use an adjective." This is probably sound advice for anyone who automatically attaches an adjective to every noun and so produces what has been called "adjective-benumbed prose." But adjectives can help a writer describe his subject as he sees it, and if he chooses the right ones, they'll make the reader see it too.

Compare **Adverbs and style.**

Adverbials

Phrases and clauses that function like adverbs can be classed as *adverbials:* He came *in the morning; After the exam* he quit; *When it was time to go,* she didn't know what to do. Words like *home* in "He went home" and *days* in "She works days" are nouns in form but can be defined as adverbials in function.

Adverbs

As a grammatical category, "adverbs" is a ragbag containing a variety of words that modify verbs, adjectives, other adverbs, and whole clauses and sentences.

1.   Forms.   Most adverbs are formed by adding *-ly* to adjectives or participles: *badly, deservedly, laughingly, surely.* Some have no special adverbial sign: *now, then, here, there.* A number of adverbs have the same form as adjectives, including these:

bad	doubtless	hard	much	slow
better	early	high	near	smooth
bright	even	late	new	straight
cheap	fair	loose	right	tight
close	fast	loud	rough	well
deep	first	low	sharp	wrong

Most of these unchanged adverbs are matched by forms in *-ly,* with which they may or may not be interchangeable. See **Adverbs and style.**

Most adverbs are compared, either by adding *-er* and *-est* to the positive, or base, form or by preceding it with *more* and *most.* See **Comparison of adjectives and adverbs.**

2.   Functions.   Adverbs are typically used in two functions:
a.   To modify single words, phrases, and clauses: He left early (*early* modifies *left*); They were practically in the street (*practically* modifies *in the street*); Fortunately no one was home (*Fortunately* modifies *no one was home*). In direct and indirect questions, *when, where, why,* and *how* perform adverbial functions: *When* did he leave? Do you know *why* he left?
b.   To connect separate sentences or the independent clauses of a compound sentence (see **Conjunctive adverbs**):

> We found the dormitories empty, the classrooms silent and deserted. *Nevertheless,* we continued the search.

> They agreed to call the matter closed; *however,* they were by no means convinced.

See **Adverbials**.

adv Adverbs and style

Correct the form of the adverb marked, change its position, or reconsider your choice.

1.   Use the standard form of the adverb.   You can say "He sang loud" or "He sang loudly"; both are standard. The short form is often preferred in general and informal English, the *-ly* form in formal English. (Cookbook compilers, who ordinarily use general English, are nevertheless addicted to chopping finely and slicing thinly.) The choice is a matter of style. But in some situations standard English doesn't permit a choice:
a.   Omitting the *-ly* ending. When adverbs are formed by adding *-ly* to the adjective *(considerably, regularly, suddenly),* the form without *-ly* is nonstandard: It hurt *considerable;* He did it *regular.* Use the *-ly* ending unless your dictionary also treats the form without *-ly* as standard.
b.   Adding an unnecessary *-ly.* Even when an adverb has two forms, they're not always interchangeable. Though you can say "Drive slow" or "Drive slowly," you can't replace *close* with *closely* in "That shot hit too close."

After a linking verb, use a predicate adjective, not an adverb: The breeze smelled sweet (*not* sweetly). And don't use an adverb-adjective combination when the adjective alone can do the job: Like many of that breed, her dogs were high-strung (*not* highly strung). Compare **bad, badly.**

Don't add *-ly* to a word that already ends in *-ly (kindlily* for *kindly).* To make an adverbial from an adjective ending in *-ly (leisurely, orderly, worldly),* put the adjective in a prepositional phrase ending with a noun like *way* or *manner:* He approached us *in a friendly way;* She handled the problem *in a scholarly manner*. Words in *-ly* that indicate time may function either as adjectives (an hourly schedule) or as adverbs (the bus departed hourly).

2. Placing adverbs for clarity and style.   Many adverbs can occupy different positions in a sentence:

> Tom had *never* liked pizza. Tom *never* had liked pizza.

> *Patiently* she explained. She *patiently* explained. She explained *patiently*.

When you have a choice, first of all place the adverb so that it makes your meaning clear: not "She answered the questions that the students asked patiently" but "She patiently answered the questions that the students asked"—if it was the answering and not the questioning that was patient. Other considerations are rhythm and emphasis. Some writers hesitate to insert an adverb between the parts of a verb: instead of "have easily seen," they write "have seen easily." But "have easily seen" is smoother and more idiomatic. See **only, Split infinitive.**

3. Making adverbs count.   The use of adverbs should at least be precise and if possible should contribute to the impact of the sentence. Adverbs hurt rather than help when they're used unnecessarily and redundantly (Truck horns blast *threateningly;* automobiles career *wildly;* buses lumber along *heavily*), when they qualify excessively (the *seemingly* difficult problem of controlling inflation), and when they set up a flutter of *-ly*s (as in this sentence). Sometimes writers use an adverb to shore up an imprecise adjective or verb when more compact expression would do the job better:

> Scholarships should be kept for *those who are academically industrious* (the studious).

> When no one was looking, I took the goggles and *swiftly made my way* (hurried) out of the store.

adverse, averse

Be careful not to confuse these two words. *Adverse* is an adjective meaning "unfavorable" or "hostile" (adverse conditions). *Averse,* also an adjective, means "opposed" (We would not be averse to such legislation). Both have a formal tone.

advise

Besides meaning "to give advice," *to advise* is used to mean "to inform, to give information." In this sense the verb is commonly used for informing that's rather formal: Reporters were advised by an administration spokesman that. . . . In all other situations simple *tell* is more appropriate: Peter tells (*not* advises) us that he won't be back next term.

affect, effect

Affect is used most often as a transitive verb meaning "influence" (This will affect the lives of thousands) or, rather formally, "put on" (He affected a stern manner). The noun *affect* is a technical term in psychology. *Effect* is most common as a noun meaning "result": The effects will be felt by thousands. But it's also a formal verb meaning "bring about": The change was effected hurriedly.

aggravate

In general and informal usage *aggravate* ordinarily means "annoy" or "irritate": The higher he turned the volume, the more aggravated I got. Formal rules still limit *aggravate* to the meaning "make worse," as to aggravate a wound or a situation: Friction between faculty and administration was aggravated by cuts in the budget. The same division occurs in the use of the noun *aggravation*.

agr Agreement

Make the verb or pronoun marked agree in form with the word to which it is related—its subject if it is a verb, its antecedent if it is a pronoun.

When used together, certain parts of speech agree, or correspond in form in such a way as to express relationships of number, person, or gender. This pair of sentences illustrates several instances of agreement:

> *This* habit, which in *itself is* harmless, *is* likely to lead to *others* that *are* decidedly harmful. *(This, itself,* and *is* agree with the singular *habit. Are* agrees with the plural *others.)*

> *These* habits, which in *themselves are* harmless, *are* likely to lead to *another* that *is* decidedly harmful. *(These, themselves, are,* and *are* agree with the plural *habits. Is* agrees with the singular *another.)*

In English, agreement is largely a matter of linguistic etiquette. If you used *is* after *habits* in the sentence above, your readers would have no trouble figuring out your meaning, but they'd frown at your carelessness. Understanding the causes of mistakes in agreement will alert you to what to look for when you proofread your papers and help you avoid lapses in grammatical good manners.

1.   Subject and verb agree in number (Those *birds were* seen; That *bird was* seen). There are four main causes for problems in subject-verb agreement: (a) phrases or clauses between subject and verb, (b) collective nouns as subjects, (c) compound subjects, and (d) dialect differences in verb forms.

a.   Most mistakes in agreement occur when a writer makes the verb agree with a word that's not the subject and that differs from the subject in number. Often the word is the noun at the end of a clause or phrase that comes between the true subject and the verb: An *analysis* of the extent to which audio-visual aids are used in schools *make* me conclude that books are no longer the chief tools of education. The singular subject *analysis* calls for the corresponding verb form *makes,* but the plural noun *schools* immediately before the verb, and perhaps also the plural *aids are,* confused the writer. The same trouble may occur in a very short sentence: "But only one in 100 patients die" *(Newsweek).* In such situations take the time to make sure what the subject of your verb is.

b.   The first question with collective nouns as subjects is whether to treat them as singular or plural. If you're thinking of what the noun names as a unit, make the verb singular: The last *couple* on the floor *was* Janet and Tom. If you're thinking instead of the individuals that make up what the noun names, use a plural verb: The *couple* next door *were* disagreeing noisily, as usual.

Once you've made this decision, be sure you use the verb and any related pronoun consistently. If the team *was* very much on edge, the reason was that *its,* not *their,* big game was only a week away. Sometimes the pronoun will determine the verb form: When we found ourselves near where the old couple *were* living, we dropped in to see *them.* "We dropped in to see *it*" would be impossible, even after *was living.* So the sentence demands the *were-them* combination. See **Collective nouns.**

c.   Problems with compound subjects sometimes arise because the writer is uncertain whether to treat the subjects as plural or singular. Some compound subjects name a unit that calls for a singular verb: Bacon and eggs *is* my favorite breakfast. Other compound subjects represent a unit to one writer, separate things to another:

Her loyalty and patriotism *was* unparalleled in the history of her people.

Her loyalty and [her] patriotism *were* unparalleled in the history of her people.

Before deciding to use a singular verb with a compound subject, be sure your readers will not only recognize your intention but accept the logic behind it. Only subjects that are closely allied *(loyalty* and *patriotism)* can reasonably be thought of as a unit. This principle rules out "Her beauty and dishonesty *was* apparent even to me," which readers would see as an error in agreement.

When both elements of a compound subject connected by the correlative conjunctions *either . . . or* or *neither . . . nor* are plural, the verb is naturally plural; and when both elements are singular, the verb is usually singular. When one subject is singular and the other plural, the traditional rule is that the verb should agree with the nearer subject:

> Neither the ideas nor the style *is* satisfactory.
>
> Neither the style nor the ideas *are* satisfactory.

Although usage varies, this is a sensible rule to follow. See **Compound subject, Correlative conjunctions.**

d.   Some American dialects, notably in Black English, lack an ending in the third-person singular, so that *do* and *see,* for example, are treated like standard English *can:* he can, he do, he see). Writers for whom this is the natural grammatical pattern have a double problem when they use a variety of standard English: they must add the ending to most present-tense, third-person-singular verbs *(starts, stops, sees)* and not add it elsewhere, as in plural verbs (they *stop*) and past-tense forms (I, you, she, we, they *stopped*). See **Principal parts of verbs 2.**

2.   **A third-person pronoun** agrees with its antecedent in number and gender. If the antecedent—the noun it refers to—is plural, the pronoun is *they, their(s),* or *them,* depending on its use in the sentence. If the antecedent is singular, the choice of pronoun is more complicated because gender enters in. Generally, if the noun refers to a male, we use *he, his,* or *him;* if to a female, *she, hers,* or *her.* Otherwise, including situations where the sex is unknown or irrelevant, we use *it(s):* The baby dropped *its* rattle; The dog was looking for *its* master.

Problems sometimes arise when the antecedent is a noun referring to a member of a group that includes both sexes (each member of the class) or when it's one of the indefinite pronouns, like *one, anyone, everyone, no one, anybody, everybody,* or *nobody.* The question of which possessive pronoun to use with an indefinite may be solved by the context: No one in the Girl Scout troop looked forward to *her* test (though *their* might be used here if everyone was taking the same test). More often both sexes are referred to (No one at the dance . . .). The problem then is whether to use *he, he or she,* or *they.* Some grammarians assert that *they,* like *you,* has both singular and plural functions and that in indefinite reference it is usually a singular pronoun. But conservatives reject *they* as a singular. Though the use of a form of *they* to refer to words like *everyone* (Everyone in the class turned in their paper) is now firmly established in informal English and is increasingly accepted in general English, it is strongly resisted in formal English, where a form of *he* (his paper) would be expected. Using a subject that's clearly plural avoids any problem: All the students handed in their papers. See **Sexist language, they.**

3.   **The demonstrative adjectives** (or determiners) *this, that, these, those* usually agree in number with the nouns they modify: *That coat* is expensive; *These shoes* cost more than my old pair did. See **kind, sort.**

agree to, agree with

One person agrees *to* a plan and agrees *with* another person. One thing agrees *with* another. Other idioms: I agree *in* principle; We agreed *on* a plan of attack; He agreed *to* fly or *on* flying or *that he would fly*.

ain't

Though in speech millions of Americans use *ain't* regularly as a contraction for *am not, is not, are not, has not,* and *have not,* it never appears in formal writing and rarely in expository prose except when a speaker is being quoted. In general writing, use of *ain't* is almost always a deliberate attempt to suggest informality or humor or down-to-earth common sense:

> It will never reach the audience Welles might have and should have reached, because there just ain't no way.—Pauline Kael, *New Republic*

> Those tiresome people with their tiresome quotes from Socrates about the fact that youth is going to the dogs are just trying to reassure themselves that it's all just a little bit more of the same. It ain't.—John M. Culkin, *New York Times*

See **Divided usage.**

all, al-

Note the spelling of these words and phrases:

1. *all ready* (adjective phrase): At last they were all ready to begin.

2. *already* (adverb of time): They had already begun.

3. *all together* (adjective phrase): We found them all together in an old trunk.

4. *altogether* (adverb, equivalent to *wholly*): That's another matter altogether.

5. *all right* (adjective phrase): The seats seemed all right to me.

Alright now appears frequently enough to be accepted as a variant spelling in some dictionaries. Others specifically label it a misspelling, and many authorities consider it nonstandard.

Alliteration

Alliteration is repetition of the same sound, usually at the beginning of several words in a series. Besides possibly appealing to the reader's or listener's ear, alliteration binds the phrase, or sometimes a series of phrases, into a unit: "carried by wind and water and soil and seed" (John F. Kennedy). Alliteration is appropriate in some formal prose but distracting in ordinary exposition unless it helps reinforce meaning. Check your first drafts to break up any string of words that begin with the same sound for no purpose. Compare **Assonance.**

all of

In many constructions with *all of, of* can be omitted: All [of] the milk was spilled; They passed all [of] the candidates; You can't fool all [of] the people all [of] the time. Usage is divided. With personal pronouns and the relatives *who* and *which, all* may follow the pronoun (we all), or *all of* may precede it (all of us). *All of whom* and *all of which,* as subjects of relative clauses (four attempts, all of which failed), are more formal than *who all* and *which all* (four attempts, which all failed).

all that

"It wasn't all that bad" and similar uses of *all that* are informal and imprecise. See **not all that . . . , not too. . . .**

all the farther

In some parts of the country *all the farther* is common in informal and general speech (This is all the farther I'm going), but standard written English uses an *as . . . as* construction: This is as far as I'm going.

Allusion

Loosely, an allusion is a brief reference to something that's not a part of the subject under discussion. Strictly, an allusion differs from a reference in that it doesn't name the event, person, or place but mentions it indirectly. "This latter-day Paul Revere calls us to arms against home-grown revolutionaries" is a reference to Paul Revere. "His signal is always a single lantern in the church steeple" is an allusion to Revere that leaves it to the reader to make the connection through knowledge of Longfellow's poem ("One if by land, and two if by sea"). Like other aspects of style, allusions should fit the rhetorical situation.

allusion, illusion

Allusion, discussed in the preceding entry, should not be confused with *illusion,* a misapprehension or a misleading appearance (Smoking a pipe can create an illusion of wisdom).

almost

Most for *almost* is informal. See **most, almost.**

also

Also as an adverb ordinarily stands within a sentence, not at its beginning: "They also serve who only stand and wait" (John Milton). But inversion may shift an *also* to initial position: Also defeated was the party's candidate for mayor. As a loose conjuction meaning "and," *also* is a weak sentence opener:

> He subscribed to eight magazines. Also he belonged to the Book-of-the-Month Club.

In many cases the information introduced with initial *also* should be included in the preceding sentence: He subscribed to eight magazines and belonged to the Book-of-the-Month Club. See **Conjunctive adverbs, Inversion, plus.**

alternative

Alternative comes from the Latin *alter,* "the second of two." For that reason some formal writers restrict its meaning to "one of two possibilities," but the word is regularly used to mean one of several possibilities (Another alternative would be to . . .). Dictionaries record this broader meaning.

although, though

Although and *though* introduce adverbial clauses that qualify the main statement:

> Although (*or* Though) the rain kept up for almost three weeks, we managed to have a good time.

> We managed to have a good time, though (*or* although) the rain kept up for almost three weeks.

In these examples there is no distinction in meaning. The choice between the two words may be based on sentence rhythm. *Although* is slightly more formal.

Often one of two clauses connected by *but* can be turned into an *(al)though* clause for a slight change of emphasis or for sentence variety:

> We had rehearsed time and again, but we all missed our cues the first night.

> Although (*or* Though) we had rehearsed time after time, we all missed our cues the first night.

Though is also used as a less formal *however:* He did it, though. See **but.**

alumnus, alumna

A male graduate is an *alumnus,* a female graduate an *alumna.* Two or more male graduates are *alumni,* two or more female graduates *alumnae.* The graduates of coeducational schools—males and females together—have traditionally been called *alumni,* but *graduates* itself is a satisfactory, and sexless, alternative. Also sexless is *alums,* the plural of the clipped word *alum.* See **Sexist language.**

a.m. and p.m.

These abbreviations for *ante meridiem,* "before noon," and *post meridiem,* "after noon," are most useful in tables and lists of times. They're also used in general writing for specific hours, usually with figures: from 2 to 4 p.m. (*not* I went there in the p.m.). Though *m.* is the abbreviation for noon (12 m.), *12 noon* is more common. Midnight is *12 p.m.* The twenty-four hour system used in Europe and by the U.S. military makes *a.m.* and *p.m.* redundant: 9 a.m. = 0900, 9 p.m. = 2100. See **Hours.**

amb Ambiguity

Make your meaning unmistakable.

An ambiguous word or phrase or sentence is one that can be interpreted in two or more ways. Though the context usually shows which of the possible meanings was intended, the reader is confused at least momentarily. The most common sources of confusion are these:

1. Inexact reference of pronouns, especially in indirect discourse: He told his father he had been talking too much. Who is the second *he,* the father or the son? Rewrite as: He admitted to his father that he had been talking too much. Or as: He criticized his father for talking too much. Or recast as direct speech. See **Indirect discourse, Reference of pronouns 1.**

2. Modifiers that can be misinterpreted.
a. Modifiers should not be so placed that they can seem to refer to either of two words or constructions: The governor dismissed those officeholders who had opposed him ruthlessly. Does *ruthlessly* refer to the dismissal or the opposition? Rewrite as: The governor ruthlessly dismissed those officeholders who had opposed him. Or as: The governor dismissed those officeholders who had ruthlessly opposed him. See **Squinting modifier.**
b. Modifiers should be clearly identified as restrictive or nonrestrictive.

Setting off a restrictive modifier with commas or failing to set off a nonrestrictive modifier changes your meaning: Out-of-state students [,] who were delayed by the blizzard [,] will not be penalized for late registration. With commas, the sentence means that no out-of-state students were penalized; without commas, it means that only those delayed by the storm were excused.

c. Modifiers shouldn't mislead even momentarily. In revising a first draft, be on the lookout for puzzlers like the headline "Police Repair Man Killed by Car." See **Hyphen 5.**

3. Incomplete idioms, especially in comparisons: "I liked Alice as well as Will" might mean "I liked Alice as well as Will did," "I liked Alice as well as I liked Will," or "I liked both Alice and Will."

4. Confusing coordination, as in: The movie deals with student protests against war and sexual experimentation. Repeating *with* after *and* would limit the target of the protests.

5. Ambiguous words. When a writer uses the wrong word—say *incredible* for *incredulous*—the result is confusion but usually not ambiguity. Ambiguity occurs when a writer uses a word that has the meaning he intends but another meaning as well—for example, the dialect word *cookie* for *doughnut,* or the word *rhetoric,* which has unfavorable connotations for many but favorable connotations for some. Instances of divided usage are particularly troublesome. Readers who find *disinterested* where they expect *uninterested* are likely to be not so much confused as outraged. See **censor, censure; convince, persuade; disinterested, uninterested; Divided usage; imply, infer; incredible, incredulous; rhetoric; Wrong word.**

See also **Comma 6.**

American

Because there's no simple adjective that corresponds to the United States of America (as *Italian,* for example, corresponds to Italy), *American* is ordinarily used. It's obviously inexact, in that all the other inhabitants of the Americas have as much right to the term as we do. Many Latin Americans refer to themselves as Americans and to us as North Americans. But the use of *American* as the adjective ("the American economy" for "the economy of the United States") and as the noun for a citizen of the United States is standard.

Americanism

An Americanism is a word or construction in English that originated in the United States *(hydrant, zipper, realtor)* or was first borrowed here, as from an African language *(goober, juke, okra)* or an Indian language *(hominy, caucus, mugwump)* or from Spanish *(canyon, rodeo, lariat). Americanism* also refers to a sense of a word that was added in the United States *(campus, carpetbagger, creek).* And it may be extended to include words that have continued to be used in the United States after becoming obsolete in England *(loan* as a verb, *gotten)* or any item of usage characteristic of the United States and not of other areas of the English-speaking world. The label *American* or *chiefly U.S.* in dictionaries identifies Americanisms.

among, between

Between is used with two, *among* with more than two. But see **between, among.**

amount, number

Number is used of countable things: a number of mistakes, a number of apples. *Amount* is preferred with mass nouns: a small amount of snow, a certain amount of humor. Distinguishing between the two words often makes writing clearer. See **Mass nouns.** Compare **fewer, less.**

Ampersand

An ampersand is the & sign. Because its primary use is to save space, the ampersand belongs only where abbreviations are appropriate. Otherwise, write out *and*.

Analysis

The term *analysis* is applied to a wide range of intellectual undertakings— attempts to grasp the nature of a thing or a concept, to separate a whole into its parts, to discover the similarities and differences between two or more things, to investigate causes, to attribute effects. The aim of analysis is to increase understanding of the subject. A writer may also use analysis as a guide to action. That is, he may analyze an assignment in order to decide how to arrange his material or what details to include or what arguments to use. See **Logical thinking.**

and

1. Appropriate uses. *And*, the conjunction we use most frequently, should join two or more elements of equal grammatical rank:

> *Adjectives:* a *pink* and *white* dress; a *blue, green,* and *white* flag
> *Adverbs:* He drove *very fast* and *rather carelessly.*

Nouns: trees and *flowers; trees, shrubs,* and *flowers*
Verbs: I *picked up* the book and *opened* it.
Phrases: in one ear and *out the other*
Dependent clauses: While the children were swimming and [*while*] *the old folks were resting,* we took a walk.
Independent clauses: The first generation makes the money, and *the second spends it.*

2. Inappropriate uses. In careless writing, elements that are not grammatically equivalent are sometimes connected by an unnecessary *and:*

Main verbs and participles: The men *sat* on the edge of the lake with their backs to the road, [and] apparently *watching* the ducks.
Independent and dependent clauses: A contract has been let to install new copper work on the post office [and] *which will give it the facelifting it needs.*

Besides being used where no connective is needed, *and* sometimes appears where some other connective would show the logical relationship more clearly: "Shah was a founding member of the Club of Rome and [but?] while he retains his membership, he did not attend last fall's gathering in Berlin" (Elizabeth Hall, *Psychology Today*). See **Coordination 2, Shifted constructions.**

3. To begin sentences. In current writing of all varieties, *and* can be used to begin a sentence, signaling a link with the preceding sentence or paragraph. Used sparingly, it will also contribute to the movement and emphasis. Overused, it will damage both, as well as bore the reader.

4. Omitted or repeated. *And* can be omitted in a series (Cousins, uncles, [and] aunts—all the relatives were there), but if it's omitted again and again, the result is a telegraphic style that's inappropriate in general writing. *And* may also be repeated between the items in a series, as an effective way of giving emphasis to each: "I do not mean to imply that the South is simple and homogeneous and monolithic" (Robert Penn Warren, *Southern Review*).

and etc.

Etc. is the abbreviation for Latin *et cetera,* in which *et* means "and." So *and* before *etc.* is redundant. See **etc.**

and/or

And/or is used primarily in legal and business writing. Its use in general writing is objected to by some readers because *and/or* looks odd and because *and* or *or* alone is often all that's needed. But it's sometimes useful when there are three alternatives—*both* the items mentioned or *either* one of them: inflation and/or depression; "that fear and awe we all feel in the presence of greatness and/or dingbats" (Hughes Rudd, *TV Guide*).

angle

Angle means "point of view" or "aspect" (from an economic angle) in standard general English, but it carries a strong suggestion of jargon. In the sense of "scheme" or "plan" (What's his angle?), *angle* is informal. See **Jargon.**

ante-, anti-

Don't confuse *ante-* "before" (antedate) with *anti-* "against" (antipollution).

Antecedent

An antecedent is the word, clause, or sentence that a pronoun refers to. It usually stands before the word that refers to it, but not always: We did not hear their call again, and when we found the Thompsons, they were almost exhausted. (*The Thompsons* is the antecedent of the possessive pronoun *their* and of *they*.) For relations between antecedents and pronouns, see **Agreement 2, Reference of pronouns.**

Anticipatory subject

In sentences like "It was Ann who found the food stamps" and "There are more important things than graduating," *it* and *there* are anticipatory subjects. See **it; there is, there are.**

any

1. Uses. *Any* is used primarily as an adjective (Any job will do) but also as a pronoun (Any will do). The pronoun *any* takes either a singular verb (Any of them *has* a chance of winning first prize) or a plural verb (Any of them *have* a chance of ending up in the top ten), depending on the sense of the statement.

In comparisons of things in the same class, use *any other:* He shaped the university more than any other president in its history. *Any* alone is always used when different classes are compared: I like a movie better than any book.

2. Compounds with *any*.   *Anybody, anyhow, anything,* and *anywhere* are always written as single words. *Any rate* is always two words: at any rate. *Anyone* is written as one word when the stress is on the *any* (Anyone would know that) and as two when the stress is on the *one* (I'd like any one of them). *Anyway* is one word when the *any* is stressed (I couldn't go anyway) and two when the stress is about equal (Any way I try, it comes out wrong). If the word *whatever* can be substituted for the *any* (Whatever way I try, it comes out wrong), *any way* should be written as two words.

3. Pronouns referring to *anybody, anyone*.   *Anybody* and *anyone* are singular in form and take singular verbs: anybody (*or* anyone) feels bad at times. They are referred to by *he, his, him* (Anybody knows what he deserves) or, since they often apply to a person of either sex, by *he or she, his or her, him or her,* or a form of *they* with the same meaning: "It is not usually possible to achieve intimacy with anybody in the back seat of a car; you have to live with them in every sense of the phrase" (Edgar Z. Friedenberg, *New York Review of Books*). Formal usage insists on a singular pronoun. See **Agreement 2, he or she, Sexist language, they.** Compare **every.**

4. Other forms.   *Anyways* is regional for the generally used *anyway,* and *anywheres* is nonstandard for *anywhere.* Though many object to it, *any more* now frequently appears in print as one word: "They want to protect all those traditional events whether or not they mean something anymore" (Herbert Warren Wind, *New Yorker*). *Any more* (or *anymore*) in a strictly affirmative context meaning "now" (Any more they do as they please) is a regional idiom.

Anyplace (now usually written as one word) has become a general synonym for "anywhere": "You will hear bitter attacks on the United States for subverting Chile, but not a word about Soviet subversion in Afghanistan or anyplace else" (Jane Rosen, *New York Times Magazine*).

apos Apostrophe

Insert an apostrophe where it belongs in the word marked; or take out an apostrophe that is incorrectly used.

Typical mistakes in the use of the apostrophe are *mans* for *man's, mens'* for *men's, it's* for the possessive *its,* and *their's* for *theirs.* Review the following uses:

1. In possessives.   The most common use of the apostrophe is in spelling the possessive case of nouns and indefinite pronouns (*anyone, nobody, someone* . . .): Dorothy's first picture, the companies' original charters, everybody's business is nobody's business, the boys' dogs. An apostrophe should be used in singular possessives (or genitives) of time and value even though they carry no idea of possession: *a day's hike, this month's quota, a dollar's worth.* In formal writing an apostrophe is also preferred in plural possessives of this kind (*two week's work*), but usage is divided (*teachers college*). For special examples of possessive form, see **Possessive case.**

2. In contractions. The apostrophe shows the omission of one or more letters in contractions: *can't, I'm, I'll, it's (it is).*

3. In plurals. An apostrophe was formerly expected in plurals of figures and letters (*three 4's, two e's*) and plurals of words being discussed as words (*the first of several that's*), but current usage is divided. Decades in figures are often written without an apostrophe: *the mid-1980s.* Using an apostrophe in writing the plural of a family name is an error: *the Smiths, not* the Smith's.

4. In representing speech. An apostrophe may be used to indicate that the speaker omits certain sounds represented in the conventional spelling: " 'Lily,' he pleaded, 'I swear t'God, you'll get it back on pay-day. You c'n meet me up at the barn if you wanna' " (I. J. Kapstein, *Something of a Hero*). Because too many apostrophes are distracting for the reader, it's better to indicate pronunciations of this sort occasionally than to try to represent all of them.

Apostrophes should not be used in the possessive forms of the personal pronouns *(his, hers, its, ours, theirs, your)* or introduced into words that don't have them *(till,* not *'till* or *'til).*

Apposition, appositives

Beside a noun or noun-equivalent in a sentence, you can put another nominal expression called an appositive: *My aunts, Mary and Agnes, moved to Boulder in 1969.* The noun and its appositive refer to the same person(s) or thing(s). Typically, the appositive is set off by commas, but sometimes no punctuation is needed: *He caught so many fish that we called him Jim [ ] the fisherman.* See **Nominals.**

Don't use appositives unnecessarily. For example, if you use the President's name, there's no need to identify him as the President, and if you refer to "the President," there's no need to tell the reader what his name is.

Arabic numerals

Arabic numerals are the ones we normally use: 1, 2, 3, etc. See **Numbers 3.**

arise, rise, get up

In referring to standing up or getting out of bed, *arise* is formal and poetic, *rise* is slightly less formal, and *get up* is the general idiom.

around

Around, like *about,* can be used to mean "approximately." See **about 1; round, around.**

Articles

Traditionally *a* and *an* are known as indefinite articles, *the* as the definite article. See **a, an; Nouns 3c.**

as

Among the meanings of *as* are "while" (As we walked along, he told us stories) and "because" (His speed is amazing, as he weighs 260 pounds). *While* is preferable to *as* if the emphasis is on the time of the action (While we were walking along, he told us stories). And though *as* is used to mean "because" (or "since") in all varieties of English, many readers dislike the usage. It can easily be ambiguous. In the sentence "As we have continued responding to erratic changes in Asia, our position has inevitably become more complex," *as* can mean either "because" or "while." See **while**.

For the growing tendency to use *as* where *like* would be expected, see **like, as.**

as . . . as

1. *As I* or *as me.* In a sentence like "He admires her as much as I/me," meaning determines whether the nominative *I* or the accusative *me* is used. If you mean "as much as I admire her," use *I*. If you mean "as much as he admires me," use *me*.

In a sentence like "They sent for somebody as big as I/me," the choice doesn't affect the meaning. Both nominative *I* and accusative *me* are good English.

For a third type of sentence—"He is as big as I/me"—in which there's no preceding noun or pronoun in the accusative position, usage has always been divided. The nominative *I* is preferred in formal contexts and is insisted upon by many word watchers. See **Accusative case, Nominative case.**

2. Omitted *as*. Writers frequently omit the second *as* in a comparison of equality (as large as) when it's joined by *or* or *if not* to a comparison of inequality (larger than): It was as large or larger than last year's crowd. But many readers and writers insist that only the complete form is correct: It was as large as, or larger than, last year's crowd. Whenever possible, move the second comparison to the end of the sentence: It was as large as last year's crowd, if not larger.

3. *As . . . as* and *so . . . as*. *As . . . as* is much more common than *so . . . as* in simple comparisons of degree (as small as that, as late as you like). Both *as* and *so* are used to begin the phrases "— far as I know" and "— far as that's concerned." Many handbooks have urged that *as . . . as* be used only in affirmative statements (She's as clever as any of them) and *so . . . as* in negative statements (She's not so clever as she thinks), but the distinction has never become established in practice.

as far as

In using the phrase *as* (or *so*) *far as . . . is concerned* (As far as tuition is concerned, I don't think we're getting any bargain) many speakers and some writers drop the verb: As far as tuition, I don't think we're getting any bargain. The reduced phrase makes no more sense than "As far as I" for "As far as I'm concerned." Often *as for* can be substituted for the longer phrase: As for tuition, I don't think we're getting any bargain.

as if, as though

In formal English the subjunctive mood of the verb is commonly used after *as if* and *as though:* He acted as if (*or* as though) he *were* losing his temper. In general English the indicative mood is usual: He acted as if (*or* as though) he *was* losing his temper. See **Subjunctive mood.**

as, like

As is the conjunction (He voted as he was expected to). *Like* is the preposition (He voted like the rest). See **like, as.**

Assonance

Assonance is the repetition of vowel sounds in words having different consonant sounds, as in *brave-vain* and *lone-show*. Assonance is characteristic of verse and also occurs in prose, especially in poetic styles: "that ideal country of green, deep lanes and high green banks" (Osbert Sitwell). Like unintentional alliteration, unintentional assonance can be distracting.

as though

As though is commonly followed by a verb in the subjunctive mood in formal English but not in general English. See **as if, as though.**

as to

As to is often a clumsy substitute for a single preposition, usually *of* or *about:* Practice is the best teacher as to (*better:* in, for, of) the use of organ stops. In some locutions it should simply be omitted: [As to] whether college is worthwhile is a question we all must try to answer. But for introducing subjects, *as to* is better than more cumbersome expressions like *as regards, as concerns, in respect to:* As to the economic value of going to college, the effect on earning power is clearly established.

as well as

When an *as well as* phrase between subject and verb gives a strong impression of adding to the subject, some writers treat it as part of the subject and let it influence the number of the verb: The singer as well as four members of the outstandingly successful band were arrested in Moose Jaw. In such cases the phrase is seldom set off by commas. But according to traditional rules the phrase is parenthetical, should be enclosed in commas, and has no bearing on the verb: "This volume, as well as others, consists of a collection of basic articles" (Robert R. Wilson, *ISIS*).

at

Forget the old vogue phrase "where it's at." People and things are where they *are:* When she called home from the airport, her father wanted to know where she was (*not* where she was at).

at about

At about can be reduced to either *at* or *about*. But see **about 3.**

athletics

When the collective noun *athletics* refers to sports and games, it usually takes a plural verb and pronoun: Our athletics *include* football, basketball, and baseball. When athletics refers to a skill or activity, it usually takes a singular verb and pronoun: Athletics *is* recommended because *it* contributes to good health.

author

An author writes books. But does a writer author books? *Author* as a verb is widely used (by publishers, among others) but also widely disapproved. It may be most defensible when it's used to refer to publication by a group (the report was authored by a presidential commission) or to the participation of a celebrity in producing an autobiography "as told to" a professional writer.

Auxiliary verbs

A verb used with other verbs to form tenses or, in the case of *be,* to change the active voice to the passive is called an auxiliary verb or helping verb. The most common auxiliaries, *be* and *have,* are used in forming the progressive and perfect tenses and the passive voice: I *am* going; He *has* gone; They *were* shot. *Do* is used in questions (Do they care?) and contradictions (They do not care) and for emphasis (Yes, they *do* care). The modal auxiliaries—*can, may, shall, will, must, ought to, could, should, would,* and *might*—are used to refer to future time *(shall* and *will)* and to suggest obligation, necessity, or possibility: You *should* reply; She *must* leave; He *could* break the record. See **Modal auxiliaries, Tenses of verbs,** and entries on individual verbs.

awful

In formal English *awful* means "awesome." In informal English it's a convenient word of disapproval meaning "ugly," "shocking," "ridiculous," "very poor" (an awful movie). In informal and sometimes in general writing, the word is also used to intensify meaning: ". . . delusions that are being chosen by an awful lot [that is, a very large number] of people in preference to standard, orthodox explanations" (Elizabeth Janeway, *Atlantic*). This use of either *awful* or *awfully* (an awfully long wait) is, of course, deplored by word worriers.

awhile, a while

Awhile is an adverb: They talked awhile. *While* is a noun: She was gone for a long while. Strictly, prepositional phrases with the noun *while* should be in at least three words (in a while), but *awhile* after a preposition is increasingly common.

B

bad, badly

Bad is ordinarily used as the adjective (a bad apple) and *badly* as the adverb (They sing badly). But though the grammatical rule calls for a predicate adjective after a linking verb, the linking verb *feel* is frequently followed by *badly* instead of *bad:* I feel badly about it. Both *feel bad* and *feel badly* are generally accepted as standard. Formal stylists prefer *bad*. Usage is divided.

Badly meaning "very much" (He wanted it badly) is standard. As a group adjective, *badly off* is general: "But we are not Satan. Fallen though we are, we are not that badly off" (John Morris, *American Scholar*).

Bad as an adverb (I played bad all through the game) is informal.

See **Hypercorrectness.**

Bad grammar

Bad grammar is applied as an expression of disapproval to all sorts of lo-cutions, from "I ain't got none" to supposed confusions in the use of *shall* and *will*. As criticism the label is too vague to be helpful. See **grammatical, ungrammatical.**

basically

Basically is one of many words we use in conversation without meaning much of anything: Basically it was a good course. Don't use it in writing unless you're making a contrast, either expressed or implied: [On the surface they seem carefree and irresponsible, but] basically they're very concerned about getting established in jobs with a future.

be

Be is the most common linking verb, joining a subject and a predicate noun (Jerome was the secretary) or predicate adjective (She is energetic). When it joins a subject and a pronoun, the pronoun is in the nominative case in formal written English (It was *he*), in the accusative in informal (It was *him*). "It's I" is formal for the general "It's me." See **it's me.**

When the infinitive *be* has a subject and complement, both are in the accusative case: I wanted *him* to be *me*. When the infinitive has no subject, formal usage has a nominative as the complement (I wanted to be *he*). General usage more often has an accusative (I wanted to be *him*).

Be has more forms and a greater variety of forms than any other verb in English:

> *Present:* I am, you are, he is; we, you, they are
> *Past:* I was, you were, he was; we, you, they were
> *Infinitive:* be
> *Present participle:* being
> *Past participle:* been

See **ain't, Subjunctive mood.**

because

Because introduces an adverbial clause that gives the reason for the statement in the main clause: *Because we were getting hungry,* we began to look for a restaurant. *Since* and *as* can be used to introduce such clauses, but they're less definite.

Because also is used in general-to-informal styles where a more formal style would use *for*—that is, where what is introduced is not the cause of an effect but the premise for a conclusion:

> *Formal:* Komarov clearly had some control over his ship, for he was able to orient it well enough to accomplish re-entry.—*Newsweek*

> *Less formal:* Komarov clearly had some control over his ship, because he was able to orient it. . . .

See **as, for, reason is because.** For **because of,** see **due to.**

beg Beginning

Revise the opening of your paper so that it will lead more directly and smoothly into your subject or so that it will do more to stir your reader's interest.

The best advice for beginning a short paper is "Get on with it." An elaborate windup is silly when the pitch is no more than a straight throw in a backyard game of catch. And an opening that indulges in philosophizing (Since the days of Plato's Academy, violence and learning have been alien entities) or announces a grand strategy (In the paragraphs that follow, I shall attempt, first by analyzing and then by synthesizing, . . .) is just as silly in a two-page paper on a campus controversy.

Ordinarily, the first step is to let your reader know what you're writing about—not by telling him what you're going to discuss but by discussing it: "We think of the drug addict as unwilling or unable to work, but he works harder to get his dope than most of us do to get our daily bread" (*Psychology Today*). This doesn't rule out a personal approach. There may be good reason for you to tell why you've chosen your topic or how you're qualified to discuss it. It does rule out beginnings that fail to begin.

Besides getting the paper under way, the opening paragraph or two should make a reader want to continue reading. But straining for humor or excitement or cuteness or sentiment is no way to arouse interest. As imitations of the techniques used by professional journalists, such attempts are likely to fail. The humor doesn't amuse, the excitement doesn't stir, and so on. Instead of trying out gimmicks, move into the subject and treat it with the interest *you* feel. If it doesn't interest you, your chances of making it interest your readers are slim. If it does interest you, and if you write about it as honestly and directly as you know how, your readers will keep on reading.

For long papers—from five to ten pages, say—somewhat more elaborate beginnings are sometimes necessary. But getting on with the discussion remains fundamental. If you provide the historical background of the problem you're dealing with, make sure that this material contributes to the solution you propose. If you announce what you're going to do in your paper, be sure you do it.

beside, besides

Beside is used chiefly as a preposition meaning "by the side of," as in "beside the road," "beside her." It's used figuratively in a few rather formal idioms like "beside the point," "beside himself with rage." *Besides* is used as a preposition meaning "in addition to" (Besides ourselves, about a dozen students came to the meeting), and as an adverb and a conjunctive adverb (He didn't think he ought to get into the quarrel; besides, he had come to enjoy himself) meaning "in addition."

between, among

Among implies more than two objects: They distributed the provisions among the survivors. *Between* is used of two: They divided the prize between Kincaid and Thomas. But attempts to limit *between* to use only with two items have failed. When the relationship is between individual items— participants in discussions or negotiations, for example—*between* is the word to use no matter how many items there are: "This is so . . . of some part of the debate between Einstein, Bohr, Wolfgang Pauli, and Max Born" (George Steiner, *Atlantic*).

When treating a group as a collective unit, use *among:* Divide the books among the poor.

between you and me

Though *you and I* as the object of a preposition or a verb is frequently heard and has a long history in written English, those who know better are likely to regard anyone who says or writes "between you and I" as only half-educated. *Between you and me* is always correct. See **Hypercorrectness.**

bi-

Some time words beginning with *bi-* cause confusion. *Bimonthly* and *biweekly,* for example, may mean "every two . . . " or "twice a . . . ." *Biennial* means "every two years," but *biannual* means "twice a year." When the context doesn't make the meaning clear, it's safest to use phrases like "every two months," "twice a week," "twice a year."

Bible, bible

When it refers to the Christian Scriptures, the word is capitalized but not italicized: You'll find all that in the Bible. In the sense of an authoritative book, the word is not capitalized: *Gray's Manual* is the botanist's bible. The adjective *biblical* is seldom capitalized.

black

Since the 1960s the term *Negro* has been replaced in most writing by *black,* usually not capitalized. *Afro-American* is also used.

bloc, block

Leave off the *k* only when you're writing about a common-interest group—of senators, for example—whose members can be expected to vote the same way on legislation affecting the interest they share: The amendment was defeated by the farm bloc.

born, borne

In most senses of *bear,* the past participle is spelled with a final *-e,* but the spelling *born* is used in the sense "brought into being" in the passive voice. Thus "She has borne three children," but "Three children were born to her." *Born* is also used in the sense "determined by birth," as in "He was born to be hanged."

both

Both is used to emphasize two-ness: The twins were both there; Both Harry and his sister went. Though neither of these *boths* is necessary, each gives a legitimate emphasis. In "They both dressed alike," on the other hand, *both* adds nothing but awkwardness. "The both of them," a fairly common spoken idiom, should be avoided in writing.

both . . . and

When used as a pair (both the tire and the tube), the coordinating conjunctions *both* and *and* are called correlative conjunctions. See **Correlative conjunctions.**

Brackets

Brackets have specific uses in scholarly writing. Their main function is to enclose alterations and additions within quoted material:

> The story answers precisely . . . to that told in the third paragraph of Curll's *Key:* "But when he [Thomas Swift] had not yet gone half way, his Companion [Jonathan Swift] borrowed the Manuscript to peruse."—Robert Martin Adams, *Modern Philology*

In brackets Adams has identified for the reader the "he" and the "Companion" referred to by Curll.

Sic in brackets indicates that an error in the quoted material is being reproduced exactly: New Haven, Connecicut [sic]. Brackets may also be used to insert a correction: Cramer writes, "In April 1943 [the month was July], Jones published his first novel." And brackets function as parentheses within parentheses, particularly in legal documents and scholarly footnotes.

If your typewriter keyboard doesn't have brackets, draw them in by hand.

bring, take

Bring implies motion toward the speaker or writer (Bring it with you when you come). *Take* implies motion away from (Take it with you when you go). When the speaker or writer is doing the moving, he's glad he *brought* his camera along. When he's returned, he's glad he *took* his camera and *brought* it back. When the point of view doesn't matter, either term can be used: Potatoes were brought (*or* taken) from Ireland to France.

bring up

Bring up, like *raise,* is general usage for the more formal *rear* or *nurture* (That's the way I was brought up). It also means "to introduce" a subject: Having brought it up, he couldn't stop talking about it. See **raise, rear.**

British English

British English and American English differ noticeably in spelling. The British prefer *-re* to *-er* in ending words like *center* and *theater,* though they use both forms. They keep *-our* in a number of words where Americans use *-or.* They use *x* in a few words like *inflexion* where Americans use *ct.*

They double more consonants, as in *traveller* and *waggon*. And they spell some individual words differently, including automobile *tyre* for U.S. *tire*. They use more hyphens than we do and the opposite order of double and single quotation marks. Differences like these occur just often enough to show that a book is of British rather than American origin—certainly not enough to interfere with comprehension.

The grammar of the popular levels of British and American English differs somewhat, though less than the vocabulary. Collective nouns referring to institutions are more likely to be plural in British usage (the government intend). British writers differ in small matters like the position of *only*, the proper preposition with *different*, the use of *shall*, and various idioms. It would be possible to assemble a fairly long list of such minor differences, but their importance shouldn't be exaggerated nor their occurrence allowed to obscure the fact that the resemblances far outnumber the differences and that the speech of the two countries represents two strands of the same language.

Usages that originate in Great Britain frequently become vogue expressions in the United States: *early on* and *a good read* are recent examples. These soon become tiresome, as home-grown vogue words and phrases do. But some Americans treat them with special contempt as evidence of affectation. Such hostility to Briticisms represents an attitude almost as old as the Republic. So does its opposite—an eagerness to embrace all things British, including Briticisms. British attitudes toward Americanisms are similarly divided.

Broad reference

A pronoun referring to the idea of a preceding clause rather than to a particular antecedent is said to have broad reference. See **Reference of pronouns 2.**

bug

Both as a noun for an electronic listening device and as a verb for the planting of such a device (They bugged his home phone), *bug* has become established in general English.

bunch

In formal English *bunch* is limited to objects that grow together like grapes or can be fastened together like carrots or keys. Used of people, *bunch* is moving into the general vocabulary: ". . . another monumental American myth—that Washington is run by a bunch of cynical, untrustworthy fools" (Nona B. Brown, *New York Times Book Review*).

burglar, robber, thief

All three take what isn't theirs, but the robber uses violence or threats, and the burglar breaks into a building. See **rob.**

burst, bust

Burst is the unchanged past tense and past participle of the verb *burst*. *Bust* (with *bust* or *busted* as past tense and participle) is a nonstandard variant of *burst* in its literal meaning: dams and balloons burst, *not* bust.

In contexts where the meaning is figurative, *bust*—frequently with the adverbs *up* and *out*—is now common, though still somewhat informal: That interception busted the game wide open. Broncos and trusts and noncommissioned officers are *busted; burst* can't be substituted in these senses.

Business letters

Business letters include not only the correspondence sent out by companies and corporations but also the letters of individuals to business firms, colleges, government agencies, newspapers, civic organizations, and so forth. When you write a letter to apply for a job or a scholarship, to obtain information, to request assistance, or to register a complaint, the recipient is more likely to give it serious attention if you have done your best with the packaging as well as the content.

1. Materials and appearance. Use good-quality white paper measuring $8^1/2$ by 11 inches. If at all possible, type your final draft. Keep a copy of every business letter you write.

Most business letters are now written in block style without indentions, as shown in the sample. Convention calls for one line of space between inside address and salutation, between salutation and body, and between body and close. Three lines of space are usually left for the signature. Other spacing depends on the length of your letter. In your drafts—and you may need to write several—work for an attractive, balanced page, with generous margins and plenty of space at top and bottom.

If you can sensibly do so, limit your letter to a single page. When you write more than one page, number the additional pages.

2. Heading. Give your full address and the date. Unless you use the abbreviations adopted by the Postal Service (which are not followed by periods), write out the names of states. Note that there's no comma between state and ZIP code and no punctuation at the ends of lines. If you use stationery with a letterhead that provides the address, type the date beneath it.

3. Inside address. Give the name and full address of the person you're writing to, just as it will appear on the envelope, beginning each line at the left margin. How far down the page you start the inside address depends on the length of your letter. For good balance, begin a short letter lower than a longer one.

Whenever possible, direct your letter to an individual or at least to an office (Personnel Director) or a department (Personnel Department).

4. Salutation. When you're writing to a person you can name, the best greeting is the simplest:

> Dear Ms. Nash:
> Dear Mr. Mahoney:

Note that a colon follows the name. When the circumstances call for special formality, "Dear Sir" or "Dear Madam" is the right choice. If you're addressing an organization or an anonymous individual, the traditional greeting is "Dear Sirs" (or "Gentlemen") or "Dear Sir." If you're writing to a women's organization, the plural of "Madam" is "Mesdames."

5. Body. Your first paragraph should make the subject of your letter clear. Let the reader know immediately why you're writing. If you're replying to a letter, answering an advertisement, or writing at the suggestion of someone known to your reader, say so. By making your purpose clear from the outset, you help your reader concentrate immediately on what you have to say.

Your paragraphs will usually be much shorter than in a college paper— often no more than two or three sentences. Use a new paragraph for each item or each subdivision in your message, so that your reader can quickly identify the specific requests you're making or the facts you're providing and can refer to them in his response.

The style of a business letter should be clear, direct, and as brief as clarity and completeness permit. The tone should be brisk without being brusque. You don't want to waste your reader's time, but neither do you want to insult him. And while being concise, be careful not to confuse or mystify him. Provide all relevant information, especially if you're complaining about defective merchandise, outlining a proposal, or seeking a job.

Finding just the right tone to use in your letter may require some effort, since you'll often have little notion what sort of person your reader is. Under such conditions, trying to make your writing seem personal may instead make it sound insincere. On the other hand, if you make no attempt to speak to the reader as an individual, your writing is likely to sound cold and aloof. The best technique is to address the reader as a stranger who is intelligent, respected, and probably short of time.

Don't make the mistake of trying to write in what you may think of as business style. The good business writer of today uses general English, avoiding both the clichés of commerce *(contact, finalize, angle, and/or)* and pretentious words like *ameliorate* for *improve, terminate* for *end.*

6. Close and signature.   Begin the close at the left margin, in the middle of the page, or aligned with the heading, depending on overall balance. Follow it with a comma. For most business letters "Sincerely" or "Sincerely yours" is appropriate. If you're writing as an official—as purchasing agent for a campus co-op, for example—give your title under your typed name:

```
Leslie Archer
Purchasing Agent
```

In typing her name, a woman may or may not choose to indicate her marital status:

```
Dorothy Olson

(Ms.) Dorothy Olson

(Miss) Dorothy Olson

(Mrs.) Dorothy Olson

Dorothy Olson
(Mrs. Henry Olson)
```

7. Mailing.   An envelope measuring 4 by $9^{1}/_{2}$ inches is best for business letters, but an envelope measuring $3^{1}/_{2}$ by $6^{1}/_{2}$ inches can be used. Repeat the inside address on the envelope, and give your own name and address in the upper left corner.

Heading	431 University Place Madison, Wisconsin 53706 November 12, 1981
Inside address	Mr. Dwight Morrison Program Director WSTR Television 546 Main Street Madison, Wisconsin 53703
Salutation	Dear Mr. Morrison:
Body	Members of the Sociology Club at the University of Wisconsin have been examining the influence of the University on the surrounding community, and we believe that some of our findings may be of interest to your viewers. In order to assess the importance of the University to local business, we have talked with many shop owners about the products they carry to attract student customers. We have looked into the way political opinions in some Madison neighborhoods have changed since students began taking an active role in local elections. And we have found that a tutorial project started by students has begun to change some people's attitudes toward the University. Members of the Sociology Club would like very much to discuss with you the possibility of using our study as the basis of a special program. Two or three of us could arrange to meet with you at your convenience.
Close	Sincerely yours,
Signature	*Marilyn Thompson* Marilyn Thompson President Sociology Club University of Wisconsin

but

But is the natural coordinating conjunction to connect two contrasted statements: He left, but she stayed. *But* is lighter than *however,* less formal than *yet,* and, unlike *(al)though,* doesn't subordinate the clause that follows it.

1. Connecting equals. The locutions connected by *but* should be of equal grammatical rank:

> *Adjectives:* not *blue* but *green*
> *Adverbs:* He worked *quickly* but *accurately.*
> *Phrases:* She finally arrived, not *at lunch time* but *in the early evening.*
> *Clauses: The first day we rested,* but *the second we got down to work.*
> *Sentences: The Rio Grande defied the best engineering minds of two countries for a century. But $10 million in flood-control work harnessed the treacherous stream.*

See **which 3** for comments on **but which.**

2. Connecting statements in opposition. The statements connected by *but* should be clearly opposed:

> He knows vaguely that the nation is not much good any more; he has read that the crust of the earth is shrinking rapidly and that the universe is growing steadily colder; but he does not believe that any of the three is in half as bad shape as he is.—James Thurber, *My Life and Hard Times.*

In "The blisters on my feet were killing me, but the road seemed to go on forever," there's no real opposition. What's needed is a second clause like "but somehow I hobbled the last long mile."

3. Beginning sentences. *But,* like *and,* is often used to begin a sentence. Separation emphasizes the contrast with the preceding sentence. Be careful, though, not to follow a *but* clause with another *but* (or *however*) clause, or both the contrast and a measure of sense will be lost:

> The magazine they founded lasted only four years and was a financial failure, *but* its influence was enormous. *But* that was not the only contribution they made to literary history.

4. Punctuation. Two clauses connected by *but* should ordinarily be separated by a comma. The contrast in ideas makes punctuation desirable even when the clauses are relatively short: I couldn't get the whole license number, but I know it began with AOK. Though writers frequently use a comma after an initial *but* (But [,] it was too late for the aging man to regain his lost skill), no punctuation should separate *but* from the clause it introduces.

but that, but what

But that as a subordinating conjunction after a negative is avoided in formal styles but appears often in general and informal styles: I don't doubt but that she will come. *But what* is sometimes used in the same construction. *That* alone can be substituted for either *but that* or *but what:* I don't doubt that she will come.

but which

If you write a clause that begins with "but which," be sure it's preceded in the sentence by a *which* clause. See **which 3.**

C

can, may (could, might)

1.   To express possibility, both *can* and *may* are used. *Can* is the only choice for simple ability: "I can swim" meaning "I'm able to swim." For feasibility ("I can swim today" meaning "There's nothing to prevent me from swimming today") *can* is less formal than *may:* "The Introduction only hints at the many paths the reader may follow" (Anna Benjamin, *Classical Philology*). Repeated use of *may* in this sense sounds excessively tentative or uncertain.

Could and might are used chiefly to convey a smaller degree of possibility than *can* and *may* or a shadow of doubt: She could be here by Saturday; I might have left it in my room. But *might* is also commonly substituted for *may,* with no difference in meaning. (*Might could* for *might be able to* is regional.)

2.   In requesting permission, *may* has a cool politeness appropriate to formal occasions: May I add one further point? Informally, *can* requests permission: Can I borrow the car next Sunday? *May* is also the formal choice in granting or denying permission. Except when the sense of institutional authority is central (Students may not attend class barefoot), *can* is more common: "After forbidding the Colonel to speak of love to her, she . . . tells him he can" (Henry Hewes, *Saturday Review*).

See **Divided usage.**

cannot, can not

Usage is divided. *Cannot* is more common.

can't hardly

Can't (or *cannot*) *hardly* should be changed to *can hardly,* since *hardly* means "probably not." See **Double negative.**

can't help but, can't seem to

Can't (or *cannot*) *help but* and *can't* (or *cannot*) *seem to* are established general idioms:

> The reader cannot help but question whether they, indeed, were so universally excellent.—Peter Walls, *Annals*

> What they can't seem to tolerate is unemployment, the feeling of being use-less.—Alfred Kazin, *Saturday Review*

Even so, *cannot help but* is avoided by some conservative stylists, who prefer *cannot help* followed by a gerund: cannot help saying. In formal usage *seem unable to* is the alternative to *can't seem to.*

Cap Capital letters

Capitalize the word marked.

Almost everyone uses capital letters at the beginning of sentences and proper names and for *I.* Some other uses of capitals are matters of taste. Formal English uses more capitals than general English, and newspaper style cuts them to a minimum. The best policy is to capitalize in accordance with well-established convention and not to capitalize in other situations without good reason.

1.   Sentence capitals.   Capitalize the first word of a sentence.
a.   Capitalize the first word in a complete sentence that you enclose in parentheses and place between two other sentences. But don't capitalize if you insert it in parentheses within a sentence or if you set it off with a dash or dashes.
b.   Capitalize the first word in a sentence following a colon if you want to emphasize the sentence (He promised this: The moment agreement was reached, the trucks would roll).
c.   In dialog, capitalize the first word of what a speaker says but not the second part of an interrupted quoted sentence: "Well," he said, "it (*not* It) was nice to see you again." Except in dialog, don't capitalize parts of sentences that are quoted: "Stressing that legal restrictions on surveillance are few, he rallied the assembled with the intelligence that 'the challenge is wide open' " (David M. Rorvik, *Playboy*).

2.   Proper names.   Capitalize proper names and abbreviations of proper names: names of people and places, months, days of the week, historical events (the Civil War, the Council of Trent, the New Deal), documents (the

Emancipation Proclamation), companies and organizations, trade names, religious denominations, holidays, races and ethnic groups (but see **black**), languages, ships, named planes and trains, and nicknames. See **Course names.**

a. Capitalize *north, south,* and so on when they denote particular regions (the Southwest, the East) but not when they indicate direction (They started west in 1849).

b. Capitalize *army, navy,* and so on when they appear in full titles (the United States Army) and when they stand for the teams of the service academies. In other cases usage is divided: the American army (or Army), their navy (or Navy).

c. Capitalize *college* as part of a full title (He went to Beloit College) but not as a level of schooling (Neither of them went to college).

d. Don't capitalize proper nouns that have become common nouns: *tweed, sandwich, bohemian, plaster of paris,* and so on. Many proper adjectives in senses that no longer suggest their origins are not capitalized *(india ink, diesel engine)* but others usually are *(French cuffs, Xerox copy, Bibb lettuce)*. Follow your dictionary.

e. Don't capitalize the names of the seasons except in *Fall term, Spring semester,* and so on, or for stylistic reasons.

3. Titles of books, articles, etc. Capitalize the first word and last word (and the first word after a colon), all nouns, pronouns, verbs, adjectives, and adverbs, and all prepositions of more than five letters: *With Malice Toward Some; Social Humanism: An International Symposium; Now Don't Try to Reason with Me;* "Biological Clocks of the Tidal Zone"; "Computer Control of Electric-Power Systems." See **Titles.**

4. Titles, positions, relatives.
a. Capitalize personal titles before proper names: President Taft, Ambassador Clark, Senator Lodge, Sergeant York. "The President" for the President of the United States is still customary. Otherwise, usage is divided when an individual is referred to by title alone: The Colonel was there; The senator spoke at length.

b. Capitalize the names for family members when used as proper nouns: We had to get Father's consent. Don't capitalize when they are used as common nouns: My mother is a better dancer than I am.

5. Deity. Capitalize the name of the Supreme Being *(God, Jehovah, Allah), Jesus,* and nouns such as *Savior.* With pronouns referring to God and Jesus, practice is divided: *He, Him, His* or *he, him, his.*

6. *Street, river, park,* and so on. Capitalize such words as *street, river, park, hotel,* and *church* when they follow a proper name (Fifth Avenue, Missouri River). Abbreviations of these words should also be capitalized: 2319 E. 100th St.

7. Abstractions. Usage is divided. Abstract nouns are likely to be capitalized in formal writing (less often in general) when the concepts they refer to are personified or when they refer to ideals or institutions: The State has nothing to do with the Church, nor the Church with the State.

8.   Quoted lines of verse.   Follow the poet's capitalization exactly.

Writers once used capitals as a form of emphasis, to stress certain words or call attention to them. Now when such initial capitals appear, the purpose is usually to amuse. If what you have to say isn't funny to begin with, capitals won't help.

✗   Careless mistakes

Correct the obvious mistake marked.

Careless lapses are inevitable in hurried work. But a college paper shouldn't be hurried work. Comma splices and fragments, mistakes in the forms of verbs and pronouns *(broke* for *broken, it's* for *its),* missing words, and similar slips are likely to occur if you give too little time or too little attention to the final stages of preparing a paper.

Train yourself to proofread carefully. Check your manuscript for such elementary mistakes as these:

Letters omitted (the *n* of *an,* the *d* of *used to,* a final *y)*
End punctuation omitted (including the closing quotation marks after a quoted passage)
Words run together (a/lot, in *a/while)*
Words confused (affect, effect; principal, principle; quiet, quite; than, then; there, their; to, too; whether, weather; whose, who's)

Check also for the unnecessary repetition of a preposition or a conjunction: It is only natural *that* with the sudden change in the administration *that* people are worrying about what new policies may be introduced.

If you're uncertain about the spelling of a word, consult your dictionary. If you're unsure what word, word form, construction, or punctuation to use, consult this *Index.*

Caret

The inverted *v* called a caret points to the place in a line of manuscript where something written above the line or in the margin should be inserted:

```
                                                    because
There was no reason for them not to get good grades,∧ all
they did was study.
```

This is an acceptable way to revise papers as long as the revisions are few and completely clear.

A caret used by an instructor as a correction mark indicates that something has been omitted.

Case Case

Correct the mistake in case.

The case of a noun or pronoun is one indication of its relationship to other elements in the sentence. (Another indication is word order.) The subject of a verb and the complement of a linking verb are in the nominative, or subjective, case *(Who* is *she?)*. The object of a verb or a preposition is in the accusative, or objective, case (I introduced *them;* He walked behind *her)*. Certain modifiers of a noun are in the possessive, or genitive, case (*his* hat, the *dog's* bone).

Except for the spelling differences in the possessive singular *(dog's)*, the possessive plural *(dogs')*, and the common plural *(dogs)*, the case of nouns presents no problems. The same form is used in both subject and object positions: Your *dog* chased my *dog*. Pronouns have more forms— especially the pronouns we use most often. And when we're in the habit of using a few nonstandard forms in speech, the case of these pronouns may cause some problems in writing.

Most of the problems involve the six pronouns that change form to indicate all three cases: *I, he, she, we, they, who* (and its variant *whoever)*. Thus: *She* sings (nominative); The song pleases *her* (accusative); It's *his* song, not *hers* (possessive). Note that four of the pronouns have a second form of the possessive, used when the pronoun doesn't precede a noun: *mine, hers, ours, theirs*. The pronouns it and you change their form only in the possessive: *its; your, yours*. These pronouns, as well as the indefinites (like *some/one, any/thing, each*), have the same form whether they are subjects or objects.

Here are the basic conventions to observe in standard written English:

1. Use the forms *I, he, she, we, they, who(ever)*
a. In subject position: *She* and *I* played on the same team; *He* asked *who* wrote the play (*who* is the subject of *wrote,* not the object of *asked)*; *Whoever* wrote it had a good ear for dialog.
b. In apposition to a noun or pronoun in subject position: The winning couple, Phil and *I,* got a trip to Disneyland; We, Phil and *I,* got a trip. . . .
c. After a linking verb: It is *he* who should pay the bill. (But see **it's me.**)

2. Use the forms *me, him, her, us, them*
a. In object position: The song reminded Jack and *me* (object of verb) of our high-school graduation; College is harder for *him* than for *me* (object of

preposition—see also **between you and me**). The object of an infinitive is often in the accusative case (I wanted to be *him*) in general writing and always in informal. But the nominative case (I always wanted to be *he*) is the rule in formal writing.

b. In apposition to a noun or pronoun in object position: Prizes went to the top students, Mary and *me;* The prizes went to us, Mary and *me*.

3. The special problem of *whom(ever)*. The object form *whom(ever)* is regularly used after a preposition: To *whom* was the remark addressed? But speakers and writers sometimes deliberately shift the preposition to the end of the sentence and use *who* for its object: *Who* was the remark addressed to? In general usage *who* at the beginning of a sentence is also increasingly common for the object of a verb: *Who* do we ask for advice? Even among formal stylists, usage is divided. See **who, whom**.

4. Use the possessive case of nouns and pronouns to indicate possession and the other relationships discussed in **Possessive case 2,** except when the *of* phrase is customary (the end *of the street,* the roof *of the house*): It was the other *man's* hat, not *his;* the mixup resulted from *their* putting them on the same hook. "*Their* putting" illustrates the standard form for a pronoun that's the subject of a gerund. When a noun is the subject of a gerund, the common form is usual in informal and general English and is the choice of some formal writers: He complained about the *book* (more formal: *book's*) going out of print. See **Gerunds 2**.

Avoid the nonstandard *hisself* for himself and *theirself* or *theirselves* for *themselves*.

See **Pronouns 1, 4; Possessive case**.

catholic, Catholic

Written with a small *c, catholic* is a rather formal synonym for "universal or broad in sympathies or interests." In general American usage *Catholic* written with a capital *c* is taken as equivalent to *Roman Catholic,* both as a noun (She's a Catholic) and as an adjective (Catholic labor unions).

censor, censure

When we *censor,* we delete or suppress. When we *censure,* we condemn or disapprove. To make things more complicated, the adjective *censorious* refers to censuring.

center around

Precisionists condemn it as illogical, but *center around* (The story centers around the theft of a necklace) is standard idiom:

> We could sometimes look out on shooting and fights that seemed to center around this saloon.—Edmund Wilson, *New Yorker*

. . . accompanied by a propaganda war centered around her rightness and fitness for the throne.—Kerby Neil, *Modern Philology*

In some formal styles *on* or *upon* may be substituted for *around,* or *revolve* may be used instead of *center*. See **Logic in language.**

Centuries

The first century A.D. ran from the beginning of the year 1 to the end of the year 100. The present century began on January 1, 1901, and will end on December 31, 2000. Thus, to name the century correctly, add one to the number of its hundred except in the last year, when the number of the hundred is the number of the century, too. We live in the twentieth century.

For clarity, the hundred can be named, even in formal writing: Dr. Johnson lived in the seventeen hundreds. Similar practice—with and without the centuries—is standard in naming decades: the nineteen twenties, the sixties.

chauvinist

Until recently *chauvinist* was used almost exclusively to mean "superpatriot" or "jingoist." Then feminists began to use the label *male chauvinist* to describe a man whose attitudes were dominated by sexist prejudice or, more loosely, a man who was prejudiced against women. Now *chauvinist* is often used alone with this second meaning. Outside of feminist circles, the only sure way to avoid confusion is to specify what sort of chauvinist you're writing about.

Circumlocution

A circumlocution is a roundabout way of saying what could be expressed more directly. See **Wordiness.**

Cities

If you refer to a city in a paper you write, locate it by state or by country only if it's a city your readers aren't familiar with or if it's not the city they might assume it is: Paris, Texas, but not Paris, France; Athens, Georgia, or Athens, Ohio, but not Athens, Greece.

claim

Used in the sense of "say" or "declare," *claim* suggests to many readers that the assertion should be regarded skeptically: He claims to be opposed to gun control. Using it as a mere variant of *say* (He claimed he was taking Chemistry 301) can therefore be misleading. See **say.**

Clauses

Each combination of a complete subject, like *he*, and a complete predicate, like *came home*, is traditionally called a clause. "He came home" is an independent clause. Grammatically it can stand alone. "When he came home" is a dependent clause. In ordinary prose a dependent clause does not stand alone as a sentence but is preceded or followed by an independent clause: When he came home, he looked for the cat.

1.   The clause structure of sentences.   The sentences that follow in **a, b, c,** and **d** both define and illustrate. Simple subjects and simple predicates are italicized. *IC* in brackets introduces an independent clause, *DC* a dependent one.

a.   [IC] A simple *sentence* (like this one) *consists* of a single independent subject-predicate combination.

b.   [IC] A compound *sentence has* two or more clauses of equal grammatical value; [IC] these *clauses are joined* by a coordinating conjunction, by a conjunctive adverb, or (as in this sentence) by a semicolon. [IC] A *writer may decide,* for reasons of emphasis or rhythm, to break a compound sentence into two separate simple sentences, [IC] and in such cases the only *difference* between the compound sentence and the separate sentences *is* punctuation.

c.   [IC begun] A complex *sentence,* like the one [DC] that *you are* now *reading,* [IC continued] *has* at least one independent clause and one or more dependent, or subordinate, clauses, [DC] *which function* as nominals, adjectivals, or adverbials.

d.   [DC] As the hyphenated *term indicates,* [IC] a compound-complex *sentence* (again illustrated by the sentence [DC] *you are reading*) *combines* the features of both compound and complex sentences: [IC] *it contains* two or more independent clauses and one or more dependent clauses.

See **Adjectivals 1, Adverbials, Noun clauses, Relative clauses.**

2.   Reduced clauses.   Though the typical clause as traditionally defined has an expressed subject and a predicate with a full verb, many constructions lack one or the other of these elements and yet function in sentences as typical clauses do. Reduced clauses are of two types:

a.   Elliptical clauses, in which a full verb can be reconstructed because it occurs earlier in the sentence:

> I don't *believe it* any more than you [*believe it*].
> They can *speak Russian,* and so can Bill [*speak Russian*].

b.   Abridged clauses, in which the reader must rely on sense to fill in the missing subject and a form of *be:*

> While [*I* was] waiting, *I* read the newspaper.
> When [*he* was] sixteen, *he* went to work.

Though [*she* was] a rapid reader, *she* disliked books.
After [*they* had been] standing in line for an hour, *they* left.
Though [*we* were] tired, *we* kept on working.

When the omitted subject isn't the same as the subject of the main clauses, the result is often a dangling modifier.

See **Dangling modifiers, Elliptical constructions, Restrictive and nonrestrictive modifiers.**

Cliché

A cliché is a worn-out word or phrase (like "white as snow"). See **Triteness.**

Clipped words

Ad[*vertisement*], *disco*[*theque*], *porn*[*ography*], and [*tele*]*phone* are clipped words. See **Origin of words 3c.**

ꝏ Coherence

Make clear the relation between the parts of this sentence or between these sentences or these paragraphs.

Coherence—the traditional name for relationship, connection, consecutiveness—is essential in expository writing. It's essential because you can't count on the minds of others working the same way your mind works. You must guide your readers from one idea, from one sentence, to another. To make a coherent presentation you have to arrange your ideas so that others can understand them.

Though careful planning in the prewriting stage will help you make clear the relationship of your ideas, testing for coherence must come after you've written a draft of your paper. To see if it hangs together, try to read it as your readers will—as if the content is new to you. Ask yourself if the relationship between statements is clear, if it's possible to move easily from one clause or sentence or paragraph to the next without losing the thread. For a passage like the following, all the logical connectives were probably in the writer's head, but that didn't help readers who tried to make sense of what was on paper:

> Disco isn't usually written to express a deep emotional meaning. All over the world people like a rhythm they can dance to. Sometimes they get such crowds that they have to turn people away.

There are many words and phrases that signal the relationship between sentence parts, sentences, and paragraphs. These signs, and suggestions for establishing coherence, are discussed in **Conjunctions and style, Prepositions, Reference of pronouns,** and **Transition.**

Collective nouns

A collective noun is a noun whose singular form names a group of objects or persons or acts. Here are some familiar examples:

army	couple	group	offspring
audience	dozen	herd	orchestra
class	faculty	jury	public
committee	family	majority	remainder
crowd	gang	number	team

Some collectives have regular plural forms *(army–armies)*. Some do not *(offspring)*. The plural of a collective noun signifies different groups: The *audiences* of New York and Seattle differed in their reception of the movie.

Some collectives are typically used in the singular *(committee is)* and some typically in the plural *(police are)*. Most are singular in one context, plural in a different one, depending on the way the writer thinks about the group. When it's the group as a whole, the collective noun takes a singular verb and a singular pronoun: "A *group* of . . . the stories *features* characters whose lives have become misshapen through means other than self-assertion" (Welford Dunaway Taylor, *Sherwood Anderson*).

When it's the individual units of the group that the writer has in mind, the noun takes a plural verb and plural pronoun: "Psychologists asked a *group* of young men and women what sex *they* wanted *their* first child to be" *(Psychology Today)*. With this example, compare "Now that John is back, the *group has its* old solidarity."

Trouble occurs when a writer treats a collective noun inconsistently. He begins by treating the word as a singular, and as long as the verb follows it closely, he makes the verb singular: The inner *circle has* great influence. But if a plural modifier comes between the collective noun and the verb, he thinks of the members of the group rather than of the group as a unit, and he shifts to a plural verb: This inner *circle* of ambitious men *pose* a serious threat.

A writer is also likely to be inconsistent when his way of thinking about the collective comes into conflict with the meaning of a sentence he's writing. He may want to keep a collective noun singular, but if the meaning calls for a plural construction, he'll often make the shift unconsciously, sometimes in mid-sentence:

The entire *congregation troops* into the church, *seats itself,* and *remains* for a good two hours, while an aged curé berates *them* [consistency demands *it*] for *their* [*its*] sins.

In making your constructions consistent, you may find that it's the collective subject that needs to be changed, rather than the pronouns. In the example just given, beginning the sentence with "All members of the congregation troop into the church, seat themselves . . ." would avoid the problem.

Casual shifts in number are common in speech, but they're likely to attract unfavorable attention in general writing, and they're almost certain to in formal writing. When you read over your papers, be sure you haven't treated the same collective noun as both singular and plural.

See **Agreement 1b; each, every.**

Colloquial English

Usage that's characteristic of the way we talk is called colloquial. Though the division between spoken English and written English isn't nearly as sharp as it once was, some spoken usages may be inappropriate in all but the most informal writing *(You know? Terrific! Unreal!),* just as some features of written English are inappropriate in all but the most formal speech.

Dictionaries sometimes mark words *Colloq.* to indicate that they're more common in speech than in writing. Many readers mistakenly take the label to mean that the dictionaries' editors frown upon these words. In fact, colloquial words are often accurate and expressive and are used freely in good general writing. Because misinterpretation of *colloquial* is common, the label is avoided in this book. If a usage is more common in speech than in writing, that fact is stated. If the word or expression is standard English but rarely appears in general or formal writing, it's labeled informal.

See **Spoken and written English.**

Colon

Use a colon here. Or reconsider the use of this colon.

The colon is a mark of anticipation. It indicates that what follows the mark will supplement what came before it.

1. Introductory uses. Use a colon before a series of words, phrases, or clauses when the series is not preceded by an introductory word or phrase or when it's formally introduced by a set phrase like *as follows* or *including the following:*

> There are two modes of thinking, two poles by which one can orientate one's life: politics and religion.—H. Saddhatissa, *The Buddha's Way.*

> Classifying the poetry written from 1500 to 1900 in accordance with this distinction, we discover a sequence which runs as follows: predicative, then balanced; predicative, then balanced.—Josephine Miles, *PMLA*

Don't use a colon after less formal introductory words *(like, such as)* that make what follows a part of the clause: The shop carried a lot of ethnic recordings, like [:] West African, Moorish, Egyptian, and Arabian. And don't use a colon between a verb and its object or complement: The reason I went broke freshman week was that I had to buy [:] books, furniture, and tickets to a lot of things I knew I'd never go to; My three immediate goals are [:] to survive midyear exams, to get to Colorado, and to ski until my legs wear out.

When appropriate, use a colon to introduce quotations in factual writing, especially if they run to more than one sentence. The colon is more common in formal than in general or informal writing, and its appropriateness depends in part on the way you introduce the quotation. If it's built into the sentence, a comma is usual. If it's more formally introduced, a colon fits the context. Both situations are illustrated in this example:

> For example, the report cannot say, "It was a wonderful car," but must say something like this: "It has been driven 50,000 miles and has never required any repairs."—S. I. Hayakawa, *Language in Thought and Action*

2.   Between clauses.   Particularly in a formal paper, you may decide to use a colon between the clauses of a compound sentence when the second clause illustrates, restates, or amplifies the first:

> The supposition that words are used principally to convey thoughts is one of the most elementary of possible errors: they are used mainly to proclaim emotional effects on the hearers or attitudes that will lead to practical results.— H. R. Huse, *The Illiteracy of the Literate*

This is the one use in which the colon and the semicolon are sometimes interchangeable. Never use a semicolon to introduce a series or a quotation.

3.   Conventional uses.
a.   After the salutation of formal letters: Dear Sir:
b.   Between hours and minutes written in figures: 11:30 a.m.
c.   Between Bible chapter and verse: Genesis 9:3–5.
d.   In ratios and proportions when the numbers are written as figures: concrete mixed 5:3:1. Two colons are used instead of an equals sign in a full proportion: 1:2::3:6.

4.   Stylistic use.   Sometimes you may use a construction that calls for a colon because you want to spotlight what the colon introduces: "It is a common dream: To stand beneath sun and blue sky, harvesting your own . . . fruits and vegetables" (*New York Times*). Both "A common dream is . . ." and "To stand . . . is a common dream" would be much less emphatic.

5. Capitals following. To begin an independent clause after a colon, either a capital letter (as in the last quoted sentence with a colon) or a small letter can be used, but a small letter is much more common. (See the example in **2.**) Use a capital after a colon only when the clause is long or complicated, with internal punctuation, or when you want to give it special prominence: ''Beneath the surface, however, is the less tangible question of values: Are the old truths true?'' (*Newsweek*).

comma Comma

Insert or remove a comma at the place marked.

''Should there be a comma here?'' is the question most often asked about punctuation. The general advice of this book is to use commas wherever established conventions demand them and to use them elsewhere if they'll help the reader. When there's a choice, your decision should be based on appropriateness: the complex structures and deliberate pace of much formal writing call for more commas than the simpler, brisker sentences of general English.

Uses of the comma

The following list of uses of the comma outlines the treatment in this article. The numbers and letters refer to sections and subsections.

1. To separate independent clauses
a. Between clauses connected by a coordinating conjunction
b. Between clauses connected by *but*
c. Between clauses connected by *for*
d. Between clauses not connected by a coordinating conjunction

2. With preceding and following elements
a. After a dependent clause or long phrase preceding the main clause
b. Before a dependent clause or long phrase following the main clause and not essential to its meaning

3. To set off nonrestrictive modifiers

4. To enclose interrupting and parenthetical elements
a. Around interrupting elements
b. Around conjunctive adverbs within clauses

5. In lists and series
a. Between units in lists and series
b. Between coordinate adjectives

6. **For clarity**

7. **For emphasis and contrast**

8. **With main sentence elements**
a. Subject and verb
b. Verb and object
c. Compound predicates

9. **In conventional practice**
a. In dates
b. In addresses
c. After salutations in all but formal letters
d. After names in direct address
e. In figures
f. With degrees and titles
g. With weak exclamations
h. To show omission

10. **With other marks of punctuation**
a. With parentheses
b. With dash
c. With quotation marks **(Quotation marks 4b, 4c)**

C_1 1. **To separate independent clauses.**
a. Use a comma before the coordinating conjunction when the clauses are rather long and when you want to emphasize their distinctness, as when they have different subjects:

> For all its impressiveness, Monks Mound is only a part of the even more impressive Cahokia group, and Cahokia in turn is only one, albeit the largest, of 10 large and small population centers and 50-odd farming villages.—Marvin L. Fowler, *Scientific American*

When the independent clauses are short and closely related in meaning, the comma is often omitted: ''Who will live and who will die?'' *(Time)*. But there's no rule that forbids using a comma to separate the clauses in a compound sentence, no matter what their length or relationship. Many experienced writers automatically place a comma before the coordinating conjunction and so guard against the momentary confusion that a sentence like this one invites: ''A crowd of spectators lined the walkway to see him [ ] and the President, in standard fashion, passed along the crowd'' *(New York Times)*.
b. Use a comma between two independent clauses joined by *but,* regard-

less of their length, to emphasize the contrast: "His achievements in office have been difficult to assess, but they have been formidable" (John David Hamilton, *Atlantic*).

c. Use a comma between independent clauses connected by the conjunction *for* to avoid confusion with the preposition *for:* They were obviously mistaken, for intercollegiate sports are always competitive. Without the guidance provided by the comma, a reader might stride through "They were obviously mistaken for intercollegiate sports," then stumble and have to begin all over again.

d. Use a comma in place of a coordinating conjunction when you have a good reason for doing so and when doing so won't confuse or annoy your readers. In most cases such punctuation represents a comma splice (see **Comma splice**), but under certain conditions a comma can appropriately stand between independent clauses that aren't joined by a coordinating conjunction:

> The intellect gets busy, means and methods are studied, purposes are assessed.—Gerald Warner Brace, *The Stuff of Fiction*

> This writer is not merely good, she is *wickedly* good.—John Updike, *New Yorker*

The clauses here are short, parallel in form, and closely bound together in meaning. Semicolons could be used instead of commas, but they'd slow the pace and make the style more formal.

Sentences punctuated like these are increasingly common in print. Not all of them are successful. If the clauses are neither short nor similar in structure, and if one or more of them contains internal punctuation, the reader may have a hard time grasping the meaning. In "The strongest and luckiest private constituencies win, social needs get pushed aside, as in the 50s, to explode a decade later" (Bill Moyers, *Newsweek*), a reader who assumes that the writer is building a series (The strongest and luckiest private constituencies win, social needs get pushed aside, and the gulf between haves and have-nots widens) is brought up short and forced to reread the sentence.

Between two independent clauses, then, you can put a coordinating conjunction (with or without a comma or a semicolon before it), a semicolon alone, or a comma alone. The choice is a matter of style. But you need to take convention into account. Before using a comma alone, consider your audience. Some very conservative readers invariably look on such punctuation as incorrect. If you can assume that your audience won't automatically condemn the practice, then be sure you're using the comma for a purpose. And, most important, be sure that your use of a comma alone won't make your reader's task more difficult.

See **Fused sentence, Semicolon 1.**

C₂

2. With preceding and following elements.

a. Use a comma after an introductory dependent clause or a long introductory phrase:

> Since encouraging women to spend money was the main point of magazines directed at us, they had distinctive characteristics.—*Ms.*

> Far from being a neutral instrument, the law belongs to those who have the power to define and use it.—Michael Parenti, *Democracy for the Few*

Often when the preceding phrase is short or when the dependent clause has the same subject as the independent clause, the comma is omitted:

> During my convalescence [ ] I will meditate on a few items.—Goodman Ace, *Saturday Review* (short phrase)

> Although Grant ignores such details [ ] he is shrewd not only about his colleagues but about his former colleagues.—Gore Vidal, *New York Review of Books* (subjects the same)

But some professional writers put commas after all introductory clauses and after all introductory phrases that contain verbals. In that way they establish a consistent pattern and avoid risking the confusion that may result from the absence of punctuation.

b. Use a comma before a dependent clause or long phrase that follows the main clause if the subordinate element isn't essential to the meaning of the main clause:

> And as I said earlier, the rear ones should probably be snow tires, even if you get the truck in May.—Noel Perrin, *First Person Rural*

> Again and again they tried to start the engine, with the breeze freshening and the tide beginning to turn.

C₃

3. To set off nonrestrictive modifiers.

Use a comma to set off word groups that don't restrict the meaning of the noun or verb or clause they modify. The italicized word groups in the following sentences are nonrestrictive:

> From where I was standing, *almost directly above the trunk,* I could see many of the articles that had been lost.

> Pigeons breed in the spring and the hen lays two eggs, *one of which usually hatches into a hen and the other into a cock.*

A modifier that restricts the reference of the word it modifies (as "that has been lost" restricts "articles" in the first of the preceding sentences) is essential to correct understanding and therefore is not set off by commas.

See **Restrictive and nonrestrictive modifiers.**

C₄   **4.   To enclose interrupting and parenthetical elements.**
a.   Use commas around a word, phrase, or clause that interrupts the main structure of the sentence:

Next summer, no matter what happens, I intend to go to Africa.

The joke, I suppose, seemed funny at the time.

My uncle, unfortunately, stopped for a drink on his way home from work.

Enclosing calls for two commas. Forgetting the second one can cause confusion: "If factory workers and farmers became more efficient, Soviet citizens were told this week [ ] they would get more domestic goods, food, housing, hospitals and schools" *(Newport Daily News)*.

Usage is divided over setting off short parenthetical expressions like *of course*. Enclosing them in commas is more characteristic of formal than of general writing. There's often a difference in emphasis as well as tone depending on whether or not commas are used:

And of course there are those who talk about the hair of the dog.—*Providence Sunday Journal*

The question, of course, is not whether the family will "survive."—*Time*

b.   Use commas around a conjunctive adverb that stands after the first phrase of its clause: It was this ridiculous proposal, however, that won majority approval. At the beginning of a sentence, conjunctive adverbs may or may not be set off: Therefore [,] I have decided to withdraw my application.

When *however* is used in the sense "no matter how," it should never be separated from the words it modifies: However [ ] strongly you feel . . .; However [ ] tired you are. . . . Similarly, *but* and other coordinating conjunctions are a part of the clauses in which they appear and should not be set off: But [ ] a solution must be found.

C₅   **5.   In lists and series.**
a.   Use commas to separate the units in lists and series: "He has read everything he could lay his hands on, manuscripts and printed, that was written during the period: plays, sermons, ballads, broadsides, letters, diaries, and, above all, court records" (Edmund S. Morgan, *New York Review of Books*).

See **Semicolon 2.**

Usage is divided over the use of a comma before the conjunction in a series: "letters, diaries, and records" or "letters, diaries and records." A comma is often a safeguard against boners: "He had small shoulders, a thick chest holding a strong heart [ ] and heavy thighs" (Richard Mandell, *Sports Illustrated*). See **Series.**

b.   Use a comma between adjectives modifying the same noun. In the sentence "Though it was a hot, sticky, miserable day, Mrs. Marston looked cool in her fresh gingham dress," there are commas between *hot* and *sticky* and between *sticky* and *miserable* because each stands in the same relation to the noun *day*. "Hot *and* sticky *and* miserable" would make sense. There's no comma between *fresh* and *gingham* because *fresh* modifies *gingham dress*, not just *dress*. "Fresh *and* gingham" would not make sense.

Some writers today use no comma when only two adjectives modify the noun: a hot sticky day; the tall dark woman. There's no loss of clarity, but if you never use a comma between such adjectives, you deprive yourself of a rhetorical resource. By separating, a comma provides emphasis. Compare these two versions:

> His long, greasy hair hung down to the shoulders of his worn, faded jacket.

> His long greasy hair hung down to the shoulders of his worn faded jacket.

In the first, *greasy* and *faded* stand out as separate modifiers of their nouns.

C_6

6.   For clarity.   Use a comma to help a reader interpret a sentence correctly as he goes along, so that he doesn't have to go back over it to get its meaning. A comma between clauses joined by *for* makes it clear that the word is being used as a conjunction rather than as a preposition. Similarly, a comma can prevent a reader from even momentarily mistaking the subject of one verb for the object of another:

> When the boll weevil struck, the credit system collapsed and ruined both landowners and tenants. (*Not* When the boll weevil struck the credit system. . . .)

> Soon after the inspector left, the room was crowded with curious onlookers. (*Not* Soon after the inspector left the room. . . .)

> While I was surveying, the ice, which was sixteen inches thick, undulated under a slight wind like water (Henry David Thoreau, *Walden*). (*Not* While I was surveying the ice. . . .)

A comma can also make immediately clear whether a modifier goes with what precedes or with what follows: A great crowd of shoppers milled around inside, and outside hundreds more were storming the doors. (*Not* . . . milled around inside and outside. . . .)

In all the preceding examples there is justification other than clarity for using a comma. In the following sentence commas would simply make reading easier: "Another positive stop would be to require as many people as are able [,] to work for a living [,] and to find or create jobs for them," (Carll Tucker, *Saturday Review*). And a comma helps when a word is used twice in a row: What he does, does not concern me.

C 7

7. For emphasis and contrast. When *and* connects two words or phrases, there's no need to set them apart with a comma. But because a comma tends to keep distinct the elements it separates and to emphasize slightly the element that follows it, you may sometimes want to use commas for these purposes alone: "Savannah was a port, and a 'good town' as he remembered it" (Stanley Dance, *The World of Earl Hines*).

Here a comma is used for emphasis, and irony: "Midge Decter is disappointed, again" (Jane O'Reilly, *New York Times Book Review*).

C 8

8. With main sentence elements.
a. Subject and verb. Though it sometimes occurs in old-fashioned formal prose, don't use a comma between a subject and its verb: "All that democracy means [,] is as equal a participation in rights as is practicable" (James Fenimore Cooper, *The American Democrat*).
b. Verb and object. Don't use a comma between a verb and its object. (Words and phrases that must be set off by pairs of commas may, of course, come between subject and verb and between verb and object. See **4.**)
c. Compound predicates. Use a comma between the verbs of a compound predicate only when the sentence is so long and involved that it's difficult to read or when you feel a need for special emphasis or contrast. This is a sensible rule and one that many writers, teachers, and editors insist on, though in published prose the verbs in a compound predicate are frequently separated by a comma when no need for aid to the reader or for special emphasis or contrast is apparent: "Works by other writers in the past few months have reflected this fascination with language, but have delved deeper into the mysterious origins of words" (*Time*).

C 9

9. In conventional practice.
a. In dates, to separate the day of the month from the year: May 26, 1981. When the day of the month isn't given, a comma may or may not be used: In September 1846 *or* In September, 1846. If a comma precedes the year, punctuation should also follow it: In September, 1846, the government fell.
b. In addresses, to separate small units from larger: Washington, D.C.; Chicago, Illinois; Hamilton, Madison County, New York; Berne, Switzerland.
c. After salutations in all but formal letters: Dear John,
d. To set off names in direct address: Spin it, Henry.
e. In figures, to separate thousands, millions, etc.: 4,672,342. In some

styles no comma is used in figures with four digits: 2750. A comma should never be used in naming a year: 1812, *not* 1,812.

f.   To separate degrees and titles from the names they follow: Donal O'Brien, D.V.M.; William Lamb, Viscount Melbourne. The comma before *Jr.* after a name is now sometimes omitted: Charles Evans Hughes [,] Jr.

g.   After a weak exclamation like *well, why, oh:* Oh, what's the use?

h.   Sometimes to show the omission of a word that's required to fill out a construction: He took the right-hand turn; I, the left.

C 10   **10. With other marks of punctuation.**

a.   When parentheses come at the end of a phrase or clause that's followed by a comma, put the comma after the *closing* parenthesis: After returning from Italy (in 1978), she lived in Oconomowoc.

b.   Use a comma or a dash, not both.

c.   For the use of commas with quotation marks, see **Quotation marks 4b, 4c.**

cs   Comma splice

Revise the sentence marked by changing the comma to a semicolon or a period, or by inserting an appropriate conjunction, or by rephrasing to make a more satisfactory sentence.

A comma splice (comma blunder, comma fault) occurs when, without good reason, a comma alone is used to separate the independent clauses of a compound or a compound-complex sentence: He stared at his visitor, it was too dark to see who it was. Occasionally sentences punctuated in this way are deliberately constructed for an intended effect, like this series: "I was awed by this system, I believed in it, I respected its force" (Alfred Kazin, *A Walker in the City*). The term *comma splice* refers to uses of the comma that are not justified either by the matching structures of the clauses or by the close relationship of their content or by any rhetorical impact.

There are various ways to correct a comma splice:

1.   Replace the comma with a period or semicolon.

He stared at his visitor, it was too dark to see who it was.

Revised: He stared at his visitor. It was too dark to see who it was.

This is the simplest remedy but not always the best one. Inserting a period in the following sentence would simply produce two weak sentences in place of one:

I think Americans should read this book, they would get a more accurate picture of problems in the Middle East.

Revised: I think Americans should read this book; they would get a more accurate picture of problems in the Middle East. (For a better revision, see **3**.)

2. Join statements that belong together with a conjunction that makes their relationship clear. If you choose a coordinating conjunction, you should probably keep the comma (see **Comma 1a**). If you choose a conjunctive adverb, replace the comma with a semicolon (see **Semicolon 1b**):

> An increase in student fees would enable us to balance the budget, this is clearly not the time for it.

> *Revised:* An increase in student fees would enable us to balance the budget, but this (*or* budget; however, this) is clearly not the time for it.

3. Rewrite the sentence, perhaps subordinating one of the clauses, perhaps making a single independent clause. Work to produce a good sentence, not just to correct the comma splice:

> I think Americans should read this book, they would get a more accurate picture of problems in the Middle East.

> *Revised:* I think Americans should read this book because it would give them a more accurate picture of problems in the Middle East.

> One cell receives the stimulus from outside and transmits the impulse to the cell, this is known as the dendrite.

> *Revised:* One part, known as the dendrite, receives the stimulus from outside and transmits the impulse to the cell.

If you can make a sure distinction between an independent clause and a dependent clause, you should find it easy to spot any comma splices in your sentences. Look first to see how many independent subject-verb combinations you have in each group of words punctuated as a single sentence. If there are two independent clauses, see if you have a connective between them. If there's no connective but only a comma, you've probably produced a comma splice. For exceptions, see **Comma 1d.** Compare **Fused sentence.**

Commands and requests

Direct commands are also called imperatives: Hurry up; Shut the door; Fill out the coupon and mail it today. Punctuate emphatic commands with an exclamation mark: Stop! Let's go! Punctuate less emphatic ones with a period: Stop at the next gas station.

Commands and requests are often expressed in the form of questions. Use question marks after those that you intend as questions: Would you be willing to take part in the program? Use periods after those you mean to be orders: Will you please report no later than 9:15.

committee

Committee is a collective noun, usually construed as singular. When the logic of the sentence makes it clear that you're not thinking of the committee as a single unit (The committee, men and women alike, were bustling around, collecting their papers and other belongings), it's better to use "the members of the committee."

Comparative form

Thinner and *more happily* are the comparative forms of *thin* and *happily*. See **Comparison of adjectives and adverbs.**

compare, contrast

Compare with *to* points out likenesses: He compared my writing to Allen's (said it was like his). *Compare* followed by *with* finds likenesses and differences: He compared my writing with Allen's (pointed out like and unlike traits). *Contrast* always points out differences.

When the things compared are of different classes, use *to:* He compared my stories to a sack of beans. In the common construction with the past participle, use either *to* or *with:* Compared with (*or* to) Allen's, mine is feeble. *In comparison* is followed by *with:* In comparison with Allen's, mine is feeble. *Contrast* ordinarily takes *with:* He contrasted my writing with Allen's. But *contrast* sometimes takes *to,* and *in contrast* usually does: In contrast to Allen's, my writing is magnificent.

Comp Comparison of adjectives and adverbs

Correct the fault in comparing the adjective or adverb marked.

To express degrees of what is named, adjectives and adverbs are compared—that is, their forms are changed by adding *-er* or *-est* to the root, or base, form *(long, longer, longest)* or by preceding it with *more* or *most (beautiful, more beautiful, most beautiful)* or with *less* or *least.*

1. Choosing the form. We say "a longer walk," not "a more long walk." We say "a more beautiful picture," not "a beautifuller picture."
a. To the root form (the positive degree), some adjectives and adverbs add *-er* to make the comparative degree, *-est* to make the superlative degree.

	Positive	*Comparative*	*Superlative*
Adjective	early	earlier	earliest
	hoarse	hoarser	hoarsest
	unhappy	unhappier	unhappiest

	Positive	Comparative	Superlative
Adverb	fast	faster	fastest
	soon	sooner	soonest

b. Other adjectives make the comparative and superlative degrees by preceding the root form with *more, most.*

	Positive	Comparative	Superlative
Adjective	exquisite	more exquisite	most exquisite
	afraid	more afraid	most afraid
	pleasing	more pleasing	most pleasing
Adverb	comfortably	more comfortably	most comfortably
	hotly	more hotly	most hotly

Three-syllable adjectives and adverbs are ordinarily compared with *more* and *most,* one-syllable adjectives and adverbs with *-er* and *-est.* Two-syllable adjectives and adverbs are usually compared with *more* and *most,* but many can take either form: *able–abler, more able–ablest, most able; empty–emptier, more empty, emptiest, most empty.* When you're in doubt, *more* and *most* are the safer choices. In earlier times it was all right to use both methods of comparison at once, as in Shakespeare's "most unkindest cut of all," but double comparatives and double negatives are no longer standard English.

Some points of usage raised by irregular forms of comparison are discussed in **former, first–latter, last** and in **last, latest.**

2. Using the comparative. The comparative expresses a greater or lesser degree (It is *warmer* now) or makes specific comparison between two people or things (He was *kinder* [or *more kind*] than his brother). The things compared must be truly comparable:

> *Comparable:* His salary was lower than a shoe clerk's (salary). *Or* . . . than that (*or* than the salary) of a shoe clerk.

> *Not comparable:* His salary was lower than a shoe clerk.

(This rule holds true when the root form of the adjective is used: His salary was low, like a beginner's. *Not* . . . like a beginner.)

Logic calls for *other* with *any* in comparisons between a single unit and the group it belongs to: She's a better dancer than *any* of the *other* girls. But the comparative is frequently used when no actual comparison is involved: *higher education, older people, the lower depths.* In advertisements the job of providing a comparison is often left to the reader or listener: *cooler, fresher, stronger, faster, more economical*—than what?

3. Using the superlative. In formal writing and in most general writing, the superlative is used to indicate the maximum or minimum degree of a quality among three or more people or things: She was the *calmest* one there; That's the *loudest* tie in the showcase. Informally, the superlative is common with two, and this usage isn't rare in general writing: Roy and Joe do push-ups to see who's *strongest;* Russia and China compete to see which can be *most critical* of the other's policies. Use of the superlative as a form of emphasis is also informal: She has the *loveliest* flowers; We saw the *best* show!

Don't use *other* to complete a superlative: Television won the largest audience for Shakespeare's plays that they had ever attracted in any (*not* any other) medium.

4. Comparing absolutes.   Logicians raise objections to the comparison of *black, dead, excellent, fatal, final, impossible, perfect, unique* on the grounds that there are no degrees of deadness or blackness or impossibility. But competent writers frequently compare these words: a *more equal* society, a *more complete* victory, a *more impossible* situation. And the Constitution speaks of "a more perfect union." Many absolutes are used figuratively with meanings that naturally admit comparison: This is the *deadest* town I was ever in. When applied to people, *black* and *white* are obviously not being used in a literal, absolute sense. See **Divided usage.**

Complement

In grammar, *complement* refers to the noun or adjective that completes the meaning of a linking verb and modifies the subject: He became *the real head of the business;* She was *busy*. See **Linking verbs, Predicate adjectives.**

complement, compliment

As a noun, *complement* means "that which completes or is called for" (a full complement). As a verb, it means "to make complete" or—of two things—"to fill out each other's lacks" (the scarf and blouse complemented each other perfectly). *Compliment* is the noun (He received many compliments for his work) and the verb (He complimented her on her victory) having to do with praise and congratulations.

Compound predicate

Two or more verbs with the same subject, together with their objects and modifiers, form a compound predicate: Ruth *wrote* and *mailed three letters*.

Compound predicates help make writing economical and can give it a brisk pace, as in this account of catching a fly ball: "I spun back to the wall, reached up, and pulled it in" (Robert H. Zieger, *Harper's*). See **Comma 8c.**

Compound subject

Two or more elements standing as subjects of one verb make a compound subject: "Flake knives and scrapers, large core choppers, and one-handed grinding stones . . . characterize the tool kit" (Dorothy K. Washburn, "The American Southwest"). The verb following a compound subject is usually plural: Inflation and recession occurring simultaneously create stagflation. See **Agreement 1c.**

Compound words

Compound words are combinations of two or more words, usually written as one word or hyphenated: *doorknob, notwithstanding, quarter-hour, father-in-law, drugstore.* Some compounds continue to be written as separate words: *White House, high school, post office.* For the spelling of particular compound words, consult your dictionary. See **Group words, Hyphen, Plurals of nouns 5.**

comprise

Traditionally, *comprise* means "consist of" or "include": The whole comprises (*not* is comprised of) its parts. In current usage the nearly opposite senses of "constitute," "compose," and "make up" are very common: "The four states that at one time comprised French Equatorial Africa . . . " (Harold G. Marcus, *American Historical Review*). But many writers, editors, and teachers insist that *comprise* be used only in its traditional sense. Since it's a relatively formal word, the more general *make up* is a better choice in most contexts: The four states that at one time made up (*or* comprised) French Equatorial Africa . . . ; French Equatorial Africa was made up of (*or* comprised) what are now four separate states.

concept

Concept as a vogue word is often used where *idea* would be more appropriate, as in "concepts for TV shows." See **Vogue words.**

Concrete words

Concrete words name things that can be seen and touched: *box, building.* See **Abstract language.**

Conditional clauses

A conditional clause states a condition (If she knows what she's talking about) that is necessary if what is expressed in the independent clause (there'll be more jobs next term) is to be true. Or it specifies an action (If the ransom is paid) that is necessary if what is expressed in the independent clause (the hostages will be freed) is to take place. *If, unless,* and *whether* are the subordinating conjunctions that most commonly begin conditional clauses. Somewhat more formal introductory words and phrases are *in case, provided, provided that, in the event that.*

1.   For real or open conditions—statements of actual or reasonable conditions under which the main statement will hold true—use the indicative verb forms:

> *If the red light is on,* you know a train is in that block of tracks.

> He will be there *unless something happens to his car.*

> *Whether they come or not,* Kate will go just the same.

2.   For hypothetical conditions—theoretical but still possible—use *should . . . would* or the past tense: *If he should offer another $100,* I would take it. Or *If he raised his offer,* I would take it.

3.   For contrary-to-fact conditions—those that can't be met or are untrue—use the past tense of the verb if you're writing in a general style: If he *was* here, we would have seen him by now. In formal English, the plural form of the past tense, usually called the subjunctive, is firmly established in the first-person singular (If I *were* you . . .) and isn't uncommon in the third-person singular (If he *were* here . . .).
See **if, whether; Subjunctive mood.**

Conjunctions

Conjunctions join words, phrases, clauses, or sentences. In this *Index* conjunctions are further defined and discussed according to their conventional classification:

> *Coordinating conjunctions* (*and, but, for,* etc.)
> *Correlative conjunctions* (*either . . . or, not only . . . but,* etc.)
> *Conjunctive adverbs* (*however, therefore, consequently,* etc.)
> *Subordinating conjunctions* (*as, because, since, so that, when,* etc.)

Conj   Conjunctions and style

Make the conjunction marked more accurate or more appropriate to the style of the passage.

1.   Conjunctions and meaning.   In everyday speech we get along with a relatively small number of conjunctions—*and, as, but, so, when,* and a few others—because we can indicate shades of meaning and exact relationships by pauses, tones, and gestures. In writing, we don't have these means of relating ideas, and we need to use connectives more thoughtfully.

Choose your conjunctions with care. Don't toss in *but* when there's no contrast between your statements (see **but 2**). Decide whether your meaning can be conveyed better by a coordinating conjunction or by a construction that uses the corresponding subordinating conjunction—*but* versus *though,* for example. And note distinctions between subordinating conjunctions. *As* can mean "because," but it's a weak *because* (see **as**). *While* can mean "although" or "whereas," but the core of its meaning is related to time. Sometimes, if your thinking has been logical and you've reproduced it on paper without skipping essential steps, the relationships are apparent, and a *therefore* or an *accordingly* will be unnecessary and unwelcome. See **Transition** and the articles on the particular conjunctions.

2.   Conjunctions and style.   Conjunctions should be appropriate to other traits of style. Often simple *but* is a better choice than *however:*

> The trail is easy walking as far as the canyon; from there on, however, it's no route for Sunday strollers.
>
> *Better:* . . . the canyon, but from there on. . . .

See **Conjunctive adverbs 1.**

Repeating a conjunction at the beginning of each item in a series makes each item distinct, avoids possible confusion, and gives the sentence strong rhythm and clear-cut parallelism:

> I took an old shutter and fixed a sort of porch roof on it, and nailed it to a locust tree nearby, and set the nest with the eggs carefully in it.—Wendell Berry, *The Long-Legged House*
>
> The tribal chants echoing from the seats were always fitting accompaniments to Mick's grunts and wails and hoots.—Robert Mazzocco, *New York Review of Books*

On the other hand, omitting *and* before the last element in a short series may build a strong climax:

> The most important of these, the most characteristic, the most misleading, is called *Some Glances at Current Linguistics.*—William H. Gass, *New Republic*

Or it may suggest that the series is only a sample, not a complete list:

> Many were the Northerners who, during and after the Civil War, went south to train, to educate, to rehabilitate Negro refugees and freedmen.—William H. Pease, *Journal of Southern History*

See **Conjunctive adverbs, Coordinating conjunctions, Correlative**

conjunctions, Subordinating conjunctions. See also **Coordination, Subordination.**

Conjunctive adverbs

Conjunctive adverbs are used as connectives after a semicolon between independent clauses or after a period to introduce a new sentence. These are some of the most common:

accordingly	furthermore	moreover
also (see **too**)	hence	nevertheless
anyhow	however	otherwise
anyway (informal)	incidentally	still
besides	indeed	then
consequently	likewise	therefore

All these words are primarily adverbs. They become conjunctive adverbs when they join together, or provide connection:

Adverb: When they got back, he was *still* waiting.
Conjunctive adverb: The results were poor; *still,* we were not disheartened and set to work on the next batch with undiminished determination.

1. Style. Because conjunctive adverbs tend to be heavy connectives (*however,* for example, is much heavier than *but*), they're most appropriate in formal writing and in sentences of some length and complexity. In general writing they're more likely to serve as transitional devices between sentences than to connect clauses within a sentence. If you load your papers with conjunctive adverbs, you won't produce simple, straightforward English that's easy to read.

Note these appropriate and inappropriate uses:

The armored saurians, the dodo, and a few other extinct creatures are supposed to have become unviable through their exaggerated specialties; usually, however, such excesses are not reached.—Susanne K. Langer, *Philosophical Sketches*. (Appropriate with the formal sentence structure and vocabulary.)

In the morning I still felt sick; *nevertheless,* when the bugle sounded, I got up. (Inappropriately heavy in this simple context. Could substitute *but.* Better to rewrite as a complex sentence: Though I still felt sick the next morning, I got up when the bugle sounded.)

2. Position. By placing conjunctive adverbs inside their clauses instead of at the beginning, you give the initial stress to more important words. See the first example in **1.**

3. Punctuation. When a conjunctive adverb is placed inside a clause, it's often set off by commas. Whether it introduces or comes inside the second independent clause of a compound sentence, the two independent clauses are separated by a semicolon. See the second example in **1.**

consensus

Consensus is a troublesome word. It's easy to misspell, and it tempts users to add *of opinion*. Since *consensus* means "agreement," *of opinion* simply repeats what the word already conveys. So let *consensus* (spelled with three *s*'s) do the job on its own.

Construction

A construction is a group of words that stand in some grammatical relationship to each other, like that of modifier and word modified (black cat), preposition and object (to the roof), or subject and predicate (They walked slowly). Any grammatical pattern may be spoken as of a construction.

contact

As a verb, *contact* means "get in touch with" (I was told to contact the superintendent). Like *get in touch with, contact* covers all means of communication (face-to-face, telephone, letter, cable, CB radio, etc.), and it's more economical—one word instead of four. But stylistically the word outrages some readers, perhaps because they continue to associate it with business jargon. See **Jargon.**

Context

The word *context* is used in different ways.

1. Verbal context.   In writing, a sentence may provide the context for a word, a paragraph may provide the context for a sentence, and so on. The context is the setting—the combination of content and style—that gives meaning to what's being said and determines its appropriateness. Context is extremely important in conveying the sense in which a word is being used. For example, dictionaries record forty or more senses in which people use the word *check*, yet when *check* appears in specific contexts, as in the following sentences, we have no trouble understanding it:

> They were able to *check* the fire at the highway.
> The treasurer's books *check* with the vouchers.
> He drew a *check* for the entire amount.
> I like the tablecloth with the red-and-white *check*.
> He moved his bishop and shouted *"Check!"*
> She had difficulty holding her temper in *check*.
> *Check* your suitcase through to Seattle.

A great many words are used in more than one sense. To convey the particular meaning he intends, a writer must—and usually can—rely on the context. And besides establishing the denotative sense of the word (as illustrated with *check*), context gives clues to its connotation. We recognize this when we say, "By itself that remark might seem insulting, but in the context it couldn't possibly give offense."

2.   The context of quotations.   An honest writer makes sure that the quotations he uses are true to the context in which they originally occurred and that they accurately represent the ideas of the people who wrote or spoke them. Complaints by government officials that they've been quoted "out of context" are often justified.

3.   Rhetorical context.   Every piece of writing occurs in a rhetorical situation, or context, which includes the writer, the subject, the writer's purpose, and the audience. The choice of material, the organization, and the style of a good paper all reflect the writer's sense of the rhetorical context.

continual(ly), continuous(ly)

In the sense "uninterrupted," with reference to time, formal stylists prefer *continuous(ly)* (For weeks we observed the almost continuous eruption of the volcano), but *continual(ly)* is also used. In the sense "occurring rapidly and often," the situation is reversed—formal writers insist on *continual(ly)* (The governor broke his promises not just repeatedly but continually), but *continuous(ly)* too is standard.

Contractions

In writing, contractions are forms that show pronunciation, usually by the substitution of an apostrophe for one or more letters of the standard spelling: *can't, you're, I'm, don't, they've*. They occur regularly in informal usage but rarely appear in formal writing. In general usage a writer should use them or avoid them just as he makes other rhetorical choices, considering the rhythm of the particular sentence, whether the occasion calls for a relaxed or a restrained style, and how much distance he wants between himself and his readers. (In this book contractions are used, in part, to show that writing about a serious subject doesn't call for a style that keeps the audience at arm's length, if not out of reach.) Contractions are necessary in representing actual speech, as in dialog (but see **Apostrophe**). See **have 3.**

contrast, compare

Contrast points out differences; *compare to* points out likenesses; *compare with* does both. See **compare, contrast.**

controversial

Controversial (a controversial person, a controversial book) labels the subject a source of disagreement, of argument. But there can be disagreement about almost any subject, and no one needs to be told that certain subjects (abortion, capital punishment) and individuals are controversial. So use the label sparingly, and don't use it as a warning. Controversy is often what makes a subject interesting enough to write about.

convince, persuade

For a long time some uses of *convince* and *persuade* have overlapped: She persuaded (*or* convinced) me of the necessity for action; She convinced (*or* persuaded) me that I should act. *Convince* is now common in still a third context, where *persuade* is traditional:

> It must have contributed to the general merriment when later it was written . . . that the invasion failed because Adlai Stevenson convinced the President to cancel the air strikes so vital to the success of the invasion.—Ward Just, *New York Times Book Review*

The use of "convince . . . to" instead of "persuade . . . to" (persuaded the President to cancel) is deplored by many conservative stylists.

Coordinate

Two or more grammatically equivalent words, phrases, or clauses are said to be coordinate: *bread* and *butter; in the sink* or *on the stove; dancing, singing, laughing; When he lectured* and *when he prayed,* everyone listened; *He wrenched his back,* and *she broke her leg.*

Coordinating conjunctions

The coordinating conjunctions, *and, but, for, nor, or, so,* and *yet,* are used to connect two or more elements of equal grammatical rank:

> ***Words:*** books *and* papers; books, pamphlets, *or* magazines

> ***Phrases:*** in one ear *and* out the other

> ***Dependent clauses:*** She . . . wrote to young Lewis Rutherford cheerfully enough that his sister looked lovely *and* that the new baby was delightful.— R. W. B. Lewis, *Edith Wharton*

> ***Independent clauses:*** There is no evidence that Elizabeth had much taste for painting; *but* she loved pictures of herself.—Horace Walpole, *Anecdotes of Painting in England*

Sentences: Perhaps I should wish that I had liked him better. *But* I do not wish it.—Renata Adler, *New Yorker*

See **Conjunctions and style, Coordination, Series.**

Coord Coordination

Correct the faulty coordination.

Faulty coordination is not a lapse in grammar or usage. It's a failure to make logical relationships clear. Coordination is faulty when, in a particular context, the material calls for a relationship or emphasis different from the one implied by the writer's use or arrangement of independent clauses.

1. Faulty coordination may result from joining two statements that don't belong together: The condition of the house is deplorable, and the dining nook seats six comfortably. Revision should put the two statements in separate—and separated—sentences.

2. Sometimes faulty coordination can be corrected by turning one of the independent clauses into a dependent clause. "He went to France for the summer, and his novel was published" suggests a causal relationship between his going to France and the publication of his novel. In some contexts this might make sense. But if the only relationship is a temporal one—two events happening at the same time but not otherwise related—the sentence needs to be revised: "During his summer in France, his novel was published," or "At the time his novel was published, he was spending the summer in France," or in some other way.

3. Coordination may be confusing or misleading as in the example above. Sometimes it's simply ineffective:

When I reached the intersection, I found a group of people gathered around a wrecked car. The left front tire had blown, and the car had gone out of control and run into a tree, and the driver was obviously dead.

The independent clause "the driver was obviously dead" needs to be taken out of the coordinate relationship and made into a separate sentence. Left in the series, it implies that the death of the driver had no more importance than the blowout and the crash.

See **Subordination.**

Correlative conjunctions

Some coordinating conjunctions are used in pairs: *both . . . and, either . . . or, neither . . . nor, not only . . . but also, whether . . . or.* Of

these correlatives, *neither . . . nor* and *not only . . . but also* show more
conscious planning than is common in informal or general English: "The
attack not only had left him blind, and in need of plastic surgery which
would require years to complete, but also had deprived him of his sense of
smell" (Joe McGinniss, *Going to Extremes*).

Like coordinating conjunctions, correlatives normally join elements of
the same grammatical rank:

> *Nouns:* He said that both *the novel* and *the play* were badly written.

> *Adjectives:* She must have been either *drunk* or *crazy*.

> *Prepositional phrases:* They can be had not only *in the usual sizes* but *in the outsizes*.

> *Verb phrases:* The wind scoop not only *caught the cool breezes* but also *picked up the captain's conversation*.

> *Clauses:* Whether *Mitch thumbed a ride through the mountains* or *Jenny made the long bus trip*, they were determined to be together during the vacation.

Like similar rules, the rule that constructions built on correlative conjunctions must be strictly parallel should be broken when it gets in the way
of natural, rhythmic expression.
See **Shifted constructions.**

could(n't) care less

Formerly (and too frequently) a lack of concern was expressed by "I
couldn't care less." Recently the negative has been dropped, and "I could
care less" is used to mean the same thing: "kids who never heard of Little
Richard and could care less" (Ellen Willis, *New Yorker*). Neither form is
suited to college writing, except perhaps to point up triteness in dialog.

Count nouns

Count nouns name things that can be counted as separate units. See **Mass
nouns, Nouns 3c.**

couple

The primary meaning of the collective noun *couple* is "a pair, two persons
or things associated in some way," as in "a married couple." In general
and informal usage *couple* is equivalent to the numeral *two* (a couple of
pencils) or to *a few* (a couple of minutes). The *of* is frequently omitted in

speech and informal writing and sometimes in general: "Re-established as a teacher, he brought forth a couple more essays on education" (Wallace Stegner, *The Uneasy Chair: A Biography of Bernard DeVoto*). Omission of the *of* before a noun (He wrote a couple essays) offends many more readers. See **Collective nouns.**

Course names

In general discussions, only the names of college subjects that are proper nouns or proper adjectives are capitalized. In writing a list of courses that includes one or more of these terms, all the course names may be capitalized for consistency, but usually the distinction is kept: I am taking biology, chemistry, European history, English composition, and French. Names of departments are capitalized (the Department of Psychology), and so are the names of subjects when accompanied by a course number (History 347).

credibility

In journalese, *credibility* ("believability") was joined to the vogue word *gap* to refer to public loss of faith in President Johnson's statements about the Vietnam War. In the Nixon administration the gap became a gulf, and *gap* went out of vogue. But *credibility* moved into officialese and flourished. Both writers and readers should remember that *honesty* and *credibility* are by no means synonymous. In college papers it's better to say that a person's word isn't trusted, or that he lies, than to say he lacks credibility.

criterion, criteria

Criteria is heard so often, particularly in college classrooms, that it's possible to forget the singular form *criterion*. As a result we run into references to "this criteria" or read that some criteria "is important." Base your judgment on *a criterion* or on *several criteria* (or *criterions*).

cupfuls, cupsful

Cupfuls is usual. See **-ful, full.**

curriculum

Curriculum (the courses offered or the courses required in a field of study) has the Latin plural *curricula* and the English plural *curriculums*. The adjective is *curricular*. The compound adjective with *extra* is usually written as one word: *extracurricular*.

D

dm Dangling modifiers

Revise the sentence so that the expression marked is clearly related to the word it is intended to modify.

A phrase is said to dangle, or to be misrelated, if its position makes it seem to modify a word that it can't sensibly modify or if, in a context that demands an explicit relationship, it has no clear relation to any word in the sentence.

In the sentence "Looking farther to the left, we saw the spire of a church," *looking* obviously modifies *we.* If the phrase "looking farther to the left" is turned into a clause, *we* is the subject of the verb: [*We* were] looking farther to the left. That is, the reconstructed subject is identical with the subject of the main clause. When the phrase does *not* refer to the subject—that is, when the phrase has a different subject from the subject of the main clause—then the modifier dangles.

In the sentence "To get the most out of a sport, the equipment must be in perfect condition," reconstruction of the subject of the introductory phrase would produce something like "[For *someone*] to get the most out of a sport, *the equipment* must be in perfect condition." But since *someone* is different from *equipment,* it can't safely be omitted. If the sentence "At eleven, my family moved to Denver" is reconstructed, it reads "[When *I* was] eleven, *my family* moved to Denver." *I* doesn't equal *my family,* so *I* should not be left out.

In the following examples, try to reconstruct the subject of the introductory phrase:

Upon telling my story to my adviser, he stopped and thought.

Born in England in 1853, John MacDowell's seafaring activities began after he had migrated to this country.

In both the examples, the introductory phrase dangles. In the second, the phrase refers to a noun—*MacDowell*—that is represented only by its possessive form. This type of dangling modifier frequently appears in print.

Modifiers that dangle may also follow the independent clause: Many signs read "Visit Our Snake Farm," driving toward the city.

You should avoid dangling modifiers in your writing chiefly because educated readers don't expect to find them. As a rule there's no real question of the intended meaning of the sentence, and in context the dangling phrases are not apt to be conspicuously awkward or as nonsensical as they appear in isolation. But they're distracting in any writing that's meant to be read carefully. And by sometimes forcing the reader to search for or guess at the related noun, they can make a piece of writing needlessly difficult.

Such dangling constructions shouldn't be confused with absolute phrases, in which the phrase has its own subject. Here, for comparison, are an absolute phrase, a correct modifier, and a dangling modifier:

> *Absolute phrases:* The car paid for with my last dollar, I was at last out of debt.
>
> *Correct modifier:* Paid for with my last dollar, the car became my first piece of personal property.
>
> *Dangling modifier:* Paid for with my last dollar, I drove the car away.

Though prepositional phrases sometimes dangle—"As an institution, he cordially detested the Spanish Church" (Scott Donaldson, *By Force of Will: The Life and Art of Ernest Hemingway*)—the phrases that cause most trouble are those that begin with participles or infinitives or that contain gerunds. So in revising your papers, examine every verbal phrase. If you continue to have trouble relating such phrases to the words they should modify, you might try giving them up and using clauses instead.

See **Absolute phrases, Gerunds, Infinitives, Participles.**

Dash

The dash—typed as two hyphens without space before or after—can be used singly to link a following word or word group to the main structure of the sentence or in pairs to enclose a word or word group that interrupts the main structure. Use enclosing dashes when you want greater separation from the core of the sentence than enclosing commas would provide but less separation—or less formality—than you'd get with parentheses.

If used sparingly, the dash suggests a definite tone, often a note of surprise or an emphasis equivalent to a mild exclamation. If used regularly in place of commas, colons, and semicolons, it loses all its distinctiveness and becomes a sloppy substitute for conventional punctuation. At its best the dash is a lively, emphatic mark.

1. Before a kicker. The single dash is often used to throw emphasis on what follows, which may be dramatic, ironic, humorous:

> The old nations still live in the hearts of men, and love of the European nation is not yet born—if it ever will be.—Raymond Aron, *Daedalus*

> For that matter, none of the Doyles of Chris's generation had children—including my mother.—Hugh Leonard, *Home Before Night*

2. Before a summary or illustration. The dash is used singly or in pairs with word groups that summarize what's just been said or provide details or examples:

> It takes a cataclysm—an invasion, a plague, or some other communal disaster—to open their eyes to the transitoriness of the "eternal order."—Eric Hoffer, *The True Believer*

> He was strongly in favor of peace—that is, he liked his wars to be fought at a distance and, if possible, in the name of God.—George Dangerfield, *The Death of Liberal England*

3. Between independent clauses.   A dash is sometimes used to link independent clauses when the second expands, develops, completes, or makes a surprising addition to the first. In this function a dash is less formal than a colon:

> Bessie was no longer the Queen of the Blues—she was the Empress.—Chris Albertson, *Bessie*

> In one respect, Welles was unique among the Cabinet members—he did not think himself a better man than the President.—Margaret Leech, *Reveille in Washington*

4. Enclosing interrupting elements.   Dashes are used to set off words and word groups, including complete sentences, that break with the main structure of the sentence:

> Fitzgerald's people believed in their world—it really mattered who won the Princeton-Harvard game, it really meant something to appear at the theatre or the opera—and because they believed in their world they owned it.—Frank Conroy, *Esquire*

data

Formal usage follows the Latin, treating *datum* as singular and *data* as plural. In general usage *datum* is rare, and *data* is treated as a collective noun. So used, it takes a singular verb to emphasize the whole—"Data so far available makes it seem doubtful" (John Mecklin, *Fortune*)—and a plural verb to emphasize the parts—"There were still a good many data in the 33–page report" (William H. Honan, *New York Times Magazine*).

Dates

The typical American form of writing dates is "August 19, 1983." The form "19 August 1983" prevails in British usage and American military usage and is gaining popularity in the United States. If the full date is given within a sentence, the year is usually set off by commas. If the day of the week is also given, it's separated from the month by a comma: The legislature met on Wednesday, December 13, 1905. When only month and year are given, no commas are necessary (In August 1983 he died), though formal stylists often use them.

The year is not written out in words except in formal social announcements, invitations, wills, and some other ceremonial situations and at the beginning of a sentence—and most writers manage to avoid beginning sentences with the year. Expressions like "January in the year 1885" waste words: "January 1885" is enough. In business writing and references, months having more than four or five letters are often abbreviated: Jan. 3, 1970.

In writing dates in figures only, American practice is month-day-year: 9/17/76. European practice is day-month-year, sometimes with the month in Roman numerals: 17–IX–76.

Deadwood

Words or phrases that add nothing to the meaning or effectiveness of a statement are deadwood. See **Wordiness.**

Declension

As applied to the English language, *declension* means the list or listing of the forms of nouns and pronouns to show number, gender, and case. See **Case, Gender, Inflection, Nouns, Number, Pronouns.**

Deep structure

Transformational grammarians distinguish between the surface form of a sentence and the more abstract relationships in its deep structure. In the five sentences "Bill bought Jane a stereo," "Bill bought a stereo for Jane," "Jane was bought a stereo by Bill," "A stereo was bought for Jane by Bill," and "It was a stereo that Bill bought for Jane," the surface subjects are *Bill, Bill, Jane, stereo,* and *it.* But at a deeper level all the sentences have the same subject, or agent—Bill—since Bill did the buying regardless of the form the expression of the fact is given.

Such a concept of sentences may enlarge your view of the sentences you write. You can experiment with ways of expressing the same deep grammatical relationships through different surface structures, noting the varying rhetorical effects. The sentences about Bill and Jane and the stereo offer an example. Each of these could also be embedded in a larger structure in various ways:

When Bill bought Jane a stereo, he surprised her.
Bill's buying Jane a stereo surprised her.
Jane was surprised by Bill's buying her a stereo.
That Bill bought Jane a stereo surprised her.
For Bill to have bought Jane a stereo surprised her.
The buying of a stereo for her by Bill surprised Jane.

These are only a few of the possibilities. Usually such considerations as focus, tone, transition between sentences, and the rhythm of the sentence in its context will help you choose between one surface structure and another.
See **Clauses 2, Grammar 3c.**

Degrees

Ordinarily, academic degrees are not given with a person's name except in college publications, reference works, and articles and letters where the degrees offer proof of competence in a particular field, as in a physician's comment on a medical matter. When used, the names of the degrees are abbreviated, and the abbreviations are separated from the person's name by a comma. In alumni publications they're often followed by the year in which the degrees were granted:

Harvey N. Probst, A.B. (*or* B.A.)   Harvey N. Probst, A.B. '38
Jane Thomson, Ph.D.   Jane Thomson, Ph.D. '81
Royce Walton, M.B.A., was master of ceremonies.

As a rule, except in reference lists, only the highest degree in an academic professional field is mentioned. If the institution granting the degree is named, the following form is usual: George H. Cook, A.B. (Grinnell), A.M. (Indiana), Ph.D. (Chicago).

Demonstrative adjectives and pronouns

This, that, these, and *those* are traditionally called demonstrative adjectives or demonstrative pronouns, according to their use in a sentence:

Adjectives: *This* car is new. *Those* people never think of others.
Pronouns: *These* cost more than *those. That*'s a good idea.

See **Determiners; kind, sort; Pronouns 6; that; this.**

Dependent clauses

A dependent, or subordinate, clause has a subject and verb but can't normally stand alone as a sentence: If he comes today. (In some contexts a dependent clause can stand as a sentence: If we had only called!) See **Clauses.**

det Details

Develop the passage or the topic more fully by giving pertinent details.

The symbol *det* is shorthand for "Give an example" or "What's your evidence?" or "Make this specific" or "Don't just *say* the house is in bad condition; make me *see* that it is." In revising a paper so marked, you need to supply particulars that will make your ideas or impressions clearer, your argument more convincing, or your essay more readable.

The details of a physical object are its parts (the *webbed feet* of a duck) or its attributes or qualities (*scorching* wind, *smooth* leather). The details of an abstraction like pride are the words and attitudes and actions that justify our saying that someone is proud. The details of a novel are specifics of plot, character, style, and so on. Thus the details of any subject are its particulars. In a good paper they fit together, making a pattern, leading to a generalization, or encouraging the reader to draw an inference. Besides giving substance to a paper, details make writing lively, so that it captures and holds the reader's interest.

Determiners

Some grammars apply the label *determiners* to a group of words, other than descriptive adjectives, that precede nouns. The group usually includes what traditional grammars call articles, demonstrative adjectives, and possessive pronouns (or adjectives), as well as such words as *some, few, several, many, each, both, half, first,* and *last.* In the phrase "*the first two* installments," the three italicized words are determiners.

Dialects

A dialect is the speech (sounds, forms, meanings) characteristic of a fairly definite region or group. It is speech that doesn't attract attention to itself among the inhabitants of a region (regional dialect) or among members of a group (group or class dialect) but that an outsider would notice immediately. All of us speak dialects of one sort or another.

The term *dialect* is also applied to written expression: there are written dialects as well as speech dialects. Standard written English, based on educated middle-class usage, is the appropriate dialect to use in college work.

1.   Dialects and style.   Though most of the writing you do in college will follow the rules and conventions of standard written English, you shouldn't set out to rid your writing of all the words and word forms and phrases of the regional dialect or other group dialect you grew up with. The guiding principle should be appropriateness. What are you writing about? Who's your audience? If you're reminiscing about your childhood or describing your homesickness, don't resist an impulse to use dialectal expressions. If your instructor and your classmates are familiar with the dialect you grew up using, you may also use it successfully in other papers. The more formal and impersonal your topic and the broader your audience, the less appropriate dialectal usages will be. In any circumstances, avoid those that are likely to mystify your readers or strike them as simply ungrammatical. See **grammatical, ungrammatical.**

2.   Dialects and standardization.   In modern times English has undergone two developments that at first seem contradictory. On the one hand, large groups of English speakers have migrated from England, and new national varieties of English have arisen in North America, Australia, New Zealand, India, and Africa. But none has diverged far enough from the parent language to be considered a separate tongue, as English itself separated from its Germanic ancestors. The reason history failed to repeat itself is the second major development in Modern English—standardization. In England a relatively uniform dialect spread to all parts of the island kingdom. In other English-speaking nations similar tendencies toward standardization have kept the separate national varieties basically alike.

American English has never diverged far from the parent language, partly because of cultural contacts, partly because of standardizing processes. Growing nationalism after the Revolution led Americans to predict, and eagerly expect, a new American language, but concern for preserving national unity checked the growth of American dialects. "A national language is a band of national union," wrote Noah Webster, and as textbook writer for the new nation, he pushed a standard of general—that is, national—custom.

American standardization has tended to concentrate on the written word and to pay more attention to grammar than to pronunciation. The country has never had an official standard of pronunciation, based on the speech of a single locale or class. Southern, Northern, and Western speakers may sound different but still speak standard American English. The same is not true of the Southerner, Northerner, or Westerner who says "He don't never do that."

Class dialects do exist in the United States. When we use the terms *standard* and *nonstandard* English, we refer to the social status of the speakers of each, not to good or bad qualities inherent in the dialects themselves. And while it's true that standard English in the United States has been flexible and tolerant of regional variation and of importations from nonstandard, dialect conflict has emerged. Heavy migration to Northern cities, particularly from the South and South-Midlands, has brought Northern and Southern speakers into close contact. Because many of the migrants have been poor and ill-educated, their speech—regional in origin—has been taken as indicative of their class. Thus in many Northern cities, Southern speech is equated with nonstandard speech. Hostility toward the new migrant, toward his class or race, attaches easily to his language. In return, the migrant may see in Webster's "general custom" only the values of an oppressive class.

⍺   Diction

Replace the word marked with one that is more exact, more appropriate, or more effective.

Diction means choice of words. Good diction is exact, appropriate, and effective. Faulty diction either doesn't convey the writer's meaning fully or accurately or in some other way fails to meet the reader's expectations.

1.   Choose the exact word.   The exact word is the one that conveys better than any other the meaning you intend. Some mistakes in word choice result from confusing two words that resemble each other in some way: *delusion* for *illusion, predominate* for *predominant*. Others result from confusing two words that, though similar in basic meaning, are not interchangeable in all contexts. We can speak of a *durable* friendship or a *lasting* friendship, but though we may describe shoes as *durable,* we don't say they're *lasting*. Idiom allows "the oldest existing manuscript" but not "the oldest living manuscript."

In some instances, finding the exact word means looking for a more specific one (*complained* is more specific and may be a better choice than *remarked*). Often it means settling for a simpler expression. If you reach for a fancy phrase, you may come up with one that has nothing to do with your meaning: Because of pressure to do well on examinations, a *disquieting aura pervades* me even when I am relaxing. See **Idiom, Meaning, Wrong word.**

2.   Choose the appropriate word.   The words you choose should fit both your subject and your relationship with your audience. If your subject is technical, complex, serious, and if you're addressing readers who know something about it and want to learn more, you'll probably use a rather formal vocabulary. If your subject is light or humorous and if you know your readers well or want to establish a sense of intimacy with them, you'll express yourself more informally.

Though a style can certainly be too informal, probably the most common fault in college papers is inappropriate formality—"big" words selected more to impress the reader than to express meaning. "Big" words needn't be long; *deem* for *think* is as "big" as *domicile* for *house*. They're "big" in the sense of "pretentious"—too fancy for the writer or the audience or the subject. Such words as *ignominious, cantankerous, lachrymose, inscrutable, mortified,* and *chronicled* can be "big" in one context and not in another.

You can catch the "big" words in what you write by reading your papers aloud. If you've used words that you'd be unlikely to speak in or out of the classroom, reconsider them. See if you can't substitute words that are just as precise but more natural to you.

Though formal, general, and informal English overlap and are frequently mixed in print, you can seriously weaken what you write if you mix them carelessly. When informal name-calling interrupts a thoughtful paper on welfare, when high-flown poetic clichés break the mood of an honest piece of descriptive writing, when *know-how* is applied to a great artist's technique or *finalize* to a composer's efforts, readers will be distracted and disturbed. If you mix usage deliberately, have a good reason for doing so— to amuse or startle your reader, perhaps, or to emphasize the point you're making. Keep your audience in mind, and avoid overkill. If you find yourself being criticized for mixing usage, read and reread your papers before turning them in, and maybe ask a friend to read them, too, with an eye open for sore thumbs and an ear cocked for sour notes.

See **Dialects, "Fine" writing, Formal English, Informal English.**

3.   Choose the effective word.   If your words convey your meaning accurately and if they're appropriate to the rhetorical situation, your diction will be competent, and it may be effective as well. But you'll probably move beyond competence only if you pay some attention to style. Effectiveness in writing factual prose nearly always means choosing words that convey your meaning directly and economically. But that isn't to say that you should always pick the shortest, plainest words you can find and use them in the simplest way. In a particular writing job you may find it effective to repeat a word or put it to a new use, or to choose a word for its sound as well as its sense.

Using words well often means using them imaginatively. The challenge is to avoid the trite and tiresome without making your prose so fancy that your reader pays less attention to what you're saying than to how you're saying it. See **Abstract language, Adjectives and style, Adverbs and style, Conjunctions and style, Imagery, Nominalization, Repetition, Style, Triteness, Vogue words, Wordiness.** See also articles on individual words: **claim, contact, drunk, finalize, hopefully, however, massive, relate, viable,** and so on.

different from, different than

Formal usage prefers *different from:* The rich are different from you and me. General usage is divided between *different from* and *different than:* "The young TV generation has a completely different sensory life than the adult generation which grew up on hot radio and hot print" *(Newsweek).* *Different than* is especially common when the object is a clause: "The story would be different for an investigator who accepts the verdict of the court than for one who doesn't" (Meyer Shapiro, *New York Review of Books).*

The formal alternative would be the longer, wordy expression: . . . verdict of the court from what it would be for one who doesn't.

dilemma

Dilemma has a range of meanings. The narrowest is "a choice between equally unpleasant alternatives." A broader meaning is "any difficult choice." And finally there's "any difficult problem." Since *dilemma* is a rather formal word, giving it so broad a meaning as this last is likely to be criticized.

Direct address

In direct address the audience being spoken to is named:

> *My friends,* I hope you will listen to me with open minds.
> What do you think about his coming home, *Doctor?*

Words in direct address are usually set off by commas. See **Indirect discourse.**

Direct objects

In "Dogs chase cats," *cats* is the direct object of the transitive verb *chase*. See **Objects 1, Transitive and intransitive verbs.**

discreet, discrete

Here's a case in which a mistake in spelling can result in a change in meaning. *Discreet* means "prudent, circumspect": They were so discreet in public that no one suspected a thing. *Discrete* means "separate, distinct": Further analysis revealed that the issue could be divided into discrete parts.

disinterested, uninterested

From its first recorded uses in the seventeenth century, *disinterested* has had two senses: "indifferent, uninterested" and "impartial, not influenced by personal interest." But the first meaning gradually disappeared from educated usage, and its revival in this century has met strong opposition. Restricting *disinterested* to the meaning "impartial" sets up a distinction between *disinterested* and *uninterested* and thereby prevents ambiguity. Ignoring the distinction creates ambiguity. So even though *disinterested* in the sense "uninterested" is established in general styles, a writer who uses it in that way should know that he risks upsetting some readers: "I began to hate someone once who habitually said 'disinterested' when he should have said 'uninterested' '' (Alexander Cockburn, *New Statesman*).

Divided usage

Usage is said to be divided when two or more forms are in reputable use in the same dialect or variety of English. *Divided usage* doesn't apply to localisms, like *poke* for *sack* or *bag*, or to differences like *ain't* and *isn't*, which belong to separate varieties of the language. It applies to different practices in spelling, pronunciation, and grammatical form by people of similar educational background. In addition to hundreds of instances of divided usage in pronunciation, most dictionaries record forms like these:

In spelling: buses or busses, millionaire or millionnaire, catalog or catalogue

In past tenses: sang or sung, stank or stunk

In past participles: shown or showed, proved or proven

The point about divided usage is that each of the alternatives is acceptable. A person who's learned to say "It's I" doesn't need to change to "It's me," and one who says "It's me" needn't change to "It's I." When there's a choice between variants of equal standing, choose the one that you use naturally, that's appropriate to your style, or the one that's customary among the people you want to reach. Before criticizing anyone's usage, make sure that it's not a variant as reputable as the one you prefer—which is usually the one you're used to.

The entries in this *Index* include divided usages and give fair warning when one or the other of two acceptable variants is likely to disturb some readers or listeners and arouse emotional attitudes. For examples, see **can, may; different from, different than; disinterested, uninterested; dove, dived; due to; enthuse; farther, further; like, as; Principal parts of verbs; reason is because; Sexist language; slow, slowly.**

div # Division of words

Break the word at the end of the line between syllables.

To keep the right-hand margin of a manuscript fairly even, you have to divide some words at the end of a line with a hyphen. When you're not sure how to divide a word, consult a dictionary. Here are the basic rules:

1. Both the divided parts should be pronounceable. The break should come between conventionally recognized syllables: *mar gin, hy phen, chil dren, hi lar i ous, ad min is tra tive*. Words of one syllable (*matched, said, thought*) shouldn't be divided.

2. Double consonants are usually separable *(ef fi cient, com mit tee, daz zling, bat ted)*, but they're kept together if there's no syllable break *(im pelled)* or if both belong to a root that a suffix has been added to *(stiff ly,* not *stif fly; yell ing,* not *yel ling)*.

3. A single letter is never allowed to stand alone. Don't divide words like *enough*.

4. Words spelled with a hyphen *(half-brother, well-disposed)* should be divided only at the hyphen, to avoid the awkwardness of two hyphens in the same word.

dock

A few people will have conniptions if you write of tying up to a dock. A dock, they'll tell you, is the waterway between piers. But *dock* now also means the pier or wharf you tie up to.

doctoral, doctor's, doctorate

Doctoral is an adjective, *doctorate* a noun. A person who has earned a doctorate has earned a doctor's degree (a Ph.D.) in a doctoral program.

don't

Don't is the contraction of *do not*. It is universally used in conversation and is often used in writing when *do not* would be too emphatic or when the shorter form gives a more comfortable rhythm. Until about 1900 *don't* was the usual third-person singular *(he don't, it don't, that don't)* in informal speech, but that usage is now nonstandard.

Double negative

In nonstandard English two or more negatives are very often used to express a single negation: There ai*n't no*body home; Could*n't no*body find the body; I do*n't* have *no*thing to lose. But standard English insists on a single negative in such constructions. Instead of "They could*n't* find it *no*where," use "They could*n't* find it anywhere" (or possibly the formal "They could find it *no*where").

Sometimes a concealed double negative occurs with *hardly* or *scarcely*. When *hardly* means "almost not" or "probably not" and *scarcely* means the same a little more emphatically, "There's hardly nothing in the campus paper" should read "There's hardly anything," and "For a while we couldn't scarcely breathe" should read "could scarcely breathe."

The objection to a double negative is not that "two negatives make an affirmative.'' They don't. In early English two negatives were used in all varieties of the language. The objection is simply that the double negative is not now in fashion among educated people.

Double prepositions

The *of* in a double preposition like *off of* is unnecessary. See **Prepositions and style 2.**

Doublespeak

Doublespeak is the use of language not to express but to obscure, disguise, or deny the truth. Dwight Bolinger has suggested that the label be applied to ''jargon that is a sophisticated form of lying.'' Doublespeak is common in the pronouncements of governments and government agencies, corporations, and special interest groups of all kinds. In some cases doublespeak in the form of euphemisms is used to protect the feelings of the old, the poor, the mentally retarded, the crippled, or the criminal, but the inaction encouraged by bland doublespeak does more harm than hurt feelings. See **Gobbledygook.**

doubt

After the verb *doubt* used negatively, a clause is introduced with *that:* I don't doubt that he meant well. After the verb *doubt* used positively, a clause is introduced by *that, whether,* or, less often, *if:*

> But there is reason to doubt that this is so.—Wayne F. LaFave, *Supreme Court Review*

> A couple of days ago, Walter Heller . . . said that he doubted whether that level could be reached.—Richard H. Rovere, *New Yorker*

> I doubt if this was ever a really important reason for his leaving London.—George Woodcock, *Esquire*

For *doubt but,* see **but that, but what.**

dove, dived

Both *dove* and *dived* are acceptable as the past tense of *dive.*

drunk

It seems to take courage to use the word *drunk.* We either go formal *(intoxicated),* or grab at respectability through euphemism *(under the influence, indulged to excess)*, or try to be funny with one of dozens of slang expressions like *looped, bombed, smashed*. But *drunk* is the word.

due to

No one complains when *due* (followed by *to*) is used as an adjective firmly modifying a noun: "The failure was due to a conceptual oversight" (William Jaffé, *Journal of Political Economy*). But there has been strong objection to the use of *due to* in the sense "because of" to introduce prepositional phrases functioning as adverbs: Due to the coal miners' strike, a lot of stores were sold out of long underwear. Although this usage has been standard for decades, prejudice against it persists. As a result some writers hesitate to use *due to* in any context.

each

1. The pronoun.   Though the pronoun *each* is singular (To each his own), we use it to individualize members of a group (each of the joggers). As a result, it attracts plural verbs and pronouns:

> Each of the stages in child development produce typical conflicts.—Selma Frailberg, *New York Review of Books*

> Each of these people undoubtedly modified Latin in accordance with their own speech habits.—Albert C. Baugh, *A History of the English Language*

In cases like these, the writers have treated *each* as a collective because the plural idea has been uppermost in their minds. The practice is common in informal English and increasing in general English. But in formal usage *each* is ordinarily singular, and conservative stylists insist that it must be: "Each of them was asserting its own individuality" (John Hingham, *American Historical Review*).

Sometimes when *each* refers to both men and women, a writer will use *they* rather than *his* as one way of avoiding sexist language: Each of the weekend guests brought their own climbing gear. See **Agreement 2, Collective nouns, every, Sexist language.**

2. The adjective.   As an adjective, *each* does not affect the number of the verb or related pronoun. When *each* follows the plural subject that it modifies, the verb and related pronoun are also plural: "The editions that

have appeared since World War I each have their weak and strong points''
(James McManaway, *PMLA*).

each other, one another

Some textbooks have insisted that *each other* refers to two only and *one
another* to more than two, but writers regularly ignore the distinction. See
Pronouns 3.

Echo phrases

An echo phrase calls to mind a passage in literature or a popular saying.
See **Allusion.**

Editorial *we*

Traditionally the anonymous writers of editorials use *we* and *our* (We believe that . . . ; It is our recommendation that . . .) rather than *I* and *my*.
This is because editorials supposedly speak not just for the individuals who
write them but for the publications in which they appear. See **I, we.**

educationese

Educationese is the label applied to the jargon of professional educators by
those who find many of their speeches painful to listen to and much of their
writing almost impossible to read. See **Jargon.**

effect, affect

The common noun is *effect,* meaning ''result.'' As verbs, *effect* means
''bring about'' (The shortage has effected a change in driving habits), and
affect means ''influence'' or ''put on'' (She affected a Southern accent).
See **affect, effect.**

e.g.

E.g. stands for the Latin words meaning ''for example.'' The best way to
avoid possible confusion with *i.e.* is to write out *for example.* See **Abbreviations 2, i.e.**

either

Though in speech a plural verb is common after *either* (I don't think either of them are going), in writing of any formality a singular verb is expected (Either of them was almost certain to reach the Pole).

either . . . or, neither . . . nor

When one element of a compound subject joined by *either . . . or* or *neither . . . nor* is singular and the other is plural, make the verb agree with the nearer subject. See **Agreement 1c.**

elder, eldest

These forms of *old* survive in references to the order of birth of members of a family—"the elder brother," "our eldest daughter"—and in some honorific senses like "elder statesman."

Ellipsis

The three periods—each preceded and followed by a space—that are used to indicate the omission of one or more words in a quotation are called an ellipsis: "Four score and seven years ago our fathers brought forth . . . a new nation . . . dedicated to the proposition that all men are created equal." When the last words in a quoted sentence are omitted, the end punctuation comes before the ellipsis—"Four score and seven years ago our fathers brought forth on this continent a new nation. . . ."—just as it does when the omission follows the sentence.

The omission of a line or more of poetry is generally indicated by a full line of spaced periods. The omission of a paragraph or more of prose is traditionally indicated in the same way, but current practice often uses only an ellipsis at the end of the paragraph preceding the omission.

Don't use ellipses when you're quoting only a phrase: It is worth asking whether we continue to be "dedicated to the proposition." (*Not* ". . . dedicated to the proposition. . . .")

In dialog an ellipsis indicates hesitation in speech. It may also be used as an end stop for a statement that's left unfinished or allowed to die away: "The town was poor then. And like so many who grew up in the Depression, we never expected we would have real jobs. There was no place for us in the world. It was depressing . . ." (John Thompson, *Harper's*).

Elliptical constructions

An elliptical construction omits a word or two that can somehow be supplied, usually from a neighboring construction: I work much harder than you [work]. The choice between longer and shorter forms is a matter of style. Formal English uses relatively few elliptical constructions. General and informal English use them freely. Compare **Clauses 2a.**

else's

In phrases with pronouns like *anyone, nobody,* and *someone, else*—not the preceding pronoun—takes the sign of the possessive: The package was left at somebody else's house.

empathy, sympathy

Both *empathy* and *sympathy* refer to a sharing of another's feelings (often of distress) or convictions. *Empathy,* the more fashionable word, suggests a particularly close identification with the other person.

emp Emphasis

Strengthen the emphasis of this passage.

Rightly used, emphasis indicates the relative importance of the points you're making, so that your reader recognizes the most important as most important, the less important as less important, the incidental as incidental. If you don't provide emphasis, you fail to guide your reader. If you place it where it doesn't belong, you mislead or confuse him.

1. Proportion. Ordinarily, allot space on the basis of importance. Give the point you want to emphasize the space and development its significance calls for. If you write a paper at the last minute, you may give the preliminaries more space, and therefore more emphasis, than they deserve and then, realizing that you're running out of time, leave your major point undeveloped and unemphatic. Budget your time so that you won't mislead your reader in these ways.

2. Position. As a general rule, the most emphatic position in a sentence, a paragraph, or a full paper is the end (hence the danger of leaving the final point undeveloped). The second most important is the beginning. Don't waste these natural positions of emphasis. In writing term papers and answering examination questions you'll often want to use both—stating your thesis in the opening paragraph and, after presenting the arguments that support it, restating it in your conclusion. In any case, don't let your major point get lost somewhere in between, and don't announce it at the beginning and then fail to get back to it. See **Beginning, Ending.**

3. Separation. To emphasize part of a sentence, lightly or heavily, set it off with a comma, a colon, or a dash. Or begin a separate sentence or a new paragraph to achieve the same purpose. See **Colon 4, Comma 7, Dash 1.**

4.   Repetition.   As long as you don't overdo it, you can gain emphasis by repeating significant words and by repeating ideas in different words. Repeating a structural pattern, such as a *who* clause, is an excellent device for emphasizing, especially in a series that builds to a climax. See **Repetition, Series.**

5.   Economy.   In the condensing that's a regular part of revision, pay special attention to the way you express ideas that deserve major emphasis. Strip sentences of unnecessary words that blur their clarity and blunt their impact. Emphatic statement needn't be brusque, but it must be direct and uncluttered. See **Wordiness.**

6.   Mechanical devices.   Using underlinings, capitals, and exclamation marks for emphasis is likely to bore, annoy, or amuse the reader. Telling him that he should be interested ("It is interesting to note") or impressed ("Here is the really important point that everyone should recognize") is likely to irritate him. "Big" words have the same effect, and the intensifiers used in speech—*terribly, extremely, incredibly*—are almost always ineffective in writing. On paper "a terribly shocking incident" turns out to be less, not more, emphatic than "a shocking incident." So earn your reader's attention. Don't try to grab it with mechanical hoots and verbal hollers.

end Ending

Revise the ending of your paper to round out the discussion.

When you reach the end of your discussion, wrap it up. Don't just stop, so that a reader wonders if the last page is missing. And don't ramble on until your audience is missing.

If your paper is long, you may want to review the ground you've covered, preferably in fresh phrasing. If the material is complex, you may need to pull together the points you've made and show how they add up and what they add up to. Short papers, as well as long ones, must add up to something.

If the reader of a paper you've written finishes the last sentence and thinks "So what?" either you've produced a paper that has no point, or—more likely—you've failed to make clear what the point is. A conclusion can't save a pointless paper by simply announcing a point, but by clarifying the essential argument, by bringing out what has only been implied, the final paragraph or two can strengthen a paper greatly.

If your paper has been a voyage of discovery in which you've tried to define your own attitudes, you may end up with something like, "What I feel now is that my parents gave too much to me without thinking enough about me." Whether such a conclusion works depends on what's gone before. If that point has been gradually emerging throughout the paper, fine. If it hasn't—if, for example, you've only told about the size of your allowance, your charge accounts, the gifts on birthdays and at Christmas—then your ending will leave the reader perplexed and dissatisfied.

Final sentences should avoid tag ends and anticlimax as well as irrelevance. They should build to a firm conclusion, not trail off into silence. They should wrap up the discussion in such a way that the reader not only recognizes its completeness but feels satisfied that the last words were the right ones.

End stop

An end stop is the mark of punctuation—usually a period, exclamation mark, or question mark—used at the end of a sentence. In writing dialog, a double dash may be used as an end stop when a speech is interrupted. An ellipsis can end a sentence that's intentionally left unfinished.

When two end stops would come at the close of a sentence, only the more emphatic or more necessary for meaning is used. Here a question comes at the end of a sentence that would normally close with a period; only the question mark is used: "When we say, for example, that Miss A plays well, only an irredeemable outsider would reply 'Plays what?' " (C. Alphonso Smith, *Studies in English Syntax*).

English language

The earliest records of English date from the seventh century A.D., two centuries after invading Germanic tribesmen from northwestern Europe—Angles, Saxons, Jutes, and Frisians—had made their homes in the British Isles, bringing with them the dialects that are the direct ancestors of the English language. Through those dialects English is connected to a prehistoric past—to an unrecorded language called Germanic, parent of the Low and High German languages, the Scandinavian languages, and English. Through Germanic, English is connected to a still more ancient and unrecorded language called Indo-European, the parent of (among others) most of the language groups on the European continent.

The history of English is often divided into three main periods: Old English (OE), c. 450–1100; Middle English (ME), c. 1100–1450; Modern English or New English (MnE or NE), c. 1450–, with this latter period sometimes subdivided into Early Modern English (EMnE), c. 1450–1700, and Modern English, c. 1700–.

See **Dialects.**

enormity, enormousness

Because *enormity* looks like a more compact way of expressing the idea of "enormousness," it's often used in that sense, as most dictionaries indicate. But this use is deplored by those who restrict *enormity* to the traditional meaning "enormously evil" or "great wickedness," as in "the enormity of the crime."

enthuse

Enthuse is a back formation (see **Origin of words 3d**) from *enthusiasm*. Though widely used in general and informal writing, the word is still not established in formal usage, and many readers object to it. The only other locutions we have for the idea are the longer *be enthusiastic over* or *be enthusiastic about*.

equally as

Though *equally as* is an established idiom (Color is equally as important as design), one of the words is always redundant. *Either* Color is as important as design *or* Color and design are equally important.

-ese

The suffix *-ese* is used to make new nouns *(journalese, educationese, bureaucratese)* that have the disparaging sense of "lingo" or "jargon": His mastery of sociologese left us impressed but uninformed.

Establishment

In the 1960s *Establishment* (sometimes not capitalized) became a vogue word for the powers-that-be:

> In the intellectuals' lexicon "the Establishment" now seems to include the federal, state, and local government, business corporations, foundations and other philanthropic organizations, Big Labor, Big Science, and the administrators of universities—Max Ways, *Fortune*.

While sometimes simply descriptive, it was more often a term of abuse, expressing discontent with the ins and sympathy with the outs. *Establishment* has remained anything but precise but continues to refer to either stuffy or sinister inner circles.

et al.

Et al. is the abbreviation for the Latin words meaning "and others." A note style may call for reducing a list of four or more authors of a single work to the first author named and *et al*. In ordinary writing, and in other note styles, use *and others*.

etc.

Though sometimes a convenient way to end an incomplete list, *etc.,* the abbreviation of the Latin phrase *et cetera* ("and the rest"), belongs primarily to business and reference uses: This case is suitable for large photographs, maps, charts, etc. In most writings, *and so forth* or *and so on* is preferable when the reference is to things, and *and others* is preferable with lists of people. The fact that a list is incomplete can also be indicated by naming the category and then using an introductory phrase like *such as:* This case is suitable for graphics such as large photographs, maps, and charts.

Ethnic labels

American English has its full share of slang terms for members of racial and ethnic groups. While the terms may at times be used with no hostile intent and may even be used by members of the groups they name, our vocabularies would be healthier without them. Besides the labels for peoples of European, African, and Latin American origins, these terms should be avoided: *Asiatic* (for *Asian*), *Jap (Japanese)*, *Chinaman* or *Chink (Chinese),* as well as words like *gook*.

every

1. *Every, everybody,* **and** *everyone* were originally singular and continue to take a singular verb: Every player on the team deserves our praise; Everybody loathes the mayor; Everyone takes the freeway. But for related pronouns that follow, usage is divided. The singular is perhaps more common in formal writing, but the plural appears in all varieties: "Everybody who has praised the inaugural address cannot possibly be as enthusiastic as they sound, unless they are merely reacting to its music" (James Reston, *New York Times*). The plural *they* is reasonable, since the reference is to a number of people. Instead of substituting *he* for *they,* formal written usage might replace *Everybody* with an explicit plural: All those who have praised. . . .

A plural pronoun is also used for clarity when the *every* phrase is the object of a verb with a singular subject: "The traditional leader then comes forward and thanks everyone for their attendance and invites them to lunch" (John A. Woodward, *Ethnology*). Treating the *every* words as collectives can sometimes prevent confusion and also avoid the awkward *he-or-she* problem. But some conservatives continue to insist that, in writing, related pronouns must be singular. See **he or she.**

2. *Everybody* is always written as one word. *Everyone* is usually written as one word, but when the *one* is stressed, it's written separately: Everyone knew what the end would be; Every one of us knew what the end would be.

3. *Every so often,* meaning "occasionally" (Every so often we have to get away from the city), should not be confused with *ever so often,* meaning "very frequently" (We went to the country ever so often in my childhood). You won't confuse the two if you give up using the exclamatory *ever so often.*

4. *Everyplace,* meaning "everywhere," is inappropriate in formal writing. *Everywheres* is nonstandard.

except, accept

Except as a verb means "leave out, exclude": In making the new assignment, the teacher excepted those who had made an honest effort on the last one. It's decidedly formal. *Excused* would often be more appropriate for the same meaning in general writing.

Accept means "receive" or "respond to affirmatively" and is slightly formal: I accept with pleasure; He accepted the position (as contrasted with "He took the job").

Exclamation mark

An exclamation mark (or point) is used after an emphatic interjection, after a phrase, clause, or sentence that's genuinely exclamatory, and after forceful commands. Clear-cut exclamations are no problem:

> Oh! Ouch! No, no, no!
> Damn those mosquitoes!
> It's the chance of a lifetime!

But many interjections are mild and deserve no more than a comma or period: "Well, well, so you're in college now." Often sentences cast in exclamatory patterns are simply statements (What a memorable experience that was), and the mark of punctuation is optional.

In deciding whether to use an exclamation mark, you should first ask yourself whether you intend to exclaim—to express strong feeling or give special emphasis. Walt Kelly said, "Using the exclamation point is like wearing padded shoulders." But when used sparingly, to signal genuine emotion, the mark can serve the writer as the raised voice or dramatic gesture serves the speaker:

> *The Sun Also Rises* is a major work, brilliantly constructed and colored— though last year I was taken aback to hear some students complain that Jake Barnes indulges himself in too much self-pity. How imperious the young can be when judging the victims of disasters they don't even trouble to learn about!—Irving Howe, *Harper's*

Exclamations

What distinguishes an exclamation from other kinds of utterance is its purpose: emphatic expression. In form, an exclamation may be a declarative sentence (She's late again!), a question (Can she be late again!), a command or request (Be ready when I call! Please be on time!), a verbless sentence (How terrible for you!), or an interjection (Ugh!). See **Exclamation mark.**

expect

In general and formal writing, *expect* is ordinarily limited to the senses "anticipate" (He expects you to be a great success) and "require as reasonable" (Winsock, Inc., expects its employees to arrive on time). In American usage the sense "to suppose, presume, believe" in reference to past or present (I expect there were times when Lincoln was heartily fed up) is likely to be limited to informal contexts.

fact

The fact is often deadwood and should be deleted: The study demonstrates [the fact] that workers can become affluent. Sometimes phrases with *fact* can be replaced by single words: in spite of the fact = *although;* due to the fact that = *because. True fact* is redundant. Omit *true.*

factor

Windy phrases with *factor* should be deleted: Determination and imagination [were the factors that] brought the program its popularity. *Factor* itself, meaning "something that helps produce a result," can often be replaced by a more precise or expressive word: A major factor (stimulus? influence? resource?) in creating the system was the artisan class. Used in the plural, it may give the reader no specific information and arouse suspicion that the writer doesn't have any: Many factors were responsible for the war (or the depression or the fuel shortage or the birth rate).

famed

Dictionaries accept *famed* as standard English, but to some readers it smacks of journalese. *Famous* is a safer choice—though in most cases the audience doesn't need to be told that what you've called famous is. See **Journalese.**

farther, further

Some careful writers make a distinction between *farther,* referring to physical distance (Farther north there was heavy snow), and *further,* referring to more abstract relations of degree or extent (Nothing could be further removed from experience). But the distinction is not consistently maintained, even in formal English.

feel

Though one of the accepted meanings of *feel* is "think" or "believe" (I feel that Barnum was right), *feel* shouldn't replace those verbs. Readers need to be reminded now and then that a writer thinks and has convictions.

fellow

Fellow is general and informal when used to mean "man" or "boy" but formal in the sense "associate." In writing, the word is commonly used as an adjectival: his fellow sufferers, a fellow feeling ("a similar feeling" or "sympathy").

female

In current usage the noun *female* seems most appropriate in somewhat formal or technical contexts: "Each female is assigned a number of social security quarters at the beginning of the simulation" (James H. Schulz, *Yale Economic Essays*). It's usually a poor substitute for *woman*. As an adjective *female* has more usefulness but also focuses on classification by sex, whether human or nonhuman. See **Sexist language.**

fewer, less

The rule is that *fewer* refers to number among things that are counted (fewer particles) and *less* to amount or quantity among things that are measured (less energy). Formal usage ordinarily observes the distinction. In general writing *less* is applied to countables fairly often—"I suggest they sell two less tickets to the public" (Dwight Macdonald, *Esquire*)—but it grates on some readers' ears.

field

The phrase *the field of* can almost always be omitted: He has long been interested in [the field of] psychiatry.

Figures

Figures are the symbols for numbers. See **Numbers.**

fig Figures of speech

This figure of speech is trite, inconsistent, or inappropriate. Revise the passage.

A good figure of speech can add color, humor, interest, or information and may convey meaning more economically than its literal equivalent. But literal expression is always preferable to a figure that doesn't work.

1. Replace trite figures.   Use figures of speech that represent your own perceptions. Many figures that once were fresh and vivid are now clichés: *cool as a cucumber, a ribbon of concrete, sick as a dog, fresh as a daisy, Old Man Winter.* The writer who thinks about what he's setting down on paper either avoids them or at least tries to give them a new look. "A cucumber-cool manner" might get by where "cool as a cucumber" would bore the reader. But there are dangers in trying to disguise clichés. Though "a lot of water has flowed under the bridge" takes on some new life in "all the water, and war, that had flowed under the bridge" (Karl Miller, *New York Review of Books*), some readers may feel that water and war don't mix.

Whenever possible, offer the reader an original figure, likes James Thurber's road "which seemed to be paved with old typewriters." If you can neither freshen an old figure successfully nor invent a new one that works, stick to a literal statement of your meaning.

2. Untangle mixed figures.   Sometimes, instead of coming up with no image at all, you may come up with too many:

> The noise, like an enthusiastic roar from a distant sports stadium, yet as insistent as the surge of distant surf, grew till it was galloping up the quadrangle in massive waves.

Here sports fans, the ocean, and horses create a catastrophe. To catch such incongruous mixtures before the final draft, read what you've written as objectively as you can.

More difficult to spot are the mixed figures that involve dead metaphors. Keep in mind that a figure that's dead in most contexts may revive in certain relationships, with ridiculous results. In the first of the following sentences, the student invents a figure that's apt. In the second, the word *faces,* which is regularly used to stand for "people," simply won't work with *sitting* or with suiting up:

> As we dressed, comments were tossed about the room as casually as the rolls of tape we were using to tape our ankles. The familiar faces, sitting in their usual corners, were all getting into their uniforms.

Don't just read what you've written before you turn a paper in. Think about what it *says*. When your figures of speech call up pictures of physical impossibilities or other absurdities because you've mixed images, they're likely to distract your readers from the point you're trying to make. If in speaking figuratively you seem to be speaking foolishly, your figurative language needs to be overhauled or abandoned.

3. Replace inappropriate figures.   A figure of speech may be inappropriate to the audience, to the subject, or to you as the writer. Whether used to explain or to amuse, similes, metaphors, and analogies drawn from biology or trout fishing or from the folklore of your home town won't work with readers who know nothing about these things. Describing bluegrass music with figures of speech appropriate to a discussion of Beethoven's symphonies, or vice versa, makes sense only if you're trying, rather desperately, to be funny. And using figures that don't match your own attitudes or temperament—poetic metaphors, for example, when your natural style is down-to-earth, or hard-boiled similes when you're typically gentle and thoughtful—gives them an off-key prominence that will disturb readers.

A figure of speech can be judged good or not good only in a context, a rhetorical situation. When you write your final draft, judge each of your figures by its appropriateness to the audience, the subject, and your prevailing tone. If you decide that a figure doesn't fit, replace it with a suitable figure or with the literal equivalent. But don't discard a figure simply because it startles you when you read over what you've written. In the context of your paper, "the moon crashed through the clouds" may be just right.

finalize

Finalize has been in widespread use for more than a generation. Its near-synonyms, *finish, complete,* and *conclude,* lack the connotation "to make official" that gives *finalize* its usefulness in some contexts: "Before they finalize new guidelines they will consult listeners in East Europe to make sure the proposed changes are having the right effect" (Mary Hornaday, *Christian Science Monitor*). But no writer can afford to be ignorant of the prejudice against *finalize*. It was included in Maury Maverick's original list of gobbledygook in 1942, and some consider it gobbledygook today.

"Fine" writing

The adjective *fine* is generally applied to writing that's too pretentious for what's being said. "Fine" writing uses "big" words and strained, artificial figures of speech. If you write more to impress your readers than to express your ideas, you're likely to produce "fine" writing. See **Diction, Figures of speech.**

fix

In formal usage *fix* means "fasten in place." In general usage it means "repair" or "put into shape": The TV had to be fixed. As a noun meaning "predicament," *fix* has passed from informal to general: "In some respects economic theory is in the same fix as biology was years ago" (Henry M. Boettinger, *Harvard Business Review*).

flaunt, flout

Flaunt, to "wave, display boastfully," is frequently used with the sense "treat with contempt, scorn," the meaning traditionally assigned to *flout*. Readers aware of the traditional distinction deplore the confusion.

flounder, founder

Flounder, meaning "stumble about, wallow," is probably the word you want. In an extended sense, *founder* means "fail, collapse," but it's not a general synonym of either. Ships founder when they sink, horses when they go lame.

Folk etymology

When people are puzzled by an unfamiliar word or phrase, they sometimes try to make it more regular or more meaningful by rephrasing it from familiar elements: from *aeroplane* they made *airplane;* from Spanish *cucuracha,* English *cockroach;* from *saler,* "a salt-holder," first the redundant *salt-saler* and then *saltcellar,* which has no more to do with a cellar than the *sir-* in *sirloin* has to do with a knight (the *sir-* in the cut of beef is *sur,* "above"). See **Origin of words 1.**

folk, folks

In formal writing *folks* is uncommon. *Folk* is used in the senses "the common people" (usually of a certain region) and "people" (of a specified type). In general writing *folks* for "people," often with the connotation "ordinary, everyday," and for "relatives, parents" is carried over from informal.

Footnote form

When you use footnotes in a paper, triple-space between the text and the first footnote on each page. Single-space the footnotes, leaving a double space between them. See pp. 311–17 for a discussion of documentation and examples of endnotes.

for

When *for* comes between clauses, it's classified as a coordinating conjunction. But coordinating *for* may mean the same as subordinating *because:* He was exhausted, for he had gone two nights without sleep. A comma is usually needed between clauses joined by *for* to keep it from being read as a preposition: The tutors must love the work, for the pay, which is only $300 a year plus room and board, can't be very attractive. The comma prevents the misreading: The tutors must love the work for the pay. As a conjunction, *for* is rather formal. See **because.**

Foreign words in English

1.   Anglicizing foreign words.   English has always borrowed words and roots from other languages, and it's still borrowing (from French, *boutique* and *discotheque*). Words usually cross the threshold of English with their foreign spelling, perhaps with un-English plurals or other forms, and with no established English pronunciation. The process of anglicizing brings them more or less in line with English usage, though they may keep some of their foreign quality, like the *i* of *machine,* the silent *s* in *debris,* the *t* where we are tempted to put a *d* in *kindergarten.*

The speed and degree of anglicizing depends on how frequently the word is used, the circumstances in which it's used, and the people who use it. Formal writers and conservative editors keep the foreign spelling longer than writers and editors of general English. If the words come in through the spoken language, like those of the automobile vocabulary, they're anglicized sooner than if they come in by way of literature: *coupe, chamois, chauffeur, garage, detour.* Words that come in through and remain in literary, scholarly, or socially elite circles change more slowly, in both spelling and pronunciation: *tête-à-tête, faux pas, nouveau riche, laissez-faire.*

2.   Using borrowed words.
a.   Italics. Words that have not been completely anglicized are usually printed in italics in magazines and books and should be underlined in the papers you write. Consult your dictionary. Words on the borderline will be found sometimes in italics, sometimes not. Formal writers use italics more than general writers.
b.   Accents and other marks. In books and magazines, words recently taken in from other languages are usually written with the accent marks they have in the language of their origin. After a time the accents are dropped unless they're needed to indicate pronunciation. But publications for the general public are more likely to drop accent marks (*expose, detente*) than are publications for limited, scholarly audiences (*exposé, détente*).
c.   Plurals. English usually brings borrowed words into its own system of conjugation and declension (*campuses,* not *campi*), though some words

change slowly, especially those used mainly in formal writing (*syllabi* or *syllabuses*). See **Plurals of nouns 4.**

See **Origin of words 2b.**

form Formal English

The word or passage marked is too formal for the subject or for the style of the rest of the paper. Revise, making it more appropriate.

Formal written English is appropriate (though not mandatory) in discussions of ideas, in research papers and other scholarly works, in addresses to be delivered on ceremonial occasions, and in literary essays intended for well-educated readers. It's usually not appropriate in accounts of personal experience, in papers about campus issues, in comments on current books, movies, TV shows, or popular records, or in other writing intended for general readers.

The vocabulary of formal style includes many words not used in general written English. *Form* in the margin of your paper may refer to a word that's too formal for the context: For a while it looked as though the bad habits he had picked up were irremediable (*better:* could never be corrected). Or it may point to a sentence pattern that suggests the deliberate pace of formal English and therefore mixes poorly with sentences that suggest the spontaneity of speech:

> In addition to being younger than my classmates, I had retained, along with the babyish habit of sucking my thumb, a tendency to cry when I was not allowed to have my own way, thereby turning them against me.

> *Possible revision:* Besides being younger than my classmates, I still sucked my thumb. This irritated them, and I made things worse by crying when I didn't get my own way.

See **General English, Informal English, Standard English.**

former, first–latter, last

Traditionally, *former* and *latter* refer only to two units: "the former called the latter 'little prig' " (Ralph Waldo Emerson). Tradition holds for *former,* but the use of *latter* with more than two is common enough to be standard. Even so, some conservative readers would prefer "the last named" in references like this one: "The list of products . . . could include potassium, bromine, chlorine, caustic, and magnesium. The latter might become a very important lightweight metal" (Glenn T. Seaborg, *Bulletin of the Atomic Scientists*).

First and *last* refer to items in a series, usually more than two:

The first president had set up a very informal organization.
His last act was to advise his family on their future.

Latest refers to a series that's still continuing (the latest fashions). *Last* refers either to the final item of a completed series (their last attempt was successful) or to the most recent item of a continuing series (the last election). See **last, latest.**

Formulas

Every language has some fixed phrases that have become customary in certain situations: Once upon a time, Ladies and gentlemen, Good morning, Best wishes, Yours truly, How do you do? Such phrases are too useful to be called clichés, and unlike most trite expressions they're not substitutes for simpler locations. When called for, they should be used without apology. See **Idiom, Subjunctive mood 2a.**

Fractions

Fractions are written in figures when attached to other figures ($72^3/_4$), in a series in figures ($^1/_2$, 1, 2, 4), or in tables or reference matter. In most running text they're written in words: In the local newspaper three fourths of the space was given to advertising, one eighth to news, and one eighth to miscellaneous matters. Hyphens may be used between the numerator and denominator if neither part itself contains a hyphen (seven-tenths), and hyphens should be used to avoid confusion: though *twenty seven eighths* probably means "twenty-seven eighths," it could mean "twenty seven-eighths." But hyphens are less common than they used to be and are now omitted when the numerator functions as an adjective, as in "He sold one half and kept the other."

Decimals are taking the place of fractions in factual writing, because they're more flexible and may be more accurate: .7; .42; 3.14159.

See **Numbers.**

frag Fragment

The construction marked is not a satisfactory sentence. Revise by joining it to a neighboring sentence, by making it grammatically complete, or by rewriting the passage.

A sentence fragment is a part of a sentence—usually a phrase or dependent clause—that's carelessly or ineffectively punctuated as if it were a whole sentence. You can usually correct a fragment by joining it to the preceding or following sentence or by otherwise making it grammatically complete. But sometimes rewriting is the best solution.

Below, with suggested revisions, are three common types of fragments.

1. **A prepositional phrase punctuated as a sentence:**

   The northern part of the city is mainly residential. On the eastern outskirts are the oil refining plants. And to the south beaches and parks.

   Revision: The northern part of the city is mainly residential. On the eastern outskirts are the oil refining plants and to the south beaches and parks.

2. **A participial phrase punctuated as a sentence:**

   For sixteen years I did pretty much what I wanted to. Being distrustful and avoiding anyone in authority.

   Revision: For sixteen years I did pretty much what I wanted to, distrusting and avoiding anyone in authority.

3. **A dependent clause punctuated as a sentence:**

   I still remember him as the best teacher I ever had. Because right then he sat down and helped me work all the problems.

   Revision: I still remember him as the best teacher I ever had, because right then he sat down and helped me work all the problems.

   In an unexpectedly heavy turnout, over 80 percent of the citizens voted. A fact that shows how strongly they felt about the issue.

   Revision: In an unexpectedly heavy turnout, over 80 percent of the citizens voted—a fact that shows. . . . Or: . . . voted. This fact shows. . . .

The deliberate setting off of a phrase or dependent clause for rhetorical effect is common in print. Used sparingly and skillfully, it can do good service as an organizational road sign that briskly points the reader toward the next topic—"But first, the new troops" (Lucian K. Truscott IV, *Harper's*)—or provides informal notice of the progress of the discussion—"Which brings us back to the absurdity of the backlash accusations" (Letty Cottin Pogrebin, *Ms.*). The parallel fragments in these two paragraphs point up a contrast:

   The prevailing view is that all our options have narrowed. I don't believe it. There is a sense of being trapped—the feeling that nothing we do makes much difference. Which leads to frantic group pressures and single-issue politics, or to the cynical rejection of all forms of public life and to a wallowing in our egos.

Let's face it. We used up our resources, polluted our environment and laid staggering burdens on our government. Which means we must now place limits on our desires, needs, greeds. The historians call it the Age of Limits. —Max Lerner, *Newsweek*

And fragments of some length can sometimes be used effectively to pile up details in descriptive writing:

Prairie wool blue-green, spring wheat bright as new lawn, winter wheat gray-green at rest and slaty when the wind flaws it, roadside primroses as shy as prairie flowers are supposed to be, and as gentle to the eye as when in my boyhood we used to call them wild tulips, and by their coming date the beginning of summer. —Wallace Stegner, *Wolf Willow*.

See **Clauses, Phrases.**

freshman, freshmen

The modifier is *freshman,* not only before nouns with an obviously singular reference (a freshman dorm) but before plural and abstract nouns (freshman courses, freshman orientation).

-ful, full

When the adjective *full* (a full basket, a basket full of apples) is used as a suffix to nouns of measure (*basketful, spoonful*) or of feeling or quality (*peaceful, sorrowful*), it has only one *l*. The plural of nouns ending in *-ful* is usually made with *-s: spoonfuls, basketfuls*. With the adjective *full,* the noun is made plural: *full baskets, baskets full*.

further, farther

Both *further* and *farther* are used in referring to distance. See **farther, further.**

Fused sentence

Fused, or *run-on, sentence* is the name sometimes given to two grammatically complete sentences written with no mark of punctuation between them: If you ask me why I did it, I can only say that at the time it seemed the right thing to do [ ] that is my only explanation. To correct the error, begin a new sentence or insert a semicolon. Compare **Comma splice.**

Future tense

English verbs don't inflect, or change their form, to express future time. Some of the means we use to refer to the future are illustrated in these sentences: I am leaving next week; He sails tomorrow; She is to speak on Saturday; He is about to resign; When I am elected, I will make an investigation; They will try to be on time; She is going to refuse; Shall I take this to the cleaners? See **Tenses of verbs.**

Gender

In speaking of gender in modern English, we're usually talking about choice of pronouns—*he, she, it, who, which*—and about the meaning of the words that govern that choice. See **Agreement 2, he or she, Sexist language.**

General English

General English is the core of standard English. Spoken general English is what we hear in most talks for general audiences, in news broadcasts, and in the ordinary conversation of educated people. Written, edited general English is what we read in newspapers, magazines, and most books. The main focus of this *Index* is on writing general English. See **Formal English, Informal English, Standard English.**

Genitive case

The genitive, or possessive, case is indicated by the apostrophe, with or without *-s;* by the possessive form of the personal pronouns; and by the relative *whose*. See **Possessive case.**

Gerunds

1. Form and function.   A gerund—also called a verbal noun—is the *-ing* form of a verb used as a noun. It can serve in any noun function: as subject or complement of a verb *(Seeing* is *believing)* or as object of a verb or preposition (He taught *dancing;* The odds are against your *winning).* Like a noun, a gerund can be modified by an adjective (Good *boxing* was rare) or used as a modifier (a *fishing* boat, a *living* wage). Yet, like a verb, a gerund can take a subject and an object and can be modified by an adverb: The critic despaired of the author (subject) ever (adverb) *constructing* a really forceful play (object).

A gerund may be in the present or the perfect tense and in the active or passive voice: *seeing, having seen, being seen, having been seen.*

Though it has the same form as the present participle, the gerund is used differently:

> **Gerund:** *Running* a hotel appealed to him. (*Running* is the subject.)
> **Participle:** *Running* a hotel, he prospered. (The participle phrase modifies *he.*)

2. Subject of a gerund.   The subject of a gerund is sometimes in the possessive case and sometimes in the accusative, or objective (in nouns, the "common"), case. Formal writing uses the possessive more than general writing does: "Such a view leads to the metaphor's becoming a brief poem in itself" (Alex Page, *Modern Philology*). General is likely to use the common case: "The Vice President's humorous remarks about Hofstra not picking up this ball are somewhat offset . . . by the record" (Clifford Lord, *College Board Review*).

When the subject is a personal pronoun or a proper noun, the possessive is more usual than the common case in both formal and general: They wanted to discuss *my going* AWOL; We overlooked *Joe's swearing.* When the subject is a personal pronoun and begins the sentence, the possessive is required: *Our* (not *Us*) *worrying* won't solve anything; *His* (not *Him*) *lying* deceived nobody.

3. Phrases with gerunds.   Gerunds are often used in phrases that function somewhat like dependent clauses: *In coming to an agreement,* they had compromised on all points; *By refusing to sing,* she embarrassed her mother. The relation of the gerund phrase to the word it modifies should be clear. The reader shouldn't have to pause to make sure just what the writer intended:

Dangling: In coming to an agreement, campaign promises were ignored.

Revision: In coming to an agreement, both sides ignored their campaign promises.

Dangling: After sleeping sixteen hours, my headache was finally gone.

Revision: After sleeping sixteen hours, I was finally rid of my headache. *Or:* After I slept sixteen hours, my headache was finally gone.

See **Dangling modifiers, Idiom.** Compare **Infinitives, Participles.**

get up

In general English you get up when you stand up or get out of bed. See **arise, rise, get up.**

go

Go in the sense "become" is used as a linking verb in a number of idioms. While some *(go broke, go native, go straight)* are informal to general, others *(go blind, go lame)* are fully established in all varieties of usage. *Go and,* as an intensive with no actual motion implied, is common in speech and turns up in some general writing: "He has gone and made a genuine commercial film" (Joseph Morgenstern, *Newsweek*). *Going for* in the sense "working to the advantage of" is general: "when women in England didn't have much going for them" (Emily Hahn, *New York Times Book Review*). Neither *go and* nor *going for* in these senses is appropriate in formal writing. See **Idiom, try and.**

Gobbledygook

Maury Maverick, a congressman from Texas, coined the term *gobbledygook* for wordy, pompous, overweight prose that confuses and irritates more than it informs. Although government bureaus have earned their reputations as producers of gobbledygook, business, the military, the social sciences, and the humanities have shown an equal weakness for such jargon. Frequently gobbledygook serves the purpose of disguising the truth. See **Diction 2, Doublespeak, Jargon.**

good, well

Good is usually an adjective in standard English. *Well* is either an adjective or an adverb. "I feel good" and "I feel well" (adjectives) are both usual but have different meanings. *Good* implies actual bodily sensations; *well* refers merely to a state, "not ill." In nonstandard usage *good* takes the place of *well:* He played good; She sings good. Adverbial *good* is also heard in informal speech and frequently appears in printed representations of speech: "She's running good now," the mechanic said.

got, gotten

Either *got* or *gotten* is usually acceptable as the past participle of *get*. But *got*—not *gotten*—is often added to *has* or *have* to emphasize the notion of "possess" (I haven't got a cent; She's got a letter from home) or of "must"

(You've got to lend me a dollar). Though seldom used in formal writing, the emphatic *got* is fairly common in general writing: "A lot of adults are bored by Bach because they haven't got the faintest idea of what music is about" (Marya Mannes, *TV Guide*). *Got married* is particularly distasteful to some formal stylists.

gourmet

A gourmet is a connoisseur of food and drink. As a vogue word, the adjective *gourmet* is regularly applied to food, restaurants, and cooking that a gourmet couldn't stomach. (It's even applied to cutlery.) If you mean "foreign," "expensive," or "fancy," use those words. To express general approval, *good* is available.

graduated

The idiom *to be graduated from* an institution has generally gone out of use except in formal and somewhat old-fashioned writing and has been replaced by *graduated from:* He graduated from high school in 1904. Omitting the *from*—She graduated college in 1980—is a common usage that causes violent reactions in some quarters: ". . . to say 'I graduated college' . . . is to be a language slob and a discredit to whatever learning factory mailed you a diploma" (William Safire, *New York Times Magazine*).

Grammar

Grammar has several different senses. Just as *history* can mean a field of study, events in the past, or the book that describes those events, so *grammar* can refer to a field of study, a set of abilities in our brains, or the book that describes those abilities.

1. Philosophers in Greece had begun speculating about language and words long before the Stoics in 300 B.C. singled out grammar as a field of study separate from rhetoric and poetics. Since then scholars have continued to study the structure of language, not only because language is the central defining characteristic of the human race but because it seems possible that the very foundation of our knowledge and thought—perhaps even perception itself—are shaped by the grammatical structures of our language. Grammar thus becomes an entry to the study of the mind.

2. *Grammar* may also refer to the ability every normal human being has to speak and understand sentences. We all have a grammar in our heads.

We can all understand an indefinite number of new sentences we've never heard before. We can distinguish between grammatical and ungrammatical sentences (see **grammatical, ungrammatical 1**). We can recognize sentences that are ambiguous. We also understand that some sentences are related to others, as this sentence is related to the next two.

> That some sentences are related to others is also understood by us. It is also understood by us that some sentences are related to others.

The goal of a linguist, a scholar who studies grammatical structure, is to describe in a written grammar this internalized grammar that we all share.

3. The history of linguistic study in the last hundred years falls very roughly into three schools.

a. Traditional. Although this label is applied to a great variety of approaches, most traditional grammars start by describing parts of speech and the inflections associated with them: nouns are names of persons, places, and things, and so on. Once the parts of speech have been described, the grammar describes functions: subjects, predicates, objects, modifiers, and so on. The definitions are illustrated by examples. The reader of the grammar is expected to understand the labeling through the descriptions and examples and then to use his native knowledge of the language to apply the label in any new sentence that might contain the pattern. For example:

> A sentence adverb modifies a whole sentence rather than any individual word or construction. It usually stands at the beginning of the sentence, though it may occur elsewhere: *Fortunately,* he left; He is *allegedly* still here; No one cares, *obviously.*

Confronted with the sentence "Apparently, she left," you could identify *apparently* as a sentence adverb on the basis of the explanation and examples. Such descriptions require the ability of a native speaker to make them work.

b. Structural. In the early part of this century a new approach to grammar emerged. Structural linguists tried to devise objective techniques for discovering the structure of a language without relying on the meanings of words (as traditional grammars do). They began by cataloging the sounds produced by native speakers, then identifying the smallest units that seemed to have meaning (morphemes), and then arranging these units into larger classes, not according to their meanings but according to their customary relationships with other units. Once the parts of speech were classified, sequences of different parts were identified (noun-verb, verb-noun, preposition-noun, adjective-noun, etc.) and then further described functionally (subject-predicate, verb-object, modifier-head, etc.).

c.   Generative-transformational. Through the 1940s and most of the 1950s, structural grammars were thought to be the new wave in English language education. Then in 1957 Noam Chomsky, a linguist at the Massachusetts Institute of Technology, published *Syntactic Structures* and revolutionized the study of language. Chomsky turned linguists toward a model of language that tries to account in a formal set of rules for the ability of native speakers to produce and understand an infinite range of new sentences. Grammarians of the generative-transformational school assume the existence of a grammar in the mind of the native speaker. They seek to account for what all languages have in common, as well as for the peculiarities that distinguish English, say, from German; and they try to deal with the full range of language, from sounds to meaning, in an integrated theory.

Chomsky's initial formulations of generative theory have been considerably modified and revised, and there are adherents of other theories of language description—tagmemic grammars, stratificational grammars, dependency grammars, and others. But for at least two decades the dominant models for research into the structure of English and other languages were generative-transformational.

4.   So far, we've ignored the most common meaning of *grammar*. This is grammar in the sense of "good grammar"—making the "right" choice between *who* and *whom,* not using *like* for *as,* avoiding sentence fragments, and so on. It concentrates only on those areas where usage varies from one social class to another or from the way English teachers believe educated people should speak to the way their students actually do speak.

How we communicate depends on our social class, our geographical roots, the social situation we happen to be in, and our mode of communication—speaking or writing. What most schools teach as grammar are those features that allegedly distinguish written, fairly formal, supposedly upper-middle-class usage from other varieties. It's a serious mistake to assume that this form of grammar alone defines "correct" usage.

Thus when we use the word *grammar,* we have to distinguish a variety of senses:

Grammar is a field of scholarly inquiry dating back to ancient Greece.

Grammar is the knowledge of our language—whatever that language may be—that we all have in our heads.

Grammar is a set of rules for a language that can be written down and that will generate the sentences of that language along with a description of each sentence. The object of this grammar is to "model" or explain grammar in sense 2.

Grammar in the sense of "good grammar" is concerned with certain usages that are supposed to characterize the practice of upper-middle-class speakers and writers. A grammar of good usage consists of the prescriptions found in grammar books—usually fewer than twenty or thirty—that allow someone who wants to be a member of the "educated" community to speak and write as those already in that community allegedly speak and write.

This last sense of *grammar* is, unfortunately, the sense most familiar to American students. The associations that cluster around this grammar make it very difficult for linguists to communicate the excitement of discovering something about grammar (sense 2) that he can write down in a grammar (sense 3) that reveals the elegantly complex organization of human linguistic knowledge.

grammatical, ungrammatical

Sentences can be grammatical in either of two senses:

1.   Sentences are grammatical when they meet the structural requirements of the grammar used by an individual speaker. "Can't nobody tell me what to do" is ungrammatical for some speakers, but it's grammatical for others, if the grammar they've incorporated into their nervous systems allows them to construct that sentence in ordinary conversation (see **Grammar 2**). "Nobody can tell me what to do" might be ungrammatical for those speakers who habitually say "Can't nobody tell me what to do" but grammatical for those who don't.

In this sense, *grammatical* simply describes the structure of a sentence that's normal for use by a particular person in ordinary speech. The made-up sentence "I know the man who and the woman left" is ungrammatical for all speakers of English.

2.   In common usage and school usage, sentences are said to be grammatical when they meet the requirements set by those who are in a position to enforce standards of usage—teachers, editors, employers. In this looser sense, "Can't nobody tell me what to do" is said to be ungrammatical for everyone, and a person to whom the construction is normal and systematic with reference to an internalized grammar (see **Grammar 2**) is said to be speaking ungrammatical English.

Such usages might more accurately be termed "socially acceptable"— meaning "acceptable to those who are concerned about the rules of 'good grammar' " (see **Grammar 4**). In many cases, advice based on this sense of *grammatical* is accurate. Most educated people in this country don't say "Can't nobody tell me what to do." In writing, most make their subjects and verbs agree. Most avoid *ain't* in all but relatively informal situations. On the other hand, rules for usage that's grammatical in the "socially acceptable" sense also involve a good deal of folklore, as many of the articles in the *Index* make clear.

See **Usage.**

Group words

In English many groups of two or more words (that is, phrases) function like single words. Examples:

> *Nouns:* hay fever, back door, holding company, home run, sacrifice hit, school year, baby blue
> *Verbs:* dig in, hold off, look into, flare up, follow through, follow up, close up, show up, blow up, back water
> *Prepositions:* according to, in spite of, in opposition to, previous to, due to

In this book we usually ignore the superficial difference between a part of speech written as a single word and one that's written as a group of words. *Noun* (sometimes called *noun phrase*) or *verb* or *preposition* refers to both single words and to group words functioning as noun or verb or preposition.

guess

Formal usage limits *guess* to its sense of "conjecture, estimate, surmise": "The employers can only guess whom the victims will choose to sue" (Henry L. Woodward, *Yale Law Journal*). But in general and informal usage *guess* is common in its looser senses of "think, suppose, believe": "They were foolish, I guess, in trying to hold history still for one more hour" (Larry L. King, *Atlantic*).

had better

Had better is the usual idiom in giving advice or an indirect command: You had better take care of that cold; You'd better go. Running the *d* in *I'd, you'd, he'd* . . . into the *b* of *better* produces the informal construction without either *had* or *'d:* "But I better get with it if I'm going to be a TV viewer" (Goodman Ace, *Saturday Review*).

half

Though *a half* is traditionally considered the more elegant, there's little distinction between *a half* and *half a/an* in current formal and general usage.

For example, both "a half century earlier" and "nearly half a century removed" occur in a single issue of the *American Historical Review*. *A half a/an* (a half an hour) is an informal redundancy.

The noun accompanying *half* or *half of* in a subject determines whether the verb is singular or plural: Half of the *book is* . . . ; Half of the *men are*. . . .

hanged, hung

In formal English people are hanged, pictures are hung. In general and informal usage *hang, hung, hung* is often used in all senses: "Of course, McCarthy hung himself at the hearing" (Isidore Silver, *New Republic*).

hardly

When *hardly* means "probably not" or "almost not," don't add another *not*. See **Double negative 2.**

have

1. Independent meaning. As a verb of independent meaning, *have* has a range of senses *(have a good time/a fight/a baby/a cold/breakfast)*, with "own, possess," both literally and figuratively, the most common: They have a new car. Because *have* occurs so frequently as an "empty" auxiliary word, its meaning as an independent word meaning "possess" is often reinforced by *got* (see **got, gotten**).

2. Auxiliary. *Have/had* functions as a signal of tense:

> *Perfect tense:* They have come.
> *Future perfect tense:* They will have gone by then.
> *Past perfect tense:* They had gone before we arrived.

See **Tenses of verbs 2.**

3. Contractions. *He, she, it has* contract to *he's, she's, it's:* He's got a long beard; It's rained for a week. (The contractions with *is* are identical: *he's, she's, it's.*) *I, you, we, they have* contract to *I've, you've, we've, they've.* Omitted *'ve* (You['ve] been gone too long), a speech habit carried over into writing, is nonstandard. Both *had* and *would* contract to *'d:* They'd already spoken; She'd already be waiting.

Would have, wouldn't have are sometimes written *would of, wouldn't of,* a nonstandard transcription of what's spoken as *would've, wouldn't've.*

4. Had ought, hadn't ought. *Had ought* (He had ought to take better care of himself) is a common nonstandard idiom, sometimes heard in informal speech. *Hadn't ought* (She hadn't ought to lie like that) is regional and informal.

For *have got,* see **got, gotten.** See also **had better.**

Headword

A headword, or head, is a word modified by another word, especially a noun modified by one or more adjectives (his first long *sleep*), a verb modified by one or more adverbs (*walk* carefully), or an adjective or adverb modified by qualifiers (very *old,* more *intelligently*). The headword of a construction is the word around which the rest of the construction is built: very old *men* in raincoats who had been waiting outside.

healthful, healthy

The distinction between *healthful* "conducive to health" (places and foods are healthful) and *healthy* "having good health" (persons, animals, and plants are healthy) is observed in formal and some general writing, but by and large *healthy* is now used for both meanings.

help but

Conservative stylists usually avoid using *can't* (or *cannot*) *help but.* See **can't help but, can't seem to.**

hence

Hence is primarily an adverb, but it's also used as a rather formal connective. See **Conjunctive adverbs.**

he or she

Traditionally, the masculine pronoun *he* is used with indefinite pronouns like *anyone* and *everybody* and with noun antecedents that may refer to either men or women: Every *student* must accept responsibility for *his* acts. But feminists find this usage a prime example of sexist language and prefer *he or she* (or *he/she* or *s/he*) and *his or her.* Sometimes antecedents make a masculine pronoun inappropriate and the double pronoun convenient: "In enabling a young man or woman to prepare for life in a shorter period of time, we direct his or her attention to other values" (Edward H. Litchfield, *Saturday Review*).

For writers and readers to whom avoiding *he* and *his* after a sexually indefinite antecedent isn't a matter of principle, *he or she* and its variants often seem unnecessarily awkward: "Any individual who is a candidate for promotion or tenure should her/himself make sure that records are complete" (Committee recommendation). When *he* or *his* is inappropriate, *they* is a frequent choice in general writing: In helping a young man or woman to prepare for life, we must direct their attention to other values. Switching to "young men and women" would avoid the problem. See **Agreement 2, Sexist language.**

himself, herself

Himself and *herself* are used in two ways, as reflexive pronouns, referring to the subject of the sentence (George has always taken himself too seriously; She looked at herself in the window) and as qualifiers, for emphasis (He told me so himself; The senator herself told me so).

historic, historical

Historic and *historical* ordinarily have quite different meanings. *Historic* usually means "important in history," "noteworthy," "famous": "a historic act: the toast to the French fleet by which the archbishop . . . urged French Catholics to abandon royalist opposition" (James E. Ward, *American Historical Review*). *Historical* is much more neutral, meaning "based on the facts of history," "having occurred in the past," "suitable for study by historians or using their methods": "This autobiography . . . provides a wide range of historical persons and events" (Heinz E. Ellersieck, *American Historical Review*).

hopefully

From an adverb with the established meaning "in a hopeful way, full of hope" (The dog waited hopefully for a handout), *hopefully* became a vogue word meaning "it is hoped": "Hopefully, they will reveal the thickness of the planet's ice cap" (Jonathan Spivak, *Wall Street Journal*). Sometimes it means no more than "with luck": Hopefully she'll be down in a minute. As long as it's kept away from the verb and set off by commas, there's little chance of real ambiguity. The *hopefully* vogue has faded, giving the violent opposition it aroused a chance to cool. The usage is standard though still unacceptable to some.

Hours

In formal writing, hours are often spelled out in words: at four o'clock, around five-fifteen. In newspapers and much other general writing, figures are used, especially if several times are mentioned and always in designations of time with *a.m.* and *p.m.:* at 4 p.m., just after 9 a.m., around 4:30 p.m., from 10 to 12.

however

However is particularly appropriate as a connective in the fully developed sentences of formal style. It is also the most common conjunctive adverb in general writing, where it typically serves to relate a sentence to what's gone before rather than to connect main clauses within the same sentence:

> Murder is usually reported, and 86 percent of all reported murders lead to arrests. Among those arrested, however, only 64 percent are prosecuted. —Ramsey Clark, *Saturday Review*

However can either introduce the clause it modifies (However, among those arrested . . .) or, as in the example, follow the words the writer wants to emphasize (Among those arrested, however, . . .). To begin a clause the simpler *but* is often the better choice.

See **Conjunctive adverbs.**

hung, hanged

In formal English, pictures are hung, people are hanged. See **hanged, hung.**

Hyperbole

We all use this very common figure of speech—obvious and extravagant overstatement—when we describe our troubles as *incredible,* our embarrassments as *horrible,* our vacations as *fabulous.* Such efforts to dramatize and intensify fail through repetition. Like other figures, hyperbole works well only when it's fresh.

Hypercorrectness

Hypercorrect forms are used by speakers and writers who work so hard at being correct that they end up being wrong. Perhaps the most common example of hypercorrectness is the use of *I* for *me* in a compound object: It is a wonderful moment for my wife and I; They invited Bill and I; between you and I. Other common hypercorrect forms include *whom* for *who* (He is critical of the other members, whom he feels spend more time making accusations than solving problems), *as* for *like* (I always tried to behave as a gentleman), the ending *-ly* where it doesn't belong (She looks badly), some verb forms (*lie* for *lay*), and many pronunciations.

Hyphen

In *Manuscript and Proof,* stylebook of the Oxford University Press, John Benbow wrote, "If you take the hyphen seriously, you will surely go mad." To ward off madness, adopt a recent dictionary or stylebook as your guide and follow it consistently.

1. Word division. The hyphen is always used to mark the division of a word at the end of a line (see **Division of words**). Other uses are in part a matter of style.

2. Compound words. Some compound words are written as two words *(post office),* some as one *(notebook),* and some as a combination of words joined by hyphens *(mother-in-law).* The trend is away from hyphenation, toward one-word spelling. Even when a prefix ends and a root word begins with the same vowel, the current tendency is to write the word solid: *cooperate, reelect, preeminent.*

A number of compound adjective forms are conventionally hyphenated when they precede the noun: *clear-eyed, able-bodied, first-class.* Compounds consisting of an adverb plus a verbal are hyphenated when the adverb doesn't end in *-ly:* a well-marked trail (*but* a plainly marked trail).

3. Noun phrases. Usage is divided on hyphenating noun phrases used as modifiers, as in "seventeenth century philosophy." A hyphen is more likely in formal styles: seventeenth-century philosophy.

4. Miscellaneous uses. A numeral as part of a modifier (5-cent cigar, nine-inch boards) is hyphenated, and a hyphen is used between a prefix and a proper name: pre-Sputnik, pro-Doonesbury. A "suspension" hyphen may be used to hold together a spread-out modifier: the third-, fourth-, and fifth-grade rooms; both fourteenth- and fifteenth-century records.

5. To avoid ambiguity. Occasionally a pair of modifiers is ambiguous without a hyphen. "A light yellow scarf" may be either a scarf that's light yellow or a light scarf that's yellow. *Light-yellow* makes the first meaning clear; *light, yellow* the second. Similarly, "new car-owner" and "new-car owner" prevent misunderstanding.

I

I

The notion that *I* (always capitalized) shouldn't be the first word in a sentence is groundless. *I* should be used wherever it's needed. Circumlocutions to avoid the natural use of *I* are usually awkward. "My present thinking is that nuclear power projects are unsound" is a clumsy way of saying "I think now [or "I think" or "I have come to think" or "At present I think"] that nuclear power projects are unsound." See **it's me, myself, we.**

id Idiom

The expression marked is not standard idiom. Revise it, referring to an article in this *Index* or to a dictionary if you are not sure of the correct form.

Idioms are established phrases that are not easy to explain grammatically or logically. Some examples are "come in handy," "strike a bargain," "look up an old friend," "many's the time," "make good," "in respect to." We learn these phrases as units, and if we're native speakers, few of them cause us trouble. No native speaker is likely to say "hit a bargain" or "look down an old friend" or "the time is many." Idioms are often completely frozen. You can use thousands of different words as subjects and verbs of sentences, but you can't substitute any other adjective in the phrase "in good stead" (Her advice stood me in good stead).

We have trouble with idioms we haven't learned, and the most common trouble is choosing the right preposition. Because we know "conform to," we may be tempted to speak of a policy that's "in conformity to public opinion"; but the idiom is "in conformity with." In using the formal word *arise,* we might attach the preposition *off* instead of the *from* that idiom calls for. Because logic is no help, the prepositions must be learned in the phrases. Dictionaries sometimes show the preposition that's conventionally used with a particular word.

Some words are idiomatically followed by gerunds, others by infinitives. For example:

Gerunds	Infinitives
can't help *doing*	compelled *to do*
capable of *painting*	able *to paint*
the habit of *giving*	the tendency *to give*
an idea of *selling*	a wish *to sell*
enjoys *playing*	likes *to play*

With many common words, either is used: the way *of doing* something, the way *to do* something.

See **ability to; acquiesce; agree to, agree with; compare, contrast; Diction 1; different from, different than; it; Prepositions and style 1; Subjunctive mood 2a.**

i.e.

I.e. is the abbreviation for the Latin words meaning "that is." It's appropriate only in scholarly writing. See **Abbreviations 2.**

if, whether

Writers have a choice between *if* and *whether* before interrogative clauses (indirect questions) and clauses expressing doubt or uncertainty. *Whether* is almost always chosen in formal contexts: "It is appropriate to ask whether these decisions are to be considered a victory for those who champion individual right" (Wayne F. LaFave, *Supreme Court Review*). Both words are used in general writing, but *if* is more common: The survey asked people if TV had influenced their vote.

illiterate

Illiterate and *literate* are used to refer both to the ability to read and write (There were few schools, and most of the peasants were completely illiterate) and to familiarity with what's been written (Any literate person should know the name Kafka). Usage called nonstandard in this book is often loosely referred to as illiterate in the second sense—that is, uneducated. The label *illiterate* is applied most freely by those who demand that others use language precisely.

ill, sick

Ill is the less common, more formal word. See **sick, ill.**

illusion, allusion

An illusion misleads, an allusion refers. See **allusion, illusion.**

image

Image meaning a public conception or impression (He was criticized for not projecting the image of a President) has moved from the jargon of the public relations man and the advertiser into general use. Image makers are experts at doublespeak. See **Doublespeak.**

Imagery

An image is a word or group of words that makes an appeal to one of the senses: sight *(shiny, ghostly, mist, light green, thick brown hair);* hearing *(creaking, faraway shouts, the pounding of surf);* taste *(salty, dry, a pickled pear);* smell *(jasmine, fresh paint, a blown-out candle);* touch *(smooth, glassy, razor sharp, a stubbly beard);* or the muscular tension known as the kinesthetic sense *(squirm, jerky, jogging heavily along).* Though an image may appeal to more than one sense *(a rough, angry sea),* in a specific context one sense is usually dominant.

Studying the images in a writer's work will reveal what has impressed him in his experience and what appeals to him—colors, lines, odors, sounds. Your own writing will be richer and stronger if it includes images drawn from your own experience and based on your own taste. A borrowed image is likely to be a dead one. An image from personal experience is a live image; and a live image is like a good photograph: it reveals something of the photographer as well as showing what he has photographed.

Imperative mood

The form of the verb used for direct commands and requests is in the imperative mood: Bring the tapes when you come; Run! See **Commands and requests.**

implement

The catchall bureaucratic verb *implement,* meaning to "give effect" to policies or ideas (It's a great scenario, but who's going to implement it?), might often be replaced by *fulfill, execute, put into practice,* or *carry out,* if only for variety.

imply, infer

A writer or speaker *implies* something in his words or manner, suggesting a conclusion without stating it. A reader or listener *infers* something from what he reads or hears, drawing a conclusion from the available information. Having a word for each of these acts contributes to clear communication, and careful writers make the distinction.

But for centuries *infer* has also been used to mean "imply," and today many dictionaries recognize this meaning (as well as the traditional meaning) as standard. So when clarity is essential, the safe course is not simply to distinguish between *imply* and *infer* but to provide a context that underlines your meaning: From the President's words, I infer that he. . . .

Incoherence

Writing is incoherent when a relationship between parts (of a sentence, of a paragraph, of a whole paper) isn't apparent. The cause may be that there actually is no relationship between the parts, or it may be that the writer has failed to make the relationship clear. See **Coherence, Transition.**

Incomplete sentence

Punctuating a phrase or a dependent clause as if it were a complete sentence is often the result of carelessness. See **Fragment.**

incredible, incredulous

A story or situation is incredible ("unbelievable"); a person is incredulous ("unbelieving"). One way to avoid confusing the two is to refrain from using *incredible,* a voguish example of trite hyperbole (I'm taking this incredible course!) unless you mean it literally (His claim to have read *War and Peace* in one evening is incredible).

Indention

To indent in manuscript or printed copy is to begin the first line of a paragraph some distance to the right of the left-hand margin—an inch in handwritten copy, five spaces in typewritten copy. Hanging indention is indention of all lines below the first line, as in bibliography entries, each main section of an outline, and many newspaper headlines. If a line of poetry is too long to complete on one line, the part brought over to the second line should be indented. For indenting quotations, see **Quotation marks 1d.**

Independent clauses

An independent clause (like this one) can stand alone as a simple sentence. See **Clauses.**

Indicative mood

Verb forms that make assertions or ask questions are said to be indicative or in the indicative mood. The indicative is the mood of most verbs in English sentences: They *sat* on the porch even though it *was* late October; *Will* you *come* if you *are* invited? Compare **Imperative mood, Subjunctive mood.**

Indirect discourse (indirect quotation)

In indirect discourse a person's words are reported in paraphrase or summary instead of being quoted exactly:

> *Direct:* He said, "I won't take it if they give it to me."

> *Indirect:* He said he wouldn't take it if they gave it to him.

An indirect question restates a question at second hand:

> *Direct:* "Is everyone all right?" he asked.

> *Indirect:* He asked if everyone was all right.

See **Commands and requests, Questions, Quotation marks 2b, Tense 3b.**

Indirect objects

An indirect object names what or whom something is given, said, or shown to: She gave *him* a prize. See **Objects 2.**

infer, imply

The writer or speaker implies; the reader or listener infers. See **imply, infer.**

Infinitives

Infinitive is a Latin grammatical term for a verb form expressing the general sense of the verb without restriction as to person, number, or tense. In Modern English the root form of the verb is the infinitive, often with *to* before it.

1.   The *to* infinitive and the bare infinitive.   More often than not, an infinitive is used with the preposition *to:* He's the man *to see;* He was glad *to come;* She likes *to be visited.* But *to* is seldom or never used after the modal auxiliary verbs or after some full verbs: I can *see;* She must *carry* it; We let him *go;* They can't make her *talk;* I heard them *sing.*

2.   Functions of infinitives.   Infinitives serve as subjects, as objects, as complements, and as modifiers. They in turn may have subjects, objects, complements, or modifiers.

> *Subject: To sit and read* was his idea of a holiday. For you *to do* that again would be a serious mistake.
> *Object:* She prefers *to wait* until Tuesday. The police tried *to hold back* the crowd.
> *Complement:* He seems *to be* happy.
> *Modifier:* My friend is the man *to see.* Jane is the person *to do* that. He was reluctant *to stay* longer. They're trying *to find out* what happened. *To avoid* colds, [you] stay out of crowds.

Infinitives and style

1.   Infinitives in a series.   In a short, unemphatic series, there's no reason to repeat *to:* He decided to shower, shave, and dress. When the series is complex or when separate verbs deserve emphasis, *to* should be repeated: These were her goals—to escape the city, to avoid routine, and to find contentment.

2.   Case of pronoun with infinitive.   For the pronoun after the infinitive of a linking verb that has no expressed subject, general English usually has the accusative case: I always wanted to be *him.* Formal favors the nominative: I always wanted to be *he.* But unless there's a reason for giving the pronoun prominence, another phrasing might be preferable: He was the person I always wanted to be.

3.   Dangling infinitives.   Infinitives that function as absolute phrases (to tell the truth, to be sure) are sentence modifiers and as such present no problems. But an infinitive, like a participle or a gerund, will dangle if it seems to be related to a word that it can't sensibly modify or if, in a context that calls for an explicit relationship, it has no clear relation to any word in the sentence:

> *Dangling:* To swim well, fear of the water must be overcome.

> *Revised:* To swim well, the learner must first overcome fear of the water.

See **Absolute phrases, Dangling modifiers.**

4. Split infinitives.   In a split infinitive a word or phrase (usually an adverb) comes between *to* and the verb: to actively pursue. Some infinitives shouldn't be split; some should be, because splitting them makes the sentence easier to understand and more pleasant to read. In still other contexts it's a matter of choice, with more splits occurring in general English than in formal. See **Split infinitive.**

Inflection

Inflection refers to the change of word forms to indicate grammatical relationships, like singular and plural number for nouns or past and present tense for verbs. See **Case, Comparison of adjectives and adverbs, Plurals of nouns, Pronouns, Verbs.**

Informal English

The word or passage marked is too informal for the subject or for the style of the rest of the paper. Revise, making it more appropriate.

Informal written English is appropriate (though not mandatory) in letters to close friends and to members of your family and may be the style you use in a diary or journal. Its casual, intimate tone makes it unsuitable for most college writing, though informal usages may be successfully introduced into papers written in general English if they're chosen with taste and judgment.

You'd be unlikely to use the informal *pretty* (pretty big, pretty soon, pretty old) in a chemistry report or a psychology examination, and you probably wouldn't describe Robert Frost as ''a pretty good poet'' in a paper for a literature course. But in writing for an audience of classmates, you might call a local hero ''a pretty good quarterback.'' Whether or not *inf* appeared in the margin of your paper would depend on the context. If your style was relaxed and conversational, *pretty* would be appropriate. If your style placed some distance between you and your readers, *fairly* would be a better choice.

As applied to sections of papers or to whole papers, *informal* usually implies sloppiness—rambling sentences, vague references, trite slang, repetition, incoherence. If something you've written has been so marked, the best solution is to rethink what you want to say and rewrite the passage, aiming for clarity and precision.

See **Formal English, General English, Standard English.** See also **Agreement, Colloquial English, Repetition, Slang, Spoken and written English, Triteness.**

in, into, in to

In usually shows location, literal or figurative: He was in the house; He was in a stupor. *Into* usually shows direction: He came into the house; He fell into a stupor. But in informal and general usage *in* is common when direction is meant: "Twice a week we get in the car, and drive down the Parkway" (Richard Rose, *St. Louis Post-Dispatch*).

The *in* of *in to* is an adverb and the *to* a preposition (They went in to dinner) or sign of the infinitive (They went in to eat).

Intensifiers

Intensifiers are words like *very, greatly, terribly, much,* which intensify the meaning of adjectives and adverbs: He is much older than she; She ran very fast. See **Qualifiers.**

Intensive pronouns

Reflexive pronouns—the personal pronouns plus *-self* or *-selves*—may be used as intensives: We ourselves are responsible. See **myself, Pronouns 2.**

Interjections

Interjections are expressions of emotion like *oh, ow, ouch, ah.* See **Exclamations.**

Interrogative pronouns

Who, whom, whose, which, what are interrogative pronouns. See **Pronouns 5.**

Intransitive verbs

An intransitive verb takes no object: The money *vanished.* See **Transitive and intransitive verbs.**

Inversion

Inversion usually means placing the verb, or some part of the verb phrase, before its subject. This is the regular pattern in questions: Will she go? Did they enjoy it? Inversion is also used with expletive *there* and *it* (There was a man at the door) and in a few other situations: What a fool I am; Long may it wave; Here comes the thunder. In a declarative sentence, any part of the predicate may occasionally be inverted for emphasis: Cabbage I hate; Down he went; This I know; That she was brilliant we had no doubt.

Irony

Irony implies something markedly different, sometimes even the opposite, of what's actually said. Light irony is mildly humorous, as in the greeting "Lovely day!" in pouring rain. Heavy irony is usually a form of sarcasm or satire: "The most important argument for collecting taxes from the elderly is that it would lower the tax burden on helpless corporations and conglomerates who are struggling to make ends meet" (Art Buchwald, syndicated columnist).

irregardless

Irregardless is redundant: both the prefix *ir-* and the suffix *-less* are negative. The standard word is *regardless*.

Irregular verbs

Verbs that don't form their past tense and past participle by adding *-ed* are irregular. See **Principal parts of verbs.**

it

The neuter third-person singular pronoun *it* is used most commonly to refer to inanimates but sometimes refers to living things. Typically it replaces preceding neuter noun phrases: Have you seen *the neighbors' new car?* Yes, isn't *it* a mess? The antecedent may be a clause or a sentence: Some people say *that more money will solve the problem of our schools,* but I don't believe *it*. But sometimes *it* has no antecedent, as in impersonal statements about weather, time, distance, or events in general, and in many idioms:

> *It's* been three hours since *it* began to rain, and *it's* still five miles to camp.
> *It* isn't pleasant to live in Washington these days.
> Damn *it*, we'll have to play *it* by ear.

Though typically neuter, the antecedent of *it* may be an animal or a small child whose sex is unknown or irrelevant. *It* is also used with reference to collective nouns denoting persons (The faculty must decide for *it*self) and in sentences where individuals are identified (I'm not sure who the tenor was, but *it* could have been Domingo).

The more important uses of *it* stylistically are those in which it fills the position of a subject or object that's fully expressed later in the sentence. In such sentences *it* is called the anticipatory subject or object:

> *It* is *doubtful that he should be given so much freedom.*
> He found *it* painful *living in the same house with a person whose racial attitudes he detested.*
> *It* was *Wordsworth* who called his gun a ''thundering tube.''

The advantages of such constructions are that they offer an alternative to lengthy separation of sentence parts that belong together (He found living in the same house with a person whose racial attitudes he detested painful) and a means of assigning emphasis: ''It was Wordsworth who . . .'' emphasizes *Wordsworth;* ''Wordsworth called his gun a 'thundering tube' '' emphasizes *thundering tube.*

    See **its, it's; it's me; there is, there are.**

ital Italics

In handwritten and typewritten copy, underline words or passages to correspond to the conventions of using italic type.

In writing, words and statements that would be printed in italics are underlined. Though newspapers have generally abandoned italic type, most magazines and books use it, and in academic writing—course papers, articles in learned journals, dissertations, reference books—italics have standardized uses:

1. To indicate titles of books, plays, motion pictures, television series, and other complete works, and to indicate titles of periodicals and newspapers. See **Titles 2.**

2. To mark words considered as words rather than for their meaning: There is a shade of difference between *because* and *for* used as conjunctions.

3. To mark unanglicized words from foreign languages: Good clothes were a *sine qua non.* See **Foreign words in English 2a.**

4. To indicate words that would be stressed if spoken. This device is most appropriate in dialog.

5. To indicate key words, phrases, or sentences in an argument or explanation. Here italics should be used sparingly. See **Emphasis 6.**

its, it's

Its is a possessive pronoun and, like the possessive pronouns *his, her, our, your,* and *their,* has no apostrophe: A car is judged by *its* performance. *It's* is the contraction for "it is" (It's a long road) and "it has" (It's been said before). Like other contractions, *it's* is more appropriate to informal and general than to formal styles.

it's me

The argument over "it's me" illustrates a conflict between theory and practice. The theory—that after a finite form of the verb *be* the nominative, or subjective, case should always be used—is consistently contradicted by the practice of educated speakers. (Except in dialog, "it's me" is a usage question writers rarely have to think about. In fact, most speakers seldom run into it.) We tend to use the nominative form of a pronoun when it's the subject and stands directly before the verb, but we're likely to use the accusative in most other positions, especially when the pronoun comes after the verb—in "object territory," as it's been called. (Compare **who, whom.**) All the major grammars of English regard "it's me" as acceptable. See **be 2.**

-ize

The formation of verbs from non-Greek nouns or adjectives by adding the Greek ending *-ize* (often *-ise* in British usage) has been going on since the sixteenth century. Some readers object to the addition of verbs in *-ize,* either because the new verbs duplicate in meaning verbs that are in common use (*fantasized, fantasied; formularize, formulate*) or because the proliferation adds to the stock of advertising jargon (*customize, personalize*), much of which is virtually meaningless, or of gobbledygook (*concretize, optimize*). See **finalize.**

J

Jargon

1. Sir Arthur Quiller-Couch popularized *jargon* as the name for verbal fuzziness of various kinds—wordiness, a high proportion of abstract words, "big" words, and words that add nothing to the meaning. *Buzzwords* is a recent term for a type of jargon. *Jargon* and *gobbledygook* are sometimes used interchangeably. Russell Baker satirizes current jargon (and current attitudes) in the following passage:

"I could not love thee, dear, so much, lov'd I not honor more," the poet could write. Today he could only say, "I could not have so fulfilling a relationship with thee, dear, had I not an even more highly intensified mental set as regards the absurd and widely discredited concept known as honor."—*New York Times Magazine*

2.   *Jargon* also means shoptalk, or the specialized language of a group—doctors, printers, sociologists, photographers, chicken farmers, and so on. So defined, jargon is appropriate in certain circumstances, as when a physicist writes for fellow physicists, but not in others, as when the physicist writes for a general audience. In many groups and many situations there's a tendency to go beyond the necessary technical jargon and create jargon in the first sense. Examples of the use of language to impress more than to inform include sociologese, psychologese, educationese, journalese, and bureaucratese.

See **Doublespeak, Gobbledygook, Shoptalk.**

job, position

Job is general English for the formal *position:* He got a job at the oil refinery. The word *position* has more dignity, though what it refers to isn't necessarily better paid. Because *position* can sound pompous, many writers use *job* for all levels of employment.

jock

The history of *jock,* now informal for "athlete" of either sex, illustrates a number of processes in the origin of words. *Jock* is the clipped form of *jockstrap,* a supporter for the male genitals worn during strenuous activity. (*Jock* is also a figure of speech in which the part—the "athletic supporter," as it was less vulgarly known—stands for the whole—the athlete.) *Jockstrap* in turn was created by combining *jock,* a slang term for the penis, and *strap.* The use of *jock* first for male athletes and then, by simple extension, for female athletes as well shows what can sometimes happen when the history of a word is not known or is ignored. See **Origin of words 1.**

Journalese

Roy Copperud defined *journalese* as "all that is bad in journalistic writing." (Journalistic writing today includes not only the writing that appears in newspapers and newsmagazines but the writing that's read to us by television and radio news reporters and commentators.) Journalese is journalistic jargon, loaded with clichés, vogue words, buzzwords, hyperboles, gobbledygook, and doublespeak and wholly lacking in character and conviction. It proves that even professional, "grammatical" writing can be awful.

just

The qualifier *just* is redundant in expressions like *just exactly* and *just perfect*. Omit it.

K

kid

The noun *kid* for "child" and the verb *kid* for "tease" are established in general usage. A problem with *kid* as a noun is that it now may mean not only someone past puberty but someone past adolescence (the kids in graduate school). So loosely used, *kid* is informal. In many contexts a more specific term is needed.

kind, sort

The words *kind* and *sort* are involved in three different problems for writers.

1. Agreement. *Kind* and *sort* are singular pronouns with regular plurals. A problem arises only when singular *kind* or *sort* is followed by *of* and a plural noun. Then there's a strong tendency to treat the plural object of *of*, rather than *kind* or *sort*, as the headword of the construction and to use plural demonstratives and verbs: These sort of books are harmless; "Those kind of overhead expenses" (Lewis H. Lapham, *Harper's*). But though the construction is common in speech and there are numerous examples of its use by respected writers, strong objection to it continues. For one kind (or sort), then: *That kind of book is. . . .* For more than one: *Those kinds* of books *are. . . .*

2. *Kind (sort) of a(n).* *Kind of a(n)* and *sort of a(n)* are general idioms: "People just didn't trust that kind of an approach" (Charles Mohr, *Esquire*). Formal style would have "kind of approach."

3. *Kind (sort) of.* As adverbs equivalent to imprecise qualifiers like *rather* and *somewhat* in more formal usage, *kind of* and *sort of* are informal to general: "She was kind of plump" (Claude Brown, *Commentary*); "Everything just sort of limped along" (E. J. Kahn, Jr., *New Yorker*).

know-how

Though *know-how* occurs in every variety of English, for many readers its connotations remain commercial and technical. To speak of the know-how of a great violinist, for example, would be inappropriate.

L

lab

The clipped form of *laboratory* is now common in all but the most formal usage.

lady

The vogue use of *lady* for *woman,* as in popular songs, is out of place in college writing. See **woman, lady, girl.**

last, latest

Both *last* and *latest* are used as superlatives of *late* (his last book; his latest book). But to avoid ambiguity, formal English uses *last* for the final item in a series (His last book was completed only weeks before his death), *latest* for the most recent of a series that may or may not be continued (His latest book shows steady improvement).

latter

The use of *latter* in referring to the last of more than two items is standard, but conservative stylists prefer "the last named." See **former, first—latter, last.**

lay, lie

In standard English *lie (lay, lain)* is intransitive: He let it lie there; She lay down for a nap; The boards have lain there for months. *Lay (laid, laid)* is transitive: You can lay it on the table; They laid the keel; She had laid it away for future reference. In much spoken English *lay* does the work of both verbs; but in most writing they are kept distinct, and in college writing they should always be. The *-ing* forms sometimes give trouble, with *laying* appearing where *lying* is meant: I spent the summer laying around the house.

learn, teach

In nonstandard English *learn* is often used to mean "teach": He learned me how to tie knots. Standard English makes the distinction: He *taught* me how to tie knots; I *learned* how to tie knots from him.

leave, let

Let, not *leave*, is standard English for "permit" or "allow." See **let, leave.**

lend, loan

In referring to material things, *lend* and *lends* are preferred to *loan* and *loans* in formal writing: "those who wished to lend" (George V. Taylor, *American Historical Review*). But the past tense and past participle *loaned* is preferred to *lent* in all varieties: "About $4 billion have been loaned" (Adolf A. Berle, *The American Economic Republic*). In general contexts, *loan* and *loans* are as common as *lend* and *lends* and are entirely acceptable.

In the sense "grant, impart, furnish" or "adapt or accommodate (itself)," *lend* and *lent* are always preferred: "America always lent itself to personification" (Norman Mailer, *Harper's*).

less, fewer

Use *fewer* for things that can be counted, *less* for things that can't be. See **fewer, less.**

let, leave

A common nonstandard idiom is the use of *leave* for "permit" or "allow," meanings that standard English assigns to *let*. Both uses are shown in this sentence by a writer making a transition between nonstandard and standard: "In high school I was cured of the practice of leaving [nonstandard] notebooks go, but I fell into the habit of letting [standard] homework slide."

In standard English the two verbs are interchangeable only with *alone* and the meaning "refrain from disturbing": Leave (*or* Let) me alone; All they asked of their government was to be let (*or* left) alone.

Lexical meaning

In linguistics a distinction is often made between grammatical or structural meaning and lexical meaning. In "Birds were killed," the information that *bird* and *kill* give us is the sort provided by a dictionary or lexicon—hence lexical meaning. The information given by the *-s* of *birds* (plural), *were* (past tense, passive voice), and the *-ed* of *killed* (past participle in this position) is the sort provided by our awareness of the grammar or structure of the language—hence grammatical or structural meaning. When we fully understand the sentence, we have grasped its total meaning.

liable

In formal writing and most general writing, *liable* followed by an infinitive is used to predict only undesirable results: The effects are liable to be disastrous. *Liable*-plus-infinitive to predict desirable results appears most often in informal and casual general contexts: "Walleyes are year-round sport and . . . they're liable to hit any time of the day or night" (Roger Latham, *Field and Stream*). *Likely* and *apt* are not restricted in this way.

lie

The transitive verb *lay* shouldn't be substituted for the intransitive *lie*. You *lie,* not *lay,* down when you're tired. You *lay,* not *laid,* down yesterday. See **lay, lie.**

life-style

One way to avoid overusing *life-style,* a term as vague as it is voguish, is to distinguish between what is truly a distinctive way of life—of attitudes and behavior—and a deviation from the norm in some specific respect. If you write about a person who sleeps all day and goes to work at night, don't refer to his life-style; say that he's on the night shift.

like, as

1. As prepositions. In all varieties of English, *like* is used as a preposition introducing a comparison: The description fits her like a plaster cast; Habit grips a person like an octopus; He took to selling like a bee to clover. *As* is increasingly common as a hypercorrect form: "Hate must run off you as water off the proverbial infield tarpaulin" (Laurence Sheehan, *Atlantic*).

2. As conjunctions. In all varieties of English, *as, as if,* and *as though* are used as conjunctions introducing clauses of comparison: They moved across the floor as skaters glide over a frozen pond; He walked as though he was hurt. *Like* as a conjunction is common in speech and appears frequently in informal and general writing: "Like a typical kid his age might do, Holden does violate some rules of grammar" (James Lundquist, *J. D. Salinger*). But opposition to *like* as a conjunction remains strong, and it should be avoided in most college writing.

3. The way. *The way* provides an escape from the *like-as* thicket for writers who think *like* is crude and *as* is prissy: "Hemingway once told Callaghan, 'Dostoevski writes like Harry Greb fights.' Unfortunately, Callaghan writes the way Hemingway fights" *(Time)*.

likely

"They'll probably be there" can also be expressed as "They'll likely be there" or "They likely will be there," though some formal stylists insist that *likely* in this usage must be preceded by a qualifier like *very* or *rather*. "They are likely to be there" is entirely acceptable but expresses a bit less likelihood.

Linguistics

Linguistics is a broad discipline incorporating several perspectives from which language may be studied systematically. Linguists study the structures of languages and the universal structure of language. They study the histories and the varieties of language. They study how language is acquired and how it is used.

Linguistics differs from other disciplines devoted to the study of language by having at its center a theory of language derived from the study of formal, regular, and recurrent patterns in the structures of human languages. Theories of language differ, and therefore schools of linguistics exist; but all linguists are empiricists, sharing a desire to be as objective as possible and rejecting conclusions not based on consistent theory and verified by significant data.

See **Grammar.**

Linking verbs

When a verb like *be* functions chiefly as a bridge between a subject and another noun or a modifier, it's called a linking, or copulative, verb. A linking verb is followed by single words, phrases, or clauses that function as adjectives or nouns and are traditionally known as predicate adjectives (This bottle was *full*) or as predicate nouns or predicate nominatives (The man was a *carpenter*). Some grammarians prefer to call them complements, or subjective complements.

Many verbs besides *be* are used as linking verbs. A few of them are italicized in the following sentences:

He *became* a doctor.	The ground *sounds* hollow.
The butter *tastes* rancid.	He *appeared* to be healthy.
She *felt* sad.	The dog *acts* old.
His story *seemed* incredible.	The weather *turned* cold.
This *looks* first-rate.	She *grew* moody.

Many verbs are used both with full meaning of their own (The tree *fell* into the water) and as linking verbs (He *fell* silent). Speakers who are not aware that the same verb can function both ways and who have been taught that verbs are modified by adverbs often make the mistake of substituting an adverb for the adjective that should follow a linking verb: "She felt sadly" for "She felt sad." Such hypercorrectness also crops up in writing.

For the most common source of difficulty in using the linking-verb pattern, see **Predicate adjectives.** See also **bad, badly; be 2; Hypercorrectness; it's me; look.**

literally

Literally means "actually, without deviating from the facts," but it's so often used to support metaphors that its literal meaning may be reversed. In statements like the following, *literally* means "figuratively" and *literal* means "figurative":

> All of this is taking place in Florida at a time when the nation is literally awash in oil.—Fred J. Cook, *Nation*

> In this struggle, women's bodies became a literal battleground.—Martin Duberman, *Nation*

> [New York City] is literally hanging by its fingernails.—Walter Cronkite, *CBS News*

Taken literally, such statements create very funny mental pictures.

literate

Literate is used to mean both "capable of reading and writing" and "acquainted with what has been written—educated." See **illiterate.**

loan

In referring to possession, *lend* is more formal than *loan* in the present tense. For the past tense, *loaned* is preferred to *lent* in all varieties of usage. See **lend, loan.**

Loan words

Loan words are words borrowed from other languages. See **Foreign words in English, Origin of words 2b.**

Localisms

A localism is a word or other expression in regular use only in a certain region, like *hoagie, submarine* (or *sub*), *hero, po' boy* for the same sort of sandwich in a roll. Though appropriate in conversation and informal writing, localisms are out of place in general and formal writing except to give a regional flavor. See **Dialects.**

Locution

Locution is a handy term for referring to a word or to a phrase or clause considered as a unit. In the preceding sentence "a handy term" is one locution.

logic Logical thinking

Reconsider the logical relationship that is expressed or implied.

At some time or other everyone has protested, "That doesn't make sense" or "That doesn't follow from what you just said." Everyone, that is, has some notion of the difference between logical and illogical thinking, and when something is said or written that doesn't make sense or fails to show a logical progression, everyone's impulse is to dismiss it.

In a college paper illogical thinking is revealed in irrelevant material, faulty organization, incoherent sentences, and words that blur or skew the meaning of what's being said. More narrowly, it shows up in the faulty relationship between ideas. Often the seeming breakdown in logic is simply the result of careless writing. In taking issue with the statement "The true university is a collection of books," a student wrote, "If I were to agree that a true university is no more than a collection of books, I would graduate well-read but not socially mature." This makes no sense, because simply agreeing or not agreeing with the statement about a true university could not determine the kind of education a particular student would receive at a particular school.

Presumably the student meant, "If a true university is no more than a collection of books, and if this is a true university, then I can expect to be well-read when I graduate but not necessarily socially mature." If he intended to base an *if . . . then* relationship on his agreeing with the original statement, he might say, "If I agreed that a true university is no more than a collection of books, then I would spend all my time in the library."

You can avoid such apparent lapses in logic by carefully reading what you write—seeing what you've *said* rather than what you *meant* to say—and revising your sentences before preparing your final draft.

Much more serious are the kinds of illogical thinking that undercut a whole paper. When you write to express an opinion, defend a point of view, argue for or against something, or persuade or convince your readers, keep these recommendations in mind:

1. Limit your generalizations to what you can support with evidence.

2. Make sure that what you offer as evidence is authoritative and has bearing on the issue.

3. Make sure that you attack the actual issue instead of skirmishing around the edges or wandering off into another conflict.

4. Make sure you omit no links in the chain of reasoning that leads to your conclusion.

In reading over what you've written, take a hard look at your generalizations. Are they sound enough to support your argument? Are they based on fact and justifiable inferences, or are they no more than unexamined assumptions or expressions of prejudice?

When you find yourself saying that A caused B or that B is the result of A, think over your reasons for saying so. Are they convincing? Are there reasons for *not* saying so that you've deliberately omitted? Are your comparisons justifiable and your analogies plausible?

After enjoying the violent language you've used in condemning those who hold an opposing point of view, and after admiring the eloquence with which you've praised those whose side you're supporting, ask yourself whether the faults of the former or the virtues of the latter have anything to do with the issue itself. Unless they have, don't mistake what you've had to say for logical argument.

See **Syllogisms.**

Logic and language

Sometimes an item of usage is objected to as being illogical—for example, "the reason is because." But when the objection to "the reason is because" is elaborated, it's usually that an adverbial clause (*because . . .*) is equated with a noun (*reason*)—a criticism that has to do with grammar rather than logic.

Idiom illustrates particularly well the lack of correspondence between logic and usage. The meanings of many idioms—"hard to come by," "hold your own," "out of order"—are not the sum of the meanings of their separate words. These show, more clearly than the general patterns and rules of English, that language is a human development, the result of millions of speech situations, not a preplanned system. Language isn't illogical; it's simply alogical.

Probably arguments from logic had an influence in establishing the double negative as nonstandard English. In Old and Middle English the more negatives there were, the stronger the negation. But arguments from logic have had few such successes, and the term *logical* applies to language only in its most general, popular sense of "more or less systematic."

See **Double negative, Idiom, reason is because.**

Long variants

Some writers are tempted to add an extra prefix or suffix to a word that already carries the meaning they intend. They write *irregardless,* though *regardless* already means "without regard to," or they write *doubtlessly* for *doubtless.* Some like to use suffixes that add nothing to the meaning, like the *-ation* in *analyzation,* which means no more than *analysis.* Some other long variants that it's wise to avoid are *certificated* for *certified, confliction* for *conflict, emotionality* when only *emotion* is meant, *hotness* for *heat, intermingle* for *mingle, orientate* for *orient, ruination* for *ruin,* and *utilize* when *use* is entirely adequate. See **Diction 2, Gobbledygook, Jargon.**

look

When used as an intransitive verb meaning "use the eyes, gaze," *look* is modified by an adverb: look longingly, look searchingly. As a linking verb, equivalent to *appear, look* is followed by an adjective that modifies the subject: He looks well (*or* healthy *or* tired *or* bad). See **Linking verbs.**

lot, lots

In the senses "much," "many," "a great deal," *a lot (of)* and *lots (of)* have an informal flavor. Both are established in general usage but not in formal:

> He tells Celine to make herself attractive and buys her a lot of new clothes.—Edmund Wilson, *New Yorker*

> There is lots of talk.—*Fortune*

A lot is two words, not one.

lc Lowercase

Use a lowercase (small) letter instead of a capital.

As an alternative or supplement to *lc,* the correction may be indicated by a slant line through the capitals:

```
It was a Great Experience.
```

For the conventional use of capitals, see **Capital letters.**

M

Main clauses

Main clauses (like this one and the next) are independent clauses. They can stand alone as sentences. See **Clauses.**

majority, plurality

Technically a majority in an election is more than half the total number of votes cast, while a plurality is the largest number of votes cast for any one candidate but not more than half the total. Though the distinction is sometimes neglected, it's worth preserving for clarity.

In formal usage *majority* is applied only to groups of at least three things that can be counted. In informal and general usage *majority* is sometimes used also of the larger part of a single thing or mass: "A majority of the LP is taken up with bouncy dance tunes" (Robert Palmer, *New York Times*). *Most* is preferable.

Manuscript form

Your manuscript is not in the proper form. Revise or rewrite as directed.

Instructors usually establish their own specifications for manuscript form at the beginning of the course. Whatever the details, the goal is a clean, legible copy that can be read easily. Use white 8½″ x 11″ paper, leave adequate margins, number the pages, make corrections neatly, and observe your instructor's directions for endorsing the paper. See **Division of words, Typewritten copy.**

massive

Used with abstract nouns, *massive* became a vogue word during the 1960s: massive retaliation, massive resistance, massive inequality, massive unemployment. This usage continues. Applying *massive* only to icebergs would be a step in the right direction.

Mass nouns

Mass nouns name masses that are not counted as separate units: food, money, health, water. See **Nouns 3c.**

may, can

In requesting or granting permission or expressing feasibility, *may* is the formal choice. *Can* expresses ability and is commonly used in place of *may* in general English. See **can, may.**

mng Meaning

? **The word, phrase, or sentence marked does not make sense in this context. Replace it with one that communicates the meaning you intend.**

For a reader to question the meaning of what you've written indicates a serious failure in communication. Ordinarily the problem is not simply the use of one word for another that's reasonably close to it in sound or meaning—*comprehension* for *comprehensibility,* for example. This would be marked *ww* (wrong word): the reader knows the word is wrong because he knows what the right one is. But *mng,* often followed by a question mark, means that the reader can't, or won't, make a guess at what you're trying to say. Rethinking and rewriting are in order. Compare **Ambiguity, Coherence, Wrong word.**

meaningful

Meaningful became a vogue word in the 1960s and still hangs on, particularly among educators (meaningful learning experiences) and young people (meaningful relationships). Before using it, ask yourself whether its omission would suggest that what you're referring to has no meaning—and remind yourself that many readers consider the term excessively vague or pretentious or both.

media, medium(s)

Medium and *media,* the Latin singular and plural forms, were taken directly into English, and formal usage consistently maintains the distinction in number, while recognizing the alternate plural *mediums:* "the moral possibilities of the mediums themselves" (Robert J. Reilly, *American Literature*). But *media,* like many other Latin plurals, has tended to become singular in American usage and is frequently so used in general writing: "with help from an enthusiastic media" (Edwin McDowell, *Wall Street Journal*). Many word watchers find singular *media* (with *medias* sometimes as its plural) highly objectionable.

Metonymy

Metonymy is a figure of speech in which the thing named suggests the thing meant, as in "guns (war) or butter (peace)."

might, could

These two words express a slighter degree of possibility than *may, can:* I might go; They could turn up. See **can, may.**

Misrelated modifiers

The position of a misrelated modifier makes it seem to modify the wrong word in the sentence. See **Dangling modifiers.**

Mixed usage

Indiscriminate, thoughtless mixing of vocabularies—formal with informal, poetic with technical—weakens writing. See **Diction 2.**

Modal auxiliaries

Can, could; may, might; must; ought; shall, should; will, would are called modal auxiliaries. They differ from other verbs in having no *-s* in the third-person singular, no infinitive, no participle, and therefore no compound or phrasal forms. Instead, they themselves always occur as part of verb phrases, complete or elliptical. The generally similar *dare* and *need* are also sometimes treated as modal auxiliaries. See **Elliptical constructions.**

Modifiers

Typically, a modifier limits the meaning of the word, phrase, or clause it modifies and makes it more exact (a *green* apple). In the following illustrations the words in italics modify the words in small capitals: A *cold windy* DAY; He FAILED *miserably;* She was *truly* SUPERB; *Undoubtedly* IT WAS THE CAT WHO STOLE THE BUTTERMILK; *Coming around the corner,* WE met him head on. See **Absolute phrases, Adjectives, Adverbs, Dangling modifiers, Gerunds 1, Infinitives and style, Participles 2, Phrases, Restrictive and nonrestrictive modifiers.**

Money

1. Exact sums of money are usually written in figures: 72¢, $4.98, $168.75, $42,810. Though round sums are likely to be written in words (two hundred dollars, a million dollars), figures may be used for them, too, particularly when several sums are mentioned.

2. In consecutive writing, amounts are usually spelled out when they're used as modifiers: a million-dollar project. Informally, figures are often used: a $2 seat.

3. For amounts in millions and billions, a dollar sign followed by the number followed by the word is most common: $50 billion. Instead of "three and a half million dollars" or "$3,500,000," "$3.5 million" is increasingly used.

4. A sum of money is usually thought of as a single unit: More than $9 million *was* invested in paintings.

Months

In reference matter and informal writing, the names of months with more than four or more than five letters are often abbreviated in dates: Jan. 21, 1982; Dec. 2, 1904; *but* May (June, July) 12, 1904. In formal writing the names of months are not abbreviated. When only the month is given, or only the month and year, abbreviation is rare in any style: He was born in January 1969; Every September she tries again. See **Dates.**

Mood

The mood of a verb, indicated by its form, tells whether the writer or speaker regards what he's saying as a statement of fact or a question concerning fact (indicative mood), as a wish or an expression of possibility or doubt (subjunctive mood), or as a command (imperative mood). See **Commands and requests, Imperative mood, Indicative mood, Subjunctive mood.**

more, most

Preceding the base forms of adjectives and adverbs with *more* and *most* is one way of expressing their comparative and superlative degrees. See **Comparison of adjectives and adverbs 1.**

most, almost

In speech *almost* is often reduced to *most:* A drop in prices would suit most anybody. *Most,* used thus, occasionally appears in factual prose for general audiences, but in college writing, if you can substitute *almost* for *most* in a sentence (almost always, almost everywhere), *almost* is normally the word to use.

Ms.

Ms. is a substitute for both *Miss* and *Mrs.* Its use is favored by those who believe that a woman shouldn't be labeled married or unmarried any more than a man is. If a first name is used after *Ms.* for a married woman, the name is hers, of course, not her husband's: Mrs. John Doe becomes Ms. Jane Doe.

In writing for college courses a choice between *Ms.* and *Miss* or *Mrs.* is most often necessary when the topic is a biographical or critical essay about a woman or her work—for example, a review of the poetry of Sylvia Plath. Sylvia Plath can be called Ms. Plath or Miss Plath. (As a poet, she remained Sylvia Plath during her marriage.) She can also be called Sylvia Plath or simply Plath. The latter usage is now common in published writing about women.

must

In general English (but not in formal) *must* is accepted as a noun meaning "necessity"—"It has never been a must" (Henry Brandon, *Saturday Review*)—and an adjective modifier meaning "essential"—"This book is a must assignment for reporters" (Robert O. Blanchard, *Columbia Journalism Review*).

myself

Myself is a reflexive or an intensive pronoun referring back to *I:* I cut myself (reflexive); I saw the whole thing myself (intensive). In addition, *myself* is often used where *I* or *me* would be expected:

> The writing was then done by myself, taking perhaps fifteen days.—Hollis Alpert, *Saturday Review*

> Then the two of us, President Johnson and myself, walked out.—Malcolm Kilduff, *Columbia Journalism Review*

For the *-self* form, many stylists would substitute the regular nominative or accusative (*me* in the first example, *I* in the second). See **himself, herself; Pronouns 2; self.**

naked, nude

Naked and *nude* mean the same thing, but *nude* has classier connotations. It's "nude" in art. It's "naked" in the shower.

namely

Introductory *namely* is rarely needed in general writing: The topic was a particularly unpleasant one—[namely,] rising prices. See **that is.**

nauseous, nauseated

Nauseated traditionally means "sickened, disgusted" (I felt nauseated at the sight), and *nauseous* traditionally means "causing sickness or disgust" (The smell was nauseous). But the use of "feeling nauseous" and "getting nauseous" has become so common that dictionaries now record "nauseated" as a second meaning of *nauseous.* Those who grew up observing the distinction find this usage ambiguous. (Was he sick, or was he sickening?)

Negatives and style

When you use both negative and positive words in the same sentence, be sure the combination says clearly what you intend. "The vocational counseling office will try to increase its clients' inability to support themselves" should be rephrased either as "to increase their ability" or as "to remedy their inability."

Poor sentences often result from starting negatively what might better be put positively:

> This mob violence does not reflect the sentiment of an overwhelming majority of the students.

> **Better:** This mob violence reflects the sentiments of only a small minority of the students.

Some writers are fond of tricky negative constructions, including *litotes,* a variety of understatement in which an affirmative is expressed by the negative of its contrary: She was not unfond of him; He was not displeased. Litotes can be effective, but when overused it makes the writer sound coy, evasive, or just tiresome. See **Double negative.**

Negro

Since the 1960s *Negro* has been replaced by *black* in most general usage. See **black.**

neither

As a pronoun, *neither* is ordinarily construed as singular and followed by a singular verb. When the verb is separated from *neither* by a prepositional phrase with a plural object, a plural verb is frequently used in informal writing and sometimes in general writing: "Marx and Trotsky, neither of whom were notably gentle or vegetarian" (Dwight Macdonald, *Esquire*). But here, too, grammatical convention calls for a singular verb.

As an adjective, *neither* modifies a singular noun (neither side), and a pronoun referring to the noun should be singular (Neither side achieved *its* goal).

nice

As a word indicating mild approval (We had a nice time), *nice* is too imprecise for college writing. In formal prose *nice* is usually restricted to meanings like "subtle" or "discriminating": Kirk raises a nice point in his article on Camus.

nobody, no one

The pronouns *nobody* and *no one* take singular verbs, and, strictly speaking, a pronoun referring to either of them should be singular: No one lowered his voice. But sometimes meaning demands a plural pronoun: "No one sings; they simply listen reverently" (Ray Jenkins, *New York Times Magazine*). In formal writing the sentence might be recast: No one sings; everyone simply listens reverently.

Nominalization

Change the abstract nominalization into a concrete verb.

For most purposes the best writing is direct writing—writing that avoids three words where two will do, writing that represents an action in a verb and the agent of that action as its subject. The difference between indirect and direct writing is illustrated in these two sentences:

It seems to be the case that certain individuals in attendance at this institution of higher education are in a state of anger over recent announcements on the part of the dean in regard to a necessity for greater restrictions where the consumption of alcoholic beverages is concerned.

Some students here are angry because the dean announced that he was tightening the rules about drinking on campus.

Probably the most common source of indirect writing is the abstract nominalization, a noun that—according to transformational theory—has been derived from a full subject + verb in the deep structure of a sentence:

Tom *paid* the money ———————→ Tom's *payment* of the money
The monks *reject* wealth ———————→ The monks' *rejection* of wealth
The students *are responsible* ———————→ The students' *responsibility*

The direct subject-verb-object or subject-*be*-adjective construction has been made indirect and accordingly less lively and forceful. If this kind of construction occurs often in your writing—say once every seven or eight words—readers are likely to find your style heavy, abstract, pretentious, and possibly dishonest.

To improve such a style, first look for nouns made out of verbs:

An investigation is being made of the causes for the decline in wheat production.

When you find them (*investigation, causes, decline, production*), ask whether the crucial action is in the main verb or in one of these abstract nouns. If it's in a noun (*investigation*), change the noun to a verb *(are investigating)*, find a subject for it (*they*, referring to a specific antecedent? *scientists? agricultural chemists?*), and rewrite the sentence around the new subject-verb:

An investigation is being made of the causes for the decline in wheat production.

Agricultural chemists are investigating what has caused wheat production to decline.

Agricultural chemists are investigating why farmers are producing less wheat.

Or, if no concise subject can be stated, make a straight passive: The decline in wheat production is being investigated.

See **Abstract language, Deep structure, Passive voice 2, Subjects, Verbs 3.**

Nominals

A word, phrase, or clause that serves as subject of a verb, as complement of a linking verb, as object of a verb or a preposition, or as an appositive is functioning as a noun and can be called a *nominal*.

Nominative case

A noun or pronoun that is subject of a verb, complement of a linking verb, or an appositive to either is said to be in the nominative (or subjective) case. The form of the nominative singular is the common form of the noun, the form to which the endings for the possessive and the plural are typically added. The pronouns with distinctive nominative forms are the personals—*I, he, she, it, we, you, they*—and the relative *who*. (*You* is both nominative and accusative.) Though these are the usual forms for the nominative functions, see **it's me; who, whom.** See also **Case 1, Subjects.**

none

The use of *none* with a plural verb is still sometimes condemned, usually on the grounds that *none* means "no one" or "not one" and so must be singular. Usage is divided, but when the reference is to countables, *none* has long been used as a plural in the most reputable writing:

> Almost none [of the letters] are either thoughtful in their approach or deliberative in their style.—Louis J. Halle, *New Republic*

> None have been older than this sacramental alliance.—Sidney Hook, *New York Times Book Review*

> None of these documents afford any solid support for those historians who have viewed Pike as a tool or accomplice in the Wilkinson-Burr schemes.—Harvey L. Carter, *American Historical Review*

Nonrestrictive modifiers

A nonrestrictive modifier does not provide essential identification of the word modified and should therefore be set off by commas. See **Restrictive and nonrestrictive modifiers.**

ns Nonstandard English

Change the nonstandard word, form, or idiom to one in standard use.

"Nobody ain't got nothing," "theirself," "he do," "they knowed"—

these are examples of nonstandard English. Among the articles that treat nonstandard words or forms are **Adverbs and style; Double negative; lay, lie; learn, teach; Principal parts of verbs.** See also **Dialects 2, Standard English.**

no place

Although *anyplace, everyplace,* and *someplace* for "anywhere," "everywhere," and "somewhere" have become common in general writing, *no place* for "nowhere" is still mainly informal: An hour of arguing got us no place. It's sometimes spelled as one word.

nor

By itself, *nor* is an emphatic negative conjunction, most commonly used at the beginning of a sentence in the sense "and . . . not": Nor was Paris (And Paris was not) the only place he visited. Before the last member of a negative series, *nor* gives an added distinctness and emphasis: "I did not see him or hear him" is less emphatic than "I did not see him nor hear him."

As a correlative conjunction, *nor* is paired with *neither.* See **Correlative conjunctions.**

not about to

Not about to is not the simple negative of *about to* but an idiom that stresses the remoteness of the suggested possibility: I'm not about to go along with their weird schemes. It occurs mainly in speech but also in writing. If used with any frequency, it quickly becomes tiresome.

not all that . . . , not too . . .

Not all that . . . is heard frequently in conversations and in weather forecasts (Tomorrow will be better but not all that sunny) and is seen increasingly in print. Sometimes *much* completes the phrase: I didn't like the movie all that much. In some cases an antecedent of a sort is provided for *that,* as in "She thought she might graduate with honors, but her grades weren't all that high"—that is, weren't high enough to qualify for honors. More often, as in this opening of a book review, there's no antecedent: "Usually, the tone of a popular novel is not all that important" *(New Yorker).*

For most college writing, *not all that . . .* is unsatisfactory if only because it invites the question "all what?"

Somewhat different is the *not too . . .* we use in speaking of ourselves and others. "I'm not feeling too good" means "I'm feeling rather poorly." "Their grades aren't too high" probably means "Their grades are mediocre.'' This usage, whether intended as understatement or as irony, is well established idiom and, while hardly precise, would be appropriate in informal writing and in a good deal of general writing, as long as the context made the meaning sufficiently clear.

not hardly, not scarcely

When *hardly* and *scarcely* mean "almost not," an additional *not* is redundant. See **Double negative 2.**

Noun clauses

A noun clause is a dependent clause that fills a nominal position: it functions as a noun. Many noun clauses are introduced by *that* or *whether*, some by *what, who, whoever, whatever, why, when,* and other interrogatives.

> *Subject: That anyone could raise his grades by studying* had never occurred to him. *Whether or not she should go* bothered her for days. *Why sociology has been growing so rapidly* is a complicated question. (A noun clause as subject often suggests a formal style.)
> *Object of a verb:* He knew [*that*] *it would never happen again.* (When the noun clause is object of the verb, introductory *that* is often omitted in general English.)
> *Complement:* His favorites were *whoever flattered him.*
> *Object of a preposition:* The cost depends on *where we spend the night.*
> *Appositive:* The doctrine *that we must avoid entangling alliances* was first stated by Washington.

See **Relative clauses.**

Nouns

Nouns are best identified by their forms and by the positions they fill in sentences.

1. Forms.   English nouns may be inflected by number and case. Many have a plural ending in *-s* or *-es: hats, kindnesses, lecturers.* These and other forms of the plural are discussed in **Plurals of nouns.**

The ending of the possessive singular is written with an apostrophe and an *s: boy's, manufacturer's.* The possessive plural adds an apostrophe to the regular spelling *(boys', manufacturers')* and apostrophe-*s* to plurals not ending in *-s (men's, sheep's).* See **Possessive case.**

Some common distinctive endings make nouns from other parts of speech. They include *-er* (buyer), *-or* (advisor), *-ness* (darkness), *-th* (warmth), *-tion* (inflation).

Some nouns in English have different forms for masculine and feminine: *actor-actress, confidant-confidante, executor-executrix.* See **Gender, Sexist language.**

Nouns may be single words or compound words written solid, as two words, or hyphenated: *bathroom, bookcase, stickup, hub cap, go-getter.* See **Group words, Hyphen.**

2.   Position and function.   *Dog* and *day* are nouns by their forms: they occur with plural and possessive inflections (the dog's leash, two days' work). But since they can occur in positions normally filled by adjectives (*dog* days) and adverbs (He works *days*), they can be called, in context only, adjectivals and adverbials. Thus if we call them nouns, we define them by formal characteristics; if adjectivals or adverbials, by syntactic function. If they also function as nouns syntactically, as in "The *dog* is man's best friend" or "*Day* will come eventually," then they are nouns in nominal function. See **Nominals.**

Here are examples of the chief uses of noun phrases and therefore of nouns:

> **Subject of a verb:** *A high wind from the east* blew for three days.
> **Object of a verb:** The wind damaged *the trees, which were loaded with ice.*
> **Object of a preposition:** In *the night,* on *a frozen pond,* fishing is no sport for *a feeble spirit.*
> **Complement:** He has become *president of the firm.*
> **Attributive:** *The young woman's* partner had the grace of a *baby* hippo.
> **Apposition:** The first settler, *Thomas Sanborn,* came in 1780.
> **Modifier of a verb:** He arrived *two months ago.*

3.   Classes of nouns.   In the traditional grouping of nouns that follows, many nouns clearly fall into more than one group:
a.   Proper nouns, names of particular people and places, written with capitals and usually without *the* or *a:* Anne, Dale A. Robb, London, Georgia, France, the Bay of Naples. All other nouns are called common.
b.   Concrete nouns, names of things that can be perceived by the senses: *leaf, leaves, road, trousers, intellectuals.* Concrete nouns are opposed to abstract nouns—names of qualities, actions, types, ideals, and so on: *goodness, thievery, beauty, heroism.*
c.   Mass nouns, names of masses that can be divided but not numbered as aggregates of separate units: *dirt, oxygen, wealth.* They're used with *the* (but not *a* or *an*) or without an article in the singular, and ordinarily they have no plural. Mass nouns are opposed to count nouns, which name what can be counted as separate units. Count nouns are used with both *a(n)* and *the* (but not without an article in the singular), and they have plurals: *a boy, the stick, horses.* Some words, especially abstract nouns, can be either mass or count nouns:

| Wood is used in building. | Beauty is only skin-deep. |
| Mahogany is a valuable wood. | That boat is a beauty. |

d. Collective nouns, names of groups of things regarded as units: *fleet, army, committee, trio*. See **Collective nouns.**

nowhere near

Though in general use, *nowhere near* has an informal tone: It was a good score but nowhere near as high as we'd hoped for. Formal usage would substitute "not nearly as (*or* so) high as."

Number

Number in English grammar is the singular and plural aspect of nouns and pronouns and verbs. Number in nouns is most important, since it controls the number of verbs and pronouns. In verbs, number is indicated only in the present tense (she sings, they sing) except in the pair *was–were*. See **Plurals of nouns, Reference of pronouns, Subjects.**

number

Number, a collective noun, takes a singular verb when the group as a group is meant and a plural verb when the individual units are the writer's concern. Ordinarily "a number of" takes the plural (A number of tickets have been sold), and "the number of" takes the singular (The number of tickets left unsold is discouraging).

Numbers

1. Figures. Figures are conventionally used in the following:
a. Dates (June 29, 1918), except in formal social correspondence and some ceremonial contexts. See **Dates.**
b. Hours with *a.m.* or *p.m.*: 5 p.m. (*but* five o'clock).
c. Street addresses and highway numbers: 2841 Washington Avenue, Route 99.
d. Pages and other references: p. 761; Act III, scene iv, line 28 (III.iv.28) *or* act 3, scene 4, line 28 (3.4.28).
e. Exact sums of money: $4.98, 75¢.
f. Measures expressed in the conventional abbreviations: 15 cc., 3 km, 6″, 10 lbs., 32°F.

The plural of a figure is formed by adding either *-s* or, somewhat more formally, apostrophe-*s:* six 5s *or* six 5's; the 1970s *or* the 1970's. For the possessive, the apostrophe is not usual with figures: They imported $12,000 (*not* $12,000') worth of equipment.

Except in dates, street numbers, ZIP codes, telephone numbers, and a few other regular series, a comma is used to separate thousands, millions, etc., though it may be omitted in four-digit numbers: 2,736 (*or* 2736) bushels; $4,682,981.

2. Figures or words.   Words are conventionally used for round numbers and indefinite numbers: ten million, hundreds, a dozen, a score. Words are also customary for numbers that begin sentences—"Nineteen-eighteen did not usher in the millennium" (Henry Steele Commager, *Saturday Review*)—though the use of figures for a year in that position is not rare. Ordinal numbers like *first, second,* and *third* are normally written out, but larger ones are given in figures: the 142nd Airborne.

As a rule, newspapers use figures for numbers over ten, words for smaller numbers. Magazine and book styles (most general writing) ordinarily use figures only for numbers over one hundred that can't be written in two words: 199 *but* two hundred.

This passage illustrates a typical book style in handling numbers:

> Stage coaches reached new top speeds as their horses galloped over the improved roads. It had taken four and a half days to travel the 160 miles from London to Manchester in 1754; thirty-four years later the journey had been shortened to twenty-eight hours.—T. Walter Wallbank et al., *Civilization Past and Present*

Words and figures shouldn't be mixed in a series of numbers applying to the same units. If one of the numbers is conventionally written in figures, use figures for all: from 9 (*not* nine) to 125 days. But large numbers are increasingly written in a combination of figures and words: "$3 billion" can be grasped more quickly than "$3,000,000,000."

Numbers in two words between twenty-one and ninety-nine are usually hyphenated, though the practice is declining: forty-two *or* forty two. A hyphen is used between figures to indicate a range: The prediction was based on 40–50 personal interviews and 200–300 phone calls. *To* should be used instead if the numbers are preceded by *from* or *between:* from 40 to 50 (*not* from 40–50).

3. Arabic and Roman numerals.   Arabic numerals (1, 2, 146) are used in almost all places where numbers are not expressed in words. Roman numerals, either lowercase (i, ii, cxlvi) or capitals (I, II, CXLVI), are occasionally used to number units in a rather short series, as in outlines, chapters of books, and acts of plays, though less often now than formerly. Traditionally, Roman numerals are used for the preliminary pages in a book.

See **Fractions, Hyphen 4, Money.**

O

Objective case

The object forms of pronouns are said to be in the objective, or accusative, case. See **Accusative case.**

Objects

1. Direct objects. In the simplest kind of sentence, the direct object is a noun phrase that follows a transitive verb: Grammar puzzles *normal people;* Alice saw *the white rabbit;* The man was building *a fence.* In more complicated sentences a variety of elements can stand as direct objects: Everybody enjoys *eating steak;* Somebody said *that porpoises are smart.* The objects don't always follow their verbs: *What she meant* I'll never know. And, of course, pronouns can replace noun phrases as objects: John met *them* earlier.

Traditionally, direct objects are said to name what is affected or effected by the actions of their verbs, though this description doesn't apply in a sentence like "He received an injury in the crash" or "They experienced many humiliations."

2. Indirect objects. Indirect objects name the person or thing to which something is given, said, or shown—the person or thing affected, indirectly, by the verbal action: He gave *the church* a memorial window; She showed *him* the snapshot. Like direct objects, indirect objects are noun phrases or their equivalents. They follow a special set of transitive verbs, precede direct objects, and are synonymous, in corresponding sentences, with prepositional phrases introduced by *to* or *for:* He gave a memorial window *to the church.*

3. Objects of prepositions. The noun phrase, or equivalent, that follows a preposition is its object. The preposition indicates what relationship it has to some other element in the sentence (here, "some other element in the sentence" is the object of *to,* and "the sentence" is the object of *in*). When a relative or interrogative pronoun is the object, it may precede the preposition: *What* are you talking *about?*

Obscenity

Though the vulgar terms for the sexual and excretory body parts and functions—the so-called four-letter words—are used much more freely in print, as well as in speech, than they were fifteen years ago, in most sentences they serve either as mere fillers or as expressions of generalized emotion—

most often disgust. In either case, they don't belong in college writing. See **Profanity.**

of course

Of course should be used sparingly and fairly. It should not be used as a substitute for evidence: Of course, we all know the administration is corrupt. Nor should it be used to suggest that, for the writer, the esoteric is the everyday:

> I can name my favorite restaurant as glibly as I can name my favorite wife, country, religion, and journal of opinion. It is (I should like to say "of course," but Paone's is not widely known) Nicola Paone. . . .—William F. Buckley, Jr., *Saturday Review*

off of

The double prepositions *inside of, outside of, off of* are in general use in writing, but many formal stylists reject the *of,* particularly with *off.*

OK, O.K., okay

OK or *O.K.* or *okay* is informal and general English for "approval" (Harris gave my topic his OK), for "all right, correct" (When I checked the grounds at midnight, everything seemed to be OK), and for "endorse, approve" (If you'll OK my time sheet, I can get paid). As a verb the forms are *OK, OK'ed* or *OK'd, OK'ing* and *okay, okayed, okaying.*

one

1. The use of the impersonal *one,* referring to people in general or to an average or typical person, is formal in tone, especially if it's repeated: "the victories and defeats of one's children, the passing of elders, one's own and one's mate's" (Benjamin DeMott, *Atlantic*); One can't be too careful, can one? Because a series of *one's* can seem pretentious, many writers refer back to *one* with forms of *he:* "One can determine his own life" (J. A. Ward, *Journal of English*). But some readers would regard *his* in this context as offensively sexist. See **Sexist language.**

A shift from *one* to impersonal *they* should be avoided in writing, and while a shift from *one* to impersonal *you* isn't rare, it would be inappropriate in formal contexts and disapproved by many readers. The *you . . . you* pattern is most common in general English. See **they, you.**

2. *One* is often used to avoid repeating a noun in the second of two compound elements: Fred took the new copy, and I took the old one. The plural *ones* is also used this way, and logically enough, since *one* is not only a number but an indefinite pronoun: She had a yellow poncho and two red ones. But *one* as a noun substitute is often deadwood, taking emphasis away from the adjective that carries the real meaning: The plan was certainly [an] original [one].

one another

The reciprocal pronoun *one another* is used to refer to two as well as to more than two. See **each other, one another; Pronouns 3.**

one of those who

In formal English the clause following *one of those who* and similar locutions is usually plural because the relative pronoun refers to a plural antecedent:

He is one of those people who believe in the perfectibility of man. (*Who* refers to *people.*)

That's one of the books that make you change your ideas. (*That* refers to *books.*)

But because there's a strong tendency to regard *one* as the antecedent, a singular verb is common:

Leslie Fiedler is one of those literary personalities who has the effect of polarizing his readers.—Peter Michelson, *New Republic*

. . . one of those crucial questions that comes up again and again.—David Garnett, *American Scholar*

The more formal your context, the more necessary a plural verb.

only

According to the conventions of formal English, a single-word modifier should stand immediately before the element it modifies: I need only six more to have a full hundred. But usage often favors placing *only* before the verb: I only need six more to have a full hundred. The meaning is equally clear, and placing *only* with the verb is an established English idiom.

Even so, precise placement of *only* may be more satisfying to both writer and reader: "In this bicentennial year, let us only praise [*better:* let us praise only] famous men" (Gore Vidal, *New York Review of Books*). And as long as it isn't insisted on where it sounds stilted and unnatural, it can at least prevent silly statements like "He only had a face that [*better:* He had a face that only] a mother could love."

In this respect *even, ever, nearly, just, exactly,* and other such limiting adverbs are similar to *only.* They can be placed so that they spoil the emphasis: I'm tolerant about such things, but his conduct even surprises me [*better:* surprises even me].

Onomatopoeia

By their pronunciations some words suggest particular sounds: *buzz, bang, clank, swish, splash, whir, pop, clatter.* Such imitative words are well established in the English vocabulary. Using sounds that match the sense of a passage in order to intensify its meaning is a stylistic device known as onomatopoeia. Ordinarily the writer works with existing words, sometimes adapting them in the process: "The wire is cut into bullet sizes, the slippery bullets slide from the chopping block on a gangway of grease, they are slithering, skiddering, and slippering into one another" (John Sack, *Esquire*). Onomatopoeia may also inspire outright imitation of sound, as in Tom Wolfe's description of stunting motorcycles: "thraaagggh." Striving for words like *thraaagggh* can produce embarrassing results unless the writer's tongue is visibly in his cheek. See **Alliteration, Assonance.**

on to, onto

When *on* is an adverb and *to* a preposition in a separate phrase, they should be written as two words: The rest of us drove on to the city. The test is that *city* can't be the object of *on*. Used as a preposition, they're written solid: The team trotted onto the floor; The windows looked out onto the park. Both *floor* and *park* are objects of the compound *onto*.

on the part of

On the part of is often wordy for "by," "among," "for," and the like: The new law resulted in less wild driving on the part of (by) young people; There has been a growing awareness of political change on the part of (among) faculty members.

or

According to conventional rules, two subjects joined by the coordinating conjunction *or* take a singular verb if each is singular, a plural verb if both are plural or if the one nearer the verb is plural:

Cod-liver oil or halibut oil is often prescribed.

Cod-liver oil or cod-liver oil capsules are often prescribed.

Cod-liver oil capsules or cod-liver oil is often prescribed.

Sometimes writers use a plural verb after singular subjects joined by *or,* suggesting "either and perhaps both" rather than "not both but one or the other": Is there evidence that smoking pot or drinking beer are affecting grades? The lack of agreement would be condemned by most formal stylists. See **Correlative conjunctions.**

oral, verbal

Literally, *verbal* means "pertaining to words" and *oral* means "pertaining to the mouth." Insisting on this distinction, some writers maintain that *oral* is the one true opposite of *written.* But *verbal* is also used in the sense "unwritten" in all varieties of English: "Though written contracts were fairly often produced, a large proportion of the agreements seem to have been verbal" (Robert Sabatino Lopez, *Speculum*).

org Organization

Improve the organization of your essay by arranging the parts in an orderly sequence, or by making the movement clear through the use of appropriate signals and transitions, or both.

Every paper should have a structure that can be defined and defended. The main cause of poor organization is failure to get clear in your own mind the natural or logical divisions of your subject and the right relation of the parts of your discourse. In writing a paper, arrange the parts in an order that makes sense in terms of your purpose, and as you develop each part, take into account its place and importance in the whole scheme.

A poorly organized paper lacks direction—a logical movement from beginning to end. Or it lacks shape—proportions that do justice to the relative significance of ideas. Or it lacks unity, with irrelevant material diverting attention from the main thread of the discussion. The best way to pinpoint such structural weaknesses is to outline what you've written, reducing it to a skeleton of key statements. Then set about reorganizing and rewriting.

If rereading your paper and studying your outline leave you convinced that the organization is basically sound, examine the ways you've introduced topics and linked paragraph sequences. Even though you can justify the order of the parts of the paper, you may find you've neglected to give the reader guidance in seeing the relationships. If this is so, relatively simple repair work—improving connections and supplying transitions—should give the paper the direction, shape, and unity it *seems* to lack. Here the remedy is not drastic reworking of the entire structure but adding or rewriting sentences, particularly those at the structural joints that connect main blocks of material.

See **Coherence, Outline form, Paragraph indention, Transition, Unity.**

Originality

Original is applied to writing in two different senses. Content is original when it's gathered by the writer from his experience, from his observation of people, events, or places, or from documents like letters and newspapers. Most college papers should contain some original material. Merely rewriting a magazine article isn't a worthwhile exercise in composition. Putting together ideas taken from several such secondary sources has some value, since it requires selection and comparison. But the most useful work for improving your writing is composing papers in which a good deal of the content is original. The writing is more fun and the gain is much greater than in simply rearranging and restating what others have written. See **Plagiarism.**

Originality in expression, in style, is a different matter. The English language has been used a long time, and absolutely new words and phrases are rare. Trying too hard for originality will produce strained writing or "fine" writing, uncomfortable for writer and reader alike. Instead of trying to sound different, concentrate on telling the truth as you know it, and then, in revising what you've written, get rid of as many clichés as you can. The result should be straightforward, readable writing that carries some suggestion of your personality. When a style that deserves the label *original* appears, it's usually the by-product of an active and independent mind, not the result of a deliberate search for novelty. See **Figures of speech.**

Origin of words

1.   The study of the sources of words.   Every word has a history. Some words, like *chauffeur, mores, television, parapsychology,* are relatively new in English. Some, like *home, candle, go, kitchen,* have been in the language for centuries. Others have been around for some time but have acquired new meanings, like *satellite* (from a Latin word for "attendant," a term in astronomy which now probably means for most people either a dependent nation or a man-made object that orbits the earth, moon, or other celestial body). Etymology, the study of word origins, traces the changes of forms and combinations of word elements (as in *dis/service, wild/ness, bath/room, room/mate*) and follows the word or its component parts back to Old English, or to the foreign language from which it came into English, and so on to the earliest discoverable forms. Of some words, like *dude, stooge, rumpus,* earlier forms are unknown. Of others, like *blizzard,* the sources are debated. But the efforts of generations of scholars have uncovered fairly full histories for most words. These are given briefly in most dictionaries and more fully in the *Oxford English Dictionary* and in special works.

Words have arrived and are still arriving in English through two general processes—the making of new words, by either creating or borrowing them, and the compounding or clipping of words and parts of words that are already in the language. Then the usefulness of this new stock of words is increased as the words undergo changes in form.

2.   New words.

a.   Creation of words. Coinage, or outright creation, is rare. Even *gas,* first used by Van Helmont (1578–1644), a Belgian scientist, probably had the Greek *chaos* as well as a Dutch or Flemish word behind it. *Kodak* is a coinage, as are a good many other trade names, some familiar from advertising. Informal words like *dud* and *burble* were also creations, good-sounding words that someone made up. F. Gelett Burgess invented *blurb,* defining it as "self-praise; to make a noise like a publisher." Imitative words like *buzz, honk, swish, whiz* are attempts to translate the sounds of nature into the sounds of language. Various exclamations of surprise, pain, scorn, may have started as emotional noises—*ow, ouch, fie, phooey*—and later became regular words. Most made-up words don't stick.

b.   Borrowed words. English has always borrowed words freely, from Latin, German, and French and from other languages that English-speaking people have come in contact with. Words of quite un-English form have been assimilated: *khaki* (Hindi), *tycoon* (Japanese), *ski* (Norwegian), *hors d'oeuvres* (French), *borscht* (Russian). The various words for *porch,* itself Norman French but the oldest and most English-seeming of the group, come from various languages: *piazza* (Italian), *stoop* (Dutch), *veranda* (Hindi).

Borrowing is still going on. Some words come into formal English and remain formal words: *intelligentsia, bourgeois, chef d'oeuvre, objet d'art, Zeitgeist,* and many others with political, philosophical, scientific, or literary connotations. *Sphygmograph* and many other scientific words are recent compoundings of Latin and especially of Greek words which are not otherwise in English usage, so they may be regarded as borrowings as well as compounds. Others come in as general words, especially when large numbers of people go abroad, as during a war *(camouflage, blitzkrieg)* or when a foreign invention becomes suddenly popular, as in *chauffeur, garage, chassis* of the automobile vocabulary. Some words brought by immigrants have stuck: *sauerkraut, pronto, pizza, kosher, goulash, zombie.*

Many borrowed words are dropped before they gain any general currency. The useful words are more or less adapted to English spelling and pronunciation and become true English words. See **Foreign words in English 2.**

3.   Changes in form of words.

a.   Word composition. Most new words are made by putting together two or more elements to create a different meaning or function. The elements may be a prefix placed before the root word *(mis-related)*, or a suffix added *(foolish-ness)*, or a combining element like *mono- (mono-syllable, mono-rail)*, or two independent words built together *(book-case, basket-ball, gentle-man, space-walk)*. Group words like *high school, out of town,* though not written as single words, could be included as a type of word composition.

At first a compound has no more than the meaning to be expected from its elements: *unable = not able.* But often it will develop an independent sense that can hardly be guessed at from the meanings of its elements: *cupboard, loudspeaker, meltdown.*

b.   Blends. Informal English has a number of words that show the liberties users of language have always taken with their words and always will take. Some of their experiments have been added to the main English vocabulary.

One common type is blends, or portmanteau words, made by telescoping two words into one, often making a letter or syllable do double duty. *Squish* is probably a blend of *squirt* and *swish; electrocute,* of *electro-* and *execute; smog,* of *smoke* and *fog.* Blends are common in the names of many firms and products. Other examples include *motel, paratroops,* and a good many folksy efforts like *absogoshdarnlutely.*

c.   Clipped words. One of the commonest types of word change is clipping—dropping one or more syllables to make a briefer form: *ad* from *advertisement, bus* from *omnibus, taxi* from *taxicab* (earlier, from *taximeter cabriolet*), *limo* from *limousine, quote* from *quotation, hifi* from *high fidelity* (a blend of clips), *stereo* from *stereophonic, auto, movie, plane, phone,* and so on. Shoptalk has many clips, like *mike* for *microphone* or *micrometer.* The speech of any closely related group is full of clips; campus vocabulary shows a full line: *econ, home ec, phys ed, grad, alum, dorm, ad building, lab, exam, gym, prof, premed,* and dozens more.

d.   Back formations. *Back formation* refers to creating a new word from an older word on the assumption that the latter was derived from the former. Thus *orate* was formed by treating *oration* as if its *-tion* was a suffix that had been added to *orate* in the first place. The new word usually serves as a different part of speech, like *baby-sit* from *baby-sitter, opt* from *option, peddle* from *peddler, typewrite* from *typewriter.* Some back formations are long established *(beg, diagnose, browse)*; some are still avoided by conservative writers *(emote, enthuse, sculpt)*; some are mostly for fun *(buttle, revolute)*.

e.   Common nouns from proper names. Some words have come into general use because of an association with a person or place: *boycott,* from the name of an Irish land agent, Captain Boycott, who was so treated; *macadam,* from the inventor of the road surface, John L. MacAdam; *sandwich,* from the Earl of Sandwich; *jersey,* from the island of Jersey; *pasteurize,* from Louis Pasteur, who developed the process. In many cases the original proper noun has been lost in the common noun: the *jean* in *blue jeans* originally referred to Genoa, the *-nim* of *denim* to the French city of Nîmes.

f. Playful formations. Blends and back formations are likely to have a playful note, and so do other word shifts that can't be classified. Some of these have been quite generally used: *dingus, doodad, beanery, jalopy.*

other

In comparing things of the same class, add *other* to *any:* That movie scared me more than any *other* I've seen. See **any 1.**

outl Outline form

Revise the form of your outline to observe the conventions given below.

1. The title. The title of the paper should stand three spaces above the outline. The heads should carry their full meaning and not refer back to the title by pronouns. See **Titles 1.**

2. Thesis statement. An optional practice, but a good one, is to put a sentence stating the subject and scope of the whole paper between title and first main head.

3. Numbering systems. The most widely used numbering alternates letters and figures, as shown in the example in **7.** Avoid complicated or confusing schemes of numbering.

4. Indention. Write the main heads flush with the left margin, and indent subheads two or three spaces from the left—enough to place them clearly in a different column.

5. Punctuation and capitalization. Don't use punctuation at the ends of lines in a topic outline, but in a sentence outline punctuate each sentence as you would in ordinary writing. Capitalize only the first word of a head and proper names; an outline head is not a title.

6. Heads.
a. Heads with meaning. Each head should be understandable by itself, especially if the outline is to be shown to someone for criticism or is to be submitted with the paper. The following would do as a scratch outline but wouldn't be satisfactory for other purposes:

My Vocation

- I. The work I am interested in
- II. Why I prefer this type of work
- III. What my responsibilities would be
- IV. The chances for success

b. Heads of equal importance. The main heads of an outline, those usually marked by Roman numerals, should show the main divisions of the material. Similarly, the immediate subdivisions of these heads, usually marked by capital letters, should designate logical divisions of each phase of the subject. The same principle applies to further divisions under any subhead.

Unequal headings	*Equal headings*
Books I Have Enjoyed	**Books I Have Enjoyed**
I. Adventure stories	I. Adventure stories
II. Historical novels	II. Historical novels
III. *Walden*	III. Science fiction
IV. Autobiographies	IV. Autobiographies
V. What I like most	V. Books on mysticism

c. Headings in parallel form. Equivalent heads and subheads are expressed in parallel grammatical form. In a sentence outline, use complete sentences throughout. In a topic outline, use phrase heads only. Make all heads of the same rank parallel; that is, make the heads in one series all nouns or all adjectives or all phrases, or whatever is most appropriate.

Heads not parallel	*Parallel heads*
Hitting a Forehand	**Hitting a Forehand**
I. The stance is fundamental	I. The stance
II. The grip	II. The grip
III. Watch the backswing	III. The backswing
IV. Meeting the ball	IV. The stroke
V. Follow through with care	V. The follow-through

7. Division of main points. Since a topic isn't "divided" unless there are at least two parts, a formal outline should have at least two subheads under any main head—or none at all. For every heading marked *A* there should be at least a *B*, for every *1* there should be a *2*, and so on.

Illogical single heads	*Logical subdivision*
The Tripartite System	**The Tripartite System**
I. The executive branch	I. The executive branch
A. President and Cabinet	A. President
	B. Cabinet
II. The legislative branch	II. The legislative branch
A. The House	A. The House of Representatives
B. The Senate	B. The Senate
1. Functions	1. Special functions
	2. Special privileges

III. The judicial branch	III. The judicial branch
A. The Supreme Court	A. The Supreme Court
	B. Lower courts

When a main point can't be divided, include any necessary detail in the head. For an organization in which the president has all the executive power, this heading would be satisfactory:

I. The executive branch (the president)

8. Introduction and conclusion. Ordinarily a paper has a beginning, a middle, and an ending (or an introduction, a body, and a conclusion), but don't use such labels in the outline. They're too general to reflect specific content, and the beginning and ending can rarely be represented by heads that are coordinate with the others. The first and last topics in an outline should be drawn from the main body of material for the paper.

over, more than

There's still some prejudice against using *over* to mean ''more than'' (a budget of over $5 billion), but the usage is established as standard.

Oxymoron

An oxymoron is a contradiction in terms used as a figure of speech—for example, ''sweet bitterness,'' ''loving hate,'' ''mildly fatal,'' ''making haste slowly,'' Aleksandr Solzhenitsyn's ''literary illiterates.''

P

pair

When not preceded by a number or other plural indicator *(these, several)*, *pairs* is the preferred plural of *pair:* Pairs of figures were common in the design. Otherwise usage is divided:

These hypotheses are confounded in two pairs.—Roselle and Campbell, *Psychological Bulletin*

He found a car with one too many pair of skis.—*Time*

Paragraph indention

Indent here for a new paragraph.

No ¶ No paragraph indention

Join this paragraph to the preceding one.

1. Indent for a new paragraph.   A paragraph symbol in the margin of your paper means that you've failed to meet your readers' expectations. From their experience with magazines and books, they're in the habit of regarding a paragraph as a series of related statements, all bearing on the action being narrated, the scene being described, or the point being argued. And they expect to be forewarned by a paragraph break of any shift in focus or any turn in the course of reasoning. When they come to a stretch of writing that drifts or leaps from one topic to another, they're confused and distracted by the lack of unity and coherence.

Your instructor may have other reasons for recommending indention. A single sentence or a short sequence of sentences that makes a significant point may demand the emphasis that being set apart as a paragraph will provide. Or a brief passage that marks a transition from one stage of the paper to another may be more helpful to the reader if it's detached from the end of a long paragraph to stand on its own. And sometimes, even if the connections in the material are close enough to justify a very long paragraph, you may be advised to break it up simply to give the reader a mental breathing spell.

Though it's not uncommon to find an 800-word paragraph in a scholarly journal where a closely reasoned argument is addressed to interested readers, most expository writing receives nothing like such close attention. Indention helps break a discussion into digestible bites. In using indention this way, be sure to look for a natural subdivision within the long paragraph. Don't divide your subject at a point that will separate two closely related sentences.

In general, the development of your topic should determine the length of your paragraphs. But take into account the kind of writing you're doing: narrative and descriptive paragraphs are likely to be shorter than paragraphs of criticism or analysis. And take into account the probable interest and attention span of your readers.

2. Join separate paragraphs.   A succession of very short paragraphs, like a succession of very long ones, makes reading difficult. An unjustified paragraph break throws the reader off the track so that he loses the connection between one idea and another. In revising, combine paragraphs in which the details or ideas are so closely related that they form a single stage in the development of the paper. In the process, make sure you provide whatever transitional words and phrases are needed to emphasize the continuity.

While a transitional paragraph that moves a paper from one phase of the topic to another may be very short—perhaps just one sentence—most paragraphs are from four to ten sentences long. If you have more than two paragraphs on a typed page of expository prose, be sure you can justify the breaks. A sequence of very short paragraphs may indicate that you're not developing your points adequately, not providing enough examples or details or comparisons. Or it may be that you've failed to recognize the close logical connections that pull your ideas together into larger units. In either case, short, choppy paragraphs suggest a collection of random observations rather than the unified development of a central idea.

See **Coherence, Transition.**

par Paragraphs

Revise or rewrite this unsatisfactory paragraph.

A paragraph is a group of related statements that a writer presents as a unit in the development of his subject. It strikes the eye as a unit because it's physically set off by indention or spacing. It will also strike the mind as a unit if the statements in it are closely related, representing a stage in the flow of the writer's thought.

Here are the most common faults in paragraphs, with suggested remedies:

1. Lack of development.   Rewrite the paragraph, including details and illustrations that will lead the reader to understand and accept its central point. See **Details.**

2. Lack of unity.   Rewrite, deleting any material that doesn't contribute to the central idea, or core of meaning, of the paragraph. See **Unity 2.**

3. Lack of continuity.   Revise or rewrite so that the relation between the statements that make up the paragraph is clear. Occasionally you'll find you can improve continuity simply by altering the order of sentences. Sometimes you need to supply a transition between sentences. And sometimes you must rethink and rewrite. See **Coherence, Logical thinking, Transition.**

4. Lack of transition.   Begin the paragraph with a word, phrase, or sentence that links it firmly to the material that precedes it. See **Transition.**

5. Lack of a required topic sentence.   Provide a topic sentence to strengthen the unity of the paragraph or to make clearer to the reader the direction your paper is taking. Not all paragraphs need topic sentences; but some do, either to present the generalization that subsequent details will support, or to pull details together into a generalization, or to introduce or sum up a stage of the discussion.

paral Parallelism and style

// Use parallel structures for elements that should logically be performing the same grammatical function.

Parallelism is one of the simplest, neatest, and most economical ways of achieving clarity. The sentence you've just read illustrates what it says. The three sentences that follow express the same idea without taking advantage of parallelism:

> Parallelism is one of the simplest ways of achieving clarity. Neatness is a major contribution made by parallelism. A sentence that uses parallel structures is more economical than one that doesn't.

Parallelism is a mode of coordination. This means that as a general rule *and, but, nor,* and *yet* should match noun (or noun equivalent) to noun, adjective to adjective, infinitive to infinitive, dependent clause to dependent clause, and so on.

1. Put into the same grammatical forms and structures those words, phrases, and clauses that are alike in purpose and related in meaning (complementary or contrasting). "He was *brilliant* but *unstable*" (predicate adjectives modifying *he*) and "He was a *brilliant* but *unstable* person" (adjectives modifying *person*) both make use of parallelism. "He was *brilliant* but an *unstable* person" does not, though the purpose of *brilliant* and *unstable* remains the same: they're still describing the subject of the sentence.

Here are some sentences that use parallelism, followed in each case by a version that doesn't:

> *Parallel nouns:* Rational thought and rational behavior rarely govern either the *formation* or the *operation* of policy.—Barbara Tuchman, *Newsweek*

> *Not parallel (noun mismatched with dependent clause):* Rational thought and rational behavior rarely govern either the *formation* of policy or *how it operates.*

> *Parallel gerunds:* Sir Percy was given to *sniffing* snuff and *prattling* foolishly as a cover for the daring Pimpernel.—Thomas Middleton, *Saturday Review*

> *Not parallel (gerund mismatched with independent clause):* Sir Percy was given to *sniffing* snuff and *he also prattled foolishly as a cover for the daring Pimpernel.*

> *Parallel pairs of adjectives:* She satisfies our secret longing to believe that those who are *good and generous* are also *stylish and beautiful.*—A. Walton Litz, *Key Reporter*

Not parallel *(paired adjectives mismatched with adjective and verb phrase):*
She satisfies our secret longing to believe that those who are *good and generous*
are also *beautiful and wear the latest styles.*

Failure to use matching grammatical structures is particularly noticeable
with the correlative conjunctions *both . . . and, either . . . or, neither
. . . nor, not only . . . but (also).* A simple example is given in the first
rewritten version above. Here's an equally common type:

The rule is *not only* ignored by those it is directed at *but* those who are supposed to enforce it ignore it too.

It seems clear that the writer wants to emphasize how thoroughly the rule is
being ignored. In revising, a good first step would be to put the verb before
not only: The rule is being ignored. Who's ignoring it? Those who . . .
and those who. . . . Then, with the correlative conjunctions added, the
phrasing falls naturally into parallel form:

The rule is being ignored *not only by those who are supposed to* observe it *but
also by those who are supposed to* enforce it.

2. Do *not* make structures parallel unless the relationship of the ideas or
details they express justifies parallelism. If parallelism in structure doesn't
represent the logic of what's being said, the reader will be misled. The three
grammatical elements that end the next sentence are not parallel:

My year abroad taught me a lot about the way Venezuelans earn a living, spend
their leisure time, and their attitudes about Americans.

Making the elements parallel (. . . and feel about Americans) would produce a smoother sentence, but as far as *meaning* goes, the change would be
a mistake. In the context, the way Venezuelans feel about Americans isn't
logically related to the way they earn their living or spend their leisure time.
The best revision, then, would be to retain the first two elements in the
series but turn the third into a separate sentence. How the new sentence
would be phrased would depend on whether the writer was making a casual
addition or introducing a major topic:

My year abroad taught me a lot about the way Venezuelans earn a living and
spend their leisure time. It also taught me a lot about their attitudes toward
Americans. *Or:* More important, I learned a lot about. . . .

See **Phrases and style, Shifted constructions.**

Parentheses

Parentheses may be used to enclose a full, independent sentence that breaks away from the main structure of the paragraph in which it appears. Like commas and dashes, they are also used within a sentence to enclose words and word groups that break away from the main structure. Of the three types of enclosing marks, parentheses indicate the most separation.

1.   For additions.   Within sentences, parentheses are used to enclose words and word groups that add facts to a statement without essentially altering its meaning. The additions may be illustrations (as in this book), definitions, or information thrown in for good measure:

> The few verb endings that English now retains *(-s, -ed, -ing)* are being still further reduced in ordinary speech.

> Gresham's Law (that bad money drives out good) applies as usual in this case.

> His concerts were well received in most cities (Cleveland was an exception), but he was still dissatisfied.

When overused, parentheses create clutter. If you've fallen into the habit of using them regularly, look closely at the material they enclose. Unimportant material might better be omitted. Material worth including might better be worked into the structure of the sentence in which it appears or made into a separate sentence.

2.   With other marks.   When a complete sentence in parentheses comes within a sentence (notice the punctuation of this one), it needs neither a capital letter nor a period. Commas and other marks of punctuation in the main sentence always *follow* the closing parenthesis (as they do here and in the preceding sentence). (A sentence in parentheses, like this one, that does not stand within another sentence has the end punctuation before the closing parenthesis.)

3.   To enclose numbers or letters in an enumeration.   Parentheses are sometimes used to enclose letters or figures that mark items in an enumeration: The additions may be (1) illustrations, (2) definitions, or (3) information thrown in for good measure. Parentheses give the listed items more emphasis.

See **Brackets, Dash.**

Participles

Participles are derived from verbs but can't serve as independent predicates.

1.   Forms.   The present participle adds *-ing* to the base form of the verb: *asking, singing*. The past participle of regular verbs adds *-ed* to the base *(asked),* and the perfect participle adds *having* to the past participle *(having asked).* In the passive, the *-ed* form is preceded by *being (being asked)* and *having been (having been asked).* Many irregular verbs have special past-participle forms: *sung, having sung, being sung, having been sung.* See **Principal parts of verbs.**

2. Functions.
a. In verb phrases. Participles enter into many verb phrases: I am asking, I am being asked, I have been asked. Though referred to as present and past, participles indicate time only in relation to the context in which they're used. See **Tenses of verbs.**
b. As modifiers. When not part of verb phrases, participles function like adjectives in that they modify nouns (a *coming* event, a *frightened* cat), like verbs in that they may take an object (*Following these clues,* he soon found her). Like both, they may be modified by adverbs *(rolling crazily).*

Compare **Gerunds.**

Participles and style

When a participle is used as an adjective, it should refer clearly to some particular noun or pronoun: Having opened the envelope, she began reading the letter *(Having opened* modifies *she).* A modifying participle is said to dangle when it seems to refer to a word the writer doesn't mean it to refer to: Kissing his wife good-bye, the door slammed behind him (technically, *kissing* modifies *the door).* Errors like this occur when the subject of the participle and the subject of the main clause aren't the same. In "[*He* was] kissing his wife good-bye, *the door* slammed behind him," *He* and *the door* aren't the same. Compare a correct modifier: [*He* was] kissing his wife good-bye, *he* let the door slam behind him. *He* in "[He was] kissing" and *he* in "he let the door slam" are the same. The first subject can be deleted. See **Dangling modifiers.**

The participle-as-adjective shouldn't be confused with the participle in an absolute phrase—a phrase that's related to the whole sentence rather than to a particular word. Some of these phrases have become formulas: Judging from her looks, she's over fifty. See **Absolute phrases, Formulas.**

Don't use a participle where a subordinate clause would read more smoothly: The train was on time, necessitating our hurrying. *Better:* . . . so we had to hurry. In revising, get rid of clumsy participial phrases like this one: The plane arriving then, we boarded it. *Better:* Then the plane arrived, and we boarded it.

For *very* with participles, see **very 2.**

Parts of speech

Parts of speech are the categories linguists set up in order to describe structures in sentences and finally sentences themselves. They group words into categories and subcategories and then describe the various patterns in which these categories may occur and the ways in which they form larger structures. Linguists working with different grammatical theories create different categories based on different sets of definitions.

Traditional schoolroom grammarians, using a system much like that developed for describing classical languages, cite eight parts of speech: nouns, verbs, adjectives, adverbs, pronouns, prepositions, conjunctions, and interjections. Nouns and verbs are defined semantically: a noun is the name of a person, place, or thing; verbs show action. The other parts of speech are defined functionally: adjectives modify nouns; adverbs modify verbs, adjectives, and other adverbs; pronouns replace nouns; and prepositions relate a noun or pronoun to some other part of the sentence.

Structural linguists use purely formal definitions. Nouns, they say, are those words that can occur with plural and possessive endings or in positions after *the* and before a verb; verbs are those words that can occur with third-person singular *-s* endings, with past-tense inflections, with perfect inflections, and with progressive *-ing* endings; adjectives are those words that can occur with comparative or superlative endings, after *more* or *most,* and in the position "The (noun) is very ————"; adverbs are those words made up of an adjective and an *-ly* ending. Structural linguists put the residue of words such as *and, in, can, very, the, not, all, therefore, because, please,* and *hello* into a large category of "indeclinable" words, or function words, which is subdivided according to where these words occur in a sentence relative to the parts of speech already identified.

Transformational grammarians are much less concerned than structuralists with devising formal tests to classify parts of speech and more concerned with the most economical and general overall description. The labels for individual words are judged "correct" only if they're necessary to describe how the words behave in the context of a sentence. Transformational grammarians assume that one part of speech may derive from another, as the verb *discover* in a deep structure like "Tom *discovered* gold" becomes, in a surface structure, the noun *discovery,* "Tom's *discovery* of gold." For transformational grammarians, it's impossible to talk about parts of speech without explaining the whole grammar of a language and without distinguishing between deep and surface structures. See **Deep structure.**

With some help from structural and transformational grammars, traditional grammar serves the purposes of this text. For descriptions of the forms and functions of the parts of speech and their stylistic uses and misuses, see the following articles:

Adjectives	**Collective nouns**
Adjectives and style	**Conjunctions**
Adverbs	**Conjunctions and style**
Adverbs and style	**Conjunctive adverbs**
Articles	**Coordinating conjunctions**
Auxiliaries	**Correlative conjunctions**

pass Passive voice

Change the verb or verbs to active voice.

1. Avoiding the passive.   Using the passive voice without good reason will tend to make your sentences awkward and wordy, place emphasis where it doesn't belong, and at times leave your readers wondering who did what.

a.   Don't use the passive to avoid using *I*.

Between Laredo and Austin the driving was done by me.

Revision: Between Laredo and Austin I drove. *Or:* . . . I did the driving.

b.   Don't use the passive in an attempt to sound weighty or "scientific."

The proposals that were made by the administration have been received negatively by the student body.

Revision: Students disliked the administration's proposals.

c.   Don't use the passive to hide or obscure the identity of the source of an action.

My roommate and I were summoned by the dean because of the waterbags that had been dropped from our windows.

Revision: The dean summoned my roommate and me for dropping waterbags from our windows.

d. Don't use the passive to vary the pattern just for the sake of varying the pattern.

> After finding our way through the woods, we reached the campsite. A half-dozen trips were made to bring in our supplies. By sunset we were more than ready for a hot meal.

The shift from active to passive isn't justified. Revising the second sentence (We had to make . . .) would keep the focus consistent and make the passage easier to read.

2.   Appropriate uses of the passive.   The passive voice is appropriately used in at least three rhetorical contexts.

a.   Passives are appropriate when the agent of the action is either unknown, unimportant, or better left unidentified:

> As many as a hundred notices of teaching jobs are printed each month in a newsletter best described as a "whole education" catalogue.—Jean Collins, *Change*

> The grammars could not be dismissed as inferior or crude; they were simply different.—J. J. Lamberts, *A Short Introduction to English Usage*

> Entry was not gained, police said, though an attempt had been made to pry open the door.

> Postal rates are to be increased.

b.   Passives can be used (as in this sentence) when the subject under discussion would otherwise be the direct object: A writer can use passives when. . . . Because passives are what is being discussed in this section, the noun phrase referring to them should be the subject-topic of most of the sentences.

c.   Passives allow a writer to focus on the agent of an action by shifting the agent to the end of the sentence, where it will be stressed. This is especially desirable when the agent is represented by a fairly long and complicated noun phrase:

> *Active:* A team bigger and tougher than any you would find outside professional football defeated us.

> *Passive:* We were defeated by a team bigger and tougher than any you would find outside professional football.

Such a shift often makes it possible for the writer to build a tighter transition from one sentence to another. The element ending one sentence leads into the subject of the sentence that follows.

See **Voice.**

Past tense

For past tense, regular verbs add *-ed* to the base form: *ask, asked; answer, answered.* See **Principal parts of verbs, Tenses of verbs.**

people, persons

People has long been used as a collective noun referring to a group, but as recently as the early part of this century, it was regarded as nonstandard when used with numerical quantifiers as the plural of *person,* as in "Five people are here." Though formal usage still tends to prefer *persons, people* is now thoroughly established in all plural uses. *Person* and *persons* are frequently resorted to by writers who object to using *man* or *men,* alone or in combinations like *businessman* and *policeman,* to represent both sexes, but coinages like *businessperson* have met strong resistance. Not surprisingly, *people-persons* is a case of divided usage. See **Sexist language.**

per

Per (Latin "through, by, among") is most appropriate in phrases that are still close to their Latin originals (per capita, per diem), in commercial expressions ($250 per week, $5.00 per yard), and in some technical phrases (revolutions per minute). In less specialized contexts, *a* or *every* is preferable: a dime a dozen, a thousand words every day.

percent

In informal and general writing (but not in formal) *percent* is often used instead of *percentage* or even *proportion:* Only a small percent of the class was (*or* were) present. When it's so used, the noun in the *of* phrase determines whether the verb is singular or plural. Since *class* is a collective noun, the verb could be either.

With figures, *percent* (97.6 percent) is preferred to the percent sign (97.6%) except in technical and statistical material. *Percent* is also written as two words. It's not an abbreviation and shouldn't be followed by a period.

Perfect tense

Tenses formed with *have* and a past participle are traditionally called perfect tenses: present perfect, *has laughed;* past perfect, *had laughed;* future perfect, *will have laughed.* See **Tenses of verbs.**

Period

1. At the end of statements. A period is used to mark the end of every completed sentence that's not a question or an exclamation. Sometimes, when not really inquiring or exclaiming, a writer will use a period at the end of a sentence in the form of a question or exclamation: Would you be so good as to return the book at your earliest convenience. What a day.

2. Miscellaneous conventional uses.
a. After abbreviations: Oct.; etc.; Mr. W. Fraser, Jr.
b. Between dollars and cents: $5.66; $0.66 (*but* 66 cents *or* 66¢)
c. Before decimals: .6, 3.14159, 44.6 percent
d. Sometimes between hours and minutes in giving precise time, though a colon is more usual: 2.36 p.m.

3. With quotation marks. When a quotation ends a sentence, most American publishers place the period inside the quotation marks whether the quotation is a complete sentence or a single word:

> "The longer you put it off," he said, "the harder it's going to be." He glared at me as he said "harder."

Person

Person as a grammatical term refers to both pronoun classification and verb inflection. Personal pronouns are in the first person, the one(s) speaking (*I, my, me, we, our, us*); second person, the one(s) spoken to (*you, your, yours*); third person, anyone or anything else (*he, his, him, she, her, hers, it, its, they, their, them*). Nouns are regarded as third person, as are most other pronouns.

Except in the verb *be (I am, you are, he is . . .),* English verbs indicate person only for the third singular of the present and perfect tenses: I see, you see, he *sees;* we see, you see, they see; I have seen, you have seen, he *has* seen; etc.

Personal pronouns

The personal pronouns are *I, we, you, he, she, it,* and *they.* See **Case, Person, Pronouns 1.**

Personification

Personification is a figure of speech in which an object or animal or quality or ideal is given some attributes of a human being. Here the mall of the Smithsonian Institution in Washington, D.C., is personified: "It was a hot summer, but the Mall carried on imperturbably, hosting event after event" (Edward Park, *Smithsonian*). Personification is less common today than formerly and less common in prose than in verse. See **Gender.**

persons

With numerical quantifiers, *persons* is preferred to *people* in formal usage: five persons. See **people, persons.**

phenomenon, phenomena

Phenomenon is the singular and *phenomena* (sometimes *phenomenons*) the plural: phenomena of the mind. Originally *phenomenon* meant "any observable event," but now it also means "something remarkable," and *phenomenal* is almost always used in that sense (Her speed is phenomenal). See **Hyperbole.**

Phrasal verbs

A main verb preceded by one or more auxiliaries (will go, has left, was thinking, is considered, must have been punished) is called a phrasal verb or a periphrastic verb. A verb-adverb combination is also called a phrasal verb. See **Verbs.**

Phrases

A phrase is a group of words that functions as a unit in a sentence, a clause, or another phrase. In these examples the word that determines the classification is in italics:

> **Noun phrase:** the *plumber*
> **Verb phrase:** have *gone* to the store
> **Adjective phrase:** *old* enough to be my father
> **Adverb phrase:** more *quickly* than usual
> **Prepositional phrase:** *in* the house
> **Participle or gerund phrase:** *walking* down the street
> **Infinitive phrase:** *to go* faster

Phrases may be further classified according to their function in a sentence. *The plumber* is an adjectival noun phrase in the larger noun phrase, *my friend the plumber*. In "Walking down the street, she saw the accident," *walking down the street* is a participle phrase because its function is adjectival. In "Walking down the street is dangerous," *walking down the street* is a gerund phrase because its function is nominal. *In the morning* is an adverbial prepositional phrase in "He left in the morning," an adjectival prepositional phrase in "Breakfast in the morning," a nominal prepositional phrase in "In the morning will be soon enough."

Phrases and style

The style of a passage depends in part on how the writer combines and coordinates phrases:

```
His ideas
            about the need
                        for intellectual renewal
                                    and
                        spiritual reform
indicate the crisis
            faced not only
                        by those
                                    in places
                                                of power
            but
                        by those
                                    in all walks
                                                of life.
```

In the preceding sentence the phrases are balanced and coordinated to create a rhythm that carries the reader along smoothly to the end. In the next sentence the phrases are merely strung out one after the other, creating a heavy, bumping kind of movement that interferes with the reader's understanding of the writer's idea:

```
Our situation
            in this century
                        of turmoil
                                    in the cities
can only be alleviated
            by improving the living conditions
                        in ghettos
                                    in the central cities
which have decayed
            beyond the endurance
                        of most
                        to live
                                    in them.
```

When you pile phrase on phrase, make sure you also establish enough parallelism to give your sentence shape and movement.

See **Absolute phrases, Gerunds, Infinitives, Participles, Prepositional phrases.** See also **Dangling modifiers.**

Plagiarism

Plagiarize is defined in *Webster's New Collegiate Dictionary* as "to steal and pass off (the ideas or words of another) as one's own." Students in college courses commit plagiarism for several different reasons, including panic, dishonesty, and ignorance of what plagiarism is. Sometimes a student plagiarizes when he drifts unconsciously from paraphrasing into copying. Whatever the cause, the penalty—a failing mark on the paper and, if the cheating is chronic or flagrant, a failing mark in the course—is justified. Copying someone else's work is the most complete failure possible.

If you haven't learned how to handle material obtained from your reading, you need guidance in the fundamentals of scholarship. Anyone using published material has a twofold responsibility: first, to make the ideas part of his own thinking and, second, to give credit to the sources he's consulted. No one is *composing* when he's copying.

Digest the material you read so that you can present it in your own words (except for the brief passages you intend to quote directly). Be able to talk about what you've read before you write about it, and when you do write, name the sources of your ideas and facts, including ideas and facts you've paraphrased or summarized. This is not only courtesy but a sign of good workmanship, part of the ethics of writing. It's also part of the legality of writing, since the plagiarist who uses copyrighted material is liable to prosecution.

In an informal paper you can give credit informally, perhaps in a preliminary note: "This essay is based on. . . . " Or you can acknowledge a source in the body of the paper: "Professor Hudspeth said in a lecture . . . " or "According to an editorial in . . . " or "Here is Jackson's position as presented in last night's debate." Or you can give credit more formally in the endnotes or footnotes that are a customary part of a research paper.

Plagiarism is stealing. And besides being dishonest, it's unnecessary and unproductive. By giving credit where credit is due, you gain free and legitimate access to everything in print (though if what you write is to be printed, you must get permission to quote copyrighted material directly). And you learn to integrate the ideas of others with your own ideas. Finally, when you express what you have to say in your own words, you're not copying but composing. See **Originality.**

plenty

As a qualifier (I was plenty worried; That car is plenty fast) *plenty* is chiefly informal. In formal and general styles such established adverbs as *very (much)* and *extremely* are preferred. An *of* is expected between *plenty* and a following noun: We had plenty of time (*not* plenty time).

plurality, majority

In an election a plurality is the largest number of votes received by any one candidate but less than a majority, which is more than half of all the votes cast. See **majority, plurality**.

Plurals of nouns

The plurals of the great majority of English nouns are made by adding -*s*. Some exceptions and special cases follow.

1. Special groups in -*s* or -*es*.

a. Some plurals can be pronounced only by adding a full syllable. The spelling is -*s* if the noun already ends in a silent -*e (edges, mazes)*, otherwise -*es: birches, misses, dishes.*

b. With a few exceptions, common nouns ending in -*y* preceded by a consonant or *qu* change *y* to *i* and add -*es: beauties, bodies, soliloquies.* Words ending in -*y* preceded by a vowel add -*s: bays, boys, honeys.*

c. Nouns ending in -*o* preceded by a vowel make regular plurals with -*s: radios, studios.* Some words ending in -*o* preceded by a consonant always or nearly always take -*s: Filipinos, pianos, solos.* Some always or nearly always take -*es: echoes, potatoes, vetoes.* Some take either: *cargoes, cargos; dominoes, dominos.*

d. Some common nouns ending in -*f* or -*fe (calf, wife, half, knife, self)* use -*ves (calves, wives, halves, knives, selves).* Some have two plurals: *hoof, hoofs/hooves; scarf, scarfs/scarves.* But many nouns ending in -*f* and -*fe* form regular plurals with -*s: beliefs, fifes.*

2. Same form for both singular and plural.   Nouns with the same form for singular and plural include names for some living creatures *(fowl, sheep),* all words ending in -*ics (athletics, politics),* and some common measurements *(foot, pair, ton*—though these also have different plural forms).

3. Survivals of older forms.   Survivals include plurals in -*en (brethren, children, oxen)* and plurals with changed vowels *(feet, geese, men, teeth, women).*

4. Foreign language plurals.   Many nouns taken into English from other languages keep their foreign plurals, at least for a time. Words chiefly in scientific or foreign use keep the foreign plural longer. *Antenna,* for example, has the plural *antennae* in biology, though it's *antennas* for TV and radio. Some common words have two plurals, the foreign *(appendices, media, nuclei)* and the English *(appendixes, mediums, nucleuses)*.

5. Compound and group words.   Most compound words and group words add *-s* to the end of the group, whether written as one word or as several: *high schools, cross-examinations, bookcases*. In a few the *-s* is added to the first element: *daughters-in-law* (and other *in-law* words), *passersby, courts-martial* (also *court-martials*).

6. Plurals of figures, words, letters.   Usually the plural of a letter of the alphabet, of a word as a word, or of a figure is written with *-'s*: There are two *c*'s and two *m*'s in *accommodate*. But usage is divided: the plural of figures especially is often made with *-s*: three 2s.

See **Apostrophe 3; -ful, full; Possessive case 1a**.

plus

Plus is a preposition having the sense "with the addition of." Therefore a phrase introduced by *plus* shouldn't affect the number of the verb, but it's sometimes allowed to do so, particularly when the *plus* phrase isn't set off by commas: The committee report plus some newspaper headlines *were* all that was needed. In more formal writing the *plus* would be changed to *and*, or the verb would be made singular.

   Plus as a substitute for the adverb *besides, also,* or *in addition* (The school has a good engineering department, plus its campus is beautiful) is objectionable to many readers, even in informal contexts. It becomes more objectionable when it begins a sentence. *Plus* also occurs as a noun (a plus for the new cafeteria is its lighting) and an adjective (a plus factor). Though there are rare occasions when *plus* substitutes economically for "to which is added," college writers would do well to avoid the word except in arithmetical contexts. See **Adjectives 1**.

p.m.

This abbreviation for *post meridiem*, "afternoon," should not be used as a noun. See **a.m. and p.m.**

Poetry

When verse is quoted, it should be lined off (as well as capitalized and punctuated) exactly as written. If possible the quoted lines should be centered on the page, indented according to the scheme of the original. When so spaced, lines of verse quoted in a prose passage needn't be enclosed in quotation marks. Diagonal marks, or virgules, are sometimes used to indicate line breaks when a short passage of poetry is run into the text: It was Marlowe who wrote, "I walk abroad 'a nights/And kill sick people groaning under walls."

pv Point of view

The shift in point of view in the passage marked is illogical or unjustified.

Your point of view in a paper is the position from which you view your subject. The position may be physical—your location in space and time—or psychological—your attitude toward your subject. The correction symbol *pv* indicates that, in the context, your change in point of view doesn't work.

1. Don't make unjustified shifts in physical point of view. When you write a description of an object, a place, a process, or an incident, the reader sees it through your eyes; and if he's to understand what he's looking *at,* he must have a clear idea of where he's looking *from.* In describing a building on campus, for example, you may begin with a head-on view and then lead the reader full circle, using such phrases as "looked at from the left," "from the rear," "on the Main Street side." Or you may begin with a view from far across campus or even a bird's eye view—how the building would look if it was approached in a helicopter. The important thing is to keep the reader oriented. A description that jumps from front steps to basement lab to clock tower to classrooms is bound to befuddle.

2. Don't make unmotivated shifts in attitude. If you set out to describe your dormitory, what you show the reader, what you show in greatest detail, and what you don't show at all will depend on your feelings about the place. Thus psychological point of view may determine physical point of view. And attitude may also lead to some role-playing. Suppose you hate your dorm and want to convince your reader that it deserves hating. Can you best accomplish your purpose by stating your attitude in the opening sentence? By being sarcastic throughout? Or by adopting an objective, analytical tone and counting on the examples and details you present to win the reader to your side? The strategy is yours to choose; but once you've made your choice, stick to it. Like an erratic change in physical point of view, a switch in tone from sympathetic to contemptuous or from hostile to nostalgic will confuse and irritate your reader.

3. Don't make confusing changes in the distance between you and your reader. Point of view—physical or psychological or both—influences your choice of a *personal* mode of narration, description, or argument, in which your presence is clearly felt, or an *impersonal* mode, in which you don't seem to be present at all. The pronouns, if any, that you use to refer to yourself will signal to the reader something about the relationship that you want to establish. Heavy reliance on the pronoun *I* (or *we*) may suggest casual intimacy or restricted but personal knowledge of the subject or real authority. Use of *you* may give the impression that you hope to engage your reader in a dialog. The third person ("If one should . . . ") may lend objectivity or imply remoteness. A completely impersonal approach focuses on what's being discussed without calling attention to either the writer or the audience. Once you've established yourself in one relation to your reader, it's unwise to adopt another without good reason.

Many problems in word choice and syntax stem from failure to maintain a consistent point of view. For related grammatical problems, see **Passive voice, Reference of pronouns, Shifted constructions, Tense, you**. See also **Details**.

politics

Politics in the usual sense is treated as a singular: In almost any group, politics *is* a controversial subject. But when used in the sense of "principles," "activities," or "tactics," it may be treated as a plural: Republican politics *were* offensive to the Federalists. Avoid treating the word both ways in the same passage.

position, job

Position is the formal word for *job*. See **job, position**.

Positive degree

The positive degree of adjectives and adverbs is the base, or root, form of the adjective *(poor, high, golden)* or adverb *(slow, slowly, bitterly)*. See **Comparison of adjectives and adverbs**.

Possessive adjectives

My, your, her, his, our, their are sometimes called possessive adjectives. See **Possessive pronouns, possessive adjectives**.

Possessive case

1. Signs of the possessive.   The possessive, or genitive, function in English is shown in four ways:

a.   Apostrophe-*s* or apostrophe alone. Singular nouns that don't end in the sound of *s* as in *chess* or *z* as in *breeze* and plural nouns that don't end in the letter *s* add apostrophe *-s: boy's, one's, England's, men's, children's,* *freshmen's.* After plural nouns ending in *-s,* only an apostrophe is used: *workers' incomes, dogs' teeth, coaches' rules.*

For singular nouns ending in the *s* or *z* sound, practice varies, as do the recommendations of stylebooks, which set up rules for writers and editors to follow for the sake of consistency. The system proposed by the *Manual of Style* (University of Chicago Press) calls for an apostrophe-*s* after all singular nouns except *Jesus, Moses,* classical names ending in *-es (Socrates, Xerxes),* and words like *conscience* and *goodness* before *sake.* These exceptions take an apostrophe only.

To indicate joint possession, the apostrophe is added only to the second of two coordinate nouns: Martha and George's son. In ''Mary's and Tom's bicycles,'' separate objects are possessed, and an apostrophe *-s* is needed for each noun.

b. The *of* possessive. Most possessives formed with an apostrophe or apostrophe-*s* can also be formed with an *of* phrase: the dancer's performance, the performance of the dancer. (Exceptions include such idioms as ''a day's work,'' ''an hour's time.'') The choice between the two will usually depend on considerations of rhythm, idiom, and what fits best with neighboring phrases and clauses. Idiom calls for ''the roof of the house,'' not ''the house's roof.'' The *of* possessive is easier to work with when the noun in the possessive is modified by clauses or by other possessives. For example, both ''the car's tires'' and ''the tires of the car'' are acceptable, but if *car* is modified by the clause ''that John used to drive,'' the *of* possessive is clearer: the tires of the car that John used to drive (*not:* the car that John used to drive's tires). If we want to indicate that the car is John's, the *of* possessive avoids a succession of apostrophes: the tires of John's car (*not:* John's car's tires).

In some contexts there's a possible difference in meaning between the two forms. ''Jane's picture'' probably means a picture belonging to Jane, but it might mean a picture of Jane. ''A picture of Jane'' can only mean that Jane is represented in the picture. (The possessive doesn't always indicate possession. A picture of Jane may be owned by someone else. See **2.**)

c. Double possessive. Using the *of* possessive and apostrophe-*s* together is an English idiom of long and respectable standing. It's especially common in locutions beginning with *this* and *that* and usually has an informal flavor: that boy of Helen's; friends of my father's; hobbies of Anne's. The double possessive is useful in avoiding the ambiguities mentioned above: the meaning of ''Jane's picture'' is made clear either as ''that picture of Jane'' or as ''that picture of Jane's.''

d. Possessive of personal pronouns. The personal and relative pronouns have possessive forms without an apostrophe: *my, your, his, her, its, our, their, whose.* It's as important not to put an apostrophe in these pronouns (and in the forms used without nouns: *ours, yours, theirs, hers*) as it is to put one in a noun in the possessive. See **its, it's; Pronouns 1; which 2.**

2. Uses of the possessive. The most common function of the possessive is to indicate possession: the professor's house, Al's dog, my daughter. It also indicates a number of other relationships:

Description: a writer's responsibility, children's toys, suit of wool

Doer of an act: the wind's force, the force of the wind; the author's second novel; with the dean's permission, with the permission of the dean; the doctor's arrival, the arrival of the doctor

Recipient of an act: the police officer's murderer, the murderer of the police officer; the bill's defeat, the defeat of the bill

Adverb: He drops in of an evening.

See **Case, Gerunds 2.**

Possessive pronouns, possessive adjectives

The personal pronouns have the following possessive forms: *my, mine; your, yours; his; her, hers; our, ours; their, theirs;* and the relative *who* has *whose. Its* is the only one that regularly tempts writers to use an apostrophe, through confusion with *it's,* the contraction for "it is."

My, your, her, his, our, their are used as adjectives (and sometimes called possessive adjectives) before a noun: my car. *Mine, yours, his, hers, its, ours, theirs* are used without a following noun: Ours is better than yours.

precedence, precedents

The student who wrote, "Now that precedence has been set, the next move against our rights will be easier," confused *precedent,* meaning an action or decision that can be used to justify subsequent similar moves, with *precedence,* meaning priority or preference (The graduating class was granted precedence when seats were assigned). The sentence should begin, "Now that a precedent has been set."

Predicate

Almost all English sentences divide into two main elements—subject and predicate. The predicate of a clause or sentence is the verb with its modifiers and objects or complements. The predicate may be a single verb (The bell *tolled*), a transitive verb and its object (She *landed the big fish*), or a linking verb and its complement (The oldest member of the family *is usually the first to go*). Two verbs depending on one subject are known as a compound predicate: The men *washed* and *wiped* the dishes in fifteen minutes.

p adj Predicate adjectives

Use an adjective here, because the verb is a linking verb.

The error of using an adverb instead of a predicate adjective (The stereo sounds loudly) results from the habit of putting adverbs after verbs. When the verb is a linking verb, adjectives, not adverbs, fill that position. In addition to *be*, about sixty verbs (*become, feel, turn, look, taste,* and so on) can perform this linking function. What follows the verb relates to or qualifies the subject, not the verb. Accordingly, an adjective—known as a predicate adjective or an adjective in the predicate position—is required, even though in its other functions the same verb is followed by an adverb. Compare "He felt *tired*" (adjective, relates to subject) and "He felt the edge of the knife *carefully*" (adverb, relates to the verb).

Adjective: She acts *tired*.   *Adverb:* She acts *brilliantly*.

Adjective: She looks *cold*.   *Adverb:* She looked at him *coldly*.

The test for a linking verb is that the appropriate form of *be* can replace it: "The story rings true" is structurally the same as "The story is true." When you've identified a verb as linking, use an adjective after it.
See **bad, badly; Linking verbs; look.** See also **Adjectives 1.**

Predicate nominative

Words and word groups that follow linking verbs and function as nouns are called predicate nominatives or complements. They include nouns, pronouns, phrases, and clauses. See **Linking verbs.**

predominant(ly)

Predominant is an adjective: a predominant sentiment, a sentiment predominant in the state. *Predominantly* is an adverb: The population is predominantly Muslim. But the verb is *predominate:* The Muslims predominate there. Not surprisingly, the spellings *predominate* and *predominately* for adjective and adverb have become common enough to be recognized by dictionaries. But the surest way to avoid criticism is to stick with *predominant* and *predominantly*.

prefer

To is ordinarily used with *prefer:* I prefer Ireland to Spain; She preferred going by train to flying. But when an infinitive is used instead of a noun or gerund, *to* is impossible, and *than* or *rather than* is used: She preferred to take the train rather than to fly (*or* rather than a plane).

Prefix

A prefix is a letter or letters that can be placed before a word or root to change its meaning or function: *un*tie, *im*mobilize. See **Origin of words 3a.** See also **Hyphen 4, Long variants.**

Prepositional phrases

A prepositional phrase consists of a preposition and its object: *without hope, in a hurry, toward a better life.* In sentences, prepositional phrases are used chiefly in the functions of adverbs (She arrived *at just the right time*) or adjectives (The man *in the black coat* was gone). See **Phrases.**

Prepositions

A preposition connects a noun phrase or a pronoun or a clause to some other part of the sentence. The whole phrase is usually adverbial or adjectival in function: He showed her *to her room;* He was old *in experience;* She was surprised *at what she saw;* the click *of flying wheels.* What follows a preposition is called its object. Prepositions may be word groups (in regard to, according to) as well as single words. And many words that serve as prepositions, such as *after, but, since,* also serve as adverbs and conjunctions. See **Objects 3, Prepositions and style.**

prep Prepositions and style

Change the preposition to one that is idiomatic or less conspicuous; or supply the missing preposition.

1.   Use prepositions that are exact or idiomatic.   A number of words are accompanied by particular prepositions: we say "contented *with* conditions," "*in* my estimation." Some words take on different meanings with different prepositions: agree *with* (a person), agree *to* (a suggestion), agree *in* (principle).

Choosing the right preposition presents no problem with words you use often, because you learn the words by hearing or seeing them in their typical combinations. When you learn new words, learn how they're used as well as what they mean: *acquiesce in* (acquiesce in a decision) rather than just *acquiesce.* Dictionaries give the preposition appropriate to some words. This book has entries for a few idioms in which prepositions occasionally cause trouble: **ability to; agree to, agree with; all of; compare, contrast; different from, different than.** See also **Idiom.**

When coordinating two words that take different prepositions, include both prepositions: The first lesson he learned was obedience *to* and respect *for* his elders. *Not:* . . . obedience and respect for his elders. When both words take the same preposition, there's no need to use it twice: The box office refused to make any allowance [ ] or refund *for* tickets purchased from an agent.

2.   Avoid wordy group prepositions.   English has a number of group prepositions that take up too much space for the work they do. A reference to "recent complaints on the part of dissatisfied students" is weighed down by *on the part of* where *by* would do the job. Sometimes we carry over from speech the habit of using double prepositions: *(in) back of, off (of)*. See **as to; off of; on to, onto; prior to.**

3.   Don't   omit   prepositions   indiscriminately.   Prepositions   aren't dropped in formal writing. Some can be dropped in general writing as well as in informal: ". . . one of the best pieces written about the United States [in] this century" (Arthur Schlesinger, *New Republic*). But expressions like "a couple [of] days later," "a different type [of] girl," and "outside [of] his interest in boxing" remain decidedly informal.

4.   When a preposition falls naturally at the end of a sentence, leave it there. There's an old "rule" that a preposition shouldn't end a sentence (She is the one I did it for). But postponing the preposition has long been a characteristic English idiom, and rhythm often demands placing the preposition at the end. Attempts to avoid putting it there may result in stilted sentences: Tell me what it is to which you object (*better:* what you object to).

Putting the preposition at the end comes so naturally that if you place it earlier in the sentence, you may end up having it in both places: He brightened the life of everyone with whom he came in contact [with].

See **Phrases 2.**

Present tense

The base form of a verb *(ask, answer, buy, say)* is its present tense. In most verbs -*s* is added in the third-person singular. See **Tenses of verbs.**

pretty

Pretty for *rather* or *fairly* gives a sentence an informal tone: "[Archibald Cox] sets pretty straight . . . the real impact of the great case of Marbury v. Madison" (Charles L. Black, Jr., *New York Times Book Review*). The usage is standard.

preventive, preventative

Unless you're being paid by the letter, *preventive* is preferable in every way.

pp Principal parts of verbs

Change the verb form to one in standard use.

1. The principal parts of a verb.   The principal parts are the base form or infinitive *(ask)*, the past-tense form *(asked)*, the past participle *(asked)*. Most English verbs are ''regular''—that is, their past tense and past participle are formed by adding *-ed* to the base form. A number of the most common change a vowel *(sing, sang, sung)* in making their past-tense and past-participle forms. Some *(let, cost)* remain unchanged. Some *(bend, make)* change the final consonant. And some have less common irregularities (past forms of *teach: taught, taught).*

The trend has been toward regularity. A few verbs *(broadcast, shine, speed)* have acquired regular forms in addition to their old ones: *broadcasted, shined, speeded.* A few others *(dive, fit, prove, sew)* have reversed the trend, acquiring irregularities that are either new or revivals of archaic forms: *dove, fit* (past tense), *proven, sewn.* For some verbs *(dream, plead, show, strive, thrive)* variant pairs have long existed side by side: *dreamed, dreamt; pleaded, pled; showed, shown* (as past participle); *strived, strove; thrived, throve.*

The following list includes a number of verbs with irregular past-tense and past-participle forms. The forms labeled *NS* (nonstandard) and *D* (dialect) would not ordinarily be written. When you're in doubt, consult a recent dictionary for verbs not listed here. Usage is by no means uniform, even among speakers and writers of standard English, and neither this list nor the dictionaries record all variations.

Infinitive	*Past tense*	*Past participle*
arise	arose	arisen
bear	bore	borne
bear	bore	born (given birth to)
begin	began (D: begun)	begun
bite	bit	bitten, bit
blow	blew (D: blowed)	blown (D: blowed)
break	broke	broken (NS: broke)
bring	brought (NS: brung)	brought (NS: brung)
catch	caught (chiefly D: catched)	caught (chiefly D: catched)
choose	chose	chosen
come	came (NS: come)	come
dig	dug	dug
dive	dived, dove	dived
do	did (NS: done)	done
drag	dragged (D: drug)	dragged (D: drug)
draw	drew (NS: drawed)	drawn
dream	dreamed, dreamt	dreamed, dreamt
drink	drank (D: drunk)	drunk
eat	ate (D: pronounced *et*)	eaten (D: pronounced *et*)
fall	fell	fallen
fly	flew	flown

Infinitive	*Past tense*	*Past participle*
forget	forgot	forgotten, forgot
freeze	froze (D: friz)	frozen (chiefly D: froze)
get	got	got, gotten
give	gave (NS: give)	given (NS: give)
go	went (D: goed)	gone (NS: went)
grow	grew (D: growed)	grown (D: growed)
hang	hung	hung
hang (execute)	hung, hanged	hung, hanged
hear	heard	heard
know	knew (D: knowed)	known (D: knowed)
lay	laid	laid
lead	led	led
lean	leaned	leaned
lend (loan)	lent	lent
lie (*see* **lay**)	lay	lain
lose	lost	lost
prove	proved	proved, proven
ride	rode (D: rid)	ridden (D: rid)
ring	rang, rung	rung
run	ran (NS: run)	run
see	saw (NS: seed)	seen (NS: seed, saw)
shake	shook (chiefly D: shaked)	shaken (chiefly D: shaked)
shine	shone, shined	shone, shined
show	showed	showed, shown
shrink	shrank, shrunk	shrunk
sing	sang, sung	sung
sink	sank, sunk	sunk, sunken
sit	sat (D: set)	sat (D: set)
slide	slid	slid
sneak	sneaked (chiefly D: snuck)	sneaked (chiefly D: snuck)
speak	spoke	spoken
spring	sprang, sprung	sprung
stand	stood	stood
steal	stole	stolen (chiefly D: stole)
swim	swam	swum
swing	swung	swung
take	took (D: taken)	taken (D: took)
tear	tore	torn
throw	threw (D: throwed)	thrown (D: throwed)
wear	wore	worn
write	wrote (D: writ)	written (D: wrote)

2. Black English verbs. Linguists investigating the patterns of some Black English dialects have found a structure that is predictable and there-fore grammatical in sentences that have traditionally been called ungrammatical. An example: The teacher gone right now, but she be back soon. The lack of a *be* form in the first clause—"The teacher [is] gone"—and the apparently incorrect form of *be* in the second—"she [will] be back"— results from what grammarians call a deletion transformation. It regularly and predictably omits a form of *be* and other auxiliary verbs such as *will, would,* and *have* where standard English speakers contract their form of *be*.

(An exception is *'m,* as in "I'm going.") This sequence represents the process:

The teacher is	gone right now, but she will be back soon.
The teacher's	gone right now, but she'll be back soon.
The teacher[	]gone right now, but she[ ]be back soon.

Where speakers of standard English can't contract a form of *be,* speakers of some dialects of Black English can't omit it:

Standard English: I don't know who he is. *Not:* I don't know who's.
Black English: I don't know who he be. *Not:* I don't know who he.

See **born, borne; do; got, gotten; grammatical, ungrammatical 1; hanged, hung; lay, lie; proved, proven; set, sit.**

principal, principle

Principal is either an adjective or a noun. *Principle* is a noun only. One way to remember that the adjective is spelled *principal* is to associate it with other adjectives ending in *-al: historical, political, musical.*

Principal as a noun is probably an abbreviation of a phrase in which it was originally an adjective. The principal that draws interest was once the principal sum; the principal of a school, the principal teacher; the principal in a legal action, the principal party; the principals in a play, the principal actors. These are the only common uses of *principal* as a noun.

The noun meaning "a general truth or rule of conduct" is *principle:* the principles of science, a matter of principle.

prior to

Prior to, a rather formal preposition, is most appropriate when it adds to the notion of "before" the notion of "in anticipation of": "He urged reform leaders to work prior to the convention so as to minimize the influence of Greeley's supporters" (Matthew T. Downey, *Journal of American History*). In most contexts, particularly in general styles, *before* is the better choice.

Profanity

Using profanity—that is, referring to sacred beings carelessly or irreverently—is primarily a matter of emotional release (or simply habit) rather than a matter of meaning. In writing, it often attracts more attention to itself than it deserves. Like other kinds of swearing, profanity has no place in college writing, except perhaps in dialog. See **Obscenity.**

professor

Write: Professor Moore; Prof. E. W. Moore; E. W. Moore, a professor of chemistry; *or* E. W. Moore, Professor of Chemistry.

Strictly speaking, the title *Professor* should be given only to assistant professors, associate professors, and full professors, and not to those who haven't achieved professorial rank. When the title follows the name in an *of* phrase, exact rank is usually indicated: Professor A. B. Plant, *but* A. B. Plant, Assistant Professor of English.

The informal *prof* (my math prof) is a clipped word, not an abbreviation, and is written without a period.

Pronouns

A pronoun is commonly defined as a word that replaces a noun or another word or group of words used as a noun. The word or phrase or clause that it substitutes for, as *it* substitutes for *a pronoun* in the sentence you're reading, is called its antecedent: *it* is said to refer to *a pronoun; a pronoun* is the antecedent of *it.* Not all pronouns have antecedents. What *I* and *you* refer to depends on the identity of the writer or speaker and the audience being addressed, not on the verbal context in which *I* and *you* appear.

Like nouns, pronouns can serve as subjects and objects (though not all pronouns can serve as both). Many have a possessive form, and a few have a separate plural form. Unlike nouns, pronouns are a small, closed class of words—that is, no new pronouns are being added to the language.

The traditional subclasses of pronouns are listed below.

1. Personal pronouns.   The personal pronouns are those words that specifically indicate person (first, second, or third), number, and, in the third-person singular, gender.

		Nominative	*Possessive*	*Accusative*
1st-person	*singular*	I	my, mine	me
	plural	we	our, ours	us
2nd-person	*singular*	you	your, yours	you
	plural	you	your, yours	you
3rd-person	*singular*			
	masculine	he	his, his	him
	feminine	she	her, hers	her
	neuter	it	its, its	it
	genderless	one	one's, one's	one
	plural	they	their, theirs	them

Except for the relative pronoun *who (whose, whom),* only the personal pronouns—and not all of them—have different forms for the three cases.

Some of the most common grammatical mistakes occur because, unlike nouns, *I, we, she, they,* and *who* have different forms in subject and object position. See **between you and me; Case; it's me; who, whom.**

In some traditional grammars, personal pronouns in the possessive case are classified separately as possessive pronouns.

2. Reflexive pronouns. The reflexives are formed by adding *-self* or *-selves* to the possessive case of personal pronouns in the first and second persons *(myself, yourself, ourselves, yourselves)* and to the accusative case in the third person *(himself, herself, itself, themselves).* They are used when an object or a subjective complement refers to the same thing or concept or event as the preceding noun or noun phrase:

Direct object:	She hurt *herself.*
Object of preposition:	The road twisted back on *itself.*
Indirect object:	They made *themselves* caftans.
Subjective complement:	Ben isn't *himself* today.
Object of infinitive:	Jane wanted Betty to help *herself.*

As intensives, the reflexive forms are considered to be pronouns in apposition: The owner *himself* sold the car; The owner sold the car *himself.* See **Apposition, appositives.**

3. Reciprocal pronouns. The reciprocals *each other* and *one another* substitute in object position for a compound or plural subject when the action of the verb is directed by each member of the subject toward the other members: Tom and Bill looked at *each other;* The losers kidded *one another.* Like the personal pronouns, the reciprocals are freely used in the possessive: They borrowed *one another's* clothes.

4. Relative pronouns. *Who, which,* and *that* are relatives. (*Who* and *which* are also interrogatives.) Like the personal pronouns, *who* has different forms for the possessive *(whose)* and the accusative *(whom). Which* and *that* are not inflected for case.

Relative pronouns introduce dependent clauses:

The student *who* submitted this paper has dropped out.
The paper *that* she submitted won an award.
Her decision to leave school, *which* caused some excitement, was never explained.

When no specific referent for the pronoun is intended, the indefinite, or expanded, form of the relative is used: *whoever, whomever, whichever, whatever.* Unexpanded *what* is also an indefinite relative pronoun:

Whoever receives this will be pleased.
I will support *whomever* you nominate.
They will believe *whatever* he says.
They will believe *what* he says.

See **Relative clauses.**

5. Interrogative pronouns.   The interrogatives *who, whose, whom, which,* and *what* are used to introduce direct and indirect questions: *What* happened? He asked me *what* happened.

6. Demonstrative pronouns.   *This, that, these,* and *those* are considered adjectives when they modify nouns (*this* hat, *these* books), pronouns when they function as nouns: *This* will fix it; *Those* are too large; I prefer *these.* The demonstratives discriminate between referents close at hand *(this, these)* and referents that are more remote *(that, those).*

7. Indefinite pronouns.   *Some, any, every,* and *no* compounded with *one (someone), thing (everything),* and *body (nobody),* and other words like *all, any, some, each,* and *either,* have traditionally been called indefinite pronouns. When used as subjects, the compounds take singular verbs, and pronouns referring to them are usually in the singular: Everyone is expected to do his part.

Informally, *they* is also used for indefinite reference: They ought to do something about these roads. See **they.**

See **Antecedent, Determiners, Reference of pronouns.**

Proofreading

Checking the final copy of a paper for mechanical mistakes that may have slipped into the last draft is an essential part of preparing a manuscript. See **Careless mistakes, Caret, Manuscript form, Typewritten copy.**

Proper adjectives

Proper nouns that are used like adjectives are capitalized, and so are adjectives that are directly derived from proper names if they still refer to the place or person. After proper adjectives lose the reference to their origins, they become simple adjectives and are no longer capitalized: the Indian service, india ink; the Roman forum, roman type. See **Capital letters.**

proved, proven

Prove is a regular verb, forming a past tense and past participle with *-ed: proved. Proven* has been used for centuries as an alternative past participle of *prove* and is now established in all varieties of usage.

provided, providing

Both *provided* and *providing* are in standard use as connectives:

> You can't even argue, much, with the picture, providing you look at it only as a clever Western.—David R. Slavitt, *Yale Review*

> Anyone who can get into M.S.U. can get into Justin Morrill, provided he is willing to work.—Duncan Norton, *Fortune*

When *if* can be used in place of either form, it probably should be.

Psychologese

Psychologese, a jargon made up of words from the technical vocabulary of psychology, is used enthusiastically if inexactly by many outsiders: *instinctual* for *instinctive, operant* for *operating, motorical* for *motor*. A great many other terms from psychology—*compulsive, empathy, motivational, neurotic, paranoid, relate, traumatic*—have entered the language, become vogue words, and lost much of their technical meaning.

public

Meaning "the people as a whole," *public* is a collective noun and can be treated as either singular or plural. A plural construction is more common: The public depend on TV newscasts for most of their information. But in the sense "a group of people with a common interest," *public* is more often singular: "There is a foreign policy public that is considerably smaller than the general public" (Carl N. Degler, *American Historical Review*).

pn Punctuation

Insert necessary punctuation, or change your punctuation to conform to standard usage.

no *pn* No punctuation

Delete the unnecessary punctuation.

The basic purpose of punctuation is to mark off sentences and to link, separate, and set off elements within sentences in ways that will make the meaning clear to readers. A good rule to follow is to use all punctuation required by current convention and as much optional punctuation as you need to help your reader. Don't use unnecessary punctuation, which may make reading more difficult. And don't rely on punctuation to bail out awkwardly constructed sentences. Instead, rewrite.

1. To end sentences. Use periods to end statements. Use question marks to end sentences that ask direct questions. Use exclamation marks to end sentences (or to follow words or phrases) that express strong emotion and demand special emphasis. See **Exclamation mark, Period, Question mark.**

2. To separate.
a. Use a comma before the conjunction to separate independent clauses joined by *but, for,* or *so.* You can also use a comma before the other coordinating conjunctions in compound sentences. To indicate a stronger separation, use a semicolon. See **Comma 1, Semicolon 1c.**
b. Use a comma after a long introductory phrase or dependent clause to separate it from the main clause. You can use a comma after all introductory phrases and clauses. Don't use a comma after introductory *but, and,* or other conjunction. See **Comma 2a.**
c. Use a comma before a nonrestrictive dependent clause or phrase that follows the main clause. Don't use a comma before a restrictive modifier that follows the main clause. See **Comma 2b.**
d. Use commas to separate the units in a series and to separate adjectives modifying the same noun. To separate the units in a series that already includes commas, use semicolons. See **Comma 5, Semicolon 2.**
e. Don't use a comma between subject and verb, between verb and object or complement, or, in most cases, between the verbs in a compound predicate. See **Comma 8.**

3. To set off.
a. Use paired commas to set off nonrestrictive modifiers.
b. Use paired commas, paired dashes, or parentheses to set off interrupting elements. Commas mark the least separation, parentheses the most. Setting off short interrupters is optional. See **Comma 4a.**

4. To link.
a. Use a semicolon between main clauses when you want to link them rather than separate them with a period. See **Semicolon 1.**
b. Use a colon (*not* a semicolon) to link a series, a quotation, or other material to the sentence element that introduces it. See **Colon 1.**
c. Use a dash to link to the end of a sentence a word, phrase, or clause you want to emphasize. See **Dash 1.**
d. Use a hyphen to link syllables and words. See **Hyphen.**

5. Other uses.
a. Use quotation marks to identify direct quotations. See **Quotation marks 2.**
b. Use ellipses to indicate omission of words. See **Ellipsis.**
c. Use apostrophes to indicate possession and to indicate the omission of letters in contractions. See **Apostrophe 1, 2.**

Puns

A pun is a figure of speech in which a word is simultaneously used in two different senses (the nut that holds the wheel) or substituted for another word of similar sound but different meaning (effluent society). Deliberate punning may serve serious purposes as well as humorous ones, but unintentional puns, which may get laughs you don't want, should be weeded out in revising.

Qualifiers

Qualifiers are words used not to convey meaning in themselves but to qualify—usually by intensifying—the meaning of adjectives. They include the first words in the phrases "much older," "very quiet," "too young," "somewhat sick," "rather careless," and "quite intelligent" and adverbs of degree like *slightly*. Unless they're used thoughtfully and sparingly, qualifiers will weaken writing instead of strengthening it.

Question mark

The chief conventions governing the use of the question mark are these:

1. As an end stop. The principal use of the question mark is as the end stop of a direct question: What was the real reason?

A question mark is not used after an indirect question: He wanted to know what the real reason was.

A request that's phrased as a question is usually followed by a question mark but may not be in general and informal styles. See **Period.**

2. With quotation marks. When a sentence ends with a question mark and closing quotation marks, the question mark belongs outside the quotation marks if the sentence that encloses the quotation is the question (Did you really say, "I thought you were older than that"?), inside if the quotation is the question (He asked, "Did you really say that?"). If both are questions, only the inside question mark is used: Did she ask, "How many are coming?"

3. Within sentences. Usage is divided over a question built into a sentence: Should I quit school now [ ] I ask myself. A question mark after *now* would emphasize the question; a comma would make it less emphatic. If quotation marks were used around the question, a question mark would be appropriate: "Should I quit school now?" I ask myself. "I'm trying to decide whether I should quit school now" avoids the problem.

Questions

1. Direct and indirect questions.   A direct question is a question as actually asked, not just reported. It begins with a capital and ends with a question mark: Who killed Cock Robin?

An indirect question isn't a question as actually asked but a question as reported in another sentence. An indirect question doesn't begin with a capital or end with a question mark, and it's not set off by quotation marks.

> *Direct:* He asked, "Do you really understand what you have read?"
> *Indirect:* He asked us *if we really understood what we had read.*
> *Indirect:* He always asks us *whether we understand what we have read.*

2. Leading questions.   A leading question is one that's phrased so as to suggest the desired answer, like "You'd like to go, wouldn't you?" (*Compare* "Do you want to go?")

3. Questions as transitions.   Occasionally, but only occasionally, asking a question in a paper is a good way to introduce a new paragraph: What can we do to improve the situation?

See **Rhetorical questions.**

quot Quotation marks

Make the quotation marks conform to conventional usage.

1. Methods of indicating quotations.
a. Double quotes, not single, are the usual marks in the United States.
b. For quotations within quotations, alternate double and single quotes. Use single quotes inside double quotes and so on: "'Perry's instinct,' he says, 'soundly chose the point at which to halt the extension of the term "formula"'" (Joseph Russo, *Yale Classical Studies*).
c. When a quotation is longer than one paragraph, use quotation marks at the beginning of each paragraph but at the end of the last paragraph only.
d. If you include a long quotation in a paper, you can make it a block quotation and omit quotation marks. In a paper that's typewritten double-spaced, indent the whole quotation five spaces and set it off from the text by triple-spacing. Double-space the quotation itself. In a handwritten paper, simply indent the whole quotation.

2. Principal uses of quotation marks.
a. Quotation marks are used to indicate all passages taken from another writer, whether a phrase or a page or more (except when the quotation is indented). Any change within the quotation should be indicated—omissions by ellipses, additions by brackets. The quoted matter may stand by itself or

may be worked into your own sentence. Both methods are shown in this passage, the more formal first:

> The most that can be said for Haig was said by Churchill: he "was unequal to the prodigious scale of events, but no one else was discerned as his equal or better." (Lloyd George, more succinctly, said he was "brilliant to the top of his army boots.")—Geoffrey Barraclough, *New York Review of Books*

When brief passages of conversation are introduced not for their own sake but to illustrate a point, they are usually incorporated in the paragraph:

> I am having a drink with the manager, Yves Blais. "You don't speak French," he starts off by saying, "but that is all right because you are from Ontario, which is another country. I will speak English with you. But I have no British accent. I have a pea-soup accent." Blais volunteers the obvious—that he is a separatist. "I'm glad to be. I don't care. I refused to accept a Canada council grant of $8,000. But it has nothing to do with my shows."—Jon Ruddy, *Maclean's*

b. There are no half quotes. A sentence is either an exact quotation and therefore in quotation marks, or else it is not an exact quotation and so is not quoted. Don't present as a direct quote material containing pronouns and verb tenses that are appropriate only to indirect statements: He boasted that he "could do twice as much work as I could." The boast must have been, "I can do twice as much work as you can." The choice is between direct and indirect quotation: He boasted, "I can do twice as much work as you can"; *or* He boasted that he could do twice as much work as I could. In the second alternative the single phrase *twice as much work* could be quoted.

3. Miscellaneous uses of quotation marks.

a. Quotation marks enclose titles of poems, articles, stories, chapters of books, and, in most newspapers and many magazines, the titles of books themselves. See **Titles 2a.**

b. Words that are used as words rather than for their meaning usually appear in italics in formal writing, in quotes in general writing. But usage is divided:

> There is the ugly and almost universal use of "like" for "as."—Douglas Bush, *American Scholar*

> The word *buff* is old in the English language.—Webb Garrison, *American Legion Magazine*

c. A word from a conspicuously different variety of English is sometimes put in quotation marks, but this only calls attention to it. If you decide that such a word suits your needs, use it without apology and without quotes:

> He spurns aspirants not of his clique, thereby creating a tyranny of taste that soon will have every center of imaginative expression . . . under its cheesy [*not* "cheesy"] thrall.—Benjamin DeMott, *New American Review*

d. A word may be put in quotation marks to show that the writer is not accepting its conventional sense in the context:

> In numerous cases it is impossible to maintain on any solid ground that one pronunciation is "better" than another, as, for example, that one pronunciation of *swamp* is better than the others given.—John S. Kenyon and Thomas A. Knott, *A Pronouncing Dictionary of American English*

But putting a word in quotation marks to signal sarcasm or ridicule (The "cute" Great Dane had eaten my sweater) is on a par with putting a question mark in parentheses to get a laugh.

e. Directly quoted *yes* and *no* (sometimes capitalized, sometimes not) frequently appear without quotation marks when they're built into the sentence in which they appear: Steve said Yes, so we went to work at once. When they're not actually spoken, they shouldn't be quoted: If she had said no, I would have resigned.

4. Quotation marks with other marks.

a. When a question mark or an exclamation mark ends a quotation, it's placed inside the quotes:

> "Don't go near that wire!" he shouted.
> Later he said, "Aren't you wondering what would have happened?"

When a question mark or exclamation mark belongs to the construction that includes the quotation, it's placed after the quotes: What is an ordinary citizen to do when he hears the words, "This is a stick-up"? See **Question mark 2.**

b. American practice is to put periods and commas within closing quotation marks, colons and semicolons after them.

c. *He said* and all its variations are normally set off by commas from the quotations they introduce:

> "History," it is said, "does not repeat itself. The historians repeat one another."—Max Beerbohm, *Works*

But the quoted phrase may be so closely built into the sentence that no comma is wanted:

> Any moron can say "I don't know who done it."—Francis Christensen, *Notes Toward a New Rhetoric*

R

raise, rear

Raise in the sense of bringing up a child is suitable in all varieties of usage. *Rear* is somewhat formal. See **bring up.**

reaction

Reaction has drifted from the scientific vocabulary and is now used for nearly any response, whether emotional or mental, general or specific. Try to find a more precise term or at least a different one—*response,* for instance.

real, really

Ordinarily *real* is the adjective (a real difficulty, in real life), and *really* is the adverb (a really significant improvement; I really thought so). Both are overused as qualifiers; TV commercials and talk shows could barely exist without them, and ''in a real sense'' is one of the most tiresome of current clichés. Adverbial *real,* as in sentences like ''Write real soon'' and ''It's real pretty,'' is informal.

rear, raise

As applied to bringing up children, *rear* is the formal choice. See **raise, rear.**

reason is because

In formal writing there's a strong preference for *reason is that,* on the grounds that *reason is because* is redundant. Even in general writing, *that* is much more common when there are no intervening words after *reason* (My only reason is that I have to work tonight) or when the intervening words aren't a clause with a subject of its own (The only reason usually given for such failures in sports is that there was inadequate concentration). But when many words or a clause with a separate subject intervenes, *reason . . . is because* often occurs in both formal and general prose:

One reason why music can stand repetition so much more sturdily than correspondingly good prose is because music, of all the àrts, is by its nature least suited to the psychology of information, and has remained closer to the psychology of form.—Kenneth Burke, *Psychology and Form*

And the reason the press isn't a menace, Reston says, is because it has divested itself of so much of its power.—*Newsweek*

Even though *reason is because* has a long history in literature and is regularly used by educated speakers, writers should remind themselves that to some readers it's a hobgoblin.

Reciprocal pronouns

Each other and *one another* are called reciprocal pronouns. See **each other, Pronouns 3.**

reckon

Used to mean "suppose" or "think," *reckon* is a localism. See **Localisms.**

Redundancy

In writing, words and phrases that are repetitive or simply unnecessary are redundant. See **Repetition, Wordiness.**

ref Reference of pronouns

Change the pronoun marked (or revise the sentence) so that the reference will be clear and the pronoun appropriate to the context.

In the sentence "Because my brother loves to ski, he spent Christmas vacation in Colorado," the pronoun *he* replaces the nominal *my brother*. *My brother* is called the antecedent of *he; he* refers to the same person as *my brother*. In "He got so frostbitten I scarcely recognized him," the pronoun *I* has a referent (the speaker) but doesn't have an antecedent. Both categories of pronouns—those that have antecedents and those that don't—create some problems for writers.

1. Clear reference. If the meaning of a pronoun is completed by reference to an antecedent, the reference should be unmistakable. The reader shouldn't have to figure it out. Here are situations in which reference lacks the precision that college writing demands:

a. When the pronoun seems to refer to a nearby noun that it can't sensibly refer to:

The next year he had an attack of appendicitis. *It* burst before the doctor had a chance to operate.

Revision: . . . His appendix burst. . . . (*It* can't sensibly refer to *appendicitis*. Such slips in reference are common when the pronoun is in one sentence and the antecedent in another.)

b. When there's no noun nearby:

He isn't married yet and doesn't plan on *it*.

Revision: . . . and doesn't plan to marry.

c. When the pronoun refers to a noun used as a possessive or as an adjective:

Bill was skipping stones across the swimming hole. One cut open a young girl's head *who* was swimming under water.

Revision: . . . One cut open the head of a young girl who. . . .

Nancy longed for a chinchilla coat, though she wouldn't have dreamed of killing *one*.

Revision: . . . of killing a chinchilla.

d. When two or more pronouns are crossed so that exactly what is referred to can't be readily determined:

Businessmen without regard for anyone else have exploited the mass of workers at every point, not caring whether *they* were earning a decent living but only whether *they* were making big profits.

Revision: . . . not caring whether they paid a decent wage but only whether they were making big profits. (The sentence needs complete rewriting, but this revision at least makes both *they's* refer to the same antecedent.)

2. Broad reference.   General English uses *which, that, this,* and sometimes *it* to refer not to a specific word or phrase but to the idea of a preceding clause. Formal English avoids broad reference.

General: Her friend was jealous of her clothes and money and had taken this way of showing *it*.

Formal: . . . and had taken this way of showing her feeling.

General: The recent price jumps, then, are not primarily the middleman's fault, *which* is why he is happy no longer to be fingered in the [Consumer Price] index.—William Safire, *New York Times Magazine*

> *Formal:* . . . the middleman's fault, and this fact explains why he. . . .
> (More formal: . . . the fault of the middleman, and this fact explains why
> he. . . .)

3. Indefinite reference.   Often you'll use the pronouns *one, you, we,
he, they* in your papers to refer to your readers or to people in general
instead of specifically mentioned individuals. Which of these pronouns to
use is a matter of style, not of grammar. Once you've settled on one of
them, use it consistently: When *you* have worked a day here, *you* have
earned *your* money. With *one,* a shift to *he* is standard: When *one* has
worked a day here, *he* has earned *his* money. But *not:* When *one* has
worked a day here, *you* have earned *your* money. See **one.**

Don't substitute indefinite *one, you, he, we,* or *they* for a definite personal pronoun:

> For *me* there is no fun in reading unless *you* can put *yourself* in the position of
> the characters and feel that *you* are really in the scene.
>
> *Revision:* . . . unless I can put myself in the position of the characters and feel
> that I am. . . .

As a common-gender pronoun meaning "he or she," *he* is traditional
in formal English, *they* in informal. General usage is divided. *He* is more
conventional, *they* often more practical. See **Agreement 2, Sexist language.**

4. Avoiding and misusing pronouns.   Writers who are uncertain about
the reference or agreement of pronouns sometimes try to avoid them by
repeating nouns. The result is usually unidiomatic or clumsy: Arrest of the
woman yesterday followed several days of observation of the woman's (her)
activities by the agents.

Referent

The referent of a word is the thing or event or concept the word refers to.
In a specific context, "Carolyn Robb" and "the love of my life," referring
to the same person, would have the same referent.

Reflexive pronouns

Myself, yourself, himself, herself, itself, ourselves, yourselves, and *themselves* are reflexive pronouns. See **myself, Pronouns 2.**

relate

In the shoptalk of psychology the verb *relate* is a convenient term meaning to "have a realistic social or intimate relationship," as in "the patient's inability to relate." This sense of *relate* has passed into everyday usage, but the relationship is usually—and preferably—specified by a *to* phrase: They find it almost impossible to relate to adults. *Relate* became a vogue word in the 1960s.

Relative clauses

Relative clauses are introduced by relative pronouns *(that, which,* or *who)* or by relative adverbs *(where, when, why).* Those introduced by relative pronouns are often referred to as adjective clauses. A relative clause stands after the noun it modifies:

> The rain *that began in the morning* kept on all night.
> The coach was abused by the alumni *who two years before had cheered him.*
> The road to the left, *which looked almost impassable,* was ours.
> The first place *where they camped* turned out to be a swamp.

In general usage, when the clause is restrictive, the introductory adverb or pronoun (if the pronoun isn't the subject of the clause) is often omitted:

> He will never forget the time *you tried to cheat him.*
>
> *More formal:* . . . the time *when you tried to cheat him.*
>
> The man *I met that afternoon* became my closest friend.
>
> *More formal:* The man *whom I met.* . . .

When relative clauses are introduced by indefinite relative pronouns *(who, what,* and the compounds with *-ever),* the clauses function as nouns or as adjectives:

> The stranger at the door wasn't *who we thought she was.*
> *What actually happened* was very different from *what the newspapers reported.*
> The stranger at the door was the woman *who had moved in downstairs.*

Several relative clauses in succession make for an awkward house-that-Jack-built sentence: People who buy houses *that* have been built in times *which* had conspicuous traits of architecture *which* have since been abandoned often find *that* they have to remodel their purchases completely. See **Subordination 1.**

See **Pronouns 4; Restrictive and nonrestrictive modifiers; that; which; who, whom.** Compare **Noun clauses.**

Relative pronouns

The relative pronouns are *who (whose, whom), which (of which, whose), that, what, whatever,* and *whoever (whomever):*

> Somebody *who* was sitting on the other side shouted, "Put 'em out!"
> The Senator, *whose* term expires next year, is already worrying.
> I haven't read the same book *that* you have.

That refers to persons and things, *who* to persons. *Which* referring to animals or objects or situations and also to collective nouns, even if they refer to persons, is now standard English:

> The army *which* mobilizes first has the advantage.
> The Board of Directors, *which* met on Saturday. . . .
> The Board of Directors, *who* are all bankers. . . .

See **Pronouns 4; Restrictive and nonrestrictive modifiers; that; which; who, whom.**

rep Repetition

Get rid of the ineffective repetition of word, meaning, sound, or sentence pattern.

Repeating words, meanings, sounds, or sentence patterns is often effective in writing, giving prose clarity and emphasis. This article reviews some kinds of repetition that ordinarily call for revision.

1. Of words and phrases.   You're bound to repeat nouns unnecessarily if you don't use pronouns:

> Ann accepted the boy's challenge and proceeded to teach the boy [him] a lesson. When the boy [he] stayed at the base line, Ann [she] ran the boy [him] from one side of the court to the other. When the boy [he] charged the net, Ann [she] beat the boy [him] with passing shots.

If you write hurriedly and don't take the time to read over what you've written, you're likely to end up with careless repetition:

> I'm having financial difficulties and need to *get* out of housing. So the hassle I *got* when I tried to *get* released from my dorm contract upset me.

When you use the same word in two different senses, the result may be worse:

> After I fell only a few feet my left foot found footing.

> I would like to find a job with a concern that shows some concern for the environment.

In cases like these, the repetition is obvious enough to be caught and corrected with little trouble—either by omitting the unnecessary repetition or by substituting synonyms. But it does call for that little trouble.

Harder for writers to spot but equally conspicuous to readers is the pet word or phrase that pops up three or four times in the course of a paper. If it's a cliché or a vogue expression, as it's likely to be, it may bother some readers on its first appearance and become increasingly irritating thereafter. In going over a first draft, then, keep an eye out for expressions that recur. Some of the repeated words and phrases will be unavoidable, some desirable. But you may also spot some pets that you've repeated simply because they're pets. Sacrifice them.

2. Of meaning.   In reviewing what you've written, watch for words and phrases that unnecessarily repeat what you've already said. For example, a gift is free and a fact true by definition, so drop the adjective from "free gift" and from "true fact." If the setting of many TV plays is San Francisco, then San Francisco must frequently be the setting of TV plays. Writing "In many TV plays the setting very often is San Francisco" adds words but subtracts sense. So does "at 8 a.m. in the morning."

3. Of sounds.   Jingles and rhyming words (hesitate to take the bait, a glance askance at the dance) are distracting in papers because they draw attention from sense to sound. So are noticeable repetitions of unstressed syllables, especially the *-ly* of adverbs and the endings of some abstract nouns, like *-tion*. Reading first drafts aloud is the best way to catch such unintentional repetition of sound as "Reliance on science has led to compliance. . . ." See **Adverbs and style, Alliteration, Assonance.**

4. Of sentence patterns.   If you unintentionally use the same pattern in one sentence after another—beginning three sentences in a row with a dependent clause, for example, or writing three successive compound sentences, or using the same coordinating conjunction in a series of sentences for no rhetorical purpose—your reader is likely to begin nodding. Sometimes this sort of repetition sets up a rhythm even more distracting than the repetition of sound within sentences. Sometimes it simply begins to bore the reader; he feels that he's being led over the same route again and again. Deliberate varying of sentence patterns isn't often called for, but if you find yourself recycling a pattern, make an effort to get untracked.

Requests

Requests are often expressed in the form of questions: Will you please co-operate? Sometimes a period takes the place of the question mark. See **Commands and requests.**

rest Restrictive and nonrestrictive modifiers

If the modifier marked is restrictive, don't separate it from the word it modifies by a comma. If it is nonrestrictive, set it off by a comma or by two commas.

"Lemmon, who isn't Jewish, plays Jews who aren't Jewish either" (Pauline Kael, *New Yorker*). The first *who* clause in the quoted sentence tells us something about Jack Lemmon, but it doesn't set him apart. It can be dropped from the sentence without destroying the meaning: Lemmon plays Jews who aren't Jewish. But the *who* clause modifying *Jews* is essential to Kael's point: the Jewishness of the characters Lemmon plays is superficial and trivial. Dropping that clause would leave us with "Lemmon plays Jews," which isn't what Kael is saying. Separating the second clause from the main clause with a comma would give us "Lemmon plays Jews, who aren't Jewish," which is nonsense. The first *who* clause is nonrestrictive. The second *who* clause is restrictive.

1. Restrictive modifiers. An adjective (or relative) clause or an adjective phrase is a restrictive modifier when the information it provides about something in the main clause is essential to the meaning the writer intends.

If you speak a sentence before you write it, or read it aloud after you've written it, you can usually tell whether a clause or phrase is restrictive:

> The girl *whose book I borrowed* has dropped the course.
> The books *stolen from the library* were found in that locker.

When the modifier is restrictive, you don't pause between the word modified and the clause or phrase that modifies it.

You can be quite sure a clause is restrictive if you can begin it with *that:* The year *that I dropped out* is one *that I'd be glad to forget.* And a clause is restrictive if you can omit the relative pronoun: The year [*that*] *I dropped out* is one [*that*] *I'd be glad to forget;* The people [*whom*] *we met;* The plan [*which*] *they came up with.*

2. Nonrestrictive modifiers. An adjective (or relative) clause or adjective phrase that can be dropped from a sentence without changing or blurring the meaning is nonrestrictive and should be set off by a comma or commas. The importance of the information the modifier provides is not the deciding factor. If you write, "The bullet *which came within an inch of my head* smashed my mother's favorite teacup," the content of your adjective clause would seem to be a lot more important than the destruction of the teacup. But unless you're using the clause to specify *this* bullet among a number of bullets—unless the information in the clause is essential to the meaning of *this* sentence—you should set it off with commas.

If *which* were used to launch only nonrestrictive clauses, as *that* is used to launch restrictive clauses, *which* and *that* clauses would cause few problems. But there are times when *which* seems a better choice for starting a restrictive clause: That was the bad news *which we had been given every reason to expect. (Which* avoids the repetition of *that.)* And some clauses are restrictive in one context, nonrestrictive in another. In a different context, the clause *whose book I borrowed,* used as an example of a restrictive clause in the preceding section, can be nonrestrictive: The girl, whose book I borrowed, left soon afterward with an older woman. So can the example of a restrictive phrase: The books, stolen from the library, later turned up in a secondhand store.

Your job, then, is to know what you mean. In the modifying clause or phrase, do you mean to say something that the sentence requires for its basic meaning, or do you mean to offer information which—no matter how important—can be omitted from that sentence without detracting from its central message? If the former, the modifier is restrictive—no commas. If the latter, the modifier is nonrestrictive—commas. Say the sentence out loud. Do you make a definite pause before the modifier? Then it's nonrestrictive—commas.

You may find the same advice useful in punctuating other modifiers. Traditionally, the restrictive/nonrestrictive distinction has applied to a dependent clause introduced by a relative pronoun and functioning as an adjective. Some grammarians extend the principle to all adjectival modifiers, to appositives (see **Apposition, appositives**), and to some adverbial modifiers, including final adverbial clauses (see **Comma 2b**).

rhetoric

To the ancient Greeks and Romans, rhetoric was the art of persuasion as applied to public speaking. With the invention of printing, the term was broadened to include written argument, and some modern theoreticians broaden it still further—to something like "the art of expression." What modern rhetorics have in common with classical ones is the idea of influencing an audience: the speaker or writer of rhetorical discourse aims to bring about a change in the attitudes, beliefs, habits, or actions of the audience.

Perhaps because skill in persuasion can be turned to bad uses as well as good ones, in general usage *rhetoric* has acquired connotations of manipulation, deceit, trickery, flamboyant insincerity, or empty verbiage—"just words.'' Currently a writer can assume that most audiences other than those that are studying, or have studied, the principles of rhetoric will regard *rhetoric* as a term of abuse.

The suggestion of empty verbiage is equally strong in most current uses of *rhetorical:* ''It will be interesting to see how many men are prepared to give more than rhetorical support today to the sex from which they have, for centuries, demanded and accepted so much'' (Adrienne Rich, *Chronicle of Higher Education*).

In this book the connotations of the term *rhetoric* are entirely favorable. The use of language for dishonest purposes is condemned. To be skilled in rhetoric is to write well, and the good writer never writes ''just words.''

Rhetorical questions

Rhetorical questions are really statements in the form of questions, since no direct answer is expected: ''Who of us born before 1950 went to college burdened with the psycho-babble of the self which recurs in all three of these memoirs—'creating a supportive community' with 'people who feel comfortable with each other's needs'?'' (Francine du Plessix Gray, *New York Review of Books*). As a stylistic device the rhetorical question has its dangers: the reader may reject the answer the writer intends—in the preceding example, ''None of us.''

right

The use of *right* in the senses ''directly'' and ''immediately'' before phrases of place and time (right across the street, right after the show) is avoided in most formal writing but is established in general usage. Phrases like *right here, right there, right now,* and *right then,* though similarly avoided in formal contexts, are commonplace in general ones. Idioms like *right away* and *right off* (''at once'' or ''now'') and *right along* (''continuously'' or ''all the time'') are slightly more informal.

In the sense of ''very,'' *right* is a localism, in good standing in the South: We'll be right glad to see you.

rise

Rise is somewhat less formal than *arise,* more formal than *get up.* See **arise, rise, get up.**

rob

A person or place is robbed. What's taken in the robbery is stolen. *Rob* for *steal* (They're the ones who robbed the money) is an old usage considered nonstandard today. See **burglar, robber, thief.**

Roman numerals

Roman numerals may be either lower case (iii, v, x) or capitals (III, V, X). See **Numbers 3.**

round, around

Round is a preposition and adverb in its own right, often interchangeable with *around:* "an easy irony, good for a laugh the first two or three times round" (Stanley Kaufmann, *New Republic*). It should not be written with an initial apostrophe ('round).

Around for "approximately" (around 1920; a cast of around forty) is now found in all varieties of usage.

The general adjectives *all-round* and *all-around* are overused, particularly with *athlete*.

Run-on sentence

The label *run-on sentence* is applied variously to a sentence in which two independent clauses are run together with no punctuation between, to a sentence in which two independent clauses are joined with only a comma between, and to a sentence in which a series of independent clauses are joined with coordinating conjunctions. Unless a particular meaning is specified, *run-on* is more confusing than useful. See **Comma splice, Fused sentence.**

 S

said

As a modifier (the said person, the said idea), *said* is legal language. In general writing, *that* or *this* or just *the* is the right choice.

saint

The abbreviation *St.* is commonly used in names of places (St. Albans, St. Louis) and often before the names of saints (St. Francis, St. Anthony of Padua). The plural of the abbreviation is *SS.* (SS. Peter and Paul). Occasionally the French feminine form *Sainte* is used (Sault Sainte Marie); the abbreviation is *Ste.* Spanish forms are common in the American West: San Diego, Santa Barbara. In writing a personal name beginning with *Saint* (Camille Saint-Saens) or *St.* (Louis St. Laurent), use the spelling the bearer uses or did use.

say

Say is the usual word for "speaking" and can also be used for what's written: In his journal, Gide says. . . . In dialog repetition of "he said," "she said" is almost always better than strained alternatives like *expostulated, muttered, babbled, hissed. State,* which implies a formal "saying," is a poor substitute for *say,* whether in dialog or in ordinary text: "To be able to state this of the new work of an American poet of 50 is, to state the least, unusual" (Aram Saroyan, *New York Times Book Review*). *Assert* and similar substitutes are also unsatisfactory in most contexts. See **claim.**

Say in the sense of "approximately," "for instance," "let us say," is used in all varieties of writing: "the specialist in the literature of, say, the English eighteenth century" (Howard Mumford Jones, *Journal of the History of Ideas*).

scarcely

When *scarcely* means "almost not," adding a *not* as in "can't scarcely" is redundant. See **Double negative 2.**

scenario

Scenario became a vogue word in the 1970s and has taken on meanings having little connection with "script" or "synopsis." When you mean *plan, prediction,* or *possibility,* use that word, instead of relying on *scenario* and forcing the reader to decide which is meant.

seem

Seem is often used to qualify a statement unnecessarily: They [seem to] run with a gang that can't [seem to] keep out of trouble. Limit your use of *seem* to situations in which you must be tentative. Don't say something *seems to be* when you know it *is.* See **can't help but, can't seem to.**

self

Self as a suffix forms the reflexive and intensive pronouns *myself, yourself, himself, herself, itself, oneself, ourselves, yourselves, themselves.* These are used chiefly for emphasis (I can do that myself) or as objects identical to the subjects of their verbs (I couldn't help myself). See **himself, herself; myself; Pronouns 2.**

As a prefix, *self* is joined to the root word by a hyphen: *self-control, self-explanatory, self-made, self-respect.* When *self* is the root word, there is no hyphen: *selfhood, selfish, selfless.*

semi-

Semi- is a prefix meaning "half or approximately half" *(semicylindrical),* "twice within a certain period" *(semiweekly, semiannual),* or "partially, imperfectly" *(semicivilized, semiprofessional). Semi-* is a live element in forming new words.

Semicolon

Use a semicolon as the link between these sentence elements.

1. To link coordinate clauses.

a. Between clauses without connectives. Use a semicolon, especially in a rather formal context, to link two independent clauses whose relatedness you want to emphasize:

> Some years ago, a learned colleague who was old and ill complained to me that he could no longer read German; it made his legs feel queer. I know that feeling well; I have had it while trying to read Henry James.—P. B. Ballard, *Thought and Language*

> To stay warm, he jumped around and flapped his arms and meditated on the warmth of God; his companion, a shadowy, shrunken hobo, sat hunched in a corner with the patience of the ages.—Dennis McNally, *Desolate Angel*

b. With conjunctive adverbs. Use a semicolon to link clauses connected by a conjunctive adverb such as *however, moreover, therefore* at the beginning of the second clause:

> His popularity was undiminished; however, he no longer enjoyed the work.

> Finally, despite the hopes and prophecies described before, we do not really agree on philosophical and political values; therefore the conference, moved by the same desire for survival and development as the world at large, carefully avoided exposing the ideological differences that remain.—Stanley Hoffman, *Daedalus*

A comma before *however* or *therefore* in these sentences would produce a comma splice. See **Conjunctive adverbs.**

c.   With coordinating conjunctions. Consider using a semicolon between clauses connected by a coordinating conjunction *(and, but, for, or . . .)* if the clauses are long, if they contain commas, or if for some reason—perhaps for contrast—you want to indicate a more definite break than you would show with a comma:

> The War on Poverty was a *policy* that purported to cure America's gravest social ills; but while Johnson was raising millenial expectations, federal *spending* programs in fact were making inner-city problems worse.—T. D. Allman, *Harper's*

> I do not suggest that as English teachers we stop talking about planning and organization; nor am I saying that logical thought has nothing to do with the organizational process.—Robert Zoellner, *College English*

2.   To separate units with internal commas.   The units may consist of listed figures or words (see, for example, the cross references at the end of the first paragraph of **self**). They may be phrases or clauses. The sentences may be long or short:

> [The snow leopard] has enormous paws and a short-faced heraldic head, like a leopard of myth; it is bold and agile in the hunt, and capable of terrific leaps; and although its usual prey is the blue sheep and the ibex, it occasionally takes livestock, including young yak of several hundred pounds.—Peter Matthiessen, *New Yorker*

> Their lyrics have been for songs; Sondheim's, for scenes.—Martin Gottfried, *Saturday Review*

In the second example, the comma after *Sondheim's* makes the semicolon after *songs* necessary.

3.   Semicolon and colon.   Do not confuse the semicolon with the colon. Don't use a semicolon to introduce a quotation or a listing or to perform other conventional functions of the colon (see **Colon 3**). The one occasion when you have a choice between colon and semicolon is when you're punctuating independent clauses. The semicolon is the usual link. The colon is more formal and suggests that the second clause will explain or illustrate the first. Often the choice is mostly a matter of style.

4.   Semicolons and style.   Semicolons are usually more suitable in the longer, more complicated sentences of formal styles than in general and informal writing, except when other punctuation makes them necessary (see **2** above). In general styles commas are often used where semicolons might appear in formal writing, or else clauses that could be linked by semicolons are written as separate sentences. But this doesn't mean that, when writing general English, you should deny your prose the effects that semicolons can give it. The use of a semicolon is often as much a matter of personal choice as of correct punctuation.

Compare **Colon, Comma.**

sensual, sensuous

Both *sensual* and *sensuous* refer to the senses, but the connotations of *sensual* are more physical, of *sensuous* more aesthetic. Sensual music and sensuous music are two different things.

Sentence fragment

A sentence fragment is a part of a sentence punctuated as a complete sentence. See **Fragment.**

Sentences

1. Classifying sentences grammatically. On the basis of their clause structure, sentences are classified grammatically as simple, complex, compound, and compound-complex. Each of these types of sentences can be expanded by making subjects, verbs, and objects compound and by using appositives and modifiers. See **Absolute phrases, Clauses.**

2. Analyzing sentences rhetorically. A sentence is not only a grammatical unit but also a rhetorical unit. Rhetorical analysis of a sentence takes into account the order of elements, the repetition of grammatical structures, and the appropriateness of such ordering and repeating to the idea expressed and to the rhetorical situation. See **Phrases and style.**

3. Building sensible sentences. Build your clauses and arrange their parts so as to bring out the natural and logical relationships in your material. When properly used, for example, subordination and parallelism clarify such relationships. Misused, they blur or distort them. If reducing clauses to phrases or single words is a way of packing more meaning into a sentence, reversing the process—converting some elements into separate sentences—can lighten an overloaded sentence and improve its unity and clarity. See **Coordination, Shifted constructions, Subordination.**

Although some structures that lack an independent subject-verb combination are rhetorically effective, most sentences have at least one such combination. Generally, faults in sentence construction result from failure to recognize the difference between a dependent clause and an independent clause or from failure to show the relation between a modifier and what it modifies. See **Comma splice, Dangling modifier, Fragment, Fused sentence.**

Sequence of tenses

In some sentences the tense of a verb in one clause is determined by the tense of a verb in another. See **Tense 3.**

Series

A succession of words, phrases, or clauses that are grammatically coordinate makes a series. Sometimes the units are simply separated by commas (apples, pears, persimmons), but usually the last unit is joined to the rest by a coordinating conjunction. Usage is divided over putting a comma before the conjunction:

> He worked in an ad agency, trained polo ponies, and did landscape gardening on a Long Island estate.—Sanford J. Smoller, *Adrift Among Geniuses*

> Another patron . . . came to see the go-go boys with her mother, her sister [ ] and her Kodak movie camera.—Jeannette Smith, *Washington Post*

Though many writers, especially in general and informal styles, omit the comma, using it helps to indicate that the units are equivalent and in some instances prevents misunderstanding (see **Comma 5**). If the units are long or have internal commas, they're often separated by semicolons (see **Semicolons 2**).

For the rhetorical effects of a series, see **Parallelism and style, Phrases and style.**

set, sit

In standard English, people and things *sit* (past: *sat*) or they are *set* (past: *set*)—that is "placed":

> I like to sit in a hotel lobby.
> I have sat in this same seat for three semesters.
> She set the casserole down with a flourish.
> The post was set three feet in the ground.

A hen, however, sets (on her eggs), cement sets, and the sun sets. A large dining room table sits eight, and few city people know how to sit a horse.

Sexist language

Since the revival of the movement for equality of the sexes, there has been much criticism of discrimination against women—that is, sexism—both in current usage and in the grammar of formal English. Examples of usage that patronizes or denigrates women include labels like *working girls, coed, the little woman, the weaker sex, boss lady, woman driver*, and *lady doctor* and use of the suffixes *-ess* and *-ette: poetess, Jewess, suffragette, usherette*. Similarly offensive to many is the use of first names for women where men's full names or last names are used: Before Robert Browning came to know her, Elizabeth [Barrett] was already considered a rival of Tennyson.

Then there are the words for certain occupations and offices that seem to imply that women are excluded: *policeman, businessman, chairman, Congressman*. And most galling of all to many is the use of *man* and *men* to stand for *men-and-women (manpower, the common man, man-made, free men)* and for the whole human race *(prehistoric man, mankind,* "all men are created equal," "the brotherhood of man") and the use of *he (him, his)* as the pronoun referring to a noun that doesn't specify gender or to an indefinite pronoun *(student, citizen, spectator, person, anyone, no one)*.

Though some feminists attach relatively little importance to such usage, others see it as a subtle but powerful conditioner of attitudes toward the sexes from very early childhood. For those who are seriously concerned, the substitution of *-woman* for *-man* in the words for occupations and offices *(policewoman, businesswoman, chairwoman, Congresswoman)* is no solution to the problem. Like *lady driver* and *woman doctor*, it calls attention to gender where gender is not, or should not be, of any significance. (*Male nurse* belongs in the same category. Opponents of sexist language deplore terms that stereotype either men or women.)

Person(s), people, and *humans* or (better) *human beings* are common substitutes for *man, men, mankind* when both sexes are intended. An increasing number of writers now avoid the traditional use of *he* to stand for *he or she* by using the latter in its various forms: Everyone must turn in his or her theme. . . . But because the wordiness is easily compounded and awkwardness is almost inevitable (. . . if he or she wants a passing grade), there's a growing tendency to write in the plural (All students must turn in their themes . . .) or to treat *they (them, their)* as an indefinite common-gender singular (Everyone must turn in their theme . . .). See **Agreement 2, he or she, they.**

If you consider sexism in language an issue of overriding importance, then in your writing you'll try to avoid all the usages you look on as sexist, probably including the use of *man* for an individual of either sex and any age and the use of *he* for *he or she*. If you don't believe that sexism exists in the language, or don't care if it does, or applaud the masculine bias, you'll ignore the whole matter when you write. But if you belong to neither of these extremes, you have choices to make. Even if you're mainly satisfied with the language as it is, you should be aware that your readers may not be. You can easily avoid the more obtrusive sexist usages, such as descriptive terms that classify women physically when their looks have no relevance (the blonde defense attorney) or that suggest a general lack of intelligence and competence (a cute little pre-med student). You may also decide to find substitutes for the *-man* words (*police officer* for *policeman,* for example) and to cut down on your use of generic *he* in sentences like "When a young person says he is interested in helping people, his counselor tells him to become a psychiatrist."

How far you go will depend in part on your own sensitivities as a writer. If your sense of style makes you wince at *he or she* (or *he/she* or *s/he),* if the connotations of *artificial* prevent you from accepting it as a substitute for *man-made,* if *persons* and *humans* bother you at least as much as generic *man,* then you face much more difficult choices than those writers who can settle the problem to their own satisfaction with the rhetorical question, "What's more important—syntax or souls?" For those truly torn between the demands of feminist ideology and the demands of stylistic grace and flow, the only solution is to write and revise and rewrite until at last the conflicts are resolved and both ideological and aesthetic demands are satisfied.

In this book *he* is used to refer to *student* and *writer* not because of bias or obtuseness but in the interest of economy and readability.

shall, will

Since the eighteenth century some grammarians have insisted that in expressing determination in statements about the future, *will* should be used with first-person subjects (I will pass the course) and *shall* with second- and third- (They shall do as they're told). But practice has never been uniform. In current American usage *will* is much more common with all three persons. The same grammarians have tried to keep the single function of indicating the future distinct by urging that *shall* be used with first-person subjects (I shall be at a meeting that night) and *will* with second- and third- (You will arrive about Thursday, Joan says). But again, in standard usage *will* is much more commmon than *shall* in all persons. *Shall* occurs most frequently in legal language and is usually the natural choice in first-person requests for instructions: Shall I close the door? See **should, would.**

shift Shifted constructions

Avoid the unnecessary shift in construction.

Shifted constructions are needless changes in grammatical form or point of view within a sentence. In speech and in much informal writing, shifted constructions are common, but in general and formal prose they're avoided, because they trouble the reader. The many types of needless shifting include the following:

1.   Between adjective and noun: This book is interesting and an informative piece of work. *Revised: . . .* interesting and informative.

2.   Between noun and clause: The most important factors are time and temperature, careful control at every point, and the mechanical equipment must be efficient. *Revised: . . .* and efficient mechanical equipment.

3.   Between adverb phrase and adjective phrase: Along these walks are the cottages, some of which have stood since the founding but others quite recent. *Revised: . . .* but others for only a short time.

4.   Between gerund and infinitive: Carrying four courses and to hold down a job at the same time will either develop my character or kill me. *Revised:* Carrying four courses and holding down a job. *. . .*

5.   Between gerund and finite verb: I have heard complaints about the plot being weak and that the setting is played up too much. *Revised: . . .* and the setting being played up. *. . .*

6.   Between participle and finite verb: You often see a fisherman trying to get quietly to his favorite spot but instead he broadcasts warnings with his rhythmical squeak-splash, squeak-splash. *Revised: . . .* but instead broadcasting warnings. *. . .*

7.   Between transitive verb and copula: Anyone who has persistence or is desperate enough can get a job on a ship. *Revised: . . .* who is persistent or who is desperate enough. *. . .*

8.   Between past and present: The tanks bulled their way through the makeshift barricades and fan out across the enormous plaza. *Revised: . . .* and fanned out. *. . .*

9.   Between active and passive: The committee members disliked each other heartily, and their time was wasted in wrangling. *Revised: . . .* heartily and wasted their time in wrangling.

10. Between personal and impersonal: When one is sick, you make few plans. *Revised:* When one is sick, one (*or* he) makes. *. . .*
   . No enumeration of shifted constructions could be complete: there are too many constructions to shift.

See **Parallelism and style; Point of view; Reference of pronouns; Tense 2, 3; when, where.**

Shoptalk

Shoptalk is the words that people in the same occupation use among themselves to refer to the things they regularly concern themselves with in their work: the noun *mud* among bricklayers to mean "mortar," the verb *docket* among lawyers to mean "make an abstract."

No occupation gets along without shoptalk. All have everyday terms that may be meaningless to outsiders but are indispensable to those who practice the trade or profession. Especially convenient are short, informal substitutes for long technical terms. So a *mike* may be a microphone in a broadcasting studio, a microscope in a laboratory, a micrometer in a shop. A *hypo* is a fixing bath to a photographer, a hypodermic injection to a nurse. Many such words are metaphoric (the television *ghost*) or imitative (the radar *blip*). Much shoptalk is so specialized or colorless that it never spreads to the general vocabulary—such printshop words as *chase, em, pi, quoins,* for example.

So long as the terms from shoptalk remain narrowly specialized, they should be used only in certain contexts or technical writing. They are inappropriate in prose intended for general audiences.

See **Jargon.** See also **Gobbledygook, Psychologese, Slang.**

should, would

In indirect discourse, *should* and *would* can function as the past tenses of *shall* and *will.* "We will go" can be reported as "He announced that we would go," and "We shall go" as "He announced that we should [*or* would] go." Because *should* has a connotation of propriety or obligation that may not be intended, *would* is preferable. See **shall, will; Tense 3.**

sic

Sic, the Latin word meaning "thus," is used to indicate that what precedes it has been quoted correctly. See **Brackets.**

sick, ill

Ill is the more formal, less common word. In the United States *ill* and *sick* mean the same thing. In British usage *sick* is usually restricted to mean "nauseated": "The mere touch of the thing would make me sick or ill, or both" (Richard Jones, *The Three Suitors*). In American usage *sick* in that sense is made clear by adding a phrase: It made me sick to (at/in) my stomach. Saying that something or someone "makes me sick" is normally figurative, meaning "disgusts me."

Simile

A simile compares with *like* or *as:* He swims like a winded walrus; straight as a lodgepole pine.

simplistic

Don't use *simplistic*, which means "oversimplified," as a fancy form of *simple*. A simple explanation and a simplistic explanation are quite different. When you mean "oversimplified," *oversimplified* is a better choice than the voguish *simplistic*.

since

As a subordinating conjunction, *since* can have the meaning "because": Since we were already late, we didn't rush. See **because.**

sit, set

People and things *sit* or *are set.* See **set, sit.**

-size

Size is typical of a class of nouns *(age, color, height, shape, width, weight . . .)* that also function as apparent modifiers: *medium-size, standard-size, life-size, outsize, oversize.* The *-size* words are redundant in compound modifiers with adjectives that should modify the head nouns directly: not "small-size box" but "small box," and similarly with "round-shape table," "younger-age students," "dark-color hair," and so on. See **Wordiness 1.**

Slang

Drawing a line between slang and other kinds of informal English is difficult. Many people use the term *slang* too broadly, applying it to almost any informal word, and dictionaries have been too generous with the label, marking as slang many words that simply suggest spoken rather than written style. In fact, there is no fully accepted criterion for marking off the segment of the vocabulary that constitutes slang, as disagreement among and between dictionaries and handbooks makes clear.

Though some of the words labeled slang in current dictionaries—*lulu, corker, deadbeat*—have been around for generations, the central characteristic of slang comes from the motive for using it: a desire for novelty, for vivid emphasis, for being up with the times or a little ahead, for belonging—either to a particular social group or, more broadly, to an age group or, more broadly still, to the in-group that uses the current slang. These are essentially qualities of style, and the tone and connotation are as important as the meaning of the words. Other varieties of language have ways of expressing the ideas of slang words, but their tone is more conventional. Young people like novelty, and so do grown-ups with youthful ideas. Entertainers need it in their trade. In-groups, both legal and illegal, have their slang vocabularies, which often spill over into general English. Some of the slang of drug users *(fix, snort)* has wide circulation among nonusers.

Slang is made by natural linguistic processes. It's full of clipped words *(porn, natch, hood, vibes)* and compounds and derivatives of ordinary words *(screwball, sourpuss, cockeyed, put-on, rip-off)*. Many slang terms are borrowed from the shoptalk of sports and the popular arts, especially jazz and rock. And a great many are figurative extensions of general words: *nut, dope, egg* (applied to people), *heavy, hung up, turned on, plugged in, spaced out*. Sound often contributes a good deal, as in *barf, booboo, ding-a-ling, goof, kook, nerd, wimp, zap, zip, zonk*.

Because most slang words have short lives, any discussion of slang in print is bound to be out of date. *Skidoo, vamoose, beat it, scram, hit the trail, take a powder, drag out, shag out, cut out, split* succeeded each other within a short lifetime. Words for being drunk *(soused, plastered, bombed)* and words of approval *(tops, neat, the most, cool, groovy, out of sight, baddest, dynamite, intense)* and disapproval *(all wet, lousy, cruddy, gross, downer, bummer, shuck, turkey)* change from year to year—though some survive and some recur. Many slang words prove permanently useful and become a part of the informal vocabulary *(blind date, boy friend)* or the general vocabulary *(highbrow, lemon)*.

The chief objection to slang in writing, aside from its conspicuousness, is that it elbows out more exact expressions. A slang cliché is at least as boring as a cliché in standard English, and slang that names general impressions instead of specific ones is in no way better than comparable words in the general vocabulary, like *nice* and *good*. If slang expressions are appropriate to the subject matter and the audience and if they come naturally to the writer, they should be used without apology (that is, without quotation marks). If they're not appropriate—or if they've become tiresome vogue expressions, as slang words and phrases often do—they should not be used, with or without quotation marks.

slow, slowly

Slow is widely used in speech and in informal writing in place of slowly. In general writing its use is restricted to only a few contexts: He drove *slow; but* He drove away *slowly*. See **Adverbs and style 1, Divided usage.** Compare **bad, badly.**

so

1. *So* **and** *so that.*   To introduce clauses of purpose, *so that* is ordinarily expected in formal contexts, but *so* by itself is respectable in general use:

> [The ghost of] Patroclus comes to ask Achilles to bury him quickly so that he may pass into the realm of Hades.—Anne Amory, *Yale Classical Studies*

> I might have tried . . . to give a clearer idea of the rest of the contents, so readers could gather some notion of whether or not this kind of material might interest them.—John Thompson, *New York Review of Books*

To express consequence or result, both *so* alone and *so that* are found in all varieties of usage. *Speculum: A Journal of Medieval Studies* had these two passages in the same issue:

> The old bishop was better known as a fighter than as a churchman, so we may reasonably assume that it was prudence and not cowardice which prompted him.—Herbert L. Oerter

> He quotes frequently from the Old French, so that the reader gains a very good appreciation of the style.—Alfred Foulet

2. *So* **as substitute.**   *So* can substitute for a whole clause: I think *I will win;* at least I hope *so.*

3. *So* **as an intensive.**   As an intensive, *so* is informal: They're so rich!

so . . . as

So . . . as is an alternative to *as . . . as* in negative comparisons of degree: The gateway to nirvana is not so wide as a barn door. See **as . . . as 3.**

so-called

If you have to use *so-called,* don't duplicate the idea by putting the name of the so-called object in quotes: the so-called champion; *not* the so-called "champion."

some

1. **As a subject.**   *Some* as a subject takes either a singular verb (*Some* of the material *is* difficult) or a plural verb (*Some* of the tests *are* easy), depending on the context.

2. As an adverb. *Some* as a qualifier is informal: He's some older than she is. More formal usage would have *somewhat.* Informally, *some* is also used to modify verbs: The springs were squeaking some.

In formal writing the adverb *someplace* is still avoided in favor of *somewhere,* but in the last generation or so *someplace* has moved from informal to general usage: "I began to get some idea of what I came to call the Civilization of the Dialogue, a phrase I am sure I stole someplace" (Robert M. Hutchins, *Saturday Review*). *Somewheres* is nonstandard. Compare **any.**

3. As one word or two. The compounds *somebody, somehow, something, someway, somewhat, somewhere* are written as one word. *Someone* is one word (Someone is coming) unless *one* is stressed (some one of them). *Someday* is written as either one word or two. *Sometime* in "Drop in sometime" means "at some time [two words] in the future."

somebody, someone

Like *anybody* and *anyone, somebody* and *someone* are singular and take singular verbs. In formal writing they also are referred to by a singular pronoun—*he (him, his).* In informal and general styles both words are often referred to by *they (them, their)* in the sense "he or she" ("him or her," "his or her"): If somebody dents my car in the parking lot, I expect them to leave their name. But conservative prejudice against this usage is strong.

sp Spelling

Correct the spelling of the word marked, referring to a dictionary if necessary.

Use your dictionary, and when alternative spellings are listed, choose the one that introduces the entry. See **Apostrophe, Capital letters, Foreign words in English, Hyphen, Plurals of nouns, Principal parts of verbs.** See also **British English, Divided usage.**

Split infinitive

An infinitive is said to be split when an adverb or an adverbial element separates the *to* from its following verb: The receptionist asked them to *kindly* sit down.

Many people have been taught to avoid splitting infinitives, and sometimes there's good reason to do so. Certainly, long intervening elements are awkward: After a while he was able to, although not very accurately, distinguish good customers from disloyal ones. Such interrupters should be moved, often to the end of the sentence.

Formal writing rather consistently avoids the split infinitive, even when the adverb can't be placed at the end of the clause:

> We must have sufficient foresight and vision patiently to guide the peoples of the world along the road they have chosen to follow.—Bernard Kiernan, *American Scholar*

> The Chinese model . . . never eclipsed the local differences that made Japan always and Korea sometimes so distinct from China as properly to constitute a separate civilization.—William H. McNeill, *The Rise of the West*

But if long intervening elements are awkward, short adverbs that modify the infinitive may fit smoothly and clearly between the *to* and the verb. Split infinitives often appear in good general writing. The first of the following citations would be ambiguous if "really" were placed before "to" and unidiomatic if it were placed after "hate." In the second, "precisely to locate" might be ambiguous, and "to locate precisely enough" would invite misreading:

> To really hate the old ruling class we would have to live under it in its days of decay.—John K. Fairbank, *New Republic*

> The major mission of Apollo 10 was to precisely locate enough lunar landmarks to prevent the crewmen of Apollo 11 from dropping onto terrain for which they would be unprepared.—John Lear, *Saturday Review*

When the prejudice against the split infinitive makes a writer bend over backwards to avoid it, his meaning is often bent as well:

> She had demonstrated her inability to rear properly numerous other children.

> Myrdal replied that it would be the proper function of planning constantly to strengthen nongovernmental structures.

In the first sentence the adverb "properly" can be read as if it modifies "numerous." In the second, "constantly" might modify "planning." Both would be improved by splitting the infinitives.

Often the decision to split or not to split is stylistic. It can be based on where the writer wants the emphasis to fall. If the sentence ". . . no one expected those who have been campaigning for a greater role for women in the Catholic Church in the U.S. to meekly drop their efforts" *(Newsweek)* ended instead with "to drop their efforts meekly," *meekly* would receive greater stress.

Spoken and written English

Though talking and writing are related, overlapping skills, they differ in several respects. Speech is peppered with expressions that seldom appear in writing other than dialog: "y'know," "y'see," "right?" and all the grunts and murmurs that ask for and provide feedback in conversation. When we talk, we pay far less attention to the shape of our sentences than when we write. We're more casual about pronoun reference and agreement; we let *and* and *so* do most of the work of joining statements; we rarely make the effort to build phrases and clauses in parallel series; and we hardly ever use the nonrestrictive clause. (We might write, "Picasso, who was born in Spain, never lost his fondness for Barcelona," but we'd probably say, "Picasso was born in Spain, and he always loved Barcelona.")

The number of significantly different sounds that all of us use in speech is much larger than the number of symbols in our writing system. In talk, words are always part of a pattern involving pitch, stress, and pause, for which the marks of punctuation provide only the barest hints. Writing blurs or fails to suggest a great many speech signals, including body language— the stance, the gesture, even the slight rise of an eyebrow that may reinforce or modify the message. Whether "more" modifies "competent" or "competent men" in "more competent men" would be shown in speech by stress (heavier stress on the "more" that modifies "competent men"). To make the distinction in writing, rewording might be necessary: more men who are competent; more truly competent men.

But if we can communicate some things more directly in talk than in writing, the reverse is also true. Punctuation indicates quotations efficiently, including quotations within quotations. Spelling distinguishes between some words that are generally pronounced the same way: We'll have it; We'll halve it. Capital letters identify proper nouns and proper adjectives. Because writing can be reread, it's a surer means of communicating difficult material—detailed, complicated instructions, for example. And because writing can be repeatedly revised, it can be more precise, better organized, and more economical than talk.

In spite of their differences, written English and spoken English have a close relationship. When we say someone "talks like a book," we mean that his talk is uncomfortably elaborate or stiff. It's more often a compliment to say that someone "writes the way he talks." For most purposes we value writing that has the flavor of good talk. But having the flavor of talk and being just like talk—even good talk—are by no means the same. Even informal written English, the written English that comes closest to casual speech, has to be far more coherent, far more selective, and far less casual than casual speech if it's to be read with ease and comprehension.

See **Colloquial English.**

spoonful, spoonfuls

Spoonfuls is the plural of *spoonful*. See **-ful, full.**

Squinting modifier

A squinting modifier looks in two directions: it may refer to the word or phrase that precedes it or to the word or phrase that follows it: Getting out of bed *often* is a nuisance; The secretary I spoke to *reluctantly* gave me an appointment.

Standard English

Standard American English is the social dialect used by the American middle class. Because the educated members of that class use it, they approve it, and because they are the dominant class in the United States, what they approve is the standard. Both spoken standard English and written standard English can be divided into formal, general, and informal, as in this book, or into different and more numerous categories. But when used appropriately, all the locutions called standard are supposed to be acceptable to all educated users of the language. In fact, there's disagreement, in dictionaries, English texts, and books on language etiquette, about a good many usages. But there's agreement on the great majority, and the chief purpose of this book is to call attention to the areas of agreement and to encourage the intelligent use of standard English. See **Nonstandard English, Usage.**

state

When you mean no more than "said," don't use *stated*. See **say.**

strata

In formal usage *stratum* is singular and *strata* plural. In general English *strata* is sometimes treated as a singular, but readers who know Latin, and some who don't, condemn the usage.

Style

Style is choice. Style consists of the choices a writer makes—choice of words, choice of sentence patterns, even choice among optional ways of punctuating. If there weren't many different ways of expressing ideas, there would be no such thing as style.

Style is character. Or, in a nonsexist version of a famous aphorism, "Style is the writer." How writers attack a problem, how they arrange their material, the manner in which they make their assertions, the "voices" they speak in—all these reveal something about their personalities, their values, their characters.

There needn't be any contradiction between these two views of style if we think of style as the sum of the choices, *conscious or unconscious,* that a writer makes among the options the language offers. Such matters as basic word order in sentences and ways of forming plurals and indicating verb tenses are part of the structure of English and therefore not stylistic. But other matters—the ways sentences are linked, their relative length and complexity, the placing of those elements that are movable, the words used and their connotations and figurative values—give a passage the distinctive features we call style. Some of these features are the result of unconscious choice, reflecting linguistic habits and ways of thought that the writer isn't aware of. Some of them are the product of deliberate calculation. To the extent that style is the result of such conscious choice, it can be improved.

A style is good or bad, effective or ineffective, to the extent that it achieves or fails to achieve the writer's purpose, wins or fails to win the response he wants from his readers. One of the best ways of improving your own style is to analyze the prose of writers you admire and try to determine how, in choosing words and shaping sentences, they won your response. The more you know about the choices the language offers, the more likely you are to write with clarity, force, and grace, qualities that are the foundation of all good styles. And if you have something to say, you will—through constant writing and rewriting—find your own style, your own voice as a writer.

Because syntax, usage, rhetoric, and style are all interrelated, the great majority of the articles in this *Index* have a bearing on style.

Subjective case

A noun or pronoun that's the subject of a verb or the complement of a linking verb is in the subjective, or nominative, case.

Subjects

1.   Definition.   The subject of a sentence can be defined in a number of ways. Here are three:

a.   The subject performs an action (The dog bit the mailman) or is in a particular state of being (The mailman was unhappy). But this doesn't explain such sentences as "These socks wear out too quickly" or "He received the condemnation of millions." Neither *socks* nor *he* is the performer of any action. Instead, both are the objects of actions.

b.   The subject is the person, place, or thing that a sentence is about. This definition doesn't explain "I just heard that a car hit the mayor." The sentence is quite clearly not "about" the speaker or a car. It's about the mayor.

Both these definitions could be correct for some sentences. "The mayor defeated his opponents in three elections" is "about" the mayor, the performer of the action—defeating.

c.   The subject is the word, phrase, or clause that usually stands before the verb and determines whether the verb will be singular or plural. Where the first two definitions are based on meaning, this one is based on position in the sentence or on the relationships between inflections for number in the subject and verb: The *woman is* here; The *women are* here. In a sentence in which *there* is an expletive—adding nothing to the meaning—the subject is the noun following the *be* verb that the number of the verb agrees with: There *is a woman* outside; There *are women* outside.

2.   Subjects and style.   In direct, vigorous writing, the subject and verb usually express the central action in a sentence, and the subject is often the topic of a paragraph. Continuing the same grammatical subject from sentence to sentence, using pronouns and synonyms for variety, helps keep the focus of a paragraph clear. See **Nominalization, Passive voice.**

See **Agreement 1, Comma 8, Compound subject, Deep structure.** For subjects of gerunds and infinitives, see **Gerunds 2, Infinitives 2.**

Subjunctive mood

Traditionally, English grammar recognizes three moods of verbs: indicative, imperative, and subjunctive. In modern English very few forms can be surely identified as subjunctives, and the use of those few is so inconsistent that definite criteria are hard to set. Generally, the subjunctive is optional, a means of setting one's language, consciously or unconsciously, a little apart from everyday usage. Though not always a trait of formal style, the subjunctive is used regularly in some formal contexts, such as resolutions.

1.   Form of the simple subjunctive.   The identifiable forms of the subjunctive are *be* throughout the present tense of that verb, *were* in its past-tense singular ("if she were here" instead of "if she was here"), and *s*-less forms of the third-person singular of the present tense of other verbs that normally have an *-s* ("that he see" instead of "that he sees"). Some past-tense forms with present or future reference are also subjunctives.

2.   Uses of the subjunctive.
a.   Formulas. The subjunctive is found in many formulas, survivals from a time when it was used freely:

Suffice it to say	Heaven forbid	As it were
Long live the king	God bless you	Be that as it may

Some of these formulas are used in all varieties of the language. Some, like "Come what may," are rather formal.

b. *That* clauses. The subjunctive is relatively common in demands, resolutions, recommendations, and the like, usually in formal contexts. Ordinarily, alternative expressions without the subjunctive are available.

> *Formal:* I ask that the interested citizen *watch* closely the movement of these troops.

> *General:* I ask the interested citizen to watch the movement of these troops closely.

> *Formal:* Who gave the order that he *be* dropped?

> *General:* Who gave the order to drop him?

> *Formal:* It is necessary that every member *inform* himself of these rules.

> *General:* It is necessary that every member should inform himself. . . . *Or:* . . . for every member to inform himself. . . . *Or:* Every member must (should) inform himself. . . .

c. Conditions. The subjunctive may be used in *if* clauses when the fulfillment of the condition is doubtful or impossible: "If one good were really as good as another, no good would be any good" (Irwin Edman, *Four Ways of Philosophy*). The subjunctive *were* isn't necessary to convey the meaning, which the past indicative *was* would convey just as well by its contrast between past form and present or future sense.

A large proportion of the conditions the subjunctive is used to express are real or open conditions, not contrary to fact:

> We set up standards and then proceed to measure each judge against these standards whether he be a sixteenth or nineteenth or twentieth century judge.—Louis L. Jaffe, *Harvard Law Review*

> Stunkard recorded each subject's stomach contractions for four hours, and at 15-minute intervals asked him if he were hungry.—Stanley Schachter, *Psychology Today*

In such conditions the writer has a choice between the subjunctive and another verb form. There's no special virtue in using the subjunctive, and it should be rejected when it gets in the way of natural, idiomatic expression. See **Conditional clauses.**

Subordinate clauses

A dependent, or subordinate, clause (when day is done) has a subject and verb but can't stand as a sentence. See **Clauses, Comma 2.**

Subordinating conjunctions

The most common subordinating conjunctions—words that relate dependent clauses to independent clauses—are these:

after	before	since	until
although	how	so that	when (whenever)
as	if	that	where (wherever)
as . . . as	in order that	though	whether
as if, as though	once	till	while
because	provided	unless	why

The relative and interrogative pronouns *who, which,* and *what* and the relative *that* also function as subordinating conjunctions. See also **for.**

sub Subordination

Correct the faulty subordination.

Faulty subordination concerns the mishandling of dependent clauses—clauses introduced by subordinating conjunctions or by relative pronouns and used in the grammatical functions of nouns, adjectives, and adverbs. Three types of faulty subordination are commonly distinguished:

1.   Tandem, or excessive, subordination occurs when you write a string of dependent clauses, each modifying an element in the clause before it. The weakness is in style, not grammar:

> *Tandem:* For his teachers, he had carefully selected those who taught classes that had a slant that was specifically directed toward students who intended to go into business.

> *Revised:* . . . those who slanted their courses toward students intending to go into business.

2.   Thwarted subordination occurs when you add *and* or *but* to a dependent clause that's already connected to the independent clause by its subordinating conjunction or relative pronoun. This is a grammatical lapse, most commonly found in the form of *and which* or *but which* (see **which 4**):

> *Thwarted:* In the first semester of the course we used three textbooks, and which were continued for the second semester.

> *Revised:* . . . three textbooks, which were continued. . . .

Compare the appropriate use of a coordinating conjunction to join two dependent clauses that are parallel: Tolerance is a virtue [which] all of us praise but [which] few of us practice.

3. Upside-down, or inverted, subordination occurs when you use subordination in such a way as to make the relationship between statements seem illogical. Since it's not a blunder in grammar or style, upside-down subordination is hard to illustrate in isolated sentences. Often only the context determines whether subordination is upside-down. In one paper, "Pearl Harbor was attacked when Roosevelt was President" would be all right. In another, "When Pearl Harbor was attacked, Roosevelt was President" might be much better. Without a context, we can't be sure which statement should be put into the independent clause and which in the dependent clause.

But the nature of some statements makes the choice relatively easy. In most contexts this sentence would sound odd: While I received a salary increase that solved my financial problems, I had to report for work five minutes earlier on Mondays. Some such statement as this would be more likely to make sense: Though I did have to report for work five minutes earlier on Mondays, I received a salary increase that solved my financial problems. Ordinarily, upside-down subordination is corrected by turning the dependent clause into an independent clause and vice versa. Often, as in the example just given, some rewriting is advisable.

See **Coordination.**

such

As an intensifier, *such* is somewhat informal (It was such a hot day; I had never seen such energetic people). In formal and most general writing the construction would usually be completed by a *that* or an *as* clause (It was such a hot day that the tar melted; I had never seen such energetic people as I saw in Ballydavid), or the basis of the comparison would be indicated elsewhere in the passage:

> In spite of high winds and raging seas, they were all out in their boats before dawn. I had never seen such energetic people.

Formal usage often introduces examples with *such as,* where general usage would have *like. Such as* is preferable when the example is only loosely or nonrestrictively connected to the preceding noun: "A number of big processors, such as Campbell and Heinz, still make their own cans" *(Fortune).*

Suffix

An element that can be placed after a word or root to make a new word of different meaning or function is called a suffix: *-ize (criticize), -ish (foolish), -ful (playful), -th (warmth).* See **Origin of words 3a.**

Superlative degree

Hottest, most pleasant, quickest, and *most surely* are examples of adjectives and adverbs in the superlative degree. See **Comparison of adjectives and adverbs 3.**

sure

Sure in standard written English is primarily an adjective (sure footing; as sure as fate; Are you sure?). As an adverb meaning "certainly," *sure* is informal to general, while *surely* is general to formal:

> It's a novel interpretation, but it sure saves oranges.—Horace Sutton, *Saturday Review*

> The Art Commission said it surely did want to honor this splendid son of Italy.—Donovan Bess, *Harper's*

The idiom *sure* (never *surely*) *enough* is in general use: "And sure enough, in all the fearful discussions about computers, the question that inevitably comes up . . ." (Robert Langbaum, *Yale Review*).

Syllabication

When you're not sure where to break a word that comes at the end of a line, consult a dictionary. For general rules, see **Division of words.**

Syllogisms

A syllogism represents deductive reasoning reduced to a pattern consisting of a major premise, a minor premise, and a conclusion. If the rules of inference (after each example below) are followed, the reasoning will be valid. Good arguments must satisfy another condition as well: the premises must be true. The rules of inference are concerned only with validity.

1.   Common patterns for syllogisms.
a.   Hypothetical syllogisms:

Major premise:	If P, then Q	*or*	If P, then Q
Minor premise:	P		Not Q
Conclusion:	Therefore Q		Therefore not P

Arguments that follow this pattern will not be valid if the minor premise is "not P" and the conclusion is "Therefore not Q," or if the minor premise is "Q" and the conclusion is "Therefore not P." The major premise gives no grounds for either of these inferences.

b. *Either-or* syllogisms:

	Disjunctive	*Alternative*
Major premise:	Either A or B but not both	Either A or B
Minor premise:	A	Not A
Conclusion:	Therefore not B	Therefore B

Arguments that follow the pattern of the alternative syllogism will not be valid if the minor premise is positive—that is, "A" or "B." The major premise does not exclude the possibility of both A and B. It simply requires one of the two.

c. Categorical syllogisms:

Major premise:	All M are P
Minor premise:	S is an M
Conclusion:	Therefore S is a P

Arguments that follow this pattern will be invalid if they introduce a fourth term (in addition to M, P, and S); if they shift the meaning of a term; if the middle term (M) is not distributed (that is, if one or more of the premises in which it appears fails to affirm or deny something about the whole class the term stands for); or if a term that has not been distributed in a premise is distributed in a conclusion.

2. Testing arguments.   Although a syllogism or, more likely, a series of interlocking syllogisms is the underpinning of most solid arguments, writers don't normally construct arguments by first formulating a syllogism and then looking for evidence to support the premises. Nor does a writer present his ideas in statements that fall naturally into the pattern of syllogisms. Even so, an elementary acquaintance with the rules of inference can help a writer in at least two ways.

First, it can make him aware of the premises that underlie his argument. In "It's not a poem; it doesn't rhyme," the first clause is the conclusion and the second clause the minor premise of an incomplete syllogism that has as its major premise a proposition something like "If the lines of the passage don't rhyme, the passage is not a poem" or, to put it another way, "All poems rhyme." That unstated assertion, or hidden premise, is too controversial to be allowed to go unsupported. If the writer intends to base an argument on it, he'd better argue for it.

Acquaintance with the rules of inference can also help a writer check the validity of his line of reasoning:

Why do colleges waste time teaching students material they can understand or skills they can learn on their own? Instead of giving courses in science fiction, they should teach double-entry bookkeeping. *That's* a skill students can't pick up on their own.

This bit of reasoning might be spelled out as three syllogisms, each of which invites the reader to raise questions about the validity of the reasoning as well as about the truth of the premises. To take just one of the syllogisms:

If students can learn a skill on their own, a college shouldn't teach it. (If P, then Q)

Students can't learn double-entry bookeeping on their own. (Not P)

Therefore colleges should teach double-entry bookkeeping. (Not Q)

Quite aside from questions of truth, the reasoning is invalid. The major premise does not assert that a college should teach *all* the skills a student can't learn on his own.

See **Logical thinking.**

Synecdoche

Synecdoche is a figure of speech in which the whole stands for the part (a nation adopts a policy) or a part stands for the whole (a baseball player's bat wins a game).

Synonyms

Broadly, synonyms are words that mean the same thing. More strictly, they are words that share at least one meaning. Very few words are completely interchangeable, because no two are likely to share all their meanings and to have the same connotations. At the very least, they'll differ in sound and therefore represent different stylistic choices.

In choosing among synonyms, you need to consider both sense—connotations as well as denotations—and sound. The meaning and suggestions of the word you want must express as precisely as possible what you have to say, and the word must fit the sound pattern of your sentence.

Syntax

Syntax refers in general to the order and relationships of the elements of sentences. That the subject of a sentence ordinarily comes before the predicate, for example, is a feature of English syntax. Words, phrases, and clauses are all syntactic elements.

T

Tandem subordination

Tying a succession of dependent clauses together produces tandem subordination. See **Subordination 1.**

teach, learn

A teaches *B,* who is taught by *A. B* learns from *A.* See **learn, teach.**

Technical writing

Good expository writing conveys information accurately, clearly, and concisely. When such writing is about specialized subject matter—in engineering, for example, or physics or chemistry—it's called technical writing. More particularly, technical writing appears in reports, articles, and manuals produced by professionals in science and technology.

Whatever the subject matter or the nature of the communication, the first obligation of the technical writer is to present his information so clearly that it can't be misunderstood by his audience. In addition to presenting information, he must often analyze data, weigh alternative solutions to problems, make predictions, argue for a course of action. In every case he needs to take into account what his readers already know and what they want to find out.

1. The technical writer and his audience. The technical writer is the expert on his subject. Nobody knows as much about his project as he does. When addressing his peers—professional associates at a convention, for example—he'll naturally use the specialized terms of his profession. But when writing reports for his superiors or giving directions to subordinates, he has to gauge their probable familiarity with the vocabulary that is second nature to him. (The president of a potash firm may have been chosen for his managerial ability rather than his knowledge of potash. In reporting to him, the technical writer may have to work as hard at translating shoptalk as he would if he were addressing a general reader.) Even students in Aerospace Engineering might have trouble understanding this announcement of a lecture by an expert in the field:

> He will talk about flow visualization experiments of a turbulent water jet in a confined tank modeled to simulate certain flow conditions expected in the Anechoic Chamber/Jet Noise Facility.

Though the gap between general English and technical vocabularies is often large, what makes technical writing difficult for the reader, either layman or professional, may not be so much the terminology as the tangled syntax that results when the writer relies heavily on nominalization, passive verbs, and strings of prepositional phrases (four in the sentence quoted above). Some industrial firms and professional societies have recognized this problem. The American Chemical Society, for one, gives short courses in communication skills for chemists and chemical engineers. Notes on a recent course stressed the need for directness, simplicity, and brevity and recommended the use of the active voice and, on occasion, the first-person pronoun.

2. Technical reports.   The merit of any technical report lies in its efficiency in communicating its content to its intended audience. Its format should therefore be carefully planned.

Technical reports differ visually from other expository writing. They're divided into sections, which are often numbered. They have no long stretches of consecutive sentences. They use subheads, tables, charts, diagrams. Many, though not all, present at the beginning a summary (or abstract) of the findings, results, or recommendations. In this format, everything vital is in the summary. No crucial new information is introduced as the report proceeds through its next three or four or dozen sections. Subsequent headings depend on the nature of the report, and the order in which they appear depends on the nature of the audience. One adaptable format follows:

I.   Summary—important results, conclusions, recommendations
II.   Introduction—background, purpose, problem being addressed, scope
III.   Review of previous work—if short, a part of the Introduction
IV.   Description of present study—details of apparatus used, if the investigation is experimental; derivation of equations; procedures followed
V.   Presentation (in table or graph form) and discussion of results—comment on salient features of the data
VI.   Conclusions and recommendations—interpretation of results; inferences; recommendation of a solution, action, or future investigation
VII.   Appendices—supporting data, usually highly specialized

The technical writer who is preparing his report for several different audiences will choose a format that permits him to move from the simple to the complex in content and vocabulary. He'll begin with a summary phrased in nontechnical language and an introduction that's as uncomplicated as he can make it. He'll then proceed directly to conclusions and recommendations, again presenting them so that the least informed of his readers can follow them. The experimental section, the discussion of results, and subsequent sections will be increasingly technical, and the final sections will supply data likely to be understandable only to specialists. The advantage of this format, with its progression from simple to complex, is that each reader can continue until he has satisfied his interest or reached the limit of his understanding. Even the reader who is ignorant of the technicalities of procedures, operations, or calculations will be able to grasp the general purpose, scope, and results of the study.

See **Abstract language, Nominalization, Passive voice, Phrases and style.**

tense Tense

Make the tense of the verb conventional in form, or make it consistent with, or in logical sequence with, other verbs in the passage.

1. Use the standard form. In general English, avoid nonstandard forms like *drawed* and *had went* and dialectal forms like *drug* (for *dragged*), *throwed,* and such double auxiliaries as *might could* and *used to could.* See **Principal parts of verbs.**

2. Make the verb consistent with others that refer to the same time. Consistency doesn't demand that you use the same tense for verbs throughout a sentence or a paragraph or a paper. Choose the verb form or verbal phrase that expresses the distinction of time you intend. In a single sentence you may refer to past, present, and future time: When I *was* ten, I *planned* to be a veterinary surgeon, but now I *know* I *will spend* my working life as an accountant. Through skillful use of verbs you can interweave particular events with habitual action:

> Summers we generally *follow* a simple routine. Every day we *travel* the fifteen miles to our lakeside cabin. We *start off* at dawn, Mother driving and the kids rubbing sleep from their eyes, and we seldom *get* home before dark. Then we *fall* into bed, tired from a day outdoors. One night last July our simple routine *was wrecked.* Just before we *turned* into the driveway, we *saw* that the lights *were* on all over the house. Since we *knew* we *had left* the lights off and the doors locked, we *were* puzzled and a little frightened. My brother *offered* to reconnoiter. When he *came* back to the car, he *said* he *had seen* . . .

But though it's natural and easy to shift tense, don't make a shift unless it serves a purpose—normally, to mark a change in time. Careless shifts like the following are distracting for the reader:

> The observers unobtrusively *slipped* in the back door while the children *were* still getting settled at their desks. The class *begins* with the teacher reading a short passage from a book about Columbus, at the end of which she *asked* for comments.

To keep the tenses consistent, *begins* should be *began*. Or, if there's a reason for doing so, all the verbs might be put in the historical present: *slips, are, begins, asks.* See **Tenses of verbs 3a.**

3. Observe the conventional sequence of tenses. In certain contexts actual time takes second place to the conventions of tense sequence.
a. Between independent and dependent clauses. A dependent clause that's the object of a verb in the past tense is usually put in the past tense even though it refers to an existing state of affairs:

> What did you say your name *was?*
> They didn't tell me you *were looking* for an apartment.

But when the dependent clause describes a timeless state of affairs, the present tense is often used: He told me that I always *remind* him of my father. And when the point of the sentence is the current existence of the state of affairs reported in the dependent clause, the present tense is common:

> Simply observing the people and comparing them with those I had seen three decades ago, I was convinced that they are a lot better off materially than their predecessors.—Robert Shaplen, *New Yorker*

b. From direct discourse to indirect discourse. When a dependent clause reports something said, its verb is ordinarily shifted from present to past (He said, "I *am* leaving" *becomes* He said he *was* leaving) or from past to past perfect (He said, "I *did* it" *becomes* He said he *had done* it). But this formal sequence can sometimes be misleading. To report the statement "I'm optimistic about the outcome of the election" as "He said that he was optimistic . . ." doesn't make clear whether the optimism persists. "He said that he is optimistic about the outcome of the election" leaves no doubt in the reader's mind.
c. With infinitives and participles. Infinitives and participles express time in relation to the time of the main verb. Use the present infinitive to indicate time that's the same as the time of the main verb or later than the time of the main verb:

> I plan *to go* to Washington, and I expect *to see* her there.
> I planned *to go* last week and expected *to see* her today.
> I would have liked *to see* her on her last trip.

Use the perfect infinitive for action prior to the action of the main verb:

> I would like *to have seen* her on her last trip.

Use the perfect form of the participle to express time prior to the time of the main verb, the present form to express the same time as the time of the main verb:

Having driven safely through the worst blizzard in local history, he slid off the edge of his own driveway and, *jamming on* the brakes too fast, overturned the car.

See **Tenses of verbs.**

Tenses of verbs

1. Time and tense. In English there is no simple correspondence between tense and time. The term *tense* refers to inflection, or change in form. English verbs have only two tenses: present (he leaves) and past (he left). There is no single-word verb, no inflection, that applies only to the future. But we do have various ways of referring to future time. We use the present tense accompanied by an adverb (He leaves tomorrow) or an auxiliary before the uninflected verb (He will leave tomorrow). Or we say "He will be leaving" or "He is going to leave" or "By this time tomorrow he will have left." Some grammarians call *will leave, will be leaving,* and so on, the future tense.

2. Tense and auxiliaries. If we use no auxiliaries, the only tenses we can form are present and past. But auxiliaries enable us to refer to times in the future as well as in the past extending into the present, the past not extending into the present, and the past of a certain time already past. So some grammarians speak of six tenses, which roughly translate into the six of Latin:

Present:	He eats	*Present perfect:*	He has eaten
Past:	He ate	*Past perfect:*	He had eaten
Future:	He will eat	*Future perfect:*	He will have eaten

Still more tenses emerge if we consider the uses of *do* (emphatic tense: *does eat, did eat*) and *be* (progressive tense: *is eating, was eating*). If the past of *shall* and *will* is also taken into account, we can speak of a past future *(would eat)* and even a past future perfect *(would have eaten)*.

3. Special uses of simple present and past.
a. In addition to its basic function of referring to something going on now, the present tense is used to refer to a state of affairs that is generally true, without reference to time (Oil *floats* on water); to habitual action that continues into the present (He *writes* in his journal every day); and, when accompanied by an adverbial, to a time in the future (She *goes* to college in the fall). Other special uses of the present tense are illustrated in

I *hear* you are going to Europe.
He'll come if you *ask* him.

Thoreau *urges* us to do without luxuries.

In the 1950s all *is* buttoned down; in the 1960s there *are* rumblings of discontent.

The third example is sometimes known as the *literary present* (Thoreau died in 1862), the fourth as the *historical present*.

b. The simple past tense is normally used to refer to something that took place in the past, either a single occurrence (He *broke* his leg) or a repeated occurrence (He *skied* at Vail every Christmas). But the past tense does not refer to past time in a dependent clause that is object of the verb in the independent clause when the main verb is in the past (I *heard* that you *were* in town); in the *if* clause that refers to a hypothetical situation (If you *knew* him, you wouldn't be surprised); nor as the polite alternative in questions or requests (*Would* you send me the catalog).

See **Auxiliaries, Tense, Verbs.**

than

At its simplest level, the choice of the case of a pronoun after *than* can be illustrated by the sentences "He is taller than I" and "He is taller than me." Both are used in general writing. Conservatives favor the nominative after an intransitive or linking verb, but many writers use the objective.

When the verb before *than* takes an object, the nominative and objective cases after *than* may have different meanings: She likes him more than I [do]; She likes him more than [she likes] me. So in standard English the case of the pronoun used with *than* after a transitive verb is the case that would be used if the dependent clause were written out. Use of the nominative case where the objective case is called for, as in the following example, is hypercorrect—that is, wrong: Though the jury said we were both guilty, the judge gave my partner a lighter sentence than [he gave] I. See **Hypercorrectness.**

that

1. *That* or *which*.   Writers are often urged to use *that* to introduce restrictive clauses and *which* to introduce nonrestrictive clauses, and the advice can be helpful for those who use *which* everywhere, in the belief that it's more elegant than *that*. In practice, the choice between *which* and *that* in restrictive clauses is likely to depend on rhythm, sound, emphasis, and personal taste. If *that* has already been used in the sentence, writers may shift to *which* to avoid repetition. On the other hand, when the restrictive clause is compound, *which* may be chosen as a clearer signal to the reader that the construction is being repeated: "He had an exploratory operation for cancer which the doctors were reluctant to undertake but which he was convinced he needed" (David Halberstam, *Atlantic*). *Which* normally introduces nonrestrictive clauses in all varieties of usage.

2. Redundant *that*. When *that* introduces a noun clause in which a modifying phrase precedes the subject, there's a temptation to repeat *that* after the modifier: "It must seem to many outsiders that if there was room for honest argument [that] a reasonable doubt had to exist . . ." (Red Smith, syndicated columnist). Don't do it.

3. Clauses without *that*. A complex sentence like "The work [that] he does shows [that] he has talent" is perfectly correct without either *that*. The dependent clauses "he does" and "he has talent" are related to the rest of the sentence clearly enough to need no explicit signs of subordination, like *that*. No writer should handicap himself by thinking a *that* must be inserted wherever it will fit. *That*-less clauses are common, and many professional writers prefer them:

> He thinks that the Italians neither approved of Fascist terror nor were really terrorized by it. He thinks [ ] they became numb, resigned, apathetic, and cynical.—Naomi Bliven, *New Yorker*

> The convention [ ] we accept unthinkingly had not as yet established itself.— William Nelson, *Journal of English Literary History*

Using *that* to stress the subordination of short clauses often robs them of their force: He knows [that] I'm sorry; I'm glad [that] you're here; Take anything [that] you want.

That is necessary when the clause comes first (That she might be hurt never occurred to us) and when a clause has no other subject (There is a moral standard that has long been accepted). When a modifier stands between two clauses, *that* is sometimes necessary to show which clause is being modified: Mr. Wrenn said [ ] after the guests were gone [ ] Mrs. Wrenn should pack her bags. Depending on the intended meaning, *that* is needed either after *said* or after *gone*.

See **this**.

that is

That is is a rather formal connective that introduces the equivalent of, or the explanation of, what precedes it. When it both follows and introduces a complete statement, it may be linked to the preceding independent clause with a semicolon: The men worked continuously for three whole weeks to complete the dam; that is, they worked twenty-four hours a day in three shifts, seven days a week. Or it may begin a new sentence. In briefer constructions a comma or dash before *that is* is adequate: They used the safest explosive for the purpose—that is, dynamite. Better yet, *that is* could be omitted: They used the safest explosive for the purpose—dynamite. See **namely.**

their

Their is the possessive of *they*. *Theirs* is the absolute form: This table is exactly like theirs. Except in formal usage, *their* is often used as a common-gender singular to refer to words like *somebody, anybody, everyone:*

> Almost nobody has the words to really talk about their lives.—*Time*

> It is necessary to make anyone on the streets think twice before attempting to vent their despair on you.—James Baldwin, *Show*

See **Agreement 2.**

then

Then is an adverb of time frequently used as a connective (conjunctive adverb): The next three hours we spent in sightseeing; then we settled down to the business of being delegates to a convention.

Adjectival *then* (the then President) is common in general writing, rare in formal. Some readers find it clumsy.

then, than

Don't confuse *then,* the adverb of time, with *than,* the conjunction in clauses of comparison: *Then* the whole crowd went to Louie's; It was better as a movie *than* as a novel.

there is, there are

When *there* is used as an anticipatory subject, the verb ordinarily agrees in number with the "real" subject, which follows it: "There is still occasional sniping at the 'supersquad' and there are still lazy, indifferent, homicide detectives" (Barbara Gelb, *New York Times Magazine*). When the subject is compound and the first element is singular, usage is divided. Some writers follow the rules of formal agreement and use a plural verb, while others find a plural verb awkward before a singular noun:

> There are much good history, intelligent analysis of social problems, and good writing.—David Fellman, *American Historical Review*

There is no jargon, few footnotes, some repetition, few insights and little analysis.—Lewis A. Froman, *American Political Science Review*

Like repeated use of *it is* . . . , repeated use of *there is* . . . , *there are* . . .* constructions robs sentences of strong subject-verb combinations. See **Subjects 2.**

they

They occurs in all varieties of usage with no explicit antecedent: "One thinks of Tolstoy, and the story that all day long they had to be beating omelets for him in the kitchen" (Louis Kronenberger, *New York Times Book Review*). The indefinite reference is troublesome, however, when there's a second *they* in the same sentence: Around campus *they* were saying that *they* had a plan to boycott classes. Often impersonal *there* is preferable: There were reports around campus that they had a plan to boycott classes. *Or:* Around campus they were saying that there was a plan. . . .

Regularly in informal English and often in general English, *they,* and especially *their,* is used as a singular pronoun to refer to *everyone* and similar words. See **Agreement 2, he or she.**

thing

Thing often encourages the accumulation of deadwood in writing: [The] first [thing] you [do is to] dry out your sleeping bag.

this

Though often criticized as a sign of lazy writing, *this,* like *that,* is regularly used to refer to the idea of the preceding clause or sentence: He had always had his own way at home, and this made him a poor roommate. Confusion is caused when *this* refers only to some part of the idea of a clause or sentence or to an antecedent that's not actually expressed. See **Reference of pronouns 2.**

though

Though in the sense "however," "nevertheless," "for all that" now appears in all varieties of writing: Two things are clear, though.

thus

Thus at the beginning of participial phrases tends to encourage loose modifiers. In sentences like this one there's no noun or pronoun for the participle to modify: "D. Eldred Rinehart's term on the racing commission also is expiring, thus opening up the chairmanship" *(Washington Post)*. See **Dangling modifiers.**

Thwarted subordination

Subordination is said to be thwarted when a coordinating conjunction precedes the subordinating conjunction: By the end of the summer he had completed three reports, [and] which were accepted for publication. See **Subordination 2.**

till, until

In all varieties of writing, *till* and *until* are interchangeable both as prepositions (Wait till/until tomorrow) and as conjunctions (Wait till/until they get here). Most dictionaries don't recognize the spelling *'til*.

Titles

1.   Choosing a title.   Although a title that captures the reader's interest is an advantage for a paper, trying too hard for originality or impact is a mistake. If no striking title comes to mind, just name the subject of your paper as precisely as you can in a few words. Because the title is considered a separate part of the paper, it shouldn't be referred to by a pronoun in the opening sentence: not "This is an important issue today" but "The parking problem [or whatever you're writing about] is an important issue today."

2.   Referring to titles.
a.   Italics or quotation marks. For most purposes there's a simple rule of thumb: Italicize titles of long works (by underlining them) and quote titles of short works. Italics are traditional for titles of books, magazines, pamphlets, long poems, plays, movies, television series, symphonies, and operas. Quotation marks are usual for short stories, essays, short poems, songs, chapters of books, lectures, paintings, and pieces of sculpture.
b.   Capitalizing. General practice is to capitalize the first and last words of titles and all intervening nouns, pronouns, verbs, adjectives, and adverbs. Some styles also capitalize prepositions and conjunctions that contain more than five letters. Examples: *Wit and Its Relation to the Unconscious; Peace through* [or *Through*] *Meditation;* "Hills like White Elephants"; "Nobody Knows You When You're Down and Out." Capitals are similarly used, without italics or quotation marks, in titles of unpublished works, book series, and books of the Bible.

The is capitalized and italicized or set within quotation marks only if it's part of the recognized title: *The Yale Law Review* but the *Harvard Law Review; The American Historical Review* but the *American Sociological Re-*

view; *The New York Times* but the *Los Angeles Times*. In some styles initial *the* is never treated as part of the title of a newspaper or periodical. In the pamphlet entitled *The MLA Style Sheet,* that publication is referred to as "the *MLA Style Sheet.*"

c. Consistency. A writer should choose an accepted style for handling titles and stick to it. For example, the name of the city in a newspaper title may be either italicized or not italicized: the *Los Angeles Times,* the Los Angeles *Times*. Similarly, while strict formality may demand that a title be given in full each time it appears, current styles permit the use of short forms and the omission of initial articles when they would cause awkwardness: Hemingway's [A] *Moveable Feast* provides background for his [*The*] *Sun Also Rises*.

Many newspapers and magazines have their own rules for handling titles. Some use quotation marks around book titles and merely capitalize the names of periodicals. For the more rigid and detailed rules governing very formal writing, as in dissertations and scholarly articles, consult such treatments as Kate L. Turabian, *Manual for Writers of Term Papers, Theses, and Dissertations* (Chicago: Univ. of Chicago Press) and the *MLA Handbook*.

too

In the sense "also," *too* is sometimes set off by commas, sometimes not. At times commas are necessary for clarity. Without them, the sentence "Bob, too, frequently interrupted rehearsals to give advice" could be taken to mean that Bob interrupted too often.

Though *too* is used to modify past participles after linking verbs in all varieties of usage (She was too excited; They were too concerned), conservative stylists prefer another adverb of degree between *too* and the participle: too greatly excited, too much concerned. Objection is strongest when the participle couldn't be placed before the noun or pronoun as a modifier: He is too identified with the opposition; Priests are too removed from real life. In such cases, many writers would use intervening adverbs—"too closely identified," "too far removed"—particularly in formal contexts.

Some formal stylists would continue to criticize both examples, on the grounds that the constructions are incomplete—"too closely identified" for what? "too far removed" for what?

See **not all that . . . , not too . . . .**

trans **Transition**

Make the transition between these sentences (or paragraphs) clear and smooth.

Transitions are words or phrases or sentences that show the relationship between one statement and another, one paragraph and another, one part of a paper and another. When you write a sentence or paragraph as an isolated unit—as if nothing had preceded it and nothing is to follow it—your reader is bound to be puzzled. A lack of transition between one paragraph and another is sometimes a sign of faulty organization and sometimes simply evidence that you've neglected to provide a signpost that shows the reader where he's been and where he's going. A lack of transition between sentences usually indicates that you haven't thought through the relationship between consecutive statements.

1. Transitions as signals. The most familiar of the markers that indicate relationships and knit a piece of writing together are conjunctions and adverbs—*and, but, still, yet, for, because, then, though, while, in order that, first, second, however, moreover, therefore,* and so on.

Some of the choices available to indicate the common logical relationships are these:

a. Addition. When you want to call attention to the fact that you're adding something, *and* is the usual connector. Others that indicate equivalent, coordinate, or similar ideas are *also, again, once again, too, likewise, moreover, furthermore, then, in addition, by the same token, similarly, analogously.* You can indicate restatements with such phrases as *that is, to clarify, more simply* or by clauses like *what this means is.*

b. Contrast. When the relation is one of contrast—ranging from direct contradiction through various degrees of opposition, qualification, restriction, and concession—some of your choices are *but, yet, however, nevertheless, nonetheless, by contrast, at the same time, instead, in place of, conversely, actually, in fact, to be sure, at any rate, anyway, still, of course, on the other hand, provided that, in case.*

c. Alternatives. You can call attention to an alternative or option by using *or, nor, either, neither, alternatively, on the other hand* (often following *on the one hand*).

d. Causal relations. You can indicate a causal relationship with *for, because, since, then, as.* You can point to a result or consequence with various words and phrases, among them *so, then, therefore, thus, hence, accordingly, as a result, in consequence.*

e. Illustration. When what follows illustrates what has come before or particularizes it in some way, some of your choices are *for example, for instance, thus, to illustrate, in particular, namely.*

f. Sequence. When the relation is sequential, your transitions may indicate relationships of time or space in the subject itself, or they may point up the organization of the paper. Sample time indicators are *then, soon, after, now, earlier, later, ten years ago.* Sample space indicators are *here, there, on top, in the middle, below, on the left, on the right, beyond.* You can indicate sequence by transitions like *for one thing, for another; first, second, third; to begin with; in short, in brief; finally, to summarize, in conclusion, as we*

have seen. Other transitions bring out the relative importance of points—
more important, less important, above and beyond.

2. Transitions and style.   A transition should give an accurate indication
of the relationship you intend. Beyond that, the transition marker should be
in keeping with the style and tone of your paper.
a.   Accurate markers. *Actually* and *incidentally* are overworked as transitions. Since *actually* often introduces a correction and *incidentally* a digression, both may be signs that revision is needed. An unwarranted transition—for example, a *therefore* when what follows is not the result of what
precedes—can be seriously misleading.
b.   Apt markers. Though *first, second, third* are preferable to old-fashioned
firstly, secondly, thirdly, they're appropriate only when the material demands emphatic division. Overuse of any of the heavier connectives (*however, nevertheless, consequently*) can clog your style. Often you can make
a transition that's just as clear, less obtrusive, and stylistically more pleasing
by repeating a key word from sentence to sentence, by using a synonym or
a pronoun to echo or pick up the key word, and by binding sentences or
parts of sentences by means of parallel structures. Whether emphatic or subtle, transitions are your chief means of giving a piece of writing coherence.

Transitive and intransitive verbs

A transitive verb is used with a direct object; an intransitive verb is not so
used: The janitor put (transitive) the books on the shelf, but they soon vanished (intransitive). Many verbs are transitive in one sense and intransitive
in another: He grows corn; The corn grows well. See **lay, lie; set, sit.**

trite Triteness

Replace the trite expression with one that is simpler and fresher.

The most troublesome trite expressions, or clichés, are worn-out figures of
speech or phrases: picture of health, break of day, reign supreme, from the
face of the earth, crack of dawn, acid test. What was once fresh and striking
has become stale and boring from being used again and again with no sense
of its figurativeness. But triteness is not a matter of age. Yesterday's vogue
expression can be as boring to a reader as one that dates back generations.
In fact, a young reader may be more familiar with a new cliché than with
an old one. So if you find yourself writing down a phrase without even
stopping to think about it, stop and think about it. Think twice. Trite expression is the natural vehicle for trite ideas.

   This doesn't mean that you should mistrust everyday English. Often a
well-established phrase, with its. connotations, will express your meaning

accurately and succinctly. Going out of your way to avoid an expression only because it's been used many times before may force you into awkwardness, incoherence, or absurdly "fine" writing. The important thing is to be aware of what you're putting on paper, to be conscious of your stylistic choices and rhetorical decisions.

See **Figures of speech, Formulas, Vogue words.**

try and

The standard idiom *try and*—"Neither Congress nor the Court itself seemed prepared to try and force him to resign" (*Newsweek*)—appears regularly in general and informal contexts, but formal stylists and many general stylists prefer *try to*.

-type

The use of *-type* in compound modifiers (Polaris-type missile, family-type programs) has spread in all varieties of usage but continues to irritate many readers. Most writers choose *type of* (Polaris type of missile) or, where possible, simply omit *type* (family programs). The practice of shortening *type of* and *make of* to *type* (this type letter) and *make* (that make car) is informal.

Typewritten copy

Use only one side of the sheet, leave wide margins at both left and right, keep the type clean, and change the ribbon regularly. In first drafts, using triple space and leaving extra space between paragraphs will provide room for revision. Double space the final draft.

Indent the first lines of paragraphs five spaces. For long quotations in double-spaced copy, indent each line as in a paragraph indention and single-space the quoted matter. Use no quotation marks with these block quotations.

For the figure 1 use small l, not capital I. For a dash, use two hyphens. Leave one space after all punctuation marks except at the end of sentences; there, leave two spaces.

Transposed letters should be erased and retyped or corrected with a curved line.

Strikeovers [*not* Strikeovers] are often hard to read.

Your instructor probably won't mind if you correct a few mistakes in ink, but you should retype any page that has more than a few.

See **Caret.**

Underlining

Underlining in manuscripts is used to mark titles that aren't quoted, words used as words, foreign expressions that haven't been anglicized, and—sparingly—words or word groups that you want to emphasize. See **Italics.**

Understatement

Understating is one means of emphasizing: Eight o'clock classes are not universally popular. See **Figures of speech, Negatives and style.**

uninterested

To be uninterested is to lack interest; to be disinterested is to be neutral, which is not the same thing. But see **disinterested, uninterested.** ·

unique

In strict formal usage *unique* means "single," "sole," "unequaled" and consequently is not compared. In general usage *unique,* like many other words that once had an absolute meaning, has become an adjective of degree. As an emphatic "unusual," "rare," or "remarkable," it's often found compared with *more* or *most:* "The more unique his language, the more peculiarly his own will be the colouring of his language" (Otto Jesperson, *Mankind, Nation and Individual from a Linguistic Point of View*). Because of this varied usage, a reader may find unqualified *unique* ambiguous. The writer of the following sentence may have been guarding against that possibility: "It is a unique festival, and there is nothing like it in the world" (Harold C. Schonberg, *New York Times*). Though redundant by strict formal standards, the second clause is probably practical. See **Comparison of adjectives and adverbs.**

United States

Like many proper nouns, *United States* is often used as an attributive (that is, as an adjective preceding the word it modifies): "There are some who think that the United States attempt to overthrow the Castro government was an act of international immorality" (Richard H. Rovere, *New Yorker*). No apostrophe is needed. Since *United States* has no adjectival form, its use as an attributive often sounds awkward, unless it's abbreviated to *U.S.* In most contexts *American* is preferable. See **American.**

un Unity

Unify this passage.

A sentence, a paragraph, or a paper is unified when its parts fit together to make a consistent whole. You weaken the unity of what you write when you include material that stands outside—or seems to stand outside—the core of thought or feeling you want to communicate.

Your first obligation as a writer is to have a purpose in writing and a controlling idea to which everything you include in the paper contributes. Your second obligation is to build your sentences and paragraphs in such a way that your train of thought, and in the end your purpose, will be clear to your audience.

Failures in unity can be real, as when a writer introduces irrelevant material, or apparent, as when a writer doesn't make plain to his readers a relationship that's perfectly plain to him. The first is a failure in reasoning (see **Logical thinking**). The second is a failure in composition, especially in continuity (see **Coherence, Transition**). A sentence, a paragraph, or a paper may be coherent but not unified. It may also be unified but not coherent. Good writing is both coherent and unified.

Without the context—and here *context* means both the writer's thinking about his subject and his expression of his thought—deciding whether a passage lacks unity or coherence is difficult. But some hints can be given about ways of strengthening passages that have been criticized for lacking unity.

1.   Unity in sentences.   For a sentence that lacks unity, there are three possible remedies:

a.   Delete any phrase or clause that isn't related to the central thought. In the sentence ''Parking space on the campus, which is one of the most beautiful in the state, has become completely inadequate, and recently the city council voted to increase bus fares again,'' delete the *which* clause.

b.   Subordinate one statement to another to show the logical relationship. Even if readers of the sentence quoted in **a** can figure out a connection between the shortage of parking space and the cost of public transportation, the coordinating *and* obscures the writer's point. A possible revision: At a time when the shortage of parking space makes commuting to campus by car almost impossible, the city council has discouraged the use of public transportation by increasing bus fares once more.

c.   Separate seemingly disconnected statements, making two sentences, and bring in material that will provide a logical link between them. Between a sentence about inadequate parking space and a sentence about increased bus fares, this sentence might be introduced: But the commuting student is not being encouraged to switch to public transportation. See **Coordination, Sentences, Subordination.**

2. Unity in paragraphs. As a general rule, a paragraph lacks unity when one or more of its sentences fail to contribute to its central idea. When that idea is expressed in a topic sentence, both writer and reader can see just where the discussion slides away from the main point. So it's wise to provide topic sentences when your subject is so complicated that a reader might need help in following your treatment of it. On the other hand, you can do without topic sentences if the logic of your thought, or the strength of your emotion, creates a unified topic *idea* that the paragraph gets across to your readers.

Sticking to a subject doesn't in itself guarantee unity. In a paragraph on Robert Frost, all the sentences may be about the poet, but if two of them deal with his current reputation, one with his last public appearance, one with his marriage, and three with his poem "After Apple-Picking," it's unlikely that the paragraph will have unity. Bringing together several loosely related subjects usually means that no one of them will be adequately developed and that the paragraph will have no central focus. See **Paragraph indention.**

3. Unity in papers. Even when each paragraph is unified, the paper as a whole may not be. Each paragraph should bear on the writer's purpose (whether or not that purpose is expressed in a thesis statement), and the paragraphs should be in such an order and so linked that the reader sees the relation of each of them to the controlling idea.

A useful way of testing a paper for unity is to outline it. Questions of relevance and relatedness can be more easily answered when you've seen through the surface of what you've written to the underlying structure. Reduce each paragraph to a heading. If your paper is brief—no more than four or five paragraphs, say—each paragraph may represent a main point; but in a longer paper the paragraphs should fall into logical groups or sequences with each sequence developing a theme. Be on the lookout for a heading that doesn't logically follow the preceding heading or lead into the next one. If you find such a heading, reexamine your organization, and if there's no slot that the heading obviously fills, consider dropping the paragraph it stands for. If you find a sequence of paragraphs that strays from your central thesis, you need to do some rethinking and rewriting. See **Organization, Outline form.**

until, till

Until and *till* (not *'til*) are interchangeable. See **till, until.**

Upside-down subordination

Subordination is said to be upside-down when logically the dependent clause should be independent and the independent clause should be dependent. See **Subordination 3.**

Usage

The study of usage depends on wide observation of what people say and write in various situations. This observation serves as a basis for judging the standing of particular words, forms, and constructions. Works on usage include scholarly studies of the ways language is used, and has been used, in speech, in print, in letters, and so on; polls to determine attitudes toward particular usages; and guides to usage based in large part on the authors' personal taste. Both the polls and the guides focus on disputed usages—locutions accepted by some, rejected by others—and it is this area of usage study that has most interested the general public.

Researchers have built up a picture of what educated users of American English say and, more especially, write. But for many people who are interested in usage, what *is* is not nearly so important as what *should be*. Most of the popular guides to usage are conservative—that is, they restrict "correct" English to usages and constructions that this *Index* associates with formal styles.

Students in particular should be aware of the influence of age on what readers accept and what they reject. In *Harper's Dictionary of Current Usage,* Walter "Red" Smith, member of a panel that commented on particular usages, had this to say: "In usage I accept what I have come to accept and reject what I don't accept." All of us find it very easy to accept what we grew up with, but as we become older, accepting new words, new meanings, new forms of expression becomes increasingly difficult. One purpose of this book is to remind students that many of the usages they take for granted are offensive to some older readers. This doesn't mean that students should adopt the attitudes toward usage of the middle-aged—and certainly not of those who see the language in imminent danger of "destruction." It does mean that they should be conscious of their audiences whenever they write.

The reaction to *Webster's Third New International Dictionary of the English Language* in 1961 revealed the intense concern about usage felt by an articulate minority of Americans. The publishers of the dictionary had decided to apply usage labels much more sparingly than in the past, on the grounds that the primary role of a dictionary was to record usage, not evaluate it, and that it was often impossible to label with any precision words taken out of context. Praised by many scholars, the decision was attacked in newspaper editorials and magazine articles as an abandonment of standards. Dictionaries published since then have been more prescriptive than *Webster's Third,* and few of the more recent books of linguistic etiquette have been as liberal as *A Dictionary of Contemporary American Usage* by Bergen and Cornelia Evans, published in 1957.

The polling technique introduced into usage study in the 1930s has been adapted by commercial publishers of dictionaries and books on usage: panels of journalists, novelists, columnists, commentators, and others concerned in one way or another with verbal communication vote on the "acceptability" of items of usage presented to them by the editors, who select the panels and also the usage "problems" the panels consider. Majority opinion is almost invariably conservative. (Panel members are predominantly middle-aged and older.) Panelists tend to express their opinions as vehemently and emotionally as do those ordinary citizens who write letters to newspapers and magazines deploring the corruption and decline of English.

Such emotionalism reveals that while word watching can make anyone's reading more interesting and his writing both richer and more precise, it can also become an unfortunate obsession. It's bad enough when the watcher (and listener) insists on "correcting" the usage of others. It's much worse when he makes usage the criterion for judging not only their educational and social level but their intelligence and their character.

Like every user of the language, you must make your own choices. They should be intelligent choices, based on sound information. The best safeguard against avoidable bias is some principle of selection, and the principle proposed in this *Index* is appropriateness. There is also the intangible called taste. If, like most of us, you find some locutions too stuffy or too crude, you can simply not use them. No one can control the usage of others, but everyone can control his own.

utilize

Utilize means "put to use." The verb *use* is almost always a better choice.

verbal, oral

Though *verbal* is widely used to mean "spoken," many word watchers insist on *oral* for that meaning. See **oral, verbal.**

Verbals

The parts of a verb that function as nouns or adjectives are called verbals. For their various uses see **Gerunds, Infinitives, Participles.**

Verbs

1. Forms. If we exclude *be* and the modal auxiliaries, all verbs can add to the base form (*ask, sing, tear*) the suffix *-ing (asking)*, the suffix *-s (asks)*, and the suffix *-ed (asked)* or use some other change in form as the equivalent of the *-ed—sing, sings, singing, sang, sung; tear, tears, tearing,* *tore, torn.* *Be* has eight forms *(be, am, is, are, was, were, being, been);* *can, may, must,* and other modal auxiliaries have only one or two forms. We recognize verbs by their form and their position in a sentence even when we don't know what they mean. In "I am sure that his words will coruscate," we recognize *am* and *will* as verbs because we've already learned their forms. Even if we've never seen or heard *coruscate,* we recognize it as a verb because it depends on *will.*

Verbs fall into two classes: a closed one (no new verbs are added) whose function is primarily grammatical, and an open one (new verbs are constantly added) in which the meaning of the words is important. In "He got hurt," *got* performs the grammatical function of showing past tense and passive voice, and *hurt* carries the lexical meaning. See **Auxiliaries, Gerunds, Infinitives, Participles, Principal parts of verbs, Tenses of verbs, Voice.**

2. Function. Verbs, with their modifiers and any objects or complements, form the predicates of clauses, which are combinations of subjects and predicates. See **Agreement, Clauses, Linking verbs, Objects, Predicates, Transitive and intransitive verbs.**

Verbs and style

The rhetorical function of a verb is usually to comment on the topic of a sentence. Generally speaking, the important action in a sentence should be in the main verb after the topic-subject has been stated. In the sentence "The possibility of a decision in regard to an investigation of reasons for student transfer exists," the one verb is *exists.* It states only that the very long and complicated topic-subject is there for the reader to consider. But the important action is not that a possibility exists; it's that someone may decide to investigate why students transfer: [The president?] may decide to investigate why students transfer. This sentence has two verbs—*decide* and *transfer*—and a verbal, the infinitive *to investigate.* The crucial actions in a sentence should be represented by verbs, not in the abstract nouns related to verbs. See **Absolute phrases, Conditional clauses, Nominalization, Passive voice, Subjunctive mood, Tense.**

Vernacular

Vernacular once meant "the local language as opposed to Latin." In England the word was used to refer to natural spoken English as opposed to formal literary English, and this usage gained social and political overtones in the United States. In the 1800s Mark Twain wrote stories and Walt Whitman wrote poems in styles adapted from ordinary speech. Since then it's been impossible to flatly oppose the literary language to the vernacular language, for the vernacular has been more important to American literature than the formal or academic. See **Colloquial English.**

very

1. As a qualifier.   *Very* is so much used as a qualifier that some teachers and editors have tried to outlaw it. But as long as it's used sparingly, *very* is a much better choice than overblown intensifiers like *incredibly, terribly, fantastically,* and so on.

2. With past participles.   Some readers complain about the use of *very* before past participles that are not established in adjectival function, on the grounds that *very* ("extremely") can't modify verbals. They insist that an adverb of degree, such as *greatly* or *much,* must stand between *very* and these participles—not "very disoriented" but "very much disoriented." In general practice some past participles regularly take *very* (very troubled), some *much* (much improved), some either (very pleased, much pleased), some neither (lighted). Let your ear be your guide.

Vogue words

Particular words and expressions are constantly enjoying great popularity in one social or professional group or another, but a true vogue word is one that's moved into general usage and there become a fad. Some begin in the slang of the black ghetto or the campus and find their way into the copy of advertising writers. Others start in the professions or the bureaucracy and become clichés through the efforts of journalists and commentators. Still others are borrowings, like the British *early on.* As P. A. Duhamel has said, "The jargon of the day can so fascinate some speakers that they will repeat it mindlessly, substituting incantation for communication" *(Boston Herald-Advertiser).* Writers are not immune to this weakness.

Some vogue words and expressions have little specific meaning to begin with, in the contexts in which they appear. (For a time the word *like* was used in place of a grunt as a filler in conversation.) Through endless repetition other vogue words lose what force and meaning they had *(actually, basically, meaningful, relevant).* Still others take on so many meanings in so many different contexts as to become almost meaningless *(massive, concept, scenario).* Whether short and simple *(thrust)* or long and fancy *(counterproductive),* all vogue words have one thing in common: they've become a bore. Writers should do their best to avoid using them.

See **Cliché, Gobbledygook, Slang, Triteness.**

Voice

Voice is a term borrowed from the grammars of the classical languages, where it usually differentiates distinctive verb endings. In English, *passive voice* refers to constructions made with the past participle and some form of the verb *be* (was killed). All other verb forms are *active.*

	Active voice	*Passive voice*
Present:	he asks (is asking)	he is asked (is being asked)
Future:	he will ask	he will be asked
Perfect:	he has asked	he has been asked
Infinitives:	to ask, to have asked	to be asked, to have been asked
Participles:	asking, having asked	being asked, asked, having been asked

Get is also used for the passive, especially in informal English: If he should get elected, we'd be lost; Our house is getting painted. See **Passive voice.**

wait on, wait for

Wait on for *wait for* (She's waiting on the mail) is regional or dialectal.

wake

English is oversupplied with verbs for waking from sleep (intransitive) and waking someone else from sleep (transitive). Most common is *wake (woke* or *waked; woke, waked,* or *woken),* to which *up* is frequently added in general English. *Awaken (awakened, awakened)* is almost as common but more formal. *Awake (awoke* or *awaked; awoke, awaked,* or *awoken)* is rather formal. *Waken (wakened, wakened)* is least used.

want

Except in the rather rare sense "have need" (They want for the bare necessities of life), *want* should not be followed by *for:* I want [for] you to go. Nor should it be followed by a *that* clause: I want that you should go.

Want for "ought," "had better" (You want to review all the notes if you're going to pass the exam) is informal.

Want in and *want out* (That dog wants out) occur in general and informal writing but not in formal.

way, ways

Way in the sense "far" is established in general writing, though not in formal: "It goes way back to his red-baiting days" (T.R.B., *New Republic*).

There's some prejudice against the use of *ways* to mean "distance," as in "a little way[s] down the road."

we

We is frequently used as an indefinite pronoun in expressions like "we find" and "we feel," to avoid passive and impersonal constructions. It's also used to mean "I and others," as in writing for a group or institution. In newspapers and magazines, editorial *we* may speak for the publication; in books it can mean "you readers and I," "all of us" (with *us* ranging from a limited group to the entire human race), or simply "I, the author." And there is the royal *we* of monarchs and popes, the corporate *we* of business letters, and, particularly since the growth of radio-television "talk" shows, the *we* that can only mean "I," as in an entertainer's "We always draw well in Vegas."

We for *I* has been taken up by some ordinary citizens, with no hint of publicity agents, teammates, or bureaucratic associates, on the peculiar grounds that it's more modest. It isn't.

See **I.**

well, good

Well is either an adjective (She looks well) or an adverb (He swam well). *Good* is an adjective (a good feeling). See **good, well.**

what

When a predicate nominative connected to a *what* clause by a linking verb is singular, the verb is singular: What I want to discuss is the responsibility of students. When the predicate nominative is plural, usage is divided:

> . . . what surprises and captures the reader is the hundreds of black-and-white photographs. . . .—*Time*

> What he wanted were people who could stimulate. . . .—Anthony Starr, *Esquire*

when, where

A *when* or *where* clause is probably the standard form for defining in informal usage and occurs often in general contexts: Welding is when (*or* where) two pieces of metal are heated and made into one. But there is strong prejudice against it. The grammatical argument is that an adverbial clause can't serve as the predicate complement of a noun, which requires as complement another noun or a noun phrase or clause: Welding is the process by which two pieces of metal are heated and made into one.

whether

Or not is required after *whether* when *whether* introduces a complete or elliptical adverbial clause: Whether [he is] right or not, he deserves a hearing. In noun clauses *or not* may be used for emphasis; but it isn't necessary and many writers prefer to omit it:

> Whether readers find him successful will depend on their patience.—Charles F. Mullet, *American Historical Review*

> If the child at home wonders whether he is loved, the pupil in school wonders whether he is a worthwhile person.—Robert Dreeben, *Harvard Educational Review*

When the alternatives are spelled out, *or not* is redundant: Whether [or not] the move is good or bad is debatable.

Repeating *whether* after *or* (Whether . . . or whether . . .) can be helpful to readers when the alternatives are long and complex, as in some formal or technical contexts.

See **Conditional clauses; if, whether.**

which

1. For broad reference.   The use of *which* to refer to the whole idea of a preceding clause (They plan to tear it down, *which* is a pity) is well established, but objections are properly raised when the reference is so loose that, at first reading, the *which* seems to refer only to the preceding word: She liked the book, *which* was puzzling. Similarly, a reader shouldn't have to wrestle with two *which*'s, one of specific and one of broad reference, in a single short sentence: I worked Saturdays to earn money *which* was owed on the car, *which* pleased my parents.

2. In the possessive.   *Whose* as the possessive of *which* is older and less cumbersome than *of which* and is preferred by most writers: "a pattern whose outlines are clearly visible" rather than "a pattern the outlines of which are. . . ."

3. In parallel clauses.   When parallel relative clauses with the same antecedent are connected by a coordinating conjunction, a writer sometimes omits the relative pronoun before the first clause and then uses it before the second: "It seems to hold as much promise for American politics as the second-hand legislative reforms [ ] Sinclair propounded in his novels, and which successive Democratic administrations enacted'' (Andrew Kopkind, *New York Times Book Review*). In this example, the missing *which* could be inserted, or the *which* after *and* could be dropped.

Sometimes a single adjective *which* clause is attached to a main clause by *and* or *but:* In elementary school I became interested in ballet, not a very popular art form where I lived, and which most of my classmates thought was silly. Omitting the *and* in this clumsy sentence only creates confusion, because without it the *which* doesn't seem to have any reference at all. The mixed construction can be turned into a balanced one by inserting *which was* before *not:* In elementary school I became interested in ballet, which was not a very popular art form . . . and which most of my classmates thought was silly. See **Subordination 2.**

4. ***Which*** **or** ***that.***   For the choice between *which* and *that* as relative pronouns, see **that.**

while

The central meaning of *while* is ''during the time that'': While the rest were playing cards, he was studying. In general English *while* is also used to mean ''although'' or ''whereas'' (While the cast is talented, the play is a bore) and to introduce the second of two clauses in place of *though* or *but* (The beagle was a thoroughbred, while the rest of the pack were mongrels). Because of the several senses, *while* can create ambiguity unless you use it with care. Among formal stylists there's some prejudice against *while* when no sense of time is involved.

who, whom

In all varieties of English, *who* is consistently used for subjects except when it's immediately followed by the subject of an interrupting clause. Then what *The New Yorker* used to call The Omnipotent Whom is common, as if the pronoun rather than its clause were the object of the interrupting clause: ''children whom Taylor thinks can bend spoons by paranormal powers'' (Martin Gardner, *New York Review of Books*). As subject, *who* is the right form in such constructions.

In formal styles *whom* is consistently used for objects, but informal and general styles often break the traditional rule. General usage permits *who* in questions like these:

And who was the hard sell aimed at?—Mary McCarthy, *New York Review of Books*

Who are they trying to impress?—Bruce Price, *Washington Post*

The reason educated writers sometimes accept *who* as object when they'd reject *I, we, he, she,* and *they* is that *who* is so often in subject territory, preceding the verb. When the pronoun functions as subject, function and position are in harmony, and *who* is the natural choice. When the pronoun functions as object, function and position are at odds. In formal contexts most writers ignore position and let function determine form. In casual conversation and casual writing, position is allowed to determine form. General usage usually favors the demands of function except when the pronoun introduces the whole sentence (Who can we turn to?). In college writing, subject *who* and object *whom* are usually the appropriate choices, unless *whom* sounds unnatural in the context.

See **one of those who.**

whose

Whose is interchangeable with *of which* and often the better choice. See **which 2.**

will, shall

Whether pointing to the future and expressing determination or simply indicating the future, *will* is more common than *shall* in all three persons. See **shall, will.**

-wise

Over a long period the suffix *-wise* was used to form a limited number of adverbs from nouns (*edgewise, lengthwise, slantwise*). Some years ago it increased in faddish use, especially in an abstract rather than a special sense (*average-wise, budget-wise, weather-wise, tax-wise*) until new *-wise* words became a joke. Now both the overuse and the ridicule have died down. When a noun has no established adjectival form, a *-wise* coinage may serve a need and save space. But often the *-wise* word lacks precision (*production-wise*); sometimes it saves no space (*economy-wise* versus *in economy*); and it may simply duplicate an existing word (*drama-wise* for *dramatically*). Besides, tacked-on *-wise* incites some readers to violence.

woman, lady, girl

An adult human female is a woman. She may or may not be a lady, just as a man may or may not be a gentleman. Feminists oppose the use of *girl* for any human female who is no longer a child.

ᴡ   Wordiness

Replace the wordy expressions with more compact and exact ones.

There are two cures for wordiness—surgery and treatment. Surgery means cutting out words. Treatment means revising or rewriting.

1. **Cut out deadwood,** the type of wordiness that contributes nothing but clutter:

> At [the age of] forty he was a handsome [looking] man.
> In [the case of] television commercials, stereotypes are everywhere.
> The writer is a member of a cultural minority because [of the fact that] he is a writer.
> The architecture [of the buildings] and the landscaping [of the grounds] speak of town pride.
> [It also happened that] we were the same age.
> He kept things moving in [the field of] basset breeding throughout [the entirety of] his career.

The most common deadwood consists of unnecessary phrases like "green *in color,*" "seven *in number,*" "rectangular *in shape*" and clichés like "in the business world" and "in the field of economics," which you may use without thinking. Good writing requires thought. When you revise a first draft, look closely at every phrase. Does "green in color" mean any more than "green"? Doesn't "in business" say everything that "in the world of business" says?

Sometimes a phrase that contributes nothing to the meaning of a sentence nevertheless fits its rhythm or has some other stylistic justification. Perhaps adding "in my life" to "for the first time" provides a desired emphasis. But as a rule simply eliminating deadwood is a step toward a compact, direct, honest prose style.

2. **Compress inflated passages.**   When deadwood is involved, no replacement is necessary, but loose, unfocused expression often demands rewriting:

> The reason that I'm telling all this is because I want to demonstrate in the clearest way possible that the cultural background of my family was of such a nature as to encourage my interest in the reading of books, magazines, etc.
>
> *Rewritten:* All this shows that my family background encouraged me to read.

Using unnecessary words produces flabby writing. You can often improve a first draft greatly by reducing long-winded phrases and other circumlocutions to single words that are more direct, more emphatic, and at least as clear:

Instead of	in this day and age	today
	at this point in time	now
	during the time that	while
	in the event that	if
	at the conclusion of	after

ωɒ Word order

Change the order of words or other elements to make the meaning clear or the phrasing more natural or more effective.

The placing of words and word groups in a sentence is the most important means of showing their grammatical relationships. Word order plays a major role in style, particularly in achieving emphasis.

1.   Interrupted constructions.   Keep your subjects close to your verbs. When a word or words interrupt a construction, the effect is usually clumsy unless the interrupter deserves special emphasis:

> *Between subject and verb:* Newspaper headlines *in these trying and confused times* are continually intensifying our fears.

> *More natural:* In these trying and confused times, newspaper headlines are. . . .

2.   Wandering modifiers.   Keep your modifiers close to the words they modify. When modifiers are separated from their headwords, the result is frequently awkward, sometimes misleading:

> Bob recovered from exhaustion plus what apparently was a bug making the rounds following two days' bedrest. —Grace Lichtenstein, *New York Times*

> *Better:* Following two days' bedrest, Bob. . . .

> Her uncle, King Leopold, was even unable to influence her.

> *Better:* Even her uncle. . . .

> I decided that if I moved in the direction of the apple tree growing beside the fence calmly, I might make it before the bull charged.

> *Better:* . . . moved calmly in the direction. . . .

3.   Word order and emphasis.   Don't change normal word order unless you have a reason for doing so. As a rule an element shifted from its usual position receives increased emphasis, as when the object is put before subject and verb:

Object first: I was surprised to find Salinger's novel on the list. *That book* I read when I was fourteen.

Predicate adjective first: Lucky are the ones who need no longer worry.

See **Ambiguity, Dangling modifiers.**

world

Inflated phrases with *world*—"the business world," "the fashion world," "the world of science" (or economics or politics or athletics)—can usually be collapsed: After graduation he went into [the world of] advertising. "Today's modern world" means "today." In other cases more specific language is preferable: This is especially true in the world of jazz [*better:* among jazz musicians]. *Area, field,* and *realm* are misused in the same way.

would, should

In indirect discourse, *shall* as well as *will* is likely to be reported as *would:* She said, "We shall see"; She said that we would see. See **should, would.**

would have, would of

Would of for *would have* is nonstandard. See **have 3.**

ww Wrong word

Replace the word marked with one that says what you mean.

No word is right or wrong in itself. As a correction symbol, *ww* means that the word does not convey a meaning that makes sense in the context. In the sentence "What he said showed real comprehensibility of the problems of Asia," *comprehensibility* doesn't make sense; it's the wrong word. *Comprehension* (or *understanding*) would be the right word. In "Some people remain stagnant to the lessons of life," *stagnant* needs to be replaced—possibly by *oblivious.* In "I remember explicitly my first puff," *clearly* would be a good choice to replace *explicitly.* Errors like these occur when you use words without being sure of their meaning, when you confuse words of similar sound, or when you simply write too hurriedly and fail to proofread your work. Sometimes a spelling is so wide of the mark (*bonified* for *bona fide*) that it's marked *ww* or *mng.* See **Careless mistakes; Meaning; precedence, precedent.**

Correct the obvious error.

See **Careless mistakes.**

Xmas

X is the first letter in the Greek word for *Christ*. It's been used for centuries as an abbreviation in the word *Xmas,* pronounced exactly like *Christmas.* Today, however, *Xmas* is most likely to be pronounced *eks mus,* and for many its popularity with advertisers has given it unpleasant commercial connotations. Except for purposes of irony, *Xmas* is inappropriate in serious writing.

yet

Yet is both an adverb (The books haven't come yet) and a coordinating conjunction roughly equivalent to *but:* His speech was almost unintelligible, yet I found I enjoyed it. *But* is less formal and much more common.

you

In giving instructions, as in a how-to paper, *you* is often a good stylistic choice (Then you glue the bottom strip . . .), certainly preferable to repeated use of the passive (The bottom strip is then glued . . .). As an impersonal pronoun, *you* is more common than *one* in general usage and not at all rare in formal:

> In a sense, Richard III, as Shakespeare sees him, is a little boy who has found out that God does not strike you dead when you tell a lie.—Arnold Edinborough, *Shakespeare Quarterly*

> There are at least three ways to treat any philosophical work: (1) You may inquire into its background. . . .—Frederick Sontag, *Journal of Religion*

Writers should avoid switching back and forth between *you* and *one* and should take care that their *you, your* is clearly indefinite, not personal. "Your parents depend on alcohol and pills to get them through the day" might better be "Our parents. . . ."

See **one, they.**

youth

As a collective noun, *youth* meaning "young people in general" can be followed by either singular or plural verbs and pronouns. In American usage the singular construction is much more common: "Russian youth wants to avoid military conscription as sincerely as American youth does" (George Feifer, *New York Times Magazine*). But when *the* precedes *youth,* a plural verb is often desirable to make clear that more than a single person is meant: The increase in tuition made education too expensive for the youth who were most in need of it.

Though the collective use includes both sexes, *youth* meaning "a young person" ordinarily refers to a young man, and the usual plural is *youths.*

Youth isn't a comfortable word for either a group or an individual. *Young people, adolescents, young men and women, girls and boys, boy(s),* or *young man* (or *men*) is often a better choice.

See **kid.**

 A correction symbol indicating approval—"good idea," "well expressed," and so on.

Acknowledgments

Kenneth R. Seeskin, "Never Speculate, Never Explain: The State of Contemporary Society" from *American Scholar*, Winter 1979/80, p. 19.

From "The Tattoo Taboo" by George Leonard, *Atlantic*, July 1976. Copyright © 1975 by The Atlantic Monthly Company, Boston, Mass. Reprinted with permission.

From "Two on the Isle" by Caskie Stinnett, *Atlantic*, October 1976. Copyright © 1976 by The Atlantic Monthly Company. Reprinted by permission of the author.

A. M. Pettis, *Basic Car Care*. New York: Monarch/Simon & Schuster, 1977, p. 11.

From "Closeup: Record Has Subtle Moments" by Charles C. DuBois, *Centre Daily Times*, September 24, 1976. Reprinted by permission.

Edward Abbey, *Desert Solitaire*. New York: McGraw-Hill Book Co., 1968, pp. 52–54.

From an article by Judd Arnett, *Detroit Free Press*, October 25, 1976. Reprinted with the permission of the Detroit Free Press.

Roy Blunt, Jr., "Sports" from *Esquire* Magazine, February 1978, p. 42.

Excerpt from "The Two Faces of Vermont" from *First Person Rural* by Noel Perrin. Copyright © 1978 by Noel Perrin. Reprinted by permission.

Excerpt from "Lift Your Feet" in *Fits & Starts: The Premature Memoirs of Andrew Ward*. Copyright © 1977 by Andrew Ward. Reprinted by permission of Little, Brown and Company in association with the Atlantic Monthly Press.

"Barbed Wire" by John Fischer in *From the High Plains*. Copyright © 1978 by John Fischer. Reprinted by permission.

Text only excerpt from *Too Rich for Heroes*, by Henry Fairlie. Copyright © 1978 by Harper's Magazine. All rights reserved. Excerpted from the November 1978 issue by special permission.

Excerpt from *After Ellis Island*, by Andrew M. Greeley. Copyright © 1978 by Harper's Magazine. All rights reserved. Reprinted from the November 1978 issue by special permission.

General Index

Correction Chart

To the student: When one of these correction symbols calls attention to a weakness in your essay, look up the *Index* entry that discusses the problem, and make the revision. The symbols in the chart are arranged alphabetically; page numbers for the entries follow the instructions.

ab   Write out this word. Or use the standard abbreviation.   347

abst   Make this word or passage more concrete or more specific.   350

adj   Reconsider your choice of adjective.   353

adv   Correct the form or change the position of the adverb. Or reconsider your choice of adverb.   356

agr   Make the verb agree with its subject or the pronoun with its antecedent.   358

amb   Make your meaning unmistakable.   364

apos ⩗   Insert or remove an apostrophe as required.   369

beg   Revise the beginning of your paper to make it lead more directly and smoothly into your subject or to arouse your reader's interest.   376

cap   Capitalize the word marked.   386

case   Correct the mistake in case.   389

coh   Make clear the relation between the parts of this sentence or between these sentences or paragraphs.   393

colon   Use a colon here. Or reconsider the use of this colon.   395

comma ⸴   Insert or remove comma here: C_1 between independent clauses, 398; C_2 with preceding or following elements, 400; C_3 with nonrestrictive modifiers, 400; C_4 with interrupting and parenthetical words and phrases, 401; C_5 in lists and series, 401; C_6 for clarity, 402; C_7 for emphasis, 403; C_8 with main

sentence elements, 403; C_9 in conventional practice, 403; C_{10} with other marks of punctuation, 404.

comp   Correct the fault in comparing the adjective or adverb marked.   406

conj   Make this conjunction more accurate or more appropriate to the style of the passage.   410

coord   Correct the faulty coordination.   416

cs   Revise this sentence to correct the comma splice.   404

d   Replace this word with one that is more exact, more appropriate, or more effective.   426

dm   Revise the sentence so that the expression marked is clearly related to the word it is intended to modify.   419

det   Develop this passage more fully by giving pertinent details.   424

div   Break the word at the end of this line between syllables.   429

emp   Strengthen the emphasis of this passage.   435

end   Revise the ending of your paper to round out the discussion.   436

fig   Replace this trite, inconsistent, or inappropriate figure of speech.   443

form   Make this word or passage less formal, more appropriate to your style, subject, and audience.   447

frag   Make this construction a grammatically complete sentence, or join it to a neighboring sentence.   448

glos   See this *Index* for an entry on the word marked.

id   Replace this expression with standard idiom.   464

inf   Make this word or passage less informal, more appropriate to your style, subject, and audience.   470